Best Wi...

THE ROYAL RULER
& THE RAILWAY DJ

A double autobiography from both sides of the Iron Curtain.
by Tony Prince and Jan Šesták

LIMITED EDITION
DMC Publishing Ltd
PO Box 89
Slough SL1 8NA
England

w.w.w.dmcworld.com

First published in Great Britain in 2017 by DMC Publishing.
Copyright © DMC Publishing Ltd.

Tony Prince and Jan Šesták have asserted their rights under the Copyright
Design and Patents Act 1988 to be identified as the authors of this work.

A CIP catalogue record for this book is available from the British Library

ISBN 978-0-9956694-0-6 (cased)
ISBN 978-0-9956694-1-3 (tpb)

DMC Ltd were the original publishers of Mixmag, Mixmag Update & 7 magazine in the UK
and Mixer magazine in the USA.

The company continue to produce a weekly youth culture magazine online from Ibiza:
http://www.dmcworld.net

The company was founded in February 1983 with the world's first BPI/PPL license to produce
and dub mixes and remixes by DJ producers for the global DJ market.

DMC have been actively promoting the DJ industry (club and radio) for 34 years.

The World DJ Championships promoted worldwide by DMC are now in their 33rd year.

DMC Ltd has also produced an extensive TV documentary titled The History of DJ
http://www.dmcworld.tv

Whilst the company's publishing history is extensive this is the company's first book.

Printed and bound in the UK by
Halstan & Co Ltd Amersham, HP6 6HJ, England

CREDITS
TONY PRINCE WOULD LIKE TO THANK:

Christine for her perpetual love.

Our kids Daniel and Gabrielle, and granddaughter Bluebell, icing on the cake of life.

My Facebook friends are many, and we have shared so much together in recent years.

The millions of radio listeners who allowed me to enter their lives across the decades.

Marconi and Ronan O'Rahilly for changing all our worlds.

Alan Keen for steering Radio London and Radio Luxembourg and...me.

Darryl von Daniken for inviting my participation in the International Radio Festival each year.

The teenagers at Radio Imaginaria in Italy, long may you enjoy what you are doing.

Elvis Presley, Colonel Tom Parker and Todd Slaughter for thrills of a lifetime.

Paul & Linda McCartney for choosing me to MC your events.

Our team at DMCWORLD.COM who have served the DJ world for 34 year.

Our global agents for helping us to stage the DMC World DJ Championships for three decades.

The thousands of DJs who have been a part of DMC as producers, members or competitors.

The British Musician's Union for expelling me.

JAN ŠESTÁK WOULD LIKE TO THANK:

Beloved daughter Šárka for her support in all fields possible, including the provision of all facilities necessary for the preparation of this book.

Earl Poole Ball, Dave Hogan, Billy Edd Wheeler, George Hamilton IV who, as top American songwriters, performers, musicians and DJ, all kept me in touch with the free world of music for almost half a century.

The people and friends who you will meet in our book: František Jemelka, Michal Bukovič, Radek Rettegy, Pavel Váně, Oldřich Veselý, Michal Polák and Jaromír Hnilička who helped to keep me sane in our mad world.

Miloš Bernátek, Jiří Sedláček, Luboš Rettegy and Libor Trejtnar – the founders of Bav club in Brno, to whom the pop music population of our town owes them an eternal debt of gratitude.

The Voice of America, Radio Luxembourg, Radio Caroline and the BBC for helping us make good our escape.

The DJs of those stations for their contribution to raising the Iron Curtain and, although the static tried to hinder you, for helping to improve my English!

Classmates of our III.D class of 1966 at High school in Brno, all of whom shared the pain.

And lastly, Paul Anka, the Beatles, Elvis Presley, Johnny Cash, Eddie Cochran and the Rolling Stones...you will never know what you gave us.

PHOTOGRAPHY CREDITS

The Authors and Publishers would like to thank friends, fans and relevant record companies for their permission to reproduce their photographs in this book. Providers include the Oldham Chronicle, Colin Nichol Archive, David Porter (AB 208 Magazine/IPC), McCartney Productions, Radio Luxembourg (London) Ltd., Radio Tele Luxembourg, the MS Society, Todd Slaughter and the Elvis Presley Fan Club of Great Britain, Colonel Tom Parker and the Elvis Presley Estate, the Tony Prince Archive, Mike Knight, Jan Šesták's private collection, Svatoslav Fiala, Lynn Rothwell.

ACKNOWLEDGEMENTS

Sonya Webb for invaluable attention to proof reading (and her husband Ryan whose career as a musician was sidelined during this process).

Martin Madigan for cover design.

Rupert Smith of Halstan & Co for his invaluable support in producing the book.

Dedicated to Jan Palach

CONTENTS

CONTENTS

Tony: Today

So many things separated us, and yet our synchronous existence had one defining addiction that caused us to meet.

I wanted to be like Elvis Presley, but the Musicians' Union got in the way. Later I wanted to broadcast from a ship in the Irish Sea, only the British Government got in the way.

He wanted to listen to his radio without fear that his love for western pop would attract the Secret Police. His parents had already suffered and survived the Nazi concentration camps, so he was especially careful when listening to Radio Luxembourg

Then one night he heard the Beatles for the first time. It would be a year before he knew what they looked like, and even longer before he knew which one was John, Paul, George or Ringo.

Music was our orbit. Radio our mother ship.

From childhood, Jan Šesták was locked inside the communist system in Czechoslovakia, whilst I was locked inside the working class north of England. I used music as my means of escape. Jan had no means of escape, but music came to his rescue.

I never really appreciated what I had until one day, Jan and I met.

We should all be dipped into Jan's life for a year or so.

It would change the world.

Jan: The concentration camp wireless

The most beautiful sound was the Big Ben chimes followed by *Volá Londýn – London Calling*. We sat there appreciating the world was much bigger and much more exciting than our rather large containment compound.

My parents quite forcefully instilled in me that I must let no one know what we did each night. No one should know that we listened to the BBC, the Voice of America or Radio Free Europe, and I must control my desire to discuss the previous night's Radio Luxembourg programmes with my friends; which I did of course, but only with friends I knew well, and understood that they, too, had their ears pressed to the speaker, as none of us could chance to let the sound drift outside. Spies and turncoats were everywhere.

Because of informers, many of our neighbours and friends were sent to concentration camps and in many cases, for the sin of listening to foreign radio stations, paid with their lives!

Could this really have been allowed to happen in the 20th century? How, after being given freedom from the Nazi grip on our country in May 1945, to have embraced freedom once again and to be allowed to travel where we wished, to listen to what we liked, discuss and freely debate anything, did we, after a mere 3 years, find ourselves once again afraid to look over our shoulders?

By February 1948, Czechoslovakia was under Russian rule, and the informers who'd shaken hands with the Nazi devils resurfaced running to the communist rulers.

The Secret Police were amongst us.

If you were discovered listening to Jack Jackson's Kraft Cheese Show or Dan Dare on Radio Luxembourg, you just disappeared.

Tony: Climbing the mast

I'd been at sea five days with the likes of Tony Blackburn, Emperor Rosko, Tom Lodge and Dave Lee Travis experiencing broadcasting in a force 12 gale when, in the middle of my lunchtime show on 15 April, a cable, high above the rigging atop the 160ft (49m) mast, had worked loose in the bad weather.

It was now causing a short circuit to the transmitter.

Radio Caroline South was off the air, free radio extinguished.

Silence was not golden.

For three days we bobbed up and down like a cork in the ocean, unable to transmit and unable to make repairs, as the gale made it impossible for anyone to climb to the top of the mast.

The ship's Dutch crew couldn't care less. All they wanted in life was their strange food, their ship rations of beer and fags and a poker hand containing a full house! What else can a crew do on a boat that only starts its engine to unwind the anchor chain once every few weeks? But we, who had been smitten with silence, cared a great deal and yearned to get back to playing our part in the swinging 60s revolutions.

"I'm going up there," said Blackburn at breakfast on day four.

"You're fuckin' nuts," said Dave Lee Travis.

"You're not insured," said the Captain and went to his cabin to type out a disclaimer.

Wrapped in winter woollies and a safety harness, Tony took his first step onto the bottom rung. Above, the mast swayed drunkenly from side-to-side.

We all stood around, crew too, their playing cards fanned in their hands from an interrupted game as we all watched the breakfast show host scale the mast.

"Tony," yelled Rosko after ten rungs.

Blackburn looked down over his left shoulder.

"Can I have your record collection?"

With necks craned skywards, we watched his laborious ascent each with a hand shading our eyes from the glaring white sky, the other hand on our hips like we were about to do the Sailor's Hornpipe.

He made it to the halfway point, stopped for a few moments and started back down descending much quicker than he'd gone up.

"I need gloves," he breathed, safe on the deck.

"And a change of underpants!"

"Let me have a go," I volunteered, suddenly struck by the thought of the applause I'd receive if I could pull this off.

Rung by rung, for a few long seconds, the ascent requires you to exercise total no-net danger as you unhook the clip on the safety harness from one rung to the next. You do not dare to look down. You're shaking enough.

Halfway up, the rogue cable was clearly visible caught like a cracking whip in the vicious winds.

I arrived at the section of mast that had been welded on in an Irish shipyard to give it broadcast height.

I was just wondering what the quality of Irish workmanship might be, when I realised that the silly sods had welded rungs on that were too thick for my safety clasp.

I took five more rungs just to outdo Blackburn, no harness and no safety net beneath, just the rolling waves of the English Channel.

Below me there was panic.

The tender, which brought us to and from Harwich out here into international waters, had arrived and was trying to dock alongside.

A tricky manoeuvre, even in a calm sea. The DJs, captain and crew were all frantically pointing towards me, signalling for the tender captain not to slam alongside Caroline.

On board the tender was Ronan O'Rahilly who had come out for the express purpose of doing what we were doing.

"That climb saved you your job," he told me many years later.

Little did I know as I perched 90 feet above sanity levels, that the trouble brewing for me back at Caroline House in London had been diverted.

I made the mistake of looking down, saw the tender and promptly threw up. The tiny figures below scattered as my breakfast rained down on them. Beaten, shit-scared and bitter to the bone, I followed my bacon and eggs back to the deck, which I promptly kissed.

Before you could say 'Caroline, the sound of a nation', Norman St John was on his way.

"Norman, the rungs..." I chattered, but he couldn't hear me for the wind.

The Australian broadcaster climbed just 20 feet before returning.

"Sorry cobbers," he said. "I was making more bloomin' wind than the gale!"

Then Blackburn, warmed up and inspired knowing the guvnor was watching 30 yards off our port side, took off once again. And this time, incredibly, he went right to the top in an episode that lies somewhere between bravery and lunacy. Although he managed to release the rogue cable, it floated just 30 feet or so before it got caught again in the lower rigging. Too exhausted to try to yank it free a second time, Tony left it dangling and came down spent.

Then I went up and pulled it down, releasing it to the midship deck.

Ronan was beyond himself with gratitude.

The tender was unable to negotiate a safe docking and turned back towards Harwich up the coast. Ronan stood, a lone figure at the bow, clapping us and blowing kisses! As irritating as he can be with his annoying jokes, his silly barking dog Arnold and his failed marriage to Tessa Wyatt, which he made an entire nation share his suffering, Tony has been a hero of mine ever since that cold April day.

I was the only other person to experience the fear he felt and share the danger he was in swinging, like an ant on a metronome in 50 feet wide arcs side to side, 180 feet above the boiling sea.

This was the greatest Tony Blackburn breakfast show ever and great practice for his future appearance in TV's I'm a Celebrity Get me Out of Here, where more courage would be required of him in years to come!

Of course there are those out there who would rather he had fallen into the sea!

Jan: Pavel comes home

My musician friend Pavel Váně had disappeared out of the country during the brief interlude known as the Prague Spring, when communism went on a low burner and people could once again travel abroad. At last Pavel was experiencing the delights of the west for the first time, and was spending some time in Austria with his girlfriend and other friends. It was the first time in his life that he understood the wonders of the west and their freedoms. His girlfriend and the others made plans to immigrate to the USA and South Africa and she begged him to do likewise, but Pavel had a number of reasons to return home to Czechoslovakia.

First, he didn't want to leave his mother and sister with any bad repercussions caused by his disappearance. He wanted to complete his studies of psychology at Brno University, and his band was doing well so he wanted to keep up the momentum.

But of course, like everyone in my country, Pavel could never have envisaged then that in merely a year, the Prague Spring would once again become an extremely long winter.

Back home in Czechoslovakia things didn't seem too bad at all in the autumn of 1968, Pavel even managed to get permission to visit England. If he'd waited until summer 1969 his application would have been refused, not just because his father was a non-conformist, but after 19 January 1969, when student Jan Palach had set himself on fire in Prague's Wenceslas Square to protest against the renewed suppression of free speech, the communist authorities stopped issuing travel documents.

He didn't travel to the UK until the summer of 1969, but he'd had the paperwork for a year, so off he went to London where the swinging 60s was still in full swing.

In England all his musician dreams came true. He saw the best bands in the best clubs and had the time of his life. He even listened to Radio Caroline, real pirate radio with DJ Johnny Walker, who had stayed on board to challenge the British government's new law to make the ships illegal. He bought clothes in Kings Road and Carnaby Street, and drank pints of beer with other bands in The Ship, next to the Marquee club in Wardour Street. He dated beautiful mini-skirted girls, who'd walk with him through the central London parks and dance with him each night to hits like Marvin Gaye's *I heard it through the Grapevine*, the Rolling Stones' *Honky Tonk Women* and the Beatles' *The Ballad of John and Yoko*.

One day quite unexpectedly, Pavel broke the news to his newfound friends that he was ready to return to Czechoslovakia. They couldn't believe his decision. Everyone knew by then that all Czechoslovakia had become, was a compound, a very, very large prison.

"Stay here," they urged. "Go anywhere, but don't go back there it's too dangerous."

But he couldn't be persuaded because Pavel had a problem, he'd never missed a gig in his life and his band had a booking in Jihlava, a city 80kms from his hometown Brno. It was almost a religion with him that he did not miss a performance.

So back he came.

On 17 August 1969, when Pavel arrived back in Czechoslovakia in time for the gig, the other band members were completely shocked, unable to understand why he would ever return from England.

Four days later on 21 August, on the occasion of the first anniversary of Soviet occupation, as I worked the railways miles away from Brno, my friend Pavel stepped out onto the streets of our city to join the protest.

Tony: Beatlemania

I slipped easily into my new time cycle. No more getting up at 7am to go
to work, or hiding on the bus from fans who might recognise the kid in
scruffy overalls as 'Little Tommy', the kid they usually saw in a gold lamé
jacket when I sang with the Jasons at the Savoy.
Dad didn't slip into my new way of life as easily as I had.
"Sun's burning the house down!" he'd shout from the bottom of the stairs
by noon.
   The bandleader, Johnny Francis, wanted me to play guitar when I wasn't
singing. If it was a difficult chord sequence, he'd stop conducting the band
and saunter over to me cocking his hand to his mouth confidentially, and
advising me to turn my amplifier off!
Now I was wearing a tuxedo on strict tempo ballroom dancing nights, a
white jacket on Saturdays, the gold lamé for my Elvis medley and, a wig
and dress for my Christine Keeler impersonation!
   After my fourth night, the strange looking middle-aged man who'd
played the records in the band break didn't show. Perhaps, I felt, he had
been kept late at his day job shelf packing at Pay Less? The manager asked
me if I'd play the records for an extra £2 a night.
Five decades later, I'm still standing in for the guy.
He doesn't know what he missed!
   Soon the band got laid off on Tuesdays, which became a total record
night. The band was earning £16 a week Union rate, whilst I was pocketing
£24. I was Rockerfellow, King of Oldham.
   At Vertoma Jig and Tool, I took home £6/2s/6d if I worked overtime on
Wednesday nights and Saturday mornings!
Early in 1963 the Top Rank Astoria's manager, Dick Salem, (who years
later ran a club in Manchester for Manchester United's George Best)
called me into his office. He wanted my opinion on a group who had just
tickled the charts with their first single. They were available shortly after
their next single was released, and Salem wondered if they would be worth
£75.
"If they chart by mid-March they'll be going out for anything up to £500,"
he predicted.
   Dick delegated such decisions to me ever since I advised him to book
Susan Maughan on the strength of her *Bobby's Girl* just before it charted,
when she was booking for £50.
He filled the place: 1,000 punters at £2 admission when she was top 10.
   I'd seen the group in question on Granada TV introduced by Bill Grundy,
the same guy who the Sex Pistols told to 'Fuck off you old wanker' on their
first TV appearance 20 years later.

I advised Dick to book a group called the Beatles.

I looked forward to meeting Ringo again, and wondered if he would remember the last time we met when he played with Rory Storm & the Hurricanes at Butlins the year I entered the talent competition with hilarious consequences. But I never got near to a conversation with him. It was pandemonium, absolute chaos, as I witnessed first-hand the night we gave birth to Beatlemania, the night they charted number one for the first time!

The queue around the Top Rank was the biggest Union Street had ever seen. By 6pm the police were outside in force.

By 8pm the drunks at the Star Inn pub across the road had vacated the bar to ogle at the spectacle of thousands of mini-skirted, screaming teenage girls blocking the road.

The Beatles arrived quite late. I put on an LP, no one was dancing anyway. I visited the dressing room they were sharing with me, hanging around as long as possible enjoying their banter, the press interviews and the autograph hunters. I was in time to witness the mop tops taking on board the news in a telegram, which they had received from Morris Kinn, the publisher of New Musical Express. Paul McCartney asked for quiet, and read it to the ensemble.

"Congratulations! The Beatles Please Please Me is Number One on the New Musical Express chart!"

They were ecstatic.

They all hugged each other.

Dick Salem hugged me!

"Fuck me!" said John Lennon. "Anyone got a Prelly?"

The white Preludine tablets were passed round. John took two, dropping them with a scotch and coke, and then offered me one.

I didn't know what they were, and declined explaining that I didn't have a headache!

Lennon thought this was very funny.

Back on stage there was a carnival atmosphere in the place.

Fred Lowe, a bouncer who ran a junk store in the market during the day, had just turned away 2,000 fans whilst posting the 'full-house' sign up.

Kids had come from all over the place. We'd never witnessed anything like it in Oldham. Not even Eden Kane, Roy Orbison, Billy Fury, Jimmy Justice, Del Shannon or Marty Wilde had ever pulled such a massive out-of-town crowd.

The Astoria was brimming with strangers, all eyes on stage as I played the latest hits and still no one danced. There was no longer room to dance; Salem had blatantly ignored the capacity limits.

With no backstage entrance from the stage where I played records, once I'd

introduced them, the Beatles appeared from stage left, running heads bent through a corridor of flailing arms and forked fingernails, as the shrieking fans were held back by the Astoria's mesmerised part-time security men.
Noise? You've never heard anything like it!

Within days, the word *Beatlemania* was uttered for the first time on planet earth.

I was stuck on stage with them for the duration of their 30-minute set, perched at the side of Paul's amplifier, eyeballing Lennon who stuck his chin out as he belted out rock classics.

'Tricky Dicky', John yelled stroking six strings for a B-flat, and then the group struck up and the whole fucking world was wonderful.

Sitting close to the amplifiers, where my eardrums were threatened, I was the last person to ever hear the Beatles live, because after this, all you would hear at a Beatles concert would be screaming!

'There were bells on a hill…' Paul sang, but I had a funny feeling I was the only person who could hear him. The noise, the screams, the fainting girls dragged onto stage to save them being crushed by the human avalanche, a wave of bodies surging towards the stage. I remember the fear on young George Harrison's face, as a girl broke rank and threw herself around his neck; and Paul's sweat dripping like a tap onto his left handed bass as he nodded approval to John, whose eyeballs distended as they harmonised their final song, 'Last night I said these words to my girl…'

It was the ultimate musical experience.

Only one event ever eclipsed it for me, but that would come in 1972.

As wily girls witnessed what happened to those who had genuinely fainted, they too feigned to pass out, to be carried to the feet of their Lords on stage. Then they recovered and sat goggle-eyed, closer than fans would ever again be to the Fab Four.

It's all documented in the Oldham Chronicle and in one shot where the bouncer, Fred Lowe, is seen reaching for a girl and accidentally stripping her of her blouse, you may, if you look closely, see me little Tommy Whitehead, white-suited, acting as a bouncer in front of John Lennon!

And then came the end.

How the fuck does a DJ follow that?

Bobby's Girl? I think not! Nothing in my collection of hits seemed appropriate.

Joe Brown's *Picture of you*? Nagh!

The Tornadoes' *Telstar*? Tripe!

Subsequently I played *Please Please Me* three times, the B-side *Ask Me Why* twice, *Love Me Do* and its flip side *PS I Love You*, and then Dick Salem came on stage and told me to call it a night.

Salem along with every member of staff had become security staff for the night, and everyone from the catering staff to the manager was utterly exhausted. We had all experienced something peerless in our memories.

Back stage, bodies were strewn everywhere with a couple of Red Cross chaps in their vocational element.

I made it to our shared dressing room, which was bedlam. Half-undressed and still sweating, the group were on a high of highs. John Lennon disappeared with a fan into the adjoining toilet, whilst the others took on the Oldham Chronicle, Manchester Evening Post, Melody Maker, and... a chap from Oldham's Alexander Park area, who Paul introduced to everyone as, "an old mucker of me dad's."

In the light of hindsight and the historic measure of that evening, something quite astounding in its normality happened next.

Paul's dad's friend invited them to go to his house for a cup of tea.

"What do you think John?" asked Paul, as this future peacemaker zipped up his flies, leaving the girl behind him in the loo.

"Why not?" slurred Lennon. "Do yer 'av any cheese sarnies?"

It now seems like such a profound anti-climax, on the night the Beatles went to Number One for the first time. As their lives as normal people finally came to an end, and we felt the first tremors of a youth-quake that would echo down the corridors of time, the Beatles went to a little house in Windsor Road, Oldham to celebrate with a cuppa tea! It doesn't get more British than that.

I came to know Paul and Linda quite well in the years ahead, even visiting them in their Cavendish Avenue home where tea remained their favourite tipple, usually with a spliff.

In May 2012, almost 50 years after this event, I received a truly extraordinary communication on Facebook. The message blew me away:

Hi Tony
Thank you for accepting my friend request. I contacted you because I recently came across a book written by Michael Turner about the Beatles' gig in Oldham in 1963. In the section on you as DJ, it said you remembered them being invited back for a cup of tea by a friend of Paul's dad. That was my dad, and they did indeed come back to our house after the gig. Unbelievable but true!
I was 11 - too young to go to the Astoria but my dad made up for it by bringing them back!
I just wondered if you really did remember it?
Liz Wharf

Hi Liz
This is so exciting Liz, thank you for getting in touch. At last my long-held memory is confirmed. I can still see your Dad in my dressing room as the lads

*towelled themselves down and changed. Of course whilst it was manic that night,
who amongst us could ever have forecast quite how big they would become and
their history ahead? When you have a moment let me know what happened?
Did John get the 'cheese sarnies' he asked for?*

*Hi Tony
I remember it vividly of course. The four of them came with Neil Aspinal, whom
they called Nell. I don't recall Mal Evans being there but my brother does and I
think, logically, he must have been. George was very quiet, John very wry. Paul
was charming and Ringo was very nice to me and then fell asleep. There was a
huge heap of sandwiches – but not cheese – my mum carved up a leg of lamb as I
recall, and loads of her famous cakes, which Ringo particularly relished.
The saddest part of the tale is that we were a family of 6 children, but only four
of us met the boys. The two youngest were upstairs asleep in their beds throughout
the whole thing, (they've never got over it)!
Thanks so much for your response. It's an amazing memory to have, but weird
because it's not one that can be shared easily. Their trajectory following that
night was so meteoric, and so fast, that we couldn't tell anybody after the first few
weeks because people just didn't believe it.
All the best
Liz*

Jan: The boy who burned for our freedom

I returned to Olomouc with 260 army days left to serve. Other than an
awareness that my country had uninvited Russian guests, life was pretty
good in our *Řepčín* railway station barracks. I was an old soldier now with
an easy job, a radio and a cassette recorder to distract me from the evil that
now manifested itself in my country.

On the evening of 16 January 1969, I was in shock after hearing on
the BBC that on this afternoon, Jan Palach, a young student, had stood
in Prague's Wenceslas Square, struck a match and set himself on fire in
protest over the Russian occupation.

A student of history and political economy at Prague's Charles University,
Jan Palach, at 21 years of age, had been prepared to give his life to awaken
the Czechoslovakian people from their lethargy in tolerating the Russian
occupation.

The communist newspaper Red Law dedicated the smallest of articles,
hidden at the bottom of page two reporting this news:

'*On Thursday, around 3 o'clock in the afternoon, a 21-year-old student of the
Philosophical Faculty in Prague Jan Palach, heavily burned himself, as he spread*

an unknown flammable liquid over himself setting it on fire. Thanks to quick help the flames were extinguished and the ambulance took him to hospital.'

And that was literally all that Red Law was prepared to write about his sacrifice. No more facts, no comments, nothing, just a hidden cursory news story.

Jaroslava Moserová, the first doctor to provide care to Jan Palach at the Charles University Faculty Hospital, provided her own diplomatic observations.

"Palach did not set himself on fire to protest against the Soviet occupation, but did so to protest against the 'demoralisation' of Czechoslovakian citizens caused by the occupation. It was not so much in opposition to the Soviet occupation, but the demoralisation which was setting in, that people were not only giving up, but giving in."

Jan Palach would never learn how his action that day, was the first brick removed from the Berlin Wall in time to come. He was of course, quite right. Complacency was rife and more and more Czechoslovak people were exchanging their Prague Spring ideals for better jobs and postings.

Maybe brave Jan Palach didn't realise why such fear ruled the day amongst our population, certainly amongst the huge majority whose relatives were executed or just disappeared because they revolted, first against the Nazis and then, after the communist upheaval in February 1948, the totalitarian regime. Many were afraid to let history repeat itself, afraid to make the same mistakes as their family members before them.

Also during brief moments of liberty in 1968, various articles had been published about the friendly and peaceful and people-loving Soviet Union, like the story of Lavrentiy Beria. Beria was the oldest and most influential of Stalin's secret police chiefs; wielding his substantial influence during, and after World War II, when he organised the communist takeover of the countries of Central and Eastern Europe, including Czechoslovakia.

This great Soviet Union, presented to us as the Vanguard of Mankind, had in Beria a Chief of Secret Police, with an enormous appetite for perverted sexual depravity. When being driven through Moscow and noticing a pretty girl on the street, he would instruct his bodyguards to stop and bring the girl over to the car. She would then be taken in the car to his palatial office where he would rape her.

His charm offensive began by offering such a girl a drink of alcohol which, if she were to refuse, he would cajole her into drinking a toast to comrade Stalin. This she could not refuse, as rejecting a toast to comrade Stalin would be seen as an insult to the Russian leader, a crime that attracted the death sentence.

Beria's method of plying young innocents with vodka to obtain sexual gratification went unbridled for years, until the death of Stalin lead to his own death in a battle for power within the Soviet communist system.

Beria's successors were no better, and the seeds of his teachings were passed down to the hated Czechoslovak Secret Police (State Safety), whose horrible deeds throughout the 50s were partly revealed in 1968. So there it was, a nation ruled by perverts with no moral compass whatsoever. Such is the background that froze our people to the inactivity that so motivated Jan Palach to make his fatal protest.

On Saturday 18 January 1969, Red Law published a front page article, in which the Czechoslovak government expressed how deeply moved they were on hearing of Jan Palach's tragic deed. The newspaper reported that, according to his doctor who had spoken with him, Jan Palach was protesting against the newly introduced censorship and that his deed ended with consequences he had not envisaged.

Red Law added that his protest happened at a time when the troubled waters of our political situation had started to calm gradually, and that the efforts of the Czechoslovak government was concentrated on overcoming the country's difficult social and economic situation. On page 7, we read of the very serious condition of Jan Palach who had endured third-degree burns over 85% of his body. Then the paper warned against Začátek formuláře any distorting of Jan Palach´s deed; virtually throwing a blanket over his burning body and his message, intended to wake up his fellow citizens.

On Sunday Jan Palach died, and it wasn't until Monday that he finally achieved a full front-page article in Red Law. Even then they did not publish his picture, in an attempt to demean his sacrifice and lessen any political impact the news of his death may have had across our nation.

There were only two pictures on the front page of Red Law on Monday 20 January 1969 when it announced the death of Jan Palach. A large photograph showed an underground river promoting an article inside the paper concerning a cave. The second set of small pictures showed kids in a puppet theatre. Red Law's disrespect for our new hero sounded like thunder across the land.

The article contained a few sentences dedicated to Jan Palach´s CV, with three-quarters of the page filled with condolence telegrams to Jan Palach's mother from the president, prime minister and other government ministers.

Tony: Radio Caroline

Radio Caroline was the brainchild of Ronan O'Rahilly, an Irishman who had a small 60s record label, and a partnership in a cool Soho nightclub called The Scene on Great Windmill Street.

This was the club that helped the Rolling Stones hone down their sound, launching them to an underground fan club of purple-heart people, before they began recording, and set about becoming the greatest rock band the world has ever known.

O'Rahilly was about to play a yet bigger role in this and every other band's advancement, indeed, he was about to give Britain's entire social fabric a complete makeover. It was Ronan's ego and an amazing set of circumstances that set radio's fate.

He'd fallen for the music of Georgie Fame, and had paid for the young white blues man to record a demo, which included Rufus Thomas' *Do the Dog*, the Miracles' *Shop Around* and Booker T's *Green Onions*.

Ronan, like Epstein with the Beatles, did the rounds of the record companies only to be fobbed off because, according to the UK's top A&R men at that time, Fame was 'too black for a white', 'blues without breed'. In the end Ronan paid for a full recording session himself, and it was here where Georgie ran into and recorded a cute little original called *Yeh Yeh*.

Columbia signed Fame, but then Ronan ran into the next problem… the BBC. He soon learned that there were only two ways to get a hit in the UK, the Light Programme had to expose it, preferably on Freeman's Pick of the Pops or TV had to give it a spot, but this was unlikely for a new artist with such a non-pop style. That left Radio Luxembourg who, according to the plugger at EMI, had turned the record down.

Ronan marched to 38 Hertford Street, the most famous address in UK radio, for this was where the DJs incited people to send their letters and competition entries.

"I'm here to see Sir Geoffrey," he demanded of the receptionist.

"We don't have a Sir Geoffrey at this address," she answered.

"Yes you do, he's expecting me," said Ronan. "Sir Geoffrey Everitt."

Everitt, a former Radio Luxembourg broadcaster who had beaten the odds to become the station's managing director, was undoubtedly a Lord in young Ronan's Irish eyes.

Somehow he found himself summoned to the first floor where Joy Nichols, Geoffrey's concubine, PA, former vocalist and BBC star, ushered him into the hallowed office. Behind a huge desk sat Everitt, a man who would employ and then fire both myself and Noel Edmonds.

"What can I do for you?" he asked the grey haired object in front of him. Joy flanked him on one side and Eggy Lay, his programme controller, on the other.

"I'd like you to playlist an important new talent," said Ronan.

The group went through the courtesy of a review and then commented that even if they liked it, which they didn't, there was no room on their playlist. Everitt pointed to a wall-chart that started at 7pm through 1am.

Each 30-minute slot was sponsored either by a record label, a shampoo or a toothpaste brand.

"There are only two ways you can get played," said Sir Geoffrey. "You need Columbia/EMI to pay for it to be played, or you need to get the DJs who broadcast from 1am to 3am to do you a favour."

"A favour," gasped Ronan. "Is that how you look on the privilege to break new talent?"

The conversation slipped swiftly into mutual animosity.

"There is another way I can get my record played," said Ronan preparing to depart the exalted company.

Three eyebrows raised in unison.

Ronan placed his record back in its costly limited edition sleeve, and reached for the door handle.

"I'll start my own radio station," he said.

"How on earth do you intend to do that?" asked Everitt.

"Who said anything about earth?"

The angry Irishman slammed the door behind him.

And went to sea.

Ronan's daddy had a shipyard back in Greenore, Eire and having heard of a Dutch radio ship Veronica, the young music-mad mogul had a vision, wherein he saw the enormous potential of a floating juke box, bobbing and popping up and down on the ocean.

With his father's help, he purchased Frederica a Dutch ferry, and had her sailed round the English Channel and across the sea to Ireland, where the welders were waiting.

He flew to Dallas, Texas to buy the transmitter and on his way, saw an article in a magazine and a picture of John F Kennedy chasing his daughter around the Oval Office. Beneath the picture was the caption that inspired the name of his beloved pirate ship:

'Caroline holds up government.'

Whenever I visited Ronan in Caroline House in London's Mayfair, I was always taken by the bust of JFK on his desk. He was such a big fan of the Irish Catholic president, that he christened his new baby after the president's baby.

Back in the Greenore shipyard, workers not in the know looked on gobsmacked as something took place that they had never seen before. The ship's mast was given a 150ft extension!

Whilst casual observers around the yard wondered where on earth they would get such large sails from, the inner circle working on the ship and all sworn to secrecy, were only too aware that the extended mast would become a radio transmitter. What no one yet knew, was that the work they were embarking upon would change the lives of everyone within reach of its radio beam.

The MV Frederica was a bargain basement Danish passenger ferry at the end of its sea-going lifespan. Had this unconventional hippie Irishman not come along, it would have been sold for scrap. Never in music history did so much pop come from a can!

In her forthcoming legal lifetime of just three years and five months, Radio Caroline became loved by almost everyone in the UK. There were exceptions of course, the deaf, the dead and the politicians!

For Great Britain's teenage residents, this music tub was what they'd all been waiting for, and her zany DJs became their Pied Pipers, the buglers who led the charge towards the greatest party of all time, the *Sensational 60s*, as the period would eventually be known.

Jan: Radio Luxembourg and AFN

The girls in my class made songbooks containing the lyrics of Czech songs. There was a real competition between them to obtain the most lyrics.

It was one thing reading the words from these tunes, and quite another listening to them. I had heard another type of music years before and I'm afraid this had made Czech tunes belong to others, adults mainly, certainly not me.

The first time I had this amazing musical visitation was whilst holidaying in the Beskydy mountains where Ivan, the son of the owners of the cottage we slept in would, on the occasion of each evening, bring out a loudspeaker, point it down the valley and fill the night air with this strange, magical radio station. It played songs in another language; short songs often with a wild beat unheard of in Czechoslovakia. I was informed that the people talking and those singing, did so in the English language.

It was the same radio channel every night, and when I first had this quite amazing experience, I would have been four or five years old.

As I grew older, when no one else was disposed to want to listen, I started to search the family Philips radio until, finally, I found what I was looking for, or in this case, listening for. The dial had stopped, as if by magic, at 208 metres in the medium wave. Here were the voices I'd heard as a child in the mountains, happy voices, excited voices, nothing at all like the sleepy droning voices we endured on Czech radio.

Later I found AFN with its American DJs who, unlike the Brits on 208, broadcast during the daytime.

I *had* to learn English and started a secret private course with a little old lady who, once a week helped me to understand what Johnny Cash was singing about!

None of the old western books saved from pre-war times, described things the way Johnny Cash did. I learned that 'country boy got no shoes' was about a kid from some village who had no shoes. I'd seen enough domestic animals on my godfather's farm in my childhood not to get too excited about cattle and horses, but Johnny took me to the plains of America and introduced me to buffalo, cowboys and Indians, outlaws and sheriffs. As my knowledge of English grew, it became so much more important to me than simply learning a language. It became crucial that I understood what those amazing singers inside that magic radio were actually singing about, and I doubt few kids were ever so incentivised as I was to learn English.

Even so, Johnny Cash and his cowboy tales didn't dominate my interests once I became besotted with the female form. Suddenly there were beautiful classmates and girls I'd met at the stadium to contend with, and slowly the love songs on Radio Luxembourg started to make sense as my hormones exploded. But hormones in young men created more needs than the desire to jump on females, we needed adrenaline and much of mine came from a most unexpected source, music. This was teenage adrenaline you didn't go looking for, because one day it found you.

And it found me one April evening in 1963, when my communistic world exploded and was finally exposed as complete and utter bullshit!

I was fiddling with the Philips radio, which my father had brought home as a souvenir from his five-year internment in Dachau concentration camp. One of its valves regularly came loose and had to be pressed back into its socket inside the back of the wireless, an operation I could do blindfolded by now.

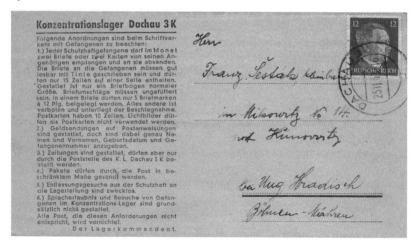

A letter from Jan's father in Dachau

Whether it was the distraction of the song that suddenly came on I'm not so sure, but my hand lost its orientation, missed the socket and 220 volts threw me across the room.

I sat up listening to the tune, the music and the singer. Only a river hurtling down the Beskydy mountains had ever projected so much drive and energy.

I sat there mesmerised until Paul McCartney had finished singing '*She was just seventeen, you know what I mean...*'

I looked at the Philips. The DJ spoke. Another song came on.

But not before he'd told me they were called the Beetles.

Just like almost every teenager in the world, I had the bug!

From that Beetles moment on, I no longer wished to live the socialist life and whenever I tuned to Radio Luxembourg hoping to hear them once again, I escaped to a completely different planet.

Back in my real world, the old lady who taught me English advised me to buy the English newspaper, the Daily Worker, as a reading exercise. So even though it was a bit more expensive than an ice cream, I would buy it from time to time and struggled alone to read and understand the articles. I enjoyed pretending to be a smart boy reading an English paper on the tram, and was lucky enough that nobody addressed me in English when doing so, because then I'd have had a problem for sure, as I was still learning words and struggled with the grammar. Thankfully there were no foreigners riding in trams around Brno during that time, with the exception of September, when the annual International Trade Fair was held in my city.

After buying the first few copies of the Daily Worker, I was very disappointed to find that they wrote far too much about the Soviet Union, in the same way our own communist party papers did. It was an even greater shock when I discovered that the Daily Worker was also a communist newspaper published by British communists. I became concerned that communism existed in this free state… but on the day I discovered their article that featured the group's photograph, I pardoned them for everything and absolutely loved the British commies!

What revelations it contained! They were not called the *Beetles*! Throughout the article they referred to them as the Beatles! I wondered if this was some kind of a Czech joke with words, because even the Czech BBC broadcasts had referred to them as Beetles.

I had, of course, already checked the English meaning of beetle and was quite satisfied that they were calling themselves after the insect variety. Once I had read the article in Daily Worker I returned to my secret dictionary but could find nothing spelt as BEATLES. The closest was the word 'beat', which had a number of Czech meanings, including 'drumming' and 'to out-do someone'. That must have been it, as no doubt the incredible Beatles surpassed all else.

For the first time, the article revealed the accurate names of each member of the group, and the song titles and other interesting facts I either never knew, or had misunderstood. I went through everything with a fine-toothed comb and with the help of my English/Czech dictionary, writing down unknown words, learning their meaning and storing them away per chance I would have the opportunity to translate the article for someone in the future. Translation proved to be unnecessary, as I soon discovered a great Beatles apathy amongst my friends, who perhaps didn't share my nocturnal listening habits and had yet to hear the Beatles for themselves.

Of course I could never tell them of Radio Luxembourg as that was our family secret, and one which could put us all in prison. But when I showed some of my friends the Beatles' article and they didn't respond in any way at all, I learned from their negativity that they probably did not listen to any western radio broadcasts.

I was only sorry not to have a tape recorder and to be able to record my favourite songs from Radio Luxembourg. What a dream that would be to be able to play the programmes including the Top 20 anytime I wanted. Instead I had to wait and hope each night that the DJs would play the Beatles, which they did more frequently as the group became more and more popular in the west.

For now, I had no complaints. Each night 208 was a place to hear some of the most amazing songs in the world, played by young exhilarating musicians and singers. I was not permitted to in the Communist manifesto, but I really did thank God for bringing me Radio Luxembourg.

Tony: The gorillas

Two of the best record pluggers were Colin Forsey and Louis Rogers, (Irish singer Clodagh Roger's younger brother) from CBS (later to become SONY).

In '73 they were coming out to Luxembourg with David Essex to plug his single *Rock on*. A week before their arrival, they had phoned me in Luxembourg to outline a scam in which my colleague, Kid Jensen, would be the central player.

On the Friday of their arrival, I discovered there was a circus in town, a great coincidence and one I used to plant key thoughts in Kid's head. No one knew what was going to happen later, but I gave my DJ colleagues food for thought as we all opened our mail.

"Did you hear about the animals that escaped from the circus?" I asked casually in the office.

"What?" asked Kid, taking the bait.

"Yes, they're looking for the buggers all over town; gorillas, a lama and a fucking seal would you believe?"

After a splendid dinner with him, I interviewed Essex and we all finished up at the Blow Up discotheque ready to party the night away. At 11.30pm Colin and Lewis slipped away unnoticed. At 12.00 it was time for Kid to leave for the late show at 1.00am. I offered him a lift and an Australian lad tagged along to watch Kid at work, oblivious to the unusual show he was about to participate in. David Essex, by then, had retired to his hotel.

"Where's Forsey and Rogers?" asked Kid from the back seat of my Daimler.

"They've gone back to their hotel to get some new records for you," I answered convincingly.

Christine, my wife, who knew of the plans, sat quietly in the front seat, shivering with grave expectancy.

As we reached the top of Avenue Marconi my car appeared to stall.

"Fucking banger!" I cursed, turning the key whilst keeping it in gear.

"Let's leave it Kid, I'll call the Auto Routier from the station."

The four of us advanced down the slope in the darkened park that led to the gates of the station car park, and the porter's lodge beyond.

Christine was ahead of our straggled convoy, almost running.

"Why are you running Chris?" asked Kid.

Her answer came in an incomprehensible gurgle.

"Hey," said Kid conversationally to the Australian guest, "Did you hear about the animals that escaped from the Circus?"

It was an unbelievable piece of timing.

Now Christine was safe as she passed the gates and broke into a canter across the car park to the radio station's front doors.

We were a few yards from the gates when Kid thought he saw or heard something. I stood one step behind them.

"Wassat?" Kid whispered signalling us to stop.

He peered into the darkness of the park, and then a rustling to our left caused each of us to look up to the first bough of an old oak.

The bough moved.

Another sound to our right established another tree, an elm hanging from which, very clearly in the moonlight, was the silhouette of a gorilla.

The three of us tried to make the 10 yards to the gate, but a thud beneath the oak was followed by a second gorilla, who cut us off standing there swaying from side to side in the road.

I heard two very loud farts and followed in hot pursuit of the two backsides that had released them.

Check-mated to the left and ahead, we flew past the elm just as the second animal dropped onto the grass. We were being chased through the park by the two gorillas whose knuckles scraped the ground as they bowled along. Kid was screaming. The Aussie was crying. I disguised my uncontainable laughter feigning a guffaw of fear, like a madman beyond hope.

After one minute of solid running we were halfway round the Villa Louvigny, above us, the lights of the English studio on the second floor.

Unbeknown to us, Paul Burnett who was coming off news duty had overheard the kerfuffle. DJ Dave Christian was on the air and they both clearly heard someone in the park below scream "gorillas!"

Paul strained to see figures running, and then looked on in horror at the outline of two apes bounding along behind them. He had no idea it was Kid Jensen and the Royal Ruler running for their lives below him. Turning to Dave Christian he said, "You've no idea what I've just seen!"

"Stop!" said Kid, as we both ran into his outstretched arms.

"I just remembered something."

We both looked up at the tall young Canadian.

"They smell fear!"

I couldn't believe his tactic. The gorillas were seconds away and here he was trying to calm us down!

"Listen cobber," said our Australian running mate. "That's not fear they can smell, that's my fucking trousers!"

He farted, as if to demonstrate his point. It ignited us, as once again we took flight.

Finally we had circumnavigated the park and the gates were again in sight, but the gorillas had fooled us and were approaching the elm from the opposite direction. We entered the car park, Kid's arms pumping like pistons.

Inside the radio station, Burnett had arrived at the porter's lodge to tell him to call the police. Through the window he saw figures advancing and ran to the large glass and metal doors to let them in. But he hadn't counted on Christine who had bolted the door and stood x-shaped forbidding him, complete fear disguising her beautiful face.

"Christine... people are..."

But the words melted in his mouth as he stared incredulously beyond my spread-eagled wife as he recognised Kid, myself and a stranger, followed by the advancing animals now breathlessly pumping clouds from their nostrils in the cold midnight air.

"Christine open up," Kid pleaded clawing at the glass door.

"Christine, open up for God's sake," cried Paul, pleading for our lives from the other side of the door.

Then, just as we all arrived at the impregnable porter's lodge, one of the gorillas stumbled over the chain link fence that established the director general's reserved car space. The gorilla rolled over four times stopping in a ball as the other gorilla turned, hands on hips to watch him.

"My leg! My fucking leg," cried the decked gorilla, hugging his shin.

"Dopey cunt!" cried Louis Rogers, from inside the hired gorilla suit.

The Aussie went straight back to his hotel without visiting Kid's show, saying that he needed to change.

We never saw him again.

Jan: Treasure mountain

In June, as the summer sunshine once again invested itself across Czechoslovakia, our school organised a three-day trip for my class to visit the High Tatra mountains in Slovakia. Here we gaped at the beautiful and majestic views before us, as we saw the world for the first time from 2,000 metres. But the bigger thrill for all was to find we were visiting a foreign country for the first time in our lives. The High Tatras formed the border between Czechoslovakia and Poland, and for two hours we had technically escaped into Zakopane, a ski resort on the Polish side.

We entered the town in awe, having meandered down the beautiful mountain paths leading into Zakopane. Here were shops so full of goods, so colourful, each so very different from anything we had in Brno. A great silence overcame our group as we ventured forward seeing the individual signs over each shop, indicating a family ownership. It was as though we had stepped back in time to the days our parents had described the Czechoslovakia before communism, and the scourge of Hitler before that.

The shops were like Aladdin's caves, with products never before seen by our eyes. Chewing gum claimed much pocket money, as we invested our Czech crowns without the need to change them to Polish zlotys, as the good people of Zakopane spent them in the Slovak side of the mountain, where basic products were that much cheaper.

Then came a miracle of sorts as I wandered into a tobacconist shop which displayed newspapers, no Daily Worker, not so much as one communist publication.

I gazed, mouth wide open in disbelief as first I looked as though hypnotised, and then snapping out of it, I reached for the International Herald Tribune.

I had always been fascinated and drawn towards everything printed, even when at summer camp at the age of 10, and because there were no newspaper sources in the areas we visited, my mother would mail me the weekly sports paper so I could keep abreast of things back home. I knew of the Herald Tribune, only through the occasions when Red Law mentioned their slights and slanders against the Soviet Union and other socialist countries.

So there I was buying my very first non-communist English newspaper and although it wasn't cheap, it had to be one of the most exciting items I'd ever bought, until I noticed a box of postcards.

My heart stopped beating as I browsed through the postcards, I was sure I'd caught sight of the word 'Beatles'. I rifled away until I found it, but what staggered me was there were grooves in the back of the brown coloured card, and the words Beatles *'Rock and Roll Music'*, beneath which was the name Chuck Berry.

Next I found a similar green card with the name Rolling Stones *'Congratulations'*.

I was alone. My classmates had preferred chatting up the girls rather than investigating a tobacconist shop, and I now wondered what I was holding, how much they would cost me and what on earth I would do if I didn't have enough money left to buy them?

The shop owner was friendly. Polish is a Slavonic language, as is Czech, and so it was possible to make myself understood, and I learned that the cards could be played like a real record on a record player. Now I was really excited. He didn't have a record player in the shop so I took him at his word, but then something else happened to me that had never before happened. To buy both record cards I was a little short of money, so the shopkeeper kindly gave me a discount. No one in any shop in Brno, for as long as I had lived, had ever given anyone I knew a discount. It just simply never happened, money was so tight.

In hindsight, never in my life had I been so lucky as the day I found, and purchased, my first Beatles and Rolling Stones records in the Polish mountain town of Zakopane!

I then rushed to our meeting point to break the news to my classmates. I had hidden the Herald Tribune in my bag, as I didn't want anyone inheriting any problems this possession may attract. I basked in my popularity as my friends reviewed my purchases and chatted excitedly about the find. Some asked if there would be any more in the shop, but I reassured them that these were the only ones. The first and the last, and *I* was the proud owner.

A close friend wondered what the border guards might have to say about me taking English pop music into Czechoslovakia, but I had my answers ready. I would ask why, if they could show British singers like Cliff Richard and Helen Shapiro in our cinemas, should I not be allowed to buy records by other British singers?

But explaining the purchase of the imperialistic Herald Tribune might not be so cut and dried, and as we approached the border search station, my anxiety grew.

We were allowed a couple of kilometres into Poland without passports, and at the border crossing stood a few soldiers and members of Public Safety. My luck stood strong; there was no searching, no questions. I had become a successful smuggler.

Only later did I start to wonder how come it was that Poland, also a socialist country, had so much more freedom than Czechoslovakia?

There and then as we left this country, I was the centre of attraction, allowing each of my classmates to hold and study my trophies. One suggested the station master might have a record player as part of his announcing equipment, and could play the records to us over the loudspeakers on the platform, but we convinced ourselves that he would not have wished to risk his job by playing English pop music to everyone in the station.

Someone wondered if we folded them into funnels and then used a pin, would they play the music? A mad idea, but it demonstrates how eager we all were to hear these precious items, the first Beatles and Rolling Stones records ever to enter Czechoslovakia! The whole class wanted to come home with me when we arrived back at school, but I persuaded them it wouldn't be wise, but they could all have an opportunity to visit me in the days ahead.

I rushed home, straight to the record player, and to my absolute joy the quality was just fantastic, and so much better than Radio Luxembourg, with all its static interfering with the music. I played *Rock and Roll Music* and *Congratulations* over and over, either in repeat mode, or changing one after the other, for hours and hours. At last, I could play my beloved music anytime I wished, and as many times as my heart desired.

These two recordings set me above two music camps that were now establishing themselves, the Beatles' fans versus the Rolling Stones' supporters, who maintained the Beatles were too neat and the Stones were harder musicians.

Of course, my opinion was formed during the personal brainwashing I had put myself through with the two cardboard discs, and I thought both groups were on an equal plateau.

In any dispute, when a Rolling Stones' fan suggested the Beatles were too soft, I told them to listen to *Rock and Roll Music*, and when a Beatles fan suggested the Rolling Stones were too hard, I directed their listening toward the slow ballad *Congratulations*.

I always maintain 'you'll never get a second chance to make a first impression', and I'd grown to love the Stones as balladeers, whilst fully appreciating through hearing their other work on 208, how hard rock they really could be. As the Rolling Stones themselves said, "You can't judge a book by looking at the cover!"

As a matter of interest, I'm told my little cardboard, plastic-grooved records are very valuable these days on the record collector's market.

Tony: The birth of radio

The marriage between music and radio was not easy to consummate. Before they could co-exist, it would take a 100-year battle for radio's potential to be established and music's freedom to be achieved, and both would meet resisting forces. Radio itself would attract many enemies, and amongst these were the newspaper barons, who saw this great instant method of communication as the death knell for their publishing empires.

Governments wanted control of such a marvelous propaganda machine. The BBC wanted it all to themselves, whilst the record companies wanted to exploit it. The Musicians' Union, meanwhile, resisted the promotion and expansion of recorded music, by telling the BBC how many (how few actually) records they could play each day. Across the road in Tin Pan Alley, the music publishers rubbed their hands, as they negotiated payments from broadcasters who would have to pay a fee whenever their recorded copyrights were played on the wireless.

In hindsight, it was a miracle Guglielmo Marconi wasn't assassinated before he could get his invention to market.

The newspaper proprietors successfully lobbied that broadcasting of the news was restricted till after 7pm and, unbelievably, this news vacuum was upheld by the BBC until after the war.

It was suggested that the BBC broadcasters plummy accents would eventually breed a nation of plum-talkers, an end to dialect and accents, the ethnic cleansing of our character.

As radio offered more concerts, parlour music and religious programming, such as Choral Evensong and The Week's Good Cause, vicars feared their flocks would wander. That's when the churches got involved.

The government knew the wireless was too powerful to leave to the welfare of the broadcasters, and they knew that one governing body would be much easier to control than multiple licensed stations, as would happen in America.

The USA was enormous. Britain was cosy, containable and the government intended to keep it that way, so the wireless broadcasters came under their intense scrutiny.

Whilst a few stations were developing around the UK, Marconi himself launched 2LO in May 1922 in London, and his engineer PP Eckersley, became the world's first DJ by introducing gramophone records with impromptu comments. Let's imagine what it must have been like to plug into the electricity, and have a voice come through a box into your home.

It must have been the most fantastic and incomprehensible invention ever. A housewife, washing the dishes listening to a man talking to her from a box! A family, having bathed in a tin bath in front of the fire, now gathered round the box listening to a play about monsters from another planet. It must have been akin to a miracle to the common folk.

The first BBC DJ was Compton McKenzie, a novelist who introduced a stack of records, and was knighted for his efforts long before HM the Queen bladed Sir Terence Wogan and Sir James Savile.

If you wanted to tune in to the phenomenon, a UK license to own a wireless box cost 10/-, or 10 bob, as we called a half of one-pound sterling back then. This put wireless ownership well out of the grasp of the working class, and allowed it to develop into a very highbrow content.

Marconi, the inventor of the wireless had his own monopoly curtailed, when the British government licensed broadcasting newcomers Metrovick and 2ZY in Manchester, 5IT in Birmingham and 2WP in London. A UK radio network *almost* developed, but then towards the end of that remarkable breakthrough year for broadcasting, the fate of British radio was sealed, this great new media's growth stunted as the Postmaster General permitted an unholy monopoly.

An amalgamation of 200 businessmen, all with radio connections or commercial broadcasting interests, was granted a license. They christened their big baby the British Broadcasting Company. And so it came to pass that the land of free press, the fortress island that boasted a Speaker's Corner in its capital, had decided to limit its broadcasting choice to just one company. The British government managed to do this whilst, at the same time, remaining critical of communism and the doctrines of Karl Marx.

Throughout the evolving years of radio, whilst the USA licensed stations on limited regional signal strength, Britain was treated to a national network controlled by Lord John Charles Walsham Reith, a dour man, the son of a minister, who singularly decided what was good and what wasn't good for the Great British public. I think he thought that the Lord's Prayer was about him! Reith was a broadcasting demagogue with the license to kill light entertainment. We were in trouble.

But not nearly as much trouble as the Czechs!

Jan: Gestapo, Nazis and Secret Police

When I first learned that Liverpool was the hometown of the Beatles, I was left almost breathless, as my Uncle Josef had been to Liverpool twice during World War II.

The first time was 1940. He was a lieutenant in the Czechoslovak army, and after the Munich treaty and following the occupation of Czechoslovakia by the Nazis, he had to flee his homeland. This was all very dramatic for him, as it was for both my parents.

When Nazi troops invaded Czechoslovakia in March 1939, they got hold of some documents concerning our army that had not been destroyed quickly enough. This led to the Nazis searching out Czechoslovak soldiers for, as they rightly thought, they could become a threat to them as part of an underground movement.

In August 1939, the Gestapo visited my father's flat in Brno. They were looking for his brother Josef, and asked my father in menacing terms to tell them where his brother was.

Fortunately enough, the brothers had already counted on these possibilities before. In his own handwriting Uncle Josef had written several postcards showing him to have been visiting different places in the Czech Republic. The postcards were sent from these places by Antonín Horsák, an inspector of Czech railroads, from Uherské Hradiště. He consorted with other members of the Czech underground to post them to my father from different parts of the then Protectorate of Bohemia and Moravia, which was what remained of the former Czechoslovakia, now under Nazi rule.

So my father could tell the Gestapo that he knew nothing about his brother Josef's whereabouts, but could tell them that he had been in Olomouc recently, as he had received a postcard from him. It was quite convincing, the Gestapo believed his story on this first occasion.

The Gestapo visited my father again in November and December 1939, but once again he had legitimising postcards ready to show them that his brother Josef was in Prague and Vysoké Mýto, which made the situation easier for my father and confused the Gestapo, who were not at all sure where Josef could be.

One snowbound day in December, the Gestapo visited my father to cynically inform him that they had captured his brother. My father was devastated until he visited his mother, my grandmother Rozalie, to impart the news. But it was my grandmother who gave him the news, showing him a postcard she'd received from Josef under the name of a false uncle from America, who was in Europe on a business trip.

The 'uncle' was safe and sound in Split, Yugoslavia.

All these visits and investigations resulted in the Gestapo's focus turning on my father who was imprisoned on 11 September 1940, together with a group of employees of the Brno Public Street Transportation, for activities against the German Empire. They were found guilty of distributing anti-Nazi leaflets and of supporting the families whose members had been sent away to concentration camps. All these crimes were considered to be high treason. He was put into a jail that had formerly been student dormitories in Kounicovy koleje in Brno, as in 1939 all Czech universities were closed down.

Whilst in jail, from October 1940 until 3 May 1941, my father organized the smuggling of uncensored letters out of jail for the other prisoners.

To receive a note from your loved one in this manner, letting the family know he was alive, was a godsend to these families.

The letters were written with a graphite pencil on toilet paper, (not the soft material we have today). He used tiny letters and because of this, his fellow prisoners nicknamed him 'The Postmaster'.

The messages were brought out of the prison by my mother Emilie, who had by then been courting my father for three years and would visit him in the Brno compound as often as possible. She was a beautiful 25-year-old blonde girl at the time, and she had to smile at SS guards, talk to them, be nice so they would let her in more often than was normally permitted and, more importantly, didn't search her thoroughly when she was leaving. This was the method my mother and father used to get the messages from prisoners to underground movements and families.

Being a pretty young woman, she sometimes experienced troubles rejecting offers and advances from SS men, but she always managed to talk them round, by reminding them it might not be good if they were to be seen with the fiancée of a prisoner. How much my mother went through, only she would know. But one thing is very clear, my mother was extremely brave.

On 3 May 1941, an informer shopped my father. The Gestapo now knew he was organizing the trafficking of uncensored letters out of the prison. On her next visit on 6 May 1941, my mother was arrested and sentenced to 30 months in prison; a light sentence for a treasonable act, perhaps brought about because she was so young. The Nazis may have thought that she could be re-educated during that time. It may seem strange, but Germans really did keep their word on such matters, Mother was sent to Ravensbrück, the notorious women's concentration camp 90 kilometres north of Berlin, where she was imprisoned until 17 February 1944 when she was sent home to Brno, after having served her time precisely to the day.

My mother was trained as a tailor, and was chosen in Ravensbrück to take part in the production of uniforms for German troops. She recalled to me with great glee, how they would put a needle into completed trousers or coats, and how the thought that they may have contributed towards some pain, or at least some discomfort for a Nazi soldier, would make the female prisoners smile to one another.

Mother saw fellow prisoners dying every day, mainly caused by lack of food and water. Many were executed, including children, many of whom were born within the prison. There were 20,000 women incarcerated with my mother in Ravensbrück, including gypsies and Jews from every part of German-occupied Europe. Most would never see life beyond this concentration camp.

Between 1939 and 1945, over 130,000 female prisoners passed through the Ravensbrück camp system.

The worst memory for my mother was a daily roll call at four or five o'clock each morning on Appel Platz (Roll Call Square, as it became known), where all the prisoners had to stand outdoors for a long time, regardless of the weather, as they were counted. Since that time my mother was constantly cold, even 50 years after the war, I always heard her complaining of being cold.

After her release from Ravensbrück in February 1944, she disembarked from the train in Prague, wearing the same summer frock she'd worn when entering prison on a sunny day in May in 1941.

Life in Prague was pretty normal with people going to the movies, living and working for the German Empire, oblivious to the fact that Winston Churchill was already planning D-Day and the Normandy landing, which would end Hitler's grip on the world, free my country, making it ready for the hammer and sickle brigade!

As my mother disembarked from the train, people looked at her like she was crazy. Prague in February is a bitterly cold place to be, even when dressed properly, so it never entered anyone's head that here was a young woman who had just been released from a concentration camp. My mother recounted this experience to me with a smile, recalling that summer frock on that winter's day, and everyone on Wenceslas Square looking at her as though she was a mad woman, when in fact she was a free woman.

My father had followed my mother to Germany in August 1941, transported to Munich and then to a concentration camp in Flossenbürg. Whilst in Flossenbürg, he was injured and got blood poisoning in his finger, and with no medicine available, they simply cut his finger off.

In October 1942, he was transported to Dachau and there he was very lucky as his friend Karel Karnet, who was already there, helped him to get into a working unit plantation as an electrician. With three other friends, they constructed a primitive shortwave radio receiver, and thus were able to receive broadcasts from the BBC and other foreign stations. This team were the Dachau inmates' source for news of the war's development. Being a Dachau war correspondent was a very dangerous occupation, and they had to devise ways of hiding their receiver whenever a German guard approached. The main hiding place was under the wooden paving in the toilets.

They had constructed a good antenna by using Dachau's own electricity wires, which then looked just like a wire bringing current to their workshop. Having thus sacrificed electric wires for the antenna, they had to get the electricity from another source, which was fed underground from a nearby greenhouse. The danger in this activity was such, that you would surely invite the death sentence for *all* prisoners who took part in it, which proves what an incredible thing a radio receiver could be, that people would put their life on the line just to be able to listen in.

Maybe in a sense, I inherited my love for radio from my father. Although I was not risking my life as much as he had when I was listening to Radio Luxembourg or the pirate ship Radio Caroline, a lot of similarities exist. Firstly, this was my only connection to a free world, just as the BBC was for my father and other Dachau prisoners during the war. I also had to choose well whom I could trust with the knowledge that I was listening to such stations, and know also when to be quiet.

Around the beginning of 1944 as my father wrote in his report about Dachau, SS men had started coming to their workshop asking prisoners to repair their own broken radio receivers. Although it was plainly not allowed, somehow it was tolerated, thus giving prisoners in the workshop the chance to listen on better radios with better signals, whilst making all kinds of delay tactics to the owners, telling them that they needed to obtain certain valves or other items. Thanks to this, after Dachau was liberated by the American army, my father got hold of a Philips radio receiver which one SS man left in his workshop for repair, but never had the chance to pick up.

With this very same radio, I spent endless hours in the late 50s and throughout the 60s, listening to Radio Luxembourg and the pirate ship Caroline and, to my shame, never realising that in the 40s, my father risked his life daily when listening to this beloved radio in Dachau.

The only excuse I can give for this blind oversight of mine was the fact that the music of Elvis Presley, the Beatles and the Rolling Stones was so strong, so enveloping of my teenage senses as I dipped in and out of that nightly free world experience, that it obliterated all other thoughts.

Tony: The 1950s

1953 arrived with some real treats in store.

Cinerama theatres were going up everywhere and some clot invented 3D movies, which made you cower or drop your little cardboard glasses, as the Red Indians' horses threatened to trample you.

Marlon Brando came into our lives in The Wild One, whilst TV had us glued to the first big US cop series Dragnet.

Mount Everest was being conquered for the first time.

I'm pleased for Sir Edmund Hillary that he wouldn't live to learn that there'd eventually be climbing holidays for hundreds of novice mountaineers, and that on the 50th anniversary of Hillary and Sherpa Tenzing Norgay's amazing achievement, 350 climbers would scale the peak to celebrate! It's easier now. There have been so many climbers going up over the past 50 years, there's now a path leading to the summit!

In America, years ahead of anything comparatively brilliant in the UK, American Bandstand with DJ Dick Clark was already celebrating its first birthday as America's most popular daytime TV show. This show had 'em all. It was to America what Top of the Pops became to Great Britain, and not one single artist in America made it big without going to Philadelphia where the TV show was shot.

Dick Clark, the show's DJ host, became best pals with Bobby Darin, because Bobby thought American Bandstand had broken Dream Lover for him. I would have corrected Bobby had I ever met him, for it was the Rock and Jive Ballroom at Butlins Pwllheli, North Wales in 1958 where the record was broken. I know, I was there; I saw the audience reaction whenever it got played. Though there was no DJ then, the records just appeared out of speakers.

One channel British TV, under the influential doctrines of Lord Reith, the founding Director General of the BBC and son of a minister, had not even thought of giving an outlet to pop music on their precious TV station.

Few people in the north of England owned their television. We rented from a company called Granada, who reinvested our payments into our very own TV show, Coronation Street!

When you turned your TV on in those days, you waited five minutes for it to warm up. There were valves in the back covered in dust that you had to have replaced when the box went on the blink.

You had to have a technical mind too, and went behind the telly to access the vertical-hold and horizontal-hold buttons you fiddled with, to stop the screen going round. As these buttons were at the back, you needed someone else in the room to tell you when the picture had settled, or you set a mirror up placed strategically in front of the box.

If this happened during the Lone Ranger young boys would be round the back of the telly in a flash. When it happened during In Town Tonight, they just let the picture revolve until dad fixed it.

Panorama was the daddy of all things monotonous to us kids. This current affairs programme was created by the BBC as a thank you to the government for giving them their monopoly license, for politics and politicians were Panorama's prime content.

If it *wasn't* a back-hander to parliament, then this programme was developed as a parental aid to get kids in bed early and, if that wouldn't work, they devised What's My Line, a quiz show, where the panellists talked like no one I'd ever met, and spent 30 minutes trying to discover what people did for a living.

4 February 1953 was a big day.

Sweets finally came off ration.

Uncle Joe and Auntie Lucia had a pub where my parents, Kath and Frank, enjoyed drinking after closing time. As a kid approaching my teenage years, I was allowed to play with Uncle Joe's Philips tape recorder and microphone. Here in the living area, as my parents enjoyed their late night gin and tonics out in the pub, I started my lifelong affair with music, recording Radio Luxembourg through the microphone, and adding my own voice where once there had been Pete Murray's voice. It was a reel-to-reel recorder and I learned how to record the track, cue the tape to the announcement and substitute my own voice. It became a party trick. Once I had perfected a sequence, I'd haul the recorder into the pub where my audience would applaud my work, unknowingly encouraging the DJ in me waiting to escape.

Uncle Joe's brother, Uncle Raymond played rugby for England's Under 21 All Comers, and displayed the cap in the front room bureau, where my dirty-faced friends and I ogled it like the crown jewels.

Ray would babysit me, and I'd creep down stairs to listen to the music on Radio Luxembourg and to watch him kissing his girlfriends.

Far Away Places by Bing Crosby was my lullaby, and I'd creep back up the stairs to sleep and dream of *'strange sounding places, calling, calling me'*.

In the early 50s, whilst we were only just heading towards a second TV channel, TV was taking over from radio in America, as the advertisers moved from audio to visual selling. It was widely believed then, that radio would not survive TV's assault, in the same way that some people thought newspapers and theatres would not survive radio's arrival. Or in the 21st century vernacular, the way the record industry would not survive internet downloading.

Radio people were in panic mode, but then along came its saviour. It came on their turntables. It was called a lot of different names, but no one had yet called it *rock 'n' roll*.

Just as I was listening to Bing, the world's most influential DJ had started to play R&B records on a small station in Ackrin, Ohio. His name was Alan Freed, the future King of the Moondoggers.

Jan: My hero uncles

My parents' experiences in Nazi concentration camps started when the Gestapo began their search for my father's brother in 1939.

Uncle Josef got safely to Split in Yugoslavia, and left there on 3 March 1943 as a member of the 13th Transport Division heading for Marseille. Then he was moved to a gun division and, within it, he took part in the retreating battles of the French army on Marna, Seine and Loira.

Next he was evacuated via Gibraltar on the ship Rod el Farag to Great Britain, where he landed in Liverpool, becoming a squadron commander to a battery of gunners. After a certain time, because of the lack of posts for officers, Uncle Josef was transferred as a backup officer between 27 September and 27 December 1940. With simply too many Czechoslovak officers in England at that time, my Uncle Josef, together with about 100 others, applied when General de Gaulle appealed for Czech officers.

Fifteen officers received permission from the Czechoslovak President, Beneš to serve in the French army, so off he went to fight in Libya, Morocco and Tunis. At the end of May 1944 Uncle Josef boarded the British ship Capetown Castle, together with the Second Armoured Division in Mers-El-Kebir, and embarked for Great Britain, arriving in Liverpool on 31 May. Two months later he found himself transferred to Portland, and on 2 August 1944 following the landing in Normandy, went with the 2nd Armoured Division and General Leclerc, directly to Paris.

When the final battles for Paris were over, my uncle took part in the final French battles close to the German borders, and onto the final battles of the Second World War within Germany.

After the war, Uncle Josef continued serving in the French army, landing in Saigon in former Indochina on 6 January 1946, where he was now a French army major, responsible for the takeover of British war supplies for

French units.

Returning to Czechoslovakia at the end of 1946, once again he became an officer in the Czechoslovak army. But after the communists took power in 1948, he found himself in constant conflict with them, and so finally decided to escape again, this time not because of the Nazis, but because of the communists.

It was the early 50s when he once again found himself in Indochina, where he finally gave his life. This came about because of a French general, who sent his army into a battle that was impossible to win.

And so it came to pass with both my father and Uncle Josef's anti-communist actions, our family were closely watched by the shadowy secret police, right up until the day the Mauerspechte (Berlin Wall woodpeckers) freed us all in November 1989.

Although Uncle Josef left us when I was only a year old, I have felt his presence ever since, either from stories told by my parents, or when studying his English–French–German dictionary, which I inherited. In those days under the communist flag, this type of literature was not seen in Czech households. I knew this book was the answer to many things and would lead me to a better place, than speaking only Czech would. It was an escape route to one of two places, the world or a concentration camp!

And then there was my other uncle, Uncle Franta.

It was one of those early summers, and as usual I went to spend some time with my Uncle Franta in a small village where my father had grown up. As soon as I arrived and unpacked I left at a canter to join my country friends. After playing cards, we set off night fishing to a branch of the Olšava.

The Amazon rainforest could not have offered more adventures than this place so far from city life, wherein flew majestic dragonflies and hooting owls, patiently waiting for their supper as night began to arrive, offering the day's final light-show as spears of sunlight shot through the bows in the forest. The spectacular laser show had its own soundtrack, provided by a frog-chorus and catfish that plopped in and out of the water, where fierce pikes hunted their prey beneath the gently rippling river.

I finally rushed home to dinner to be confronted with the most awful sight I could imagine. My auntie was weeping. I had never before seen her crying and it broke my heart. Everyone was sad and I noticed there was no Uncle Franta amongst them. I was very confused, until I was given the information that he had left suddenly for a working group in the mines of Jáchymov.

I told them I had learned from my eighth grade schoolmates that recruitment to the mines of Ostrava wasn't too bad at all. The miners had a lot of fun and earned a lot of money, they did sports in their free time and, I assured them that dear Uncle Franta would be fine. But no one was interested. On the contrary, they pushed me out of the room and encouraged me to go back to play.

I quickly took a cheese sandwich from the kitchen. As I left I could still hear their discussions about farming concerns and harvesting without my uncle.

It was becoming quite dark as I set off back to the river where we had all agreed to congregate again after dinner. I mentioned Uncle Franta's departure for the job in Jáchymov, which, I explained to my audience, on the one hand it was bad, as my auntie would have to manage all the harvesting by herself and yet, on the other hand, Uncle Franta would earn a lot of money in the mines.

Tonda, one of the older boys, took hold of me around the shoulders and broke the news to me.

"Your uncle was taken to Jáchymov as a prisoner not as a worker, but don't you worry little Jan, he's a strong man and he'll be back sooner than you know."

I was deeply shocked and told them I would not be fishing with them on this evening and set off home alone, struggling to understand the reason for Uncle Franta's imprisonment.

Passing the alders reminded me of the time I had once spotted two hares and how, after recounting this excellent discovery to my uncle, he had wanted to know exactly where I had seen them. Then, as if by magic, the next day two skinned hares appeared hanging by hooks in the pantry. Even if Uncle Franta had poached them, that was surely no good reason to be imprisoned, and I recall that the hares disappeared down our stomachs before anyone could have even known about them.

I thought about how he often listened to illegal radio stations such as Voice of America, the BBC and Radio Free Europe, but nobody within the family would have spread the word, so this could not be the reason either. Going to church was also a crime, but Uncle Franta found this as boring as I did. I went there only because of Grandma Rozalie, influenced perhaps by the ten crowns she gave me every summer.

In truth it was probably half my grandma and half the money that took me to church. Gran cared about my spiritual welfare, she was the one who explained to me the doctrines of communism and the values of sharing fairly. Depending on how many people need to share something, the one who makes the divisions must ensure all parts are equal in order that the last in line receives the same portion as the first.

Grandma Rozalie taught me it is best when people actually want the best for each other. That is sharing, as sharing was meant to be. It all sounded so feasible and reasonable; however, it wasn't working out that way in the society I had inherited.

Uncle Franta had a problem with priests, noting that often they would not practice what they preached. Although he was neither a practising communist nor a Christian, my uncle did not impose atheism on anyone; however, he sometimes mentioned, quite assertively, that if God was so powerful, why had he allowed such horrors in the name of fascism and communism? Indeed it was said in the village that when Uncle Franta agreed to come to the church for a wedding or a funeral, that the church must have collapsed.

This was my childish reasoning to convince myself that my uncle was at work and not in any jail. They had no evidence he was a poacher, nor that he listened to illegal radio stations, or that he did not support the communist law lords.

Continuing my journey home, preoccupied with thoughts of my uncle's disappearance, I consoled myself that prison was quite out of the question for a man so admired within his community. I didn't know it until I was much older, but the admiration for him, so evident throughout my visits, was because he bravely protected the bridge over the Olšava, preventing it from being blown up by the retreating fascists at the end of the war.

After the war, the villagers wanted the bridge to be named after him, but he refused to give his permission.

Uncle Franta was a devout pacifist, and had demonstrated this to me when he saw me playing soldiers with a friend as we shot at each other with wooden sticks. My uncle got angry and chastised me with words that influenced me throughout my life. "You must never, ever point a weapon at any human! Not even in pretence!"

Much later I learned that he had to shoot a fascist while rescuing the bridge, and even though there had been no other option, he struggled to cope with the incident for the rest of his life.

I took these thoughts with me as I journeyed home. Would they imprison such a man? But of course, he was refusing to enter *kolkhoz* as the last man in the village to place his property into the sharing programme. This didn't stop him working hard in his fields and fulfilling all his farming duties. The truth would evade me for years, but as I arrived home on this evening, as no one would say exactly where my uncle was and why he had had to go, I climbed the ladder to a hayloft where I had dozed with him so many times over long wonderful summers. Tonight, however, it was a place of enormous sadness.

Tony: Blackpool & rock 'n' roll

The journey to Blackpool, took us past Hollingworth Lake and out along the East Lancashire Road passing Burton the Tailors' head office, (funny the things you remember). It should have taken a couple of hours; however, there were no drink-driving restrictions then.

It never took less than five hours by which time I and whichever friend I was taking with me, had consumed four ginger wines, six packets of Smiths crisps, a lemonade, peanuts, cheese and biscuits with silver skin onions, a bitter lemon, a jar of mussels and a Dandelion and Burdock. Every time Dad made a pit stop, we were included in the round.

By Rochdale they had done the Artisans Rest, the Junction Inn, the White Horse, the Ship and the Halfway House. The latter was 30 minutes from our front door. We'd been on the road, off on our holidays, for two and a half hours.

We made headway finally when the pubs shut at 2.30. But dad knew one or two pubs between Rochdale and Blackpool whose doors weren't as closed as they seemed.

I also slowed progress, stopping regularly to either pee or be sick.

Two gastronomic experiences in Blackpool continue to inevitably take me back to their moment.

The first time I ever tasted a real pineapple was with Grandma Whitehead on the Central Pier. I not only flip to the time whenever I taste a pineapple, but I stand in front of the vendor, I see him, a youngish man with a sailor's hat and I see grandma rolling her eyes in ecstasy, and I remember her saying to me, "We haven't had these since the war Tommy!"

Next, on top of the pineapple, Carrie (my grandmother) really tested my courage and showed me how to slither a full oyster off the shell, straight down my throat. God bless her memory.

They say how much courage the first person to eat an oyster must have had. It's true. I was that person!

Over the years, whenever I arrived in New York I headed straight for the wonderful Oyster Bar in New York's Central Station to wallop a dozen Blue Points. Wherever I am, as I swallow an oyster, my grandmother's ecstatic expression on Blackpool's promenade those many years ago is manifested in my taste memory.

We always stayed at the Seaview boarding house. Digs we called them. Full board already, breakfast, dinner and tea!

Frankie Lymon's *I'm Not a Juvenile Delinquent* almost put me off rock 'n' roll forever.

Across the road from my bedroom was an amusement arcade with a jukebox. It was Oldham Wakes 1956.

Sam Phillips had sold Elvis' Sun Records contract to RCA for $35,000. *Heartbreak Hotel* was out.

And so were the teddy boys.

And I couldn't read my Dandy and Beano comics for Frankie fucking Lymon & the Teenagers!

Jan: Grand Prix and the free world

I was 10 when my father took me to the International Machinery Exhibition in Brno in September 1958. This event later became the International Trade Fair linked to the trade fair in Leipzig, in the German Democratic Republic, which were the two most important trade fairs in all of Eastern Europe, until the fall of the Berlin wall in 1989.

I was quite astonished to see so many beautiful products from the western countries on exhibit. Even heavy industrial machines seemed attractive to me, and above all I could walk amongst marvellous cars that I could never dream of seeing on the streets of Brno. As we toured around I picked up leaflets in many languages and fell in love with Mercedes, Alfa Romeo, BMW and Jaguar, learning the names of these beauties by heart immediately. I was also very impressed by my father's ability to address some exhibitors in the German language, and appreciated it very much when his discourse with the sales teams led to me receiving souvenirs like ballpoint pens, badges or plastic bags, filled with colourful brochures and information.

Here was the moment when I first realised how useful it could be to understand a language other than my mother tongue. Actually, that isn't quite true. I had this thought before, whenever my parents spoke in German together so that my sister and I couldn't understand things we were not supposed to hear. But this was a more profound experience in valuing another language, and comprehending what a wonderful qualification it would be to be able to communicate with a real foreigner who did not speak Czech.

It was my second direct and live encounter with the free world in just two weeks, having recently attended the World Motorcycle Championship Grand Prix of Czechoslovakia, also held in Brno. The most important race here was the 500cc category, in which the outright winner was Dickie Dale from Great Britain. Even the Czech communist party newspaper, Rudé právo, informed its readers about Dale's victory in a long article with large headlines.

It was very thrilling for me to read in the paper about an event I'd been able to watch in person, and unusually to read about a winner who came from another part of the world. Banner headlines and long articles in our communist newspaper, were usually only reserved for successful sportsmen and women from the Soviet Union and other socialist countries.

I was sorry that my father didn't speak any English other than *thank you* or *good morning*, and such sound bites even I knew. His discussions with foreigners were always in German, which frustrated me, as my head was full of daydreams that we might meet Dickie Dale and ask him so many questions, which might be impossible if we didn't speak in English. Another reason I preferred English was the fact that as a stamp collector, I liked very much the stamps from British colonies, such as Kenya and Tanganyika, which were full of colours and had only English words on them. Uncle Josef spent a lot of time in Africa, Gibraltar and Aden, transporting war material on ships to England. I inherited a great stamp collection and spent lots of time wondering about these other countries.

As I grew older and had learned to read, my parents insisted I keep my uncle's items top secret and never to mention to anybody, not even to my cousin, that we kept items from a western army soldier, who had escaped from Czechoslovakia. It was drummed into me in the most serious tones, just how dangerous it would be should this information ever leak out.

In the beginning I couldn't get my head round it. Hadn't Uncle Josef fought against the Nazis, risking his life just like my grandfather who died in Buchenwald concentration camp, and my brave mother and father who spent many years in Ravensbrück and Dachau? It just didn't stand up in my young mind why I couldn't mention my Uncle Josef at all? In time, of course, I grew to understand these political matters, and became the gatekeeper to our family secrets.

Accordingly, I never broke this rule, although at times it was difficult. Like for example, after Dickie Dale's victory when I was bursting to tell the world he was from England, and that my Uncle Josef spent some time in this country during the war. But keep it to myself I did, and now looking back, I can be quite proud of myself, for what kid can keep a secret when it gives him such bragging rights?

Tony: Skiffle

Another type of music accompanied us down Blackpool's Golden Mile - Skiffle.
Lonnie Donegan's *Rock Island Line* had been around all year and was joined on the jukeboxes by his *Lost John* single.
This was the year rock 'n' roll came to centre stage.
Elvis was treading on Carl Perkins' *Blue Suede Shoes*, and although Carl had penned this Teddy Boy's call to arms and was a stable-mate with Elvis at Sun Records, both their versions were released at the same time.
The King romped home with his follow-up to *Heartbreak Hotel*; Carl's

version nibbled the UK charts for one week. I would think Carl made a couple of million bucks out of that one song alone during his lifetime, and when I saw him playing on stage with his sons in London a couple of months before he died, Carl came across as a man who had made more out of Elvis than Elvis himself, spiritually that is.

It was a confused chart in 1956, and the positions were based on sheet music sales, not record sales.

With three chords and a few daft words making up a rock 'n' roll tune, it's a wonder any of them charted at all. If you could play C, F and G, you could play 95% of rock 'n' roll's portfolio.

Bill Haley shared space in the Top 20 with the *Carousel* soundtrack album. The Goons had two top 20 hits, but Lonnie Donegan had three, and the third caused a whole lotta rockin' – at Number 20, his EP *Skiffle Session*.

Although skiffle really was a passing trend, music genetics owe a great deal to it.

Most importantly, skiffle captured young men's imaginations when they saw how you could form a group, by just nailing a broom handle to a tea chest to make a one-string bass.

The 2i's Coffee Bar in London saw the birth of one of the most successful Skiffle bands, the Vipers whose two big hits were *Don't You Rock Me Daddy-O* and *Cumberland Gap*.

The band members were Tommy Steele, Wally Whyton, Hank B Marvin, Jet Harris and Bruce Welch. Whilst the latter three went off to form The Shadows, Tom went off to try on the King's new clothes, and Wally did children's shows such as the Five O'Clock Club working with puppets such as Pussy Cat Willum. I'm not sure but I think he was the inspiration behind the expression, 'What a fuckin' Wally!'

He also became a BBC DJ, hosting Country Club for 20 years.

Another major bloodline to Skiffle was Richard Starkey, who first did a paradiddle with a Liverpool skiffle group, before moving on to Rory Storm & the Hurricanes and finally, the Beatles.

I suppose John and Paul's Quarrymen also had skiffle influences.

The teddy boys adopted skiffle as part of their musical arsenal and they were stocking up with Gene Vincent's *Be Bop A Lula*, Elvis' *Hound Dog* and Bill Haley's *See you later Alligator*, all of which according to some were 'gimmicks and passing trends'.

Amongst rock 'n' roll's greatest foes was none other than the 'King of Skiffle', Lonnie Donegan who, as Frankie Lymon broke my ears, tried dramatically to distance himself from the whole damn lot of 'em.

In the 1 September 1956 edition of Picturegoer, Lonnie wrote an outrageous article headlined: '*Rock 'n' roll – It's a Swindle*'.

In it he nailed his colours to the mast:

'Stories of big swindles hit the headlines daily – and one of the biggest is happening right now on Tin Pan Alley's own doorstep. You won't find it publicised as such but I'll name it: rock 'n' roll.

Yes I know rock 'n' roll is red-hot pop music news. But it's also big business for the music moguls. That's why I say the rock 'n' roll fans are being taken for a ride. And who are the fans of rock 'n' roll? I'll tell you. Youngsters whose musical taste is undeveloped, or those who frankly come into the 'tin-ear' category.

Harsh words? Anyone with an atom of musical appreciation would endorse them to the hilt. But just let me go on record as saying that rock 'n' roll has no musical value, no variety in sound, nondescript lyrics and a rhythmical beat about as subtle as that of a pile-driver.

Moreover, the majority of the rock 'n' roll exponents can't even sing in tune. Yet this is the 'music' that is sweeping both the United States and Britain.

Rock 'n' roll is a menace in one sense. Musically, I mean. The mums and dads of today's fans had their crazes. But at least they listened to men like Benny Goodman, Harry James, Duke Ellington. Good musicians all of them.

What sort of musical appreciation is a generation brought up on rock 'n' roll going to develop? A pretty debauched one, I can tell you.

There's one ray of hope, though. Rock 'n' roll is a gimmick.

It is sure to die the death. Let's hope it will happen soon.

Well, I've let off steam. Just let me have one final blast. Nothing makes me madder than to be bracketed with those rock 'n' roll boys.

I'm a folk singer. And I intend to stay that way.

No rock 'n' roll gimmicks for me!'

Lonnie's first hit the following year was *Don't You Rock Me Daddy-O*.

His lack of respect for the lyrics of rock 'n' roll suggests to me that he'd never heard Eddie Cochran's *20 Flight Rock,* and had not yet run into Chuck Berry or rock 'n' rolls poet laureates, Leiber and Stoller.

Donegan's own hits were pure prose and set such a high standard of course like, *Does Your Chewing Gum Lose Its Flavour (On The Bed Post Overnight?),* and the award winning *Any Old Iron*, the first ever heavy metal track.

Tin Pan Alley, London's square mile of music publishing houses, was the training ground for debauchery within the music industry, but Lonnie didn't see it that way. These were the people who found him his hits, as usual by scouring the USA for ideal songs for him to cover.

Lonnie forgot that US publishers and record labels had sent DJ Alan Freed, America's founding father of rock 'n' roll, to the retirement chair through their debauchery.

The residents of Tin Pan Alley now entering panic-mode, told the DJs to stay true to 'top melodies'.

None were investing in rock 'n' roll as the lovin' up storm clouds appeared above them. In the same paper that Donegan let rip, the publishers warned disc jockeys that they would incite teenage riots, 'as in the United States', if they gave too much air time to rock 'n' roll!

Of course Alan Freed used a cow-bell as a riot-alarm and drummed out a carnal call on a telephone directory to start the teenage charge, whilst like-minded Murray the K (Kaufman) incited teenagers to do sex with his coded 'known-only-to-teenagers' messages such as, 'Let's go Submarine Race Watchers!'

Tin Pan Alley needed to ensure that these rock 'n' roll invaders were not introduced into British society, and so they publicised their warnings to DJs David Jacobs, Pete Murray, and Brian Matthew, who weren't listening, they were out to lunch with Lonnie Donegan!

'Tin Pan Alley will urge British singing stars to record songs-mainly ballads-that have a more sustained appeal. Make no mistake, Tin Pan Alley HATES rock 'n' roll and is preparing to kill off the craze.'

Les Perrin from Southern Music gave a forceful opinion: "There are indications that rock 'n' roll is losing its grip. Sinatra's LP Song for Swinging Lovers is a top selling disc; the LP from the show My Fair Lady is also strong."

He then played his race card: "The British market for rock 'n' roll is really too small to make it an important musical factor. In America, the Negro population is so big that a vocalist could easily sell more than a million rock 'n' roll discs to them."

In New York, in the famous Brill Building just up from Times Square, an entire skyscraper, housed America's large and small publishers. Unlike their UK counterparts, they were funding tomorrow's rock and pop writers. Young men and women entered this building as a place where they would mix and meet other songwriters to craft their style. Neil Sedaka, Paul Anka, Jackie De Shannon, Carol King, Leiber and Stoller, were amongst the work force.

In 1960 Lonnie wrote this on his EP sleeve notes *Yankee Doodle Donegan*: *Junko Partner is an old blues introduced to me by Leiber & Stoller. These two talented young men have been responsible for many record successes in the USA. Not the least of their triumphs was the composition and supervision of Hound Dog and King Creole by Elvis Presley.'*

Lonnie was like the Dutch kid who put his hand in the hole to stop the dyke from flooding his village. The minute Lonnie saw the flood coming, he started to swim with the tide!

Jan: The record player

My mother was a ladies' dressmaker, and after World War II she had a small salon with two young lady apprentices. The salon was nothing more than a third room in our flat.

After the communists took power, she had to close her traditional salon so as not to exploit her apprentices or, indeed, herself. So she stayed at home taking care of me and my elder sister, occasionally making dresses for friends to make a little extra money, for times were really hard back then. However, luck shone on my mother when a friend told her of a vacancy for a job as a governess in a boarding house for female apprentices. She applied and got the job, and in September 1958, she started to work in the afternoons. The young girls had come to Brno from all over Czechoslovakia to learn various professions connected with telecommunications. It was the only school of its kind in the country, and was situated just a 20-minute walk from our flat.

One Sunday afternoon in the autumn of 1958, Mother asked me to come to visit her and to bring a towel with me so I could take a shower whilst there. Although we rented a very nice centrally heated flat, we were only supplied with hot water once a week because of a coal shortage.

Mother was alone when I arrived as the girls were supposed to arrive from their homes later in the day. After a quick tour I was stationed in her small cosy office, which I immediately grew to like the moment my eyes fell on a huge radiogram in the corner with a record player and a number of records, all items I had never before seen, other than in pictures.

I found a record with a picture of a blonde lady on the cover and four song titles beneath. It mentioned Miss Gery Scott and the Gustav Brom orchestra. Gustav Brom was a conductor who lived in Brno, together with the members of his orchestra.

Not knowing how to use a phonograph, I asked Mother to play the record for me. It was a rather expensive device in those days and a simple one would cost almost 300 crowns, which made it a real luxury item in a household. Mother, for example, earned less than 800 crowns a month and father, just 200 crowns more.

Until then I had no interest in owning a phonograph as songs played on our state radio stations were sleepy tunes, with just one boring tune after another. In Czechoslovakia during 40 years of communist power, radio stations were state-owned, like all other companies, so their miserable, cheerless music became the perfect soundtrack for the austerity in which we lived.

The EP caught my attention immediately and I still can see it in my mind's eye. The picture of the blonde lady was only in black and white, but so full of action with Gery Scott singing close up to a microphone. Holding this EP in my hands was a very big moment in my life, with enormous consequences for me.

I seemed to know intuitively to be very careful and respectful of the vinyl as I studied this amazing grooved plastic. The titles, *Alexander's Ragtime Band* and *Chicago* featured on one side, and *When the Saints go Marching in*, and *Some of these Days* on the other.

Mother started the record spinning on the turntable, and, although I didn't understand a single word of what she sang, I became totally lost as Gery Scott began to sing *Alexander's Ragtime Band*. Gery Scott's style of singing carried me away as, for the first time in my life, I experienced how music alone could help me to escape out of our grey, mirthless country.

Gery became my first audio love, a love that would never die but grow into my passion for western music. Another damned secret I would have to keep or risk the wrath of the secret police!

How Gery Scott happened to come to Brno to record with Gustav Brom and his orchestra was quite an accident. In the spring of 1957, Brom and his orchestra were invited to play in Leipzig, East Germany, during the International Trade Fair, held there every year. Whilst there, Gustav made a short visit to Berlin, which was not yet a divided city with the building of the dreaded Berlin Wall just four years away. Here in West Berlin he met Gery Scott, and when he learned, that she also recorded for the East German label Amiga, he invited her to come to Brno to record some songs with his orchestra. Because she had already made records in the Eastern Bloc, the Czechoslovak Ministry of Culture did not hesitate to give permission for Gery to come to Brno in the summer of 1957.

She was indeed like that famous proverbial swallow, bringing to Czechoslovakia an entirely new musical experience and referring openly in the media to American jazz and mainstream popular music of the 20th century. So Gery Scott became the first ambassador of the style of music from the Anglo-American territories, singing songs from the golden repertoire of jazz and pop music, all performed in the English language. Because many of her recordings on the Czech Supraphon label were exported in big numbers to other so-called socialist countries, Gery Scott's influence throughout Eastern Europe can never be understated.

Any of the great songs which came from the pens of music's great western writers, via the voices of American and English singers, were plagiarised on a massive scale, covered by lesser vocal mortals into the native language of the eastern countries.

Even today you can play an original Frank Sinatra song to a Czech, who will stand back in amazement once they learn that his, and not the Czech-sung version they bought back in the day, was the original version!

In 1962, Gery was signed to the UK's Parlophone label by George Martin himself, around the same time he signed the Beatles!

One of Gery Scott's trumpeters, 25-year-old Jaromír Hnilička, became very famous in April 1961 when writing the music to recognise Russia's Yuri Gagarin´s first space flight.

In 1968 Jaromír relinquished all rights to the royalties he could have earned in protest of the Russian invasion of our country. This may be the only case in the history of pop music, where a writer disassociated himself with his biggest hit for political reasons.

The track following *Alexander's Ragtime Band* was *Chicago*, which I especially liked, but of course I had absolutely no idea what a '*toddlin town*' might be! As I played, the girls began returning from their homes. Some of them chatted with me a little but I realised their chatter was them being polite to their governess, by showing an interest in her son. Still I enjoyed the sojourn enormously.

One particular girl who was talking with Mother seemed to notice how attentively I listened to Gery Scott, raising the turntable arm immediately *Alexander's Ragtime Band* ended, to make it play once again without delay. This girl turned out to be Jana Vorlová, and she asked me why I liked that song so much that I played it over and over, whilst ignoring the remaining three songs? My mother laughed and recounted the time when she was a kid in pre-war times, when neighbours in the house where she lived, bought a phonograph with only one 78rpm record. The entire house heard the tune played over and over for a solid month. One day someone brought it to their attention that it was possible to turn the record over where they would find a second song, as 78s had one on each side. Jana and I joined in Mother's laughter, and 15 years later Mother still reminded me of this encounter with Jana.

In the early 70s, I wrote to an American magazine saying that I'd be interested in exchanging records that were not available in Czechoslovakia, offering in exchange, either Czech classical music, cut glass, dolls in native costume or whatever might be of interest.

Although I recognised that my country manufactured very little else that might interest an American, my letter was published, and among the people who responded was Dave Hogan, a country music DJ from Asheville NC, and Earl Poole Ball, who later played piano in Johnny Cash's band for some 25 years, accompanying such giants as Gram Parsons, Carl Perkins, Rick Nelson, and the great Marty Robbins.

Both sent me promotional copies of singles that had the same song on each side, a record industry tactic to stop radio DJs being tempted to play the flip side, which could weaken their promotion campaign of the chosen song.

This initiative of mine was something to come later in my life but now at the age of 10, I was spinning the very first record in my life, whilst trying to explain to Jana why I loved *Alexander's Ragtime Band* more than the other tracks. She then informed me that she played the guitar a little and asked if I'd be interested in listening to her. I was left breathless. What a day I was having! My first phonogram, and now a beautiful long-haired girl about to serenade me. How happy I was that I hadn't rejected Mother's invitation in favour of playing with the boys in the yard.

After a while Jana returned with her guitar and started to play and sing a popular song at that time, but whilst the tune would have been familiar, few in America would recognise it from the original. The words in Czech translated as follows:

'People say about her that she's unfaithful in love,
But she has only one boy in her heart secretly,
She will be dreaming alone forever,
She will never find peace of mind - beautiful, naïve Diana.'

It was of course the Czech version of Paul Anka's greatest hit, with lyrics hardly as perfect and expressive as Paul's were. The reason for this wasn't a poor translation by some Czech lyricist, but rather that Paul's Diana contained inferences that were banned by the communist cultural censor:

'When you hold me in your loving arms,
I can feel you giving all your charms,
Hold me, darling hold me tight,
Squeeze me baby with all your might.'

The communist cultural censors guarded proper education and upbringing of young people, also making sure only movies with satisfactory content were shown in cinemas. They also ensured that western books, containing what they considered to be bad influences, were never published.
Welcome to communist Czechoslovakia!

During the long summer vacations, together with kids from all over Czechoslovakia, I would go to summer camps, the best of which were in the mountains.

Here we would exchange stories, and the kids from Prague always seemed to upstage us with tales of what they got up to in the capital, for Prague was indeed an exciting place to live. But then it was my turn to spout yarns, and I told them about the World Championship Motorcycle race coming to my hometown, they would be silenced and you could sense their envy as I recounted how the world came to Brno. Telling my tales of previous years

and anticipating the coming Grand Prix, I felt like a king. Prague could
not compete with Brno!

Although after February 1948, the Bolshevik had destroyed most
everything of value from the old order including freeholders, schools and
boy scouts, they left two important events in Brno, the September Trade Fair
and the Czechoslovakian Grand Prix Motorcycle World Championships.
Because of this annual event, Brno boys were probably the only
schoolchildren in totalitarian Czechoslovakia who actually looked forward
to the *end* of the summer holidays.

We had much to anticipate. A whole world of exciting foreign people
descending on us, fences to climb to gain free access to a world of new
western vehicles, and world-class brands that would fill our dreams once
the events had ended.

The Russian propaganda machine was hardly seen at these events, their
exhibitions were easy to avoid, and there were no Russian motorcycles to
be seen in the Grand Prix.

I cannot express how jealous we made those non-Brno schoolboys at
the summer camps with our anticipation of the events to come after the
holiday.

Like all the years before, our anticipation in 1962 was no exception.
The posters around town announced the Grand Prix of Czechoslovakia,
describing it as 'A Friendship of Nations!' How wonderful it would be to
see a sporting event with no Russians dominating, and a few Hungarians
trailing in last!

Of course we all hero-worshipped our own František Šťastný and willed
him to do better than the previous year, but we knew that his Jawa bike
hadn't got a chance against the Nortons.

Our heroes came from lands beyond our confines, lands that sent us
wonderful sportsmen on incredible machines. They came from Italy,
Switzerland, Rhodesia and they were Luigi Taveri, Gary Hocking and Jim
Redman, and we watched as they negotiated the Brno route, their knees
scraping the road as they leaned bravely into the bends.

Back in summer camp, the boys from Prague had stamp collecting, but
we had heroes to worship as each year we watched the bravest, most daring
men in the world revving up their engines, polluting our air with a smell I
can still recall in my imagination.

And what was so special, there was not a Russian on the podium... ever!
And this meant no Russian hymns to sing in celebration of the success of
athletes from the People's Democracy.

When the older boys explained to us the meaning of a People's Democracy
and its method of governing its people with fears and restrictions, we
looked on the newspaper articles written by comrades about the governing

of people as pure bullshit. Our seeds of discontent began to surface. But you had to choose the people you would discuss these issues with quite carefully.

I had an extra instruction, *never* to mention Uncle Franta, who was imprisoned in the Jáchymov uranium mines for more than three years.

Comrades were not forgiving of my godfather for resisting communist rules, so better he was not mentioned in discussion.

I could never understand how we should be afraid of our governors. What kind of governing was it, when older people worry so much about avoiding trouble, and why we responded so enthusiastically to the slightest sign of revolution?

My best friend Lad'a came across such a sign on a trip to his grandpa's in Roštín, where overnight some brave revolutionary had written on the main road asphalt in large white painted letters a rhyme, which seemed to praise Hitler...

Under Hitler Czechs had meat
At this time they all could eat
But now we've got a smaller piece
On Sunday only we have our feast

Of course in the Czech language, this rhymed beautifully.

We all agreed that we liked someone having the courage to mention on a road that we were better off under Hitler during the 2nd World War.

The graffiti caused chaos in the region as the Public Safety Department conducted a witch-hunt for the perpetrator. The Public Safety crowd were the State organised cops, so named by the communists, as they didn't want to call them *policemen*, because that sounded too western.

In reality, Public Safety was the new Gestapo!

The rhyme that caused all this fuss, inferred that Hitler was better than our Russian hosts, even though 50 million people had been killed under Nazi occupation, and even though I was sent to queue for hours to buy meat when I could have been playing football!

Meat or no meat, during the war with Germany, Uncle Franta was a partisan and hid in the forest for years, whilst in the Communist regime he spent several years in prison without committing a crime. It just didn't add up.

The rhyme on the road wound Public Safety up good and proper.

No one had yet been convicted for this rhyme-crime, but everyone was being questioned, and then I started to grow fearful thoughts.

Surely once they had finished questioning the grown-ups it would be our turn, and who amongst us might mention that Lad'a was in Roštín visiting his grandpa just at that time, and who might mention Lad'a was the one who told them of the rhyme? And if they came to me first and I denied everything and then they found out Lad'a had told me, where would that leave me? In prison, undoubtedly.

I was shit-scared as I had seen two Public Safety officers come to our school for some investigations. Fortunately enough, we were not the reason for them.

Tony: Art school

It was 1957 in Memphis. Elvis was buying Graceland and had just made his last of three appearances on The Ed Sullivan Show, the TV show where they weren't allowed to show him from the waist down.

The art teacher at Henshaw's announced an examination was taking place to enter Oldham Municipal Art School. She thought I should give it a crack. (In hindsight, I think she wanted to get rid of me for the day). Somehow, God only knows how, I passed the exam.

For me it was a day off school, a day out, legal hooky.

But I passed and this success resonated in me.

I used to be good at painting country scenes, a brook, a house, a lane, a hill and a sky with clouds and Lowry type figures scattered where the paint fell. But here's where my portfolio ended.

From the age of thirteen I bypassed two very important educational years, painting and drawing and coming bottom of the class.

But I did meet Alan Walsh and Harry Mills who thought they were funnier than me and once, at school dinners, because I took the piss out of them, threatened to shit on my head directly the meal was finished.

There was nothing veiled about their threat, and so I spent the rest of my lunch break on the run evading them around Oldham market.

Harry's dad had a newspaper wholesalers business, a rich source and supplier of Harrison Mark's latest photographic nude studies.

As I was entering Oldham Municipal Art School, pop music was arriving in our living rooms. By 1957, most of us had a telly and if they hadn't, in February of that year when Six Five Special was launched on the BBC, every kid in the country beseeched their parents to get one.

Two great DJs introduced the artists on this show, namely Jimmy Henney (who finished up in music publishing) and Tony Hall, (who had a show on Radio Luxembourg sponsored by Decca Records who he worked for before leaving to manage two funky British bands, the Real Thing and Loose Ends).

Six Five Special wasn't Britain's first pop television. In 1952, the same year that New Musical Express launched its record charts, the BBC treated those lucky enough to have a TV to Hit Parade, whereon artists such as young, smiling Petula Clarke and Dennis Lotis covered the hits of others (mainly American hits). These included *Zing A Little Zong* by Bing Crosby and Jane Wyman (the ex-wife of Ronald Reagan) and Mario Lanza's, *Because You're Mine*, the first ever 45 rpm record to be released into a 78rpm world.

Outside of art school, my muckers were still the Egerton Street gang of my childhood. George Brierley was from the posh end of Egerton Street, at the bottom of Jones Street.

You knew when kids were posh, because their parents wouldn't allow you in their house, and their fathers came home in clean overalls.

But, by 14, we must have got past the unacceptable stage for his parents as we started to convene in his living room, the only living room around greater Egerton Street with a multi-stacking Dansette record player! The legend amongst record players!

Not only did George have big shiny 78s, but the Elvis Rock n Roll album too, which we never stopped playing!

This was my first stage of puberty.

When Elvis went to that party in the county jail, the adrenaline coursing through my body was sufficiently explosive to blow down the prison gates.

As we rejoiced over the fact that Elvis' hits just got better and better with each release, across the Atlantic the Memphis draft board's 60-day deferment to allow Elvis to film King Creole had come to an end.

The King entered the US army on 24 March 1958 and was sheared without mercy the following day. We witnessed this sheering on Pathe News in the cinema; it was uncomfortable viewing.

George Brierly also had Bill Haley, Pat Boone, Lonnie Donegan and other miracles of life but, when Elvis started spinning, I was a gone hip cat! At last I came to understand what the long mirror in Mum's bedroom was made for. Quiffed up with Brylcream to the gills, shirt collar pulled up to a point, it then only took a curl of the lip and I was He.

The cricket bat, which had scored me so many runs at rounders down on Blanche Street, was now a guitar.

And all life's aims funnelled towards having a real guitar.

Then came the bombshell.

"How's about this?" said Harry Mills one disastrous morning.

I was looking at his personal membership card to the Elvis Presley Fan Club.

It wasn't cool to copy. Harry had beaten me to it. I could not now join the club as much as I wanted to.

I was all shook up, devastated by complete envy.

Little did I know then what amazing events the future held in store for me with regard to Elvis!

Fred, our form teacher who had sold Alan, Harry and I down the corridor to the head master, for developing our awareness of the Harrison Mark's female art form, was not popular.

"We can't have every Tom, Dick and Harry looking at naked ladies in class", admonished the head. How could we not laugh? I was with Harry and my full name was Thomas Richard! Even the headmaster laughed.

I took my first guitar to a class party just before the '58 Christmas half term, when you could take games and have a free period.

Inevitably we put some Elvis records on a Dansette and I mimed to *Good Rockin' Tonight*.

Fred suddenly turned off the volume to demonstrate to everyone that I couldn't play a chord to save my life.

I was consumed with embarrassment and thoughts of revenge.

We went to the Oldham Public Library across the road from the Art School to meet a Careers Development Officer.

"What would you like to do when you leave school?" he asked.

"I'd like to be a reporter on the Oldham Chron," I offered.

"Well we don't have any details on that kind of job Tommy, are you sure you wouldn't like to be a carpenter?"

It was suddenly obvious that the bugger had looked at my exam results.

"No, I'd like to be a reporter," I confirmed.

And so he tried to put me on the right line... "Ever thought of a job on the railway?" he asked.

But he didn't pull my cord.

Sandra did. She was a horse-mad classmate

For years people had said to me, "Th'shud be a jockey Tommy!"

If I'd heard that once...

I was fast approaching 5ft, with 4 inches ahead of me.

So it was, that Sandra gave me the names of a number of stables to which I applied for a job as an apprentice jockey.

My previous equestrian experiences were on Billy the goat, who we owned when my parents had been landlords of the Bulls Head, a pub out in the countryside, and Brandy the cart horse I would ride at the farm in Delph owned by my Uncle Lees and Auntie Lucy. Both animals could bear testament to my talent, and becoming a jockey seemed a better prospect than the long list of vocations suggested to me by the Careers Officer.

The first name on the list replied within days offering me a four-week trial in Middleham, Yorkshire at the Gerald Armstrong stables.

Other than a one-length free style race at a cub's swimming gala, this was my first personal accomplishment. The whole family and everyone on

Egerton Street were buzzin' at my prospects.

End of term and the last day at Art School finally arrived.

It was revenge time.

The moment Fred left the classroom, Harry Mills, Alan Walsh and I invaded the exercise book cupboard.

For two years we'd been aware of a quarter bottle of brandy that Fred hid behind a box of pencils.

Harry and Alan drank the lot. The deal was that they would drink it and I would refill it.

I slipped out to the toilet where I filled the bottle with vintage Tommy Whitehead pee returning to replace it in the cupboard.

Revenge in place.

Slightly warm, but good as new.

Fred couldn't comprehend the laughing and sniggering when he returned. We were leaving his dominion today, so when he told us to stop laughing we laughed more.

"Try and turn that volume down you nasty, bald bugger!" I thought.

All my life I've wanted to be there when he reached for his nip, and to hear his classroom filled with laughter once more.

In January 1959, whilst I was writing my application to Gerald Armstrong, another world away 22-year-old Buddy Holly, one of pop music's greatest influences, (Paul McCartney rated him higher than Elvis) was sick of spending hours on the road in the tour bus. Being quite the wealthiest of the rock n roll ensemble, having just split from the Crickets to go solo, he chartered a plane to get them out of Mason City, Iowa.

His final song on stage that night had the lyrics, *That'll be the day, when I die.*

And indeed it was. The plane crashed on take-off killing Buddy, Ritchie Valens (La Bamba and Donna) and the Big Bopper (Chantilly Lace).

In years to come I would work with Paul McCartney on an annual Buddy Holly week celebration, I would sing with the Crickets and Paul McCartney, keeping the Buddy Holly legend in the spotlight.

But there was a lot of music and life to get through before then.

Jan: The transistor radio

As a nation, we were neurotic, for all the right reasons!

But now all worries were packed away for another day. I had the motorcycle race to concentrate on and how to get into the circuit without paying, as in previous years.

At the age of 13, we were victims of the economic circumstances. Ten crowns pocket money was no longer enough even to buy Travex (weed killer), the substance we used for our rocket fuel experiments, an irresistible pastime, until our childhood hobby started to bankrupt us.

As we became teenagers, our economic situation was dire, but we were as wily as kids anywhere in the world when needs must. Whilst our schooling taught us that the peace-bloc would undoubtedly win the economic struggle against the capitalists, we had shortcuts to bring our personal income to an acceptable level by exploiting other people or at least, to make money with little effort.

The turning point came when we ran into the Car Collectors Club, specifically the anoraks who salivated over cigarette cards, matchboxes, stickers, badges and the like. They had their own marquee during the trade fairs. Here's where they bartered, where kids and grown-ups became equals, their status depending on their sticker collection wealth.

A local scrap merchant offered stickers as part payment for scrap items people brought to him, and we began working for him in exchange for the stickers he would dish out in handfuls to us at the end of each day. I studied which stickers had the higher values amongst the traders and so became an entrepreneur.

I advanced to badges earning two or three crowns for company ones, and a great deal more for the harder to find western car brands. The collectors sold them individually for more than we had sold them, but we were wholesalers and business was good.

In Czechoslovakia around this time, a shop known as Tuzex, appeared in Brno and other big cities; Tuzex came from *tuzemský export* (domestic export). In this store you could buy western items, but you could only do so if you had special Tuzex vouchers, which had to be bought with foreign currency or Czechoslovak koruna on the black market. It was altogether mysterious to my friends and I, a little cloak and dagger, and somewhat dangerous, because here was the west we had been bred to hate, selling goods in a communist state. Very weird.

One day in the Tuzex window I saw something I coveted, something I'd dreamed of owning, a beautiful transistor radio.
I started to visit that window like some teenager going by a girl's house just to get a glimpse of her.

There was never a queue inside the Tuzex shop, but there was always a crowd ogling the window display outside. Unfortunately there was also a hard-faced porter at the door who you would never get past, unless you had your vouchers.

We dealt with porters at the cinema quite cleverly because at the entrance there were always two taking tickets. The trick was to look towards the one on the left as you passed the one on the right, giving the one on the right the impression you had handed your ticket to the opposite porter. We saw lots of free movies this way. But we hated the Tuzex porter even more than the Public Safety officers, because they were over zealous and literally stopped us 'going to the west', which is what we would be doing by browsing the products inside Tuzex.

We had an anti-commy joke about this magical shop, whereby a cop won the 'Idiot of the Year' competition, when he jumped over the counter in the Tuzex shop and claimed political asylum!

We were too young to question why such stores and such vouchers existed for certain people, but as you can perhaps surmise, the rich somehow found ways to obtain the vouchers, and visiting foreigners brought with them their currencies which they could exchange for Tuzex money.

The transistor was my obsession. A dream too far just then, but something I would one day hold to my ear in my own bedroom with an earplug beneath my pillow, when I was supposed to be sleeping. For now though, I shared the electric concentration camp wireless with my parents, and Radio Luxembourg and AFN were not stations they would tune to very often with the thought-police sniffing around every neighbourhood.

Tony: The jockey

The tunnel was dug.
Mum and Dad were taking me to Yorkshire in the Velox.
Sing Something Simple was escaping from the car radio, and I was escaping my birthplace.
We drove slowly down the St Stephen's Street cobbles. Uncle Ray stood leaning against the Egerton Arms window, the pub at the bottom of my street, where my Grandma Whitehead had been a single mum wartime pub landlady.
He looked melancholy but managed a smile as we cruised by.
Jack Smith had waved at me like I was the heroic one.
People stood at their doors like they were waiting for the Oldham Carnival Parade.
But there was only the Velox.
Dad stopped the car for my grandmas who each, in turn, reached inside to squeeze and kiss me. Grandma Whitehead pushed a five-pound note into my palm, and Grandma Hart gave me four half crowns. They were both crying.
Ray leant in the car last.
"See you in the Derby Tommy," he said stuffing a fiver in my top pocket.
The car turned left down Egerton Street. Dad was taking us via the Bull's

Head and Garner's Farm, and on over the moors to Yorkshire.

I recall looking at Daniel my son when he was 15. Although he was taller than I had been at that age (which wasn't too difficult!), I could not imagine such a young thing being put to work away from home.
But such was my strange choice.
"You don't have to go," my Mum beseeched as my Dad applied the brakes to let the 59 bus pass by.
"OK, great, LET'S TURN BACK DAD!" My thoughts screamed.
As if he'd heard me Dad looked at me through the rear view mirror.
"Tommy, you can still change your mind you know."
"OK, it was a silly idea. I don't even want to be a jockey. Take me home," my mind created the script.
But all that escaped were tears, which I hid by turning to wave a last farewell to Uncle Ray.
You see, once people found out that I had been accepted for trial at a top stable, I became a personality. People would stop and talk to you about it. Your mates revered your escape plan. The people around Egerton Street were relying on me. THEY WANTED ONE OF US TO ESCAPE!
And the humiliation caused to my family, were I to turn back now, as much as I wanted to, was unacceptable.

The Cliff Adams Singers medley increased in tempo as they sang, '*I love to go a wandering… valderee valdera…*'
The Velox engine groaned like my soul.

Gerald Armstrong greeted us at the door to his manor house, which flanked the stable yard.
He was a dapper man who spoke posher than I had ever heard.
In his office he explained the terms.
"We don't spoil our boys with money, although we do furnish them with a new suit each year, shirts, underwear, riding boots etc."
He then told us how much he wasn't going to spoil me by.
"For the four week trial period Thomas will be paid 2/6d per week. Once he's accepted we will increase his payment to 4/6d and, for the duration of his six year apprenticeship, he will be given a one shilling a year increase."
2/6d, the old half crown, was in millennium terms around 12p. One packet of Park Drive cigarettes, a Bounty bar, packet of Spangles and 2ozs of lemon sherbets and I was stony broke.

Like all the apprentices at Armstrong's Dickensian unit, I relied on my parents for weekly parcels and envelopes with 10-shilling notes from Uncle Ray and my grans.

There were 10 midgets with whom I shared two bedrooms in a house on a slope, north of the biggest pile of horseshit you've ever seen in your life!
The house was donated to the apprentices by Ted Larking, one of Gerald's

success stories. Christ knows what he'd had to live through to inspire such generosity to his unknown successive apprentices!

Armstrong reared an even bigger success story. As a lonely apprentice, it was the wit and humour of Willie Carson that got me through many moments of homesickness and teenage depression. Willie, a couple of years older than me and therefore on 6/6d (33p or 45c) a week, tried to show me how to 'push' a horse using a buffet as his nag. He'd obviously got that right, because for 30 years whenever I've watched Willie riding for the Queen or winning The Derby and every other conceivable Classic, when his arse is in the air and he's scrubbing away in that last furlong, I can still see him on the buffet in Middleham.

Like most teenagers, we each had our own transistors and a pillow under which we would escape. Elvis was still going strong with *One Night*, the horniest record ever released and he'd followed it up with *A Fool Such as I*. He was doing well with Uncle Sam too, having been promoted to private first class. I hummed his tunes all day and used the pitchfork as a microphone.

We arose at 6am to muck-out and feed the horses. By 6.10am I had a sack three times my size and eight times my weight loaded on my back, staggering in a full crouch position towards the muck pile.

"*Hi Hoooooe,*" we sang like the eleven dwarfs.

Halfway to the muck pile, the horse's pee would seep through the sackcloth, and through your clothes and trickle down your back and down the crack of your bum.

In 1959, apprentice jockeys did not smell good, unless of course you liked thoroughbred's excreta. We carried arm-wrenching buckets of water to specified animals, each apprentice having at least two horses that were allocated to his care. I left most of my water down the yard and always seemed to find, in my knackered state, that the troughs were just too high for me to reach. The stable architects worked on a horse's dimensions, not those of an apprentice jockey.

The thoroughbreds were fed twice a day, when we would fill their nets with hay and their mangers with oats mixed with honey, treacle and glucose, which Tom poured from huge bottles that glugged their gooey contents onto 10 extended forefingers, before reaching the oats.

Horses scheduled to race were treated to a bottle of Guinness mixed in with their feed, which they'd smell as you came up the yard. Entering their box with its freshly laid straw, their heads would strain in their head collar, the rope pulled tight, their eyes popping wide with mouth-watering anticipation.

I often wonder what those horses would make of Budweiser!

Some of the stallions had erections and would be masturbating as you walked into their box. This wasn't regarded as good for them if they were near race-day, and so it became our job to dissuade them. Not an easy task for lads who could limbo dance under their belly, without so much as bending!

So the way we did it was by flicking a tea towel at their willy as it slapped against their undercarriage. These willies, as they fantasised about their favourite filly, were larger than my right leg!

I couldn't help wondering how wonderful it must be to be able to do it without hands!

As the 'last lad', it fell to me to light the fire in the house, collect firewood from the nearby forest, which contained a massive rookery that scared me shitless. I also had to run errands to the tuck shop at the adjoining Fawkus' stables across the meadow.

But worse, by far, I inherited Silver!

Silver was one of two ponies owned by Armstrong's youngest daughter. No one told me it kicked.

Tom, the Chief Lad, and the other apprentices took great pleasure in keeping such facts to themselves, and waiting for the new lad's initiation.

As I came flying through the air out of Silver's stable, the entire ensemble stood in the yard roaring and applauding my indoctrination.

And more humiliation awaited me.

My first time riding to exercise on Middleham moor was an exciting occasion, even though I was sitting many hands below my colleagues, on board Silver.

The racehorses and their pilots towered above me as I clip-clopped happily alongside them.

Winter was upon us and we'd all wear the warmest garments, three or four jumpers, two pairs of thick woolly socks, balaclavas, caps, scarves and, unashamedly, long-john underwear. But it was no protection from the wind that penetrated all our storm proofing on that brutal Yorkshire moor. It took an hour of walking and trotting from the stables to the jockey-filled gallops, and we were all ready for the cantering to begin in an effort to kindle our blood in our frozen veins.

"Awaaaaygh!" yelled Tom, from atop his steed and the cavalry charge began.

Pete McMahon on Magic led the field, Geordie on Clover, Willie Carson on the magnificent Pappa's Image.

One by one the 10 Armstrong apprentices and Tom the Head Lad aimed their mounts in the direction of a watery moon and, with exhilarated cries, our iced ears were forgotten. Now it was balance, head down, and knees gripping like fuck!

And the 12th passenger was me, caught in the back draft of 11 thoroughbreds. The Lone Ranger, at last!

After a mile, the horses ahead broke from full stretch to a canter, their energy spent. Silver, beneath me, galloped on towards them two furlongs behind. My cap flew off, lost on the moors forever, together with the tears that were forced from my squinting eyes and my knuckles were bone-white clenching the reins.

Still ahead of me, the apprentices slowed to a trot, bending forward majestically slapping their animals steaming necks. Silver galloped up to them. I pulled hard on his reigns but there was no response. The brakes weren't working!

We drew level with the posse, and ever onward full pelt past them.

I was leaning back in the saddle at 45 degrees, using my stirrups and reins to get the message through to Silver that it was over.

Behind me, mixed in with the howling wind, I heard guffaws.

It was an old trick. Silver would tongue the bit in front of his grass-green ivories and simply smile, his brakes redundant.

"*Sod it!*" I cried and kicked him in the rib cage.

If that's what he wanted, I was ready to show my audience that here was a future winner of the King George!

And that was his cue to stop, all four hooves sliding across the frost-hardened moor, his nose almost scraping the ground.

Seat belts for ponies had not been invented but, thankfully, there was no windscreen - just the morning air through which to fly! I soared in a perfect somersault straight across his arched, silver mane landing, first past the post, in a pile of grade 'A' manure!

The 10 potential course and distance winners surrounded me with their chortling riders.

Not for the first time I thought, "*What the bloody 'ell am I doing here?!*"

Jan: The good boy

Radio played such a big part in my family's lives. My father used it as a means of survival whilst in Dachau concentration camp, I used it as a counterbalance against the communist education and philosophies that tried to own my spirit. My mother and father had the Nazis to contend with, whilst I inherited the Russians. Take your choice they were both cancers within our society.

In 1963, our teacher at the People's Academy of Science, Technology & Art lectured us on how we would become better citizens within our lovely commune. It took a whole page in my schoolbook to write them all down and topics included:

1. Towards communism
2. Educating the new man
3. What makes a man of art?
4. Discussions with the young ones
5. Production modernisation for a better future

I was speechless as I viewed this list, wondering what on earth they were trying to achieve? What communism do they want that would thwart our pleasures so?

I considered 'Educating the new man' and asked myself *who* educates him? Would it be those greasy party bosses who we saw once a year, lauding it over us on their May Day parade tribune, waving to the poor workers?

As for the 'Man of art', the closest art that I could see were the sculpted statues of Marx, Lenin, Stalin, and our own Gottwald, the largest of the world's Big Brothers.

I pondered the subject 'Discussions with the young ones'. Nobody had ever talked to me about *my* needs, and by the time I reached Production Modernisation, they were talking to my hand!

I doubted anything on their list could deliver a better future, and I knew beyond any doubt, that their better tomorrow was not a thing that interested me.

What I wanted was a better *today*, which for starters would have records by the Beatles, Elvis, the Rolling Stones and Johnny Cash and a radio station like Radio Luxembourg, the Station of the Stars!

It was September 1963. The Russians were still running the show in Czechoslovakia, even down to insisting our first language was Russian, a torture we endured from the 3rd grade.

Now, after nine years, my primary school days were coming to an end, and I was happy and excited anticipating high school after the summer holidays.

The entrance exams in spring had been quite easy, and I was grateful the government hadn't made family trees a part of the qualifications, because I would have failed.

If Uncle Franta's long years spent as a political prisoner in the uranium mines of Jáchymov hadn't scotched my chances then Uncle Josef, fighting bravely in Indochina after he had emigrated from our country, would have been totally unacceptable as he became a major in the French army!

My family lineage was contaminated with anti-communist genes. As history will show, most Czechs hated the regime and waited for the day when we would rise against it. But for now there didn't seem a hope in hell. I'd joined the Young Pioneers (Pionýr, a youth organisation for 8 to 15 year olds), after my parents were convinced by their friends that this was my best chance of gaining admission to High School.

My friend Pepek said I was a fool joining, after resisting to join for so many years. But I actually enjoyed the Pioneers' meetings and walks with kids, and I adored our leader Dagmar, who was a sister of my favourite classmate Eva.

I wore the white shirt and blue neckerchief with pride, and whilst I was not a socialist, I was very much a social animal.

High School gave me wider social wings and I relished the thought of making lots of new friends, maybe some who loved music as much as I did. I enjoyed talking about my future with friends, but was aware of envy, which I feared since Pavel's experience.

Pavel Srnda was just two years older than me, and the bravest cyclist I ever knew. He was a victim of a drug similar to thalidomide as a child, having been born with a part of his leg and his hand missing.

To counter this, he had the handlebars on his bike turned round the opposite way. Of all of us daredevil kids, his skids on the sand were absolutely the best. Neither was he afraid to ride off the Brno tram platforms at full speed. We watched in pure horror and excitement, but his bravado never once let him down.

Pavel Srnda was friendly to everyone and once, when explaining the circumstances of his birth, he drove us all to tears when he confided they had all wanted to let him die at birth because of his malformation.

When he was admitted to High School two years before me, someone commented, "He's only been admitted because of his handicap."
Such envy. It was a disease in my country.

And so, when talking to someone training to be an apprentice, I hid my joy at the thought that my destiny would not lead to becoming a worker even though, according to the commie manifest, you could aspire to nothing greater.

There were mottos and catchphrases everywhere bigging-up our state, which was a state of workers and farmers who were the leading force amongst our population.

I felt remorse for friends whose lives would become manual, nine to five for all the workers I knew seemed dissatisfied with their lot. If they weren't complaining about the work, it was the poor pay in comparison to those whose advantage was their membership in the omnipresent, yet quite invisible, Communist Party.

I knew not what the communists thought of their lot, because I had never knowingly met any other than through newspapers, newsreels or May Day stands. I knew one thing, their slogans just couldn't be true, *no way* was the land worker the leading force. *No way* was a land where transistor radios were unreachable to the common worker, yet instantly available for the well-advantaged, a place of equal rights with a superior factory and farm worker populace.

Take my dear auntie, worn down with the work on the Collective Farm, getting by as her husband, Uncle Franta served his time in jail, living in a house with an earthen floor in the hall, one room and a kitchen smaller still than a cow stall. *This* was *the leading force?*

My eyes were wide open, as were my ears. Neither I, nor my friends, could be fooled by newspaper propaganda but we ignored their bullshit, never discussed it and just accepted it as our lot. But one thing was certain to me, you could achieve far more with your brain than with your hands!

And so I was looking forward to high school and, for the first time in my life I was not sorry that the holidays had ended, far from it. The first week was not even school, apart from day two when we received our textbooks. For the rest of the week we all joined in the harvesting of grain in farms in rural Brno.

I did have a concern however. My textbooks did not contain one English book. In my last days at school I got quite excited about learning my favourite language, so that I could fully understand what those DJs were saying on Radio Luxembourg.

Things immediately became more fantastic than I could ever have envisaged right from day one. I made new friends who loved music as much as I did, and a few took me into the bosom of their friendship when they confided in me that they, too, listened to Radio Luxembourg!
We had plenty to talk about.

But this was the quiet before the storm for many of us, as just before our time in rural Brno with the working class and cooperative farmers ended, for whatever reason they'd seen fit to send us on this enjoyable agricultural sojourn, someone broke the news that we were to be split into two language classes. One half would learn English, whilst the other half would study Spanish.

To a man, we had requested English as our preferred lesson alongside Russian, which was mandatory.
I was numb. I was speechless. I was angry. I was frightened to death. Spanish? Who the hell needed Spanish? Do they speak Spanish on Radio Luxembourg? Do the Beatles sing in Spanish? Of course not! So why should I study Spanish?
I was devastated,

The explanation finally came. It was because the Cubans led by Fidel Castro had won their fight for peace (communism) in Cuba. Like Czechoslovakia who had this amazing advantage for 15 years, Cuba was our new neighbour in the community of peaceful and socialist countries. Fucking Spanish!!!

It became apparent once again as our whispered saying went: '*The fight for peace is about the same as to fuck for virginity!*'

The day of the language barrier arrived. Half of us would be learning Russian and Spanish, half Russian and English, a mini-Iron Curtain was about to be erected.

40 textbooks arrived, 20 Spanish and 20 English.

I threw my head into my hands as the teacher began to reel off name by name, those who would be in the English class.

Cheer after cheer went up, but my hands continued to cover my eyes. There were just two names left. I felt tears welling in my eyes beneath my sweaty palms.

And then my name was spoken, and then Mojmir the very last. I wanted to throw my school papers in the air to celebrate, half the class did too, but we only had to look at the sad faces around us not to rub so much salt into their literary wounds.

The only exception to the sad group was smart Helena, who had already got the command of English, French and German from secret private tuition. Spanish would be less of a problem for her than the English teacher Mr Machander who, because the directive from Prague insisted on Spanish lessons and because we had no Spanish teacher, poor Machander had to learn the language himself.

He must have been one of only a few teachers in the world who was just one lesson ahead of his own pupils!

Tony: Five foot Elvis

Everyone smoked in this land of midget weight watching apprentice jockeys. It suppressed appetites.

We all looked forward to the letters from home with their 10 bob notes (50p/66c), but some looked forward to better benefactors. The horse's owners!

Tom would tip the apprentice off when a pending visit was anticipated, and special grooming was implemented.

The horse's mane would be plaited and the brush-down would leave creative criss-cross designs on their hindquarters, and their hooves would be painted black and every ounce of shit would be painstakingly removed from horse, stable and jockey.

The smart apprentice would stand stiffly at the stable door as Gerald Armstrong chaperoned his client down the yard.

Pete McMahon, who coincidentally also came from Oldham, was the longest serving apprentice and looked after Magic. Her owner usually gave him £50 on his biannual visits. Everyone aspired to muck-out Magic!

Middleham village was like Lillyput, filled with midget humans wearing elfin suits. At the top of the village was a blacksmith's stable with bellows and anvils, and sweating, muscular men wielding hammers that yanked out old nails in warn, or damaged racing plates.

The midget jockeys would hold the horse's reigns close to the bit as the animal chewed cud, like a smart guy in West Side Story. Occasionally the thoroughbreds would toss their head with a loud whinny, lifting the apprentice six inches off the ground.

The fearful eye whites looked like scallops, popping out of their sockets staring sideways at the blacksmith with grave mistrust, as he bent their leg back at the knee, holding it in a death grip between his arm and thigh. Then the blacksmith went to work attacking the hoof with his clawed hammer and a mouthful of rusting nails.

There were pubs where I'd take Mum and Dad, and their friends from Egerton Street who'd accompany them, on the great occasion when I would give them my official tour of the yard.

Naturally, they'd all ask for hot tips.

Our Saturday nights began with a four mile walk across Middleham moor to the cinema or the barn dance. Most times we'd finish up in a large house just off the village square, where the doors were thrown open to us by a wealthy land owner, who enjoyed our company and set up card tables in front of a huge crackling log fire. Maybe he was gay, but the thought never crossed my mind in those days, and I have no evidence to support such a malicious thought.

My dreams of getting rich quick were confounded by two realisations.

Firstly, Armstrong would only give each apprentice three or four races in their six years with him. If you didn't push yourself first past the post; if you didn't succeed in that handful of tottering minutes, you were mucking out for the rest of your life.

Secondly, the thought that one would win with 'insider information', you know, from the horse's mouth as it were, was also dashed when everyone of us placed an on the nose week's 'wages' on a cert from the Fawkus stable. The horse came last of five. I was broke, and so, too, the myth.

For seven days a week, this backbreaking work never ended. The bit of free time on Sunday was spent earning an extra shilling (5p) doing odd jobs for Gerald and *odd* they were.

One Sunday, he gave me a can of Crown High Gloss blue paint and had me paint his daughter's old Austin car!

He'd heard I came from an art school.

Each afternoon, instead of siesta like the rest of us, the apprentices due a race ran round the fields returning to the house, bolting up the stairs and throwing themselves under as many blankets as they could borrow. This was the forerunner of the sauna. I once helped to pile 22 blankets on top of Willie Carson; he almost suffocated for the sake of losing an ounce.

Eventually I was given my first proper horse to look after. She was called *Clover*, a 10-year-old filly at the end of her uneventful career.

Ginger, a likeable apprentice, was to be given his first chance to ride in a race, and Clover her last. They were both entered into the 3.15pm, a 5-furlong apprentice race at Ripon some 20 miles away from Middleham. I was as excited as Ginger, my first day at the races where I would walk Clover around the paddock, Mum and Dad watching me like I'd won the Derby.

Ginger's mum, a widower from Sutton Coldfield, was also proudly watching as the owners and Gerald Armstrong entered the parade ring circle, followed by her dapper son all kitted out in his silks. I gave Ginger a leg up. He was shaking like jelly.

"Keep her well covered until the last two furlongs," instructed Gerald Armstrong. I held the bridle tightly until we were on the racetrack; Clover whinnied with excitement, jerked from my grip, raised her front hooves in a classic 'Hi ho Silver' and they were off, both chasing their careers.

We watched from the vantage point reserved for stable boys adjacent to the winning post.

The flag went up, no starting stalls in 1959.

"They're under starters orders," a metallic voice announced from the tannoy. "And they're off!"

But Clover wasn't. She dwelled. Idled. Had second thoughts, or whatever horses think. Then, making up her mind, off she set, 30 lengths adrift of the pack.

No schoolboy ending to that tale I'm afraid.

Clover and Ginger were retired!

"You'll never ride for me again," scolded the furious trainer, with anger he hoped would appease the grim-faced owners, or at least sidetrack the blame from himself.

It was a wasted day for everyone, except Ginger's mum who now strode into the unsaddling enclosure, eyes blazing.

"C'mon love," she said dragging Ginger by his silks. "Take no notice of 'im, we'll get you that job in't brewery!"

"You must let him weigh in or else we'll be fined," called old Armstrong.

"Tek it out of 'is bloody wages you tight bugger!" she screamed in her final flight.

My humour and my ability to sing any of the current hits kept me popular around the stable. I'd challenge them to name any Elvis song and, at night, I'd stand on the bed my parents had bought for me, and I'd swivel

my hips holding a shovel guitar and churn out the tunes.
An imaginary King, in the land of small lads.
I grew by the verse.

Jan: The Young Ones

The music lovers amongst us had all miraculously got through to the English lessons. We had so much in common and derived so much joy discussing music and musicians, singers and the latest tunes we had heard on Radio Luxembourg.

Then we heard something quite amazing. An English musical was to be shown in our cinema. Cliff Richard and the Shadows, the Young Ones! It was the talk of the campus. We all rushed to buy tickets as soon as they became available.

Actually this wasn't to be the first pop musical to be shown in Czechoslovakia. Five years earlier, people saw an excerpt from a Bill Haley concert at the Berlin Sportpalast. It was only 30 seconds long, but people had the chance to see a 30-second excerpt of Rock around the Clock in newsreels in all our cinemas. Some people went many times just to see this 30-second part of a film.

A communist, anti-western culture, journalist reviewed this newsreel clip along the lines of, '*Capitalist culture grows worse as crazy young music fans go wild for their hero Elvis Presley!*'
The uninitiated who couldn't tell the difference between the voice who sang *Heartbreak Hotel*, and the voice who sang *Rock around the Clock*, went through life for a number of years believing Bill Haley to be Elvis Presley!

We who listened to the outlawed 208 on the Medium Wave (AM) knew differently. We knew the man who sang *Rock Around the Clock* and, the man in the newsreel was Bill Haley, a man with a kiss curl haircut who looked old enough to be Elvis' father! Commie journalism! They'd have you believe that black was red! Now Cliff was coming to town in a complete film, and I cannot explain how thrilling it was to anticipate, especially in those last few days.

To be honest we found it a little anti-climatic, as it certainly wasn't a rock 'n' roll movie like we'd come to expect from the guy who sang *Move it*. Whilst we were a little disappointed, we agreed it was ok especially the title song, which we already knew from Radio Luxembourg.
But, here was the thing: the film had subtitles, which meant we could perfect our English, not a bad reason to see the film a dozen times!

I couldn't for one minute see our Prague rulers allowing *Blackboard Jungle Jailhouse Rock* loose on our society. Needless to say the Czechoslovakian radio stations didn't play anything from movie soundtracks at all, it all had to come from Luxembourg, our light at the end of the communist tunnel.

And so it came to pass that Cliff Richard and a handful of friendly DJs taught Czechoslovakian kids how to speak English and use it in context and, for us, Cliff became the very first singer singing in English on the big screen. He made a lot more impact in our part of the world than perhaps his fan club newsletters give him credit for!

I celebrated New Year's Eve 1964 in a great frame of mind. I felt I had left the kid in me behind at the door to high school six months earlier. I was so keen and enthusiastic; I had become one of a group of students who arrived at school one hour before the official opening time of 8am, or 7am for gymnastics. Often we would arrive ahead of the janitor.

There was much to discuss before lessons began, unfinished homework had to be copied from the more diligent and studious amongst us who understood and supported our distractions. I, for example, played ice hockey and practised light athletics, including shot put and discus throwing.

Others amongst us had formed a group they called the Stamping Heels featuring three guitars and drums, just like the Beatles, but nowhere near in their league in any way whatsoever.

I was sorry that I had been unable to join the group, but the only instrument I had ever held was the violin my parents had gifted me for Christmas when I was 10. They purchased it quite cheaply from family friends and, whilst I was delighted to have received it, I would have much preferred a guitar, an instrument I'd enjoyed hearing older boys playing at summer camp by the fire in the evenings, when everyone would sing along with them.

But the violin was equally beautiful and I occasionally strummed its four strings without a fiddle stick, making believe it was a guitar, if on the small side. Playing the violin as a guitar one day, I broke a string. To my young mind, this was the end of the world and would mean more trouble for my parents, something I had vowed to avoid. I had no idea new strings could be purchased individually, for I had never so much as stepped foot inside a musical instrument shop.

What I did know was that both my parents had suffered in concentration camps and that their mental state was not as strong as it should have been, and I had, at all times, to be a good and caring boy for them.

The broken violin string was a major calamity, and the words of our close family friend Auntie Lída flooded my mind. Auntie Lída had a tattoo long before it became fashionable; her's was a number on her elbow, a Nazi memento of her many years in Auschwitz, the worst concentration camp of all.

"Now Jan," she would say taking me into a room alone after I had argued loudly with my sister, "You must be a good boy for your mother and father who have suffered enormously in their lives in the concentration camps. They must now have your love and respect, will you do this for them?" "Yes auntie," I would reply, my head bowed, my eyes looking to the ground in shame. "I'll be a good boy."

Strangely enough, my parents never used this emotional blackmail to get the best behaviour out of me; it was only Auntie Lída's initiative. Indeed my parents rarely mentioned their time in the concentration camps, and when they did it would be to recall happier moments, such as the time my mother received a coloured postcard depicting dancers in native costumes from my father's family in Moravian Slovakia. She took great joy in managing to keep this card throughout her days in Ravensbrück with the stamp depicting Herr Hitler long torn away. Somehow this card had returned home with her and was a precious and cherished item in both my parent's lives. I suppose it was a postcard that first broke into, and then escaped from that inhuman prison camp.

Now, to give them the news that I had damaged the violin, was as difficult a message any 10-year-old had ever had to deliver. To this day I still recall the trepidation. But when they explained that new strings were easily bought and not so expensive to replace, I was so overwhelmed and wept with relief as my dear parents consoled me.

From the age of 12, for one year, I attended weekly violin lessons but with all my other preoccupations, my sports, books and Radio Luxembourg, I found little time to practice and eventually gave it up. Luxembourg rarely featured anything with violin, with the exception of the *Luxembourg Waltz* that featured nightly at the start of each evening's broadcasts.

The guitar remained out of my reach and the more I listened to the great music brought to me each night on Radio Luxembourg, the more I appreciated how many great guitarists there were in the world, and how little my contributions would have meant, had I taken up this instrument. Whilst I did learn a couple of chords on a friend's guitar, this was not sufficient musicianship to join my classmates in their group. But I was their strong ally, bringing them good ideas for songs, and helping them to transport their equipment around to places they could rehearse.

I was as happy and as excited as the band members when they got their first gig. A Bratislavan high school came to Brno to challenge us at sports, and The Stamping Heels were given opportunity to perform during the evening get together. This was the first concert I had seen in my life, and I was more than delighted to be closely connected to the stars of the evening, and to have provided them with lyrics to the tunes they now performed, including Paul Anka's *Crazy Love* through to Little Richard's *Lucille*, and plenty Beatles songs of course.

In Czechoslovakia in those days, groups playing such music were all called *big beat* groups after Fats Domino's hit, *The Big Beat*. Unknown communist influences created this description as *rock 'n' roll* and its variations such as a rock group were considered far too subversive.

Subsequently right through to today in my country, *rock* is still referred to as *big beat*. Little did I know that across the Atlantic the man who coined the phrase Rock 'n' Roll, DJ Alan Freed, also used the name BIG BEAT for his live rock 'n' roll concerts.

Tony: The rock 'n' roll DJs

In 1959, around the same time that Elvis was arriving in Bremerhaven with the Second Armoured Division, back in America, DJ Alan Freed stood in front of a Congressional hearing in a payola scandal that rocked rock 'n' roll.

Back in the UK, billeted at the Gerald Armstrong stables, like all the kids in the land, I'd listen to 208 Radio Luxembourg beneath my pillow, and we'd gather round the small transistor on Sunday nights, listening to the brand new Top 20 with DJ Alan Dell, Barry Alldis or Don Wardell.

Jimmy Savile, (deemed a saint during his lifetime, demonised in his death), invited us to join the Teen and Twenty Disc Club and his Under the Bedclothes Club. Sam Costa's voice followed the jingle 'Oh it's Sunday... Yeeeees it's Sunday'. One night a new voice followed the 208 'gong' which pre-empted time checks! His name was Alan Freeman.

The entire population of Great Britain nodded off listening to those '*Ovaltinies, Happy Girls and Boys...*' or Horace Batchelor's advice on how to win on Vernon's Football Pools in the days before a National Lottery existed. If you wrote to old Horace at Keynsham, a town outside Bristol, (which everyone in Europe knew how to spell, because Horace spelt it 12 times a night for years), he'd let you into his secret winning formula.

As I crossed exhausted into the arms of Orpheus each night, I started to feel that the tunnel from Oldham had surfaced in the wrong place.

Before I finally resigned my career as a jockey, due to the comradeship we'd developed through living, laughing and freezing our tiny balls off on the Yorkshire moors, one of my great transgressions in life took place.

I was a devout non-drinker and because of my childhood experiences had vowed purely to myself, that I would never in my life drink alcohol.

It was the eve of our only annual two-week Christmas break and a 10/6d bonus provided by our benefactor. The horse world dealt in guineas then and this represented a half a guinea (just over 50p/75c).

Dressed to kill in a farewell frame of mind, we lined the bar in the White

Swan, one of Wensleydale's finest pubs. Here there was no underage drinking. No one here in Lillyput could tell if you were 15 or 50, and the pub was packed with elflings, midgets, dwarfs, pixies and the odd five-foot hobbit.

"Eleven rounds should get as all well pissed," said Willie Carson whose future as the Queen's jockey, could we have known, would have had us in awe of the fun-loving Scot.

Tonight, however, he was one of 11 tiny lads telling jokes and celebrating our forthcoming return to civilisation and the big people.

Someone decided we should have vodka and blackcurrant, followed by straight shots of Dimple whisky. Peer pressure won me. I went along with the craic, packet of salted crisps at the ready to dowse the flame and kill the spirit.

Five packets of Smith's crisps later, and I was no longer in Yorkshire.

I was no longer.

Whisky became my drink for the rest of my life, but mixing vodka and blackcurrant on that Middleham night was a bad decision!

I have only two memories of the evening; one was Willie Carson sitting astride another apprentice, and racing Pete McMahon and his human mount, around the pub in our own Xmas Derby.

It was Willie's first winner.

The other memory is miserable.

I'm sitting stooped on a war memorial in the village square, searching through my vomit for my lost two-toothed denture. And then there was Mick, who I haven't seen to thank from that night to this, carrying and dragging me the four miles across Middleham moor to our abode.

The next day was the first day of the rest of my hangovers. I carried my two heads and my suitcase down the lane to the waiting Velox. The birds sang joyfully and unsympathetically. Behind me, Willie Carson reminded me that during our fortnight's absence, the Armstrong family created a deep-bed for the horses, which meant they simply put dry straw on top of the horseshit.

"We'll be mucking out for a week non stop when we get back," he chortled.

I didn't like the odds.

The prospects were grim.

Life was tough and each day seemed grey.

I'd signed my life away. At 15, my 21st birthday seemed a lifetime away. It was time to swallow my pride.

Kath and Frank were delighted I would not be returning, and suggested this was the greatest Christmas gift they could imagine. My family doctor gave me a note saying I had unsuitable health for the work involved.

Gerald Armstrong wrote back releasing me from my contract: '*Providing you don't work for any other stable until the age of 21!'*

In the six months since leaving school at the tender age of 15, I had become a drinker, a gambler and now, a contract breaker!

Rock 'n' roll was my soundtrack; there was music to hear and fun to be had. My life was about to begin, as in one week's time, so were the Swinging 60s.

1960 would be the year Elvis left the army. The year he would appear on the Frank Sinatra TV show, and the year he asked Colonel Joseph Beaulieu if his daughter Priscilla, could spend Christmas with him at Graceland! Change was in the air.

Jan: It's Trad Dad

Things were beginning to thaw somewhat in Czechoslovakia. Around the beginning of 1964, a Czech section of Radio Free Europe started to broadcast special music programmes for young listeners between 3pm to 6pm on short wave.

The reason for this was quite simple, although Radio Free Europe's signal was jammed in Czechoslovakia and quite illegal to listen to, it was a well-known fact that, when you listened, you hopped along the radio dial as Radio Free Europe constantly moved its frequency making it difficult to jam the signal. Radio Free Europe broadcast in both the Czech and Slovak languages, and although we were constantly twiddling the radio dials, it was a godsend for us all, a breath of fresh air, literally!

Some progressive employees in the Prague-based state radio woke the commie controllers up to the fact that young people were interested in the music of Elvis Presley and the Beatles etc suggesting that it would be better were this music made available to them on a Czech network, rather than tempt them to listen to RFE.

The experiment was a great success. The programme was called Mikrofórum and it commenced at 3pm, just as the Radio Free Europe youth programme started. With a strong signal that remained in one place and a policy to avoid politics and to play popular western records mixed with some national pop tunes and interviews with people like Miloš Forman, you would discuss these events in school the following day.

Radio Prague started to win the teenagers of Czechoslovakia away from Radio Free Europe.

For the first time in my life, I was hearing new music in superior quality. As much as I loved Luxembourg and would continue to do so for many years, the signal on the AM frequency was not reliable, especially in the summer months. At least the young Mikrofórum announcers avoided the rigid traditional political correctness and ideological vocabulary and bullshit we were served with, beyond this oasis of a programme.

My problem was I couldn't get past my love for western music and I hated the Czechoslovakian and Eastern European attempts to emulate the music I listened to on Luxy every night, especially when they attempted a cover version of a song I liked. At times I was forced to reach for the radio knob and switch off the likes of our very own Karel Gott, who had the audacity to try to cover the Beatles, *From Me to You.*

I had two problems with Karel Gott, firstly he was far too old at 25 and secondly, he was a favourite within the communist regime. He was also one of the reasons I didn't yearn for a television as, according to my friends who had one, he was on our one and only channel constantly.

So in the afternoons after school, I would tune in to Mikrofórum until 5pm, and then immediately switch to RFE for their Gott-free final youth hour. By then I only had one hour to survive before the Station of the Stars came on 208 metres at 7.30pm.

The most important thing about Mikrofórum for me, personally, was the relief I felt that I could avoid falling into a trap set by any communist inquisitor, who might wonder how I knew so much about western music?

This was a constant worry for me and I was neurotically on my guard over who I dared to discuss the latest Beatles' tune with. It was tough when I'd heard something fantastic on Luxembourg, like the latest Rolling Stones' release, and wanted to shout from the school rooftops just how great it was! I was constantly on my guard due to the deep-seated fears established by Auntie Lída's brainwashing, that my subversive radio listening could cause more problems for my parents.

Now at last, because Mikrofórum played Beatles and Anglo-American songs, they had, in effect, legalised my illegal listening activity and I was no longer afraid of being discovered. I had my cover.

From the age of 15, Auntie Lída no longer worked on making me a good boy. It was quite obvious to her that she had done a good job.

In March 1964, another musical milestone was reached in Czechoslovakia. For the first time since the Communist upheaval in 1948, with the exception of the black spiritualist singer Paul Robeson, who stopped by in Prague on his way to Moscow some years earlier, it was announced that an American singer would visit our country, and would even be appearing in Brno.

His name was Pete Seeger, and we knew nothing of him, save that I had never heard him on Luxembourg, and he played a banjo. For these reasons we avoided wasting money on someone we were quite unsure about, and most of us stayed home. This was a bad decision. When they later released an album of his live Prague concert, I knew I had made a mistake. The LP included American standards like *T for Texas, Irene Goodnight, Careless Love* and *We Shall Overcome*, a song that became my mantra, for I was convinced this was a reference to us overcoming communism someday.

I liked Pete Seeger's songs of the old west we knew of from well-thumbed pre-war books that still secretly circulated amongst my friends. His songs reminded me also of our campfire songs which we sang in the mountains in summer camp.

His sleeve notes disturbed me. He was quoted as saying that his songs were not the America of Coca Cola fame, now being churned throughout the world in enormous quantities by the music industry, but songs he had inherited from local folk singers as he travelled around America. What he didn't appreciate perhaps was that Czechoslovakia was not tarnished by the Coca Cola America, nor were we, or other Eastern Bloc countries, serviced by this mighty music industry he referred to.

It was a pity he never found time to visit a record shop whilst in Czechoslovakia or Russia. He might have appreciated America's Coca Cola world a little more.

Having missed Pete Seeger in March, just two weeks later my music-mad friends and I had a new and amazing experience, and all down to an almighty error within the communist censorship authority. We had seen in a Brno cinema programme a film called Jazz Review was scheduled. Jazz did little to move us, and we would have let it bypass us had it not been for my friend Radek Rettegy who had been to see it, and reported that here was a film that virtually brought Radio Luxembourg to life. There was some jazz, but it was of the Dixieland style, whilst the rest of the music was mainly by well known UK and American pop stars. He further reported the concept of the storyline was so like what we were going through in Czechoslovakia, with authoritarian denial of the music young kids wanted to hear, that we could not comprehend for a moment how this film made it through to the largest of our cinemas in Brno.

Here they came on screen one after the other, Chubby Checker, Gene Vincent, John Leyton, and Helen Shapiro who played a main character. Del Shannon also performed although, unfortunately, not the wonderful *Runaway* as we had hoped. The actual jazz was Dixieland served up by the likable Acker Bilk and Chris Barber. There is no doubt that it was because these tracks were featured in the film, that the censorship board permitted the film, as the general feeling with the communist-minded police was that jazz came from the underprivileged, poor American Negro populous, and was not therefore dangerous to young people's minds.

We had theories. Someone quite progressive within the Prague censorship office wanted western pop to penetrate, and created a title to divert attention from his superiors. Or someone saw only the jazz extracts when reviewing the film, and didn't quite understand the beatnikish title, It's Trad Dad, and so created Jazz Review, a title that would be better understood amongst the Czechoslovak public. Either way, it worked in our favour, and for one week it played at our biggest Brno cinema after which, rather strangely, it went to the smaller cinemas in the suburbs.

Again there were whispered theories amongst my schoolmates which suggested that the big communist boss in Brno had been to see it, freaked out and sent it to the outskirts of the city as, having been passed by Prague, he had no power to ban the film altogether.

We'll never know. But once we had seen it six or seven times, we began to understand that the actual plot, rather than the pop lyrics, was the real challenge to our communist officers.

The mayor tries to ban the music and has the police stop their concert, the kids revolt, the mayor capitulates for the sake of his own popularity and, as the final words in the movie go, '...so the boy and girl and the mayor lived happily ever after' we always left the cinema feeling wired to the world at large, if somewhat frustrated.

The story could never happen in Czechoslovakia where we have no mayor, a place where the chairman of the communist party would never support rock 'n' roll for a moment. On the contrary, ever since the emergence of rock 'n' roll they smothered it in my country. Kids dancing to rock 'n' roll jive-style were taken out of ballrooms by Public Safety, and actually portrayed in the communist press as bad examples amongst our nation's youth. Some were even expelled from their schools as censors from the Cultural Authority maintained their vigil, seeking out those who did not show complete loyalty to the red flag. Musicians, newly forming groups and bands were told not to play rock 'n' roll, otherwise the State-run agency would not find them work and they would be blacklisted in all the nation's music venues.

A mere 10 years had passed since 1948, when thousands of students had been taken out of universities for not supporting the communist party.

To our big brothers in the ruling party, rock 'n' roll was the thin end of the wedge, the seed of rebellion that had to be stamped on before it could be fertilised.

But this strange little pop movie gave us real hope. If young people in England could endure these types of problems and eventually win the day after struggling to do so, one day our chance would also come. Maybe…

Tony: The holiday camp

I still have my five Butlins Pthwheli badges.

I'd holidayed there five years in succession, first with mum and dad in 1957, then with Jack Smith, and later Oldham's greatest rock 'n' roll pianist Ian Fenn.

It was during my third year that I bumped into my vocation.

I'd finally got a 'proper job' as an apprentice toolmaker, having rebounded from the stables straight into the radio department of the Oldham Co-op. How ironic that I should be selling radios.

I was 16. Hormone city.

I'd wandered into my favourite place on the entire camp, the Rock & Jive Ballroom. I sometimes think that this was my true birthplace, where my bottom was really smacked and where I first gasped life's air, my ears opened and there was *Little Darlin* by the Diamonds.

There wasn't much to interest me in the afternoons. A knobbly knees competition for the dads, Glamorous Gran, Bonny Baby, family stuff.

At night, I'd drown in the tunes.

My holidays at Butlins can be traced through the hits I danced to.

In 59 it was Bobby Darin's *Dream Lover* and Cliff's *Mean Streak*. In '60, I bopped to Johnny Preston's *Cradle of love*, and Jimmy Jones' falsetto on *Good Timin'*. 1960/61 gave me Jerry Lee Lewis *What'd I Say* and Billy Fury's *Halfway To Paradise*.

In the summer of 1960 I preferred the resident group to the one in 1959, which had been Rory Blackwell's band. This year it was Rory Storm and the Hurricanes.

Rory seemed to be a popular stage name.

One afternoon I noticed the drummer who wore lots of rings and cowboy boots sitting alone at a table spitting and polishing the boots. I sat next to him with a milkshake.

"I like the group," I offered.

"Ta!"

"I like yer boots."

"Thanks la."

"Do you know the best song Rory does?" I quizzed.

"What would that be now?" He asked daubing white cream on the boots pointed toe.

"Baby I Don't Care!"

"Gerraway."

A fag hung from the corner of his lips burning his left eye, he still hadn't looked up from his preoccupation.

"Whole Lotta Shakin's' good too! ...Specially when he starts shaking like a silly bugger!"

Then, finally, he surveyed me.

This was Ringo Starr.

We small talked as he smoked and polished and I drank my milkshake. I told him I knew all the songs.

"Well Tommy," he said straining to put his left boot on. "We've got a talent

competition tomorrow night why don't you give it a crack?"
He made to walk away his cigarette ash falling to the floor.
"I will." I said.
"If you'll lend me your cowboy boots!"

Before the competition my pals Jack Smith, Ian Fenn and I fuelled up
at the Pig and Whistle pub, I'd knocked back two whiskeys dousing them
with a packet of Smith's crisps. By 9.30pm I stood confidently at the side
of stage. Ringo eventually caught my eye between numbers and pointed
his drumstick across the stage at a mangy pair of cowboy boots.
"Thanksh a lot." I yelled to all three of him.
Wingo rinked at me.
"What you singin?" asked Rory Storm leaning down his blonde locks
almost touching my face.
"Be-Bop-A-Lula," I said.
And then he was on the microphone, a big silver thing.
"Ladies and gentlemen," he announced. "The next competitor is Tommy
Whitehead from Oldham."
The Oldham Wakes crowd drowned him out with their football chant of
the time, "Zigga zagga, zigga zagga, Oi! Oi! Oi!!!"
"And he's gonna sing the Gene Vincent classic, *Be Bop a Lula!*"
"What key?" asked Johnny Guitar as I ambled towards him in the boots
that were four sizes too big.
I searched my pockets and offered him my chalet key, thinking you needed
to show it for some reason.
The band pissed themselves.
Rory explained what a key was.
"I've no idea, any key you like. I'm not fussy."
They chose C.
"*Weeeeeeeeeee*"... I stretched it out, the group waiting patiently as I milked
this big moment..."*eeeeeeeeeeell.*"
I tilted the mic stand back to a full 45 degrees, cupping it with two hands
like you do on a frosty night. Like Gene Vincent did.
And then I let it go.
"*BeeeeeBopalula she's a mah baby...*"
Johnny Guitar wrenched a chord out of his Fender Stratocaster right on
the 'Beeeeee' and we were rockin!'
The first verse, chorus, verse, went fine until the guitar solo, where I had a
surprise lined up for them.

At this stage, Gene Vincent kicks his leg across the angled mic stand,
finishing up with the stand behind his back rocking his body, moody like.
I'd practised with a brush in front of mum's mirror many times.
"*My baby doll, my baby doll, my baby doll.*"

The verse ended and I looked at Johnny Guitar taking one hand off the mic and pointing at him.

"Go Johnny Go!" I yelled.

My leg shot skywards and two things happened. The right boot flew off into the audience and landed on a tough looking teddy boy's head; my leg didn't make it over the chrome stand and… I fell arse over tit right off the stage.

The audience were confused for that moment. Some watched the boot like people at a tennis match as it travelled through the air, whilst others popped open their mouths watching me as I fell into the front row, the mic booming feedback.

The group couldn't play for laughing. Johnny Guitar sat on the stage crying, Ringo's head hit the snare drum, whilst Rory hammered his fists against the wall.

They all loved it. I came second. A boot polish kit!

And that was my first taste of the drug called audience.

I was a singer.

To qualify that, a bunch of lads came to me explaining that they were a group from Oldham looking for a singer.

This was the founding of the Jasons although they weren't called that yet, they were called the Silver Dollars, which identifies the levels of creativity and originality, which existed in the band at that time.

On this momentous night, two things happened, I got drunk for the second time in my life, and Jack Smith got laid for his first.

At dawn the next morning I awoke to the sound of Welsh birds singing, intermingled with loud Lancashire laughter. Then the Butlin's Tannoy public address system spoke like God to Moses,

"Good morning campers…"

I forced my eyes to squint open, listening to the morning's planned activities, whilst the cackle of mirthful tee-hees persisted around the head that had once been mine. As my eyelids strengthened to expand their squint, I noticed how exceptionally high the ceiling was.

Then I heard my second applause within 12 hours, and I sat bolt upright remembering last nights victorious rock 'n' roll performance and the subsequent celebration at the Pig & Whistle. And then it dawned.

I was surrounded by campers who, ignoring their hunger pangs, had halted to view the spectacle that was I, as they made their way to the first sitting of breakfast.

My *friends* had pulled my mattress out of the chalet and left me to sleep between rows 14A and 14B!

Later, I salivated as Jack told me about the much more memorable night he'd had. I'd been getting legless, while he'd been getting his leg over.

Whilst I was getting drunk, he was in the bunk. Here was my life-long friend, a boy who I'd tried to out-masturbate in our early development as sexual animals, confiding that he'd just beat me at becoming a man.

"I took that girl from Leeds back to her chalet," he began. I was niggled that he assumed I recalled *any* girl from *anywhere* last night, but let him continue with his bawdy tale.

"I'm just about to 'do it' when the door opens and in walks her mate with... guess who?"

He wanted a guessing game.

"Give in," I said, after going through Elvis, Sgt Bilko and Mick McManus, the famous wrestler.

"No," he said lighting up a Park Drive cigarette.

"Give fucking in!" I cried for the third time. "Who was it?"

"Rory Storm!" he said rolling the Rory bit like Jackie Wilson rolls Reet Petite and knowing I'd be well impressed.

"I was fucking with Rory Storm!"

I wanted to hear more about Jack on the bottom bunk. I wanted to know how quickly she let him undo her bra and details, such as what *it* was like, but he was far more keen to tell me about the action on the *top* bunk.

"He fucks like a rabbit, all bloody night, and guess what...guess what?"

"Not again please..."

"He stutters!"

It was true. Whilst bleached-blonde Rory had the most profound stutter, it never affected his singing. But it affected his confidence.

When Ringo Starr left Rory Storm and the Hurricanes to join the Beatles a couple of years later, it just about finished the singer off.

He had a quite good record out called *Dr Feelgood* but he became infamous as 'the singer who lost the drummer to the most successful group in history'.

A shit claim to fame.

Iris, his sister, is a good pal of mine these many years later. She married another chum, Shane Fenton, who became Alvin Stardust. Iris went to her mum's one day to find her brother dead in one bedroom, and her mother in another. When she'd found Rory she was so overcome with grief; mum, too, took her life.

Iris is a class act who rose above the worst the world and the music industry had to offer. In 2010, I took Iris back to her old school and the Cavern Club in a TV series I made called Rock 'n' Rollmance. This gave me the opportunity to make the world aware of her special story back in the day when George Harrison and Paul McCartney fought for her affections.

Jan: The Beatles

It's Trad Dad was a real boost to morale; a sign of an undercurrent taking place moving us towards that better world Helen Shapiro lived in.

In the spring the communist paper Red Law featured a big article on the Royal Shakespeare Company from Stratford-Upon-Avon, who were performing King Lear in Prague, as part of a 16-country European tour. I knew nothing of Shakespeare. Our school's curriculum had never featured his work, as our literature learning was biased towards Soviet writers.

Red Law praised the brilliance of the English actors, stating that Czech actors could learn a lot from them. Surely this was another sign that things were changing, and that the English were not so hated by our benefactors as much as they once were.

It was a far cry from my mother's friend who worked in a department store with a colleague, who was learning English with her. One day they were talking on the internal telephone to each other practicing their English, little knowing the phone was tapped. Both women were immediately fired.

So now, according to our national communist newspaper, English wasn't so bad after all. What a change! What hypocrisy! What a confusing world in which to grow!

Suddenly, the red light that had shone so aggressively on all things English or American since communists took power in 1948 seemed to be diminishing. Cliff's Young Ones, It's Trad Dad and Royal Shakespeare actors had all happened within a few short months of each other, and seemed to me to be tiny lights at the end of a very long tunnel.

1964 was an exciting year for youth culture in the UK and USA, with the Beatles doing their first live show at Carnegie Hall and the Rolling Stones headlining their first tour with the Ronettes in tow. But there was so very little reporting on Western culture in Czechoslovakian media. Almost nothing at all, until 1 October of that year.

On this day someone came to school with a copy of Red Law. They were excited, and when we read the page dedicated to cultural reports, we were in a state of euphoria. The huge area of the page featured two main stories, one regarding the manifestation of the relationship between Czechoslovakia and Hungary; with the second feature covering the 15th anniversary of the founding of the People's Republic of China.

Beneath these two dominant articles, a quarter page told of something quite miraculous, a festival of English films would be touring the country starting in a Prague cinema on 9 October. The festival would last nine days and would tour through four cities including Brno. Red Law listed the film Tom Jones as the first of the selected films that would play firstly in Prague, from where the film was to be transported to the next city and so on. It explained that a delegation of British filmmakers would be present, although it didn't list any names.

What it did name, was so unbelievable to us devout Radio Luxembourg listeners, it seemed beyond belief. The list of film titles over the nine day festival were written in Czech and beneath one of them we read: Richard Lester, A Hard Day's Night with the Beatles.

We anticipated a stampede to buy tickets from the Brno cinema, where it would play three times on one day at 3.30pm, 6.00pm and 8.15pm. The selected Brno cinema was our biggest; constructed before the war when it was known as Scala (later renamed Moscow), it housed 750 seats.

A whole posse of us charged downtown after school to the Moscow only to be devastated by a card taped to the main door, which read... 'BEATLES SOLD OUT!' I'd wanted three tickets, one for each showing, now I would have none. It didn't seem possible that I would be in the same city as the Beatles, and would not be one amongst the 2,250 who would bask in this glorious experience.

Our friend Jarek Gardáš' mother was an usherette at the Moscow, so we quickly learned what was going on and how the cinema and the city administrators were working ticket allocation. These would go to the factories that had reached targets before others, and the farm workers whose crop quota had exceeded the minimum requirement set by the communist overlord directors.

The factory and farm managers had a deal with the cinema to purchase blocks of tickets cheaply, which were then gifted to the workers as a bonus. Workers, of course, continued to be the Kings in the dominion of a communist society. The favoured benefactors cared nothing for western music, gave out their bonus tickets to people who had never even heard of the Beatles and probably didn't even understand English!

It now looked seriously like we, the secret Beatle-mad society, would stand by the cinema exits trying to hear the soundtrack.

The management at the Moscow who so valued this factory business, would ensure the tickets went to their best customers. You couldn't blame them I suppose, they were forced to feature week-long Soviet films attended primarily by young lovers who wanted somewhere private to do their necking, during a movie that would offer no distractions. Or the odd old couple who hadn't yet got a TV set and had been given Soviet film tickets by some trade union worker neighbour, who would have otherwise binned them.

Of course the People's Militia and Trade Unionists would not have wanted to see the Beatles' A Hard Day's Night movie, but they would have wanted them for their kids, which underlines the acute hypocrisy that existed within the communist system.

Until this time, the Beatles had been featured a couple of times in the newsreel film, which preceded the headline film in our cinemas. The bulletin showed mainly screaming girls at Beatles' concerts, flashes of the band performing or running the gauntlet, and a commentator who brought our attention to the crazy and fanatical fuss the Beatles stood for, and how it had nothing to do with cultural value.

There was no mention of all the fun everyone seemed to be having, or the freedom kids had to express themselves. Whenever we heard a Beatles news clip was showing in our cinema, no matter what crap film was being shown, Soviet or otherwise, we would attend for what amounted to a 15-second thrill. Our Beatles fix.

We would discuss the clips on the way home and point out to each other the flaw in the commentator's sanctimonious statement, that these were little kids yelling for the Beatles.

What we hadn't perhaps realised then was that priority cinema and theatre tickets were the tip of the iceberg. The sons and daughters of communist members and administrators also gained admission to universities easier and obtained the better jobs. Everything in their lives was that much easier, purely based on how well their parents had played the game.

The kids living in this privileged communist cocoon had no motivation to march and scream for their freedom, as did many anti Russian protesters. When their parents fired their weapons against us during the first anniversary of the Russian invasion in August 1969, killing two young protesters who had a brick and a book in their hands, they remained at home. Afraid such activity would tarnish their parents' reputation.

At our age we had no way of evaluating all these social politics. We were a handful of school kids who illegally listened to a foreign radio station to hear the music we loved; music we discussed in whispers in the playground with a gathering of friends we could trust.

We stood before the Moscow cinema doors utterly devastated. One of the privileged within our circle, was Jarek Gardáš, who helped us to understand that all communists were not bad apples, in just the same way that my own father had impressed upon me that not all German people were Nazis. Jarek's father wasn't only a communist, he was an officer in the Secret Police as part of State Security.

The family lived very near to our school and so we visited with Jarek regularly who, when his parents were out, showed us the Secret Police newsletters which described criminal events that were never discussed in our newspapers.

Jarek's trust in showing us these documents was reciprocated. We knew had we leaked any of these stories in open discussion, it could have had dire consequences on his father and his entire family.

Jarek often told us how unhappy his father was working for State Security because he simply couldn't trust anyone, not one single person.

Jarek gave us another lesson; we now understood that not every communist or indeed son of a communist was necessarily a full-badge wearing commy. I learned also that as Jarek played lead guitar together with Lad'a Kubíček in our school band The Stamping Heels, you could always trust a genuine fan of Anglo-American music.

The most important day since our birth arrived, and on this day Jarek's mother proved to be a Goddess. Her job as an usher at Moscow led to our little group following her instructions to be outside the cinema no later than 3.30pm, as the afternoon matinee would be the easiest for her to smuggle us inside. Later shows would be infested with supervisors from the Communist National Committee of Brno and other dangerous people.

Twelve of us arrived at 3pm to find the foyer completely full and people spilling onto the road. I wasn't hopeful of getting in as I witnessed this bedlam. It looked to us like the entire city of Brno had come to see the Beatles. Thoughts gushed through my mind. Did anyone comprehend what this meant? Did the power brokers in our government have a chance to witness this western earth tremor and the influence of music, this divine impact of the Beatles? And, damn it I thought, *why* when they can show The Young Ones and It's Trad Dad, were they not able to let A Hard Day's Night run everywhere for a week or more?

There were now hundreds asking for tickets with none available, and by 3.20pm everyone who had a ticket was sitting down ready to watch the movie.

I was literally shaking, there was no sign of Mrs Gardáš, her son looked at me with sad eyes; he too had lost hope.

At exactly 3.30pm we heard the most dreaded sound imaginable coming from inside the cinema. It was the mighty first chord of the film's title song *A Hard Day's Night*. What should have been the greatest intro to any song in musical history, was now laughing at us. This was Czechoslovakia; you don't get a chance to see a film like this tomorrow or even next year. It was a one-off chance in communist hell.

Then the angel of mercy arrived, the door to the cinema opened and there stood Jarek's mother with her torch bidding us to come towards her, placing her index finger to her lips and shushing us inside.

Twelve of us did as we were told and finished sitting in the most wonderful seats imaginable, we were on the floor, and we were watching the Czechoslovakian premier of the Beatles' A Hard Day's Night.

Our Beatles experience was limited to hearing them on Luxy. Not one of us had ever seen a Beatles' face or a Beatles' picture sleeve, neither did we know then which one was John, Paul, George or Ringo; but here we were about to find out.

Their unbridled energy which we had all felt through their music, now enveloped us with their images and soundtrack.

Never before and never since have any of us felt so much emotion in a cinema. I can state with complete conviction, that this experience for each of us, was much stronger than that amazing experience of being with a woman for the first time.

After seeing A Hard day's Night we each understood that music was the way we would make it, and for the next 25 years this proved to be the case until, finally, after so long, we found our freedom.

There is not doubt that Jarek's mother took enormous risks with us, and in more sophisticated times we would have at least sent her some flowers of gratitude.

Forty-five years later, I finally had my opportunity to thank her for getting us in to the Moscow cinema to see the Beatles. The memory drew a smile to her face on the sad day of Jarek's funeral.

Tony: The Jasons

Prior to this fateful holiday and meeting the Jasons, I had established a social life in Oldham, which, unbeknownst to me, found me at the foot of my career ladder playing records at The Princess dancehall. This was a venue run by orchestra leader Harry Robinson, who did a lot of TV work at the time with vocalist Janie Marden. Managing the Princess and leading his orchestra was his day job. Well, a night-time day job.

He paid me Gerald Armstrong's equivalent of two weeks' wages to play the records on Saturday nights when his orchestra had a break. This was performed from a corridor out of sight of the audience as if Harry was ashamed of my activity, which he was, because my job substituted three members of a live trio at union rate. Harry and his band were Musician's Union affiliated.

Generously, he also gave me free admission, which as he pointed out, on a Saturday night, was worth a half a crown. I conned him really. I'd have gladly paid *him*.

The Log Cabin was another quantum leap for Oldham's burgeoning teenage society.

Cona Coffee had arrived, frothy coffee, together with a feed station for the jukebox at every table, which to me was space-age wizardry, sponsored by heaven!

It was here I first fell in love with Ray Charles' original version of *What'd I say* and... Christine Hall the love of my life.

The first time I plucked up courage to speak with her was at a 'beatnik' club called Flintstone's Cave, a paper maché cave-like joint that looked like Barney Rubble's living room.

Christine Hall had the most fabulous eyes, and hair, and body and smell and voice and ears and ankles and legs and finger nails and... *slap!*

I remember her smacking me across the left ear like it was yesterday.

Christine was my total teenage love, but she was as popular as she was beautiful and the competition was extreme. So I worked hard on her, and once I started doing gigs with the Jasons at the Savoy, Oldham's premier venue, I would seek her out in the audience and sing to her Jack Scott's *What in the world's come over you*, which always drew the audience to the stage as everyone waited to see if I could reach the high note at the end of the song.

'*Onleeeeeee...onleee real love!*'

We rehearsed mainly in Alan Maudsley's living room, in his mum and dad's terraced house on Chadderton Road.

Alan was our lead guitarist. I couldn't help noticing how much in love his parents were. His dad was a bus driver whose bus route ran straight passed their terraced house on Chadderton Road. Mr Maudsley would always stop the bus at his door and sound its throaty horn, whereupon the extremely diminutive Mrs M would go bounding out of the house, climb up the double-decker's mud flaps and purse her lips as her husband, leaning down from his cab and holding her tightly around her waist in case she fell into the traffic, kissed her passionately.

I watched in amazement as the rush hour traffic built up behind the number 6 bus as Alan's mum and dad had their smooch!

Alan was our Hank B Marvin; he studied the Shadows and taught the rest of the group how to walk the routine around their winkle picker shoes without tripping up, in true Shads style.

He could play a chord of 'F' with a full index finger barré. As we progressed, he bought not only a Fender guitar like Hank's, but also an identical pair of black-rimmed glasses! He played *Apache, Kon Tiki, The Frightened City* and *FBI* note perfect. Duane Eddy's *Pepe* was no problem, and the Venture's *Walk Don't Run*, he perfected in one afternoon.

Alan was an accountant.

Trevor played rhythm guitar and sang ballads better than me, although I was the lead singer and Trev couldn't rock like me. Thankfully Trevor mainly sang Pat Boone songs which left me free to handle *Tell Laura I Love Her, Dreamin, I'm Just a Lonely Boy,* and all the great rock n' roll songs covered by the chords C, F & G, including *Mean Woman Blues, Whole Lotta Shakin'* and Eddie Cochran's *20 Flight Rock*, which we'd string into a medley. I sang the long chorus of *What'd I Say* standing on my head, and only came down when my face was blood red and snot was running down my throat.

Trevor, our perfect Pat Boone sound-alike and rhythm guitarist, was a fireman. He sang Speedy Gonzalez climbing ladders and saving lives.

The drummer I hated. Malc Yates would stand at the bar after the gig with the girl I'd been giving the eye to all night. He didn't do this once; he did it often! I was still a virgin. Malc wasn't. There was obvious conflict. But he was a great drummer, and I loved it when we reached the point in the show where I would let each of the instrumentalists loose in the group's decathlon of solos, and stretch Malc to his limit.

We always left the drum solo till last because the audience always went wild. Malc needed me to come back on stage before his drum solo was completed.

If I didn't show, he'd just have to continue.

When I really hated him, I stayed off stage as long as possible.

The sweat would drip from his long nose, and he'd look at me gratefully as I returned to the microphone.

He couldn't maintain timing. His solos would start at 140 beats per minute and would be a ballad tempo when I returned. Malc was a plumber. I bought him a metronome for Christmas!

We had various bass players. Harold Jones who I first met at the Butlins gig, played bass on a normal six string guitar until he was replaced with a proper bass player.

Alan and Trev judged them on merit. Malc and I judged them on how competitive they were with the ladies. The uglier the bass player was, the better we liked him.

I changed my name about this time. Tommy Whitehead didn't quite work in the rock 'n' roll garden of Eden's, Dion's, Jet's, Rory's and Fabian's. But I thought Tommy was OK and the band became known as Tommy Prince and the Jasons. Or as Tommy Smith, the owner of the Savoy used to advertise in the Oldham Chronicle, '*Little Tommy, everybody loves him!*'

I found our road manager on a lathe at Vertoma Jig and Tool engineering factory, where I had managed to get a proper job as an apprentice toolmaker.

Cyril Salt had a small Thames van, and once talked us out of buying a new Vox amplifier because it wouldn't fit in. Things were so tight in that small tour vehicle that, had we introduced so much as a tambourine to augment our sound, he'd have had to invest in a roof rack!

We were resident at The Savoy on Monday and Thursday nights. Thursdays featured guest groups such as Manchester's Freddie and the Dreamers, the Playboys, Pete McLean and the Clan, Deke Arlon & the Tremors, Wayne Fontana & the Mindbenders and the Hollies.

Sometimes the owner Tommy Smith would splash out on a bigger name from far afield, Shane Fenton and the Fentones, the Barron Knights and Sounds Incorporated.

Bernard Manning owned two major cabaret clubs in Manchester. The Embassy and The Palladium.

The Jasons were doing well, and one night we had a double booking at both his clubs.

At the second club, The Embassy, we ran into Bernard Manning for the first time. Bernard compèred the whole evening, telling his dirty jokes between each act.

We were readying ourselves for the second gig, when the rotund legend himself walked into our dressing room, shook hands with each of us then, striding over our guitar cases and belongings, proceeded to pee in the sink.

We were topping the bill. Jerry Dorsey was second on the bill and had just brought the house down with his tariff of Frank Sinatra, Tony Bennet and Sammy Davies standards. He was now just 5 years away from being rechristened Engelbert Humperdinck.

We went on and gave them Elvis Presley, Buddy Holly and Little Richard. I did Ray Charles' *What'd I say* and did the final chorus standing on my head as usual. It became my party trick for the next 50 years.

After the gig we were getting changed, and the sink turned out to be the only back-stage plumbed facility.

The toilet was out front through the audience, accordingly we dehydrated into the sink following Bernard Manning's example.

Bernard walked in and caught our drummer Malc mid-pee.

"Well done lads," he said. "Now what was the damage?"

"Eighty quid to you Bernard," I said towelling myself down.

"Hold on," said Alan Maudsley, our lead guitarist and accountant. "There's only 75 here."

"That's right," said Bernard. "There's a five pound fine for peeing in the sink!"

"But," we all chimed. "YOU peed in the sink!!"

He was halfway out the door and peered back at us.

"It's my bloody sink lads!"

He winked, beamed at us and returned to centre stage to deliver more blue repertoire.

Orange cordial with lots of ice was my main tipple at gigs. Scotch and coke however was soon to secure my affection after the Beatles popularised the mix.

I'd never even heard of the other coke. Kids were doing pills called purple hearts but I didn't need substances, Elvis was enough of a drug for me.

I eventually followed all the other Mop Top fashions such as the haircut, their rounded collared jackets and, their greatest idea, Beatle boots. These put me up to 5'7". I was eternally grateful to J, P, G and R, and continued wearing them long after they'd gone out of fashion.

As I was standing on my head around Manchester, the Beatles were in their Hamburg phase. Brian Epstein, running his family NEMS record shop in Liverpool, had yet to meet his fate.

When the Beatles were playing the Cavern, Litherland Town Hall, New Brighton Pier, the Jasons were performing at the Twisted Wheel, Lee Road Social Club and, every group's target gig, The Oasis.

Irlam, a village near Warrington, was a fair hike for us all cramped in Cyril's van. Trev had advanced to his first wheels, three of them, a red Bond that opened like a clam from the front and had an engine about the size of my first Hornsby train. He, his girlfriend Dorothy and his guitar case would follow Cyril's van; behind them our cavalcade would be completed with Malc, who rode a Lambretta scooter.

So, although Malc in particular didn't like the long hike on his scooter, we were about as popular as you could get at the Black Swan, Irlam and were given residency each Sunday night.

It was here that I first experienced the look of lust. Unfortunately though it was on the face of Fran Matulko, who was on the arm of the toughest teddy boy in Irlam.

But it was there all right, an eyeball laser zapping me from across the pub. As her dark, mascara-eyes devoured me, my loins responded to the release of the testosterone she'd caused.

One Sunday, when her teddy-beau was in the loo, she slipped a piece of paper with her telephone number into my hand. I took it home, savouring it like a penny black. The two electric words she whispered in my ear as she passed me the paper kept repeating themselves.

"Anytime, anywhere!"

The Jasons split up.

We'd been offered a season at Butlins, but the boys didn't want to resign their careers. Alan the accountant, Trevor a fireman and Malcolm the plumber.

Suddenly I was a solo artist.

I entered a talent competition in a Manchester theatre and found myself up against a 10-year-old pianist who played a classical interpretation of *Three Blind Mice*. He was followed by a fellow who sang *Mardi Gras*, and did a percussive solo with a pair of ivory rickers held between his arthritic fingers.

Two competitors sang Bing Crosby's/Ronnie Hilton's/Gracie Fields/ Mantovani's *Around the World I Searched for You*, and no less than three women duplicated their performances with Peggy Lee's *Mr Wonderful*.

I was also challenged for position in the event by a man who wanted to keep 14 plates spinning at the same time, but the theatre props couldn't find a table big enough, so he had to settle on spinning six, which he seemed to find quite easy. His act under-ran by two minutes.

I won first prize.

I was made.

£10 cash.

The judge, purported to be Adam Faith's manager, came up to me in the wings. I thought he was going to suggest he manage me but, instead, he gave me some sound advice to help my career.

"Don't get big headed Tommy," he cautioned, and walked away, forgetting to give me my contract.

I was catching up with Elvis and Ray Charles fast. This was how their careers began winning talent competitions. Ray won in Georgia in 1945, Elvis came only second the same year at the Mississippi-Alabama Fair and Dairy Show, and I came first in Manchester.

Then came the big night when my star took up its most influential position in my life at that time. Two things of major ecological and physiological proportion were about to happen. A new ballroom, the Top Rank Astoria Suite was opening in Oldham. And so too was Fran Matulko!

Fran had caught three buses on a 20-mile journey from Irlam to Oldham, where I met her off the Number 59 bus on Egerton Street.

Timed like a military manoeuvre, so that I could be sure my mother and father were secure in their respective positions in the Egerton Arms, Fran held my perspiring hand as we walked up my street, through the door of number 8, onto the settee and, at lifetime last, up the creaking stairs.

I was in great pain. John Thomas had never been back so far.

She thought I was in ecstasy, but I was in agony. After three minutes, I could bear it no longer and made out I had... made out.

Technically, therefore, I was still a virgin.

But, even so, at 18 going on 19, for the first time in my life I was six feet tall.

The fatefulness of that evening continued unabated. I had tickets to the opening night of the Top Rank Astoria Ballroom, formerly the Gaumont cinema, now a dancehall downstairs, bowling alley above.

With Fran on my arm, I walked into the ballroom feeling a little taller than usual. Beyond the dance floor, the stage featured the 15-piece Johnny Francis Orchestra. Johnny used to play alto sax in Tommy Smith's band when I had been resident with the Jasons at the Savoy. We knew each other well.

During the band break a very un-cool looking chap played very cool records. Chubby Checker's *Let's Twist Again* and Little Eva's *Locomotion* filled the venue.

"How you doin' Tommy?" asked the bandleader waiting for his pint of lager.

And so it was that with a glass of orange cordial in one hand and Fran on my arm, I followed the yellow brick road.

"I'm desperate for a male singer, how do you fancy it?" he asked.

"Sorry Johnny," I answered. "I prefer girls!"

And then he told me how much I'd earn.

The next day I handed in my notice at Vertoma Jig & Tool, giving my micrometer to my old road manager Cyril.

I then descended into the factory cellar and burned my overalls.

Nothing I would ever achieve was greater than this.

I was a full time professional musician.

Jan: The Voice of America

I took a big chance and could have been swatted like a fly by the Secret Police.

Trying my luck with the radio dial, I came across the Voice of America and a broadcast in special English. The programmes were as normal, news and topics but delivered by the presenter at a slower pace, not using such difficult words in a vocabulary that was easy to follow. I felt like a King, as I no longer relied on Czechoslovak sources for my world news. It was a rather incredible feeling to know that I was listening and understanding fully a programme in English, as were millions of other people around the world. It was a mini escape from the forces around me.

One day the announcer invited me to write to them if I would like a free book of Special English Words, and I wasted no time bypassing my parent's permission in my all-consuming desire to own my first English book.

It arrived just in time for Christmas, a great gift to myself. Published in June 1964 by Voice of America – United States Information Agency, Washington, DC 20547. It soon became my bible. Inside was an English dictionary, words and pictures in some cases, maps of the United States and pictures of all American presidents, together with the Declaration of Independence.

I knew as I studied this precious book for the first time, I would, if I practiced hard, one day understand English in its most fluent form and enjoy my radio programmes so much more.

I'd understood that my name would be in their naughty book at customs as someone who listened to the Voice of America, but the book's arrival indicated a lightening in attitude. Only a few short years ago I'd have been interrogated and imprisoned for these crimes.

Then Jack Allen, the Czech programme announcer at the BBC, asked me a silly question, would I like a free autographed picture of the Beatles?

This also arrived safe and sound, and I spent many years arguing with my envious friends about how genuine the signatures were. They insisted they were stamped or printed into the photograph. In the end we agreed that perhaps they did one real signature on each photograph to give authenticity and to save the Beatles so much signing. The John Lennon signature looked somewhat different than the others, with grooves on the reverse corresponding with the signature, that seemed to indicate some weight was used.

We could have spent hours each day discussing and fantasising about the Fab Four. Radio Luxembourg, a constantly renewing source of escape materials, had become more precious than ever.

We no longer needed a train or plane to escape our communist landscape. A Beatles record transported us away quite nicely.

Anyone who hasn't lived in a communist-controlled society will never really understand the fear that constantly pervades a non-communist.

Imagine now that your country has been won over by the communist party, not because they got most votes from your fellow countrymen, but because a huge dominant communist force (Russia in our case), has imposed its politics on your country, handing political control to the communist party.

Now imagine your street has neighbours who are devout communists, many of whom take up new and influential positions of power. They might replace a non-communist manager of a factory, move into key positions in local government, become judges and lawyers, whilst known non-communists start to lose their jobs or just disappear.

Now, because you can't trust anyone on your street, you button up, hiding your anti-communist opinions, towing the party line because you are afraid, not just for yourself, but for those around you, who you love. Your life becomes totally controlled and you live by strict disciplines and rules. Break the rules and *you* will be broken. From 1948, the whole of Czechoslovakia became like that street. Only the closest of friends could share their repulsion of the position the country had got itself into, but first ensuring that they were well out of earshot.

You had to listen closely for clues to your neighbour's political leanings in the exact opposite way that a communist would listen for clues that you were a traitor, anti-red, someone to report to the Secret Police or Public Safety.

Tony: Musicians' Union

In late 1963, Rank moved me and the band, lock, stock and barrel to their latest showpiece venue, the swanky Top Rank Suite in Bristol.

A new tunnel faced me. I was 19 and had no hesitation in exiting my hometown.

On my last night sitting in the Egerton Arms having a farewell drink with my family, I was called outside. Christine had come to say goodbye, it was a teary farewell, but we were both pretty young and agreed we would see each other whenever we could.

"Goodbye Tommy," she said after we kissed goodbye.

We wouldn't see each other again for five years, by which time I'd changed my name. But the next time we saw the Egerton Arms together would be on the occasion of our cheap and cheerful wedding reception. I had a lot of 60s to get through until then.

"You should change your name to Tony, Tommy," said Garry Brown Top Rank's entertainment guru who had selected us for the brand new Bristol Top Rank Suite.

"Tony Tommy, sounds daft," I said.

"No, Tony Prince! Leave Tommy in Oldham," he beseeched.

I lived in digs with Johnny Francis and Pat Taylor the band's female crooner who would one day in the future give birth to the actor Max Beasley.

I used to hide under her bed watching her disrobe, it became my hobby, and she'd scream and chase me out of her room.

Pat was wildly jealous of me because I sang all the songs people wanted to hear, and she sang stuff that the band wanted to hear like *Love for sale* and other classics from an almost extinct era.

I got, *She Loves You, I Like It, Glad All Over*. Johnny Francis loved to introduce me singing the Dave Clarke hit.

"And now folks here's Tony again who's feeling glad all over, lucky lad!"

He also liked to give silly prizes.

"The first girl up here with a pair of green knickers," he'd announce between tunes before being inundated with underwear, whilst the prize went to the girl who proffered a pair of one pound notes, which pre-Euro, we nicknamed nickers!

The band liked it. They always laughed at Johnny's jokes. He paid their wages.

My first meeting with the Musicians' Union looked like being a profitable affair. In those days, when a band opened in a new venue, the local MU secretary came to see them to check that they were all members, and that their terms were up to MU standards. Ken Lewis was his name. You remember certain names, especially when they change your life.

"You play the records as well as sing and play guitar," he observed, to which I concurred.

MU rate for the band was £18 a week. I was on £24, plus £6 for Tuesday's record night. I did 2-hour lunchtime sessions Monday through Friday and three sessions on Saturday.

"You should be on more than that son for the hours you're working," said Ken. He fed me avarice.

Two weeks went by before I received an official looking Musicians' Union envelope. I opened it to see if I could now buy my first car.

It read:

'Dear Tony,

It's been brought to my attention that you are breaking Union rules. The Musicians' Union is opposed to records being played in dancehalls as they are putting trios out of work.

I have to ask you to refrain from playing records, or you may have to resign from the Musicians' Union.

Ken Lewis.

(Secretary, Musicians' Union, Bristol).'

The *extreme* hierarchy in Top Rank's head office motored down the A4 from London like Stirling Moss. The team included my mentor Garry Brown and John Jarvis, who in time, would become Chairman of one of the world's most successful hotel chains, Ramada/Jarvis. Back then, John was batting for me.

I sat in the Bristol Suite General Manager's office and listened as they outbid the Musicians' Union.

Garry Brown took the floor. A former trombonist with one of the world's greatest Jazz bands, the Johnny Dankworth Orchestra, and later a bandleader in his own right for Mecca and Butlins and the future Entertainment Consultant for the QE2 liner, now addressed me by the name he had given me.

"Tony, we need you to go to a Musicians' Union meeting to fight for your rights as a musician to play records."

"What if I lose?" I posed.

"We'll still pay you your present salary as a disc jockey," chimed Mr Whittle, the Chairman of the whole Top Rank Leisure company, who had also joined the meeting. His presence served to strengthen my resolve.

"So my career as a vocalist and musician will be terminated if I fail to win?" I asked the trio of executives who sat before me.

"Tony, I don't know how to put this," said Garry Brown.

"You're a good singer, but you're the best fucking live DJ I've ever seen!"

The night before this meeting, I'd discussed the possible reasons for this unexpected Head Office visit with Johnny Francis, whose family I now lived with. Over tea and toast with raw tomatoes, our favourite supper, Johnny and his wife Sheila, made me aware of the star now hovering above me, and indeed over the leisure industry.

The economics of records versus Musicians' Union trio rates, taken across the Top Rank and Mecca ballroom networks was phenomenal.

Johnny then dropped the bombshell.

"Did you never wonder why the musicians didn't give you a hard time when your record night took a night's work off them?"

I had a mouthful of tomato and toast, so couldn't reply. Johnny continued: "The whole band got paid for this night off!"

It became clear that if the MU shut me down as a vocalist, Top Rank's Princely scapegoat would pave the way for incalculable corporate savings and, more importantly, ensure full houses, because records by the original artists played through high decibel, high quality speakers, was what the public wanted.

The Musicians' Union had already severely blocked records on BBC radio, what little radio we had in those days, now they were muscling in on the record-starved 60s generation in their clubs and dance halls.

Bands such as Bob Miller & the Millermen, the Steve Race Orchestra, Joe Loss, Edmundo Ross and Victor Sylvester with his satanic smile and his fucking 'Slow, slow, quick, quick slow' were absolutely coining it! All at the price of teenagers' sanity!

We worked it out in Johnny's kitchen that I was all that stood in the way of Top Rank, saving in excess of £1m a year in musician's wages, together with new levels of door-take, and of course, the equally ginormous Mecca Leisure and countless independent venue owners would also reap the rewards that vinyl discs could bring.

I currently earned £30 a week.

I was a big chip.

I faced the three friendly head office Directors witnessed by Johnny Hilliard the venue manager, and Johnny Francis my bandleader, who had advised me totally in my own interest and not his own. I always loved Johnny for that.

"So you will continue to pay me around £30 a week to only play records, but I have to be prepared to change my career?" I probed.

"Yes" – "Yes" – "Yes" the trio harmonised along the lines of *She Loves You*.

"But my career as a singer would be over?"

"Well… yes." one of them muttered as they each averted their eyes from direct contact with mine.

"May I point out that although I'll be working less during an evening, I'll still be there all night?"

Silence reigned.

I drew a breath and pitched:

"How about £100 a week should the MU expel me?"

They looked like three fairground sideshow heads, where you put a table tennis ball in their gaping mouths as the heads move from side to side, and you aim for the channel that gives the best score, and the top prize on the top shelf.

I got the prize.

"Yeah, yeah, yeah," they harmonised.

Then I went for the top shelf.

"Plus, every night we hit capacity I get a £20 bonus. Is that fair?"

Six weeks later I was called to a Bristol Musicians' Union meeting at the Spa Hotel. The local Union secretary, Ken Lewis, put forward his case, the same MU secretary who had suggested I *should* be paid more money, was inadvertently about to make it happen.

Unashamedly, I made him look very foolish by addressing the meeting with the story of how, the last time I met him, Ken had promised me a pay rise because I did the record breaks.

I wasn't taking any prisoners.

Lewis shrunk with embarrassment, hiding behind a pitcher of water that he drank rapaciously throughout the 30-minute hearing.

I'm sure I lost his vote.

Top Rank's bosses, up once again from London for this crucial meeting, presented their observations to the gathered members.

Johnny Francis stood up, a towering six foot two of a man, a life-long MU member and superb bandleader, saxophone and clarinet player and devout knicker collector. He took the microphone into his hand and began:

"If you throw Tony out of the Union, I promise you we will be down to a four-day week within months, down to a six piece within the year! Currently we are being booed when we come on stage, whilst Tony is cheered when he starts playing his records!"

There were 86 votes for me to be expelled, and 14 to keep me in the Union. For some reason my vote wasn't allowed, just as well really because then there'd have been 87 expulsion votes!

I was elated. The Bristol musicians had just voted me a massive pay rise, at the same time tolling the bell for big bands.

Back in 1964, by default, I became the world's first full time, wage earning, club DJ and eventually the first person to be on their payroll with my National Insurance describing my employment as *Disc Jockey*.

Top Rank gave me my own dressing room, which the band started to call my undressing room. At the age of 19 on £100+ a week, in a city called Bristol well, what would you expect?

Within weeks of the MU meeting, Tuesday nights record night reached the capacity 1,750 along with Saturday and Sunday night.

And so it remained until I left in 1966.

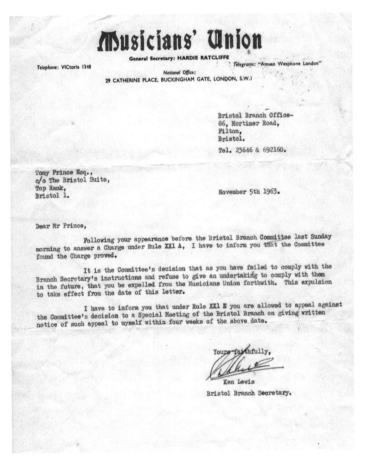

Jan: Learning English

We were given a new teacher in High School who specialised in our new subject, English Conversation. It was due to the teaching of Mrs Alena Hladká that we found ourselves speaking in English together for the first time. Our previous teacher had us copying phrases but never actually uttering them.

We assumed she had never been to the United Kingdom or any of the English-speaking countries, and had probably never spoken with someone whose mother tongue was English.

She would never know that our secret teachers were the DJs of Radio Luxembourg.

Students who listened regularly to Radio Luxembourg and were taught by Mrs Alena Hladká, became well advanced in how to string English into comprehensible sentences. OK, we may have inserted the odd '*Guys and gals*', but that was Jimmy Savile's fault!

Every one of us spent several hours each night making our escape to the Station of the Stars!

The move towards more western-produced movies continued into 1965 and we were treated to the type of English lessons we preferred, subtitled movies such as A Kind of Loving and This Sporting Life from the UK; the Mustangs with Marilyn Monroe and David & Lisa from the USA.

Then, right out of the blue, I received a post card depicting Trafalgar Square posted from London, and sent to me by a girl named Audrey.

Although my father had retired, from time to time he helped his former public transport company as a tram driver. I'd totally forgotten about his story the night he came home and mentioned the young English girl who was lost on his tram and who he had helped to find her way. Although they didn't have a long conversation he said they had understood enough for him to explain to her that I was studying English and how much I would appreciate a postcard from the UK. Audrey said how kind my father had been and that it was a pleasure for her to send me the postcard. Our textbooks didn't feature any pictures of London. Now, pasted inside mine, was a wonderful colour picture, the envy of all my friends in English class.

Pavel Kroupa and I teased each other constantly. We were great classmates. Each day we came to school with a new English word we had learned the previous evening. The game was to come up with one the other didn't yet know. It was a great way to accumulate even more vocabulary, and Pavel loved English as much as I.

One day, just before the school holidays, Pavel brought me details of an opportunity we both jumped at, a week-long intensive English course in the highlands, some 50kms from Brno. The idea of a whole week studying English was nothing short of a dream. The course was the first of its kind in our country, and I was lucky Pavel had come across it and we had completed the application straight away because it was an immediate sell out. But the problem was the cost.

Six hundred and ninety crowns were equivalent to two weeks' average salary, but I found a part-time job that came about, because of the panel homes people were building at that time. To buy one of these self-construct homes, the buyer had to put their hands to the plough and give several hundred hours to lay the building site. But some people, such as doctors, didn't like the concept of bricklaying and as this was all above board, advertisements appeared in the papers seeking surrogate labourers and I quickly became one for six or seven crowns an hour. My parents promised to make up the deficit, and so July became one of those dates you wished your life away for.

I counted the days to what I called our 'Paradise of English', but even before Pavel and I set sail on this literate journey, we decided to meet every other day and brush up on our English together, so that when we arrived we would look smart.

Tony: Discs-a-Gogo

I'd become friends with a local Bristol beauty queen called Heather Innes who had tickets to a TWW television show where we danced as part of the audience in a Cavern-style coffee bar setting. This was Discs-a-Gogo, an exciting audience participation pop show, established long before Ready Steady Go was launched.

We mingled, danced and looked as hip as we could around cameras, cables, and the artists miming their hits who included Peter and Gordon *World Without Love*, the Swinging Blue Jeans *Good Golly Miss Molly*, the Applejacks *Tell Me When,* and the Four Pennies singing *Juliet*. It was stimulating stuff.

After the rehearsal came a camera break prior to the actual 30- minute recording. I was sitting in a canvas chair pondering how the hell I could get the resident DJ Kent Walton's job when a fellow from a previous generation approached me.

"You're sitting in my chair," he said.

"How can it be yours? I've been here 15 minutes."

"I've been sat in it for four years. Read what it says on the back."

I stood and looked...'PRODUCER', it screamed at me!

"You must be Chris Mercer," I said offering my hand, which he reached down to accept.

"And who might you be tiny one?"

Golden words fell from my mouth, life-changing words.

"I'm Tony Prince DJ from the Top Rank Suite. I can do better than Kent Walton if ever he ever gets a sore throat!"

The show's producer laughed at my arrogance. I gave him his chair and we talked music.

And that was it for then. I left the studio having glimpsed heaven. Now I wanted the golden gates at TWW to open, but I wondered if I'd over-stepped the mark with Kent Walton, another Radio Luxembourg legend and a man who doubled DJing with wrestling commentary on television every Saturday afternoon.

Shortly after this momentous expedition to TWW, Heather blew me out; she also blew her parents out. At 16 and never had a nipple kissed so far as I knew, she took off with one Peter Walsh an ageing, debonair, smooth talking bastard who managed the Tremeloes. Heather's mum and dad were mortified; I was mystified. Peter Walsh must have been 40.

Eventually Heather married Peter and had kids, but by the time I became a friend of Peter's years later, they were divorced and I haven't seen her from the night of our last kiss to this day. But Heather Walsh née Innes definitely placed a large paving stone in my lengthening yellow brick road the day she took me to Discs-a-Gogo. I was thrilled at meeting another DJ legend, bigger even than Kent Walton because this one was the man who presented my favourite TV show Juke Box Jury. David Jacobs, a most unlikely Radio Luxembourg star, came to the Top Rank to compare a fashion show at a private dinner dance.

As usual, when the band finished I played the records.

Whilst spinning the Honeycombs' *Have I the Right*, I noticed David Jacobs on the balcony talking to Johnny Francis.

In those days there was no console. The two turntables sat atop plastic drums, which displayed swirling colours. There were ten feet between each drum and after I'd cued up the next record, I danced to the music along with the audience.

I was the first DJ to stand up to do the job miming to every record and playing air-guitar. Who could stand still with all that great Motown and soul music like Sly & the Family Stone's *Dance to the Music* or the Showstoppers' *Ain't nothing but a House party?*

Today no club DJ sits behind the console. Today's DJs are far too cool to dance, they just lurch over the records lifting the stylus, or pressing the controller, one hand pressing their headphone tight to their ear, working out the mix point. There are the odd exceptions such as America's Junior Vasquez and the UK's Carl Cox, who like to be one with the crowd but generally, David Guetta, Fat Boy Slim and the big money spinners, just wave their hands in the air. Personality DJs in clubs are in recession, now it's all about the music and the drugs that rock the house.

Later, on Radio Caroline, Radio Luxembourg and Capital Gold, I continued to stand throughout my broadcasts unless I had a hang-over of course. How the hell can you sit down when you're doing such an exciting job? Accountants sit down for God's sake! I'd take a leaf out of my old bandleader Johnny Francis' audience games, changing the format slightly. "Anyone with a pair of green knickers?"

"No? OK, white ones'll do…"

When a pair materialised, I'd put the panties over my head like a blindfold still dancing around the stage. Then I'd stretch the elastic, placing the knickers in my mouth like a sword swallower. A slight of hand, palming them into my pocket, tongue pushed into the wall of my mouth giving the impression I was still chewing them, and down they'd be gulped with a grimace on my face and a look of sheer horror on the face of the knickerless girl at front of stage! Draughty dancing for her for the rest of the night, but boy did she get a lot of guys asking her what she wanted to drink?

I'd mime to a record by Mr Murray (Mitch Murray) called, *Down Came the Rain*, where I finished up drowning myself with a jug of water.

People loved to see a drowned DJ. It's all well and good kitting yourself out in the latest fashions and poncing around to please the girls, but the minute they see you're prepared to make a prat of yourself, the guys start to like you too, and I wanted everyone to like me.

One night the staff went too far and threw a full bucket of water over me from the balcony fusing the sound system, prematurely terminating the evening and their jobs.

I'd dress up to the nines in a 60s mini-skirt and bra, and mime to *My name's Christine*, as political hooker Christine Keeler. I'd trip, fall off stage, finishing up arse over tit with the mic lead wrapped around my ankles in Houdini style, laid out on the dance floor enjoying thunderous applause.

Then I'd take things one step further and peel off my dress to David Rose's *The Stripper*. The bra came off last of all revealing two baby's feeding teats stuck to my chest with strips of plasters. The symptoms of class comic syndrome affected me all my life, I might have become a comedian had music not possessed me so. I wasn't satisfied just playing records. The singer and the clown, established deep within my Whitehead family genes, both needed an outlet.

And so it came to pass that the top BBC and Radio Luxembourg DJ, David Jacobs, came towards me as the band started their quickstep session. David was a charming English gentleman who was just as you saw and heard him on the media, but don't ask me how he got into *teenage* radio because this was one square fella in a very round world. He had all the bases covered, BBC Light Programme, Radio Luxembourg and the most important pop music show on television, Juke Box Jury.

I was thrilled to pump the legend's hand, voted BEST DJ every year in the NME readers poll. In between signing autographs, he asked me if I had an agent? Then he suggested that his own agent might be interested in me. It sounded to me like lots of yellow bricks.

Jan: Stalin's monument

In 1949 Stalin had openly demanded respect for the liberation of Czechoslovakia and immediately comrades laid an enormous foundation stone in Prague, and had the nation's architects conceptualise the biggest statue our capital had ever seen; it was simply enormous.

The building of the Stalin statue with the mighty Chairman of the Council of People's Commissars of the Soviet Union, standing firmly at the head of a flag waving line of farmers and workers, began to take shape in 1952 and was unveiled by 1955. I don't think Russia, itself, had built such a fine statue to a leader.

Those arse-lickers who had commissioned this granite elephant, hadn't allowed for what happened in 1956. This was the year when President Khrushchev told everyone what he thought of Stalin, and what he thought of Stalin was far removed from the media and educational tenet we had been served. If we were to believe Khrushchev, Stalin was now a *'brutal despot'*. And believe him we did. His picture was taken down in classrooms, offices and factories throughout the land.

Russia's new leader's condemnation of Joseph Stalin caused ripples right across the eastern block creating unrest in Poland, and a revolution in Hungary.

In Czechoslovakia we hadn't revolted since 1953, when the money reform led to 50 units being devalued to 1. One minute a farmer was earning one hundred crowns a month, next he was earning two! The Czechoslovakian communists knew how to smokescreen us, it was their speciality. Khrushchev's denouncement of Stalin was given the explanation with phrases that explained everything and nothing. They were good at this; they'd had lots of practise in dismantling policies as one thing after another failed.

But what they couldn't hide was the monstrous statue in Prague. Stalin stared out from behind a queue of granite people that had become known as *'the queue for meat'*!

Stalin's image stared down on the residents of Prague from Letná Hill, an acute embarrassment to its commissioners and a painful memo to everyone that they got it wrong.

Finally, in 1962, as the Beatles were playing in Hamburg, the decision was made to destroy the Stalin statue. But how to demolish a 15.5 metre high granite ensemble that is set on a 15 metre reinforced metal and concrete pedestal… *without* telling the people?

The first thing Public Safety did was cordon off the area surrounding Letná Hill and then forgot to mention anything at all was happening. They guarded the area day and night and photography was strictly forbidden.

So the fact that photographs eventually surfaced is a minor communist miracle, it clearly shows the destruction taking place including the detonation of explosives and clouds of smoke, which happened on a regular basis.

Whenever an explosion was heard across the city, students and young kids screamed their delight no matter where they were and eventually the whole non-communist population joined in, so it sounded like a goal had been scored by FC Praha in a Cup Final.

For the first time in their lives, students were able to express their hatred for the regime without Public Safety being able to do anything about it. No one could ask them 'What are you laughing at? Why do you dance on that table?' because, from Public Safety's point of view, it was top secret that the monolith was being demolished. So no one could be punished for something that never happened.

Whilst this farce made fools of the communist government in front of the whole nation, still they would not admit that black was black. In this case, the event was so black and white all they could do was say nothing at all.

Tony: Bunny Lewis

Five weeks later David Jacobs was as good as his word, and accompanied his agent Bunny Lewis from London, exclusively to see me on my Tuesday night full-house record session.

Next I was invited to London to talk with the DJ *agent of agents* in his Knightsbridge offices, where he shared space with his wife Janique Joelle, who ran a subsidiary model agency.

Sitting waiting in reception with all those beautiful models going in and out, I was already signed!

"We'll have to take 25%," Bunny slipped in as I scanned his desk for a contract.

"We normally take 20%, but as David discovered you, we'll want to reward him with 10% so we'll only take 15% not 30%."

I wasn't at all interested in their percentages. I wanted fame.

"Very generous Mr.Lewis," I bantered ignoring the mathematics.

"Will I have a contract?" I asked.

"Don't worry about a contract son," he smirked, "Even Katy Boyle doesn't have a contract with us and she does the Pink Camay soap ads!"

"It's just that..."

"What?"

"Well Mr Lewis, I once broke a contract and wondered if it would have any effect, as I won't be released from it until I'm 21?"

"What contract was that," he asked, seeing his 25% slipping away.

"With Gerald Armstrong, the horse trainer. I broke my apprentice contract and they won't let me work as a jockey anywhere else until the end of 1965."

He guffawed.

"Don't worry son," he said his huge shoulders pumping with mirth.

"We won't book you for the Grand National commentary!"

My mentor wasn't at the meeting, but if you believe in such voodoo as the Celestine Prophecy, then, how about this...

Towards lunchtime, I was walking down Oxford Street for the first time in my life, taking in the hustle and bustle of the capital, just killing time until I had to catch the train back to Bristol, when a car horn sounded. I turned from admiring a large display of Beatle boots in a shop window to see a Daimler Sovereign pulling up beside me at the curb.

Behind the wheel of his swank wheels beckoning me to join him, was none other than David Jacobs, the one and only person I knew in London! Just how spooky was *that*? He was on his way to the BBC for his Midday Spin programme, and bade me jump in the car. First time in London, first time in a Daimler, first time in Broadcasting House, this was heady stuff for an Oldham kid and my feet hovered half an inch above the ground, long before David Blaine did it!

Little did I know it, and not that I would have believed it with so much ambition coursing through my veins, but this would be the only time in my professional DJ life that I would sit in a Broadcasting House studio. Years later I would be interviewed on the Steve Wright Show a couple of times, and be featured in a half hour BBC TV documentary titled Farewell Fab 208 but this, for now, was the nearest I would ever get to a BBC microphone.

I can't tell you how thrilling it was.

Ten minutes into his show, with me sitting right by his side as he broadcast, the producer's metallic voice came over the speaker system.

"Anyone got a loud watch on?" he asked.

It was a Timex, which my mother and father had bought me for my 16th birthday from HR Samuels, the Jewellers, in Oldham. It was expensive for a working class couple in 1960, and therefore something of a treasure.

But it was too noisy for the BBC.

I suppose that in the production room on the other side of the studio window it went like... '*And welcome (tick) to the show everyone (tock). I'd like to begin with a (tick) new platter presentation (tock) from the Helmut Zacharias Orchestra (tick) which is aptly entitled (tock) Tockio Medley!*'

Everything David uttered was on a script in front of him and, horror of horrors... he didn't even play the records! This was done in the next room beyond the double-glazing, where no less than three men and a secretary controlled the output.

I was gob smacked that Mid Day Spin was all so pre-ordained.

For me it was a *Dis Mayed Sin*.

Later still, when I visited Radio Luxembourg's studios in Hertford Street with David where he introduced me to my Lords and Masters, Pete Murray and Alan Freeman, I was astounded to learn that they ALL worked from scripts all apart from "*ooooo000Ooooo, howzabout-that-then*", Jimmy Savile, whose incredible funeral I would attend some 47 years later, and whose fall from grace as a perverted paedophile was only revealed after his death.

I would soon be playing my part in ridding our airwaves of all the pre-scripted bullshit, but there were no pirate ships at sea yet, and the entire nation still had to wait until 7.30pm every night to hear non-stop pop music. If you became a radio DJ in these days, you were one of a mere handful who became household names on 208.

The BBC Light Programme still offered very little pop and that was dominated by the likes of David Jacobs.

My first ever agent said I needed to be in Equity, the actors' union, as I was no longer in the Musicians' Union. In Bunny's office a few weeks later, David Jacobs and pop singer Craig Douglas (also handled by Lewis) proposed and seconded me, as we filled out my Equity application.

Whilst I bore no animosity towards David and have to recognise that it was wonderful to be 'discovered' and to be appreciated by an icon in my younger days, in later years I learned that he had also 'discovered' my colleague Stuart Henry. Stuart also gave a 10% tithing to the David Jacobs' Foundation for David Jacobs for many years. When I revealed this to his close colleague Pete Murray in 2012, he was abjectly shocked and dismayed that David would stoop so low for the sake of money he hardly needed.

I did two audition tapes, one for Radio Luxembourg at Radio Luxembourg, and one for the BBC at the BBC. Both shows were scripted for me by Bunny Lewis, who put words into my mouth that *he* thought I should be saying:

'There goes Elvis Presley with his groovy new single (You're the) Devil in Disguise. I was only talking to the King the other day and he said to be sure and send Radio Luxembourg listeners his best wishes!'

The script bore no resemblance whatsoever to me, myself or I, and I knew I had jumped through no hoops at all.

The responses from those in power were imparted to me by Bunny a few days later. They said I needed to *'practice a little more and try to stop sounding like Jimmy Savile.'*

Bunny suggested we make some more tapes in a few weeks time, which I did

but beseeched him to let me perform scriptless. This time we experienced a strange kind of approval, which Bunny announced in a letter:
'Your tape has been accepted by the BBC. What this means is that if anyone wishes to use you, they may do so. We now have to find someone to use you.'
I looked forward to being used.

Within a few months, with no work or further auditions forthcoming simply because there was nothing else to audition for, I grew tired of having an agent who was neither earning for me, himself *or* David Jacobs! A proper contract had yet to see my signature and, for some reason, I put great store on the idea of having a contract with my manager. Money meant very little to me, certainly not as much as it did to David Jacobs.

Jan: Katka

As soon as the school holidays of Summer 1965 began and, as planned, I committed to working on a building site to raise funds for my next trip. What a wonderful experience it was to get dirt beneath my fingernails, to become fit and to earn money through good old-fashioned hard graft that would produce the funding to my Paradise of English.

The journey began for Pavel and I by train, which took us some 50 kilometres into the mountains, to a highland village called Chlébské, which sat about 600 metres above sea level, with rather steep inclines and romantic views leading to an old war-time hotel that civilisation had bypassed.

Pavel and I were put in separate classes, which, after two years of being seated together in our English class, was no wrench for us. I found myself amongst a friendly group of Bratislavan students and had a lot of fun with all of them. One however, a girl named Katka, constantly caught my eye. I couldn't see enough of her and, as I gazed at love for the very first time, my heart exploded.

We had been advised by the teacher to speak in English to one another throughout the week, including late afternoons when lessons ended, and we played volleyball, table tennis or went for walks together. You could hardly call them lessons, we were having so much fun making grammar in the wide outdoors, lounging in the beautiful hilly countryside, chatting in the shade of a tree as we escaped from the hot summer sun. I had been right all along. This was my Paradise of English, and especially now I had met Katka.

We learned new songs and sang them a great deal, all in English but not all English songs, rather traditional songs from England, Scotland, Ireland and America. We joined voices on *You are my Sunshine, South of the Border, It's a long way to Tipperary* and *Auld Lang Syne*.

All the teachers were excellent, but we liked Miroslav Berka the best, as he told us of his times in New York some 17 years earlier. He was one of the last Czech students after World War II who managed to go to America before the gates closed in 1948. After this time, studying a language in a western country was prohibited by the Czechoslovakian authorities.

Mr Berka had been teaching in Cairo University in Egypt, a comradely nation with our country. His weekly teaching on the Summer English Course was part of his vacation, after which he would return to Cairo. We were extremely grateful to the fate that ordained we should speak with a man who had studied in the United States, the same fate that would see us in the open air, singing American and English songs at the top of our voices, and speaking of life in the west with our teachers and like minded school chums.

But the most amazing part of all this was that we could do all this without fear. It was law in Czechoslovakia that every restaurant and hotel subscribed and made available to their guests the communist rag Red Law. The hotel had a copy so I glanced through it to see what they wanted me to love today? Then I saw it. The announcement, that from 9 July 1965, the Beatles' Hard Day's Night was coming to the Jalta cinema in Prague. There was no mention of Brno, but it was always so, that Prague had the premiers and our city would follow in the film distribution system.

Now I had something to look forward to, which eased the pain growing in my heart, as my Paradise week was drawing to a close. But the best was yet to come on the final night, when we threw a party in one of the rooms with a little wine and a lot of music. Ivan Havel was one of our study group - we didn't know it then, but he was the brother of our future president, and Ivan had something amazing, a tape recorder with plenty of Beatles tapes. Before long, someone suggested that the best way to listen to the Beatles was in the dark, and we unanimously agreed.

For the first time in my life I was able to enjoy the Beatles in top studio quality without the usual Luxembourg static and fading, and with one Beatles track followed by another and another. This never happened on 208 metres, because the DJs mixed the music so that a Beatles track would be rationed across each evening.

When the lights went down, Katka moved closer to me and we listened together and drew even closer so that we could whisper in English until words were no longer needed, and we spoke in the language of love as Paul McCartney sang '*She was just 17, you know what I mean?*' I knew what he meant alright, but Katka was 16 and *the way she looked was way beyond compare!* And just as things were getting really interesting, the reel to reel tape would come to an end, the lights would go on, the tape turned over, the lights turned off and away we would go again until the morning arrived, and although none of us had slept, not one of us felt tired. We were all charged with teenage juice.

And so the time came to sing our final *Auld Lang Syne*. Then, as I left to catch my train, Katka and Andrej my new Bratislavan English-speaking friends invited me to visit them later that summer, and without hesitation I promised I would.

Tony: The haircut

Back at the Top Rank, Bristol, I had learned to milk the local tabloids for publicity and was filling the place week-in week-out. Even on the Saturday morning under-16 sessions, which mums used as a great baby-sitting device whilst they did their shopping, we had 1,600 under 16s doing the *Twist* with Chubby Checker and the *Shake* with Sam Cooke and I had them all *Shouting* their lungs out with Lulu.

'*WeeeEeeeelllllllll...you know you make me wanna...*'

Then a quick cleaning of the joint between 12 and 2 after which, in excess of a thousand teenagers came to dance in my afternoon matinee.

Roger Cook and Roger Greenaway, aka David & Jonathan, seminal writers of countless hits including *I'd Like to Teach the World to Sing* for Blue Mink, told me years later that they were in my Saturday audiences every week being musically influenced, as the hits just kept on coming on that Bristol dancefloor.

At 7.30pm we were off again, non stop till 1am, by which time I had worked three sessions for over 4,400 customers.

Saturdays were long days, what with all the female distractions and dressing room action, packed into a 15-hour gig which I have no doubt the M.U. would not have permitted me to do!

In the UK at that time, you had to be a club member to attend licensed dance premises on a Sunday. Sunday Club was by far our most popular night in Bristol, with the manager illegally allowing in excess of 2,000 paying customers. Together with the Sunday crowd, 1,200 on Friday nights, a full house on Tuesdays, and 4,400 admissions every Saturday over three sessions, the Bristol Suite was the jewel in the Top Rank crown.

My budget for purchasing records was a mere £10 a week, for which I could buy perhaps 20 singles and a couple of albums. This budget was equivalent to 20 or so admissions! With 1,750 admissions on my Tuesday record-only nights, Johnny's prediction of the live orchestra's doomsday was now coming about, with the Monday 'strict tempo' session down to a mere 150 shiny-shoed punters, who glided by Johnny's once big band, now down from 15 musicians to 10.

On this night when the band had a break I played waltzes, quick steps and fox trots, and as the toffee nosed couples glided by me, I counted the seconds before Johnny and the band returned.

I soon began pocketing the record budget, giving myself a weekly bonus. The local record store wanted exposure, and I was the man with the microphone, and the means to secure free records from them in exchange for the odd plug. It could have been translated as a form of payola, but the record shop didn't direct which records I played, so they got their nightly name checks and I even did an occasional show in their shop window, which was promotion for all of us.

Receipts at the till for my record sessions alone were in the region of £10,000 a week, and I suppose I was going through what Alan Freed went through in America. The 'payola' stopped the DJs asking for a pay rise!

Walking outside the Rank one morning with Garry Brown who was up from London for a visit, we saw a ladder protruding from a manhole in the middle of the Broadmead shopping centre's main road. Garry turned to Johnny Hilliard, our rakish Irish manager, (who Garry later discovered was shagging the girl in the pay box, and fucking Top Rank at the same time) and asked him if there was a sewer beneath the road?

"To be sure it's a sewer," he answered. "Runs turds straight into the river Avon!"

Within 30 minutes Brown had borrowed a fishing rod from a local sports shop, purchased a salmon from a nearby fishmongers whilst Hilliard, under Brown's instruction, had pulled a photographer out of the Western Daily Press whose offices were directly across the road.

I posed, coming up the ladder from stink-town below with the fish on the end of the line.

The next day the picture took up an entire page in the local rag with the caption: '*DJ pulls something fishy from Broadmead sewers!*'

Garry Brown taught me the value of how good ideas attracted media interest, and the full-page publicity fired me into a publicity-seeking frenzy.

We had some trouble when Frank Lord took over from Johnny Hilliard as manager. A dapper, traditional manager from strict-tempo land who, like the MU, had still to come to terms with records and DJs. Frank and I had a love-hate relationship. His main problem was, he thought he was the boss! He also thought I might have been intimate with his new girlfriend Mary, which was true. Although we were the exact same height, we didn't see eye to eye.

"You'll have to get your hair cut Tony, look at this," said Frank Lord-God-Almighty offering me the Bristol Evening Post.

On the letters page, a punter who had been refused admission because his hair was too long, sighted the hypocrisy of the Top Rank: 'For having a DJ,

Tony Prince, with hair twice as long as mine!'
"You'll have to get it chopped," Frank said coldly.
"You'll have to fuck off Frank," I replied.
"Then you're fired," he said and walked away.
I walked into his office the following day with my proposal.
"I will get my hair cut Frank, but it will have to be on a Tuesday night, on stage, before the audience!" Frank agreed, I'd got him out of a stew.

Come Tuesday night when the local barber arrived, the Top Rank Suite was rammed. If the police had raided, Frank Lord would have been busted for over-capacity. There were 2,500 kids in a 1,750 capacity ballroom, it seemed that every kid in Bristol wanted to see the scalping live on stage.

I announced my fate, and faded the record as the hairdresser arrived on stage. Sitting in a chair, he threw his white sheet around me and reached for his scissors.
That was when the riot began.

Incensed members of the audience dragged the barber off the stage, even before he could make his first snip. The stage was invaded by scores of Beatle-haired lads and mini-skirted girls. I was about to be saved by a generation who were challenging archaic rules of entry, which demanded boys have a short back and sides hairstyle, wear a suit, sport a tie and don't dance together.

On stage I was surrounded in an impregnable human fortress, as the bouncers tried to re-establish a semblance of a dancehall, that had become anarchistic bedlam in a matter of minutes. The police, whose headquarters were conveniently across the road from the Rank, joined the fray.
Chairs were thrown from the balcony as fights broke out between rival Bristolian gangs, who now used the revolution as a smoke screen for yobism.
I'd returned to my turntables, and started playing the Supreme's *Baby Love* in an attempt to get them dancing and restore order, but I was knocked sideways and the needle gouged into a groove playing a dramatic 'kerklunk', 'kerklunk'. A perfect sound-effect for the hostile scene around me, which in 40 years' time would have been regarded as a hip-hop scratch, which people would have danced to and rapped over.
There were 32 arrests.

Frank Lord, the dapper manager who still used Brylcream on his extremely short back and sides, took the microphone, his right arm raised in the air, fingers outstretched calling for calm.
The kids dragged me off stage, and carried me shoulder high around the dance floor. I know what it's like to be the only scorer in a World Cup Final!
As I was carried shoulder high around the Top Rank, my pleasure levels

were at a zenith, my arteries firing pure adrenaline.

"The hairdresser has left the building, calm down now, calm down please!" announced Frank.

"Tony will not be having his hair cut!"

The cheers lifted the roof.

The *No Long Hair* rule was dropped from that day forth throughout the Top Rank circuit. Ties were no longer necessary and you didn't have to wear a suit, providing you looked clean and tidy.

The 60s decade was getting into its swing.

Jan: Pirate Radio Caroline

I returned to Brno still full of the amazing night before with Katka, and the incredibly romantic musical experience the Beatles had provided. I had been spoiled somewhat by the high quality of the tapes, now I had to settle back into music covered in static, music that would fade depending on the atmospherics. But my enthusiasm for Radio Luxembourg and its DJs was as strong as ever as I tuned in at 7.30pm to see what new tunes might have arrived in my absence?

As I listened to the station that night, my thoughts jumped from Katka to the tape recorder. I loved Katka and I coveted the tape recorder. I had to have both.

One was a phone call away. The other was a lot of saving away.

A tape recorder was now available in the shops as Tesla, a state company was producing the Sonet Duo but unfortunately the price was 2,300 crowns, some six weeks' wages for the average worker, and I wasn't a worker.

Earlier that afternoon, I had called my new Bratislavan friend Andrej, who told me that his parents had confirmed I could visit and stay with him anytime.

Before I went to sleep I had made up my mind.

I would go the very next day.

As Bob Dylan said, *The Time's they are a Changin'* and nowhere more than in Czechoslovakia. Two years ago, I would not have been able to make such an impulsive decision. To travel, you needed permission. Two days in another city, and the first thing you did was visit the municipal offices to log in. The communists wanted to know *everybody's* whereabouts.

When we went to the Beskydy Mountains with our parents each year renting a room there, immediately upon our arrival we had to let the local authorities know we had arrived and how long we would be staying. It was a time wasting, boring ritual.

For the first time in my life I was travelling alone to see friends, and not to summer camps or relatives. I was starting to feel quite mature, and what a wonderful moment when I climbed down off the train to be met on the platform by all my new Slovak friends. We'd only parted company two days earlier, but the reunion was like we were long lost friends. They made me feel like a celebrity.

As part of Czechoslovakia, Slovakia wasn't a foreign country in the usual sense, as perhaps Wales is not so foreign to an Englishman, even though, like the Czech Republic and Slovakia, they have two different languages.

What thrilled me most was the trust we gave each other after only a matter of days since we had met in the hills. The trust came from the common ground, learning English together and learning we all loved the Beatles, the Rolling Stones, the Kinks and Radio Luxembourg. This united us. This gave us hope for our future and each of us felt there was a definite change in the air. The nature of our friendship instilled optimism where hope had no portfolio. So we talked and talked in an atmosphere of freedom I had never before known, speaking openly, loudly and fearlessly critical of our totalitarian world and the communist ideology we were living.

Our little group had arrived at an age where we could ask questions, questions we'd not yet understood but needed to be asked, because our parents kept political discussion off the agenda for our welfare.

With these new friends I grew brazen and joked with them, but I also inherited knowledge and an awareness of things my parents had never mentioned to me. It was explained that we would not get the good jobs unless we were members of the communist party, and that my chances of gaining a place at university were slim to non-existent, for the same reason.

I shared with my friends the story of the Stalin monument's destruction, and the detonations that caused applause around the city of Prague. I was amazed that they were completely unaware of what had happened.

Having recounted the story, they all shared my belief that this was yet another sign that our communist government were reaching the end of their life expectancy.

Our thoughts were 25 years premature.

Then I told them about the Beatles' A Hard Days Night, and how unfair it was that it had been in Prague and Bohemian cities since July, whilst in Brno and Bratislava there was no sign of a release.

The very next day we had some consolation when we went to the movies. The newsreel came on, and we stared in disbelief as a 30-second Beatles clip came on the screen.

A voice talked over them singing I Wanna be your Man, and we all gawked at the screen as he said:

"The real Beatles are quite different from their exaggerated images and people's perception. Above all they are superb musicians and write many of their songs. What is even more interesting is that they are politically progressive as they were involved in the British elections in the winter of 1964 when they openly supported the Labour Party, which eventually won. The real Beatles have our full admiration!"

Walking home we discussed what had happened with the Beatles news clip. Normally this wouldn't have got anywhere near passing the censor. We fantasised that 'one of our kind' must work in the Cultural Department news editing facility, a bright spark perhaps who loved the Beatles as much as we. Our secret ally who knew just how to write a script that would impress the film censorship board members, probably the very same person who had worked it for A Hard Day's Night to have a public release. Our unknown hero ensured that the Beatles' clip came to our towns.

This then was the consensus of opinion as we chatted and laughed, and put the world to rights on our way home after seeing the Beatles.

I said farewell to Katka and now looked forward to returning with Andrej who had shown me an Elvis EP called *Kid Galahad*. Tonight he would play all six tracks for me. Like the Beatles in the mountains, I now experienced Elvis in high quality; it felt as though Elvis was with us in Andrej's room.

I really appreciated Elvis' voice for the first time and wished Andrej had some real gutsy Elvis rock 'n' roll to play such as *Jailhouse Rock* or *Hound Dog*, but after six plays I started to love the tracks and realised, as I caught the words, one of the songs was all about me.

'*The rich man wants the Princess - The poor man just wants the girl - But the man who can sing when he hasn't got a thing - He's the king of the whole wide world!*'

Then the next song came on, and suddenly Elvis was speaking of our situation in Czechoslovakia, like a philosopher...

'*It's good to laugh and sing - Don't worry about a thing - Wear a happy smile - Cut loose and run a mile - If you relax and just enjoy it all - Life has got to be a ball.*'

If I wasn't feeling good now, the next thing lifted me to another level altogether. Andrej pulled out his radio receiver, and due to optimal atmospheric conditions in the area we were able to listen, not just to Radio Luxembourg but also to the exciting new arrival Radio Caroline, the pirate ship both clear as a bell.

Caroline seemed even more cool than Luxy. We listened to Tony Prince, who seemed like, well, like *us*. The Radio Luxembourg DJs were great but somewhat smooth and perfect, Tony sounded a great deal younger, like the kid next door. Pirate radio brought a new dimension into our lives. I never would believe that anything could be better than Luxy but here it was, the next generation of DJs.

Tony spoke quickly. Sometimes we couldn't keep up with him and yet we

understood everything. He was speaking a language we understood and
although we didn't fully comprehend what Radio Caroline was about, why
a boat would become a radio station, we recognised the language instantly;
it was a language we wanted to hear every day.
It was the language of freedom.

Tony: The gang chase

I ate regularly at a cafe near the Rank called The Pegasus, owned by a
wonderful Greek called Paul Lazarides and his honey-friendly wife Maria.
Paul had got himself involved with an ex-catering manager from the Top
Rank called Jeff Hubbard, who'd persuaded him to release some of the
restaurant's profits from bacon and eggs into a management company.
Frustrated as only a youth can become, developing gloom from impatience,
I was ripe for the plucking.
Paul and Jeff wanted to manage me and put me in front of a group.
  I called Bunny Lewis. He wasn't in so I spoke with Tom, his assistant
who expressed their profound interest in me, and advised me to give things
time. But time was sand in a bottle, and it was flowing far too fast.
"Even Alan Freeman doesn't have a contract with us and he does the
OMO washing powder commercials!" It was like a script they worked
from. In the end I left the Lewis agency on the grounds that they hadn't
procured any work for me during the five months I'd been with them. A
couple of audition tapes was all they had funded with negative responses
from Luxembourg and the BBC.
  A few years later, when I called him to see if we could kiss and make up,
sweet Bunny told me not to bother him again.
"And tell your mother to stop sending me her pathetic letters!"
A man obviously bitterly scarred by a kid who would walk away from his
stewardship.
  Years later still, during a telephone conversation with this man with an
elephant's memory, still miffed by my rebuff, Bunny told me with vengeful
undertones that he'd planned to do for me what he did for Simon Dee.
With Lewis as his agent, Simon had blazed his way from Radio Caroline
to the BBC and primetime TV with Dee Time on Saturday nights.
  He could have become a real hero, an icon amongst DJs. He could have,
but he didn't because Simon grew into a megalomaniac, a supercilious
manager's nightmare.
"What a shame for both of us Bunny," I said in response to this revelation.
Now however, I was talking to him in my position as Programme Director
of Radio Luxembourg discussing a programme for the Emperor Rosko,

who he now managed.

"By the way," I asked, "Whatever happened to Simon Dee?"

He gave a guttural choking sound.

Paul and Jeff persuaded me to resign from the Top Rank, paid me a small retainer and found me a group of head-bangers from Liverpool called the Mersey 4, who we promptly renamed the Tony Prince Kombo, (with a 'K' to be Kool)!

I ignored the Musicians' Union, because I would never ever pay a £50 fine to rejoin. Strangely no one ever asked me if I, or my band, were in the Musicians' Union and had they done so, they would have learned that I was a paid up member of Equity.

I was back in the gold lamé suit!

"*Weeeeeeeellllllll, Be bopalula…!*"

It was a strange decision, passing up the potential of doing future Fairy Snow washing powder TV commercials, in preference to singing *Hoochie Coochie Man* in half empty village halls in Gloucestershire.

I could have cleaned up, been top of the soaps!

The group was a nightmare. Great rock n' rollers but utterly mental! The Mersey 4 were Robbie, (bass), Pete (drums), Carl (lead guitar) and Tony (rhythm guitar). The four moved into my two-bedroomed flat and proceeded to dismantle my brain cells.

Example: One day I reached for a bottle of ginger beer someone had left opened. I swallowed day-old piss! – *You* feel sick? How do you think *I* felt?

The drummer, Pete, came out of the toilet displaying a turd wrapped in toilet paper, steaming like a hot dog and proceeded to aim it through the window at a group of my fans, who had gathered below. Thankfully, he missed the fans, but it remained plum centre of my car roof until the next torrential downpour.

I worked it out. They'd heard the story that John Lennon had once pissed on a nun's head off a balcony on the Reeperbahn in Hamburg, and to emulate him was the route to success!

Womanising in a pub up the Gloucester Road, we found ourselves surrounded by a dozen local babes who were enamoured with their Scouse charm. Beyond this pretty circle of adulation were their boyfriends, tough, hard, Bristol teds. By closing time they had sounded the war drums, and 100 teds gathered from various watering holes lying in wait for us in the street.

The landlord, who knew on which side his bread was buttered, refused to either call the police, or let us escape through the back door.

We ran the gauntlet to the group's van, parked behind my turd-capped banger.

Women screamed, men put the boot in, passersby ran for cover, windows opened and quickly closed.

I made it into my car trying to persuade the local girl who had followed me to sod off, as I fumbled with the keys. She climbed inside, just as someone who looked like he had some claim on her, arrived with three large friends. I locked the door, turned the key and the engine churned unsympathetically with a flooded carburettor caused by my impatient foot.

Six inches from my face, the uninvited passenger's boyfriend showed me the tread on his boot sole, but the window held. Behind me, gauntlet run, the group somehow made it into the van.

I wasn't concerned about them but Robbie, the bass player, held our mascot, a small kitten we named Kombo, who he had decided to take with us for the night. Kombo was to blame for everything. In the pub, pussy had attracted pussy, which started the whole unhealthy liaison.

We were chased in convoy, me in my Vauxhall Victor, the van containing the Mersey 4, followed by five angry ted-filled cars. I hoped that taking the Gloucester Road at 90mph with my horn blowing might attract the police. No such luck! As we all well know, they're never there when you need them.

And brother did we need them now!

I stopped on a dual carriageway at the edge of the city, witnessing the unbelievable scenes unfolding in my rear view mirror. Three cars overtook the van blocking its path, two pulled up behind. Tyres screeched to a halt Hollywood-style, I could see the blue smoke.

I looked over my shoulder a safe distance down the road from the attack, my passenger screaming, "They're going to kill them!"

I watched as the mob literally ripped the van door off its hinges pulling Tony the rhythm guitarist out, and to the ground. As some advanced to pull other members from the vehicle, two of them lifted the door off the road, raised it above their heads and smashed it through the windscreen.

"Go, go, get away," screamed the girl.

I had to do something, anything and to flee for help didn't seem a life-saving option.

"Drive to Broadmead! Get the police," she urged.

"Not yet," I breathed slamming the gears into reverse. Keeping one hand on the horn, the other trying to steer, I reversed the 50 yards, my tyres screaming as loudly as my unwelcome passenger. The gang scattered as I made impact with the lead vehicle. Crunch!

The distraction worked, they were spitting blood, but now they were after *me*!

With their bumper mating with mine creating a flare of sparks in my wake, it took five minutes to reach the sanctum of Broadmead Police Station.

Running inside I was lucky enough to find Cliff Smith, a sergeant I knew well from the Top Rank riot days.

By the time we came out of the station the cavalcade had arrived. The ted, whose Ford Capri I had wrapped in a Vauxhall Victor, approached with angry bloodshot eyes.

I hid behind three cops as *he* accused *me* of dangerous driving!

The group's van, its door still posted firmly in the former windscreen, limped to the back of the queue as eight mascara-streaked molls poured out, with what used to look like the Tony Prince Kombo.

The teds, as it transpired, had more willing witnesses than us, and probably friends in low places.

No charges were made by either party.

Bristol became a dangerous place for me and the band.

Still known as a DJ in the region, our management company put their toes into the piranha-infested 'promoter' pool, and asked me to compare a show with various bands they'd booked for a theatre in nearby Cheltenham. Gene Vincent was topping the bill and I savoured the prospect of meeting him but at the back of my mind was the knowledge that the *Be-Bop-A-Lula* man wasn't totally reliable, and had failed to turn up on two previous occasions in this town.

On the night, the local surviving teddy boys remained faithful to the Yank ex-pat who brought us the unforgettable *Bi-I-Bickey-Bi, Bo-Bo-Go!*

Sadly, for the crepe-soled, draped species, here in the 60s, the surviving 50s teddy boys were suffering a massive population decrease caused by marriage, getting older and fashion's evolution. Their music belonged in the decade departed.

Accordingly, the theatre was only half-filled with sideburn-sporting teds, who also wore customised knuckle dusters, some with their drape jacket pockets bulging with their lavatory chain weapons.

My gold lamé jacket won them over, and I started to introduce the support bands.

First a couple of local outfits followed by Screaming Lord Sutch and the Savages, a group who had the world's only hit about a serial killer, Jack the Ripper!

It was a fated show. Lord Sutch traditionally arrived on stage from a coffin, but the lid got stuck. His band had played two numbers before we could get him out. He almost suffocated and could hardly sing *I'm a hog for you!*

Johnny Kidd and the Pirates preceded Shane Fenton & the Fentones, and then the sickening interval where, back stage Jeff Hubbard told me flatly through tight, colluding lips, that Gene Vincent had once again failed to show!

"You have to tell them," he insisted.

"Like fuck!" I said.

"It's your job Tony," he said firmly. "Now get out there and tell them!"

I parted the heavy velvet stage drapes, and stood before the microphone facing the impatient audience who were now anticipating Vincent's leather-trousered stance, and egg-eyed delivery of his rock anthems.

Something akin to a war chant erupted from them. I felt my bladder seeking an outlet.

Trepidation is a word that comes to mind.

"Shhhh! Shhhh," I said, both hands extended in a mid air press-up

They stopped chanting.

The silence you could hear. Some arsehole put the house lights up.

They read me...

They knew what I knew.

They'd been here before!

"Vincent hasn't shown," my voice boomed around the smoke filled auditorium.

"I'm as bloody sorry as you, you know!" I offered as the silence turned to rumbling, grumbling and then a mass muttering, which I knew would, within moments, turn to a call for bloodletting.

Standing there I knew how a fox felt when the trumpet blew.

Suddenly, before the riot could ignite, from the corner of my eye I saw a solitary figure limping from the front row towards me.

Gene Vincent himself stood below me, leather jeans and all!

And a snarl on his lips.

"You're a fucking liar man!" he screamed at me.

Then, turning to his fans, each frozen, agog, fuelled but not yet aflame, he continued to scream in their midst.

"The sons of bitches won't let me go on because I wuz 10 minutes late!!"

I didn't wait to help Gene to work out a denouement.

Backstage Hubbard had already scarpered.

The other groups were legging it with their guitar cases and drum kits, vacating their dressing rooms like they had just heard an announcement from the captain of the Titanic. The stage behind me was already full of people with greased quiffs as I exited the stage door.

Then came the wrecking ball, by which time I was headed for the A38. As a promoter, Hubbard had employed the standard rule of the day. If the receipts don't meet the costs, cut your budget!

I'll never forget that look on Gene Vincent's face as he approached me. Nor the shiver in my heart. Or the movement in my trousers as I gazed on the guy whose song I'd sung with Ringo Starr at Butlins!

Failing miserably, having spent Paul Lazarides' bacon and egg takings, Hubbard disappeared, leaving us with a Greek restaurant owner managing us.

At least we got fed.

"Guess what?" said Paul beaming whilst frothing me a coffee one Bristol morning.

"I've got you a month at The Star Club in Hamburg!"

Horror!

Four weeks with my band pissing off balconies held no appeal.

Ten-hour gigs, seven days a week with low nutritious turd dogs, and ginger ale piss was not what I had in mind!

But Paul was holding me to the very contract I had so longed for. He had to recoup some rashers.

The night before our embarkation, God moved in his strange protective way by striking me down.

We were playing a hall in Gloucester.

"Here's the one and only," Carl announced, "*Toneeeeeee Prince!*"

The band started a rock n' roll version of *Over the rainbow*, our answer to the Beatles '*Till there was you*' and Gerry's '*You'll never walk alone*'.

I strode from the wings to centre stage, taking hold of the microphone.

'*There's a place for us...*'

And then I rainbowed my Pegasus Café lunch over the first three rows of punters.

An ambulance was called and I was rushed to hospital with suspected appendicitis. The following morning, I escaped and returned to my empty flat, by which time the van and the Mersey Four were half way across the English Channel.

I slept for two days in what could loosely be described as a coma. I awoke with blankets covered in strange green vomit. The room was stifling, and the stink compelled me to close my eyes and sleep for another day.

It was at lunchtime on the third day when Paul Lazarides arrived with a doctor.

Only when the group had arrived in Hamburg did they phone him, to make him aware that his lead singer was not with them.

At the age of 21 I gave birth to my baby, a beautiful duodenal ulcer. Through the following 30 years my baby kept me company. Nothing could separate us, not barium meal, diet, Zantac, Tagamet nor Losec.

But this strange gift from God has undoubtedly kept me alive by limiting my candle-burning ability, and I have no doubt that had I had the stomach for it, whisky would have totally scotched me!

The band reverted to being the Mersey 4 and I never saw them again in my life; although 20 years later, I received a nice letter from Robbie who informed me that they'd all got proper jobs and families. More recently, Carl called the Steve Wright Show on Radio 2, after Steve had interviewed me on the anniversary of Elvis' death. They took his phone number, but I lost it, and I'm sorry I did because I'm curious to know if any of them work in a car wash and did they take Kombo the cat to Germany?

Jan: The Elvis gift

The next day my friends continued showing me their Bratislava. We practiced our rowing on the lake, and in the evening they threw a party in my honour at Katka's cousin Eva's apartment. Eva too had attended the summer English course, but in a different student group to ours.

Never in my life had I, or anyone I knew, been to a party quite like this. There was constantly a couple of dozen guests, with some leaving, new guests arriving, a real party.
In Brno we never had parties like this. I was only 17 after all, and the best that ever happened would be when I invited them, or they invited me to play chess, or discuss a stamp or badge collection.

We avoided parties in Brno for one reason and one reason only – fear. Fear, that the janitor would notice so many people gathering in one place and report you to the Public Safety. And what was the inspiration to throw a party? So we could discuss the output of the processing plant, or get excited over the coming public march through the city? Fear ruled our social life completely, compounded by avoiding making yourself conspicuous in the eyes of authority.

But here, tonight in Eva's apartment, I felt the earth move. To begin with, as the only non-Slovak there I became the centre of attraction, and as we chatted away, the tape recorder played all the music your heart could wish for, in high quality.

I noticed records in the apartment also, but was too social to browse through them, and of course Katka constantly had my eye. Party guests wanted to know more about events across the Morava River, where Slovakia was divided from Moravia and Bohemia, and I was urged to repeat the Stalin monument story, that once again caused both mirth and disbelief.

They also loved another story that came to mind after my second glass of wine, a story my mother recounted to me some time ago. It concerned her friend, who was visited at work by a communist boss, who threatened to report her to the communist party committee because she didn't comply, or satisfy, his requirements.
She remained calm and eventually addressed him as *comrade*, even though she was not a communist at all.
"Comrade," she began. "You threaten me with the communist party and all because I keep to my duty and regulations. I find your attitude very bad

indeed, and actually I find your behaviour very dangerous because you are damaging the good name of our communist party. It is you, I should be reporting to the communist party committee, for making the people afraid of our beloved communist party."

The communist boss shot his mouth off, turned and left. Everyone in the office applauded her performance!

These were such golden words, and I used the same phrases many time in the next 25 years, when I faced similar confrontations and threats. To beat communists with their own weapon was something quite inspiring from my mother's friend.

Throughout this magic night, Katka remained by my side, introducing me to her friends, bringing me food and drink and generally taking care of me. Our relationship had established itself so quickly, so naturally. I started to feel it would always be this way.

Later we started to discuss my favourite topic, music and I must say I had never heard such a question from a 16-year-old girl before: "Do you like Fats Domino?"

That was it. That was when I knew without any doubt that Katka was my girl!

Shortly after midnight we set off to walk down to Bratislava where Andrej and Katka lived. It was a long walk, no public transport at that time, but time flew by as we walked beneath a full moon through beautiful Bratislava.

It brought to mind Curtis Lee's rock 'n' roll classic *Under the Moon of Love*. I wished the walk would never end.

The following day I accompanied Andrej to a bank. I had never before been in a bank, and I had never before seen a US one dollar bank note. Andrej collected coins and swapped the note for quarters and dimes. What impressed me was that he was quite well known by the girl who attended to him.

Afterwards we went to meet Katka as we had scheduled, but after waiting for half an hour or so we returned to Andrej's home, from where he called her.

As he spoke into the phone, he looked preoccupied by the conversation. Cupping the mouthpiece, he explained to me it was her mother who wanted to know why her daughter had come home crying a while ago. I was shocked and waited now as he spoke to Katka herself.

Then it was resolved, we had confused our meeting place. It must have been the wine!

As we walked to a new rendezvous, my mind was alive with an amazing realisation. If Katka was this upset, it could only mean one thing. Katka loved me! Why else would she be so upset that she would go home crying?

We had never mentioned the four-letter word before, even though our affection for one another was plain to see. But I was very, very inexperienced in matters of the heart and reaching for this word, until then, was beyond my heart's vocabulary.

The Four Aces song lyrics played in my head, '*Love is nature's way of giving a reason to be living, the golden crown that makes a man a king*'.

The three of us walked through Bratislava old city, until Andrej excused himself, as he had to run an errand for his mother. At last the moment I had been waiting for since arriving in Bratislava, I was alone with Katka.

We decided we would go to the cinema and decided to watch a French movie Le Rat d'Amerique with Charles Aznavour. I can't tell you anything about the film. I didn't see any of it!

I accompanied Katka home, and broke the news that tomorrow I must return to Brno. Two days before, my mother had returned from a train trip she had taken with two friends to Bulgaria, and I had promised to be back for her return.

The authorities were at last relaxing some of our travel restrictions, and as my mother, at the age of 50, had never in her life seen the sea, she was off to warm her bones in the sunshine by the Black Sea. Bones that Aunt Lída had so often reminded me had once frozen on the Appel Platz in Ravensbrück. I was now anxious to know she was fine, and that her trip had gone well.

The next day as I got ready to leave, Andrej handed me one of his most valuable possessions, Elvis' *Kid Galahad* EP.

"This is for you Jan," he said. "I have seen how much you love Elvis."

I held the vinyl in my hand, speechless as he apologized for keeping the sleeve for himself. The music was what was important to me, for the first time in my life, I was the owner of an Elvis record.

As we all walked to the railway station, I couldn't get away from the thought that I now had a record collection! I had the Gery Scott EP, two plastic singles on post cards by the Beatles and the Rolling Stones, and now six tracks from the King. With a dozen songs in total, I could create a discotheque in my home for my friends, and become a real DJ. Why my record library would run to 30 minutes in total!

I waved my Bratislavan friends farewell, and watched Katka's eyes brimming with tears, as the locomotive's departure whistle drowned out our goodbyes. We had all agreed they would soon visit me in Brno, but my mind told me I would much prefer to stay with them here in Bratislava, where life was so good.

I sat back in the train and thought – this must be what it is like living in the west!

Back in Brno, my thoughts changed from missing Katka and my new friends, to looking forward to telling my closest friends of my adventures, and the wonderful world of Bratislava.

I hurried home to see how mother had enjoyed her first trip to the sea. She would be only the second member of my entire family to see the sea!

Here in 1965 something was afoot. A liberal wind was in the air, and so my mother and her two friends took full advantage to fulfill their dreams. I walked through the door, to be met with a very upset mother and Auntie Lída's voice rattled through my brain even though she wasn't there.

"Where have you been for so long, and why didn't you meet me at the railway station as you were supposed to?"

Father had been driving a tram. My sister thought I would return on schedule, but of course I had over-stayed, and my poor mother had no one to meet her to carry her luggage. If you had put me in front of a firing squad, I could not have felt any worse.

My stories from Bratislava had to wait. Firstly, once her anger had abated, mother had to tell me all her stories from her first trip to the sea. I decided to wait for another day to tell her of my adventures, and of my Bratislavan princess.

The next day, after playing the *Kid Galahad* EP 20 times, I phoned František who gave me the incredible news that from 1 August, A Hard Day's Night would start to be played at our 3,000 capacity Summer Cinema on Lenin Street.

We laughed at the thought that last year it played in our Brno cinema, called Moscow, and this time on a street called *Lenin*! In this amazing way, although they didn't know it, the Beatles were fighting communism on our behalf, and right under the noses of the dreaded Secret Police whose headquarters were directly opposite the cinema where soon, thousands of Czechoslovakians would march by to digest the most powerful anti-communist device the west ever sent our way.

The Fab Four.

Tony: The TV audition

I was offered a partnership in a new discotheque. Vito, another ex-pat Greek, who owned a Casino in Bristol, was opening the Monaco Rooms in Bath, a small club flanked by his new Casino. I had 50% of the door take, and the solitary one-armed bandit.

I would receive my payment nightly and then, once the club had closed, enter the Casino which stayed open all night, promptly giving my earnings back to my partner.

Baccarat was a hell of a game.

Keeping late nights at the Rank, moving in pre-dawn circles, some of my best friends were croupiers.

One night on one of their regular visits, I took mum and dad to a Bristol Casino. Dad sat facing Mike the dealer, who threw the cards around the green baize like the seasoned pro he was. Dad sat in the middle of a clutch of local hoods playing three-card brag no deuces wild. His holiday money was almost gone.

Mike caught my eye as the players fanned out their hands.

A wink.

I watched over dad's shoulder as he opened the three cards cupped possessively in his hands. Three of hearts... three of clubs...

Three three's!

No deuces floating.

Unbeatable.

Dad won back his holiday money.

Never trust a croupier, unless you've bailed him out once or twice when he was broke.

I was a night person in the grip of the after-dark society, feeding my addiction for adrenaline in exactly the same way that a vampire lusts for warm blood. Same time-cycle, same dawn curfew.

Within two months the Monaco Room's roulette wheel had me hocked, maligned and stinkered.

I owed Vito so much in advance of potential income, that I was almost incapable of escape.

Almost...

I put my last coins into the deserted club's one-armed bandit and pulled three bells! Luck at last.

With enough money for a tank of petrol, I gathered together my record collection, threw the gold lamè in a suitcase and took an early bath! It was dawning as I journeyed back through the tunnel, north, to the sanity of my hometown.

After a few weeks convalescing in the womb of family warmth in Oldham, I returned to Top Rank. For my sin in leaving them, they banished me to Rank's equivalent of Outer Mongolia, the Leeds Top Rank, the town, where some five years earlier, Savile was discovered playing records at the Mecca by Decca Records.

At the Top Rank right in the city centre, I provided plastic refreshment as support to strict-tempo king, Irving Tidswell and his Orchestra, some of the last note-reading heathens on a vinyl planet.

It was a very old ballroom with very old punters, so old in fact that they booed *me* when I came on, and cheered Irving's lot when his baton once again struck the air.

I had been sent to Musicians' Union Shangri-la!

I knew what Rank was up to; they wanted me to scuttle Tidswell!

I was dedicating myself to doing so, but then the telegram arrived.

I was called to Cardiff, headquarters of TWW, Television for Wales & the West.

Canadian DJ Kent Walton, famous nationally for his wrestling commentaries, smoking Kent cigarettes, (sponsored freebies which he blatantly smoked on camera), and his Radio Luxembourg programmes, had been contracted to cover the wrestling at the 1964 Olympic Games.

"This is Kent Walton bidding you farewell and whether you're at home or on the highway, thank you for tuning my way..." was how he closed each show.

It was a sunny day and four of us were called to the audition including Millie, who had a hit with *My Boy lollipop*, the first for Chris Blackwell's Island Records.

Chris Mercer gave us each a script, a half hour to digest and rehearse and then, one at a time, he called us outside onto the sun-kissed lawn, where he proceeded to listen to us make our shot.

It only takes a few seconds to change entire lives. These were my seconds.

I was crap.

I was asked to read an old Kent Walton script.

"I thought you told me you could do better than him?" Chris chided.

"Do I have to use a script?" I asked.

"Not at all."

I threw the script to the ground and made out I was introducing Elvis.

Seconds well spent.

"You've got the job. Four shows starting in six weeks' time. I want you to do the first show with Millie. Are you available?"

I spent two years with the show.

Chris Mercer also asked me to be his record librarian and keep my ears open for hits! This was 1964, and I was already one of the most powerful people in the music industry although I didn't appreciate that at the time.

I gave a band called Tom Jones and the Squires the thumbs up which led to the Welshman's first real TV break. *Chills and Fever*, was his debut for Discs-a-Gogo. He returned soon after with his classic number one, *It's Not Unusual*, by which time he'd ditched his band and was a solo artist managed by Gordon Mills, who took him and Englebert Humperdinck all the way.

The summer of 1964 saw me introducing: Lulu (*Shout)*, the Animals (*House Of The Rising Sun*), PJ Proby (*Hold Me*), and the sensuous Marianne Faithful with the Stones (*As Tears Go By*).

Tuesdays, the day we recorded Discs-a-Gogo were wonderful, as suddenly, the artists I played each night at the Top Rank (where I had suddenly been invited back at double my previous wages), came to life.

I had a dressing room next to Billy Fury, ate with the Kinks in the canteen, Van Morrison sat in the next chair in make-up.

When the show was in the can, we'd all shuffle next door to Arnos Court Country Club, which sported a dance floor, live band and cabaret, a casino and a bar, which we tried to deplete of stock.

It was a DJ's delight. We'd take over from the band and sing rock 'n' roll. Dave Berry and I giving stick to *Memphis Tennessee*, Cliff Bennett, hand cocked to his ear belting out *Mean Woman Blues* and me standing on my head for the chorus of *What'd I say*, and Spencer Davies held the mic to my mouth whilst in the audience, Dusty Springfield, the Barron Knights and Dionne Warwick laughed at our antics.

I worked through Christmas, as indeed I did for the following 20 years. Kath and Frank came to spend it with me, and stayed in my tiny bedsit, with dad and I taking up sleeping bags on the carpet.

Jan: Our RAF heroes

The big day was here at last, and we all congregated by the lake chattering away as excitedly as any teenage group you would see anywhere in the world.

František arrived looking like the cat that got the cream. He had something hidden behind his back, and once he was in our midst, out it came for us all to see. It was a book. One he'd been reading into the night.

So far as our little group of friends were concerned, František Jemelka was our book reviewer. He loved books and had good black market sources for literature from the west and from Czech libraries pre-1948, which were supposed to be destroyed so that we could not read anything, which upset the communist apple cart. František particularly loved poetry and was in the process of trying to write lyrics for our top group Synkopy 61.

What he held in his hand this day however was quite mind blowing to each of us. It was a book actually published legally in Czechoslovakia, and we spent the rest of the afternoon discussing the *hows* and *whys* of such a book would escape censorship? The Beatles were one thing, but Riders in the Sky by author Filip Jánský was so close to all our lives, so personal in its subject matter that suddenly, A Hard Day's Night wasn't quite as important as it had been before František's arrival.

The book was about Czechoslovakian pilots who joined the British Royal Air Force during the war. We each knew of them, their legend had been whispered about since the war.

We are still today a very young country, but in the mid 20th century we were almost newborn.

The Czech Republic began when our government was formed in 1918. Twenty years later, the Munich Agreement handed over the northern territories of our country to Adolph Hitler, even though no one from the Czech government was there to ratify the Agreement. In March 1939, even though we had a well-developed army and air force, the Nazis were able to occupy the rest of the country with no resistance.

During this period, many soldiers managed to escape including the highly skilled Czech pilots, who joined the allies in their bid to free their homeland. Many went to France via Poland or Yugoslavia, but once France capitulated, their next stop was the UK where they stood side by side with Winston Churchill, who had declared all-out war against Adolph Hitler. There was never any hesitation on their part, all their instincts told them to defend our country from abroad, and to sacrifice their lives if necessary.

Their history was never uttered in any open conversation, nor was their bravery ever taught to us in school. But the story of our Czech/RAF legends was whispered amongst schoolboys, and their glory secured in the hearts of every secret non-conformist.

After 1948, any soldiers who had been active within western armies and, who therefore may negatively influence society, were sent to prison, most of them for 20 years.

The ones who didn't go to jail were expelled from their jobs, and from that point on could only ever do menial work, all because they fought against Hitler with the Brits rather than the Bolsheviks, in order to free our country. We can only imagine how they felt.

Riders in the Sky exalted our pilots and showed them as the heroes they were. We spent the rest of the afternoon devouring as many pages as we could, each taking a turn to read or to be a listener.

We would jump from the text in the book to issues we needed to discuss. At last we had something official, something that for some crazy reason, had escaped censorship. At long last we had a book that gave us pride, an emblem of Czech courage and fortitude.

In the discussion that day, I reminded everyone that in 1949 my Uncle Josef needed to escape to avoid such fates. We discussed our school chums, Lad'a and Jura, whose father was General Machálek. He served in the Royal Air force 312th Squadron, and was expelled from the Czechoslovak army immediately after 1948, somehow managing to escape a trial.

František went to the same Open University as Lad'a, and often discussed the war with General Machálek according to whom, 1,000 Czechs joined the British RAF of which 531 gave their lives. Their average age was 20. Every one of us had links to some member of their family, who were either executed in peacetime, or disappeared forever, or endured hard labour in prisons.

We had often discussed what it must have been like having escaped your country to fight on its behalf from the United Kingdom, to have survived many battles, perhaps to have met and married an English girl with whom you have started a family. Then, with the Nazis defeated, whilst the world still celebrated, your homeland secured once again, you returned home with your new family to build a new life and to enjoy the embrace of the surviving members of your family and friends.

We knew what a wrench it must have been for those young English girls to leave their own families in the UK to settle in our country, but even they had no idea of the horrors they would inherit.

Within just a couple of years, the Russian liberators of the Czech Republic imposed their communist ideology across the East, resulting in the putsch of February 1948.

Our Spring had come to an abrupt end.

Now, far from being looked on as our liberators and heroes, the pilots who had served in western countries rather than the Soviet Red Army, were now persecuted, seen as corrupted and tainted by capitalism.

Many pilots escaped once again, whilst those who decided to stay with their families were in deep trouble. The usual communist routine was to arrest them in the middle of the night, to be held by the dreaded Secret Police, (the StB, or Státní bezpečnost) and judged, not by local courts, but rather a workers committee assisted by the StB. The replacement Czechoslovakian communist judges were new to the jobs, factory workers one day, law makers the next. Many had to go through a mere year of training before they had the power to execute people. Imagine that if you will, as did we that day by the lake, whilst reading this impossible book.

In 1962, due to Kruschev's denunciation of Stalinism, our pilots were finally given their freedom. Even then, after their many years enduring the basest of prison conditions, in typical communist bureaucratic form, not one announcement was made to the effect that they'd all been pardoned and released.

There were no speeches condemning the wrongs that had been done to these men. Not so much as one report appeared in Red Law as an admission to the sins of the state. Their prison cells were opened, they were shown the way out, and given a stipend to get them wherever their home might be. And that was that. Typically, the entire episode was swept beneath the authorities very large red carpet.

Right through to the great day when the Berlin Wall was finally toppled, no one in my country had publically acknowledged that the Communist Government had made an odious and immoral mistake. The word *sorry* did not exist in the communist vocabulary. Neither did the word compensation. All they got was their freedom.

But now the unbelievable had happened, a book confirming their contributions, a book on our shelves, not smuggled into the country to be read in secret, a book confirming once and for all what phony liars our communist bosses were.

We kept repeating… "How the hell did this get through censorship?"

No wonder we were excited. The whole damn thing had the flavour of… freedom!

Our Sunday meeting at the lake was a day when the sun shone both in the sky and in our hearts.

In our eyes, our RAF airmen had finally, truly been released because of this book, on the exact same weekend that the Beatles, A Hard Days Night, was also finally released in Czechoslovakia!

Tony: Stars come out

1964 gave way to '65, and many of the stars who made repeated visits to Discs-a-Gogo became my friends.

Gogo was a treadmill of talent. The ultimate 60s trip. Dave Berry, Mike Berry, Chuck Berry, Rockin' Berries.

Billie Davis, Spencer Davis, Ray Davies, Skeeter Davis.

Gene Pitney, Gene Vincent, the Swinging Blue Jeans.

PJ Proby, Billy J Kramer, Jay & the Americans, Peter Jay and the Jaywalkers. The list was endless, the Gogo conveyor belt packed to the hilt. It took a little time, but finally the music industry itself started to wake up to how publicity increased sales, and so it became game- on between the ever-hungry tabloids and the publicity mad music industry.

Publicity relied a lot on stunts put together by the record labels themselves. Sonny & Cher arrived at Discs-a-Gogo with *I Got You Babe*. Sonny soloed on *Laugh at Me*, and his Jewish Princess sang *All I Really Want To Do*.

Cher stood next to me on the set ready to exchange banter with me, but I gaped at her beauty and words failed me as the cameras rolled.

I wondered what such a sensational looking girl was doing with a gawky looking guy like Sonny Bono? It would be years later before she would ask herself that question, but I had known since the Gogo days, she wasn't exactly monogamous even then.

I was in the next dressing room to the American duo, and I entered their room by mistake to find her in a passionate embrace with her UK agent Larry Page, (the Rage of the Age as he had been known in his pre-mogul life as a pop star!). Apart from handling (sic) Cher, Larry also managed and produced the Kinks and the Troggs.

He came down to TWW's Gogo quite often, joining us after filming at the Arnos Court Country Club next door, where everyone would swap rock 'n' roll tales.

Larry had launched Sonny & Cher's careers in the UK with the help of publicist Keith Altham and the manager of London's swanky Mayfair Hotel.

"I'd booked them a suite," Larry recounted. "When Sonny arrived with his collar-length hair, jacket with fur lining on the outside and zebra striped silk trousers with matching boots, according to the management the Mayfair was suddenly full!"

Larry then took the couple and their suitcases across the road into Hyde Park and with the help of the record company, erected a wigwam where Sonny and Cher, much to the delight of the media, took up residence!

These were the days when tabloids were not easy to penetrate, unless you were the Beatles denouncing Christ, or the Rolling Stones taking a leak in a petrol station forecourt, or Elvis going into the army. But this stunt made the couple a household name overnight, and added to the media's growing appreciation for the record industry. After this stunt *I got you babe* shot up the charts.

Larry Page himself was one of England's pioneer pop stars touring with Lonnie Donegan, Wee Willy Harris, Don Lang and Marty Wilde.

He was born in Hayes.

If you lived in Hayes, you went to work for EMI.

He started in the packing department, carefully boxing 78s by Ruby Murray and trumpeter Eddie Calvert.

But it wasn't long before he found his own records being packed after he entered a talent competition, which saw him on TV.

The record producers of the day were stuck in a time warp with the likes of Ronnie Carol and Dickie Valentine.

The British record industry was still in 'find the next Sinatra' mode, and it was generally recognised that r&r was a fad, and wouldn't be here to degrade the music industry for very long.

At Columbia, according to Larry, "They couldn't tell their arse from their tit when it came to producing a rock 'n' roll record."

"They'd give you a demo recording and say 'learn it'. There was no discussion about royalty levels. A single sold for 7/6d (37p), I got one farthing (1/4p!) for every sale!"

It was a hard school then, and the artists earned from performances, not record sales.

There were no charts to aim for yet. You _had_ to get on Radio Luxembourg, the Station of the Stars. Not impossible when all the majors paid for plays, or had their own sponsored shows, in which they blatantly exploited every bit of crap they released.

The trick, performed only when you were a Columbia priority, was to get your mug on TV's Six Five Special or The Jack Jackson Show.

Then you'd be billed outside the venue as: *Larry Page the Rage of the Age*, Direct from the Six Five Special TV Show!

Then you had queues around the block.

One day, Larry's producer gave him a demo of an American song. The honchoes at Columbia had passed on it. They didn't like the production; it was too basic, too thinly produced in their opinion.

"Learn it," Larry was told.

And EMI produced Larry's fuller, luscious instrumental version.

The artist they passed on was Buddy Holly with the Crickets!

The song, *That'll be the day*. A track which influenced a young Paul McCartney.

When Larry met Buddy, he was afraid he would be pissed off that it was Larry's picture on the sheet music in the UK.

In England there were five versions of the song released. It was the music publisher's job in those days to attract as many cover versions as possible, because they were working the song which paid dividends not only when the record sold, but each and every time the tune was played on TV, radio or in a supermarket.

As a songwriter, Buddy Holly was laughing all the way to the bank. No wonder Paul McCartney was pissed off when Michael Jackson bought publishing rights to a load of early Beatles' tunes. The members of the bands who wrote the songs in the 60s were the ones who would have pensions for life, in Paul's case rather than become a millionaire, he would become a billionaire. This is why Dolly Parton smiled when she heard that Whitney Houston had recorded *I will always love you*; and Reg Presley as songwriter of *Love is All Around*, was blown away when Wet Wet Wet's version, nestled at number one for three months, a quarter of a century after Reg wrote it for his group the Troggs!

The Yardbirds with God's incarnate, Eric Clapton and Jeff Beck, (soon to be replaced by Jimmy Page) arrived at Discs-a-Gogo to perform *Still I'm Sad*.

Chris Mercer, the show's producer, staged a moody set that had the band marching mournfully around the arches of the Discs-a-Gogo coffee cellar. On reflection it was a very camp scene, and probably contributed somewhat to the band splitting up shortly after this appearance.

With the Yardbirds gliding ahead of us, I followed leading our entire studio audience each holding candles as if TWW's electricity bill hadn't been paid. Standing watching this off camera was the former 2i's Coffee

Bar bouncer, now their manager, Peter Grant.

Soon he would start a new Yardbirds with Jimmy Page, bringing in three new band members and junking the name in favour of Keith Moon's suggestion... Led Zeppelin.

Jan: My first DJ gig

The party in Bratislava had inspired me, to be so social and speak so openly was something I wanted to experience more often. I convinced my closest friends that on New Year's Eve, when my parents left to celebrate the end of 1965 with their wartime friends, we should gather in our flat to see if we could turn the arrival of 1966 into something special.

It turned out to be a great night. Everyone in the apartment block was celebrating, so František could play his guitar and sing as loudly as he liked, and we all joined in.

This night in 1965, with just six records and one old record player, I finally became a disc jockey. My audience amounted to nine people, each of whom lived for the music we heard on illegal Luxembourg, and now Radio Caroline the pirate ship that had sailed into our lives.

Of course, with only six records things did get a little repetitive, but no one paid any attention, because we were doing what we knew our western counterpart teenagers did anytime they wished. We were, on New Year's Eve 1965, teenage escapees.

It was the night when I first realised how great it was to share your music with others, and what a great vocation it was to be a disc jockey. I felt enormous energy from just being able to play each record from start to end, and then back to the start, or to change the record or turn it over. I had a record collection *and* I had my first audience.

From this night onwards, throughout my DJ career, my love for the English language paid dividends in Czechoslovakia. The Radio Luxembourg DJs didn't have to explain the meaning of the lyrics, because of course their listeners already understood them. We, who became DJs in Czechoslovakia on the other hand, had an obligation to explain to an audience who were fascinated to learn all the nooks and crannies of the words and meanings in the hits they loved.

But there was a downside to knowing the original British and American tunes too well, as I began to realise how poorly the Czech cover versions were, and how much was lost in translation.

Even today when I play my Oldies but Goldies disco show, and I explain in Czech the meaning of the lyrics in the song my audience had just been dancing to, people come up to me to express their surprise. Having loved an original English song all their lives, only now had I revealed to them what the song was about.

As I became more and more familiar with the English language, so I grew to hate cover versions with a passion. Dressed in their new Czech lyrics, completely plagiarised and bastardised and divorced from the original, I could no longer listen to them.

As western music became more successful in our country, so more and more cover versions were released by our state owned record label. Can you imagine hearing Don McLean's *American Pie*, and then hear a Czech version where the singer is singing about *cooking*?! So I was tormented throughout my teenage years by poorly translated hits and poor standards of production.

That night as I tested my right to party, I had absolutely no idea whatsoever that there were such things in the world as dancehalls, where *only* records were played. All our music venues had live bands without a record in sight. The word *DJ* did not exist.

Neither could I imagine a day, when the communist-controlled radio station in Czechoslovakia would allow anything other than a thoroughly researched, out and out communist member to work there. To imagine a DJ playing and saying exactly what he wanted, as they did on Radio Luxembourg, was so far from likely, that it never so much as entered my head. DJs nattering and having fun, was free-world stuff.

Yet whilst I accepted life's straightjacket, I was now beginning to understand that dreams are all well and good, (dreaming was an essential survival device in our circumstances), but for one night in Bratislava I had stopped dreaming. I had stopped being compliant to those who handed out the straightjackets and did all our thinking for us.

At midnight, tuned into Luxembourg as Big Ben chimed in 1966 I suddenly felt I was a part of the world. For the first time in my life I felt an emotion I wasn't familiar with.

I felt optimistic.

Tony: Cilla Black

Paul Simon arrived at Discs-a-Gogo pre-Garfunkel to perform his delicate solo debut, *I am a Rock*, and I had no concept that this man, who I could look directly in the eye without standing on my tip toes, would soon record one of the greatest albums ever recorded, Sounds of Silence.

I found Paul, too, was a big Elvis fan, and although you wouldn't believe it looking at the small thin-haired folk singer then, he started out copying Elvis after first hearing *That's alright Mama*. Whilst I once had a tailor copy the gold suit on Elvis' Golden Records album for my stage show, Paul had searched the length and breadth of New York to find a lavender shirt Elvis had worn on an album.

Big Barry McGuire, the world's most unlikely protest singer, came along with the doomy, *Eve Of Destruction*, his only hit after which he bombed. A year before I was introducing her on Discs-a-Gogo, I disturbed Cilla Black's slumber.

Today, 40 years after the event, I remember with stagnant guilt the very moment I woke Cilla!

She was playing Bristol, working her first single *Love of the Loved*, which the Beatles had written for her as a thank you for tending their coats at the Cavern. Myself and a couple of mates were chilling out back in my flat after a night at the Top Rank.

"She's staying at the Grand," said one of the guys.

"Give her a ring Tony, invite her round for a drink."

Seemed feasible.

"Grand Hotel good evening."

"Ciller Black pleeze," I said in my best Liverpool accent.

"Miss Black is on do not disturb."

"That's alrise. I'm her manager, Brian Epstein."

I mustn't have heard Epstein talk because I'd assumed he had a typical Scouse accent that exchanged 't's for 'esses' at the end of certain words. Anyway it would seem that the receptionist hadn't heard him speak either.

"One moment sir," he said politely.

Pause.

"'Ello Brian, Ciller 'ere."

Sleepy voiced.

I bottled out and hung up!

Now, here in the TWW TV studio, I was thinking of apologising to her, but instead asked lamely, "Is that your boyfriend?" I looked across the studio at blonde Bobby, who'd flanked her like a shadow all afternoon.

"Mind yer own business!" she said brutally. This was the only conversation I ever had with Cilla.

I made friends with lots of people, but was attracted to nutters and fun seekers.

I made friends with Steve Marriot, who was the brilliant lead singer with the Small Faces. I first saw him perform live at Gogo. His eyes closed, his voice a growl, his guitar slunk over a shoulder and his arm flying smashing out chords... '*I want you to know that I love you baby...*'

I wondered if the arking arm guitar strumming came from him or Pete Townshend first? Marriot was the better of the two from the waist down – dancing I mean!

Years later, Steve came to my home in Luxembourg and tried to persuade my wife Christine to smoke some pot.

Her single drag ever!

"Tastes like bloody gas-tar," she coughed.

"What's gas-tar?" asked Steve.

"That is!" she coughed, pointing at his joint.

Years and years later, Steve died in a house fire and was found seeking refuge from the flames in his wardrobe.

Jimmy McCullough made a great buddy, we could see eye to eye. Diminutive Jimmy was in Thunderclap Newman, and in the late 60s after their hit with *Something in the Air*, we partied a lot in London's Speakeasy, and later still I followed him to Wings concerts when he, Denny Laine and I would empty one hotel room's drink cabinet after another.

Jim OD'd in a bath. It was inevitable, even Paul and Linda McCartney couldn't pull him back.

One of my treasures is a photograph of he and I larking about, which Linda took and featured in her 1977 photography diary.

Keith Moon and I looned from time to time. He was one of the few I couldn't keep up with, especially when he was in the mood to party and on speed which was actually every time I saw him.

Keith had terminal party disease, like me he got on the slide at an early age, but never ran into a Christine Prince to pull him off.

I'd like to mention just what a nice, normal guy Moony was when sober, but then, who of us was sober in the 60s?

Certainly he wasn't sober the night we caught a ferry out to a boat housing an Elton John party in the middle of the River Thames, so held where the police couldn't raid, as they were prone to do in clubland.

A long queue at the inadequate ship's toilet caused Keith consternation.

"I want a genuine shit!" he yelled at the stoned queue. Two minutes later, I found myself holding him at the back of the ship, bum over the side having an extremely dodgy-looking bowel movement.

Keith OD'd in Harry Nilsson's London apartment, conveniently placed between Radio Caroline and Radio Luxembourg's offices off Curzon Street.

I once interviewed Ringo Starr there. It wasn't a lucky gaff. Mama Cass died 'on her own vomit' in the same bed in which Keith died.

A man who could be dead from alcoholic poisoning is Eric Burdon. One night at Arnos Court Country Club in Bristol, he inshishted I stay with him whenever, and if ever, I came to London.

"You'll always find me at The Revolution or Scotch of St James if I'm in town," he slurred.

I remembered this now as I drove with Billy J Kramer & the Dakotas down the A4, pre-M4.

I had a new agent, London's Phil and Dorothy Solomon, who Chris Mercer encouraged me to sign with.

They handled the Bachelors, but I forgave them for that as they also handled Van Morrison's Them and Twinkle or Twink as we called her.

Twink wrote a little song called *Terry* about a biker who died. Her dad knew Phil Solomon, and sent a demo to him with a view to the Bachelors recording it. Silly daddy!

I, for one, would have loved to have heard the Bachelors singing about their dead motor-biking boyfriend, it didn't quite fit their repertoire!

Dorothy subsequently put Twink in a white plastic cap and white calf-high boots and had her record it herself.

It went to number 4 for three weeks.

Now Dorothy had called me to the big city to audition for Rediffusion's Ready, Steady, Go and I had to get to TV House in London's Kingsway the day after we'd recorded Discs-a-Gogo. I shook with anticipation.

Rediffusion was a giant corporation capable of networking shows nationally, compared with TWW who couldn't muster interest in Gogo either from Rediffusion, (Greater East Enders), or Granada, (Greater Coronation Street).

So with TWW's networking limitations made clear to me by the Solomon's, I turned turncoat.

A year earlier, Rediffusion had asked Chris Mercer to send them three samples of recent Discs-a-Gogo, 'for their consideration'.

In the end, they stole, or at best adapted the format by using Discs-a-Gogo and American Bandstand from the USA, as the blueprint for a music show of their own. They took Mercer's concept, which put live bands and singers in a coffee-club cellar, surrounding them in close proximity by the audience who danced around them, and created their own version, which they called Ready Steady Go. The show was launched and networked on 9 August 1963.

Because regional channels didn't want two similar shows, or didn't wish to burden us with too much music, Gogo started getting axed from schedules.

A shrinking audience meant inescapable extinction for the UK's forerunner of live audience participation pop TV.

Cathy McGowan and Keith Fordyce linked the raunchy proceedings. RSG's status as a networked show gave Rediffusion the muscle to book the Beatles, the Rolling Stones and big US stars, such as James Brown.

It was completely live, more electric and exciting than Gogo, and I hungered to be a part of it.

Now I was on my way.

No point in being loyal to a show that was in terminal decline.

I'd known the Dakotas from my days in Manchester with the Jasons. Then they were known as Pete McLean and the Clan, before Billy J Kramer and Brian Epstein took them from Pete.

I had intended going on the train to London, but Robbie McDonald the Dakotas' bass player and Mick Green the brilliant lead guitarist, insisted I pack myself in the transit with them.

It snowed.

And it snowed.

By Chippenham, we were snowed under.

"This is where Eddie Cochran died," said Billy J Kramer cheerlessly.

Driving back to London after a West Country gig, Eddie Cochran's car crashed killing him, and badly injuring Gene Vincent.

A young trainee policeman was one of the first on the scene dragging the man who had warned us all about the *Summertime Blues* from the wreckage. The young lad who packed in being a cop became Dave Dee, fronting his little team of pop dwarfs, Dozy, Beaky, Mick and Titch!

At around 2.30am DJ Don Wardell played their *Little Children* on Radio Luxembourg which brought them all to life.

At 3.00am Don played *At the End of the Day,* Luxembourg's traditional closing theme. We were left with static, which hung in the cold night air as the station went off the air. The entire Medium Wave/AM frequency was as if Armageddon had taken place with only France and Germany surviving.

It was 4.30am when the roadie turned off the engine; the van was almost out of petrol. Anyone trying to sleep soon woke up cold to the bone.

By 5.00am we huddled together.

"It's like a three-dog-night," said Mick Green explaining the phrase was based on Eskimos sleeping with their huskies, using them like extra blankets the colder it became.

I faced a five-Dakota-night.

Ahead of us a Jaguar, windows steamed up, its passengers settling down for a warm night, reminded us of how warm life used to be. Our teeth rattled, our hands turned red, our ears felt like they had terriers hanging from them. Then our bass player had a brain wave.

"Get the fuckin' stage clothes out," said Robin.

The travel bags were ripped open and Billy J Kramer passed me one of his gold lamé jackets.

Dawn's light brought council workers trudging car to car, telling occupants that the bulldozer's were on their way and, if we wished to brave the drifts, a cafe with long-distance driver-sized mugs of hot tea, eggs, bacon, fried bread and sausages, was a cold mile away!

We climbed from the van walking forward slowly and unsteadily, the entire group in stagewear, the bleached A4 stretching before us like the Antarctic. As we passed the Jaguar, the driver forced open his igloo door, pushing against the four-foot mound of snow that had piled up during the night.

Heat billowed from the car like a health club sauna. We stood up to our waists in snow, staring inside the Jaguar at the ever-twinkling eyes of singer Anita Harris and her manager boyfriend.

"Good morning boys," she cried like it was 1 August in Montego Bay! She, too, had been on Discs-a-Gogo the previous night.

"You should have said," she frowned, responding to our frozen response to her presence.

"You could have taken turns warming up with me on the back seat!"

Tut, bloody tut!

"Or you could have used my two gallon can of petrol to keep your engine running," said her manager, leaning across her.

I eventually arrived at Rediffusion in London, having been given a lift in a police car from the Dakota's snowbound van to the local railway station, using most of my cash on a train ticket to Paddington. I now contemplated Eric Burdon's invite to stay with him.

At the audition, Keith Fordyce was particularly friendly towards me, and after I recounted my horror trip, he bought me a meal in the canteen.

Many years later, when his star was on the wane and I was dishing out work, I returned this long-remembered kindness, by contracting him to a show on Radio Luxembourg.

Later still, at a party to mark the closure of the famous 208 Station of the Stars, I saw Keith for the last time.

He'd opened a small aircraft museum, which had failed in the recession.

"I'm labouring on a building site," he'd told me cheerfully. "Had to get my sleeves rolled up or we wouldn't eat."

I often wonder why antediluvian characters like Jimmy Young, Pete Murray, David Jacobs and Alan Freeman's careers went on forever, when someone as nice as Keith failed to go the distance?

The RSG audition was a swift affair and I knew I'd failed it. Dishevelled and exhausted and wondering where I'd sleep that night with so few funds remaining, I crashed like a computer until

I suddenly saw Eric Burdon in the RSG studio and everything started to work out fine.

"See you tonight in the Scotch of Saint James. Just tell 'em yer with me and they'll letcher in," said my Geordie pal.

And so they did.

I spent my last few shillings on a couple of scotch and cokes with no idea what I was going to do if Eric didn't show. There were no cash points back then and I knew no one who would change a cheque.

As I waited, I found myself smack in the middle of the 60s revolution. The club's DJ announced, "Please welcome the cast from Hair, a new London musical starting soon!"

I sat there gawking at a man who walked on stage stark naked.

'This is the dawning of...'

Insanity?

'Harmony and understanding...' I honest to God expected a police raid any minute. It called for another scotch and coke.

Eric would change me a cheque I was sure.

The naked cast having gone well over the top from the version the world would shortly see, waved goodbye to a rapturous, star-studded audience.

It was then that I saw Eric, pissed out of his head in a corner of the club, hugging a bottle of Johnny Walker and flanked by bookend women.

I approached the comatose one.

He didn't recognise me from Adam.

At 3am I stood outside the club, deep snow last night, deep shit tonight. A snowdrift, a failed audition, and now no cash and no in at the room!

Eric weaved his way out with a blonde boiler on either arm, the bottle of Johnny Walker scotch grasped firmly by the neck. The trio climbed into a black cab, I followed.

"Who the fuck are you?" screamed one of the bookends.

"I've nowhere to stay, Eric said I could..."

Eric was sprawled out, dreaming he could sing like Howling Wolf.

The girls kicked me towards the cab's open door, I resisted, they screamed to someone outside and that was it, I was dragged onto the pavement and the pummelling commenced. I curled in a ball to avoid any further deprettyfying of my face, covering my head with my arms as the boots went in.

Boots to the rib, fists to the head, kicks up the arse, there was nowhere to run as Martha Reeves might have said. I heard the cab pull away, my lodgings for the night disappearing with it.

On the point of oblivion, I heard a good Samaritan protesting somewhere way above my cowering self. I felt myself lifted from the horizontal. Now I was running, being supported by strong arms. Running down the strange streets of London, blubbering like a baby and quite wretched.

"Fucking bitches," cried my saviour translating my thoughts.

"Fucking thugs-for-bouncers!"

Finally, "Don't worry, we're almost there."

I was badly battered, and remember little of the first 36 hours as I fell into a fevered sleep. In the middle of the second night I heard his voice again, and felt warm breath on my neck, and his hands where I didn't want his hands to be.

I groaned in protest, coming out of my fevered sleep.

He misinterpreted it.

I felt my back passage being smeared with gel or whatever it is they use. I was about to be raped.

"No! No!" I moaned making one great effort to push the groping hand away from my sphincter.

And God heard my prayer.

He backed off.

"I'm sorry," he whispered in a shaky voice.

"I thought you were... 'alright'."

"I am now," I thought, falling back into my semi-coma.

The next day I awoke to find myself in a cosy apartment covered in book-filled shelves and art.

"Ah! My Prince awakes!" said my saviour, host and molester in an affected voice.

I sat up and looked at him as he handed me a cup of tea.

He was a waiter from the Scotch of St James.

"You've been very ill," he said.

"Yes," I agreed.

"But am I still a bloody virgin?"

I still wonder!

Jan: The commies and the cheating

The New Year dawned and it brought to mind the Rolling Stones' version of *Route 66*, and I hoped sincerely that we would get our kicks in year 66! There was every reason to be optimistic. It looked like the communist chiefs were finally slowing down their compulsions, which they'd had since 1948, to prevent people adapting anything at all that looked western. Even in high school the teachers seemed to have got off their high horses about our superiority. The source for everyone's valedictory was the weekly Red Law newspaper. In this first week of 1966 it posed the question: *How do new members enrol into the Communist Party?*

The article indicated there had been a meeting with young people, who asked a series of questions concerning the basic principles of the party.

It suggested that the young people had wanted to know:

Why had the party stopped accepting new members?

Is it true that only workers and members of co-operative farms can join the party or can members of other classes join?

Who decides which new member can join?

The underlying theme of the article of course, indicated that young people were really interested in joining the party. To a man we could smell Red Law crap. It blocked our nostrils.

The Beatles' A Hard Day's Night had been running and selling out in our cinemas for five months, it was obvious every kid in the country had been to see it at least once. How did they think for one minute, that *these* kids who had seen *this* film, wanted to join *that* party? I saw straight through the Red Law's article, the questions and responses were pure fiction, communist propaganda at its finest.

As 1966 took hold, we looked back on the past 18 years in which to join the communist party was to jump into a social status elevator. Just sign on brothers and you would have jobs, free homes and be permitted to travel without the restrictions endured by the rest of the population.

No matter how bad the reputation of the communist party under this system of Russian cronyism, there would always be those who would join simply to reach for better living conditions and opportunity. I think the music industry called this *payola*!

My parents rejected communism and its party benefits outright. They loved democracy and so, instead of living in a fine house with no rent to pay, they selected a life in a rented flat owned by the State. This was their choice. This was their wonderful influence over my sister and I.

But my parents did remain friends with František and Marie. I even called them auntie and uncle as their daughter Hanka called my parents. Concentration camp friendship is a hard seal to break, and something so strong it survives the political differences, even in a totalitarian society, like Czechoslovakia was during those terrible years.

František Bláha can be described as a good communist, a description that may seem oxymoronic but he was open, friendly and had great charisma, the type of person who would wrong no one. He originated from Uherské Hradiště where my father was also born, so you can see they had a stronger concentration camp bond than most.

To František, a totalitarian regime was good, and why would it not be for a communist party member who had risen to become the Director of Malba, a huge state company in Brno that painted and decorated the flats, hospitals and offices across the city.

My father, on the other hand, had a job as a clerk in a State Health insurance company, until in 1948, he was sent to work as a repairman for the tram depot in a job hardly suited for a former Dachau resident for five years, now suffering from poor health.

With the new job came lower pay, and suddenly the rent on our apartment went up to 200 crowns, whilst his friend František paid zero rent for a large house. That's the way it worked, and why my parent's friends, the Bláha's, could afford a TV set or a tape recorder, items we could only dream about.

It may seem strange to admit it now, but there was no animosity felt for the communist party members who lived amongst us with their better status, more comfortable homes, better health care and benefits. It was just accepted that that was how things were.

We had a saying in Czechoslovakia. *'All citizens of a socialist country are equal. But some are more equal than others!'*

It has to be said, however, that this preferential treatment wasn't something that only grew from communism in our society. The former concentration camp inmates, who had survived the death camps, were absolutely clicky and tried to help one another.

This is why we had one of the best-painted flats in our block, Uncle František made sure of this!

I understood as I grew up, that it was impossible for my parents to join the party even though it would have seen us living in relative luxury for the rest of their lives. But we knew it wouldn't have lasted because of the perceived sins of our family. Because Uncle Josef had fled the country after 1948, and Uncle Franta was sentenced to prison in the dreaded Jáchymov uranium mines for not supporting the cooperative farming system, the house would have been taken away from us, and we would have been demoted.

Whilst the Czech men in Dachau all stuck together, communists or not, it wasn't like that with the women in Ravensbrück, where hard-line female communists went head to head with non-communists in a most aggressive way.

My mother befriended inmate Margarete Buber-Neumann, a former German communist who lived with Heinz Neumann, a leading German communist in the Soviet Union, after the Nazis took power in 1933.

In 1937 during Stalin's Great Purge, whilst staying in a Moscow hotel, Heinz Neumann was arrested, taken away and executed. Margarete Buber-Neumann was sent to a labour camp until in 1940, after the Nazi-Soviet Pact, she was handed over to the Nazis and sent to Ravensbrück concentration camp where the friendship with my mother awaited her. Before she died, she managed to write a book about her experiences titled Under Two Dictators: Prisoner of Stalin and Hitler.

These poor women of Ravensbrück would have laughed at the restrictions we, their children, bellyached about. Comparisons are indeed odious.

Cliff Richard in the Young Ones, Helen Shapiro's Trad Jazz together with all the tunes we heard nightly on Radio Luxembourg, had revealed to us what teenage freedom could be like. We'd seen it, we got the message.

Manfred Mann had performed live in three Czechoslovak cities, and now the Beatles had won the hearts of everyone who had seen them, and it certainly seemed like everyone *had* seen them!

Tony: A pirate's life

The song was *Don't get off that train.*
The singer was DJ Tony Blackburn.
He got off the train at Bristol's Temple Meads station and changed my life. Tony made half a dozen records during his career each selling less than the last. I'd suggested that Chris Mercer book him for Discs-a-Gogo, not because he was a good singer, but rather because I wanted to know more about his day job as a pirate DJ on the off-shore vessel, Radio Caroline.

We couldn't receive the station so far west as Bristol, but I'd read a great deal about Radio Caroline and Radio London in the NME and Disc and Music Echo.
As I read these reports, so I would salivate. I could taste the excitement and smell the sea air.

Whilst teenage-only DJs had established themselves in the USA, in the UK, the nearest we had before the pirate ships, were the DJs on Radio Luxembourg who were trying hard to emulate their American rock and rolling counterparts. Where they failed was that they read scripts, sounding somewhat sterile, like those Musician Union bands who read music rather than play from memory.
The transistor radio also came into our lives at this time. It was a portable radio, small enough to tuck beneath your pillow!
208 was our light at the end of a tunnel – we all listened beneath that pillow, especially to the Top 20 show on Sunday night. With our small plastic ear plugs pressed firmly in one ear, we would each fall asleep awakening after 3am when only the disturbing static filled the air, and all the 208 sounds had stopped falling from the sky.

In 1964, as the weekend arrived, Irishman Ronan O'Rahilly, put us out of our misery and played his hand creating, on that historic day, a whole new Good Friday with the arrival of the pirates of the airwaves. The 'Boat that Rocked' had dropped anchor.

Radio history has us believing that Simon Dee was the first pirate DJ to broadcast from 199 Radio Caroline, but in fact it was a person called Chris Moore who made the first test transmission announcements. The same Chris Moore who was later to give me a job, and a whole lot of trouble.

Neither did Simon Dee stay very long on the ship for, whilst the publicity was phenomenal for Radio Caroline, Simon thought it was all about him. He thought he was God when in reality he was, at best, a very fortunate selected disciple.
Ronan was God, of course.

Simon had a whirlwind career from that point. Launched on the good ship Caroline, with the help of top DJ agent Bunny Lewis, he was soon fêted at Broadcasting House where a peak-time BBC chat show took him into every home in Britain. Remember at this time we had only BBC 1 & 2 and ITV and were only just getting used to colour TV! Simon, a man of high personal esteem who lacked the currency of talent to support his arrogance and petulance, moved from peak to peak to trough in no time at all.

Many years later when I had become Programme Director, I gave Simon a chance to re-launch his career on Radio Luxembourg. Sadly, even then as a man entering middle age, he remained on ego autopilot, missing recording schedules and letting people down.

We had one last telephone conversation wherein he informed me that his grandfather had died, and left him sufficient money that he wouldn't need his broadcasting career any more. So off he went to where he had come from – a real nowhere man.

Within the first few weeks of broadcasting, Radio Caroline stole 7 million listeners off the BBC according to Gallup Research, who hadn't even polled the under-17s! This extraordinary survey result obviously only took into account the area of southern Britain where Caroline could be heard.

In London's Regent Street, just north of Oxford Street, Auntie BBC's monopoly game had finally come to an end. There were now other players on the board and the Musicians' Union had been given a 'Go to Jail' card.

Ronan O'Rahilly had sparked a very real music revolution, inspired by the BBC's poor entrepreneurial make-up, and made possible by the union's intransigence as they tried doggedly to plug the damn of vinyl's progress.

In September 1965 in the Discs-a-Gogo television studio, Tony Blackburn filled my ears with pirate tales, feeding my enthusiasm for an exciting new commercial media.

Whilst many radio DJs, both then and now, aspire to television, by instinct I felt radio was my realm, I'd done TV, it was no big deal.

On Tony's advice I applied to Chris Moore, (the first voice of Caroline), who by then had become the Programme Chief based in Caroline House in Chesterfield Gardens, a mews cul-de-sac off London's Curzon Street. The fact that I was coming *from* television impressed Moore especially as Simon Dee had left them to do the opposite.

"When can you start?" he fired.

"Discs-a-Gogo ends in four weeks' time," I answered.

We shook hands and he walked me to the door.

"Have you got an agent by the way?" he muttered as a last thought.

"Solomon, Phil and Dorothy Solomon," I replied like the name would impress him.

It didn't.

He shut the door almost trapping my fingers.

"Sorry, there's no job!"

My mouth caught flies.

"Not if you're with Phil Solomon," he said apologetically. "I can't deal with the man!"

I wondered what Phil had done to upset the guy? He managed various artists like Ireland's Them, featuring vocalist Van Morrison, and Twinkle had recently signed to the agency. He also had a record label, Major Minor. Maybe Chris hated him for releasing David McWilliams *Days Of Pearly Spencer*?

Or maybe he hated *anyone* who managed the Bachelors?

I back-pedalled ferociously.

"Look, they haven't got me any work in six months; I don't have to be with them. I'm here because of Tony Blackburn, not the Solomon's."

I was panicking, this wasn't the way I'd seen it at all. I admitted to him that I had a management contract with them.

Then my potential pirate life began to materialise again.

"Don't worry about the contract, our solicitor will handle it for you."

A couple of weeks later, I was told by Moore that Solomon didn't object to releasing me. I was strangely miffed. I received a very nice 'release' letter from Dorothy wishing me success in the future.

I liked Dorothy very much, but Phil was something different. A classic Jewish face, featuring spectacles with jar bottom lenses, over which he would look at you mirthlessly. He gave you the impression you were working for him!

Whilst I was glad to see this person out of my sphere, I was somewhat sorry to be leaving Dorothy. And very happy indeed to become a Caroline Good Guy!

Moore made a mistake sending me to Caroline South, which bobbed up and down, three miles out from Frinton off the south east coast of England.

I should have been sent to Caroline North off the Isle of Man where people could understand my accent delivered at a zappy-60s-radio-DJ speed. And of course I called it 'Putney' instead of 'Patney', which meant that the London cabbies couldn't understand me at all.

"What the fuck is he saying?" enquired the prematurely grey-haired Irish man inside Caroline House.

The God-like Ronan O'Rahilly held a transistor in front of Chris Moore's nose. He was pointing at my voice.

"He's talking Oldhamese!"

Suddenly, as he wagged his index at my accent the radio went dead in his hand.

"Fuck sweet Jesus," said the Irishman. "What now?"

It was always going to be risky living and working on a tub like Radio Caroline. Only a couple of months back Caroline South had beached in a storm. Now we took our lives in our hands, rung after freezing rung as we, the DJs, climbed, unharnessed and uninsured, to put our station back on air. I don't believe there is one radio station in the world today that could motivate a DJ to rise to this level of insanity, and apart from the 60s pirate ships and good old Radio Luxembourg, there never was a station DJs would die for.

Jan: The free NME

To cheer myself up I tuned to my beloved Luxy and Radio Caroline now available 24/7 when its signal would allow. What a great development the pirates were, but why had they arrived I wondered? There was no news source to explain this phenomenon.

Then I heard The Who's *My Generation*, and I had to lie down and let my heartbeat return to normal. I didn't have too long to wait before it was played again and again, and I wrote the words down as quickly as I could each time it came on the radio.

'People try to put us down...just because we get around (Talkin' bout my g... g... generation)'

Maybe I didn't catch all the lyrics right away, but I knew immediately by the singer's voice that this was about dissatisfaction, probably frustration with the older generation.

But I couldn't get it into my head – *why the UK?* Why on earth would the British kids *'hope to die before they got old'*?

To be honest it frightened me a lot. There was much cause to be pissed off with the older generation in Czechoslovakia, but did whoever wrote this song, not understand how brilliant the free world was?

Thank God the Beatles came along and saved the day with *We Can Work it Out*. There it was, whatever problems the British kids had, John, Paul, George and Ringo reassured them that things could all be worked out. My mind was much easier, although I greatly doubted we could adopt that philosophy in my country.

Then came one of the greatest advertisements I ever heard on Luxembourg:

'Send us your name and address and we will send you a sample copy of the New Musical Express to show what kind of a music weekly you can subscribe to.'

I didn't need any more persuasion, are you kidding!

It took two weeks to arrive and I regarded it as a miracle. Why would they send me a free copy, knowing that a Czech kid could never subscribe?

Someone had a very big heart and I'm told it was Maurice Kinn, the publisher, who one day had agreed to make the free offer on Luxembourg, which, he claimed, saved the paper from extinction!

I ran to my bedroom with the precious consignment and unfolded it and devoured every picture, slowly reading each article. Here was a Top 20 Chart, record advertisements and a feature on the Who. Now I knew that the man who sang *My Generation* was Roger Daltrey, and I knew exactly what he looked like. As I turned each page, the music of Radio Luxembourg poured out like the fountain of life.

The next morning I took my NME to school, and once again it was my turn to be the class hero. The teacher even allowed us to read and discuss two articles in the paper. What a lesson!

What a giant leap in just one year. Only last June I had been afraid to smuggle a copy of the Herald Tribune from Zakopane, now, here we were discussing in open class this great British music journal.

During the Easter holidays I had a call from Hanka, the daughter of my parents' friends, František and Marie. I had spent many hours with Hanka during my parents' visits; she was in the same school stream as me, only in a different class. She could play boogie-woogie on the piano and loved western music as much as I did, and failed miserably to teach me some piano chords. Now she informed me she was popping over to see me with her penpal, a French girl called Martina.

The majority of this visit was spent standing over my record player, listening to my massive six-record collection with the entire conversation in English; the first time I had conversed socially in anything other than Czech. I was quite proud of myself, but not as proud as my mother, who had been listening in from time to time. The fact that Hanka's parents had welcomed a western capitalist to stay with them was yet another sign of what special communists they had become.

At the end of the war when General Patton and the American's pulled up in Pilsen just 300 kilometres from Brno, and a few kilometres from the German border, František and my father watched helplessly as the west gave way to Russia.

In hindsight I suppose František was not a devout communist. After the Jalta Agreement, which separated Europe and decided our fate for the next 40 years, František must have made the decision to stay within the communist party for the sake of a better life, and who could blame him. He and Marie had, after all, survived the Nazi concentration camp which I'm sure would weaken anyone's political resolve.

Nothing I ever saw of him made him look or act like a communist, and nothing I ever saw showed him to compromise his kind nature, especially demonstrated now in allowing a capitalist friend of his daughter to stay in his home for several days.

What a great father to risk so much for his daughter's happiness.

Tony: The great 208

By the end of the 50s, Elvis had been crowned King and too quickly abdicated, as the Colonel contracted him to Hollywood, entering the MGM lot in Culver City and taking early rock n' roll retirement and musical decline.

When the incredible Beatles came along, and then Radio Caroline sailed into their lives, the 60s teen generation's time to party got underway.

What a mix! Pirate ships providing their soundtrack, a media eager to whip things up and, the ingredient which made it all work, accommodating parents.

The unbridled teenagers weren't going to miss a beat!

Beatles hair-cuts, Rolling Stones no-haircuts, Beatle suits and boots, James Bond, the mini, (cars and skirts), Mary Quant, Twiggy, George Best, Carnaby Street, were all British developments. There were influential pills on the scene too, a pill to stop pregnancies, and pills to get you high and dancing or making out all night long!

Then something that had never been allowed, men dancing together! It had never happened before, indeed if you tried that in the rock 'n' roll era you'd be thrown out on your gay arse!

Girls *always* danced together, they had to because the men didn't appear until just before last orders in the pubs. Chatting up girls too soon was a costly matter. It was usually during the last 30 minutes of a dance when there'd be a mad scramble for the girls, which led to an extended smooch session just before the DJ brought the night to a close.

Straight men dancing together was a part of the move in the culture, and a realisation that dancing was something men could enjoy and not simply regard as an instrument to find a girlfriend.

The track that took them there was *The Shake* by Sam Cooke, and other dance crazes that didn't require you to hold a partner such as *The Twist* and *Let's Twist Again* from Chubby Checker or Little Eva's *Locomotion*.

Now the boys could dance alone, and we waited for the girls to ask us if we'd like a drink. But the circle didn't quite complete.

Who could explain the phenomenon that we would inherit an amazing new pill, an amazing new radio station and the greatest group the world would ever know, each arriving at *exactly* the same time?

For the first time in history, teenagers were entertaining teenagers. The 60s kids swiftly took self-control, spurred on by a generation of parents who had gone nose to nose with Hitler and won a valuable freedom. It was a freedom they would pass on to their children as a gift they had earned for them.

The 60s kids were the beneficiaries of failed Nazism.

Until that fateful day when Radio Caroline with her extended mast sailed up the Thames estuary, there had been a musical drought across the land. The problems came from my old friends at the Musicians' Union, who imposed 'needle-time restrictions' on the BBC, the UK's *only* radio station! Imagine that? All that great music going unheard, it was almost... communism.

I often say to today's young DJs and the kids I meet, "Can you imagine life with only one station and only a half hour of new music played every day?"

Of course they can't, it's inconceivable to them in a day and age where you can't move for music and the further we've got away from those early 60s, the less believable it seems that such a situation could have ever existed.

In the years BC (before Caroline), teenagers everywhere had struggled to stay awake to hear the night-time-only Radio Luxembourg pop programmes. Although without precedent, it required much delicate fine-tuning of our wireless receivers to bring out the stars. When you found them, they lurked, ducked and dived within the static which emitted from 208 metres on the medium wave or AM as it is known today.

Millions of music lovers and our parents before us, put up with this every night, whilst millions more pop parched teenagers around Europe also pulled up nightly, at the 208 watering hole.

Radio Luxembourg was, without any doubt, the greatest radio station the world has ever known. And at this time, I had no aspirations whatsoever to work there.

Radio Caroline had captured my heart.

Jan: Vladimir's birthday gift

On 2 March 1966, the Red Law daily drew our attention to a problem. Countryside dwellers, farmers and workers were leaving the fields for the inner cities, where they could find better jobs and better working conditions. A big flaw within the red system had started to reveal itself.

Worse still, whilst mechanisation on the cooperative farms was keeping pace with industry, the brains required to run things weren't coming through at an academic level. Academia didn't want to know agriculture. Farming had a brain drain.

The article strengthened my convictions and confirmed that my decision to enter the Brno University of Agriculture was the right one.

With a poor family record like mine, I knew the communist barriers would be set against me and that, no matter how well I did, my chosen career would be stifled and the big jobs given to the *cleaner* communists. But the Red Law comments gave me hope. The countryside needed brains as well as brawn, and I loved rural life.

I'd flirted with reaching for a degree in law, but soon realised that law students were only studying how to maintain the status quo for the Czechoslovakian Communist Party and the welfare of Public Safety, the Secret Safety Police and the Czechoslovakian People's Army.

I'd considered trying to go for a university ticket with English but no more than 10 students per year were admitted, all selected from staunch communist families, something I thought was strange when true-reds realistically should have wanted degrees in Russian, not the hated English. Communist or not, it was a strange society for a pubescent to get to grips with. On the one hand, we were bred to despise the west and all it stood for, and yet it was clear the government wanted us to remain in touch with them.

This was very apparent with the state tourist agency Čedok, who had suddenly started to advertise a most amazing cruise in Red Law. Here was the opportunity to visit Holland, France, Italy and Spain, a 24-day cruise and all you needed was 8,000 crowns.

There were just two things in our way. Firstly, this was equivalent to six months' salary to an ordinary worker. Secondly, there was no doubt you would have required a perfect communist family pedigree to get anywhere near the liner.

So I looked towards a life in agriculture away from the inner-city socialist culture, where theatres staged only progressive plays from Eastern nations. What I liked about the countryside was the lack of radio signal jamming and clarity of signal, so that as my Uncle Franta had so enjoyed Radio Free Europe, my own pleasure in listening to Radio Luxembourg was also enhanced. Yes, a degree in agriculture seemed the right route for me.

It was a tough time, end of school exams mixed with the agriculture exam-swatting, and then a real let down when to my great sorrow, I wasn't nominated for either the high school basketball team, nor the volleyball team that would be visiting our friendship school in Bratislava. A chance to see Katka again had been more important to me, than being selected for the team. But never mind, I consoled myself with the knowledge that the next time I met her, I'd be a university student.

So I did my serious studying at night, whilst taking strength from either Radio Luxembourg or Radio Caroline.

One fine sunny afternoon, after school, I diverted to downtown Brno to do a little window-shopping and had the biggest shock of my life.

Suddenly, Radio Luxembourg, as clear in signal as I had ever heard it, appeared to be playing right there in the high street. It could only be Radio Luxembourg because only 208 had ever played the tune we were hearing and yet, I looked at my watch, it was too early for the station.

I followed the music, drawn down the high street until my heartbeat started to slow down at the Supraphon record shop, a dark uninviting shop that played orchestral dirges and communist opera, a place I rarely frequented for these reasons.

But now I was drawn inside as Chris Andrews sang first *Yesterday Man* followed by *To Whom it Concerns*.

Mesmerised, I approached the source of the music, a record player at the end of the counter. Surely, I thought, someone must have received a gift from someone in the west, has called into the shop and asked to hear what was on the record. That was my first theory but then I saw the label as the logo went round and round. Above the name of Chris Andrews was the name of the shop Supraphon.

My mind was in turmoil. I wanted to ask the shop assistant what magic was there here? Was the record for sale? Did she know it had been to the top part of the Luxembourg charts?

The problem remained, I could not reveal my expert knowledge on western pop music, I had to play dumb, just as I had a week earlier on a tram ride...

Sitting across from me was a boy about my age blatantly and proudly holding in his hands the Beatles' *Help* album. I had never seen a Beatles album before; I had heard the odd track on 208 but had not been indulged with the other pleasures contained within the grooves of what I now stared at. I wanted to ask him to let me hold it but didn't. I wanted to tell him I had a copy of the New Musical Express, and brag that I had been amongst the first in Brno to see A Hard Day's Night. What would I have said if he had been friendly towards me, and offered to loan me this amazing vinyl so that I could record it on a tape recorder?

I grew angry as my mind asked how the communist party had brought me to this stage where I couldn't borrow this boy's Beatles album, because they had made tape recorders available at last for 2,300 crowns, for which a worker would have to toil for six weeks to be able to buy. I let the boy leave the tram unhindered by my dreams, and I watched him walking down the sidewalk as he started to admire the sleeve of his priceless LP. Then we pulled off in the opposite direction, and I was left abjectly frustrated.

The memory of this incident returned as I watched Chris Andrews spinning round.

I was now flanked by three school friends, who had also heard the music out in the street and entered to investigate. Each of us were profoundly aware we were standing at a moment in history, witnessing change, containing our excitement at the wonder that was taking place before our eyes and in our ears.

Then, casually, as though I wasn't so very interested, I asked the lady behind the counter, "How is it you play a western record even in the street from the speaker above the door? This is very unusual in Brno."
Her answer sustained my feelings of shock. The record was actually released for sale in Czechoslovakia on the Supraphon label, and had arrived that very morning.
The million-dollar question… "And how much will this record cost?"
When she told us she had ten copies, my 12 crowns appeared on the counter quicker than you could say "Thank you Lord!"
When we left the shop, she had six copies left.

We talked excitedly as we headed homewards, each studying our acquisition. We agreed it was a great shame Supraphon hadn't released *Help* or *I Can't Get No (Satisfaction)* our favourite Luxembourg plays in the year gone by. But then my friend Vladimir made a very good point, "Maybe this is just the start! Maybe Supraphon will release more western hits!"
Like four madmen, we hugged one another right there in the street, formed a circle and danced around singing loudly, *I'm her Yesterday Man*!
It had taken us three years before we could genuinely respond to Martha & the Vandellas' *Dancing in the Street*.

Vladimir called me one day, his calmness hiding an amazing secret.
"You must come here to my home," he said. "I have to show you something."
I didn't hesitate, Vladimir never understated anything and I was intrigued to know why he was so keen that I should visit him, and why he was insistent that I take my record collection along?
His apartment door opened and there he was singing *Happy Birthday* to himself, whilst escorting me by the arm into the living room.

If the four Beatles had been standing before me, I could not have been more excited at what I now gazed upon. Here was a brand new Sonet Duo tape recorder, the dream of every kid in my class. "Happy birthday Vlad," I said my mouth dry, my mind numb. I walked around it. I drooled over it. I touched it, stroked it almost. An amazing Saturday afternoon took place, where we recorded our voices for the very first time, and listened to the tape containing 60 Paul Anka songs. I could have listened to Paul Anka all that day and the next, but after *Crazy Love* and then *You are my Destiny* and then *Lonely Boy*, I could see that the birthday boy grew impatient to record my own precious records, which we did to our great delight.
From Elvis to the Beatles, the Stones, and now my latest acquisition, Chris Andrews.

Little did we know we were violating the law and, with no alternative, did so for the next quarter century. Printed on the Elvis EP was the copyright warning: *Unauthorised public performance and copying of this record is prohibited.* On the Chris Andrews *Supraphon* record was the sentence: *All rights of the producer and authors for public performance and radio broadcast reserved.*

Supraphon could well have omitted their warning, there were so few tape recorders in Czechoslovakia and, with little choice but to ignore the small print on our records, the tape recorder became the most important item a music-loving Czech kid could own other than their radios.

But, whilst I was yet to own my own, my dear friend Vladimir loaned me his from time to time, and so began my Sunday night ritual, when I would record the Radio Luxembourg Top 20 with DJ Barry Alldis.

Now, for the first time, I could hear 208 during daylight hours. Now also I could repeat and repeat a recording, until I fully comprehended the lyrics and the meaning of the DJ's introductions.

Once again I became the focus of my classmates when I arrived, not only with the lyrics of a currently popular tune which they all knew from Radio Luxembourg, but, on the opposite page of my school exercise book, the lyrics translated into our own language.

Tony: Kenny has an orgasm

After a few weeks on Radio Caroline South I came ashore knowing I'd found my vocation.

I travelled from Harwich to London on the train with the Emperor Rosko and his mynah bird Alfie. From rival Radio London our companions included Kenny Everett and Tony Windsor. The latter was in a drinking competition with his archrival newsreader, Paul Kaye. The competition ran for almost three years!

Kenny was worried. He'd been called ashore prematurely by his boss at Radio London, Alan Keen.

Years later, when Alan was my MD at Radio Luxembourg he recounted the story to me.

"What's your game coming out with such language on my radio station?" he asked the funny little DJ.

"What language boss?" he asked eyebrows furrowed.

"How dare you talk about 'coming' on air!"

"Coming? Come again boss?"

Alan slammed a finger into a cassette player. Kenny's voice filled the room.

"Oooooooooo!" it began over the strains of the Beatles' *Michelle.*

"That record gives me an orgasm!"

He then was heard to segue smoothly into Len Barry's *1,2,3* but Alan's finger hit the stop button before Len got to '2'.

"Well?" he said dramatically, "What have you got to say for yourself?"

Kenny looked nonplussed.

"What's wrong with that? If I love the record, it gives me orgasms, so what boss?"

Keen scrutinised the diminutive DJ who sat cross legged, a mile of executive desk separating them, and then it dawned on him. As unbelievable as it seemed, it *had* to be the answer.

"Kenny," he said like a kindly father.

"What does the word 'orgasm' mean?"

Ken looked back at him, a picture of naive innocence.

"Err... it's like when something excites you."

"Let's go to the pub," said Alan throwing his arm around Kenny's shoulder, "We need to have a little talk."

Tony Windsor (TW) was the chief DJ on Radio London. He was Australian and had a voice to die for, *literally*.

Back in Sydney, he had been known as DJ Tony Withers.

He grew restless with the breakfast show on Sydney's top radio station and wanted to see the world, so he dreamed up a scam.

He announced to the media that he was diagnosed with a terminal illness. He was just sorry that his dream, to see a bit of the world, would not be possible.

Subsequently the station got the listeners to contribute to a fund to send him on a round the world trip. His trip ended in London when he heard the pirate stations, and applied for a job on Radio London.

Thirty years after his adoring Australian public chipped in, he was still as fit as a fiddle apart from a little alcohol abuse.

Every pirate DJ can recount numerous hearty yarns from their days on the high seas.

Paul Burnett takes great pleasure in recalling his adventures on board a small tub called Radio 270 off Scarborough Bay in Yorkshire. The DJs set up what was to become known as 'the self-raising affair'.

The DJ on air didn't notice the studio door inching open, nor the nozzle of the vacuum cleaner that pointed at him like a Dalek ready to '*Exterrrminate!*'

The DJs and crew took up vantage positions outside the studio's windows ready for the next time he opened the microphone.

Halfway through his first sentence a DJ whose name was never revealed, turned on the vacuum from 'suck' to 'blow' and the room filled with 4lbs of McDougall's self raising flour.

All the listeners could hear was coughing and spluttering, followed by obscenities from his gagging throat, as the *abominable snowDJ* felt his way blindly out of the studio to sweet fresh air.

The gag backfired. It took two days to get the studio equipment back to normal. The culprit was never revealed and so avoided walking the plank.

A broadcaster breaking up during the news on the BBC is a very rare occurrence. Understandably, you can't tell the nation the Queen's corgi has died, or a serial killer has struck again and then start to titter.

Sometimes though, it happens, either through the reader's own doing or by a third party prank.

Both the pirates and Radio Luxembourg used people like me, untrained journalists, to transcribe the BBC's news broadcasting almost identical stories 60 minutes or so after Auntie had broadcast the original version. For me, trained as I was in reeding and riting at Oldham Art School, it was a terrible responsibility.

The instruction of course was not to copy the Beeb's version verbatim by changing the odd noun here or an adjective there... or was it an adverb here and a pronoun there?

I recall the late Dave Christian on Luxembourg covering the Lebanese problems of the day and reading, '*Lesbian forces are advancing*'.

Tony Brandon on Radio London announced, "The great French resistance leader and Army Chief has died..."

Then it was Brandon's turn to die as Kenny Everett and Dave Cash slowly appeared over the top of his news sheet, with two pieces of white chalk hanging from their nostrils, like two lunatic cross-eyed walruses.

Brandon was the best in the pirate business at not breaking up, so he became a target and a challenge for one and all.

DJ Mark Roman entered the studio during Brandon's news and proceeded to undress him. Tony maintained a smooth delivery even when he heard his zip zipping open, and felt his trousers pulled down by hands beneath the desk, his presentation was immaculate.

Stark naked, Brandon continued po-faced.

"And finally, the weather..."

And that was when Roman started to pour an ice-cold pitcher of water over his head.

Brandon finally broke up right on, "...wet weather is expected". Other self-inflicted break-ups included David 'Kid Jensen' on Radio Luxembourg who delivered, "Militant prostitutes tonight marched into Belfast!"

The Catholics would have loved that one.

Kid too, was a difficult customer to break. Many DJs have claimed other DJs did this to other DJs over the years, but I can vouch for this one because I saw it happen...

Our Radio Luxembourg colleague, Mark Wesley, found a way to crack Kid up, by bringing a step ladder into the studio as our young Canadian friend read the 9pm bulletin which, in those days, arrived in Luxembourg on a telex from the Daily Mirror in London.

Mark placed a plastic bucket in front of Kid, climbed the ladder and just as Kid arrived at the weather, proceeded to pee from high into the plastic bucket! The forecast was for rain followed by severe gales of laughter from a completely broken Kid Jensen.

Newsreaders laughing? DJs mis-reads? It was all a part of what made the pirate stations... piratical and 208 great.

Jan: The milkman

By the middle of May all my class had passed our exams with flying colours. Then came the entrance exams organised by the various Universities, with me optimistically heading for the University of Agriculture.

Immediately after this I became a lorry driver's mate at Lacrum, the state enterprise producer of the nation's dairy products. We delivered milk, yoghurt and cream to shops, hospitals, factories and even to Brno's Bohunice prison, a place that, in just a couple of years time, would host the company of my friends, including guitarist Pavel Váně, and the kids who faced-off against the Secret Police in protest of the Soviet occupation, which was now just two years away.

How different things might have been if only these authoritarians had permitted us to freely purchase the Beatles and the Rolling Stones records, and to allow our radios to play whatever we wanted to hear, wherever we directed the dial. Rebellion, anarchy, protest almost always emanates from students whose brains are still flowing like freshwater streams, unpolluted by life and filled with hope and dreams.

I have never doubted that Radio Luxembourg and the Beatles influenced the Dubček uprising in the Prague Spring of 68, when our newly elected First Secretary of the Communist Party of Czechoslovakia, stretched his political arm too far for Russian liking. He wanted reforms to include an end to media restrictions, freedom of speech and travel.

But all this was two years later. Back then, in 1966, I was still busy enjoying my own newfound freedom with a friend's tape recorder. The biggest political decision I had to make each day was whether to record Radio Luxembourg, or the exciting new pirate ship Radio Caroline?

The job I had taken really got in the way of my listening. I had plenty of time during the day with no school but having to rise at 2.30am, as the Radio Luxembourg closing theme took the station to 3am, I was already at the dairy loading our lorry ready to distribute our products to the city by

6am. Now, however, thanks to Vladimir's generosity, I often spent the day with his tape recorder, which he so very generously loaned to me. Now I could press the red button and go to sleep safe in the knowledge that my daylight hours could now also be filled with 208 and 199 programmes.

There were other advantages to working from 3am. By 10am in the warm days of summer, I'd jump on my bike and ride to the lake enjoying a freedom like never before. Then I learned more about the communist system thanks to my wily driver. Because we started work at 3am, you could guarantee the bosses didn't show their faces until after 6am, by which time we were loaded and doing our rounds. Every morning somehow we'd find slightly more products than were listed on our schedule.

These fresh creams, milk and yogurt went into bakeries and came out looking like fresh loaves or croissants. Tubs of whipped cream would enter butchers shops and materialise as delicious salami, which the driver would then carefully slice with his knife and share with me along with the still warm oven breads, that had recently been swapped for a tub of delicious whipped cream. I ate the finest breakfasts in the land all washed down with the sweetest, freshest milk our countryside could deliver. Within 12 hours of the cow giving up her milk, it was in my stomach.

Over 25 years, I saw many examples of how the communist system worked. It was exactly as Karl Marx had ordained, "From each according to his ability, to each according to his needs." Cheating in our totalitarian state, was a way of life, corruption ran like a seam from the very top to the very bottom of our society.

And so it was that I embraced the system, so that as I ate my free kefir, yogurt, cheese and bread by the lake, I would gaze at the blue sky above me and start to believe that life wasn't too bad at all.

But then one morning, I suddenly came down to earth.

We'd just unloaded our shipment of milk at St Anne's hospital, always a very pleasant stop as so many beautiful nurses and kitchen staff greeted and flirted with the driver and I. By 4am we were making tracks through to Bohunice prison via Gregor Mendel Square, so named after the scientist who had become an Augustinian friar, gaining posthumous fame as the founder of the new science of genetics. From 1843 till his death in 1884, Mendel lived and worked in the Abbey of St Thomas, which was situated in the square named after him.

After all those beautiful girls at the hospital, to enter such a beautifully tranquil, historic setting where normal traffic was not allowed, became a feature of the early morning pleasures.

But now something caught my eye and I begged the driver to stop the lorry. I jumped out of the cab and ran back to where I had seen a large poster, which I now stopped in front of to make sure I hadn't been mistaken or dreaming, as one often is so early in the morning.

And there it was, in letters larger than me, PAUL ANKA appearing in BRNO!

The poster was still wet with paste. I would be the first amongst my friends to bring this news to them. We could rush to buy tickets, be amongst the first, maybe ever get front row seats for this historic event, where the first ever global pop star was coming to perform live in Brno.

I couldn't wait for the shift to end.

Whilst František was every bit as excited as I, our other friends were not exactly overwhelmed, saying that Paul Anka was a yesterday man, it was the Beatles they wished to see. I hid my anger. They couldn't associate with my own level of involvement with Paul Anka since I first heard *Diana* at summer camp now a decade ago. And didn't Jana Vorlová play this song just for me in my Mother's dormitory? And wasn't it Paul Anka's entire song catalogue we enjoyed when I first played a tape on a tape recorder?

No, they obviously did not have the same threads that held me close to Paul Anka and his *Diana*, but what no one appreciated was the fact that, as they yearned to see the Beatles in live concert, the Beatles were finished.

Their London concert on 1 May 1966 was their last ever in Great Britain, other than their Apple rooftop performance in 1969 seen by passersby and, thankfully, a camera crew.

In just a few days' time, three concerts in West Germany would be their last ever in Europe. Then the most valuable tickets in the world would be for their concerts in Manila, then Tokyo, Canada and certain American cities until, on 26 August 1966, the Beatles final concert ever took place in San Francisco's Candlestick Park.

We would know none of this in Czechoslovakia. We would never be able to mourn the end of an era because, for us, such an era had never even started.

The very next day, although we were first in line at the theatre, undoubtedly due to bloody communist favouritism again, the best tickets we could buy were in the 7th row. Our close friends may have poo-poo'd Paul Anka, but the citizens of Brno must have been Radio Luxembourg listeners to a man. The concert was sold out, with hundreds gathered at the entrance on the big night begging to purchase our tickets. My soul would have been cheaper for them to buy!

Even after all these years I cannot express the pleasures I experienced that night as Paul, who came across like a lifelong friend, sang and spoke to us as if we were sitting in his living room.

"Do you want to hear Crazy Love?" he asked.

I was shouting "Yes" at the top of my voice, and then suddenly realised something quite remarkable. Everyone in the theatre wanted to hear it, and suddenly it seemed that everyone could understand and respond in English!

After the concert, high on endorphins and adrenalin we stopped for a couple of beers, which was when I revealed to the others that I had access to a tape containing 60 Paul Anka songs whereupon, helped by the persuasive alcohol and the amazing after-concert atmosphere, I promised each of them I would gladly dub the tape for each of them, providing they bought the blank tape.

The next day I had 8 tapes brought to my door, and only then did I realise to complete my task, I needed a *second* tape recorder.

And so it was that I became inspired to work every extra hour God gave me, to earn and save from my summer-break milk job, to buy that very machine.

Tony: Radio Caroline North

In February 1966 I experienced my first flight. Cambrian Airways to the Isle of Man. Little did I know that for the next eighteen years my career would find me on an average of one flight per week!

By my side on this exciting journey were Ugly Ray Teret and Mick Luvzit whose imagination for stage names was extremely challenged.

We were driven by Caroline's chauffeur, a gentle Manx man named Bob who drove us over the hill from Douglas to Ramsey Bay passing over the Fairy Bridge, where our Manxman driver insisted we each greet the fairies or walk the rest of the way.

Bob explained to us the local folklore, wherein many Manx years ago a cat had angered the fairies, and to this day no cat on the Isle of Man had a tail. Now that's what I call a *real* fairy tail.

"Startin' them from school are they?" asked the custom's officer who'd boarded our tender to check our passports.

I was 21, and looked 15. The team of DJs already gathered on board had never been so happy to see reinforcements. I was the new recruit who would ensure those due shore leave would return with the tender.

The standard rota was two weeks on, one week off, although my first period on Caroline South had taken me through Christmas and well into New Year.

Now Ronan had shipped me north where he thought people could better understand me!

It just didn't seem like work for which most of us were paid £25 a week including the week off and flights to and from the mainland to either London, Manchester or Liverpool.

I decided to call myself Tony Prince the 'Royal Ruler', having been enamoured with the powerful style of Caroline South's 'Emperor' Rosko, who remains a dear friend right to this day.

I arrived on the ship, completely unaware of the personalities who had developed their popularity on Caroline North. I didn't know them and they didn't know me, although the ones who travelled to London for their week off, had heard me broadcasting on the south ship.

"What's Blackburn like?" they wanted to know. "Is DLT coming to the North ship?"

After the super-egos of Caroline South and Radio London's DJs, I found myself sharing the microphone with the zaniest set of personalities imaginable. You could not dream up these characters!

The Fredericia was the original Radio Caroline vessel, an old Dutch ferry with enough cabins to provide each DJ with their own nest in which to sleep and answer their fan mail.

I was met and welcomed on board by Jerry 'Soopa' Leighton, who hosted the wonderful Leighton-early show from 6am-9am, a show I'd set my alarm for each morning to learn from and to enjoy.

I would never be a DJ like Jerry. He had that off the cuff ad-lib magic humour gifted to a few human beings. He had the ability to make a joke out of anything, and did.

Jerry, in my opinion, was a major omission from the BBC Radio 1's original line-up.

They went for the safe, tabloid friendly Blackburn rather than the lightening wit and intellectually stimulating Jerry Leighton.

Radio Caroline North listeners will know exactly what I mean. Jerry was, in my estimation, one of the greatest DJs ever, a smart Jewish lad with his profound sense of humour, which continued from studio to dining table. Jerry admitted to us all that he had previously sold contraceptives by the gross to London's prostitutes. He wasn't joking.

"I sold them whoresale," he'd tell us.

'Daffy' Don Alan was a Canadian who died in 1996 in Ireland, the country that inherited his unique verbal garbage to their airwaves, after the pirates had finally been sunk.

One day, after weeks locked in his room giggling, (I lived in the next cabin and became curiouser and curiouser), he invited all of us down to view the fruits of his labour, a redecoration of his cabin. Every inch of his four walls and ceiling was covered in bosoms from Playboy and Penthouse, and his stable of fans who obeyed his on-air requests.

Don held down the traditional housewife hours of 9am–noon where, for weeks, he'd encouraged female listeners to send him 'sexy' photos to add to the beautification of his domain. Approximately half of Lancashire had disrobed for him!

It was bad enough fantasising you were back on shore during those long fortnights at sea, but it must have been sheer hell in Don's cabin!

Many moons later, I heard from a die-hard pirate radio fan who'd been to look round the old MV Caroline, lying, dying in a Dutch shipyard, confirming to me that this famous cabin remained a testament to Don Juan Alan's amorous adventures.

Bob Stewart, a handsome Scouser with a Texan accent, also welcomed me on board.

Bob's mother died giving birth to him. His father was taken in the Second World War, so he had been brought up in Liverpool by three elderly aunts who he adored.

Somewhere along the line, Bob focused his kid-brain on American movies and TV shows and, at 16, had begun to sound like Hoss and Lil' Joe's dad in Bonanza, the Lorne Green of Fazakerly!

Whilst my young friends and I pretended to ride horses, slapping our thighs and prancing home from the Kings Cinema on Saturday mornings, Bob was playing similar games in Liverpool, but when we said to our enemies, "Yer dead 'I shot yer right int 'thart," Bob was yelling, "Yer dead buddy, lie down you son of a bitch!"

He almost became a Beatle.

Bob was a close friend of Pete Best, whose mother transformed the basement of their large house in Liverpool's West Derby district into a coffee bar so that Pete, his brother Rory and their mates, wouldn't have to go to the awful Conservative Club, where nothing but trouble lived.

Pete's inner sanctum of pals helped to build the coffee bar, and became founding members of the famous Kasbah.

Some of the friends had guitars.

Johnny Guitar, who would go on to form one of Liverpool's first ever groups with Rory Storm and Richard Starkey, was amongst them. Johnny Gustafson, soon to be one third of the Big Three, frequented the 'Kas' and Billy Hatton, a founder of the Foremost, was a regular. Two other novice guitar players were John Lennon and George Harrison, who would sit through the night with Bob and Pete listening to Carl Perkins and Chuck Berry tunes on the jukebox, learning the lyrics and fathoming out the chords.

"I was offered a job in the band if I'd get a leather jacket and black jeans," Bob reminisced with me on deck one night as the ship bobbed in a gentle Irish Sea swell.

Pete Best might well have regarded Bob as a potential competitor for the vacant drummer's gig, which history shows he held in the Beatles before Ringo made him the world's most famous sacked person.

To take Bob out of the running, sneaky Pete recommended him to Brian Kelly a local promoter who needed a DJ and that, according to Bob, "Was the Beatle's loss and Litherland Town Hall's gain."

Here Bob played the records he liked and introduced great Liverpool groups like Faron's Flamingos, the Dennisons, Rory Storm and the Hurricanes, the Undertakers, Lee Curtis & the Cruisers. Then one night he found himself introducing his old friends when the Beatles' circus came to town.

Bob met another DJ at Litherland Town Hall, Mike Ahearn who one night told Bob he was leaving the gig because he'd got a job on Radio Caroline.

"Radio what," asked Bob, who hadn't even got a radio.

Soon afterwards he invested in a transistor radio and tuned in to Mike's show. When Mike signed off Bob knew Litherland Town Hall had lost two DJs.

It only took a phone call to Radio Caroline's Chris Moore for his deep American accent to impress the Head of Programmes.

"I love your voice," said Moore. "We only pay £15 a week though, err I don't know how much that is in dollars. When can you come over to England?"

"England?" queried Bob, "I'm from Liverpool!"

Bob had a wicked sense of humour, and was a big enough lad to be as funny as he wanted to be.

To wake me, he'd lean over the side of the ship and throw fish through my porthole, landing them on my bed. We called them shit-fish because they hung around the ship in their thousands, eating *anything* we discarded.

It was an alarming wake up call.

I'd be soaping down in the communal showers to find my towel had been borrowed and, as I attempted to negotiate the corridors back to the safety of my cabin, 'Baby' Bob would appear with a posse chasing me naked round the ship, threatening to throw me over the side.

This was timed to coincide with the tourist boat arriving at high tide from Ramsey Bay, just as it circled the good ship Caroline, filled with two shilling paying pirate radio fans.

I hid from the Mersey madman and his cohorts in the engine room, my breathlessness masked by the groans of huge throbbing cogs and pulsating pistons, behind which I cowered.

I spent the remainder of my time on board scrubbing thick black oil off my hindquarters.

'Ugly' Ray Teret decided to use this self-defacing suffix when Bob had explained to the listeners just how ugly he was.

Like I say, Bob could say this kind of thing without fear of reprisal.

Whilst most Caroline DJs received a sack of letters delivered by the tender twice weekly, Ugly Ray got *three* sacks of sympathy mail!

His snivelling self-pitying characterised his show. As self-effacing and nauseous Ray was, Bob's gag backfired, because it gave Ray a career and a hook to hang his ugly DJ hat on. The girls loved him, ugly or not! Many years later Ray Teret became embroiled and arrested in the Jimmy Savile paedophile investigation, and is now in prison for the rest of his life.

Like America's rock 'n' roll pioneering airmen, DJs came up with the most imaginative names.

Graham 'Spider' Webb was an Australian who taught me a great deal about the serious nature of voice projection and presentation, but it was a Canadian who joined us on Caroline North, who blew us all away with his on-air name.

He called himself Mick Luvzit, the DJ who got married to Jan, Ray Teret's sister, on board Radio Caroline.

Ship-bound on Caroline for two weeks at a time, was a great environment to develop your DJ style and broaden your broadcasting knowledge.

I had my own 6pm-9pm show and stood in on the breakfast show when Soopa Leighton was on leave, or I'd do 9am-noon when Daffy Don was away. On a few occasions we found ourselves working 3 x 3 hour shows a day.

After the Midnight Surf Party ended at 3am, we'd go off air for a couple of hours to let the transponder cool down.

We'd each reserve the studio to make our jingles and programme features, or simply practice.

Like an ant's nest, Caroline was always active. DJs with metal spools of tapes and records heading upstairs to the studio or record library, DJs with bacon butties, DJs playing cards and telling jokes, DJs getting drunk or just simply trying to watch TV.

We had a television in the dining room, which also served as our lounge in the evenings but as the vessel was continually circling the anchor chain with each tide change, we had to use a contraption directly behind the telly, which descended from the top deck just like a periscope.

As the ship moved, so the picture quality deteriorated every few minutes. Throughout the evening we took it in turns with members of the crew, to jump up, reach for the contraption and change the aerial's direction.

When I first joined Caroline North, 'Murph the Surf', (Jim Murphy), was the Chief DJ. Jim was a 6'6" Texan who double-dwarfed me.

He was a bearded creature, a stick insect who wore his Chief DJ title like a Lonsdale Belt, ordering everyone around. I couldn't understand a word of his muffled Texan drawl, and I don't believe the listeners could either.

Accordingly, he called you certain names, the level of insult only he understood, but you got the gist by his self-congratulatory laughter that lit up his bearded face.

We were trying to watch the TV one night when, in front of everyone, Murph shouts to me, "Hey you little shitfucker, give that goddam handle a turn mumble, mumble, hah, hah, hah!"

I'd understood him clearly for once. Everyone in the room had.

Following his orders, I arose from my seat and headed towards the telly. Halfway across the room, I took a flying British rugby tackle at his legs, bringing him to the deck where I proceeded to climb on board him.

Texas 0 - Little Shitfucker 1. Bob Stewart pulled me off him.

One night, during a ferocious North Sea storm, I found myself on the aforementioned late show. In these circumstances the studio tilted from side to side increasing in degrees as the storm built until, eventually, the stylus arm would lift off the record. The rule was to switch to a reel-to-reel tape of pre-recorded hits using the remote to inject any voice-overs.

At storm force 12 with Caroline at a 45° tilt, I cut from turntables to the Revox recorder standing to attention, coffin-sized against the studio wall to my left.

I jammed my feet hard against the side of the console, knees under my chin so I wouldn't capsize.

At precisely 48°, the Revox broke its mooring from the studio wall, staggering forward like a drunken steel cabinet, and then back as the ship rolled and then, once again, lurching towards me like an alien metallic monster looking for blood.

At 50° it finally gave in to earthly gravity smashing to the floor, just as a rack of records behind my head spewed out its Top 50 black vinyl frisbees, each seeking me out on the floor.

Having just made ready to comment on the tumbling tape recorder, the microphone was wide open.

The late night listeners heard everything.

It went, "Ouch! Fuck! Agh! Jesus!"

The Revox dead.

The Royal Ruler dethroned!

On 20 January 1966 during one of my first weeks on board Caroline North, we looked in disbelief at the television. Radio Caroline South (the Mi Amigo) had run aground after dragging its anchor in the same storm. We watched open-mouthed as the TV news showed the beached Caroline South with my friends Tony Blackburn, Dave Lee Travis, Tom Lodge, Norman St John and Graham Webb, being winched ashore by breeches buoy.

Not one of us ever considered the dangers we faced, not even then!

Jan: Death sentence

After Nazi troops occupied parts of Czechoslovakia and formed the
Protectorate of Bohemia and Moravia in March 1939, by September
of that year, a law was introduced making it illegal to listen to foreign
stations. Anyone found doing so risked a prison sentence or the more
severe concentration camp. The new law also stated that in certain cases
where someone was found to have circulated propaganda from foreign
broadcasters they would, in serious cases, receive the death penalty.

Hundreds finished up in concentration camps for not having followed
orders to take their radios into an official workshop to take the short
wave receiver out. Every radio receiver had to have a card fixed it with the
inscription:

*'Remember that listening to foreign broadcasting is punishable with a prison
sentence or death.'*

We each had our track records, an invisible license-to-live containing our
perceived misdemeanours, compiled by, recorded and maintained within
the vast files of State Safety, like a driving license with endorsements.

If someone was found to have been listening to Radio Luxembourg or
music programmes on AFN or the BBC World Service, onto their file this
would go. Worse still, if this person was heard to be praising or promoting
these broadcasts amongst their contemporaries, it would be entered onto
their file and remain there as a black mark forever.

The law was, of course, a hand-me-down from the Second World War
when anti-Nazi propaganda was high on broadcasters' objectives. As I
grew into a pop radio fanatic, these ancient wartime laws remained within
our new classless, farm-sharing totalitarian society.

There was no doubt that I got away with my radio listening because,
firstly I was careful, and secondly, the authorities couldn't get too heavy
with people listening to harmless pop music. What little they knew! Had
they appreciated just how anti-communist the promotion of the free world,
which we heard portrayed in the lyrics by the likes of John Lennon, Bob
Dylan and Johnny Cash, could be? Had they sussed this out so they would
have burned every radio in the country. Understanding western disc jockey
banter as we did, we soon understood clearly what a black and white part
of a colourful world we occupied.

The anti-communist propaganda emitting from the Station of the
Stars was the most potent force imaginable, one that our dark overlords
were totally unaware of. Little did they grasp there were secret messages
contained in the songs we heard, an influence from the other side of the
iron curtain, which would ultimately herald the end of communism.
They had clues.

In 1964, Yvonne had scored a massive hit with her version of Brenda Lee's *I'm Sorry* sung in Czech, and loved by the whole population of Czechoslovakia across the generations. In the year it was released, it became so popular that word spread around the country like wildfire that Yvonne was to perform the song on a Saturday TV show.

My parents had friends who, because they had no kids, had enough resources to buy a television set and we were invited to watch the programme with them. We were far from the only family visiting friends to see our new singing star performing her hit on that Saturday evening. Across the nation on the streets, everyone seemed to be going somewhere; the trams were packed.

Those lucky enough to have a television were about to discover just how many friends they had!

Clues don't come any bigger but Yvonne's version of Brenda Lee's *I'm sorry*, (an American written song!), was viewed with the same enthusiasm by all employees of the Police and Specific Tasks Departments, all gathered around their televisions with their families. Little did they know that we avid Radio Luxembourg listeners had enjoyed the original version some four years previously when it scored so big with Brenda Lee herself, across the entire free world.

Of course the announcer didn't mention that the song Yvonne would sing was, in fact, an American song with Czech lyrics, which complimented the original quite well on this occasion.

In later years once our records became public domain and we could see what had been going on, the archives revealed certain young people had attracted Public Safety's attention and were registered for listening to and promoting radio stations like Luxembourg and were under the scrutiny of the Secret Police.

After 1948 they didn't put people in prison for listening to foreign radio stations, but many were locked away for passing the news from these stations to other people. The most dangerous in the 50s would be to utter what you'd heard broadcast on Radio Free Europe. I'd decided the risks of mentioning Luxembourg's Teen & Twenty Disc Club wasn't something I should worry too much about, but of course, I had to protect my parents, who still regarded such subversive activity as dangerous. I was therefore far more concerned about my parents discovering I was a 208 Clubber than the Secret Police!

All western radio stations broadcasting in Czech or Slovak were jammed by special jamming transmitters, spread throughout the country creating artificial static. In the 60s it got better, although Radio Free Europe remained enemy number one (founded by the US Congress in the Cold War) they stopped jamming the BBC, Voice of America and Deutsche

Welle. Radio Free Europe was jammed until 1988, and it's quite remarkable and astonishing to me that this station, (which I never had any interest in as their broadcast was jammed too much in big cities), moved its HQ to Prague in 1995. How things change!

Tony: Sacked

I went home to my parents in Oldham with sacks filled with fan mail. The listeners had welcomed me to their wonderful radio station, and I couldn't wait to get back on board to be with them again.

Some DJs couldn't be bothered to reply to their fan mail, but I wrote to each and every one, not wasting a moment of time on board. And a good thing too.

Putting my shilling coins into an Egerton Street pay phone I was responding to a telegram asking me to call Caroline South DJ Tom Lodge, who'd recently been posted to a management position in Caroline House. "I'm afraid we won't be sending you back to the ship," he announced coldly. "Are you kidding?" I asked. "I have three sacks of mail. Where's Chris Moore I want to talk to him!"

"Chris is no longer with the company. We have a new boss..."

I waited for him to deliver the two little words that turned my palm that gripped the phone damp.

"Philip Solomon!"

I couldn't believe my ears. I had to hand in my skull and crossbones the victim of my ex-agent's revenge. I understood now why he hadn't held me to contract, this way he saved on solicitor's bills!

I got the job on Radio Caroline without Solomon's Agency influence and arranged the interview myself. Had Solomon gone to Chris Moore on my behalf, I would not have got the job because Chris hated him for some reason.

Little did I know however, as I boarded my first ever flight, that at the same time Phil Soloman was about to become a prime shareholder in the nation's favourite radio station.

Ronan wouldn't take my calls. No one would.

I had been to heaven and was now standing outside the Golden Gates, barred like a fellow outside the Top Rank without a tie! It was chilly outside heaven. I stood sobbing in Oldham hell, a telephone box on Egerton Street.

By the time I'd walked home I had my resolve. I wouldn't give in, and neither did I apply to other ships for work. There was only one ship for me, and I wanted my cabin back.

With my few savings I bought reams of stationary and stamps, and set about writing to the fans whose letters I'd brought home with me.

It was a monumental task for someone who spelled spelt spealt.

I must have written a couple of thousand scrawly hand-written letters explaining my sacking, and beseeching my new fans to write to Ronan asking for me to be reinstated.

After a few weeks on shore I received a telegram from my old boss Garry Brown at Top Rank Leisure. That was how it worked in the days when few homes boasted a telephone. People sent you short cryptic telegrams, 'Call Garry Brown... Stop... Urgent.'

Back in the phone box.

"I believe you're doing very well up there Tony, do you fancy doing a one night appearance back at your old stomping ground in Bristol?"

I confided my news about Caroline to Garry, who immediately offered me a full time job.

"Give me a week to think about it," I said.

Within the week I got a letter from Ronan's PA Delia, asking me to call him urgently.

"You've got more fans than Tony Blackburn," he announced, as if this was something bordering on an Olympian fête.

I booked my flight back to the Isle of Man.

1966 was a blur of happiness. People say today's DJs aren't as good as the pirates, but from what I've heard on archive recordings, we were a bunch of lads having a laugh finding ourselves in the right place at the right time. People talk about 'the 60s' as though there were 10 years of debauchery, youthful revolution, protest, music and flower power. To me the *real* 60s lasted three years, 1965 to 1967, and the 60s ended when Harold Wilson and his Labour government had their wicked way with the pirates on 14 August 1967.

I always went to London on my week off Caroline North sharing a twin bedded room at the Winton Hotel, Inverness Terrace, Bayswater with the Emperor Rosko aka Mike Pasternak.

Whilst he went off on exotic trips to broadcast for RTL in Paris, (he spoke fluent French), I was given charge of his battered Citroen can of a car, together with his pet Mynah bird, known to listeners throughout the south, as Alfie.

Rosko featured Alfie on his show, and travelled to and from the ship with him much to the customs officer's amusement.

"Morning Alfie!" yelled the Emperor.

"Morning Rosko!" Alfie squawked on cue.

During Rosko's absence one week, after I'd grown weary of my feathered friend's monosyllabic conversations, I decided to expand his vocabulary.

Back on board Radio Caroline Alfie was perched in his cage close to the microphone when Rosko bade him his usual cheery good morrow.

"Morning Alfie!" said the Emperor.

"Fuck off Rosko!" the bird replied.

Alfie's broadcasting career was over and done. Rosko made him hang up his headphones and banished him to birdland.

The Winton Hotel on Inverness Terrace, Bayswater was the place to be all right. Because we DJs were in residence, the out-of-town artists started using it too, and the groups and record company people resident in London frequented the hotel bar nightly.

One summer's evening in 1966, Johnny Walker, then on Radio England, had brought two mini-skirted damsels into my room, a gift of sorts so that I might put in a good word for him with Ronan.

Johnny and I talked radio and music all night, boring the knickers off our pretty guests.

"You hear what Blackburn and your lot did this morning?" Johnny asked.

Radio England was a new arrival in the Thames estuary, an American-backed pirate ship. It had not yet officially come on air but was making test broadcasts. The owners hadn't even made bunks for the DJs. It was chaos. A hundred yards away across the waves the Caroline DJs listened with envy at the newcomer's brand new PAMS jingle package, the best jingles that money could buy.

The DJs on board Radio Caroline South recorded Radio England's test broadcasts and within 24 hours had edited them to sound like Radio Caroline jingles!

It was a terrific coup and one of the most piratical events on the high seas. Walker told me that Radio England's American solicitors had been banging down Ronan's door at Caroline House!

Jingles by PAMS of Dallas were very expensive and copyright protected.

I phoned Jimmy Houlaghan, Ronan's Irish bodyguard, to ask what our boss was doing about the matter?

Jimmy answered with a guffaw.

"Yer man Ronan welcomed them to England and asked them if they knew what a pirate radio station was?"

Johnny Walker was pleased to be employed as a pirate, but longed to make the leap to Radio Caroline, Britain's most popular station. He made the leap in October 1966, and was one of the few English DJs to stay on after the Marine Offences Broadcasting Act had been introduced, staying until March 1968.

Johnny came via Radio England to Caroline where his show started to feature his Kiss in the Car, a nightly event where lovers were invited to park on the Frinton coast and flash their car headlights to him out at sea. It made an incredible sight, the power of the DJ seen through a thousand headlights, demonstrating just how popular Johnny Walker had become. The population in the Frinton area today is partly due to Johnny Walker's Kiss in the Car!

One very late night at the Hotel 'Wanton' as it was now called, I descended to the lobby seeking the cigarette dispenser when my great friend, Chas Chandler, former bass player with The Animals, greeted me.

"Tony, I want you to meet someone I'm managing," he bade.

A black guy with short hair and big teeth pumped my hand up and down like he wanted to see water flow from my mouth.

Standing at reception just three hours in from the USA, via the Cromwellian Club, was Jimi Hendrix!

No moustache yet, and not a solitary bead.

A rather plain dude for a God, with very long fingers.

They'd literally landed at Heathrow and gone straight to the Cromwellian club where Jimi had jammed with Brian Auger performing *Hey Joe* to an audience who didn't know him from Adam.

At night, when the mass of bands arrived back from their gigs, we'd drink and sing to acoustic guitars in the hotel bar whilst the wonderful receptionist Maggie, (Nell Gwyn in a previous life) plied us with ale.

The Righteous Brothers, the Four Tops and Hendrix jamming with the Dakotas, the Merseybeats, Billy Fury and Keith Moon.

It was Top of the Pops after hours!

With no MU around to protest, I joined in with the Crickets, singing the Buddy Holly songbook.

The next time I would sing with the original Crickets would be 30 years later, with Paul McCartney sharing the microphone with me!

You can dream it - or you can just do it!

Rosko was loaded. His father, Joe Pasternak, had produced the Elvis movies, Girl Happy and Spinout.

This alone made me his lap dog.

He took me shopping for made to measure footwear at Anello & Davide's on the Tottenham Court Road. Rosko flamboyantly ordering five pairs of cowboy boots peer-pressured me into ordering two pair of Beatle boots.

I loved Beatle boots, they made me two inches taller.

Although I was the poor relation, the personal appearances and club gigs at ten times my weekly Radio Caroline wages, were helping me to keep up with the Emperor's lifestyle.

Money was for spending, and Rosko taught me well. He taught me about riders in contracts. Rosko always had a bottle of Bacardi rum and Coca Cola waiting in the dressing room. It followed him on stage. There was never any left by the end of the gig!

At night we'd slip down to the Speakeasy where we'd order Jim Carter-

Fey's delicious spare-ribs, which we'd eat laughing with nutters like Keith Moon, or the bands in town from Liverpool.

The only time the conversation lulled was when a Beatle, or a Stone, or someone worthy entered the restaurant.

George Harrison's arrival with Patty Boyd was well worth a pregnant pause.

Another favourite haunt for the chart establishment was the Cromwellian Club on the Cromwell Road, but you had to avoid the Casino upstairs, which I didn't find easy. I was good up to the fifth scotch and coke; by the sixth I was broke. But who could resist playing Blackjack with the likes of Brian Epstein and Sean Connery sitting next to you?

Sometimes, as Caroline's northern office was based in Lord Street, Liverpool, I'd spend time with Ronan's Irish managers, Jimmy and Kevin, the wonderful Dougan brothers.

I tried to persuade them, they were all screwing up the radio station by making us play Solomon's Irish brother Mervyn's Emerald Records, and Solomon's own diseased Major Minor vinyl, or the Bachelors who were managed by Solomon.

It was the beginning of the end for Radio Caroline, months before Harold Wilson's government struck.

Suddenly, in between brilliant tracks such as Cat Steven's *I'm Gonna Get Me a Gun*, the Young Rascals' *Groovin* and Traffic's *Paper Sun*, you'd hear the Dubliners' *7 Drunken Nights* and Bridie Gallagher's latest *hourly*!

The listeners actually thought we liked that shit because we played the Dubliners so often and never bad-mouthed them!

Jimmy and Kevin who monitored the station in Liverpool for Ronan and Phil sympathised. But of course Phil's brother Mervyn could hear us all hours across the ocean in Belfast.

"Drop the fuckers after midnight," suggested Kevin. "Fuckin' Solomon's in bed for 10 with his hot chocolate!"

It wasn't an answer to the damage to the image pirate radio had earned and dismantling of Caroline's status in the land which was now sliding inexorably back towards the Mid-Day-Spin days of the BBC Light Programme!

Now, as the Marine Offences Bill got nearer to statute, the men behind the pirates observed no respect for either the listeners or the fine media legend we had all contributed towards.

In that last year, we fought like crazy to get on the playlist-free Midnight Surf Party just for our own individual sanity and credibility, as we selected music that was right for the millions of fans who relied on us to get it right! Down on the South ship, my buddy Rosko was sacked by Phil Solomon no less than three times, for feeding his vinyl to the shoal of 'shit fish' who spent their life around Radio Caroline waiting for such rubbish!

Jan: The Beatmen

I recognised change in the air when the Beatmen from Bratislava came to Brno to give a concert with a few other groups including Synkopy 61, for whom my great friend František had started to write song lyrics. This connection proved to be advantageous, as František smuggled me inside without having to pay. Miloš Bernátek, (who in only a couple of years' time would launch what would become the famous Bav club Šelepova), was the promoter of this concert and had created an exciting anticipation of the event with huge posters all around Brno without any legal permission to do so. On the posters was a provocative title challenging the status quo of Prague based group Olympic, it read: *THE BEATMEN... BETTER THAN OLYMPIC?*

There was now enormous anticipation. Could the Beatmen possibly be better than Olympic? The whole town turned out to see if this was so.

This was the Beatmen's first ever performance in Brno, not even Paul Anka had achieved this level of anticipation around town. When Bratislava's Beatmen came onto the stage and started '*Tell me whyyyyy you cryyyyy*' the entire audience stood up as one, and remained so for the rest of the concert. It was the very first, and probably the last time in Brno that chairs were not necessary during a concert, the vivid answer to the question posed on the posters.

The Beatmen continued with *She loves you* another Beatles cover, this time sung in the Slovak language and then they switched to some of their own songs, each received with the same enthusiasm. It all felt like we imagined what a real Beatles concert would be like and, later, we fantasised what it would have been like if the Beatmen were actually the opening act for the Beatles?

Not one of us had ever seen or ever hoped to attend a real Beatles concert and by the time we were free, the Beatles had disbanded. But for all our lives, we who had been there would remember coming very close to it on this summer's evening in 1966.

After a couple of songs sung in Slovak, the Beatmen continued with more of their own songs in English. Their target was to break through in the west, and they were well aware that it was possible only if they sang in English. So they featured all their big hits which we knew intimately from many radio plays, but in this Brno concert they sang them in English including *Let's make a Summer*, even today acclaimed by the critics as one of the best Czechoslovak songs ever.

We were all emotionally connected, high on the knowledge that here was a group who were in the process of making good their escape via music. What I would have given to be their road manager!

Their big chance to make it in the west slipped by them just a year earlier, in the cruellest of circumstances. In the autumn of 1965, the Beatmen had opened for Manfred Mann during their two appearances in Bratislava. Manfred himself was so impressed he invited them to play support for his group on their next British tour, but the group didn't get permission to leave the country.

The rumour spread through the grapevine, that the Prague communist bosses from the Artist State Agency would only let them go on condition that the most successful Czechoslovak group, Olympic (a Prague band) were also invited to perform. Manfred's management company would have none of it. Olympic only did cover versions, and Manfred wanted a group who played originals.

Songwriting and singing in English. These aspects of breaking into the global market were well beyond the mental capacity of people within the Artist Agency and their refusal to permit the Beatmen on the Manfred Mann tour, was catastrophic for them and remains one of the greatest crimes in our cultural history.

Later, in 1966, the Beatmen were given the chance to appear in Vienna, Austria just across our border. Secretly, the band members decided they would immigrate on this tour, and spend their careers with political freedom and try to succeed in a world that had become music crazy. But, at the 11th hour, the band's leading personality and main composer, Dežo Ursiny, decided against leaving. He felt, like many young people at this time, that Czechoslovakia was his country and he would not forsake it, leaving it to the regime that was crippling us.

Dežo was replaced by another guitarist, and the group moved to West Germany where they had a single released with little success. The group eventually disbanded, whilst back home Dežo formed the Soulmen, but was only ever permitted to tour the Eastern Bloc. He went on to have great domestic success, both with his songwriting and film directing, but after becoming seriously ill in 1989, Dežo Ursiny died in 1994, without enjoying our newfound liberty. There was never any question that had he and his Beatmen been permitted to join the Manfred Mann tour, he would have had a glorious global career.

Dežo, of course, was one of hundreds and thousands, whose lives were blighted and violated within mother Russia's communist system. We'll never know all the stories. To this day, no one ever discussed the crime against the Beatmen, so we can assume there were uncountable atrocities swept beneath the red carpet of our history.

After the unforgettable Brno concert of 1966, I left the theatre knowing I had no alternative; I had to have a tape recorder. Urged on by František and his co-songwriter Oldřich Veselý of the group Synkopy 61, I became their official lyrics translator.

As a milkman, I had managed to save some money, but I had to pull together 2,300 crowns, an almost impossible sum of money for a young working class kid. I went to my bedroom, pulled out a box from the bottom drawer and gazed at my precious collection of badges, which I had accumulated as a child visiting international trade fairs with my father. Today the automobile company badges were changing hands for up to 30 crowns. I looked at them for the last time. The next time I looked they had become a tape recorder.

Tony: Pirate days

Dear Mike Ahearn was a strange character. His eyeballs moved round like records as he talked to you. Although he worked on the North ship, he managed to make his name known nationally quite unintentionally.

We ran an American tape series by veteran US DJ, Jack Spector and Mike Ahearn followed Spector on air at which time he would rib him sending the Yank up.

"Boy Spector, you're some dummy!" he'd shout as Jack's tape came to an end. Spector was on reel-to-reel, recorded weeks earlier in the USA. Mike was live.

Eventually Spector, because of fan mail, got wind of Mike's jibes on Caroline North and started to fight back in a verbal battle he could never win because Mike always had the jump on him. He would listen to Spector's recorded responses *before* transmission and had his own retorts and put-downs prepared.

Ahearn mauled him. It was like the Vietnam War, America could never win.

The listeners to Caroline South tuning in to Spector's shows had never heard of Mike Ahearn, until Spector started ripping into him.

But the more Spector rounded on Mike, the more famous Mike became in the South of England, the more it made Ronan and the bosses aware that they had a DJ out of range, who was getting lip service from their expensive US investment.

Ahearn got the call to migrate South.

Spending that final year and a half on Caroline South, Mike was in the first Radio 1 DJ line-up, a plum gig on the stations new coast-to-coast BBC station. However, within weeks Mike became one of the very few DJs to leave the BBC due to differences of programming opinion.

He moved to Australia where he became a household name but, missing the UK, Mike returned in the 90s to London's Capital Gold, where I found myself working with him for the final time.

In late 2009 we spread Mike Ahearn's ashes in the Thames Estuary where, back in the 60s, the tender would take him out to his beloved Radio Caroline.

Canadian DJ Mick Luvzit was one of those text-book, irritatingly good looking DJs who had no trouble with women, until he fell in love with Ugly Ray Teret's sister Jan, who was emotionally shattered from the death of her boyfriend in a car accident when Mick began his courtship.

Like Tony Blackburn with actress Tessa Wyatt, Mick blatantly courted Jan on air during his daily programme on Caroline North, quite overwhelming her. And yet she hesitated in accepting his proposal of marriage, still mourning the death of her boyfriend.

We were partying in captain Martin Gibb's cabin with a few crew members, including Dutch Harry who ate raw meat straight from the fridge laced with pepper. I was playing guitar and singing some rock 'n' roll with my vocal backing group, newsreader Dave Williams and Daffy Don. "Say Meeezter Prinz," said the inebriated cap'n. "Why don't you let me marry you?"

I stopped strumming my guitar.

"Say that again Cap'n," I said, wondering if I'd misheard him.

"I said, vhy don't you let me marry you," he repeated in his guttural Dutch-English.

"Because I don't love you," I answered.

He laughed loudly, and staggered across his rather large cabin to show me his certificate on the wall. Martin was the only Captain with our shipping company who was licensed to conduct wedding ceremonies on board!

One of those coiled 'idea' symbols appeared above my head. My publicity head ran through my little black book but whilst this was an incredible concept, I had no girlfriend who I loved enough to marry. But the publicity! The history!

Then I remembered Mick and Jan.

I ran down the two flights of stairs to Mick's cabin, woke him up and gave him my idea.

"You'll be the most famous pirate DJ in history," I prophesied.

Two months later Jan and Mick stood on the Ramsey quayside with their wedding guests looking out to sea. The bride wore white, in contrast to the grey vale of mist that covered the bay, obscuring any view of the ship, three miles out in the Irish Sea. With Caroline's klaxon horn sounding out, and the deck-bound DJs signaling our whereabouts through cupped hands, the voices echoed out across the totally calm, mirror like ocean.

At last, the flotilla of craft containing the wedding party appeared through the eerie grey morning mist, like a scene from a Steven King movie.

On board were Liverpool's pop elite, Tony and Billy from the Merseys, Charlie Crane and Ritchie of the Crying Shames, members of the Foremost, flanked by record company promotion men, label owners and a veritable clutch of local and tabloid journalists and cameramen. First on deck was Roy Carr, the journalist with the New Musical Express, a poacher turned gamekeeper who had once been in the Blackpool band, the Executives and with his dad co-wrote their hit *March of the Mods*.

In the lounge, Graham 'Spider' Webb, the great Australian DJ, was giving a running commentary between myself in the studio. A remote microphone was thrust under everyone's nose, as they precariously climbed the rope ladder like competitors in The Gladiators.

The Irish Sea fog and our guests lost within it added to the broadcasting dimensions.

I was on air as the wedding commenced handing over to Graham Webb down below. I'd been at sea two weeks and when a beautiful young lady journalist arrived in the studio, it was all a little too much. She'd come from from London, from which paper I still don't know. And so it came to pass that I heard most of the wedding-of-the-decade from my cabin, where I was giving a guided tour to this micro-skirted female. The last I saw of her was as the tender returned to Ramsey Bay as she stood waving her quite empty note pad at me.

The following day pirate wedding photos feature in newspapers around the world.

Mick and Jan moved to Canada and eventually divorced. They produced a lovely daughter, the only girl on earth whose mum and dad married on a pirate radio ship.

Mick remarried. I was surprised he wasn't married and divorced more times. It must have been quite disconcerting to be introduced at parties: "Do you know Mick's wife Jan Luvzit?" It would wear any wife down I'm sure!

We lost Mick in 2012, but not before we had a wonderful pirate radio reunion, which he hosted in Vancouver.

The summers were long and hot, three miles out on the bay. Days would be spent sunbathing on the lifeboat, diving like swallows into the freezing Irish Sea, swimming with the tides and waving at the boats loaded with holiday makers and fans who'd paid two shillings to come and gawk at the DJs.

One day I offered Baby Bob Stewart a race around the ship.

"You dive in on the port side and I'll start from the starboard, we'll swim up past the bow and the first one back up the ladder wins a fiver!"

"Go!" yelled our starter Gordy Cruise.

The first part of the swim is the hardest as you're pushing against the tide. At the bow you pass the anchor chain, which you can cling to and get your breath back.

I looked around the hull feeling the first glow of triumph. Stewart had either chickened out or gone round the wrong way.

I let the cold tide take me along as I breaststroked the 40 metres to the rope ladder that hung sandwiched between enormous rubber tyres, which acted as buffers for the tender.

Suddenly a purple blur appeared in the water directly in front of me. I was swimming into a Portuguese man-of-war jellyfish!

Unable to stop my advance with the strong current pulling me along, I swam directly over the sea beast. I clambered up the rope ladder quicker than Jack on his beanstalk, with entrails from the jellyfish covering me.

A bone dry Bob Stewart stood on deck laughing. In response, I pulled a slimy tentacle off my chest and threw it so it criss-crossed his smirking face!

Bob's face developed a nasty bright red tattoo. It stung him for days.

I went down with a massive fever existing in the gloom of my cabin covered in the Dutch equivalent of vinegar and brown paper for three days. Of course the DJs on-air were full of it, funniest thing in weeks.

Meanwhile, on Caroline South Tony Blackburn had decided that life seemed more secure for a number of reasons, on the much more substantial neighbouring Radio London. The station also happened to be killing Caroline in the ratings war, and they wanted Blackburn badly as someone who was holding a bigger breakfast show audience than their DJs.

There was a catch though. They wanted him to change his name to Mark Roman, but Tony had point blank refused.

A further two weeks went by with Blackburn winning the ratings, until they finally signed him to the Radio London breakfast slot as Tony Blackburn.

The next DJ who came through the door at Radio London would be christened Mark Roman, because some brain in their Curzon Street head office was keen to have a show called The Roman Empire.

All of which came to pass.

Tony Blackburn became the brunt of the Radio London DJ's wicked wit and malicious humor. He was the outsider, the new kid in town with the Number One breakfast show audience. Tony Windsor and the other disc jokers soon began to realise how gullible Tony was and proceeded to wind him up at any opportunity.

Shortly after joining Radio London, Tony Blackburn descended to the lounge where Dave Cash, Kenny Everett and Tony Windsor were confiding their thoughts appearing not to have noticed his arrival.

"Lot to learn," said Cash.

"Indeed," agreed the deep baritone voice of TW. "Voice like a woman, I don't know why he doesn't work more on lowering it. It's only exercise, I used to be like him."

Now pretending to notice the new recruit for the first time, they proceeded to look flustered and lowered their voices more confidentially.

Suddenly it dawned on Blackburn that they were talking about him. Kenny Everett, with his back turned to Blackburn, continued supposedly oblivious of his arrival.

"It's not good for the station having someone with such a camp voice," said Kenny who at that time of his life, had still to come out of the closet, thinking himself to be heterosexual.

"I'll have a word with Alan Keen next week," he chided.

Tony left the room eyes brimming with tears.

After 20 minutes, Windsor became concerned that the young man hadn't finished his meal and went to his cabin to explain the bad joke. When he couldn't find him, Cash and Everett joined in the search eventually finding him in the small production studio copying Tony Windsor's 'HELLLLoooow' into the recorder, whilst looking into a mirror creating as butch an expression as he could muster.

Whenever you heard Tony Blackburn say 'HELLLLoooow,' you could be sure he was impersonating TW in front of that mirror!

Cruel sea!

Alan Keen the boss of Radio London awoke one morning earlier than usual with a telephone call.

"*I've seen your elephant walking down Sunningdale Road,*" said a voice.

"Eh?"

They hung up with a laugh.

Alan climbed out of bed and was about to switch his station on as he did habitually every morning, when the phone rang again.

"Believe you lost an elephant? How d'you do a silly thing like that?"

"Who are you? How did you get my number?"

"Just a couple of interested listeners eating breakfast and wondering how anyone could even lose an elephant?"

Alan hung up and strode to his radio turning up Keith Skue's making a special announcement.

"A local circus has lost an elephant in the Ascot area. Anyone spotting the animal should telephone the following number giving a description of the beast."

Keen's telephone rang constantly all morning, and into the afternoon, and night, and into the days beyond 1 April 1966!

But the best April fool stunt was the 1965 one, when the competing DJ teams of Caroline South and Radio London worked a gag in unison. It started on the tender as Kenny Everett and John Peel concocted the plan with Tony Blackburn, Tom Lodge and Richard Swainson, Radio London's on-board admin manager.

Swainson took some persuading, because it would be he who would carry the can.

But persuaded he was.

Driving into London that morning, Alan Keen could have been forgiven had he collided with another vehicle as he concentrated on trying to find his radio station on the dial.

The station was there all right, but a Radio Caroline DJ was linking the music. And, worse, the commercials weren't his either!

In Caroline House, just around the corner from Radio London's Mayfair offices, Ronan O'Rahilly called in all personnel.

"Does anyone know why or how we're broadcasting Radio London on our frequency, and they on ours?"

By lunch, the switchboards of both station's offices and much of Fleet Street were jammed with confused and worried listeners.

There had been so much enthusiasm that Swainson had to let them go ahead.

"If I hadn't they would seriously have just bound and gagged me!" he maintains.

At first light of dawn a lifeboat was lowered from Radio Caroline with Blackburn and other players, complete with a rack of jingle cartridges and logs. As Blackburn and party climbed aboard Radio London, Kenny Everett and Dave Cash returned on the lifeboat to Radio Caroline.

No one dreamed in London city that it was the humans who had swapped seats. To a man they thought there had been some sort of frequency anomaly.

On the stroke of noon, the problem seemed to right itself by which time engineers from both companies were half way to Harwich to sort out the problems.

Swainson was demoted to Record Librarian until, after a few days and great press coverage, the station controllers calmed their sponsors with promises of airtime compensation and began to see the funny side of the elaborate April fool prank.

Can you imagine local competing radio stations even thinking of doing something so crazy these days?

Nah, me neither. Different days of course.

Arch pirate radio villain Prime Minister Harold Wilson was deep into plans to scuttle us, when he found himself on a train heading for Liverpool to preside over the grand 're-opening' of the legendary Cavern Club.

It was a marvelous coup getting Wilson, whose decision to cut the ribbon leading down to that sweaty cellar, was based on his waning popularity with the kids who we bombarded with anti-Labour government propaganda on a daily basis.

Behind him, this day on the inter city train, sat two strangers who were also heading for the Cavern. In front of them was a transistor radio.

As the train entered the reception area around Birmingham, the men tuned in to Radio Caroline North where everyone in the carriage heard us belting out commercials for the new Cavern every few minutes.

Harold Wilson's press officer came down the aisle and asked the men to turn off their radio, not recognising the silver-haired Irishman Ronan O'Rahilly, who also happened to be the Cavern's new backer.

A few years later I was at a reception for Nordoff-Robbins Music Therapy, as one of the original fund-raising committee members.

I was standing with Alan Keen, my boss at Radio Luxembourg and Derek Chinnery, Head of BBC Radio 1. Derek was a mirthless type, dour and serious. Lord Reith would have liked him a lot.

I left their side, relieved to get away from him, and walked over to Harold Wilson who was standing quite alone.

"Why's he bothering talking to Wilson?" Chinnery asked Keen.

"Because he can!" answered Alan laughing, as the photographers moved in on me and the former Prime Minister, as their first photo opportunity of the day materialised.

"How are you Mr Wilson?" I said shaking the hand that wasn't holding the pipe.

"Fine, who are you?" he asked looking at my paisley-patterned lurex jacket.

"I'm fine thanks for asking," I said.

"No", he said slipping the pipe from between his lips, "<u>Who</u> are you I asked?"

"I once lost my job because of you."

"A miner?"

"No, guess again!"

"Union connected?"

"No, I was with a union for a while though."

"County Council employee?" he quizzed pushing the baccy deeper into his pipe.

"No Mr Wilson, I was a pirate!"

He looked at me like I was the King of Lilliput whose language required translation.

"What's a pirate?" he asked.

"You don't remember your Marine Offences Act of Parliament?"

Harold coughed as the pipe, and his memory ignited.

"I wonder, do you remember opening Liverpool's Cavern Club in 1968?"

"Vaguely," he said vaguely looking round for someone to save him.

"I just wondered if you knew that you were opening a club which was owned by Ronan O'Rahilly. It just struck me as strange that you would do that?"

"Who's O'Rahilly?"

"Someone who did more for this country than you lot ever did," I teased.

"Who was he again?"

"He was someone who had his day, a bit like you Mr Wilson!" I teased more.

"Which party was he with?" he asked dourly.

"The People's Right to Party party," I said.

That was when Princess Michael of Kent arrived, ending our charming meeting. We all shook hands.

"Do give O'Rahilly my regards," said Harold.

In early 1967, at long last, the BBC announced they were to drop the Light Programme in favour of a new 'youth' channel they christened Radio1.

As August approached, we learned the method by which the Government intended to sink our beloved floating jukeboxes. No British subject would be allowed to work for the ships; no one could provide them with provisions, (except in an emergency) and, (the real killer), no British Company was permitted to advertise with them.

Having been run by professional businessmen who had made a proper legal killing, Radio London announced immediately that they would close down without resistance.

Caroline's bosses however, still driven by the spirit of Ronan O'Rahilly, announced that they would continue to broadcast using foreign DJs and advertisers. Furthermore, to confuse the authorities whose job it would be to implement the bill, the station officially announced that they would commence to give British companies free advertising. This way, they speculated, the Government would never be able to distinguish between free and paid for advertisements.

In future all adverts paid for on Radio Caroline had to be paid for in cash, in paper bags in either Eire or The Hague.

In future the tender, instead of a 40-minute three-mile trip from the Harwich and Ramsey harbours, would take an entire day negotiating the high seas from Amsterdam to the South ship, and from the Republic of Ireland to the North ship. Certainly, the twice-weekly trips were over, and fresh milk a thing of the hay day.

I seriously considered staying, but Caroline's controllers had taken the fun out of the station with their money lust and crap playlists. I knew it was now nothing more than a business, and the majority of my listeners urged me in my last fan mail sack loads, to lift anchor and hand in my eye-patch.

Jan: World Cup

July 1966 was an exciting time for my friends and I who were into music and
football. The Football World Championship was being staged in England
and, for the very first time, I would see the country that so inspired and
engaged me with the music originated from her shores.

But of course, to watch the TV one needed accommodating friends and,
with Czechoslovakia having become a football-mad nation since becoming
runners-up in the last World Cup, although we hadn't managed to get
through this year, invitations were like gold dust.

But something rather fantastic happened. An electrical shop in a Brno
square had taken a leaf from the record store, and placed a speaker out in
the street for all to hear. This time, with three TVs taking up the window
display, the pavement outside the store was like the touchline, the town
square like Wembley!

Red Law, for the first time I could recall, played an important role in our
lives by providing World Cup schedules and daily reports.

When the live broadcast took us to Goodison Park in Liverpool, my
mind wandered to the Cavern Club, and I wondered if my Uncle Josef had
been to this stadium during the war?

Four years earlier, in 1962, our Czechoslovak team won a silver medal in
Chile. Ladislav Novák played in that team and he was sent to England to
report on the matches for Red Law. Incredibly he was not given any status
as media representative for Czechoslovakia; he had arrived as a tourist and
attended matches with the cheapest possible tickets.

You had to read between the lines of one of his articles to fully appreciate
what had taken place. Ladislav was suffering from a back injury, whilst
his teammate from the Chile tournament, Svatopluk Pluskal, who had
travelled with Ladislav to watch the World Cup, had a leg injury, which
had happened just prior to leaving for the UK. Together they went to see a
professor Schober, the physio for the West German team.

Fortunately, both players had once played for Dukla Prague, a team that
was very popular in West Germany, the reason professor Schober knew
them and welcomed them for treatment.

In his Red Law article, Ladislav mentioned he and Svatopluk had only got
standing sector tickets for the matches, and told readers that during his
physio treatment he mentioned this to the professor, who hastily arranged
for two complimentary tickets to the VIP stands for the final matches at
Wembley.

I stored this away in a section of my mind where I had put something my
father had once said to me: "The German people were not to blame for the
atrocities of the war. Civilians in Germany were under the control of the

Nazis, just as we are now under the control of Communists. It is the Nazis we should despise, not the poor people of Germany."

Footballers and sportsmen in Czechoslovakia were treated a little differently to everyone else, other than the communists themselves. They all came under the wage-levelling system. When our two silver medal-winning footballers attended the wonderful 1966 World Cup, where England beat Germany for the 'third' time, they went as poor civilians, stayed in the cheapest hotels, ate on meagre budgets and stood in the cheapest seats. Such was our sports authority's relationship with FIFA, and our government's pathetic relationship with our sporting heroes.

The football club Dukla Prague was not very popular in Czechoslovakia itself, for the simple reason the team was an army team and considered by fans to be too pro-regime.

The national attitude changed of course, at the turn of the 50s and throughout the 60s when Dukla Prague won three American Challenge Cups in New York.

We knew when to cheer communism or not, and of course the National team was a very different matter. We didn't mind that the squad contained army team members, what mattered was our national pride in an incredibly competitive world arena.

That we could beat the Germans was a revenge we would take hot or cold!

This German doctor and Manfred Mann identified to me something that kept my spirit intact. I knew there were people beyond our borders who cared for us. Certainly these artists understood that the money they earned in Czechoslovakia was worthless outside the country. Their willingness to perform for us was generosity beyond measure.

I also believed that Radio Luxembourg was a part of that generosity. It didn't cost me a cent, and was one of the few things in life that you could say was truly free. I wondered at the time why they would aim their transmitter towards us, when they were obviously targeting the UK with their programmes? I knew nothing then off directional signals and transmitter rigs, aimed at the ionosphere that would rebound to earth in a circular coverage of their signal, in which we, and much of greater Europe and Scandinavia, were beneficiaries. I looked on 208 as a nightly gift from the west, and when, finally, one of their DJs came to play in my town and other cities, my love and appreciation for the station simply overwhelmed me.

We stood on the sidewalk outside the TV store urging West Germany on. It was the semi-final and they had drawn against mother Russia. Suddenly we loved West Germany as we watched them kick shit out of the USSR. What a result, what a noise you could hear across downtown Brno!

And then the big day arrived, Saturday 30 July 1966, and I'm sure the population of England could not have enjoyed this match more than we, who stood outside an electrical shop on Malinovský Square. This was our version of big screen television, a shop window with three televisions behind the glass. I'd arrived with a copy of Red Law. My friends showed concern, until I explained that they were actually giving great reports and information that, for the journal's first time, was talking about westerners as though they were real people with real families, not the despicable capitalists they had been depicted until now.

I read to them that England's Bobby and Jack Charlton's father had taken a day off from his mining job to watch his sons. Also, that the great Stanley Matthews had been injured in a car crash the previous day, and regardless of his broken ribs still intended to watch from the stands.

Then I read the news that Czechoslovak Radio would be broadcasting the entire match, news that would have been quite welcome had we not found Nirvana in our town square.

My friends fantasised about what it would be like if they were there. I kept my thoughts to myself because I knew they would be derided. Who else other than me would swap a World Cup Final ticket, just to visit an English record shop?

The World Cup experience, brought me so close to England my music empire, it spurred me on towards my new ambition. I had to surround my friends and I with the music of Radio Luxembourg, and there was only one way to do this. I had to be in possession of my own tape recorder 24/7. As I came to my decision in bed that night, I could barely sleep with anticipation of the following day.

I awoke to a warm Sunday morning and gathered together my cherished collection of Western Automobile factory badges, the only things of value I possessed. I headed at pace towards the weekly collector's corner situated across the road from a local Brno railway station, where people swapped and traded badges, stamps, matchbox labels and other items people loved to collect.

I'd left my most treasured badge at home, the Jaguar badge, a real iconic beauty and something to remind me of my days at the International Trade Fair, where I would collect them with my father.

As I started to trade, everyone was still buzzing from England winning the World Cup in such spectacular fashion. When the avid collectors cast their eyes on my collection, they fell silent. It was indeed one of the greatest collections they'd ever seen, with known gems constantly in demand. Slowly, one by one, they took another little piece of my heart until, at last, with 800 crowns in my pocket, I was all done.

I had no sentiment. The collection I had been building for years had finally reached a higher purpose. Tomorrow I would become the owner of a Sonet

Duo tape recorder.

As I walked home from the square, I started to sob with the pure joy of tomorrow.

Tony: Pirates walk the plank

On 14 August 1967 as the noon armistice approached, the 'Hairy Monster' DLT, Jerry 'Soopa' Leighton and the 'Royal Ruler', disembarked from Radio Caroline for the very last time.

We climbed down the rope ladder and swapped places on the tender with the new DJ team, after exchanging good wishes with each other. It was the longest journey ever back to Ramsey Bay, our wonderful tin can home growing smaller, shrinking behind us like our spirits.

A double-page centerfold picture of Dave Lee Travis carrying me off the tender in Ramsey Bay, appeared in the northern edition of the Daily Mirror the following day, the kind of publicity a DJ could only dream of. Hundreds of weeping fans stood around the dock feeling, as did we, that life was about to change for the worse. We spent time consoling them, signing autographs and finally we were driven over the mountain, passing the Fairy Bridge for the last time on into Douglas and the Palace Hotel where we would have one night to seek solace from our depression.

In the south, similar scenes were taking place. Radio London closed down at 3pm with the final statement from Ringo Starr, whose pre-recorded message was, '*Radio will never be the same, but it's just one of those things, cheerio.*'

Little did Ringo know that the Beatles would never be the same again either. Thirteen days later their manager Brian Epstein, like pirate radio, also passed away. Few of us at that time believed the official verdict that he had died an *accidental* death through sleeping tablets. Elvis sent the Beatles a telegram with his deep regrets.

A landlubber once again, the following day was lost in a hangover of enormous proportions, and a most miserable day presented itself.

Dave and I had stayed the night of the 14th at the Palace, because it had been too late to catch the last plane off the island. It was an evening that started with DLT toasting me, and ended with the croupiers roasting me. I awoke stony broke, having lost my final Caroline salary in the hotel's casino.

Gathering myself, I presented what was left of me to Alex O'Brian, the hotel's manager and someone who, with his wife Lilly, had become dear friends during my regular island stopovers. Alex tore up my hotel bill and bought me a one-way flight home to Manchester. He also slipped me two £10 notes into my top pocket.

It was the only money I had.

After a few days with a new life sinking in, I telephoned Robin Scott, the Programme Controller of Radio 1, who told me to be patient. "We'll find you something eventually," he said reassuringly.

I began what transpired to be a lifetime waiting for *eventually*.

In the 6 August 1966 edition of Disc, Beatle George Harrison, a lifetime benefactor to the causes of Ronan O'Rahilly, spoke out candidly in an interview with the great music journalist Ray Coleman:

"I can't understand the Government's attitude over the pirates. Why don't they make the BBC illegal as well – it doesn't give the public the service what it wants, otherwise the pirates wouldn't be here to fill the gap. The Government makes me sick. This is becoming a Police State. They should leave the pirates alone. At least they've had a go, which is more than the BBC has done..."

From here the treasure map led to Broadcasting House, but my outspoken, blinkered loyalty to Caroline as a concept, saw me last in a queue of DJs from the southerly ships, who were much better known to the BBC heriarchy in London than we in the north.

Together with Dave Lee Travis, I had remained on board until the final minute of the eleventh hour, "Bulova-watch-time B-U-L-O-V-A, when you know what makes a watch tick you'll buy a Bulova".

The sponsored time checks were history, as the golden days reached a dull dusk.

I sent my audition tape to Robin Scott, the very first Head of Radio 1, but I had missed the BBC boat by weeks, months, maybe. Whilst I was playing the loyal puppy to Ronan, off the south shore, the DJs had been fighting for late night studio time to cut their individual audition tapes for the BBC, months before I'd even thought of changing sides.

Johnny Walker became a true pirate DJ, by staying on the ship after the bill in his personal fight for free radio.

Caroline North broadcasters were legends across Lancashire, Ireland, Cumberland and West Yorkshire, yet not one of us was approached by the BBC, other than DLT who'd spent most of his pirate years establishing himself on Radio Caroline South.

DLT landed a god-awful live big-band show from Manchester, featuring Bob Miller and the Millermen, the kings of cover versions. This was simply a continuity of the hex placed on the BBC by the Musicians' Union.

In the early days Radio 1 remained saddled with 'needle-time' restrictions, all to make sure trumpeters could guarantee to earn a minimum £16 a week!

The MU still had not started to recognise how much their members could make from worldwide million-selling records!

Only one DJ outside the Radio London/Caroline South London catchment area was selected to be part of that first Radio 1 team. This was the beautiful Stuart Henry from Radio Scotland whose agent, mine also for a while, Bunny Lewis, had enormous influence at the BBC. I couldn't forget the letter he sent me confirming my audition tape had been accepted at the BBC and '*we just have to find someone to use you*'.

My friend from Discs-a-Gogo and mast-climbing pal, Tony Blackburn, my room mate Emperor Rosko and former Caroline North émigré, Mike Ahearn, were amongst the line-up standing on the steps of Broadcasting House for that very first press call, which produced such an iconic first Radio 1 team photograph. They looked like a successful lottery syndicate, which of course they were.

Envy engulfed me as I viewed each of my colleague's smiling faces in the tabloids and, by the time I closed the newspaper, the envy had become pure, unadulterated jealousy.

My unemployment became a prison term.

Top Rank's Garry Brown came to the aid of my sanity and gave me a residency at their Sheffield Suite, where I first befriended Joe Cocker in his Grease Band days. I'd catch his gigs at the Penny Farthing club and listen in awe at his magnificent talent and that of guitarist Henry McCullough, who years later became a member of Wings. My first 'hit-pick' on Radio Luxembourg was Joe's first release, *Margarine*.

He used to write to me at Radio Luxembourg from Sheffield, asking me for my support and asking me to be on the listen out for his next single, a Beatles song called *With a Little Help From My Friends*.

The drive between Oldham and Sheffield's dreaded A57 Snake Pass was high-risk stuff late at night at this time of year. Only cats-eyes guided your decent, as the road wound down through a God-forgotten valley protected by ferocious blizzards and deep snowdrifts. If I wanted to continue spinning those black shiny records, it had to be done. I had no intention of going back to my old engineering job at Vertoma Jig and Tool under any circumstance, and although the Sheffield Top Rank was a mighty step backwards career-wise, it had a big edge on drilling and filing metal.

In this period, I met Christine, my childhood sweetheart once again. I'd left for Bristol the last time we saw one another and in recent times trapped in my cabin, I'd revived my feelings of love for the beautiful girl who loved me when I had no claim to fame. We've been married now for 47 years.

Just as I was settling in with Christine, the Programme Director of Radio Luxembourg, Eggy Lay (honest!) called me down to London for an audition, and things started to get right back in the groove.

I was about to swap the Snake Pass from Oldham to Sheffield for Belgium's Ardennes to the Grand Duchy of Luxembourg.

Jan: The salad cheat

The Elektra shop that had provided the poor football fans of Brno with a front row seat at the 1966 World Cup, came up trumps with their marketing campaign.

On the Monday morning, I knew exactly where I would buy my tape recorder because during the World Cup half-time, I had glimpsed inside the store through the window and seen a line of Sonet Duos, one of them almost calling out to me to take it home. It was usual in communist Czechoslovakian stores for products to sell out almost as soon as they were delivered. If you wanted milk, butter or yogurt, any later than 10am, you would have to settle for black tea. There was never a loaf in Brno come the afternoon.

But the price of the Sonet Duo was such that few would afford them. At 2,300 crowns, normal workers had to pay two months wages.

Heading home on the tram, I was impatient to get back and plug my new baby in and start to use it and yet, as the tram stopped at each red light, I took great pleasure as people looked with curiosity at the young lad with such a wonder on his lap.

Once home I didn't quite know what to do first. Play my Paul Anka tape, try recording my voice or attempt recording some of my records to tape? I would wait until the evening to record Radio Luxembourg so, in the end, Paul Anka won. I sat back and started to listen to *Diana* as the feeling of freedom enveloped me. I'd never felt better, never felt so in charge of my life as the endorphins took over. No longer would I have to return a borrowed tape recorder, now anytime I wanted to record music or hear music, I was in control. I could from this day forth hear Radio Luxembourg in daylight hours. No communist could ever beat me now.

Suddenly I also understood what a blind man had told me in the cellar of an apartment block next to ours, in which they had their club where I would play chess with the residents. The blind had a small chessboard with miniature pieces, which they constantly felt whilst we had the standard board, and would tell them where we had moved. The old man was an amazing chess player, I rarely beat him and it was he who told me something, to which only now I could relate.

He'd lost his sight later in life, but insisted he preferred losing vision than his hearing.

"That would mean losing direct contact with people," he'd said.

Now it came home to me just how barren my life would have been had I lost this precious sense, and that whilst perhaps it would not be too unbearable never to see again, I could never envisage life without the songs I heard on 208, and the words of the disc jockeys who kept me company, brightening my life when I was down.

For the very first time I experienced what it was like to be a DJ, recording myself introducing the artists as they played from the radio, beating them to the vocals and moving the microphone from my lips to the radio's speaker, just as they reached the vocals.

I still used the radio my father had brought back from Dachau, a wireless manufactured before World War II, and so had no connection for direct radio to tape recording. The microphone was quite adequate for my purposes at the time, but I wonder what people in the digital-high-definition world of today would make of my recordings? I'm sure they would hold their ears with a pained expression.

I called František with the happy news, and was contracted to my first order to search and record three particular songs he was anxious to learn, so he could write the Czech lyrics for the group he was associated with.

As I waited for the evening transmissions to begin on Luxembourg, I wrote to my Paul Anka tape benefactor, Michal from Černošice in Prague, thanking him for his kindness and letting him know I was now a fully-fledged member of the Czech Tape Recorder Owner's Club. I had a devious agenda in my heart that would never have settled there, had he not previously sent me details of the 25 LPs in his record collection. These included the Beatles' *With the Beatles, Beatles for Sale, A Hard Day's Night*, an Elvis album and two Johnny Cash LPs.

It was hard not being envious. I had never in my life seen an LP from the west, other than in a picture in my sole copy of the New Musical Express. But I didn't ask, just thanked him once again for his kindness, subtly letting him know I was now in the market for any further generosity.

My long time dream began that night. No longer would I have to wait days to capture a song's lyrics and although the recording quality, together with the static left much to be desired, I was pleasantly surprised at the relative ease with which I now approached song-lyric gathering.

This first evening saw me capture what became one of my all-time favourites from this period, the Kinks' *Sunny Afternoon*. The very next morning I easily transcribed Ray Davies' classic tune, delivering the lyrics to František that evening.

I struggled with 'And I can't sell my yard' leaving a blank space. Eventually we figured he must be selling a 'yacht' not a '*yard*', but it was years later when the lyrics finally revealed to me that he wasn't in fact *selling a yacht*, but was sorry that he couldn't *sail his yacht!*

I'd failed to understand the underlying story in *Sunny Afternoon*, which was actually about the taxman taking away his wealth and then, once he was a poor boy again, his girlfriend took his car and all he had left.

There was a simple reason we didn't understand the story and had to consult our parents for clues. There was no such thing as income tax in our communist society, where the state owned every company in the country, right down to the humble shoemakers.

In the evenings I started going out to see the groups who František was working with, especially Synkopy, and we visited with the amateur groups eager to have the correct English lyrics.

That first 208 recording session also delivered the Beatles' *Paperback Writer* to us, and that posed a real problem in translation the following afternoon when František came by my home.

There was some discussion about it being about book publishing in the UK, but there was one line that foxed us.

"It's based on a novel by a man named Leer?" We threw it around, wondering if it was something to do with William Shakespeare's King Lear, with the song relating to a paperback writer who wasn't too original? Much later we learned it was actually about the Victorian painter Edward Lear, who was famous for writing nonsense poems.

Five years later, František became manager of the famous Brno Theatre on a String (Divadlo na provázku), where they staged a whole play based on Edward Lear poems. Then one night whilst listening to DJ Jimmy Savile on the radio, he told us that *Paperback Writer* came about when Paul McCartney's aunt asked him if he could write a song that *wasn't* about love?

Even John and Paul would have found it difficult writing about our books in Czechoslovakia books crammed with touching problems, like fulfilling production plans and our friendship with the Soviet Union.

We had no weekly magazines to drool over our music heroes, no pop papers with music charts, no record shops, no domestic rock stars filling concert halls or venues where we could dance the night away. It is obvious now that had John, Paul, George and Ringo been born in my country their inspiration to write songs would have been very challenged. Which explains perhaps why our first generation of groups stuck mostly to cover versions, and why I, and my Sonet Duo, had suddenly become quite important to them.

Another amazing tune captured in my first night of recording on that August night was the Rolling Stones' *Paint it Black*. The next afternoon František looked at my lyrics and listened as I played the tape. He smiled and made remarks, which flattered me, after which we threw our arms around each other's shoulders and walked down the road for a cold beer.

Beneath a large lime tree in the pub's garden, František threw a copy of Red Law on the table.

"What do you think of this?" he asked.

The headline shocked me:

'950,000 TRIPS ABROAD SETTLED'

The article announced 800,000 trips to socialist countries had been permitted, and 150,000 people had received permission to travel to capitalist countries with the majority choosing our western neighbouring countries, Austria and West Germany.

We both agreed we had never heard of anyone in our lives who had gone on such a trip, and so we wondered who might even have the 8,000 crowns in the Red Law advertisement required to take them cruising for three weeks around the Mediterranean.

A working man would have to spend the equivalent of six months' salary to go on such a trip, and that didn't account for his wife or kids!

Certainly it was obvious this was a communist party perk, and I suggested to Fran that they would surely be going on such trips to confirm their worst fears about the way the west conducted itself. František laughed and raised his glass in a toast.

"To the Beatles and truth," he proposed.

We emptied our glasses and ordered more beer as we continued to debate the complete hypocrisy of the communists.

It was patently obvious to us now that the commies were breeding a nation of liars and cheats.

My mother had a friend who worked in a buffet bar serving sandwiches and salads, who once confided in her how she creamed off twice her salary by cheating each customer who bought a salad, by adding a couple of hellers (Czech pennies) as she weighed their salads. She told my mother that no one from People's Control would ever notice, because individually it was nothing, but multiplied by 200 customers in one day, it meant she was doubling her salary.

After I heard this story, I was incensed not to be cheated by buffet workers and went out of my way to test if this was so. I visited Brno's largest buffet Sputnik (named after the first Russian satellite). I noticed immediately the woman was spreading salads across the plate making it look full, so I immediately had my suspicions.

After the woman had weighed and wrapped my salad, I immediately checked the weight on the control scales provided in all shops, where food was sold for exactly the purpose I was now using them. People were generally too busy to do this, so of course the shop worker got away with it. If they complained they would have some excuse such as a tram going by causing the scales to shake. She handed me the plate which I stared at curiously catching her attention until, with the impatient queue of people watching the drama unfold, I suggested she had made a mistake, I had asked for 20 dag of salad. I insisted she weigh it again and there it was...15 dag! She had ripped me off by a quarter its value.

Immediately she apologised and scooped what must have been 10 dag onto my plate.

So there it was, my mother's story was correct. Although her friend only ripped off the tiniest fractions of a couple of pence, the Sputnik ladies were really taking us to the cleaners.

As we enjoyed our beers and I recounted this story to Fran, it suddenly dawned on us that we were all losing our moral fibre, even non-communists had started to play the cheating game just to establish a better living for themselves.

I couldn't blame them. But then I couldn't let them cheat me, and so I spent my life weighing my meals and became an expert knowing what 20 dag of fish salad should look like. I frequented the shops where the staff didn't cheat, and whenever I entered buffets where they did, after a while of self-weighing, they too treated me fairly.

So, we agreed, these buffet cheats must be amongst the lucky 150,000 people who had used their extra wealth to pay off the bank directors, in order to obtain the hard currency they would need to go on such a holiday. It became clear to us that if you weren't a communist in a high position or a cheat from the lower non-communist populace, you'd better get your backpack on, take a tent and have a holiday camping in the mountains.

František shrugged his shoulders.

"It is what it is," he said, like a wise old owl.

"Yes," I agreed. "But let us not forget we still have people here like Michal Bukovič from Černošice who, without even knowing me, sent me the Paul Anka recording, just because he recognised how much I loved his music."

Only a couple of days later, I received a letter from Michal who now asked *me* a favour.

After his June appearances, the Paul Anka Czechoslovakian Fan Club was growing very swiftly and Michal wanted to treat everyone to a tape of his music, just as he had for me.

I immediately contacted Lad'a to see if he would loan me his Sonet Duo, to which he agreed.

Now my home became a dubbing factory, ringing to the sound of Paul Anka. Life, even without going to the west, was great. I had a wonderful hobby and a circle of friends who looked on me as their benefactor.

And I always had Radio Luxembourg and Radio Caroline to transport me out of my communist environment.

Tony: Radio Luxembourg

"Are you queer?" asked Eggy Lay, after I'd successfully auditioned at 38 Hertford Street in London's Mayfair.

Here I was sitting in the office of the man who employed the DJs on the station that had brought me Dan Dare, the Ovaltinies, the Teen and Twenty Disc Club and he wanted to know if I was gay!?

It put a whole new slant on getting *layed*.

I'd expected a written test asking me to spell Keynsham, Bristol, as in the famous 'Horace Batchelor's Famous Infra Draw Method' advert or to sing, *'Bingo! Bingo! I'm in Love'*, the tune we'd heard night after night, preceding the MECCA live Bingo game on the station.

Eggy's question totally threw me. I wondered if this was the legendary casting couch, and if my sexuality was being compromised for the sake of my career?

"No. I'm afraid not," I said, as if apologising for my genetic make-up.

"Married?" he shot back. "Steady girlfriend?"

I thought of Christine and then, like a Judas, didn't.

"No," I confirmed, afraid that to hint at my steady relationship might sway the candidacy away from me.

Eggy Lay eyeballed me over an almost smoked leafy Havana.

"You've got the job son but listen, I want you to go out there and shag everything in sight!"

I stared back at the stocky little madman who had just changed my life.

Then he explained.

DJs Don Wardell, Colin Nicol and Chris Denning had been the resident 'midnight team', each openly gay and now out on their arse!

This team's 60s-style sexuality had left much to be desired in the conservative Grand Duchy of Luxembourg.

While Don and Colin were very gentle types, (Don became 208's Press Officer when I joined, and Colin and I had worked together on Radio Caroline South) hindsight would suggest that the ringleader was Denning, who went on to join the BBC Radio 1 team. He is now serving a 14-year prison sentence in the UK for his sexual crimes. He was previously jailed for 18 months in 1985 for gross indecency, and in 1988 he received a three-year sentence for indencent assault. Because of his insatiable appetite, in 1997 he was arrested in the Czech Republic, and in 2000 he was jailed by a Prague court for four and a half years for having sexual contact with underage teenage boys.

"I want you to get out there and clean up our image," said Eggy. "We need a team of boyos out there, lots and lots of bloody heterosexuality!"

My yellow brick road now led to a Luxair Focher Friendship at Heathrow.

We taxied down the runway, and I took off on a European adventure that lasted 16 incredible years.

I arrived in Luxembourg on 1 April 1968, having fully expected Eggy Lay to meet me at Heathrow to tell me I was an April fool's victim, and to bugger off back up north.

The noisy stag beetle of a plane touched down with three heavy bounces, leaving half its Good Year's on the inadequate runway. I was met in the small airport arrivals area by former Radio London newsman Paul Kaye, a bearded Brit who, after a mere six months in the Grand Duchy as English Service Manager, was already an expert on Luxembourg's Riesling Sylvaner and sported very red-nosed credentials.

Paul shook my hand enthusiastically and led the way to his battered Taunus car, ignoring my two extremely large and heavy suitcases. By the time he got to the car, he turned to see if I'd digested everything he'd been saying, realizing suddenly that I'd been well out of earshot, still struggling across the road with my life's possessions.

Arriving at his car finally, he measured me with blood shot eyes, through which he sternly watched as I struggled to lift first one, and then the other case into the trunk, the lid of which he gallantly held open.

"You're pretty confident you'll pass the three month trial period then are you?" he asked looking calculatingly at the two large cases.

"I'd have packed less clothes if I'd been you," he said cheerfully.

Confidence boosted, we began the journey to Luxembourg's capital city, Luxembourg. After one kilometre the news-reading station manager insisted he welcome me properly in a local hostelry.

"You must try the Luxembourg nectar," he said leading me to the bar in a small dark café.

Three elderly men sat at the end of the bar playing 'Spoof', a dice game for the mentally bankrupt.

"Bonjour madame," said Paul in perfect English-French.

"Bonjour monsieur," said a small lady with a moustache, "Comment allez-vous?"

"Sorry madame," Paul coughed into his fist, "Do you happen to speak English?"

"Pardon et mois monsieur," she parleyed, "Parler vous Francaise?"

"Certainly Madame," said Kaye fluently. "Two, err... douze grande glasses of Sylvana."

"Vous voulez deux ou douze?"

It was only then that I smelled the booze on Paul's breath. It was to become his smell, as familiar around the office as the secretary's fresh ground coffee. Paul had severe *Sylvanahalitosis*!

He had started off fine with his greeting, very local, very confident. But now he had to string together a few French words in quick succession, and that wasn't easy, because my flight had arrived 90 minutes late and Paul had already reached his coherent Sylvana limit.

"Look lady," he said getting angry and breathing fumes on the small woman.

"Don't give me that vous voulez stuff, we want two glasses of Syl... Van... Argh!"

"Qu'est-ce... ?"

"*SYL BLOODY VARNA SYL VOUS PLAIT*" repeated the red-faced newsreader, bending down across the bar taking her air space.

The three dice players stopped their tossing and turned to the woman in harmonised Luxembourgish, a language I was hearing for the first time. They appeared to understand what the bearded Englishman wanted.

"Sylvana!" they sang in unison, "DEUX!"

"Oui!" chided Kaye, "Syl-bloody-vana!"

I'm convinced, in the end, it was his breath, and not his pronunciation that gave her the clue she needed to comprendre.

"Ahhh!" she cried triumphantly, "SYLVANA!"

I sprayed my first mouthful of Paul's beloved nectar over my beige suede Beatle boots. The last time I'd tasted anything this vile was in the cubs when priming a Bunsen burner.

"I'd prefer a scotch and coke," I implored.

"No way mate", he said in his British Garrison Commander's voice, "You'll be going without food if you drink scotch, it's far too expensive."

I hadn't wanted a drink. I'd wanted to get down to the studios and check out the corridors trodden by Pete Murray, Alan Freeman, Teddy Johnson, Barry Alldis and Lord Haw Haw.

It was 12 noon, and I was in the European version of the Egerton Arms!

Paul Kaye had been the very first voice on pirate Radio London, and made the brilliant closing speech when the station finally lifted its anchor. Kaye was a legend and quite brilliant as a broadcaster, until 9pm!

In those early days, Radio Luxembourg borrowed the news from the BBC, just like the pirate ships. Transposing the news and then reading what he'd written, was Paul Kaye's job. He also administrated the English Service office during the day.

Between bulletins, Paul sneaked down to the Auberge de L'Etoile and his shlurring of schpeech got worse as the night progreshed.

The 10pm news got a bit ropey, 11pm his greatest challenge.

One night I found him fast asleep slumped over his typewriter, with just one minute to go to news.

As time went by and the call of the Auberge de L'Etoile became too great, Paul would record the 8pm or 9pm news error-free, instructing us to play the recording for the rest of the night.

He rarely updated the news after 9pm; accordingly we missed floods, assassinations, air crashes and landings on the moon. If the Queen had been shot dead at 9.05pm, Radio Luxembourg's listeners would not have known about it until 8pm the following evening.

Paul Kaye was a delightful, red-bearded eccentric English alcoholic, who'd fought the Mau Mau in Kenya where he first started broadcasting. His early death in 1980 aged just 46 was sad news for radio listeners, but no great surprise for those of us lucky enough to have worked with him.

Two Australian DJs, Norman St John, who had climbed ten rungs of the Caroline mast with Blackburn and I, and Tony Murphy, (described in the NME as 'the world's worst ever DJ'), were leaving as I arrived.

Paul Burnett had already been there a few weeks and welcomed a fellow hetero Brit with open arms, well, a strong handshake under our circumstances, to butch the place up somewhat.

Both Paul and I were broke and living in frugal surroundings.

We earned the equivalent of £80 a week. A scotch and coke cost £2.00, rent about £30 a week.

The top radio gig in Europe, and we were always broke.

We were paid monthly. By week three I was back to the apprentice jockey era, looking forward to the envelope post-marked Oldham!

Radio Luxembourg on 208 was only the little brother of RTL's family of broadcasting. The German and French Services, both broadcasting 24 hours a day, were the real money-spinners. They'd had a good run on the frequency, but the Medium Wave transmission limited the station to night time, when the sun went down and the signal could bounce off the atmosphere, penetrating not only Great Britain, but an extraordinary pan-European area. Take a compass point from Luxembourg to Iceland and see where 360° takes you! Oslo, Moscow, Vienna, Rome, Madrid... halfway across the Atlantic, pilot friends of ours used to tune in.

At its peak, Radio Luxembourg enjoyed an estimated European audience of three hundred million. You will still meet French, Spanish, Scandinavian and Czechoslovakian people who learned English by tuning to 208, identifiable by the static in their vocabulary and in the way, to a man, they can all spell Keynsham due to the famous and repetitive Horace Batchelor Famous Infra Draw Method commercial!

The radio studios, television studios and Luxembourg Symphony Orchestra theatre were all housed in the Villa Louvigny, a former castle complete with moat and tunnels, with exciting catacombs that led to outlets around the gorges and valleys of Luxembourg Ville. Most of these tunnels were dug by the Nazis.

It was eerie in the basement record library, which once housed the studio for Lord Haw Haw, a man who had been employed by Adolph Hitler, and rivalled Paul Kaye for on-air inebriation.

Whilst Paul Kaye got steadily worse towards midnight, Haw Haw (real name William Joyce) grew notably more inebriated towards the end of his World War II career. Haw Haw must have been a far worse DJ than Tony Murphy, because the war tribunal hung him for his broadcasts!

In the control room below our studio were banks and banks of bays containing electronic equipment. It was Paul Burnett who drew the valves to my attention, pointing out to me that they each had a swastika emblem.

A few months after my arrival, we spied two porters heaving stacks of strange-looking black discs into the rubbish bins. They'd been brought up from the catacombs below and had suffered from dampness, many now stuck together, inseparable, welded by time. We'd witnessed an enormous archive of Nazi broadcasts thrown into some Luxembourg rubbish tip.

The records were larger than albums and played from the centre of the disc outwards, which was the back to front pre-war method and explained the over-sized turntables we used in the studio. They would have been recorded in Berlin and sent to Luxembourg for transmission.

Days later, Paul managed to separate a handful of the records, and we sat around the office playing sound tracks of Lord Haw Haw interviewing prisoners of war. A sailor, a survivor from a destroyed submarine, was heard telling 208's listeners how well 'Mr Hitler' was treating him, and went on to greet his family giving out their full names and address in Cornwall!

It was nauseous stuff to listen to and God knows what it would have been like listening to Radio Luxembourg during the war? How much that rubbished collection might have been worth to the British War Museum can only be speculated.

On 3 January 1946, Haw Haw, (Bill Joyce) the man so famous for his opening gambit, '*Germany calling, Germany calling,*' was found guilty of high treason, and executed at Wandsworth prison after judges ignored a plea that he was an Irish subject.

Like the BBC who gave birth to Radio 1 as their response, Luxy had to pull its socks up after the pirates abdicated.

Limited to night-time only broadcasting on AM, for the first time in the station's history Radio Luxembourg, Europe's most popular radio station, finally committed to broadcasting *every* show live from the Grand Duchy of Luxembourg. Scripted DJs were to become history as the brand new team of ad-libbing boys arrived.

Before 1968, apart from the voice links between shows and the live late shows after midnight, all Luxembourg's programmes were pre-recorded at 38 Hertford Street, London W1. Worse still, they were all sponsored shows! Worse, *worse* still, they were sponsored in the main by record companies.

Jack Jackson's show began, '*D.E.C.C.A ... Decca, Decca, Decca.*'

Savile played a tune a minute, not because he wanted to thrill us with all the latest hot tunes he could squeeze in, but because EMI wanted to play every piece of crap they released!

Not one DJ chose the music they played.

There were two generations of DJs on this famous station; my lot were the Second Generation. The First Generation included Stephen Williams (208's first ever DJ), Muriel Young, Geoffrey Everitt, Teddy Johnson, Shaw Taylor, Roger Moffat, Warren Mitchell, Peter Madron, Peter Carver, Sam Costa, Ray Orchard, David Gell, Don Moss, Brian Matthews, Alan Dell, Pat Campbell, Ted King, Don Wardell, Johnny Moran, Chris Denning, David Jacobs, Kent Walton, Colin Hamilton, Tony Hall, Jimmy Young, Barry Alldis, Peter Carver, Jimmy Savile, Alan Freeman, Keith Fordyce, Peter Aldersley, Pete Murray, Jack Jackson, Colin Nichol all of whom gave of their pre-recorded best on the Station of the Stars. Most of whom were out of work actors filling time!

Now it was our turn and we weren't actors, we were DJs.

Enter Messieurs Burnett, Jensen, Edmonds and Prince, 208's first live aircrew who were, in the qualified opinions of Kid, Paul Noel and I, the best DJ team in the history of radio! There had certainly never been a more enthusiastic bunch and whilst the pirates suffered seasickness, all this fab four suffered from was homesickness.

There had never been a DJ team like this, four young men ostracised from their homeland, left to their own devices in the centre of Europe, living and playing together with little else to think about other than their programmes.

Like the Italians in New York and the Pakistanis in Bolton, we formed an English-speaking conclave and set about making Luxembourg more... 60s! Within days, I was on the carpet for calling on a blonde German DJ named Heidi broadcasting live from the German studio. Pretending to get amorous with her as she read a live script, she didn't take to it very well. All I'd done was put my head on her shoulder but, alas, the Germans didn't understand pirate humour.

I was chased around the radio station by the burly Chief Engineer, Mr Mac, and was only saved by English Service Manager, Paul Kaye, who explained to Mac that I might have translated Eggy Lay's instructions to me a little too enthusiastically!

I got into trouble with the Italian Service, which preceded my early show some nights. The entire 15 minutes was a garble of Italian chat, no music at all. When it ended I came out with a mouthful of *gracias* and stuff you'd read on an Italian menu.

"Gracias senior, arrivederci, cannelloni, spaghetti-vongole, lasagna, Parmesan, finoccio!"

They liked everything except '*finoccio*'. Apparently I'd called their presenter a slang word for gay, and the sponsors didn't like it. I thought finoccio was fennel, but I must have mispronounced it.

Then I got into trouble with the Dutch station by back-announcing their DJ Felix Meurders as '*the DJ who should be murdered.*'

Paul and I were once guilty of taking a hard cash payola payment but not, as you might suspect, for playing someone's record. We'd both been brought in to do a voiceover for a new tiny pocket-sized organ called the Stylophone made famous by Rolf Harris, and used by David Bowie at the start of *Space Odyssey*. Having been given £50 each for the voiceover, an envelope arrived for both of us with an extra £50.

The note read: '*You did a brilliant job and I'm sure you'll have lots of fun playing with the Stylophone's during your shows!*'

Paul came up with the solution, "Let's never play them again then no one can accuse us of taking payola".

"Shall we send the cash back", I asked.

"Now that would be churlish", he replied.

I used to target the younger listeners in a big way, and I liked to keep folks listening by being unpredictable or off the wall.

"OK, it's end of term, no school for six weeks so I'm going to give a prize to the one out there who burns down the most schools, between now and the end of the summer holiday!"

Intro: Alice Cooper's *School's Out*.

It was trying through this joke, to show the kids I knew how much they hated school and to associate with them, especially the boys, who were always harder to win over than female listeners.

The next day a school burnt down and you know who got the blame! It made headlines in all the tabloids!

Paul Burnett was the son of Paul Burnett, the Orchestra leader, and had spent a lifetime in caravans moving from gig to gig, ballroom to ballroom. It paid off for him. In Luxembourg he lived in a shoebox bedsit and made it look like a caravan! Paul had come to 208 via Radio 270, a pirate ship off the Scarborough coast, where he spent the entire show with a bucket lodged between his knees. A great DJ but, alas, no tar.

He came ashore to join Manx Radio on the Isle of Man before getting the big break to join Radio Luxembourg. Paul, an only child like myself, was the funniest man I have ever known. Together we took on the responsibility of keeping our colleagues buoyant in our foreign surroundings.

Once we'd established ourselves on 208, the club gigs started to come along to supplement our wages.

What we earned in a month at Radio Luxembourg, we earned for a one-hour live appearance in clubs around the UK and Europe.
Each week our two days off air led to the airport.

In 16 years with Radio Luxembourg, I did an average two gigs a week catching around 1,400 Luxair flights.

The 208 Summer Road Show took us, and our huge yellow tour bus, to every cove in the UK, and inspired the BBC to launch their own competitive Radio 1 Road Show. We had a big advantage over Radio 1 in these circumstances, because we had the kids and their parents who had grown up listening to our station. The beach parties when Luxembourg hit town were really family affairs, perfect for the British resorts. Radio 1 was new and young but just the mention of the name Radio Luxembourg sent some people off into nostalgia-land. A *history*, that's what Radio Luxembourg had over Radio 1.

Jan: The girl with the banana

I had dubbed all the blank tapes into Paul Anka tracks and was packing them ready to post back to Michal, when a friend came by and asked me how much I charged for a copy? I laughed and told him I did it for fun to make other Paul Anka fans happy.
He looked at me like I had lost my marbles.
"But surely you know that some people charge 10 crowns to record just one LP, and more if it's the Beatles or the Rolling Stones?"

I explained how Michal had recorded a Paul Anka tape for me at no cost without even knowing me, because I'd shown interest in the Paul Anka fan club he was launching.

I remained very naive about the music industry. All I wanted was to make people enjoy music other than Russian music; this was my goal and my greatest pleasure. I had not even contemplated the economics of the music industry and thought surely everyone was in it for pleasure. In my unworldly circumstances, I actually thought that Elvis, Paul Anka and the Beatles did it for fun with perhaps some cost cover of their recording costs. I honestly was appalled at my friend's suggestion that I would charge money for doing this task.

The beautiful summer by the lake continued to stretch onwards, and whilst most people sunbathed or swam or played around with footballs and volleyballs, František and I wrestled with lyric translation, trying to complete them and understand them, so we could explain to our friends in groups just what the Young Rascals meant when they sang '*I ain't gonna eat out my heart anymore*'. First we had to get our English knowledge around words like *ain't*, and then we had to comprehend what eating a heart was all about?

František was about to start his second year at the Technical University in Brno, but kept telling me he didn't like it and was thinking about quitting. I wasn't surprised, he was a man of art, interested in literature, poetry and song lyrics, and his interest in engineering or machine building began and ended with audio equipment.

In a sense it consoled me knowing František wasn't happy at the university, I didn't feel so much like I'd lost out now that I realised being accepted didn't always turn out to be a great thing.

On the contrary, I had been living at an all-consuming high speed like never before.

My Sonet Duo changed my life completely. I started recording Radio Luxembourg, keeping the record button on so that no hit would slip me by. The greatest thing was being able to listen to last night's recording the following day, right from breakfast if I wished. 208 by daylight – never before in history!

This helped my English too, as I grew to understand disc jockeys banter much better after listening to a recording for the second or third time. The same also for my ability to catch the lyrics, which gained me enormous respect amongst my musician friends.

So in this way I bounced along without a communist in my hair, feeling freer than I had ever felt in my life. Recording songs from Radio Caroline and Luxembourg, editing the good ones onto a master tape, translating the lyrics of my favourite artists, there were sports to attend also; life was fine. Then my father gave me the wake up call.

Being the type who couldn't stay still for a minute, he grew tired of watching me do what he regarded as a hobby, not a vocation. I tried to defend myself.

"I'm learning English father," I offered.

Two days later he approached me again with a newspaper advertisement announcing that Brno railway station was seeking high school graduates for a special course to become train dispatchers.

My conscience got the better of me and I agreed to go. Having spent most of my money on tapes and the recorder, by the end of August I would be calling on my parents for support. I realised now that it was about time I showed them some gratitude via a wage packet.

The next day I went along with my school report, which confirmed I had graduated. I was told, almost too quickly, I could have a job, but first I'd have to work for three months as a switchman in the freight train depot to give me the experience for the job ahead. The very next day my ID card was stamped and from 1 September 1966, I became an employee of the Brno

Freight Train Depot in the district of Maloměřice.

It was important to have such a stamp in your Identity Card because when Public Safety were controlling people doing their spot checks in pubs and the venues where young people attended concerts, they arrested them and locked them up until they could prove who they were.

In 1948, a law was introduced whereby everybody older than 15 had to carry his identity card with him whenever he left home. We hated it, especially on summer days when you wanted to visit the lake in your shorts. Other than students, *everybody* had to be employed, otherwise he would be marked as a work-shy parasite in our socialist society. An investigation would discover where they were getting their money to live. If things didn't add up they'd be sent down.

We were lucky enough to have a telephone due to my mother's old job at the telecommunications company, but I stared at it every day, now unable to pick it up and call Katka in Bratislava. Her question last autumn when she wondered which university I would like to study at, kept running through my mind like an eternal echo. It wasn't that I would be embarrassed to explain I failed university and was now a railway worker, I just wanted to protect her from her friends' questioning. She'd sent me a postcard two weeks earlier telling me she was once again at the summer English course where we met the previous summer. I considered calling her in the mountain hotel to see if she would like me to visit her, but I somehow felt a failed university and a tape recorder would not impress her very much.

So I let Katka go and accepted that I was now about to enter a new world, from one where students excitedly planned their lives, to one with workers whose destiny had run out of stars.

There was one great aspect of becoming a member of the working class, a starting salary of 1,200 crowns, far more than my mother earned as a governess, not to mention my father's lowly pension. I was supplied with free working clothes, including shoes and overalls, and told to come start my training course on 1 September to understand the safety regulations everyone had to abide by on the railway.

It was impressed on us what a dangerous place a freight yard could be, with whole trains and separate wagons moving this way and that.

We learned that when a freight train arrived at our depot it was either going onwards to another destination, partly separated or being unloaded for freight forwarding. We had female workers whose job it was to check the bills on each wagon kept in a small wire container. This information was then passed to the shift leader situated on a hill. Shunters disconnected each wagon, whilst the shift leader gave instructions to the switchmen through a loud speaker, instructing down which of the 23 tracks each wagon had to be sent. When the train was complete off it went to a further destination.

The freight depot was a noisy place as the wagons rolled down the hill at different speeds, bumping finally into the previous wagon when shunters hadn't managed to stop them in time.

Sometimes there would be incorrect data on the wagon's weight, and an empty wagon came out of the turnout and down the hill much slower. If then a fully laden wagon came out too soon, it would catch up to the empty wagon but on a different rail, causing one, or both to derail with a mighty metallic thundering. All this was accompanied by the permanent sound of booming voice orders over loudspeakers, and the howling of locomotives from passing trains.

The lecturer tried to make us fully aware we would be working a hectic environment where our complete concentration had to be applied every minute of our 12-hour shift.

"A wrong step," he warned, "could be fatal."

The yard was situated on the outskirts of Brno, in a beauty spot I used to visit with my friends on our bikes when we were younger. I decided to catch a tram from a stop further up the yard so I could enjoy some of the views and reminisce a little.

As I walked up the line, all of a sudden a gentle girl's voice called out to me.

"Would you like a banana?" she enquired.

A beautiful blonde girl who had been on the training course with me was following me. I'd been too busy concentrating on the lecture to pay anyone else too much attention, but I recognised her, you couldn't help it, she was a real peach.

It was such a strange offer, for some reason bananas, oranges, tangerines etc were things you only saw at Christmastime and here was a girl on her own initiative not only offering me one, but peeling it for me!

After taking it from her, I offered the banana to her lips and she took a bite. Then, with a huge smile, this unusual girl took out another banana for herself and we continued our walk together chatting away.

It turned out that she too had failed to be accepted for university and had applied for an office job at the rail yard. Now, like I, in attending the training course and having learned what a dangerous place we would be working in, she was not too happy.

Her name was Jana and, as she was home alone, she invited me to come with her for coffee.

I had never in my life drunk coffee, and I certainly had never been invited home alone to drink coffee with a beautiful blonde creature. Coffee was made available when my parents had guests, but it was a drink I felt was for grown-ups, so I boycotted it.

Until now... well almost.

Inside Jana's apartment, instead of preparing coffee she moved closer to me. Suddenly we stopped talking and were undressing each other at a rate of knots, coffee the last thing on our minds. I was overwhelmed by the beauty of Jana's naked body and didn't know quite what to look at first. Neither did I know what exactly I should be doing other than admiring her.

Once again on this remarkable day, I was undergoing training and instruction.

It was so easy, so simple, so natural. An hour ago we didn't know each other's names, now we were lying naked together hugging each other like old lovers.

This was not like it was with Katka last summer. Katka was about feeling in love with our clothes on, but whilst there could be no love here within an hour of meeting, it had been everything else I had ever fantasised about.

After time spent caressing, kissing, sucking and stroking each other, she turned me on my back, sat on top of me and started slowly moving herself up and down so I could see all of her exquisite body, her hair framing her beautiful face, her eyes closed allowing me to inspect her without embarrassment.

In these precious moments, with the Iron Curtain nowhere to be seen, I began at last and so unexpectedly, to enjoy becoming a man.

Jana had towered over me for some time when she asked me to change positions. Just when I was getting into my rhythm, Jana uttered. "Be sure to pay attention!"

I was flattered that Jana considered me experienced enough to have such willpower and timing, but at the same time I knew that I was completely inexperienced, and that I could easily fail this challenging test of masculinity.

Suddenly I was hearing Aunt Lída´s words of old, "Jan, be a good boy and don't upset your parents. You know how they suffered in concentration camps."

I felt my loins collapsing.

What if I didn't pull out in time and made Jana pregnant? What then, what would I tell my parents who had suffered so much in life? And that was when my errection disappeared as quickly as spring snow.

I fell onto my side exasperated.

"What happened?" she asked.

It was the first time in my life that I really didn't know what to say, as I lay there breathless, putty in her hand.

If I were with Katka, it would be something I could have explained easily, but Jana was too new to understand my background and this parental weight I carried through my life.

"Did you not like it with me?" she asked with the most penetratingly sad eyes, to which I was able to answer quite enthusiastically.

"I liked this better than anything I have ever done in my life Jana," I smiled at her reassuringly leaning towards her on one elbow. "I am terribly sorry."

She asked again why I'd stopped and if I had a girlfriend? I looked for an excuse, telling her I had this girl in Bratislava, Katka, but we rarely saw each other. I wanted to ask her if she had a boyfriend, but thought better of it and decided to stroke her naked body as such an opportunity was not likely to come my way again soon. But she was through with me, and urged me to stop caressing her and get dressed, as someone might come home anytime.

Before leaving we embraced and she noticed I was awakening again.

"Go now, we'll see each other tomorrow," she said opening the door.

Wrapped in thought, I walked home. My world had suddenly changed in Jana's apartment. It was a sky-punching experience. I'm sure most boys experience the elation after having their first real sex. Life's great secret had been revealed, and it was good. I wondered if she really wanted to see me tomorrow and if this was love, because it felt bloody wonderful to me.

I had Jana in the back of my mind throughout the following day, and was concerned when she didn't appear. I'd rehearsed what I would say to her, how beautiful she was and how much I had enjoyed our time together yesterday.

I now realised how huge the freight depot was with over 30 tracks and main side tracks that took the trains from Brno to Prague, and I guessed Jana was busy with her own supervisor, checking the wagons for consignment notes.

In the afternoon I was sent to the other side of the depot to get acquainted with their system.

There was much less traffic on this side, and whilst I waited to flip the switch as soon as a freight train passed, a voice called me. I looked up to see an engineer in the cab of a steam locomotive waiting on the next rail. He looked like someone out of a fairy tale, a bearded old man with a weather-beaten face. He bade me to come closer and I approached his noisy steaming engine.

"What are you doing here boy?" he cried above the steam.

I explained to him this was my first day at work after a safety training session yesterday.

He told me he had been working on the railway for 40 years and that it was no life at all, working nights and weekends and being constantly under stress during 12-hour shifts.

He looked down at me with a kindly old face and said, "If you want to have an acceptable life, you'd better leave this job as soon as possible. Working on the railway is no life at all son."

His words remained with me, and it wasn't long before he was proved right. My social life was about to take a nose-dive.

I came home from work as the sun fell over the horizon just in time to dial 208 and prepared my tape recorder in case there would be some new songs played on beloved Luxembourg, and this night I was in for a major treat as the DJ's announced he had the 'premier play' of the new Beach Boys' single.

I pressed the record button, but just wasn't prepared for the impact *Wouldn't it be Nice* made on me. The comparison from a day of locomotive yard noises to this almost angelic Californian harmony, made my hair stand on end.

What a difference a song could make, it immediately transported me to a much better world and on this occasion, I had just recorded what was probably going to be the song of the year.

How many times I replayed this song that night I cannot remember, 60? 100? But by the end I knew the lyrics, which at that time I felt had been written for me and my girl.

'You know it's gonna make it that much better, When we can say goodnight and stay together.'

What I wasn't too sure about was which one would accompany me in my dreams tonight? Jana or Katka? Katka was out of reach, but Jana couldn't be closer.

With *Wouldn't it be Nice* repeating in my head as I went to sleep, I decided to call Jana the following morning.

She answered after one ring and I launched into how I had missed seeing her at work. Her answer stunned me.

"I've quit the railway', she announced. It was easier quitting in the first month of the so-called trial period, after which you had to give a full six-month's notice.

This was the method our socialist economy used to stop people changing their jobs too often. Jana had discussed everything with her parents, who agreed it wasn't right for a young girl to be walking through the night amongst the freight trains.

Yesterday, they had accepted her resignation.

I recounted to Jana the words of the old engineer and we both began laughing after I pointed out how smart she was to find this solution after one day, when it had taken the old man 40 years!

"We should meet tonight and finally have the coffee together," she said, but I pointed out I had my first night shift, but I would call her as soon as I came off the shift.

I'd already accepted that I would miss Radio Luxembourg during night shifts, but missing this opportunity to take up with Jana where we left off, was quite a blow.

With less work at night, there was more time to talk with my colleagues who were much older than me and married. I soon discovered we had very little in common and that these hard-working men seemed unconcerned with the communist regime.

I was soon to discover why.

The answer came at the end of the month when I received my first salary. I earned more than the daughter of my mother's friend who had just become a physician.

Now, finally, I understood the communist party system, which made sure the working class earned well and kept out of politics. I thanked God I had friends with so much in common with me, but I realised now that their friendship and my social life was about to be sacrificed for new wealth.

The meeting for coffee with Jana never materialised. The university had accepted her for the sociology course. I tried to woo her every day, but she was constantly busy making her preparations for university and 'our coffee will have to wait' became a regular chime.

Each day as the wagons rolled at work my mind was with her, as I pictured her sitting atop of me, her blonde hair thrown back, her cherry tipped breasts bouncing before me. This was not a healthy fantasy to sustain a young man over a 12-hour shift, but I could do nothing about it, I was in love or was it lust?

I had sunk to begging her for the coffee date, every day I faced and accepted humiliation as she made one excuse after another.

So I summoned up willpower from somewhere and called upon my dignity and stopped calling her. But it was a long time before I stopped calling on her image during the day she gave me a lot more than a banana.

One of the great cohesions between everyone in the yard was to allow a wagon filled with high quality coal to crash. The impact against another wagon would cause the doors to smash open and the coal to spill across the tracks. A new seal was put on the wagon, explaining that the breaks had failed and coal spilled. Then for weeks after, everyone with coal heating would bring two sacks, which would return home with them, full of the very best coal at the end of their shift.

The same happened with grain, an unusual method of an entire workforce creating their own bonus system.

My first pleasant surprise came after the first three weeks of my railway career, when I got an advance payment of 600 crowns. The balance would be paid 10 days into the following month. I could immediately buy two German quality Basf tapes and still have 300 crowns left!

My only other spend from my first wage was inviting František to discuss our lyrics in a pub as my guest, as it was an unwritten law that the first stipend had to be spent in a wet way.

When the September salary was paid out, I began to quite like being working class. I'd never seen anything like it. I was paid another 1,200 crowns more, which, together with the advance, amounted to almost double the average salary in Czechoslovakia at that time.

It got better, I was paid generous bonuses for working nights and weekend shift, overtime shifts paid even more. I calculated that for a 12-hour overtime shift working nights or weekends, I earned 150 crowns, which was quite incredible, and was equivalent to one whole German tape for just one shift!

I may have been the only worker in Czechoslovakia who was notionally paid in music, as I translated crowns into tapes.

Being such a rich man, I made another decision, I would buy a Japanese transistor radio only available in Tuzex stores, where coupons exchanged for hard currency at the bank could buy you many exotic foreign products. Tuzex shops were explained by the government, as shops created especially for foreign tourists in order to bring in hard currency, but this was only partly true, as mostly it served for black market luxury items bought by the Czechoslovakian über-riche.

Our neighbour Jura, was a man of the world and someone about to become very important to me. He was the first in our street to own a scooter at a time when he was studying medicine. Jura always had beautiful girls around him and he was always pleasant to me. So I called on him to see if he could obtain 140 Tuzex coupons for my dream Japanese Hitachi transistor radio I had admired in the Tuzex shop window.

Jura came up with the goods and gave me one Tuzex coupon for every five Czechoslovak crowns. I ran to the shop and ran back with the Hitachi and looked forward to a special nightshift with Radio Luxembourg, providing me with music while I worked the yard.

From 7.30pm that night the great TWO-O-EIGHT was with me in my work place, a bonus I had given to myself!

Tony: Paul's gig

One of Paul Burnett's best stories was when he returned triumphantly to Tiffany's in Great Yarmouth, his old pirate radio stomping ground. As a Radio Luxembourg DJ, Paul walked on stage like a conquering hero and started his act playing hits and having fun with the audience, which is what we did back then.

After 30 minutes, realising he'd left some 208 T-shirt prizes in his dressing room, he left the resident DJ playing a Motown medley, the Supremes' *In and Out of Love*, back to back with Stevie Wonder's *I'm Wondering*, cross-fading into the Four Tops' *Bernadette*.

That would give him plenty of time and the audience, heavily into Motown and Northern Soul, wouldn't even know he was gone for the few minutes it would take.

He managed to relocate his dressing room in the maze of back stage corridors however, carrying his cardboard box full of T-shirts somehow, on his return, he went through the wrong door finishing up in a back yard with the door shutting firmly behind him!

"I banged and hammered on the door," Paul grimaces whenever he recounts the story. "But no one could hear me above fucking Stevie Wonder!"

The resident DJ was already playing *Bernadette* when Burnett dropped the box of prizes and pushed a large garbage bin to a back gate. There was nothing else for it, he climbed onto the drum and immediately fell into it as the lid gave way!

This was a Sunday gig, so Paul was waist deep in all Saturday's hamburger and chips leftovers, relish and all! Yanking himself over the gate like a soldier on fatigues, stinking like a skunk, his 208 bomber jacket ripped, Paul dropped to the other side landing awkwardly and spraining his ankle. He found himself in a pitch-black alleyway, out of which he limped like Marshal Dylan's deputy in the Gunsmoke TV show. Entering a dark cobbled street at the back of Tiffany's he had to decide whether to go left or right?

Inside the venue, the DJ by now had selected his own records and wasn't questioning Burnett's absence. In their minds, all resident DJs are 10 times better than the visiting radio personalities, and this one was now diving into the biggest tunes in his collection, loving the fact that the star of the show had not yet returned. Jeff Beck's *Hi Ho Silver Lining* was playing. The floor was full. Not one person questioned where the Radio Luxembourg DJ had gone!

Out back, Paul turned right and right again... then left and right and then left and then, at last, after 10 minutes of panic, in the distance he saw the bright lights of Tiffany's front entrance.

The faint sound of Spencer Davies' *Keep on Running* grew louder as he approached.

"I hobbled up to the front door stinking of garbage and looking like John Mills on the beach in Love Story," Paul recounted. "There was a lettuce leaf on my shoe, tomato ketchup on my shirt, my jacket was ripped and I was sweating profusely!"

A very large bouncer blocked his path at the door.

"Sorry matey we're full," he announced arms crossed, his double chin inflating as he looked down at the bedraggled person before him.

"I'm Paul Burnett," said Paul Burnett.

"Yeah", the bouncer sneered. "And I'm fucking Anne Nightingale!"

Inside the DJ played Lulu's *Shout*, the audience was going wild. Outside, so was Paul.

"But I am Paul Burnett."

A variety of expressions formed on the bouncer's face until, finally, with years of experience and training in diplomacy, a smile appeared.

"Fuck off son!" he said. "Paul Burnett went on stage half an hour ago!"

Inside the venue the DJ did a nice little segue into Chris Farlow's *Out of Time*.

When he eventually joined the corporation, Paul became infamous at the BBC for playing the B-sides of records by mistake, and it may have been his scatter-brainacy that eventually lost him his Radio 1 gig, but at least he made it there, and shone at the top of our national DJ tree.

There was though, an occasion on 208 when he played more B-sides and made more gaffs than is acceptable. But it was quite explainable.

Walking to the radio station one evening he turned the corner to come nose to trunk with an elephant! Paul stood there releasing farts, trumpet to trump, toe to toe with the beasty, trying to comprehend the insanity of his situation.

Just as his bowel contents were about to wave farewell to him, the circus trainer arrived with a stick and yanked Jumbo off the pavement and back to a pack of the beasts, parading down the middle of the road. Paul had run into a promotional parade for the new circus in town.

An understandable craving for a strong tipple came over him and so, pale of face he entered the nearest café, where he repeated the story over again to the bar tender, and anyone who could understand the hyper Englishman, whose hands shook as he drank a strange foreign version of rum and coke. Three swift large ones later, his watch told him he was in big trouble, there were just 10 minutes to airtime, and he was the first DJ on the air so there would be no one to fill in for him if he was late.

Outside, a storm had arrived and the heavens were angry.

A one-kilometre sprint took Paul down the Avenue Marconi, which ran like a stream down to RTL in the Villa Louvigny. Breathless, Paul took the two flights two steps at a time to the English studio, straight to the cartridge rack for his opening jingle, then to the cupboard for play-listed records. With mere seconds to go, he pressed the button, which told the engineer beyond the glass to turn on the microphone, which he now did.

Wet from a combination of rain and sweat, tipsy from Luxembourg's far from short-shots of Bacardi, Paul started his show.

It was a sheer dishashter! He schlurred his schpeech and started to over compenshate verbally, sounding like a ventriloquist dummy. He ran the wrong commercials, gave the wrong time checks, played a B-side in error and crashed lyrics for fun. After 20 minutes abusing the listeners, the hotline rang.

There was only one person who would be ringing the hotline - the boss from London, Geoffrey Everett, the devil-incarnate who, within weeks of this event, would sack Noel Edmonds who, very quickly, went on to huge success at the BBC.

Paul let the telephone hotline light flash as long as he reasonably felt he could and then picked it up with a deep breath and a feeble, "H'lo?"

"What the fuck's going on out there?" screamed Geoffrey Everett.

Paul reached for his best option - silence.

"Why aren't we broadcasting?" demanded the irate chief.

"Not... broad-cast-ing?" Burnett stammered.

"There's nothing but fucking static on 208. What's going on at Marnach?"

Five minutes before transmission, lightening had struck a bullseye on our transmitter in Marnach in the north of Luxembourg.

Since that day, understanding that lightening doesn't strike twice, Paul has been a pre-show tea-total DJ.

Jan: Johnny Cash & Eddie Cochran

I had asked Michal in Černošice if he would be so kind as to record some more tapes for me. In reply to this he sent me a list, no less than 25 albums for me to choose from. How anyone could amass such a wonderful vinyl collection was beyond me, and my mouth watered as I looked through the titles. Right at the top of the list were the first three Beatles albums, *Please Please Me*, *With the Beatles* and *A Hard Day's Night*. There were also two albums by Elvis and I had to laugh when I saw amongst them three Johnny Cash albums, one titled Ride this Train.

When my selected music arrived I was supremely happy. At last I had the Beatles music at high quality in chronological order. I now heard my long-loved Elvis songs such as *Heartbreak Hotel* and *Jailhouse Rock* in full audio glory. But what really struck me was the album Ride this Train by Johnny Cash, as it uncovered a musical dimension I was discovering for the first time. The sounds of steam locomotives accompanied Johnny Cash´s narrative between each song, capturing the atmosphere of my own freight train depot with sounds I lived with daily.

It was much more than just 10 songs put together to make an album, and later I would learn that this type of musical grouping would be called a concept album.

Maybe this wouldn't mean so much to people in the free world, but for me it took me beyond music enjoyment, into a classroom where I could learn about America and different cultures, something we just never heard about in our media-controlled world. Johnny Cash told me stories that were several centuries old, and then sang a song related to it. I was listening to an American history book as he talked and sang about cowboys and Indians, railroad men and mainly concentrated his tales on hard-working men.

It's one thing learning English, another history and about other lives in other lands, but when you learn from a song, you don't have to revise, you just remember the tune and it's all there!

The first two lines of his song *Loading Coal* caught my attention because it corresponded with my own story:

'My pappy said when I was seventeen you're six feet tall and your face is clean
And it don't look right for a boy that old to not make a livin' loadin' coal.'

I related with this kid, and even though I was being paid more than the poor miners Johnny Cash sung about, I felt that it was not a job that I should be doing for the rest of my life.

Some of his lyrics reminded me of a very old Czech proverb which said that *'Nowhere in the world do roasted pigeons fly into ones mouth for free!'* My teacher, Johnny Cash taught me that America wasn't filled exclusively with millionaires, as was the popular belief in my country. I've spent my life being grateful for his teachings.

In offices and factories around Czechoslovakia, regular meetings, discussions and lectures followed each working day. Employees were forced to attend these meetings, and to endure communist propaganda and the process of brainwashing our subjects.

Of course this would never happen at the freight depot where switchmen and shunters, many of them former inmates, would send anybody who dared suggest such an idea to hell. The communist railway bosses left them well alone, as the year's productivity was such that their huge bonuses were guaranteed.

Whilst I enjoyed my newfound wealth, my friendship with František was suffering.

One day he called me to see if I would be joining for a Synkopy 61 concert that coincided with a scheduled night shift. I promised I'd try to exchange shifts with someone, and when I asked a fellow switchman if he would, his answer changed things quite a lot.

Instead of officially changing shifts, he proposed he would simply arrive in my place and do my work if I paid him 100 crowns in cash. If anyone found out or questioned what had happened, I would have to tell them I had fallen ill just before the shift and came to these arrangements. What puzzled me at first was the maths of the deal. I earned 140 crowns on this shift and he only wanted 100, but he confided in me that he had a lover, and his wife checked his pay slip, so this was a great way of hiding his income from her so he could spend it with his lover.

The deal suited us both, and it became a regular occurrence starting on the night of the Synkopy 61 concert.

I was surprised and quite pleased to see that Pavel Váně had become the band's new lead singer. The original singer, Pavel Pokorný, had been drafted and so the new Pavel was given the job and no wonder, he was already shaping up to be an excellent guitarist, and there was no question just how much the girls loved his singing.

As I watched him performing and the girls clambering at the front of stage, I felt a ripple of envy and my mind strayed to Jana, who still showed no interest in meeting me again. It was my fault that I didn't concentrate my efforts on females like most guys were doing at my age. I knew that my preoccupation with music and my beloved English language were the causes, and that at least this pastime had led to me becoming part of an exciting music community in Brno.

I knew that I would never become a singer and that I had no calling to play a musical instrument. But at least I had discovered the value of lyric translations, which fulfilled my spare time and gave me great status amongst my musician friends. Radio Luxembourg and my growing knowledge of English had become my contribution to the development of western music inside Czechoslovakia, in spite of all the obstacles made by the Communist regime.

The fact that Pavel Pokorný had now left to serve his two years in the Czechoslovak People's Army brought to mind that I, too, would become 19 the following year and my time would have come.

At 18 years of age, 19 seemed a long way in the future, so I gave it no further thought as it was all so unavoidable, unless I failed the medical test which was very unlikely, as I enjoyed robust health.

On 30 November, I had completed three months working for the Czechoslovak State Railways and was now eligible for hugely reduced train fares. Without delay I took advantage and headed for the big city of Prague, having been informed that the Tuzex shop stocked imported records.

I picked the card up from the depot office, and whilst there asked the Director of Human Resources how my application for the train dispatcher job was coming along, as I had now completed three months training. He seemed taken aback that I should be standing there asking this question, and uttered something like it wouldn't happen until next year. I thought it strange that my work application seemed to be on the back burner so far as management were concerned but, for the moment, I didn't consider it to be a problem, I was more interested in my imminent journey to Prague.

Once again I had called on our neighbour Jura to obtain some more Tuzex crowns, and with them now safely in my pocket, I took an early Monday morning train to Prague, having paid only two crowns for a journey that would normally have cost 15.

I was quite excited when entering the Tuzex shop expecting to see shelves lined with records like the Supraphon shop only these would be western albums. I looked around but there were none to be seen so finally, I asked the lady behind the counter if they had any records at all? She bent down beneath the counter and suddenly there they were, a box filled with LPs.

Rifling through them I became very despondent, they were all jazz and classical records, not a pop album in sight. Seeing that I had looked through the entire box the shop assistant placed another box before me, and suddenly my long journey finally bore fruit.

For the first time in my life, I gazed at a rock 'n' roll star, this was Eddie Cochran and my hands shook as I turned the sleeve to see what tracks were included. The album was titled Inédits (unpublished) with sleeve notes written in French.

Next I found an EP that had tried to hide between two LPs, and I gazed upon the Animals with four of their songs, including their greatest hit *House of the Rising Sun*. Although I had heard this great group many times on 208, before this moment I could only imagine what they looked like. Then again, you could say that about pretty much every band and artist I have ever heard up to this time.

On the back of the EP was a short profile of each member, and this time it wasn't only all in English, according to the sleeve it was actually released directly in the UK on Columbia, an EMI label. I was utterly amazed and thrilled to be holding an actual English record, and when I asked the price to be told that Eddie Cochran would cost me 28 Tuzex crowns, the Animals cost just six, my mission to Prague was complete.

I might then have considered a walk through downtown Prague, but I simply couldn't wait to get back to Brno to play my new acquisitions. I knew this was the right decision as soon as I heard *My Way*, the first song on Eddie Cochran's LP as he growled the words '*I was born a tiger, I always had my way, nobody's gonna change me, this or any other day.*'

After the umpteenth play of the album on that Monday night, I convinced myself Eddie was one of the greatest rock 'n' roll stars ever, and that his songs spoke *to* me and *for* me. To hear the Animals' *House of the Rising Sun* playing loud from a record player was another great thrill, and I understood no matter how great and convenient my tape recorder was, nothing could compare to the sound of vinyl.

Suddenly I started to feel like I was becoming a DJ.

I couldn't wait for our New Year's Eve party!

Tony: Kid Jensen

After I'd been in Luxembourg nine months, David 'Kid' Jensen joined us.

The team was almost complete.

Kid arrived as 'David' Jensen, but we soon changed that when we saw this gawky looking 19-year-old Canadian standing before us.

Apart from being a great companion who eventually lived with Christine and I, David, the Kid, was a hypochondriac of classic proportion.

Burnett and I checked him in to the Hotel Francais in the Place d'Armes, from where he would spend his first few days flat hunting.

He opened his suitcase and you couldn't see clothes for medicines.

Kid's best ever malady claim was that he once had identical symptoms to Christine's premenstrual syndrome.

I kid you not, a Kid with monthly moods!

Eventually he held down a progressive music show, Jensen's Dimensions, which the station launched in competition to John Peel at the BBC. Kid played Jethro Tull, Led Zeppelin, Thin Lizzy, Juicy Lucy and a load of shite he pretended to like by folk singers. Kid also had to host normal top 40 shows, which must have affected his prog-rock credibility enormously.

One night he'd be talking deep rock with Deep Purple's Ian Gillan and Roger Glover, or the Who's Pete Townsend, the next night he'd be playing Karen Young's *Nobody's Child*.

It got worse. At 7.30pm hundreds and thousands of old women sat in Mecca Bingo Halls waiting for their chance to win the national jackpot. At this time every night, all music stopped on Luxembourg as Kid, Paul or I read out the numbers.

It was 15 minutes of complete torture for all of us, but for Kid, who had to learn all about Kelly's Eye – Number 1 and Two Fat Ladies - 66 and then, later that night interview the Edgar Broughton Band, it was a nightmare!

Kid must have been the central character in King Crimson's, 21st Century Schizoid Man!

One of the aspects we liked about Kid's show was that his interviews were mainly live, which meant that Fleetwood Mac, Status Quo, Elton John, Phil Lynot and all the rock bands flew in on the Luxair Focher Friendship, accompanied by a manager and their record-plugger, who had a very large expense account. Both these people had very fine tastes in restaurants and wines, and all the DJs would get invited no matter who was conducting the interview.

The pluggers loved coming to Luxembourg, it meant status to them. The BBC was round the corner in Langham Place, whereas Radio Luxembourg needed a passport, wild nights in the strip bars, emptying of Holiday Inn mini-bars and much currency changing. Record pluggers never argued with you. They always told great jokes and revealed intimate indiscretions of household names in pop and rock. Pluggers were put on earth by the record companies to feed and entertain DJs and music journalists.

One of the best was David Most, Mickey's brother, who plugged all the acts on RAK Records including Mud, Suzie Quatro, Herman's Hermits, Hot Chocolate, and a few even Mickey wouldn't have cared to remember. David discovered a cheap, yet potent, form of payola when he learned that we couldn't get English sausages, or good lean Danish bacon in the Grand Duchy.

On one trip he came by road over the Ardennes with members of Mud to promote *Lonely this Christmas* and, to avoid problems with customs, cleverly smuggled the contraband beneath the bonnet of their Ford Transit. In the Radio Luxembourg car park we queued up, salivating like beggars, with plates at a Salvation Army feeding station.

The most savoury smell to ever emit from an engine greeted us as David raised the bonnet. It made quite a sight, the Wall's sausages frizzling on the manifold, the bacon welded to the sump, burned to a frizzle.

"No wonder it was sluggish over the Ardennes," sighed David.

Jan: New Year's Eve '67

New Year's Eve 1967 was unforgettable for all of us, and all because of the music captured from Radio Luxembourg on my new tape recorder. Before this evening this was a programme of western music we could only ever have dreamed of. The tape was filled with non-stop hits, the very best the 60s had to offer, one after another after another.

We had ended 1966 with the Beach Boys at the top of the charts with *Good Vibrations*, a song to establish the mood for our greatest ever party. If only Brian Wilson knew then how much his songs meant to us. If only John, Paul, George and Ringo could grasp the lifeline their tunes were to us kids in Czechoslovakia. All they needed to do was be there at this party, where they would have understood a completely different level to the value of their music. The problem until this party was, that my favourite tunes were distributed on many different spools, recorded over many different 208 Top Twenty Shows. Thanks to Lad'a loaning me his Sonet Duo, over the weeks leading up to this party, I worked slavishly to provide the occasion with music, the likes of which they could never have imagined. It was the night I delivered to them Radio Luxembourg's Greatest Hits, retaining the DJs introduction of each track, adding to the authenticity of my production, giving an impression as though we had star DJs hosting our party.

The very voices that had maintained us and nourished us, flying through the night air, across the Iron Curtain and over barbed wire fences, where my friends and I waited every single night of our teenage lives to hear them, were now here amongst us once again. Now, as I played at being a programme producer, their voices filled our room without the usual commercials to interrupt their DJ banter.

As I dubbed my recordings onto one master tape, I stopped to ponder how we would have survived without 208 and my conclusion is that it is just unimaginable. Had we never heard western pop and rock 'n' roll, we would never have become so infected. I suppose it's like audio-heroin.

At this New Year party, we danced and embraced each other, as though we realised this would be a magical memory to carry with us throughout the rest of our lives. Indeed, whilst we had no idea what the future held, we had decades ahead where music would help us to survive the regime that had been sent to plague us and diminish our quality of life.

When we felt like listening to excellent quality recordings minus the Radio Luxembourg static, I played the first three Beatles albums that Michal had recorded for me.

Then there was my first real rock 'n' roll LP with the greatest hits of Eddie Cochran, an album with a sleeve that had literally mesmerised me when my eyes fell on my very first picture of a real western rock 'n' roll star. The sleeve showed Eddie in a cool jacket with legs spread wide, whilst looking directly at me strumming on his guitar. Although I didn't realise there and then, that Eddie was mimicking his own hero Elvis Presley, I have never seen a photograph so full of action before, reflecting perfectly the mood of the songs featured on the LP.

It may be too difficult to imagine these days, that whilst the free world teenagers were enjoying live concerts, TV appearances, magazines, fan clubs and wall-to-wall rock 'n' roll radio, we had no idea what a rock 'n' roll singer looked like, not even Elvis Presley.

Here we were in Czechoslovakia 10 years after their recording, and yet, to us, they were not outdated, on the contrary, each one of us felt that Cochran and Elvis and Little Richard had provided the base level for all pop music's roots. We understood the, *Summertime Blues*, reflected how our teenage counterparts in the free world felt about *their* lives and what they were doing to change that world, it's all there in *Summertime Blues* when the boss said '*no dice son you gotta work late*', and the passion you could feel for a girl as Cochran ran us through his trials in *Twenty Flight Rock*.

No film documentary could have revealed to us more vividly what life was like in the west, better than the lyrics in the songs that had been smuggled into our lives by the Radio Luxembourg transmitters at Marnach, in the Grand Duchy.

Here and now on this 1967 celebration of the birth of a new year, we had no way of placing our own discontent onto a record, then out through a radio station, to pass our message on around the world. But this rock 'n' roll revolution gave us hope that one day, we too would have our say.

If the communist rulers could have seen us dancing to Eddie Cochran's *My way* or to the Beatles *I saw her standing there* and *Rock and Roll Music*, they might have understood that they could no longer bend us, as they had our forefathers in the war years.

Such is the power of music.

In the 40s our parents may have taken heart when Vera Lynn sang *We'll Meet Again*, but *our* spokesmen were Elvis, the Beatles, Dylan and the Stones, all of whom vented teenage frustration, openly revealing our feelings, our sexuality and offering an empathy which we, in the east, clung onto for dear life.

Tony: Noel Edmonds

Christine joined me once I'd passed my three-month trial period.

I'd hit pay dirt. Don Wardell, former 208 DJ who I'd listened to under my pillow, had been appointed as the station's Press Officer, based in 208's London HQ on Hertford Street.

I'd sent him an article I'd written, and Fab 208 magazine had not only accepted it, but also wanted me to write a weekly column.

An extra £10 a week!

I ended up doing a weekly column for years on the very next page to footballer heartthrob, George Best's column. Each month, David the Fab 208 photographer, flew to Luxembourg where we'd come up with camp or crazy DJ adventures. I have the most *fabulous* photo library of my kids growing up because of this.

It's amazing who read what was basically a girl's weekly full of Amen Corner, Love Affair, Tremeloes, David Cassidy, Donny Osmond and the Bay City Rollers.

Three-month trial completed, I drove to Oldham from Luxembourg in my Mini to collect my lady. Christine and I stayed the night in London, parking my overloaded Mini car outside the Little Mayfair hotel on Down

Street, across from Radio Luxembourg where we grabbed a few hours sleep. The next morning we found the car window smashed and our suitcases lifted, every stitch Christine had in the world was gone, my typewriter for my Fab 208 column also stolen.

We arrived in Luxembourg back at square one, completely broke. Things were tight and to help us put shirts back on our back, Christine took a job at our favourite late night haunt, Club 31. Apart from wages, her deal was that we ate with the proprietors, John and Laurie, every day at 5pm.

Here we learned to move our gastronomic boundaries from fish and chips to lobster thermidor, meat and potato pie to venison, sirloin steak to wild boar and Heinz spaghetti hoops to penne, home made ravioli and spaghetti alle vongole (with home made pasta and fresh clams). In John's hands, our appreciation of a Grand Cru wine was established.

Free grub! What an education!

But there was an added bonus to Christine's employment as the bar maid for all the DJs, and that was the size of the measures she served us each night after work, (and the odd drinks she forgot to charge us for).

Noel Edmonds was also amongst the recipients of Christine's liberalism. Arriving in the Grand Duchy in his kit-built sports car, his pride and joy, Noel proceeded to write it off in his first week with us, not having understood you must give way to the vehicles on the left at a junction, especially if they are a 12-wheeled pantechnican driven by a French man! Noel Edmonds should have died there and then. The Brit's kit was in bits but he was unscathed.

Next he escaped death at a party on the Grand Rue, when he slipped from a banister and somehow managed to hold on by one hand, like Sylvester Stallone does in the movies. Burnett and I pulled him back from a fourth-floor splat.

Noel was followed to Luxembourg by his sweetheart, an English dandelion! His mum and dad were headteachers, lovely people and his girlfriend looked very much like the school m'arm she was. She was much older than Noel and, unfortunately for her, arrived about 12 weeks after we had indoctrinated the future House Party and Deal or no Deal host into our rock 'n' roll lifestyle.

By the time she came out to visit him, Noel was in love with a Luxembourg wench, and was coming to terms with fully requited lust for the first time in his life.

His career was taking off on 208 and there is no doubt his programmes were '*multitudinously*' entertaining for his listeners, who he referred to as his '*sons and daughters*'.

Then the school m'arm arrived, and he had a few problems.

Many years later when he met Christine and I at a Dave Lee Travis party, (by which time he was a household name, complete with helicopter), fighting his way through the guests having spotted us, he indicated we have a scrum down at the corner of the bar where he whispered, "You two know too much!"

What we knew was that young Noel tried to get a life for himself, but the lass from his previous life, didn't want to give her prime catch his freedom.

She attempted suicide, an ancient method to demonstrate undying love, thereby making a prisoner for life of someone who can't reciprocate that love. Thankfully she survived her suicide attempt and took her broken heart back to her school-life in England and a society Noel now left behind, as his hormones were fully unleashed in the Grand Duchy of Luxembourg.

Jan: The bottle of rum

By now the communists no longer bothered us, we'd become immune to them and suffered them just as we would a bad teacher in school. You just had to survive until they were gone, no matter how long that might take.

At Christmas there were signs of a political lightening. Items appeared in our shops we had never before seen, western beverages and food products we had never tasted, such as bananas and oranges, which we regarded as gifts from our governing warders.

We were naive to the reality of politics, blindsided to our precious uranium ore being shipped to mother Russia, who then paid for it with bananas! But we did sense change as little shoots appeared around us.

Our only music magazine, a monthly publication called Melodie started to feature the Beatles and other groups we heard during our nightly escapes.

In February 67 things started moving with my train dispatcher's course, when I was invited to take a psychological test to evaluate if I was suitable. Such tests were unusual during this time as sociology and psychology were considered to be a bourgeois anachronism, a science not required in a socialist country.

But attitudes were slowly changing, and that was why I had to undergo the test to be accepted into the railway. I returned a few days after the test to discuss the results with a young psychologist, who revealed I had not done too badly at all.

I put my success down to the years of fun my schoolmates and I had had with word puzzles and linguistic gimmicks, with which we tried to catch each other out.

We'd hear a Radio Caroline or Luxembourg DJ come out with an English word or phrase, and store it away so that when listening to the radio, we

THE YOUNG PRINCE

Tony with Gran and Grandad Hart.

Blackpool with mum and dad.

First job as an apprentice jockey 1959
at Gerald Armstrong's stable.

THE JASONS
Trev, Malc, Bill, Alan and Tony.

THE BIRTH OF BEATLEMANIA
(picture courtesy of the Oldham Chronicle)

Stuck on stage with the Beatles at the Oldham Top Rank. Tony helps the security team throughout the Beatles entire set. (Paul McCartney left - John Lennon right)

Expelled from the british musician's union.

Tony on Discs-a-Gogo

Tommy has become Tony

THE PIRATE RADIO ERA
(1964 – 16th August 1967)

Radio Caroline North.

Ronan O'Rahilly comes on board.

60's Hippy uniform.

Tony gives Harold Wilson Prime Minister a piece of his mind.

Life on board Radio Caroline North

Live on the Caroline Countdown! Tony broadcasts from Radio Caroline North, Ramsey Bay, Isle of Man.

The DJ air crew Dave Williams, Nick Bailey, Jerry King, Don Allen, Mick Luvzit, Tony Prince and Jerry 'Soopa' Leighton.

Tony and Daffy Don Allen in the Caroline North studio.

There's no escape! The tender's not coming out till Thursday!

The pirate DJ wedding on Caroline North when Mick Luvzit married Jan Terrett live on air.

In 2004 Mick Luvzit staged a pirate reunion in Vancouver.
Back: Mel Howard Radio Scotland & Caroline
Mick Luvzit (Radio Caroline), Bryan Vaughan (Radio Scotland)
Lorne King (Radio London) Front: Steve Young (Caroline),
Tony Prince (Caroline) Ben Healy (Radio Scotland).

14 August 1967 Tony comes ashore with Dave Lee Travis in Ramsey Bay, Isle of Man. At midnight it would become illegal for a British subject to work on the pirate ships, and the real killer, no British company could legally advertise with the pirates after this day.

RADIO LUXEMBOURG
THE GREATEST RADIO STATION IN THE WORLD

The golden 50's on the Station of the Stars when all programmes were recorded in London and sponsored by the record companies themselves.

This copy of the Beatles 'Love Me Do' was played first in the world on Luxy.

The record once lived here in the Villa Louvigny home to 208 & RTL.

Noel Edmonds, the man who 'murdered' my wife!

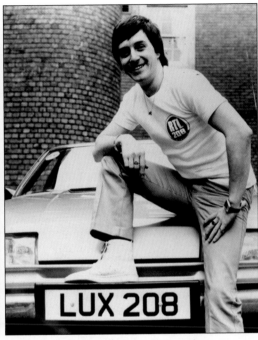

Best number plate in europe?

The Palace of Peachy Platters.

Standing in for John Lennon!

The launch of the Stuart Henry Multiple Scelerosis Appeal

Back Row L to R: *Ed Stewart, Pete Murray, Duncan Johnson, Pete Drummond, Mike Read, Dave Lee Travis.*
Middle Row L to R: *Dave Cash, Noel Edmonds, Richard Skinner, Andy Peebles, Tony Prince, Steve Wright, Anne Nightingale, Tommy Vance, Simon Bates, Keith Skues, Johnny Moran, David Jacobs.*
Front Row L to R: *Paul Burnett, Peter Powell, Tony Blackburn, Stuart Henry, Rob Jones, Alan Freeman.*

The launch of Buddy Holly Week

Paul & Linda McCartney throw a party! The Royal Ruler, seen here with Chistine, hosted the event for ten years. Guests included Eric Clapton, Elton John, Queen, 10CC, Wings, Steve Harley, Patti Boyd, Paul & Linda, Norman & Vi Petty and many luminaries of the UK music industry.

Happy Days

When Tony proposed to her on air, Christine made him promise never to do anything like that again.
Here they are having married in the Oldham town centre. In 2017 they'll have been married for 47 years,
nine of which were spent in Luxembourg with their two wonderful car washers, Daniel and Gabrielle.

Radio Luxembourg team players.

Tony Prince, Paul Burnett, Dave Christian, Mark Wesley, Bob Stewart, Kid Jensen.

Bob Stewart, Kid Jensen, Tony Prince,
Dave Christian, Peter Powell, Mark Wesley.

Barry Alldis, Mike Hollis, Bob Stewart, Tony Prince,
Rob Jones, Stuart & Ollie Henry, Benny Brown.

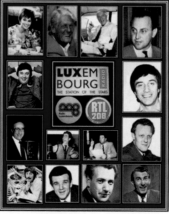

208's first live team:
Paul Burnett, Tony Prince,
Dave Christian, Kid Jensen,
Noel Edmonds.

First and second generation Luxy DJs.

Barry Aldiss, Start Henry, Chris
Carey, Bob Stewart, Mark Wesley,
Tony Prince, Peter Powell.

Sex Pistols in Luxembourg studio.   Cliff Richard in Luxy HQ.   Tony & Elvis in Vegas.

Tony photobombs the ABBA Awards.   Billy Idol joins the Royal Ruler at a Fab 208 Party.

Gaggle of girls outside 208's London HQ: Mary Stavin (Miss World) Britt Ekland, Patti Boulaye and Suzi Quatro. Flanked by promo men Willie Morgan and Gary Farrow.   Donny Osmond on tour.

THE ELEVEN BLESSED UK ELVIS FANS IN 1972

Tony's badges adorning his trousers said 'Elvis & the Colonel say 'Have a nice day'! He certainly did! The NME trophy is in Graceland's Trophy Room together with a photo of Tony & Todd Slaughter.

In 1973 Tony took Christine to meet the King.

The trophy ice bucket.

JAN'S CZECHOSLOVAKIA

Stalin's monument in Prague.

Now you see it... now you don't!

Dad with the Dachau wireless.

Jan's brave mother.

Uncle Joseph in UK.

Jan and sister Jarka.

Katka, Jan's first love.

Young Jan and his father.

Learning English (Jan on the right).

Summer camp July 1963.

Transistor radio and German nudist article shared with the mystery girl by the lake.

The good boy.

The Railway DJ on the wrong track!

Jan moving mountains in the High Tatras.

Pavel Váně chased by
Russian tanks.

Michal Bukovič, the boy with the
record collection.

Jan's parents survived
concentration camp.

Radek Rettegy (left) singing in the army in 1963.

Jan in the army railway division

Plain paper letter from
Voice of America.

The postcard from London.

Jan's DJ Certificate

Original Poster.

Spinning in Brno's Bav Club.

Tram ride in Prague.

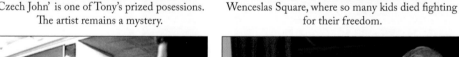

208 disc-jockey TONY PRINCE has just completed an eight-city personal appearance tour of Czechoslovakia — the first Radio Luxembourg personality ever to appear behind the Iron Curtain. Tony is pictured in Prague's famous Wenceslas Square during a break in his itinerary.

'Czech John' is one of Tony's prized posessions. The artist remains a mystery.

Wenceslas Square, where so many kids died fighting for their freedom.

Jan & František Jemelka welcome Tony to Brno minutes after his arrival.

The Railway DJ joins the Royal Ruler at the 2015 Luxembourg Reunion.

were not just enjoying the music we were harvesting our questions for our classmates.

The psychologist asked me why I hadn't entered university and had decided on the railway as my vocation?

"According to your test results," he proclaimed, "You would do very well at University."

That almost floored me. My eyes started to go moist and I had to get a grip on my emotions. We discussed my failed attempt at the University of Agriculture and the likely reasons I failed. He then suggested I apply to the University of Transportation, which had been founded in the Slovakian city of Žilina as recently as 1960.

He explained that as the university was in a small Slovakian city, not many students were eager to study in a lost corner of the country. He gave me high hopes and renewed my confidence, as I already loved Slovakia since my visit to Bratislava a year ago. An attractive advantage was that I then avoided the obligatory two-year military service, because university graduates served only one year, having had military trainings on weekends during the school year.

My parents were as excited and enthusiastic as I was about this proposal. Suddenly in spite of the unfavourable family files, which had so badly impacted on me, at last their son could become an educated man as they had always hoped.

In April I filled in the application form for the University of Transportation, and asked the Director of Cargo Railway Depot to write a letter of recommendation to accompany the application form. He wrote that I was a member of the Socialist Trade Union, a good railwayman who never missed a shift working in a three-shift operation mode, for the benefit of socialist transportation.

Missing a shift was not unusual, as quite often switchmen and shunters arrived half-drunk, and if there happened to be a check control planned, they were sent home.

Such controls weren't frequent, so it was not an exception, with certain railwaymen working half-drunk, that a number of horrific and serious injuries happened. With this in mind, the shift leader always kept a bottle of rum handy in case of an accident.

Whenever a drunken worker was lying with a leg or arm decapitated, out would come the rum, whereupon the supervisor would be informed the drink had been administered to help them with the shock. Thanks to this system, such unfortunates were saved from the State Insurance refusing to pay compensation, due to it happening whilst under the influence of alcohol.

Some of the switch-turn platforms, where one would revolve an engine or wagon, were 30–40 metres distance from one another, and many times when I had to turn the rear wagon I would jump on its footboard and take a short ride rather than walk. During the night shifts, part of the fun of the job was riding the tracks whilst listening to my transistor radio.

The coldest of winters had finally been shunted away by the blossoms of springtime. Wherever I looked, life seemed just wonderful.

And then I received the notification from the University of Transportation that I had not been accepted. It was hard to take especially as my life would now lead to a full two-year term in the army.

Tony: The Royal Command

One day I got a call from the Palace, the Grand Duke's Chef-de-something or other asked if I was capable of transforming their palace ballroom into a discotheque?

Our lovely Luxembourg office secretary, Jose, was more excited than me once she learned to whom I was talking, and what the subject matter was.

"The ballroom's no problem," I said. "But you need atmosphere and people who wanna party if you want a real discotheque. Who's going to be there?"

"Well, let me see," he began, "It's Princess Marie Astrid's birthday celebration and her guests are coming from far and wide. Your very own Prince Charles has been invited..."

I couldn't wait to tell Christine!

"You'd do better having a barn dance by the sounds of things," I laughed.

I arranged free equipment from Mike Chen, a local hi-fi dealer, and a devout royalist from China.

In the afternoon we went to the Grand Duke's principle residence, Berg Castle in Colmar-Berg, and set the rig up as two scruffy girls came to watch me doing the sound check.

"Do you work here?" I asked.

"No, this is Princess Marie Astrid!" answered the second girl, causing me to immediately fall to my knees.

"Forsooth your majesty," I said, head bowed and begging her pardon. The birthday girl and her friend's laughter echoed around the empty ballroom. As we exchanged pleasantries, I learned that the second girl, far from working at the palace, was the daughter of the deposed King of Romania, one of a couple of hundred royals in Luxembourg for the bash!

"We all listen to you in Bucharest," she said. I pretended I knew where Bucharest was and continued with my sound check.

The Grand Duke's Chef Des Affaires came by, pleased that I'd rounded up the gear at such short notice.

"Forgive me Mr Prince," he began pulling me to one side, "I forgot to ask how much we might owe you for your services?"

"Nothing, it's my birthday gift for the Princess," I said. "But I would like my wife to accompany me if that would be acceptable?"

That night Christine and I waited for the 9pm charge when the guests, all seated in the adjoining dining room, were scheduled to finish their Fondue Bourguignon, a Swiss invention with long forks, dipping dishes, boiling oil and cubes of best fillet mignon.

The first time we made one for Kid, he went around with a fork tattoo on his bottom lip for a week, not appreciating you don't eat the meat directly off the fondue fork!

The old Luxembourg Riesling must have been good, it was 10pm when the large double doors opened and I struck out with the Beatles *Twist and Shout*. I couldn't believe it; some couples started doing a foxtrot.

The former King of Romania's daughter waltzed over to us. I introduced her to Christine who said, "Is Charles here then?"

"No" she confided, bending down to browse through my records. "He's tired of the press making a romantic liaison between him and Marie Astrid!"

"Was there one?" I asked curiously.

"Are you kidding," she answered leaning up handing me a record to play. "She wants thrilling, not killing!!"

Christine and I looked at one another, both feeling a pang of hurt for our nation.

I played *In the Summertime* by Mungo Jerry, a challenging rhythm at the best of times for ordinary clubbers, and quite confusing for this lot.

My royal audience went apeshit doing tangos, quicksteps, twists and shakes, whilst the Spanish contingency somehow managed to dance flamenco. It was an extraordinary sight. Today it would have had 30 million YouTube hits!

A man with a familiar face, who I couldn't quite place, approached the DJ console.

"I think you're extremely generous Mr Prince," he said shaking my hand, "Or should I call you the Royal Ruler?"

Then it hit me. I'd only seen him on bank notes and postage stamps until this moment. I was shaking hands with His Royal Highness the Grand Duc of Luxembourg, a *real* Royal Ruler!

Once again I got down on one knee bowing my head so to avert my gaze from his holiness.

"Get up you silly kipper!" said Christine, also shaking his hand.

"Kipper?" said the Duke finding one of the few English words not in his vocabulary.

"Herring sir," replied Christine. "Or is it mackerel?"

"Poison sir," I ventured, turning the volume down so we could hear each other better. "Eaten in parts of Great Britain for breakfast and smothered in butter!"

"Have you ever eaten haggis, I was once 'treated' to it in Balmoral," he laughed screwing up his nose.

"Haven't got the stomach for it myself sir!" I said turning to cross-fade into Desmond Decker's the *Israelites*.

Blue blood is easily identified by their immaculate manners and an ability to hold conversation for ages about absolutely nothing. In Oldham the only etiquette training I ever had was Mum's, *'Say PLLEEEZE Tommy!'* The royals can disarm anyone with their charm.

"May I bring you a drink?" asked Grand Duc Jean.

At my parties, I'd just tell people where the bar was and to help themselves. Here in his palace, with butlers in long socks, balancing silver trays on three fingers wherever you looked, this wonderful man returned personally carrying two glasses of white wine.

He then excused himself as he had promised his wife, the Grand Duchess, a dance. "I hope you might be playing the Beatles later," he said smiling.

A hundred royals coasted by doing the Valetta to Chairman of the Board's *You've Got Me Dangling On A String*!

"I bet Philip wouldn't have got us a drink!" said Christine after the Duke had left.

In the end I did get paid for Astrid's party after a fashion, as my dear wife nicked one of the glasses. Well it did sport the Duchy's coat of arms and the Grand Duc's fingerprints were all over it. What a momentous memento.

At midnight, the royal mob started to pass out or slow down.

A man with a Germanic accent asked me, "You avenzee Blue Danube?"

"No, but I know one you'll like," and off he trotted happy as Larry as I played Edwin Starr's *War*!

Princess Marie came over to us next.

"Take no notice of him he's an old fashioned Count!"

I didn't say a word.

Jan: The lyric translator

At home I would puzzle over the English lyrics, to put them together as complete as possible for František Jemelka, until we got together completing the songs.

There was never a better way to learn a language.

Sometimes also Pavel Váně and his childhood friend guitarist and singer, Jan Sochor, came to consult with us over lyrics, just several months before their big break came along.

The biggest rock star in Brno was Radek Rettegy, and I was quite proud to help him with his English lyrics. Imagine someone like Bobby Darin in the USA, Cliff Richard in the UK or Johnny Hallyday in France; Radek was our version.

I'd admired Radek since I was a kid. In1958 I was on my way to visit my aunt passing through the Kartouzská Street park, when I noticed a bunch of youngsters gathered around a 15-year-old Radek who was playing guitar and singing rock 'n' roll songs in English.

Being a timid 10-year-old kid I didn't dare impose myself onto strangers, even though they were mostly young girls, so I viewed the scene from a safe distance.

In those moments Radek awoke in me the greatest gift I have ever been given. His music busking would influence my entire life and, even though the lyrics went way over my head, I knew that I was witnessing something very special.

Without realising it at that time because nothing of this nature existed, I found myself watching my very first open-air free rock concert. Admittedly a one-artist show, but what an artist! And what friends we would become in the years ahead.

I felt a rush of excitement, kid-sized adrenaline, knowing immediately that this guitar man was singing the same type of songs that I heard fading in an out on foreign radio stations whenever I played with the dial on our old wireless. To be able to listen to such songs *live* was so new and exotic, that I just stood there mesmerised.

All of a sudden, as I stood there enjoying this moment, Radek stopped singing the English rock 'n' roll song and just continued strumming his guitar, whilst looking in my direction.

So I thought that maybe my presence was not welcomed, and as I turned to leave, I looked up to see two old men behind me who had also stopped to watch Radek.

I stopped to stare at them in surprise, when they suddenly turned and disappeared over the hill. In my child's eyes I had learned something important about rock 'n' roll. It was better to keep it for young people, otherwise Radek would not perform!

From this time onwards, I looked forward to running my mother's errands to and from my aunt's, hoping once again to find Radek performing his rock 'n' roll concert in Kartouzská Park.

A few months later whilst playing ice hockey in a Brno youth hockey match, I noticed one player in a team of younger boys, who looked a lot like someone I had seen once or twice at Radek´s concerts.

He was Luboš Rettegy, Radek´s brother and once I'd established a rapport with him, I always had a front seat at Radek´s shows.

It was once I'd become a close friend to Radek and Luboš, that I learned we had to be watchful whenever playing and singing rock 'n' roll music in the open air. If an older person showed an interest, they could very well be State Secret Police informers.

One afternoon, two Public Safety police came towards us, but as we had already noticed them from a distance, Radek switched quickly to a popular Czech tune.

The two cops started to interrogate us about what songs were being played and when Radek answered "Czech favourites sir," they asked if he also performed foreign songs, as they believed young people admired foreign songs? Radek had a brilliant response.

"You are right sir, there are some great foreign songs!"

As the smug-looking cops watched, Radek struck a chord on the guitar and launched into *Katusha* a famous Soviet song, which we had all been forced to learn at school. Now we all joined in with Radek on the chorus, singing our hearts out and laughing.

The cops left without a smile, glancing back sternly, until they disappeared out of the park.

"You see everyone," said Radek, "You didn't waste your time learning Russian songs in school!"

Thanks to his quick wit, for which he became quite famous, Radek Rettegy ridiculed Public Safety cops with their own weapon, when he started that famous Soviet love story about a girl called Katusha, who was in love with a soldier guarding the Soviet Union. During the war, Katusha´s lover was defending the Soviet borders against Nazi troops, but later the lyrics were adjusted to defend the borders against Imperialists and their culture.

This time the Soviet song had helped us to defend rock 'n' roll against two stupid Public Safety cops, and it was my indoctrination into the rock 'n' roll society that paved the way for so much ahead of me.

As for Radek, there is a strong comparison and timing between his story and that of the Beatles. He was auditioning guitar players for his first group at the park in Kartouzská Street, around the same time that John Lennon was being introduced to Paul McCartney by their mutual friend Ivan Vaughn. This was the historic Woolton audition of 1957, when the Quarry Men was formed.

It was quite a different matter for Radek to discover like-spirited rock 'n' roll players, than it was for John Lennon. John would ask if they knew any Chuck Berry riffs, Radek's questioning had to be very careful indeed when he auditioned musicians for Orion, his first group.

There are quite a few things Radek had in common with the Beatles. Yet whilst they made enormous contributions to music, not one of them ever faced off against the Secret Police in defence of rock 'n' roll like he did that day. It was an event I witnessed and is something which still bring tears to my eyes when I consider such audacity and bravado, in the face of all the evil those cops stood for.

His great Radek Park Shows ended in 1962 when he had to leave for two years military service which he spent in Poprad, Slovakia, in the most faraway part of Czechoslovakia, right on the Soviet Union border.

Just as Radek arrived for military duty, the army officers received orders that soldiers had to be given cultural activities, instead of drinking their lives away in their down time. Radek used this to orchestrate an army group, which led to him taking over the hall created to indoctrinate the soldiers into the eternal friendship with mother Russia, and the Soviet fight for world peace.

Whilst his concerts featured only ideologically harmless songs under the scrutiny of the officers, in rehearsal time he and the group could let it rip. For two years, Radek rehearsed a western style set for the great day when he would be unleashed into the world outside the army and, eventually he hoped, beyond the Iron Curtain and the grip of communism.

Tony: The murder

As the British nation appreciates, Noel Edmonds likes a laugh. But it was in 1968 when we were part of his very first Gotcha for which, I may add, we never received a trophy, as did his television subjects!

One of Noel's girlfriends was an Australian waitress, who shared the bar with Christine at the Club 31.

The relationship had reached the fractious stage, and once again Noel wanted out, but she wasn't going easy. Noel was becoming slightly neurotic about women who didn't want to let him back into the playground.

At this time he was sharing an apartment with Kid Jensen, and on this night we'd been thrown out of the Club 31 and Paul Burnett, Christine and I had ended up back at their place.

We were listening to Kid on the graveyard shift, so-called because it ended at 3.00am, and he had to walk home through the darkened rues right past a graveyard.

It was 2.30am and he was playing *MacArthur Park* by Richard Harris when Noel hatched the plot.

"Let's make out I've gone off my rocker and killed her," he said, with reference to the clinging vine barmaid.

"Christine's in the same outfit and can pretend to be the body!"

It seemed feasible, quite mad, but feasible.

At the offset it was simple, Christine lying facedown, her head hidden beneath the bed with a knife, (exhibit A), placed strategically covered in tomato ketchup.

As the set began to build, I suggested Noel fake his own suicide putting his head in the oven, gas tap turned on, so Kid got a view and a whiff as soon as he opened the door.

We went over the top with the ketchup, ruining Christine's uniform, turned a chair or two over and put a picture askew on the wall.

It was 3am and Kid was playing the closing theme, *At the end of the day*, when two things happened to contribute to the authentication of our stage set.

First their temperamental central-heating system, an AGA-style stove in the living room-come bedroom, blew up. Black snowflakes rained down on us.

Moments later, I peered out of the window and spied Kid hotfooting it past the cemetery at the bottom of the rue.

In the kitchen Noel, fiddling with the oven knobs to release sufficient gas for authenticity, stumbled and knocked over the chip pan filled with Flora. The kitchen floor was now completely swathed in two litres of oil!

Now with such ominous influences on our stage, there was no way anyone opening that door would not be convinced that something of extraordinary proportions had taken place.

Beneath the bed, Christine shivered with fear.

The front door down the stairs opened.

We took our positions, Noel skated and slipped arse over bosom on the oil. Fumbling to his knees, we placed a cushion on the oven's lower grill bar on which to rest his dead head. Burnett and I then skated across the room like Torville and Dean as we made to hide in the kitchen's adjoining shower cubicle.

All our clothes, saturated in oil and ketchup, were now beyond the help of cleaners.

Now Noel laid his sniggering head on the pillow, trying to avoid death by gas inhalation. Kid arrived at the top of the stairs.

Inside the shower, behind the cheap plastic curtain, Burnett and I cupped our mouths like two school kids, lest we exposed ourselves with fits of laughter.

Inside the apartment the gas hissed sibilantly in the now stony, silent room. A floorboard creaked outside the door, and a key turned in the lock.

My eyes were watering from stifled mirth and gas fumes. Beneath the bed, Christine regretted deeply having agreed to this role. She bit her free hand and held her breath, trying to avoid going into spasms, as the door finally creaked open.

Kid's suspicion intoned voice split our united silence.

"Noel?"

His first view was the kitchen scene, the oil, the hissing gas, Noel at peace.

"NOEL?" he called nervously.

Then, the door opened wide, the lounge-come-bedroom covered in soot, the upturned chair, a picture askew on the wall, the blood and...the body, all came into the terrified DJ's view.

There was one more "Noel!" but it was from a dry throat, and in too high a key and almost inaudible. This was the point when Kid retreated throwing himself back down the stairs at three steps a time.

Inside the oven Noel, quite convincingly, continued his dying role. In the shower cubicle Paul and I looked at each other, both standing our station, not sure if we had translated the sounds of Kid's retreat correctly?

Our eyebrows arched not quite comprehending how Kid could leave his flatmate dying like this. This wasn't quite what any of us had imagined, but then there was no telephone in the flat, no one around at 3.10am and Kid's instinct, (don't knock it until you've been in a Noel 'Gotcha' of this proportion!), was to run out into the street and call for help!!

Burnett and I jumped out of the shower, colliding with a groggy Noel on the skating rink tiled floor.

Stumbling down the stairs, we ran out into the rue, the three of us yelling to Kid in as much of a whisper as we could muster, so as not to wake the neighbourhood.

Kid's reply wasn't a whisper.

"You FUCKERS!" he yelled from the middle of the road, as lights went on in windows around the rue.

It took Noel, Paul and I three hours to clean the flat.

Kid and Christine drank tea together watching us at work, waiting to stop their shaking.

Eventually I had to ask the question we all wanted to ask, "Why didn't you try to save Noel?"

"Save that murdering little swine?" answered our Canadian colleague.

Noel had been employed by a new Programme Controller, Australian DJ Tony McArthur, who went on to manage Charles Aznavour much better than he'd managed us.

But the Managing Director Geoffrey Everett, himself a former Luxembourg DJ from as far back as the 40s, for reasons only he knew, did not like Noel Edmonds.

Already Noel had almost been fired by Geoffrey, when he corpsed in the middle of a serious news bulletin about the outbreak of typhoid in Italy, where people had died, and hundreds had been hospitalised.

Then came the trip-wire.

"Authorities believe they have traced the source of the outbreak to an ice-cream vendor who has been washing his utensils in the Po!"

His weather forecast contained gales of laughter.

Hey... whose crazy idea was it to have us read serious news bulletins anyway? Tony McArthur that's who! Get rid of the resident newsreader Paul Kaye, and bring in another full time DJ. Enter Noel Edmonds.

"I'm not going to be a DJ all my life," Noel once confided in me in a state of inebriation caused by Christine's generous replenishments in Club 31.

"You're pissed," I suggested just as he fell off the barstool.

A few weeks later, unable to survive Everett's constant scrutiny and old school broadcasting ideals, Noel was invited to leave Luxembourg, walking from one Everett shadow, into a much bigger one.

Kenny Everett had been sacked by the BBC for suggesting, after a news bulletin, that an MP's wife had slipped the instructor a fiver to pass her driving test! Nobody gave Noel a dog's chance; how could anyone follow Kenny, the zaniest DJ in history?

But big shoes that needed filling were filled. Noel increased the audience by so many and so quickly, he was catapulted to stardom and the nation's most prestigious programme, the Radio 1 Breakfast Show.

Noel Edmonds murdered the ratings quicker than he murdered my wife!

Forgiving him for chasing me naked around Radio Caroline's engine room, I helped Bob Stewart to get a job on 208, which lasted him 20 years. Dave Christian was the next to augment the team, together with Mark Wesley. And so we ran for a number of years, apart from Roger Day who came from Radio England, (a pirate ship that floated up the Thames estuary *after* the Marine Offences Act, too late for battle).

After just four weeks' trial with the station, Roger decided to write to Geoff Everett telling him precisely what was wrong with Radio Luxembourg.

The boss replied with a return ticket to London!

Geoff Everett was a tyrant.

He'd arrived in Luxembourg in 1946 as a Royal Engineer to help restructure the Luxembourg army.

Once there he befriended Stephen Williams, Radio Luxembourg's resident British announcer. When the British Army football team arrived in the Grand Duchy, Williams called on Arsenal devotee Everett to do some interviews.

Geoff scored big, married a Luxembourg girl, and eventually ran the station through its precious years in the 50s and early 60s.

This was the man who came up with the novel idea of a radio show featuring the Top 20 (based originally on the best selling sheet music sales), which he launched on Sunday nights as far back as 1948.

Although he acceded to a live team after the pirates, Everett couldn't break the station's old habit of taking paid-for-plays from the record labels. Worse still, he encouraged record companies to give the station's music publishing company, (Louvigny Marquee), B-side publishing.

Once the company had acquired the B-side, we had to play it as often as possible so that every time the record sold, the publishing company copped a royalty.

We had the Power Play, right after the news, another Tony McArthur creation, which elevated him to deity level with Geoffrey Everitt.

Tony McArthur wasn't with us long, but he left a mucky thumbprint on the station. Every label wanted the Power Play and many gave up their B-side publishing to get it!

It gets worse! Everett had his own publishing company, Shaftesbury Music which, quite unbeknown to the directors of RTL based in Luxembourg, also accessed our playlist on a regular basis. I'm afraid we mere DJs didn't fully grasp our bosses' money-lust and their inability to match our own love for radio and great music.

Lord Reith, Phil Solomon and Geoffrey Everett, were businessmen who all ran into radio by accident. Not one of them cared a red cent for pop music.

What really hurt was when you heard great DJs like the Emperor Rosko playing the Dubliners' *7 Drunken Nights* or Kid Jensen having to introduce Ken Dodd's *Tears*.

Jan: Teenage freedom

The thought of missing out on the chance of a university education didn't preoccupy me, the bigger problem for me was that now there would be nothing left to do, but leave Brno for two years of army duty in God knows where?

With two months to go, I made the decision to dedicate this time to my tape recorder and my transistor radio tuned constantly to either Luxy or Radio Caroline. I shared a lot of time with my like-minded friends, solving lyric riddles that we did mostly by Brno Lake, the perfect place to spend warm summer days.

I still had to go to work that was made less bearable on pleasant warm days knowing that almost everybody, especially lucky students, were by the lake. At that time Eddie Cochran kept my spirit high with his song *Summertime Blues*, as some of the words fitted my situation perfectly.

I'm gonna raise a fuss, I'm gonna raise a holler
About a workin' all summer just to try to earn a dollar

Well my mom and pop told me, 'Son you gotta make some money'
'If you want to use the car to go ridin' next Sunday'

It was incredible how Eddie's lyrics described my situation almost perfectly.
It was, for example, only a year ago that my father had started urging me to
start thinking about finding work to earn my living. My father could not,
however, have ever lent me his car, because he never had one.
And then there was another line which related directly to my life which
went, '*Well I didn't go to work, told the boss I was sick.*'
     One hot August night shift, I took my usual wagon ride to the next
switch turn, when jumping down in the darkness, I stepped on a stone
and sprained my ankle. As I could hardly move, I asked my colleagues to
take over my duties and limped along to the office building to be the first
one there to see the depot doctor in the railway health centre when he
would come in the morning. He asked me what had happened? Thinking
quickly, because I should not have been riding the wagon, I explained that
I'd slipped on a piece of coal that must have fallen from a wagon, and I'd
had no chance to notice it in the dark. Then he wondered how come I was
wearing a pair of tennis shoes instead of the metal tipped safety shoes we
were provided with, and ordered to wear at all times?
     Again I reacted quickly, saying that I changed them before coming to see
him, as the swelling made almost impossible to have the solid boots on.
I didn't dare tell him that I always wore tennis shoes that suited my daily
bike ride to and from the depot. And so it was reported by the doctor, that
I had suffered an occupational injury, which was a relief because now I
would be paid *more* than my usual salary, as everything was calculated on
your average earning, including your overtime.
     The doctor treated my ankle with cream, which the nurse then bandaged
and sent me to x-ray, where it was identified as a sprain. Then they sent me
home for two weeks on full pay, and off I trotted, with a pronounced limp
in case the health-police were watching me, to the lake.
Now there were no *Summertime Blues* at all.
There was a slight danger that someone from Cargo Depot Health Control
might come to make sure I was following doctor's orders, to remain calm at
home so I would be fit again, as soon as possible. But I told myself to hell
with such controls, I had been working like a dog for almost a year on the
railways, risking my life daily and now with less than two months before
I joined the army, I needed to get into shape and this could not be done
at home during this warm summer. The shape I needed was more mental
than physical, and a swollen ankle's best place was lying in the grass or
swimming in the lake. It's amazing how the mind becomes so much more
relaxed looking at all the pretty girls.

So for the first time, I was cheating our communist bosses, just as they had cheated us by sending our precious uranium ore to the Soviet Union, instead of selling it to the west, which could make Czechoslovakia rich. There existed a cheating culture throughout our Soviet-controlled country and I'd now become part of it, whether it was crashing wagons so coal escaped, changing your nightshift so your colleagues could cheat on his wife, or lie by the lake in the sunshine on full pay with a not-so-dodgy ankle.

I understood the cheating culture, it gave you a sense of freedom, of victory, a feeling that you edged closer to the flower-power community Scott McKenzie sang about in his song *San Francisco (Be Sure to Wear Some Flowers in Your Hair)*.

Our local music-loving society embraced the hippy, music spirit of 'Frisco every late evening in the garden of U Šuláka, a pub hidden by a forest above the lake. Guitars rang out to the vocals of developing and established local stars, Radek Rettegy, Pavel Váně and Míša Polák and other members of Synkopy 61, entertained us.

František Jemelka tested the impact of his lyrics here whilst strumming out his creations, whilst others belted out current popular songs we'd heard on Radio Luxembourg's Top Twenty Show. I sat contentedly knowing I had contributed to the refining of the lyric translation.

Now was a time of quiet before the storm. The Public Safety cops left us alone as, unbeknown to us, a political tsunami was about to engulf us all.

After two weeks of these wonderful days and nights, I visited hospital once again to get my ankle checked, and when the doctor told me that it all looked fine and I could return to work, I made my case for the weakness I still felt and that after two weeks of non-movement, to suddenly place weight on the ankle might cause further harm.

"What is your job?" he asked me for the first time.

"I'm a switchman and occasional shunter," I replied. "I ride and dodge between 80 ton wagons and engines."

That's when he gave me another week off on full pay, and when I entered the greatest time of my teenage years. This three-week period stayed with me all my life; it was quite simply, teenage freedom

Tony: The stripper

One evening Christine and I were peckish. After 1am it was difficult to get a meal in Luxembourg, the city that *always* slept.

It might be different now with all the European Parliament and EEC and Banking fraternity ensconced there. But back then, after 1am, you either went home and fried some chips, or went to a local strip-club for a croque monsieur.

"Have you guys ever had a cheese fondue," asked my friend John Paul Gallé, whose father owned the Hertz rent-a-car franchise for Luxembourg, and subsequently drove around town in a white Mercedes saloon.

We adored JP's wealth and he, in turn adored our wild lifestyle.

"Get your passports," he urged. "We're going over the border."

The border in Luxembourg was 50 miles to Belgium, Germany or France.

We arrived in France as John Paul mysteriously chuckled.

By the French city Nancy, both Christine and I had fallen asleep.

At dawn we awoke at the foot of a snow-covered Swiss glacier, *Les Diablerets*!

In a chalet restaurant at the foot of the mighty snow-covered mountain, not far from where Jean Paul had been sent to boarding school, we ordered his fabled cheese fondue for breakfast.

"Just a cuppa tea and toast for me," said Christine, whose body clock understood it was Sunday morning.

To our host's chagrin, I hated the bread and cheese dip and ordered a coutlette de pork and chips.

We swung round and returned to Luxembourg without stopping for breath, or the Lake Lausanne or Monte Blanc, the Matterhorn and the Eiger, all of which received a cursory glance in the distance.

Jean Paul Gallé, what a daft sod he was, we absolutely loved him.

We took over the Chez Nous nightclub, a strip joint owned by Paulie, an affable French man with whom I did a deal. In exchange for bringing our pop star guests whenever they came to town, together with our rather large band of Luxembourg friends, everyone got free admission.

Better still, whenever I sang with the Jempy 4, the resident band, drinks were on the house.

Accordingly DJ's Kid Jensen, Paul Burnett and Mark Wesley became my backing singers as we medlied our way through Ray Charles' *What'd I say*, Jerry Lee's *Mean Woman Blues* and Eddie Cochran's *20 Flight Rock*.

This may sound arrogant but... we received a standing ovation every time. You could understand why when you heard what the Jempy 4 normally played!

Night after night I finished this rock 'n' roll act in the Chez Nous and sometimes in the town's other hot spot, Charley's Bar, singing whilst standing on my head. This became my party trick through life, but back then it saved me and the other jocks a fortune in free drinks.

'Free' in these Luxembourg venues was a big saving because drinks were proportionally priced to subsidise the cabaret, which included the month's guest strippers with whom, if they could speak English, we became great friends.

There were half a dozen such night-clubs in Luxembourg but Paulie had the Radio Luxembourg DJ's in his pocket and enjoyed packed houses with revellers such as Phil Lynot, Jimi Hendrix, Ian Gillan, Elton John, Status Quo, the Beach Boys, Keith Moon, John Lord, Freddie Mercury, Tony Ashton, Steve Harley, Neil Sedaka. The list went on, and we sang rock 'n' roll with all of them, becoming drunk as lords at the record label's expense!

With no Musicians' Union in Luxembourg, I was always the lead singer. Imagine, Jimi Hendrix on guitar, Moon on drums, Johnny Gustafson (Big Three/Quatermass) on bass, the Royal Ruler hogging the mic! I just couldn't be stopped. The MU had failed to keep me away from the microphone. The act always ended with me standing on my head, doing the last chorus of *What'd I Say*.

I just wish iPhones and YouTube had been around back then to capture what must have been some amazing party nights, when so many legends came out to play with us.

Some nights the visiting record pluggers and their artists would come back to our place with the strippers, who'd give us repeat performances right there in our living room. When this happened during one of my mother and father's visits my dad Frank thought he'd died and woke up in heaven.

My colleague, Mark Wesley, filmed that particular party, and I've now got a digital copy of my dad's beaming face framed within a discarded bejewelled bra!

One night, having had an excessively delicious meal at the expense of Phonogram's plugger Tim Knight and Thin Lizzy's Phil Lynot, they joined us for a late night romp.

Tiger Lily, a voluptuous German stripper had arrived for her month at the Chez Nous. She performed on a draped round dais, like an elephant would stand on in the circus. Whipping herself throughout her strip, she ended her performance laid naked across the dais, her stomach pumping air, her skin lacerated with whip welts. The dais was rolled ceremoniously to the centre of the small dance floor, Tiger Lily standing in the corridor ready for her entrance, looking like Boadicea with her enormous tasselled brassiere.

The lights went down momentarily, and a voice like Lord Haw Haw introduced her in German, French and English, giving me sufficient time and cover to sneak beneath the dais.

The archaic striptease music began as the solitary spotlight sought out the redheaded fraulein, who now danced onto the floor to applause and ribald calls in various tongues.

Beneath the dais I parted the drape and gave the V sign to Lynot, moving back into hiding each time her legs came into view.

Tiger didn't get it; she'd never had an audience laughing before.

Every time she dropped a garment, I dragged it beneath the podium, the laughter level rising each time until, finally, I grabbed her knickers in and quickly threw them out again.

Her act ended with her totally naked body sprawled above me, whipping herself with a cat-o-nine-tails, her mound of Venus pointing in a V directly at Phil Lynot, who was wet-eyed with laughter.

A last fanfare from her tape indicated her act had ended but tonight, not quite. Putting my back into the job, like a snail in a shell, I lifted my housing and walked her off the dance floor naked on the dais.

Once we were out of the spotlight, with an exhausted Tiger sprawled out and confused, her erect, red nipples pointing at the ceiling, I made my escape.

Unfortunately, however, she still had some reserves of energy and chased me round the club three times until I darted out into the street. Still she came for me, holding her whip above her head her naked bosoms bouncing navel to chin, a wonderful sight for the few late night passersby.

Two weeks later Roger Glover and Ian Gillan of Deep Purple came out for Jensen's Dimensions, and I was encouraged to repeat the joke. This time Tiger threw a number of glasses at me.

People wonder why I always smile whenever I hear Lulu's *I'm a Tiger*!

Christine was pregnant with our son Daniel, who'd finally made his way up the fallopian to claim his place on Earth. We'd decided Christine would return to Oldham to give birth as we had little faith in Luxembourg hospitals after an incident, where Christine had failed to kill me, but had managed to gash her foot trying to kick a glass door in my face in our apartment.

I'd carried her bleeding through the hospital doors and a very large nun was taking her away for stitches when Christine, scared stiff of the approaching needlework said, "Darling please don't leave me!"

"Ah! Darling!" said the daughter-of-Christ mimicking Christine's despair.

"Right then," I said lifting her off the trolley.

"Where you go?" cried the nun, as Christine dripped blood across the marble reception area.

"I'll stitch it myself!" I cried.

A tourniquet, and lashings of 12 year old Johnny Walker Black Label disinfectant, and she was as right as rain.

So Daniel would be born in England, in Oldham Boundary Park, just like all his ancestors.

Apart from the nun incident, I wasn't keen on him being born in Luxembourg, because then he would be known as a Luxembourger, which sounded a bit too much like a Big Mac for my liking. British he would be, a thoroughbred Lancastrian at that!

To celebrate our good fortune, we took off for a day by the Moussel River, planning to cross into Germany for lunch. It was a beautiful European summer's day as we headed for Trier.

Reaching the bridge to the Fatterland a small, smiling, Luxembourg customs officer saluted us gingerly without asking for our Carte de Identity. "He looks happy," commented Christine.

Over the bridge his German counterpart was not so happy, a sour Kraut, in fact who wanted us to pay for a 24-hour green card insurance for the car to enter his republic.

Discovering that there was nowhere to change our Belgian francs into their paper, we parked the car and walked back across the bridge, enjoying the sunshine and admiring the view and the vineyards that stretched for miles down the Mousel river.

The little Luxy Duane one was waving everyone through with a flourish. Christine was right, he had a perpetual grin.

Up close to him I discovered his secret, Henry Funk, a popular Luxembourg ale.

Then an amazing thing happened.

In broken French, I explained our need for change waving Luxembourg monopoly money at him.

He grabbed the wedge, pulled an antique black bicycle from beside his customs post, and bade us wait whilst he got the Deutschmarks from the village.

Off he went like a man who'd just been given early shore leave.

And that was that.

I was in charge of the border!

Inside the customs hut we sat idly waiting, when I noticed he had left his rather splendid custom's hat.

Outside a horn sounded.

I put on the cap, which didn't really go with my silk superman T-shirt and white bell-bottoms, (complimented, I must add, by shiny white Beatle boots). A ginger-haired limey in an English reg Ford Cortina had caused a queue of traffic across the bridge to Germany.

His mouth fell open as I emerged from the hut.

"Veeazit mein leiber junger vonush clift, what's up guv?" I asked in my best Luxy Cockney.

His wife, nearer to me, turned to her husband, "You sure this is Luxembourg Arfur?" she asked, as their three kids on the back seat fought for window space to gaze at me.

"Passports please, sir," I said.

Behind them, the drivers from around Europe wound down their windows. I returned to the hut and relieved myself of laughter.

"You'll get us shot!" said Christine.

Putting on a straight face, I returned to Mr & Mrs Pearson.

An intolerant horn sounded five cars back, I ignored it and waved the Pearson's on.

"Welcome to the land of 208," I said like Luxembourg was a radio station theme park.

"Are you British," asked Mrs Pearson.

"Yes, I'm a Radio Luxembourg DJ, listen tonight I'll play you a record around 8.15pm."

"But," said Mr. Pearson leaning across his wife. "What are you doing running the customs post?"

"Pin money," I explained.

I'd attended to a dozen cars or so waving them in and out of the country, posing for photos and winding everyone up before the real thing reappeared, puffing and blowing up the hill, and triumphantly slapping a handful of Deutschmarks in my hand.

I now understood why he'd been keen to go on the errand for us, the Bureau De Change doubled as a café.

I've never liked the smell of Pernod!

We let ourselves into Germany.

Life in Luxembourg was one party after another. In nine years of residence, Christine and I moved house 10 times. Not to keep up with the Jones's, but to stay one step ahead of the noise abatement society and the Gendarmerie.

Three noise complaints in Luxembourg, and you were history.

Three was too easy, what with the likes of Stan Webb of Chicken Shack, who christened our new carpet being sick, Freddie Mercury who sang opera in our place long before he'd duet with Montserrat Caballé, and our boisterous pilot friends from Air Bahamas, who thought the rules were that they were not allowed to drink 12 feet before a flight, instead of 12 hours!

Elton John arrived with his manager, John Reid, and let the side down. Jensen's Dimensions interview would be his 47th in a 10-country promotional trip. He was knackered and went straight from the plane for a nap at his hotel.

We all wanted to meet him, but he didn't show for dinner.

He came alive for Kid's interview and was then coerced to join the DJ team, all still waiting to meet him, at the heaving Blow Up where he was plonked in a corner, especially reserved for such an omnipotent.

Before the rest of us arrived, he had dozed off again.

I'd never seen anyone sleep so soundly on a 2kwt bass bin, six times their size.

Golly, the resident DJ, tried his best to wake him up as we each competed suggesting the records with the highest decibels. First Led Zeppelin's *Whole Lotta Love*, then Sweet's *Teenage Rampage*, then Slade's *Mama Weer All Crazee Now*.

It was no good, John was gone! We thought we'd got him with Gary Glitter's *Rock and Roll Part 2*.

A twitch, a repositioning of the head, but his lurexed arms remained folded across his sequinned chest, beneath the shadow of his baseball cap, his eyes remained closed.

Paul Burnett almost got him suggesting Rod Stewart's *Shake*.

He stirred, crossed his paisley trousered legs and almost knocked over our bottle of Riesling 71 with his six-inch plinths.

We all sat around waiting to be introduced, but all he did was pull his peak lower over his glittered eyelids sinking further down his bass- bin cushion.

By now, Golly was surrounded by James Brown and Motown fans in mass protest.

"Why you play sheet?" they asked.

"I'll show you how to wake him," said John Reid his manager who made his way to the DJ booth.

"Play Elton's new single Crocodile Rock," he ordered Golly.

"Sorry", said Golly glumly. "Don't have it. I'm not on DJM's mailing list!"

And that was that, Elton got his alarm call.

"C'mon Elton," said Reid shaking him, "It's time for bye-byes!"

We waved him goodbye, without so much as a hello!

Deep Purple's Ian Gillan was much more fun, although in an inebriated moment, he did confide in me that he thought DJs were parasites living on the back of the music. He might have had a point then, but DJs would change his hypothesise dramatically in years to come!

We'd all gathered in the studio for Kid's interview and had invited along our pilot pal, Jake, and his 18-year-old daughter who'd wangled a free trip to Europe from dad.

Twenty minutes before the interview, sitting around the studio, beers flowing freely, Jake's daughter asked for directions to the loo.

Two minutes later, Gillan also went to water the enamel.

"You've only got eight minutes," shouted Kid.

The Gents and Ladies were adjoining rooms at the far end of the corridor, just far enough to run, piddle and wash your hands before a record ended.

As Ian came out of the gents, he couldn't help noticing that the young American girl had absentmindedly left the door to her cubicle open.

She was just reaching for her knickers, skirt pulled up waste high, as the Deep Purple eyed her whilst drying his hands.
She looked up at him mid knicker-pull, and stopped pulling.
"Why not?" said Gillan entering her booth.
The same man who sang *Speed King* was back in the studio in time for the interview!

Jan: First flight

Then came September, and things started to move very quickly. My military draft notice arrived by post instructing me to registerZačátek formuláře
 at the barracks of the railway military unit number 1104 in the city of Olomouc, no later than 2pm on 3 October 1967.

I got a big break, I was posted to Olomouc only 75kms from Brno, and my friends and everyone I discussed it with, told me how fortunate I was to be so close to home, when many were sent to the outer reaches of Czechoslovakia. Some finished up in Slovakia, close to the distant Soviet border, the worst being Košice.

Because of my job, I landed another great break and learned that I was to be posted a railway army unit that, according to those who were experienced in army matters, was so much better than being a part of a combat unit who played at being real soldiers.

For the first time ever, I thanked my ancestors for creating such a bad family record with the commies. This meant that I would not be selected as a reliable soldier, such as those sent to protect the borders, where many young men escaped to the west. Now only those from the most reliable communist families were posted to these great escape hot-spot border posts.

Laďa, my old friend who had changed my life when loaning me his Sonet Duo tape recorder so many times, was drafted to an army-fighting unit as a tank driver. This meant that his family was considered to be more reliable than mine, and his enterprise in becoming a lorry driver had not escaped the attention of the army bosses, as so few recruits had a driving licence.

"Lucky you," I joked. "Driving around the countryside all day long, what a great job!"
Laďa and I had known each other since the age of 6 and had shared many things together. Now he hit on a great idea. With three weeks to go before we entered the army, Laďa suggested we fly for the first time in our lives.
"It's the perfect time for us," said Laďa, "If the plane crashes we will have avoided army duty and cheated the government!"

We bought advance air tickets from Prague to Brno for 60 crowns each and went to Prague by train in the morning, to return by plane in the late afternoon. Sixty crowns was four times more than a train ticket for Lad'a, and a great deal more expensive for me, with my discounted rail fare. But it was still money well spent and we looked forward to our great adventure. We arrived in Prague and before travelling to the airport, I entered a bookshop we were passing and was left breathless, in almost the same way as when I noticed the Chris Andrews single in Supraphon a year back.

On the front shelf were copies of The Joke by Milan Kundera that had been published recently, but not one of my friends in Brno had seen it. We had only heard rumours, that the book was published, but believed it was yet another item reserved for the friends of bookshops, or distributed through the back door system like bananas and tropical fruit, or like chicken and meat which you bought if you knew someone who knew someone.

Kundera´s The Joke was the most sought after book since Sky Riders by Filip Jánský, published two years ago. It was said that The Joke was the very first novel about Czechoslovakia in the early 50s. The hero was a student who was once an enthusiastic Communist Party supporter, but after 1948, certain circumstances turned him into their opposition.

Standing here in the bookshop, it was hard to believe that I had come across the book by accident. Perhaps the rumours were true that supplies and deliveries of everything were much better in Prague than anywhere in Czechoslovakia, as people often complained?

But this was the last thing bothering me as I took two copies and sauntered across to the cashier to pay for a copy for myself, and one for František, who would be over the moon with my gift, as we both had a weakness for Milan Kundera who, like us, was from Brno. Milan went to study in Prague, until eventually the Prague Film Faculty appointed him lecturer in world literature. We also enjoyed very much his first book Laughable Loves. The first poetry book I ever bought was Monologues by Kundera. I had read Monologues again recently, and one particular poem touched me and calmed me down with regard to my coming army duty.

The poem was about a soldier who also had to go for his two-year military service, leaving his girl behind and thinking of her through all the lonely nights in the barracks. After six months he received a letter from a friend back home, breaking the news to him that his girlfriend, Mary, had another man, which was when he took a gun and killed himself.

I was moved and disturbed by this poem, as it might well have been about me, if only I had a girlfriend, but then I reflected that this was not the time to have a girlfriend, which would have made the two years even more intolerable.

The shop assistant told me that because of a short supply, only one copy per person could be bought. So I'd learned the truth, that even in Prague there were supply and demand problems, but I solved the matter quickly as I brought Laďa in from outside to show that we were indeed two people, then she allowed me to buy the two books. The thing about this short supply was that when you succeeded in finding something, your pleasure was more than doubled but in truth, after so many years, it was just a bit too much and we all grew restless, appalled by a system that failed us so badly.

But there were little shoots of hope popping up everywhere now if you looked closely enough. I had, for example, bought a copy of the weekly literary newspaper that contained the speech by Milan Kundera, which he made at the Czechoslovak writers congress. It was designated a whole page, which I read with my mouth open.

In it he asserted that the reason for many recent Czechoslovakian international cultural successes, such as the Oscar winning movie A Shop On The Main Street, and other films by Forman or Menzel was happening because our writers, artists and producers now had much more creative freedom.

He went on to mention that many years ago in a letter to the French philosopher and writer Claude Adrien Helvétius, Voltaire, famous for his wit and advocacy of civil liberties and freedom of expression wrote, '*I disapprove of what you say, but I will defend to the death your right to say it.*'

Here was the first sign of a creeping freedom of speech returning to Czechoslovakia.

We were brought to the airport by the Czechoslovak Airlines bus appreciating every step of our journey, we felt like men of the world, digested into the airport atmosphere on a concourse so dynamic, compared to our railway or bus stations.

After check-in with only hand baggage, a lovely stewardess escorted us to the smallest plane on the forecourt, with a seating capacity of some 20 passengers. There were 10 of us altogether, the others being older men who with their miserable expressions, looked like they could well be communist party bosses. Who else would pay four times more to get to Brno than it would cost them by train? Other than us two of course!

The four-hour train journey from Prague to Brno now took 45 minutes; it was all such a boy's adventure.

The moment I got home I called František to tell him I had found such an amazing gift for him in Prague, that I had taken the plane back to save time, and so we should now meet in our favourite pub as I had so much to tell him. František was delighted with the book and, together with other friends who had gathered with us, contributed more signs of change they had experienced or recognised in our country. By the end of the evening we all agreed that better times were surely just around the corner.

I was only sorry that just as it was starting to improve, I was leaving Brno and all my friends for bloody military service.

"This fresh wind will not miss the army," said František consoling me.

Cula and Došin were part of our gang and had just come back home from their two years military service. To listen to them, you would think the army was the greatest place in the world where you were laughing, fit to burst every day. Došin recalled the frequent military false alarms when within minutes everyone had to be up, dressed and on parade complete with kitbag and gun. Once lined up in the barrack yard, they'd hear the sergeant order them to "ATTENTION!!" and then immediately, "FALL OUT!!" Some nights this would be repeated many times, so some of the soldiers grew wary and started keeping their pyjamas on beneath their uniforms.

Došin did not like being made to look a fool; he was one who didn't change out of his nightwear, and even slipped barefoot into his army boots. It was quite uncomfortable he told us, but he was back in bed and asleep before everyone else.

One bitterly cold winter night the sergeant changed the rules, instead of allowing them back to their beds, after the alarm was over when all the soldiers were counted, they were ordered to jump onto military trucks and went away for a two-week military exercise in the frozen snow-covered Šumava mountains. Sockless and without warm underwear, Došin had to beg and borrow filthy rags from fellow truck driving soldiers, as there was no way he could tell the officers he hadn't been in combat readiness back at the barracks.

Having such authentic first hand reports, I felt like I knew everything I needed to know about the army. Now, with a few days of paid vacation and a three-day leave provided by government so new recruits could sort themselves out, I had 10 free days before leaving home for two years. I dedicated my last free days to listening to music and meeting my friends to discuss matters of common interest.

One evening just prior to my departure, I met a lad in the pub who I knew from my days collecting badges at the railway station, and we started to discuss music. When he discovered I had a tape recorder, he begged me to loan it to him so he could copy the Beatles' *Help*. I hesitated trying to imagine a day without my beloved Sonet Duo, which, with so little time remaining now before I would not be seeing it for a long time, would be torture.

Eventually he offered to also copy the Help LP for me, and I crumbled. As he had no phone, I agreed to meet him with the tape recorder at Red Army Square, which was not far from home. On the dot of noon the

following day he was waiting, so I handed him the tape recorder and a tape
to record the Beatles for me, and we arranged to meet at the same time the
next day when he would return it to me. Just before we parted, I reminded
myself that I didn't know his surname or indeed his address so, although I
found it embarrassing to do so, I asked to see his identity card.

Feeling quite ashamed that I should doubt the integrity of a fellow western
music lover, I noted his surname and didn't bother reading the back pages
for his address. Instead I asked him where he lived just in case he couldn't
come and I had to collect it.

With that we parted company.

The next day I arrived early at our meeting point, as I didn't want the
time, which divided me from listening to the *Help* album, to be a single
second longer than was necessary.

Something was different, yesterday he came to meet me at precisely noon,
today I stood waiting for him. Ten minutes went by, and then half an hour
and he still hadn't showed. Now I'd stopped wishing for the recording, all I
wanted was my Sonet Duo back. When an hour had passed I knew I had
to go to his home as something catastrophic must have happened to him. I
took the tram to his district, quickly found his street and the house he had
indicated without a problem.

Our huge old houses contained many families in studios and apartments,
the doorbell listed the family names. But no matter how thoroughly I read
the list of tenants, the name I had seen in his ID was not listed.

I asked someone leaving the house if they knew him but the answer
was no. I asked others coming and going but none of them knew anyone
who followed his description. I knew that the address was right as it was
a well-known street, and he definitely told me the number was five, which
I remembered because this was my own house number. My stomach
tightened as the impossible started to seem possible. Had he given me a
wrong address? Could it be that a fan of western music could cheat another
such fan, when both were bonded in opposition to our ruling regime?

No true lover of rock 'n' roll ever turned out to be a communist!

I had four days left before going into the army. I quickly met František
admitting I was the fool of the year, no one in the pub where we had met
knew the cheat. There was now little I could do, I'd told the thief that I was
going into the army, so he obviously counted on knowing I would be away
and that, after two years, it would all be impossible to prove anything even
were I to find him.

My Sonet Duo was more than life itself, and I was madder than mad now
so I decided to go to the Public Safety police. But what should I tell them?
That I gave him a tape recorder to make me a copy of the *Help* album?

I was pretty nervous. What remarks might then go onto my file if I was discovered to be distributing western music, and in doing so was cheated by another similar element?

František came up with an idea, the Sonet Duo was too expensive to let matters be, and I should tell Public Safety that the thief was a friend I knew by sight from Brno Lake, and that he'd asked to borrow my tape recorder to record the voice of his mother.

The next morning I went to the local Public Safety unit telling my story to the duty officer and underlined that in just a few days I was leaving to serve my country, so that I would be wearing a uniform soon, just like he was now. He just laughed and was very kind to me and promised, that as I at least knew his surname, he was sure something could be done.

On 3 October 1967 I took a morning train to Olomouc, and in less than two hours I arrived in the ancient city that had the reputation from the olden days expressed in a saying: *If you throw a stone in Olomouc, you hit either a soldier, a whore or a priest.* There had always been numerous army garrisons and churches in the area.

First I was scalped. Then we had to strip naked and put all our belongings in a sack that would wait two years for us. No civilian dress was allowed for soldiers during your entire two years service.

We were kept busy every hour of every day, including Sundays, when there was a slight change of pace as we were shown a Soviet war film, the room in which we viewed this dirge was labelled The Culture Room.

If the day didn't fuck you, the night would. We were billeted in a 40-bedded room and no matter how tired I was, loud snoring woke me up constantly. Then we had the night alarms which Došin had warned me about, so I preferred to dress properly on each occasion, there was no way I was heading to any snow-capped mountains without my socks and underwear!

The reason our rooms were so big was that before the Second World War cavalry troops had been stationed in our barracks, and the rooms were converted from stables. Now instead of horses and riders, we members of the railway army unit lodged there, which explains why the entire garrison was without a single shower. Six hundred sweating, stinking young soldiers and only washbasins with cold water was all they were provided with. Thankfully, after 10 days, we were taken to shower in the municipal baths. We marched down the road in formation seeing girls for the first time in 10 days, Olomouc was also a university city and quite a few pretty girls smiled back at us from the pavement. By the time the boys hit the showers, they could finally stop standing erect!

Then came November and the day of our oath of allegiance to Czechoslovakia, for which my mother and father came from Brno. A lot of bullshit was spoken about how we would be ready to fight for our socialist country, alongside our great supporters, the Soviet Red Army, if called upon to do so. My father, wearing his old 1923 hat seemed proud of me wearing a similar Czechoslovak army hat that he and his brother, Uncle Josef wore before he was expelled from the army, and forced to leave Czechoslovakia forever. Afterwards we all went for a walk together and drank some coffee, where my father for the very first time aired his optimistic views telling me he felt a new political force was coming, one he believed was worthy of me continuing the family tradition of wearing the uniform. It was quite an emotional farewell afterwards as I accompanied them to the railway station and waved them goodbye. I had never loved my parents more than at that moment.

With almost two years of army service remaining, I had to cope with a severe lack of contact with the free world not having heard one minute of Radio Luxembourg or Radio Caroline.

But then, two days later, I received a military order that at the commencement of January 1968 I would go to the city of Nový Bohumín for two month of shunter training. I knew then that my Hitachi transistor radio would be there with me.

Three months without a radio was about all I could stand.

Tony: The gift from Ahmet

In 1972 Kid Jensen was excited, the Stones were touring America and he'd been invited to fly over to join the tour travelling with them to Pittsburgh, Philadelphia and New York where he would interview the band. Bill Fowler, Warner's top promotion man accompanied him to New York travelling in First Class. When they touched down at JFK, they were immediately transported to a waiting helicopter that shuttled them over to Philadelphia.

The following day Kid was to interview Mick Jagger, watch the show then join the band on their private plane, where he would wave his Radio Luxembourg microphone under the rest of their noses.

In Philadelphia, Kid and Bill had an adjoining suite. Kid was whacked, had a towel round his waist and was readying for bed, when a knock came to the door.

"Are you Mr. Jensen?" said Philadelphia's answer to Pamela Anderson.

Kid stammered his confirmation, mouth wide open as she squeezed past him, walked to the centre of the room and turned to face him opening her coat revealing, well, very little, or quite a lot, whichever way you want to look at it!

"Kid Jensen! A big welcome to the Rolling Stones Tour. I'm a gift from Mr Ahmet Ertegun and Atlantic Records!"

Kid was taking in the red tongue Stones logo tattoo at her groin, which licked tantalizingly towards the gift.

She threw her purse down and tried the mattress.

Ahmet, the founder of Atlantic Records, was obviously extremely generous, but what his American promotion team hadn't accounted for was Kid being a hypochondriac.

Anyone who knows one, will confirm that they won't go with prostitutes in case they catch some skin disease or cold virus.

"Wait there," said Kid running into the adjoining suite.

"A whaaat?" said Bill Fowler, embarrassed because Kid was embarrassed.

"You wait right here Kid. I'll sort this out!"

Such kindness.

Bill sorted her out all right!

By all accounts, it took him all night to get rid of her.

The next day went perfectly. After the concert, Kid and Bill went by limousine to the airport where the cavalcade of rock's supreme beings climbed on board their private 707, a huge Sticky Finger tongue rasping at them from the tail of the plane.

Kid described inside as bedlam as the plane set off. Instead of any announcement from the captain or stewardess, they got *Street Fighting Man* as they taxied, and *Brown Sugar* as the aircraft's nose lifted into the night sky. Not one person had a seat belt on.

The bar was the most popular place. Instead of nuts and olives, the vessels contained a variety of pills, obviously for those who suffered from airsickness. Around the plane people were snorting white powder through nose-straw dollar bills.

We were all a little vague about cocaine in Luxembourg, cut off from society as we were. Kid couldn't understand why they snorted baking powder!

Bill Fowler explained, "It's self-raising flour!"

"Bread heads uh?" said Kid.

Wherever Kid looked people toked away, the pungent aroma of marijuana filling the cabin.

Up front Charlie Watts played snap with his kids.

"I'm going for a beer," Kid announced, but Bill was making up for the sleep he had bypassed the night before.

At the back of the plane a crowd had gathered. Jagger, Wyman, Richards were clapping wildly with the touring party circle of musicians, workers and hangers-on.

"Check it out Kid," said Bill Wyman making room for the DJ to come through.

On the floor were two naked 18-year-olds giving a lesbian show for their satanic majesties. Keith Richards had just covered them in cream from a spray can, and those gathered applauded as the waifs writhed together in a naked clotted clinch.

Charlie Watts was seen to chase his curious kids back down the aisle away from the cabaret, just as a huge American member of the road crew lifted one of the naked girls into the air, eating her like a mid-flight cunnilingus snack.

This whole episode, which included a brief view of Kid conducting an interview down the cabin, was featured in the 2013 TV documentary Crossfire Hurricane.

It was only rock 'n' roll, but they liked it!

On other adventures, David Bowie invited Kid to stay with him, but Kid declined. The only DJ in history to blank Bowie because he was afraid the man would try to seduce him! Bowie persisted however, and an invite arrived for Kid to join Ziggy Stardust at a chateau in Paris.

Bowie, at this time, was the biggest rock star on the planet and too big to be fucked around, and as bisexual Bowie would discover in Paris, Kid couldn't be fucked with either.

About the same time, when everyone was putting glitter on their eyelids and walking round on plinths, (including myself), I received the first test-pressing of *My Coo Ca Choo* by someone called Alvin Stardust and I made it my hit-pic.

I always chatted to listeners who phoned in long distance, it was a kind of confirmation that we were being listened to those many moonlit miles away from home.

I answered one evening to hear a voice say, "Ello, Princely Platter Player". Then they said, "Who is Alvin Stardust really?" and immediately hung up the phone.

Later I decided it had been either Michael Levy the owner of Magnet Records, Peter Shelley the person who wrote the song, or my old pal Shane Fenton who eventually become Alvin Stardust. But I'll never really know. Whoever it was, their little ploy worked. Each time I played *My Coo Ca Choo*, I asked the listeners, "Who is Alvin Stardust REALLY?"

It became Magnet Record's first monster hit and the latest appendage to the glam 'n' glitter movement.

I've been told countless times that Shane Fenton was not the singer on *My Coo Ca Choo*, and that in fact the writer Peter Shelley sings the hit. Alvin was supposedly coerced to front it, only when the record started biting.

Alvin had various manifestations firstly, as Bernard Jewry, then Shane Fenton and finally, Alvin Stardust.

I had some wild nights with two of him, then he made his move to Christianity and you couldn't see him for halos.

That puzzled me, because he always seemed so happy as a sinner.

Michael Levy threw a party at Gulliver's a club across the road from Radio Luxembourg. He was so grateful for my support so he invited Christine and I out for dinner with his wife. The evening ended with him showing me how brilliant he was at table tennis, and how crap he was at dancing on and off his settee with his wife, Gilda.

Lord Levy became famous as prime minister Tony Blair's controversial Middle East adviser and fundraiser.

One year earlier, I'd resisted Bell Records' decision to make *Rock 'n' Roll Pt 1* by newcomer and future leader of the pervs, Gary Glitter, the side to play. I preferred the instrumental *Pt 2* B-side, simply because I'd seen the track work on the dance floor during my many gigs. I already felt that club DJs were breaking the track without any help from their radio counterparts.

I phoned Dick Leahy the boss at Bell Records, the guy who'd sent me to LA to interview David Cassidy on a number of occasions. I told him he'd made a mistake.

"We made it a double A-side so you DJs could decide," he told me.

"Oh," I groaned down the phone. "You want us to be your bloody A&R department as well as your Marketing department now do you?"

The record became a monster. Just like the singer who was busted for downloading child porn, after which he did the jailhouse rock 'n' roll!

The nation got glam and glitter crazy, make-up for guys becoming a requisite, I slapped a bit on my face at gigs.

Gary Glitter came first, Bowie followed with *Aladdin Sane*, Mark Bolan jumped out of his T. Rex outfit into something he could excel in, Roy Wood started dressing up like a bearded tart, Sweet started to dazzle us on Top of the Pops and Slade, already wearing the highest platform shoes they could balance on, released *Merry Xmas Everybody* which was number one for Xmas 1973, and was still at number one when Rudolph was back grazing in Greenland on 12 January 1974!

Glam Rock was a brief period in pop history when there was nearly as much glitter on the stage, as there had been dandruff at the end of a rock gig.

Bruce Johnston of the Beach Boys wrote to me from LA with an idea that I thought was great - Beach Boys Live in Luxembourg! It was written over two pages in longhand and I still have it. I don't care who you are, there's nothing more thrilling than getting a letter or a phone call from a superstar, using the personal touch gets them whatever they want. In this case Bruce wanted to broadcast *live* to our millions of listeners across Europe.

I talked with Warner Brothers' Bill Fowler, and together we concocted *two* mega-live shows from the Villa Louvigny in our in-house theatre, designed primarily for the Luxembourg Symphony Orchestra, with a capacity to seat a maximum 200 people.

Bill agreed to bring in the Beach Boys, providing the following week we did another live broadcast with Grateful Dead. Kid Jensen was beside himself at this development.

We, the DJs, in the Grand Duchy were given the task of inviting the right kind of audiences to the two concerts, and whilst we knew who to invite in Luxembourg for the Beach Boys, we couldn't for our lives think who in the ultra square Grand Duchy we could invite to a Frank Zappa concert?

The first event was perfect with the *Sloop John B* boys on a *Surfin Safari* with *Barbara Ann* before an audience, which included most of the strippers from the Chez Nous, Leo and his waiters from the Italia restaurant, Mickey the telephone receptionist at the American Embassy, and the Marines we played poker with at TGIF. We also invited Hank, a dark-skinned gunrunner, we'd met in some club and Lloyd, a handsome American black basketball player who was about twice my height.

It was a wide demographic, but we didn't know of any real pop fans in Luxembourg, and our distribution of free tickets was predominantly done by us at the Chez Nous strip club. On the strength of this, Pauli the owner gave us free drinks for weeks, and we promised him we'd bring the band to his club after the concert.

It was a classic Beach Boys live concert, and we all felt very privileged to witness it and get wrecked with the lads later that night at the Chez Nous. But the next concert, just one month later, turned into a complete and utter nightmare.

A French DJ had announced on the RTL French Service that the Grateful Dead concert was a free concert, which indeed it was for our 200 invitees; he just forgot to mention it was ticket-only and all tickets had been distributed!

On the day of the concert 2,500 French hippies crossed the Luxembourg border! It was a Sunday and the clouds threw down their by-product all day long.

Grateful Dead came with an army-sized road crew and enough equipment to keep NASA happy. As the afternoon broke to evening, outside the radio station, drowning French hippies started to break windows whilst inside, the two unlucky, on duty porters started to break wind.

The Director General, Gust Grass arrived, and had to battle through the Villa Louvigny park which by then was filled with pot-smoking, French zombies. Once inside the car park gates he found himself entering the radio station by the only way possible, climbing through a side window.

The gendarmes arrived, real heavy looking buggers with guns. Then, one hour to show time and Grateful Dead went on a sit-down strike.

"If ya don't open the doors, we're not opening our mouths," Jerry Garcia announced eyeballing the cops.

"And you can get them fuckin' pigs outahere," said Pigpen to me and Kid Jensen, pointing his joint at the gendarmerie.

Gus, the Director General, spoke in Luxembourgish to the cops asking them to leave the main hall, but remain on hand in the corridors. He then instructed the station's porters to allow about a hundred French Dead fans in, however 200 got through before they could close the huge metal doors, trapping 20 flailing joint-holding hands as they did so.

Inside it was now wall-to-wall sardine-frogs. The sedate auditorium, built for the Luxembourg Symphony Orchestra, had never housed anything like it.

Last month I had introduced the Beach Boys, tonight it was Kid's turn. Two minutes to show time and our young friend walked across the stage towards the microphone when a black-vested Hell's Angels roadie, leathered, tattooed and muscled, stood in his path, hand outstretched, his hairy fingers spidered out on kids fashionable white shirt.

"Get the fuck off this stage!" he said menacingly.

Paul Burnett and I stood a few feet away, shocked and helpless as the clock reached show time, minus 60 seconds.

"Errr, I'm Kid Jensen," began Kid.

"I don't care if you're Charles fucking Manson," (obviously one of his idols)... Get offa this fuckin stage!!"

Suddenly this was *his* stage. This guy had thrown people off stages from Height Asbury to Woodstock, and now it was Kid's turn in the Villa Louvigny.

30 seconds to go.

"I'm the DJ..."

Kid was now staring cross-eyed at a large flick-knife blade that had stopped just short of his nose.

"OFF Mother Fucker!"

20 seconds. The group were still tuning their equipment, no one in the band saw what was happening side of stage. The roadie pulled the knife back threateningly. Then a hand came out of nowhere and pushed him away from Kid.

"What you doin' man?" asked a more senior member of the Dead's road crew.

The angel of death stashed the knife and faded quick-as-a-flash to look for trouble elsewhere.

"Sorry about him, he's a little over protective," said the roadie guiding Kid towards the microphone. "One of those Frenchies gave him some heroin, fucking strong stuff!"

The group turned to the audience; the roadie slapped Kid on the back and apologized once again.

"Real sorry DJ. He'll fuckin' kill someone one of these days."

The microphone turned live.

"G G G Good evening f f f folks," Kid began.

It was the shortest intro Kid has ever performed.

I was back in Glasgow for a gig at Clouds, a club so huge they could hang real aeroplanes from the ceiling as decoration. Certainly public safety didn't seem an issue.

Downstairs, deep below the discotheque, was a 2,000 capacity concert theatre and tonight, it was me versus Led Zeppelin!

I lost by about 100 dB as they stretched themselves towards the 130 dB, their 1969 record for The World's Loudest Band.

The band and I were staying in the same hotel and, having met him in the lobby, their manager Peter Grant invited me to their suite after our respective gigs.

As we entered, Bonzo the drummer was sitting cross-legged on the carpet, screwdriver in hand with each piece of the telephone laid out around him. Bonzo had all the symptoms of on-the-road-monotony syndrome, a mere handful of years away from death by too many screwdrivers.

I'd had a couple of whiskeys with Jimmy Page, Robert Plant and Peter Grant when John Paul Jones entered the room.

"Mike's getting us some cabaret!" he announced. "Give us £200 Pete."

Peter snapped out the readies in four £50 notes, and Jimmy passed the money to one of their personal security guys.

Thirty minutes later we were herded into an adjoining room where two ragged-looking Glaswegian molls were already unrobing as we gathered around like men at a cockfight.

"C'mon you two, you know what's required," shouted the bodyguard, annoyed that they were just giving a straight strip.

"You want lesbian we want more money," said the peroxide one.

"Yeah, we want £200 for lesbian," chimed the other.

The bodyguard looked at John Paul and Jimmy Page and then Peter who'd given him the £200.

"I fuckin' gave you £200 you bitches," he said pointing from one to the other as they stood there confronting him in bra and pants.

"Nay yee fuckin' did'nay yee gave us £150!" snarled Miss World War.

And that was it. With his credibility on line, his bosses wondering if he'd tried to pocket £50 for himself, he swung one blow which lifted the hooker straight off her feet.

As she lay there out for the count and her friend crying, "Marie, Marie, are you all right Marie?" I really thought she was dead. Tomorrow's tabloid headline flashed through my mind, '*Zep Zap Hooker at Lezbo Party*', and my aspirations to join the BBC would finally be laid fully to rest.

The bodyguard ripped open Marie's bag and pulled out the money, fanning out four £50 readies.

"C'mon Tony', let's get you out of here," said big Peter Grant. "I think we're in trouble."

Bonham returned to his carpet game, the others split into hiding.

One hour later in the hotel lobby, I saw Peter straighten out first the cops, and then the pimps, with enough readies to keep safe the greatest classic rock band that ever strutted the planet.

Peter Grant was a sweet guy who'd risen from bouncing at the 2i's Coffee Bar to road-managing the Yardbirds, and on to managing Led Zeppelin and their Swan Songs label, which spawned the Pretty Things and Bad Company.

His image was a central character in *VINYL* the Mick Jagger/Martin Scorsese HBO collaboration.

Peter Grant was quite a manager, larger than life in every respect. The last time I spoke to him was in 1995 just before his death, when Christine and I were trying to buy Jimmy Page's old house, The Mill, at Windsor, a most beautiful Thames riverside home, which had once been owned by Michael Kane before Jimmy Page moved in.

The estate agent had said Page was bidding against me, I didn't believe him, why would he want to return to his 60s home and the memories of a broken marriage?

"Nonsense," said Peter. "There's no way Jimmy would go back to The Mill, Bonham died there, it's too morbid for him!"

Then an enormously spooky coincidence took place. The very next day I was at Cheltenham races with my kids for a Nordoff-Robbins Music Therapy charity meeting, where we found ourselves having lunch sitting next to a couple of guys in a marquee. I discovered the one next to me was a property broker for people in the music industry.

"Do you by any chance represent Jimmy Page?" I asked instinctively.

"As it happens I do, why?" he asked.

"I'm Tony Prince, the guy who's supposedly bidding against him for The Mill!"

Neither of us could believe the proportion of fate afoot placing us, not just at the same race meeting, but next to each other at the very same table in a marquee with four hundred guests. And both hungry at precisely the same time!

"I've been meaning to call you," he said.

And then I got my explanation.

"Jim only moved out of The Mill because of his new wife, who's now another ex-wife. He loved the place, he'll have it at any price, he told me to tell you!"

"Tell Jimmy I wouldn't dream of coming between him and The Mill, but if he ever leaves again, ask him to give me first option!"

We shook hands.

Whilst everyone else lost their shirts at Cheltenham, I was the only person there who'd lost a house!

Jan: Permission to roam

In the second part of November we stopped playing at being soldiers; no more did we suffer the morning warm-up ritual running around the barracks buildings. Instead of uniforms we put on our working overalls, went for breakfast, after which we rode each day to the outskirts of Olomouc, where in the Řepčín district a new railway station was being built, with a new track leading to the nearby iron foundry.

We'd now become classic manual labourers who spent the days spreading gravel onto the track with shovels and pitchforks. Compared to the exercise tortures we'd been enduring, this was like summer camp.

So far we'd been permitted to leave the barracks three times for a couple of hours, just enough time to drink a beer or two, and a means to survive the political brainwashing process that was embedded in the communist army system.

So the little pub trips and a couple of beers helped us to swill all the bullshit away.

I was experiencing radio withdrawal syndrome. Tomorrow we reached December, which meant that I had gone two months without hearing one decent song. I had endured life with no Caroline or Luxembourg at all, not even Mikrofórum on Czechoslovak Communist Radio in the afternoon.

That night I wrote a letter home, expressing to my parents how happy I was that I had completed two months already, and only had 670 days left of the 730 I was donating to the army. Subtracting a number each evening became a favourite point of the evening as we became one day closer to becoming civilians again.

During my mother's visit to attend my oath, she mentioned there was an apprentice in the telecommunication training institution where she worked, and that he was from Olomouc.

I'd warned my parents that I probably would not be allowed home for Christmas, in which case they might ask the apprentice if he could bring my beloved Hitachi transistor radio to Olomouc where I would meet him? Because both our incoming and outgoing mail was monitored, to be sure nobody got wind of my plan, I posted the letter in town.

I wasn't quite sure if we were allowed to use a private radio in the army, but was afraid to know the answer so I didn't bother asking. It was pretty obvious however, that with 600 soldiers around me, none of whom had a radio, what the answer would have been.

We were all pissed off when it was confirmed we would not be given leave to go home for Christmas. Plainly the army knew how not to spoil their soldiers, so that we would be prepared for the hardships of any future wars. However we detected that since we had started working in the area of Řepčín railway station, our officers seemed to be treating us a little better. The reason for this was whispered man-to-man, bed-to-bed. Someone had learned that the officers were in for a nice fat bonus if we worked well to schedule. So we put our backs into laying the rail tracks and were rewarded with many more chances to leave the barracks in the evenings.

Halfway through December, I learned that I would leave for my shunter´s training in Nový Bohumín after New Year's Eve on 3 January 1968, so I realised I had to act swiftly if I was to get my transistor radio. I phoned home and mother gave me the address of Petr, the apprentice. Two days later I was thanking Petr and heading back to the barracks, whilst at the same time dialling 208 Medium Wave (1440 Kilohertz). My hands were actually shaking as I connected the earphone and I looked around furtively, making sure the Military Police, who walked the streets of Olomouc all the time checking that soldiers had permission to walk outside the army base, were not around. If this wasn't confirmed in their permit book, they'd be put into a military prison to be taken out later by an officer from their garrison, after which they'd be punished for leaving their barracks without authority.

I'd made sure I had my permission all right, but I knew too well that if they came across a soldier playing a radio station with English capitalist propaganda programmes, I might be for the high jump. So in my letter to home I reminded my mother – *please do not forget an earphone cord when packing my Hitachi.*

So here I go with a little one-ear headphone after three months deprivation, a prison sentence in effect for me, but now the *Station of the Stars* was back in my life, and I knew all too well that I could now survive my time in army service.

On Wednesday 3 January 1968, 10 of us took a train to Nový Bohumín as planned, arriving in the afternoon. We were accommodated in old wooden barracks in a garrison that had seen better times before the Second World War. After what we'd endured, this was pure luxury with five of us in each of two rooms.

But the best bit came by at supper time, when our accompanying sergeant took away our soldier permit books, returning them later with the unbelievable permission to leave the barracks throughout the whole of January and February, 24 hours a day.

The document also permitted us to stay in both Nový Bohumín and Ostrava, Czechoslovak fourth biggest city, just 20kms away.

The reason for this generosity was simple. We were scheduled to attend railway regulation lectures in Ostrava every other day during the first part of January, whilst training as shunters at the depot in Nový Bohumín. After passing these exams we would be working on irregular night or Sunday shifts, which meant we would be leaving our barracks at different times and days.

In another words, we would be totally free for the next two months.

This was all a walk in the park for me as I'd already been through the Ostrava lectures and exams a year back.

Another pleasant thing was that we each received a stipend of 14,90 crowns to buy breakfast and lunch, which was paid to us each time we went to Ostrava.

You could eat quite adequately for half this amount, and when I winked and slipped two crowns to an army cook in the barracks asking for a generous piece of meat, he smiled back and gave me three pieces.

It's funny how a mere 5-crown food allowance, on top of a 75-crown monthly salary and an extra piece of meat, can make you feel like a king!

On Friday we were supposed to study in the barracks; none of us took that too seriously, and then we were free.

After lunch I took some of my fellow soldiers on a sightseeing walk through Bohumín.

The supervising soldier at the barrack gates was surprised when we saluted him goodbye, and he wanted to see our permits and to know where we were going? With what could best be described as the *joy of permit*, we confidently told him to keep cool as we did not belong to his combat garrison, but were only accommodated there and were off to do some work at the local railway depot.

Like magic, the big brother system collapsed before our eyes as he raised the barrier and saluted us. We decided it was far too cold for sightseeing and joyfully strode into the nearest pub to celebrate our liberty.

On our return journey, I noticed that Bohumín had a cinema already adapted for showing movies filmed, using 70mm negative stock; that was a big novelty, and only recently had come to Czechoslovakia. Seeing on their programme the musical *My Fair Lady* and a notification it would play 'In English with subtitles', I knew immediately how I would spend Saturday afternoon.

No one else was interested in joining me, saying that if there had been some crime or adventure movie, or at least A Hard Day's Night playing that would be something else, but they would not spend their money 'watching an opera'.

I couldn't expect them to love the English language as I did, or all types of music for that matter. What was important for me was that I had the opportunity, here in the middle of army training, to see a classical musical based on the play Pygmalion by George Bernard Shaw, whom I knew as a witty writer.

Who could resist a Saturday afternoon, sitting in a well-equipped cinema listening to beautiful English in high quality American motion pictures? Not to mention beautiful Audrey Hepburn, whom I admired since I first saw her in Roman Holiday.

As I strolled downtown that Saturday, I thought of what poor Laďa would be enduring, probably he would be bouncing around in some ramshackle tank on military exercise. Learning to kill the perceived enemy, an enemy who were about to royally entertain me.

I arrived early and was grateful I had bought an advance ticket. a queue had formed at the box office, there were obviously a lot of people in this town who wanted the enemy to entertain them.

With time on my hands, I crossed to the railway station to check the local news stand where, for the first time since joining the army, I bought a copy of Red Law to see what bullshit they were spreading today. As I paid for the paper, I noticed what looked like imported bubble gum in unusual coloured packing, shaped like a small postcard.

I treated myself to two pieces, at three crowns each they were not cheap. This was three times more expensive than Pedro, the only chewing gum produced in Czechoslovakia.

After unwrapping one piece and placing the rather large pink rectangular slice of gum into my mouth, just before crushing the wrapping ready for the bin, I noticed something firm inside the outer wrapping. I stood there transfixed to the spot unable to believe my eyes. The inner card was a full colour 6 x 9 cm picture of Paul Anka, whilst on the reverse side was a black and white picture of the 1966 Marlin fastback hardtop car.

Next to Paul Anka´s name was the number 35, so I guessed from this I was looking at a series. Without any hesitation I opened the second gum as well and there they were – the Beatles in full colour sitting at a green table!

This was the first time that I had ever seen the Beatles other than in black and white. The flip side featured the lyrics to My Bonny with one verse titled Mein Bonny translated into German. Above this was the headline TEENAGER-news HIT parade and the number 33.

So as a keen collector of almost everything since I was a little kid, I was sure that there had to be at least two different series of pop stars, one with cars and one with lyrics. I had to laugh. I'd hesitated a little before buying the gum as the price seemed a bit too high, but with such pictures, I now regarded this chewing gum as one of the greatest bargains imaginable. The gum wasn't bad either!

I started to believe that there really was something up high, a friendly angel, an ancestor, a friendly spirit charming my life. Here I was running into some foreign gum in the small city of Nový Bohumín, a city fate sent me to, a railway newsstand where fate had decided I would buy a paper and look left and see this gum, a gum I had never seen or bought before in my life. Then I would ask for two packets, the lady would select the two which I would open without appreciating they had an inner packaging and then, I, a guy from Brno who might well be Paul Anka and the Beatles biggest fan in the East, would hold these particular cards in his hand. Where do you draw the line on spooky and pure coincidence, I wondered as I meandered back to the cinema. I stopped and turned back, my curiosity burning me. First I bought another two packets of gum, and then I asked the lady shop assistant how long was she selling them and if she knew where they came from? She explained it was a rather new import that had probably come from Poland.

Poland was again my winning nation, just like when I had come across the plastic records in Zakopane a couple of years ago.

Nový Bohumín was almost directly on our border with Poland, so I told myself the gum may well have been smuggled in, the reason why it was not on nationwide distribution.

Gum runners... whatever next?!

I now had two more great pictures to add to my collection, four perhaps after I opened the two I had just bought. I decided to open them back at the barracks, once I had enjoyed My Fair Lady.

By the time I arrived the cinema had the SOLD OUT sign on the door. I'd done well buying an advance ticket and with time to go before the film started, I sat down to read Red Law, and as usual I started reading the sports section from the back. Finally, I reached what was usually a boring front page known mostly only for its phrases and communistic clichés and, with Xmas upon us, it was surely going to be full of the usual telegram greetings of brotherly communist party love from around the world.

But not this year. I looked upon a picture of an unknown man with a face that was quite different from the usual greasy, unpleasant faces of communist leaders.

In the principal article in bold letters was a report on the session of the Central Committee of Czechoslovak Communist Party. This article included an almost inconspicuous comment that Antonín Novotný, who had been the President and Party Chief for many years, was now only the

President from that time on.

The new First Secretary of the Communist Party of Czechoslovakia was newly appointed Alexander Dubček.

CVs of communist party bosses was usually the last thing that would interest me, but I made an exception this time and began to read about this man Dubček, whose face really seemed to be different from the ones we used to see in Red Law. There was a gentleness about him, a kindness in his eyes.

I couldn't believe what I was reading, sitting on a bench just outside the cinema, waiting for the film to begin. Before the First World War Dubček´s father went to the United States of America in search of work, and returned home only after the war was over. He joined the Czechoslovak communist party when it was founded in 1921, the same year his son Alexander Dubček was born. When our communist society were urged to go to the Soviet Union to help them with cooperative farming, he took his family there in 1925, and the Dubček family stayed in the Soviet Union until 1938, returning when Alexander had just turned 17.

It was sure that Alexander Dubček was another communist who had grown up in Russia for some 13 years. But the fact that his father lived several years in the USA intrigued me, and gave me hope that this pleasant-looking man might *not* be just another communist.

Surely his father had told him about the United States and that it wasn't bad at all? And that Communism under the USSR was not so good as Red Law would have everyone believe?

All in all I had a gut feeling coming close to a certainty, that the movie that was just about to start would now be followed by many more American, British, French and non-communist produced movies. Logically then, I told myself, thereafter records too would flow into Czechoslovakia from the free world, a world which all rock 'n' roll fans already yearned to be part of.

I sat there mesmerised by My Fair Lady, and Audrey Hepburn as Eliza improving her English was just fantastic experience for me. I fell in love with one phrase forever, 'The rain in Spain stays mainly in the plain!' It reminded me of how extremely lucky I had been in being in the English stream, rather than the Spanish at high school, that was a lottery that would have changed my entire life. I once again contemplated that thing in the sky I had felt today, and now realised my guardian had been at work on my behalf long before today.

When I returned to the barracks and told my friends that I had to go to see the movie again the next day and had already purchased my ticket, they just stared at me with their eyes wide open, wondering if perhaps I had lost my mind?

I lay down on my bed and switched on my Hitachi to full volume, I was in such a good mood and conserving the batteries wasn't in my mind at all. Radio Luxembourg was playing all the hits from *California Dreaming* to *Paint it Black* with the DJs babbling away 10 to the dozen. I reflected on this amazing day and only now decided to open the two extra chewing gum packets I'd bought. This time the cards featured someone called Freddy and Ria Valk, and whilst she looked lovely I had never heard of either of them. They turned out to be West German singers.

But never mind, I would have more luck next time.

My lucky day ended just then as the door opened, and in walked the Supervisory Board Officer for the whole garrison.

Petr who was the nearest of us to the door stood up, saluted and performed the obligatory military report we had to do every time an officer entered a room.

"Hello comrade major, soldiers of Olomouc railway garrison during their free time."

He did not even answer the greeting, but shouted, "What does this mean? Whose radio is that? What station is it playing? Why so loud?"

I was numb, but somehow volunteered, "It's mine Sir."

The major stormed over to me.

"Who allowed you to bring a radio here?"

There was nothing else but to throw myself at his mercy.

"I am sorry sir, nobody told me that it is prohibited."

Then he let me have it.

"We are in the army to defend our socialist country, as well as other countries from Warsaw treaty, and the world's peace camp as a whole against American imperialism, and you have got nothing better to do than to perform an American party here."

Now he hesitated for effect.

"And after a while for a change, you will listen to Radio Free Europe, won't you?"

"It's not possible," I began with a great reply. "This transistor radio has only long and medium waves, and RFE is broadcasting only on short wave."

I realised suddenly that I had gone into too much detail and quickly added: "But anyway sir, we are not at all interested in the RFE bullshit broadcasting."

But it was too late.

"How come you know so well on which frequency Radio Free Europe broadcasts?"

I was almost dead in the water, but my mind was alive and I gave my explanation almost instantly.

"In our garrison in Olomouc, we have political lectures quite often, and our political officer told us that RFE broadcasts on short wave, and that it is a stupid station with no sense to it."

The major seemed to be impressed with this, but as he was somewhat green he maintained his campaign against my Hitachi.

"And did your politruk tell you also that you should listen to American music, that our Czechoslovak songs are not good enough for us?"

I knew I had to be polite, and that there was no sense discussing such matters with a brain-washed army creature, but this was just too much and I had to defend the music, I had to fight for my dear Hitachi transistor.

"Sir" I responded, "Our politruk did not speak about music, as he concentrated only on politics. But I can assure you comrade major that some western songs are very good. Even our own radio station plays some western tunes, in the afternoon from 3 to 5, and by the way, this afternoon I went to the 70mm wide screen cinema here in Bohumín to see an American musical called My Fair Lady. The place was completely full, which means that many of our people like music other than Czechoslovak music, if it is good."

The comrade major had no answer to this, who knows, maybe his own wife had been to see My Fair Lady?

Now he attacked from another side.

"How was it that you went to the cinema this afternoon? Show me your book with permits! Who gave you permission?"

I'd put my foot right in it. Sure we could leave the barracks anytime, but only for training lectures or work. My mind worked overtime and I came up with my reply. "Sir, I had been to the railway depot to make an appointment to see the depot manager as I was going there for training to work as a shunter. I was told to come back in a couple of hour's time when the depot manager would be there. It seemed pointless walking all the way back to the barracks only to turn straight back. I didn't fancy waiting in a smoky pub either, so I went to the cinema to kill time."

He looked through my permit book, and it was only then that he realized we did not belong to his combat unit, but were part of the Olomouc railway garrison.

"Do you know how to shoot." he asked grinning.

"No sir, we haven't had shooting training yet," I replied.

"Just as well," he said making to leave. "Soldiers like you should not even wear a uniform, let alone hold a gun."

He slipped my Hitachi and earplug into his pocket and turned at the door. "I shall take this radio and pass it on to the counter espionage section, you shall hear from them." And with that spear through my chest, he left.

I was devastated. After losing my tape recorder only three months ago, I'd now lost my transistor radio in almost the same way. I hadn't dared to

ask him if he would give me a receipt, but I felt I had been conned for a
second time.
All of us were in shock, the room went terribly quiet. What a difference
from just a while ago in our happy Radio Luxembourg free-world mood.

Tony: The Pirates

Kid and I did a double show called Rock Present, Roll Past, I'd play the
up-tempo stuff from pre-1960, and he'd fight back with modern rock.
Presley vs Pretty Things, Conway Twitty vs the Edgar Broughton Band,
Little Richard vs Led Zeppelin... a no contest battle, which we both felt
we'd won each week.
We decided to do a live broadcast or two from Luxembourg's Blow Up
club. Kid's choice first, Status Quo, the best live three-chord four piece
outfit on planet E.
When they'd finished head-banging *Mean Girl*, you couldn't see the
dance floor for dandruff.
Then my choice, the Pirates, the remains of Johnny Kidd's band, reformed
years after his death, to cash in on their not insignificant name and talents.
Mick Green had been with Kidd before Billy J Kramer & the Dakotas,
before our night in the snowdrift, and had filled the gap backing Engelbert
Humperdinck in Las Vegas.
Shaking all Over vs *Release Me*, was no life for a rock hardened man like
Green, and he was thirsty to return to his pedestal as one of the world's
greatest rock guitarists.
Reforming the band with Johnny Spencer, who two years later walked off
stage at a London gig because I'd out-sung him, they were right back on
top and stroking those mighty *Please Don't Touch* chords all over Europe.
'Skull Wars!'
The Pirates were scheduled to hit the first chord of *A Shot of Rhythm and
Blues* at two minutes past midnight, and I was to introduce them as soon
as the news ended at that precise time.
At ten minutes to midnight, the gendarmes raided the Blow Up, sniffer
Alsatian dogs and all!
We were used to these periodic under-age drinker checks, but no one had
anticipated they'd do one tonight live on 208.
The clock was ticking swiftly towards broadcast time, and for some reason
the cops had no concept that Radio Luxembourg was about to broadcast
live as a truculent sergeant insisted that the club's DJ, Golly Gallagher,
stopped the music. Above the disgruntled murmuring of the audience, the
tower of Pirate Vox amplifiers hummed ready to deliver their payload.

I called our Luxembourg engineer Norbert over, his English was limited but I asked him to translate, "What the fuck's going on here?"

At five to midnight I had a dog smelling my bellbottoms and six cops on stage with me and the Pirates.

Mick Green leaned over and said to me, "I've done some fucking gigs Tone but this is a first!"

With two minutes to go, Norbert came over to the microphone where I stood listening through headphones, as Kid Jensen started the news three kilometres away in the studio!

"It's a routine age-check," said Norbert.

Diddy, the club owner's son, (whose wife shot him dead a few years later), ran round like a headless chicken.

Kids all around the club were searching for their carte de l'identité or trying to hide.

With Norbert and the Chief of Police standing by my side on stage, I made an impassioned plea.

"Tell him Norbert, if they don't bugger off in one minute and err... 25 seconds, this guitarist will send those dogs mental!"

"Tell him what 5,000 watts does to a dogs ears," confirmed Mick pointing his Fender Stratocaster at them from behind me.

Mr Turmas, Diddy's 70-year old father, the money behind the Blow Up, ran around like Charlie Chaplin on speed from one cop to another, and then we lost him as he walked into the fog machine which started to billow its contents ready for the show to commence.

"And now the weather," said Kid, oblivious of the situation three kilometres away from the sanity of his studio.

"Nous commençons la announcement en direct sur RTL Service Anglais dans dix seconds," I announced into the microphone in my best Oldham-French, desperately hoping that the cops would finally comprehend that the fuse had almost reached the dynamite.

They started to leave, but nothing like quickly enough. On air, Kid was handing over to me. I had to make the announcement.

"And now, what we've all been waiting for," announced Kid to a few million listeners. "Over to the Royal Ruler live in the Blow Up!"

I still have the recording, it goes:

"Ladies and gentlemen welcome to Luxembourg's Blow Up discotheque, where you would simply not believe what has been taking place! We have just been raided for underage drinkers by the gendarmerie who, together with six Alsatian dogs, are literally just departing the club... we must wait a moment until the dogs are out of here... one Alsatian to go... yes, there he goes... right!"

I nodded at the band as Mick Green's plectrum caressed the strings of his Fender, and a massive chord of 'C' filled the room.

"Ladeeeeez and gentlemen... mademoiselle et monsieur, meine damen unt herren... the Piiiiiirates!"

It was almost an anticlimax.

Later, in the hotel bar, Johnny Spencer vowed never to work with animals again!

Jan: Radio rescue

I decided to take supper to calm down. Weekend rations came from cans to give the cooks a rest. The cans were taken from strategic reserves and were replaced every two years with fresh cans. The first one was something like tuna fish and was rather good, but when I put the knife into a second can to open it, a huge explosion followed covering my face, my shirt and the ceiling with a disgusting smelling stew.

I saw an opportunity, and told my friends that I would go to see the major about this incident to see what he would have to say about the poisoning of soldiers under his command?

We quickly checked the remaining cans to find that two were bulging so I asked Petr to go with me to confirm that although his can did not explode, he was not feeling very well after eating the tuna. I'd then show him the bulging cans. I didn't bother to clean my face or clothing, as I wanted full dramatic effect.

We stood outside the command room and knocked on the door.

The major shouted "ENTER", we opened the door, saluted and Petr gave the standard response, "Comrade major, let us enter."

After we explained everything, I expressed our concern that had the cans contained botulinum toxin it could actually kill soldiers. Luckily I had only recently read about this deadly bacterium and had remembered its name, leaving the major suitably impressed and quite concerned. He smelled the putrid can and recoiled, I could see he was on the rack, he knew this would reflect on him and not help his career at all.

"We have a little money left from Thursday's meal major," I said, "So we will go to the pub."

"Yes," said Petr whose condition seemed to be stabilising. "A beer will help to swill the poison away."

The major turned to face me. "You mustn't mention this to anyone in the pub or indeed the garrison."

Then he suggested we bring our permit books, which he would sign to give us the required permission.

"Not necessary sir, we won't bother you, our permanent permission will be quite adequate."

With his cock in the vice, I gave it one last turn.

"Of course we will not talk about it sir." I replied and added an old Czech proverb: "What is cooked at home should be also eaten at home." And then I knew that right moment came to ask for the return of my Hitachi.

"Comrade major, I am sorry that I was using the radio without permission. In fact I wanted to use it only during Christmas time, and thought to take it back home as I was supposed to get a holiday for New Year's Eve. Then we got the command to leave for Nový Bohumín on 3rd January and I just could not send it back home by post as I could not get out. But now I have enough time so I could mail it home on Monday if you would allow."

I lied through my teeth but it had the right effect, a big weight fell from my heart as he reached into his desk drawer and pulled out my transistor.

"OK, but don't you dare to use it, even for one minute in the barracks again."

"Absolutely not," I answered almost wrenching it from his hand and uttered finally, "Comrade major, let us leave", and of course he had no problem in letting us leave, you could see the relief etched in his face.

My Hitachi was saved, and I had saved myself from any further enquiries. Petr congratulated me on a great performance, and I couldn't disagree.

On the following Monday I had a medical examination by the railway doctor.

In the army, knowing there would be a couple of lovely nurses around, you never minded medical examinations, and I was sure I'd be OK having passed both the army medical test and a medical examination, when I started work for the railway depot in Brno.

Suddenly though, a shadow of doubt crossed my mind.

Eventually our sergeant called us together and announced that two of our group of 10 had failed the sight medical.

I was sure I would be one of them.

"It's nothing serious," the sergeant explained. "But unlike switchmen, shunters have a very dangerous job running between trains and wagons so"… he turned in our direction… "Paul and Bonifác will return to the Olomouc garrison tomorrow, and as my job is now done here, I will also be leaving you."

Paul and Bonifác were on the verge of tears. They had just lost the dream job.

Within a week of passing the exam I became a shunter, working at different train depots in Nový Bohumín, where I was assigned to a specific group of north Moravian shunters.

1968 opened like the North Pole and I took care of the stove in a shed

where the shunter team came, when waiting for a new train to arrive.
Because I was a good stoker, the boys asked me to do the night shift, and
because they knew I had already worked in the Brno yards and didn't need
shunting practice, not once did they ask me to do any shunting.
I was the fire king. There was no better job in the entire army.

   I would come to the depot at about 7pm and prepare coal, coke and
wood to last through the night. Then I'd sit down and tune the Hitachi
to Radio Luxembourg just in time for the 7.30pm station opening. At
3am the closing theme would lead to *At the End of the Day*, when I'd tuck
in to the delicious cake my colleagues' wives had made for the little Brno
kid who was so far from home. At around 5 o'clock in the morning, I was
usually told to return to my barracks and so time flew by with 208, going
to the movies and buying bubble gum. By the end of my time there, I had a
collection of 30 pop star pictures including Chuck Berry, Roy Orbison and
Tom Jones, all of whom I gazed upon for the first time in my life. It was
always very thrilling to find a face in the chewing gum packet of someone
whose voice I knew for so many years, and yet I had no idea what they
looked like. I never found a picture of the Rolling Stones, and was always
intrigued to know what they looked like.

   One day I was called to the command office where I was informed that
the Public Safety police in Ostrava wanted to see me.
The major couldn't tell me what they wanted me for, but reassured me the
army was behind me if there was a serious problem.
I walked up to the police sergeant and introduced myself.
"We've found the person who stole your tape recorder," he said, and my
relief must have shown because he brought me some water, asked me to
fill out a form detailing the value of the stolen items, and if I would accept
monthly instalments from the perpetrator.
Things were picking up, when I returned to Brno I would buy a new
recorder and record my life away.

Tony: Two shit flights

I ferried across to the Isle of Wight to spin a few hits at the Carousel Club
in Ryde. The resident DJ was John Gould, who I later helped to get a job in
promotion at Magnet Records and who, later still, went on to manage his
brother's band, Level 42 becoming a millionaire in the process.
John persuaded me to return to the mainland with his brother, who had to
get so many flying hours in to obtain his full pilot's license.

   Agreeing to pay his fuel and landing charges, I looked forward to my
first flight in a two-seater prop. There were three of us in the cockpit, as I'd

been given a kitten by the landlady of my hotel. I placed her in a string bag behind my head and we took to the sky.

Crossing the famous Needles and the Solent, we skirted past Southampton and proceeded to get totally lost.

"Fuckin' bastard!" cursed my pilot, banging the dial that was supposed to tell us if we were going north or south.

It became turbulent, I felt nauseous. Pussy didn't like it either and threw up her Kitty Kat on my shoulder. Now I really felt nauseous.

"Look out for the M3," he shouted. Now I felt sick.

"How many hours have you logged?" I asked curiously.

"About 12," he shouted.

The cat had now shit too; there was no escape from the vile effluvium. I opened the window and vomited over the world below.

"I'm putting down there," he said pointing to earth with his right wing. Below us was a field, flanked by a hilly area sprinkled with motorbikes and caravans. Ant-sized kids were playing football in the field he wanted to land in, so he did a couple of flybys until some bright spark got the message, and panicky mothers shepherded their offspring's away to safety.

We missed the trees at the end of the field by feet, but not the wire fence that stopped us abruptly like a fighter jet on an aircraft carrier.

Snarled by the wire, trailing fence posts behind us, I lurched forward banging my head on the malfunctioning compass as my miserable shit-covered kitten screamed a fearful cat cry.

"You've fixed it!" said my pilot pointing to the dial that now pointed to the 'N'.

Within seconds the kids were back down the field climbing over the plane. I jumped to the ground with my string-bag-cat, who looked pale for a ginger tom, and very bedraggled.

"Anyone got some water to clean the moggy?" I asked the advancing mothers.

"Anyone tell me how far to White Waltham?" asked the pilot.

Cat washed, pilot furnished with pedestrian directions, we again took to the English skies, frightening the hell out of a rook we missed by inches, in the topmost bough of a tall oak.

We kept to the general compass directions, but because I couldn't read the map he'd given me, we occasionally dropped to 40 feet or so to read the street signs.

Somehow, God knows how, I finally found myself running with kitty across the runway of White Waltham airport. No time to kiss the ground, I was about to miss my flight at Heathrow and my 7.30pm broadcast.

A kind woman in the airport cafe stopped eating her salad, to take my offer of the £20 note I was waving for anyone who would run me the 20 miles down the M4 to Heathrow.

With moments to spare and only hand baggage, I could still make the Luxair flight LG501.

With little time to spare, I put my hand baggage and string bag on the x-ray machine and waited at the other side as the security men gathered around the screen. They'd never seen a kitten skeleton before.

Our smells got us quickly through passport control, which was as well as the new Luxair Caravelle doors were about to shut just as I arrived.

"I'm not sure you can bring that cat on board," said a familiar hostess.

"Fine," I said handing him over. "Find him a nice home, his name is Biggles."

After a short political debate inside the captain's cockpit, she returned and let us on board, the captain was a mate I played poker with, which was fortunate.

As we pulled away from the embarkation finger, I jumped into the toilet and washed kitty down for the second time that morning. Drying her with loo paper, I then sprayed Aramis over both of us and did a quick change.

There was only one seat, front left window, lots of legroom. A smart young woman stood to let me pass, the three hostesses fluttered around really pissed off with me and controlling their tempers professionally as we taxied.

"Pretty kitten," said my neighbour from behind a newspaper.

"Sorry about the aroma, she's been poorly."

I pulled the window blind down, leaned my head against it and before we left the ground both me and kitty, snuggled on my lap, had taken off for the Land of Nod.

When I awoke the flight was over. The young lady was standing in the aisle, surrounded by members of the Luxembourg military, who kept the other passengers a stride away from her. She was thanking my pilot buddy who was shaking her hand, and she turned to the hostesses saying something in Luxembourgish.

Then she turned to me and said, "Did I ever thank you for playing the music at my party?"

I had just slept with Princess Marie Astrid of Luxembourg.

By all accounts, even Prince Charles didn't manage that!

Christine had returned to Oldham, and our baby Daniel had arrived four weeks ahead of schedule. After months of infanticipation I'd missed his stage entrance.

I called Christine in England one night, and detected she was low in spirit and missing me. To lift her out of her antenatal depression, I proposed to her - live on air.

The press were on it like a rocket.

Within two days, a mini-skirted Christine was in the tabloids, pictured on the kids' swings in Stoneyleigh Park, which skirted the side of her parent's terraced house in Oldham. Inside the house, our two-week old son was being bathed in front of a coal fire by his grandma. Outside in the park, somehow Christine's smiling face disguised her anger.

"Don't you ever put me in the limelight again!" she scolded me long distance.

We married in the Oldham Registry, and had our reception at the Egerton Arms where Ian Fenn, one of Oldham's great rock 'n' roll pianists, accompanied me on the piano as I serenaded my new wife with *What'd I say*.

Christine wore a pink full-length dress with ostrich feathers, whilst the bridegroom wore white, right down to my Beatle boots.

It was a rare sight for Oldham, and half the town turned out to wish us well. We returned to Luxembourg as a family with grandma in tow, and for the next 12 months, time flowed by like a rushing stream.

We often went to the American Marine's Friday night, TGIF to mingle with others of like tongue and to pay homage to a game of poker.

Ray, the Chief Marine, a likeable Rambo type from Cincinnati, had a burning ambition to fight in Vietnam. His dad had been killed on the battlefield of World War II and he wanted to emulate him, a medal or death, there was no in-between and, of the two, I actually felt he would have preferred death.

One night, whilst Christine was in England, a marine called Chris, Noel Edmonds, Kid Jensen and I emerged from Charlie's, one of the Grand Duchy's strip bars. They call them strip bars because they strip the mugs of all their money, but we were the exceptions, the DJs were welcomed with free drinks, and the hookers didn't hassle us for champagne.

On this particular evening, as we were leaving the club, Chris bad-mouthed a quartet of Italians as we climbed into my car. One of them, whose father had probably died during the Battle of Salerno whilst wearing a Nazi armband, threw a stone at my Daimler.

I wound down the electric window on the passenger side where Chris, sat and leaned across my marine pal to beckon the boy over.

"Tony let's go," Kid urged from the back seat.

"Fuckin' finocchios!" Chris shouted.

"Oh Jesus!" breathed Noel, next to Kid in the back.

Italian stallions don't like being called gay, especially in their own tongue by a Yank.

They advanced towards the open window very un-finocchio like, until one of them bent down – tough, eyes squinting, ready for anything.

"Tony," breathed Kid.

"Drive," begged Noel.

"You speaka de English?" I asked.

"Not," he said flanked now by his three West Side Story mates.

"You know what we do with people who throw stones at cars in England?"

"Non capisco."

I showed him.

Leaning right across Chris the marine, I hit him square in the face.

And then we were out of the car, fighting like Montagues and Capulets.

The guy I'd hit was through being tough, dabbing his bloody nose. I took a second one onto the bonnet of the car, and squeezed his balls until he learned enough English to say '*Aghhhhh!*'

Meanwhile, however, Chris the marine, trained to kill, was having his jacket torn from his back by the other two.

Kid and Noel sat deathly pale in the back seat, the door lock button securely down.

I ran to help Chris, but they vamoosed taking their wounded with them. Chris' lovely suede jacket lay in tatters on the ground.

"My fuckin' new jacket!" Chris moaned in despair.

"Where were you two?" I asked, climbing back in the car angrily eyeballing the ashen-faced duo on the back seat.

"The door wouldn't open," explained Kid.

I didn't fight often, but I did still have a bit of a short fuse when pushed, and a bit of Jack Smith's training to get me by.

I had a too-close encounter with a colleague, Dave Christian at the Marine's TGIF club, and we finished up in a carpet clinch until Bob Stewart separated us.

It was something and nothing to me, but became a major incident when John Barter, the new station manager, reported me to the London hierarchy. Everett suspended me. He'd rid himself of the detestable Noel Edmonds, now it was the turn of the horrid Princely Platter Player.

John Barter's version of what he *heard* had happened was quite enough for the company's Commandant back home in Mayfair. I was fired.

Luckily however, maybe because I made them laugh a lot or got them free drinks, my other DJ colleagues and many staff at the station, rallied round and protested my dismissal to Gus Grass, the Director General, who subsequently made an impassioned plea to Everett not to sack me.

But by now, I was frustrated as hell living in the centre of Europe and, with a very black mark on my log, unloved by the boss, I handed in my notice. I had decided that, as my half dozen audition tapes sent to Radio 1 hadn't achieved anything, it was time to move to America and take my chances there.

I gave Radio Luxembourg three months' notice, but within a month I had major regrets.

Geoff Everett, one of the founding fathers of European commercial broadcasting, was history and Alan Keen the former Programme Director of the formidable pirate ship Radio London, was to become Radio Luxembourg's new Managing Director.

Geoff was asked to resign when it was discovered he'd been doing publishing deals for his own company Shaftesbury Music, rather than prioritising RTL's company, Louvigny Music.

Anyway he was leaving but so far as I was concerned, the cavalry had arrived just as the covered wagons were burning!

It brought to mind one of my all time favourite rock 'n' roll songs, Jimmy Jones' *Good Timin'*, but the Stones' *Out of Time* was playing louder.

Keen was a radio man with a fabulous portfolio, a great pianist, a visionary and a true-blooded English eccentric, all rolled into one delightful boss. My timing couldn't have been worse, or so I thought until things worsened.

Christine announced to me that Gabrielle would be joining us for the rest of our lives, which was great news for our about-to-multiply royal family, but not an event out of the Jimmy Jones' Good Timin' textbook. America with baby Daniel we could handle, but I didn't relish the chances we were about to take with Christine expecting so, with one month to go, I grabbed my pride by the scruff of its neck and asked the new boss if it was too late to withdraw my notice?

"It is too late I'm afraid," Alan Keen replied.

Everett was leaving to work for Gordon Mills (Tom Jones and Engelbert Humperdinck's manager) at MAM, but before he left Radio Luxembourg he advised Alan to get rid of me.

"He said you were a boat rocker," Alan told me years later.

I took it on the chin, turned right and looked around for new yellow bricks.

Jan: Station to station

On 2 February Red Law published a big speech by Dubček at a national meeting of cooperative farms and in spite of many of the usual socialist phrases, I was deeply impressed with the courage he showed in what he had to say:

"There were many mistakes made in our agriculture policies in the past and we should do our best to repair this, and above all we should deepen socialist democracy and get rid of barriers that have been blocking us. If we do, new roads will open for us and everybody who wants to work for our country must feel needed and must have their chance."

I knew now that I had been born just two years too soon, and that my application for Agriculture University under this Dubček would have been accepted.

In my very soul I knew that Dubček was our key to freedom.

When we embarked on the train on the last day of February to return to our garrison in Olomouc I opened a huge envelope sent to me from my mother. Inside was Time magazine. Her friend worked in the cloakroom at the Grand Hotel in Brno where she sold cigarettes and magazines. America had once again stepped foot into Czechoslovakia!

There couldn't have been better evidence that things were improving than seeing me, a soldier of the Socialist Warsaw Treaty army, on a train reading the American magazine TIME whilst openly listening to British and American songs. I was listening to Mikrofórum and I was delighted to notice they were featuring more western music than ever.

Reporting to the supervisory officer at the barrack gates, confirming that we were the squad returning from Nový Bohumín, he checked our IDs eventually signalling for us to enter. Suddenly, as I passed by, he threw an arm across my chest halting me in my tracks.

"You stay right there," he growled menacingly.

I could feel the blood draining from my face.

"What's to happen with me?" I asked, but he just mumbled something about me waiting for a GAZ jeep when he would let my commander know I was here.

GAZ was a Soviet-made army vehicle, so I sat down and started watching for it, becoming more and more nervous as each minute passed by. What could it all mean?

Contemplation of the mystery came to an end with the arrival of the GAZ vehicle, whereupon the driver came to report to the supervising officer who then phoned my commander that we were ready, "Šesták and the transport are here at the gate".

I was extremely nervous as he approached but, as he drew closer, I could see he was smiling at me. This was not a man about to deliver a court martial.

He wanted to know if I had passed the shunter exam. I told him that as I had been a qualified railway worker for more than a year, and passing the exams for switchman, I would surely be qualified as a shunter, as those exams were not too different.

"Good comrade Šesták," he said. "Take yourself off to the supply sergeant for an air mattress and bedding, he'll also give you a month's food allowance. You're off to a new railway station at Řepčín where part of our railway transport squad has been moved already."

So away I ran to see our supply sergeant who handed me 31 x 23,50 crowns food allowance, a total of 728.50 crowns. To try to save such an amount from the 75 crowns army pocket money a soldier would receive each month, would be equivalent to saving for 10 months, and here I had only a one-month advance in cash.

Talk about hitting the jackpot! Of course the money was for nourishment, but there were many ways to spend just a little without starving.

This was like a dream again. No barracks meant we'd be well away from the officers, no army alarms and drills, and overcrowded mess halls, and noisy fart-filled bedrooms.

The commander and I jumped into the GAZ and were taken to the outskirts of Olomouc, where, in a rural area called Řepčín, the new railway station was situated, I didn't know it then, but I was looking at my very first discotheque.

My fellow soldiers had already moved there in the morning with our unit commander Corporal Miloslav, a university graduate who, due to taking the compulsory army lectures during his studies, would, automatically be ranked Corporal with just one year to serve.

The other members of our little squad included two loco tractor engineers, plus Veverka my fellow shunter, and Jarek who became a train dispatcher in a course he took immediately he'd left high school.

Our commander gave a little speech confirming that our unit was now complete and that Corporal Miloslav would be our commander. He had already prepared signed permits for us to come and go from the place, and reminded us that strangers were not to enter the building, and alcohol was strictly forbidden.

Finally he informed us we were responsible for the maintenance of the station, which, as it wasn't yet a functioning railway station, would be our abode.

Corporal Miloslav proved to be a really cooperative officer, quickly becoming one of the boys.

He then gave his first commands sending Veverka and I to oil the switch turns, whilst one of us loaded the stove in the cellar with furnace coke. Jarek offered to go on a one kilometre jog through the snow to the nearest shop to bring back apple wine, which was the cheapest fruit wine available at nine crowns a bottle.

That evening we held a big celebration in what would eventually become the passenger waiting room. Right now it was our very cosy bedroom, one that would be the envy of any Warsaw treaty soldier.

Relaxing on this first night in our new abode, out came the Hitachi and on came Radio Luxembourg at full volume. As Kid Jensen introduced some quite progressive music from a new band called Deep Purple, I retold my friends the story about the stupid officer in Nový Bohumín, and when I'd finished it was generally agreed that if the officer could see and hear us now, he would have had a heart attack!

I was so happy to see that everyone enjoyed the songs and the cool disc jockeys on Radio Luxembourg. Tony Prince became a firm favourite, Paul Burnett had taken over the crucial Top Twenty on Sunday nights, and Kid Jensen, at 17 the youngest of the new DJs on 208, brought to the station Jensen's Dimensions which was popular amongst the rockers in our billet. Few understood a word of what the DJs were saying, so it fell to educated Miloslav who studied English at high school, and myself to translate DJ comments and the song lyrics that appealed most. Even so, the quick-fire chatter from the 208 DJs often went over our heads, and so we filled in our translation with the words we thought they had said, or should have said.

It really didn't matter what the DJs said, it was their speedy cadence and friendly demeanour which made them so listenable, and everyone lying around our bedroom late into the evening regardless of whether he understood just a little or nothing at all, basked in the atmosphere the radio station created in our railway station.

On this night we all felt we had beat the system and all because with my little Hitachi, we were able to invite the west into our lives.

But I still loved my country. This was the country that my grandfather died for in Buchenwald concentration camp. Czechoslovakia was the nation my mother and father risked their lives for, just like my uncles, Josef and Franta.

Every teenage rail-soldier dancing around to 208 in our new bedroom, loved our country, but boy did we hate the communists who seized power and made our country into a totalitarian regime.

Which maybe explains the feeling we had that night whilst doing something so simple like drinking apple juice, chatting away and dancing to fabulous music of the 60s. We were beating the system and outsmarting the commies.

We had also inherited the same high-level food allowance as was afforded to the privileged officers, a stipend, something you only received when you were placed outside the barracks. This was totalitarianism working in our favour, because everyone had to be treated the same in this share and share alike world. For the first time in our lives we experienced what it was like belonging to a privileged class. But the freedom we had was rather more special than the extra money.

Away from the rigid army regime in our garrison, we were basking in our unusual freedom to come and go. Our only direct officer was Miloslav, a non-commissioned officer who became our friend, someone longing to get through his army service just like the rest of us.

To make matters better still, the cinemas in nearby Olomouc were showing western films, including classic old Hollywood films we had never seen. Cleopatra with Liz Taylor and the Mustangs with Marilyn Monroe finally played in the east. We also saw The Magnificent Seven and North to Alaska with John Wayne for the first time. Then there were quite a few good Italian and French movies as well, but all the Eastern Bloc movies that only two weeks ago made up almost three quarters of the films shown in our cinemas, were nowhere to be seen.

Something was going on, but I was damned if I knew what?

Some days we'd leave one in charge, and we'd all pile into the various cinemas to catch up on the movies we should have been watching years ago. Newspapers and magazines also broadened their content becoming much more light-hearted, even Red Law had significantly started to limit its attacks on everything coming from the west.

A seismic literary wave hit us in March 1968 when, 20 years after it was banned, the weekly Literární Listy (Literary Leaves) returned to the shelves.

One of its early lead articles addressed totalitarian society maintaining it was of no use to anyone, and no one understood this better than the people of Czechoslovakia. Then the prolific writer Jan Procházka, joined the editorial team, explained the goals of the publication in a way no one could misinterpret. A reader asked him if as a literary magazine, they would be focusing mainly on community-wide issues in our society?

He answered candidly and metaphorically:

'When the ship is sinking and has a hole below the waterline the size of a barn door, a reasonable captain does not send the ship's boy to paint the mast. So we simply cannot discuss the way we are writing books or verse when we live in a continuous social earthquake.'

The metaphor about the ship made me recall the times that Radio Caroline went off air, first, in January 1966, when she lost her anchor chain and ran aground. Then shortly afterwards 199 metres just went dead for three days. When it finally came back on air, the DJs explained there had been a storm and it had taken Tony Blackburn and their newest DJ, Tony Prince, to make the climb up the swaying mast to release a cable which was causing the broadcasting system to short circuit. When I listened to the DJs recounting these dramatic events, although they spoke too quickly for me to fully understand, you couldn't help appreciate that these pirate DJs loved music and radio, just as much as we loved our country. What else could have driven them to climb 180 feet above the sea in a gale?

Jan Procházka had made us think. We could embrace matters of art and literature once we'd made the ship seaworthy again.

Sometimes it was so good we found it difficult deciding which movie to see first. Likewise, magazines and books, we'd never ever been spoilt for choice in all our lives.

We had been stationed in Řepčín railway station for just over a week, when I happened to mention to commander Miloslav that I had not been home since enlisting more than five months ago. He stared at me with disbelief, took my permit book and wrote *'three days' leave from the garrison to visit home in Brno Friday–Sunday'*.

On the Friday morning, I had my thumb in the air and decided to hitchhike rather than spend my money on a bus or train. Drivers usually picked girls or soldiers, because of course a shared ride with a young girl made for a pleasant change, whereas sympathy flowed for the poor soldiers taken out of their homes for two years with so little money. My theory proved to be right, in less than two hours after leaving the railway station, I was knocking on the door of our flat in Brno.

I felt like a returning hero as my parents enveloped me in their hugs and kisses at the door. Mother feigned annoyance that I hadn't let her know I was coming so she could have prepared the cakes she knew I loved so much.

I explained that giving them this surprise was what I'd wanted more than anything, and then I added to their delight telling them I would be staying until Sunday, so mother should begin to prepare the cakes right away.

I found both mother and father more relaxed and very happy with the new political developments, the pulse of freedom apparent through friends and neighbours openly discussing the failure of the communist totalitarian system.

As soon as I could, I went to meet my buddy František Jemelka, who filled me in with all the news concerning our friends playing in various groups. His biggest and best news was that Synkopy 61 had been to the Czechoslovak Radio studio in Brno to record some songs, with their new singer/guitarist Pavel Váně.

This was the kind of climate change I'd dreamed of, a local group known to sing American West Coast-style songs in English, afforded the opportunity to record their music. Then František took the good news to another level, informing me that the band looked like they would have a record deal.

Next František surprised me with a gift, a large metal record, the likes of which a sound studio in the centre of Brno used to produce some years ago with one song on each side cut into a metal discs that played at 78 revolutions per minute. According to František there were two Chubby Checker songs on it, and that he'd come across it when visiting a friend who said he no longer played it.

František knew someone who loved anything sung in English regardless of the speed. Now it was mine and I couldn't wait to play it.

I returned home with my prize and all of a sudden the room became one big party even though I stood alone.

'Come on everybody! Clap your hands! Ha you're looking good! I'm gonna sing my song. It won't take long! We're gonna do the twist and it goes like this…'

The fact that *Let's Twist Again* was seven years old, didn't change the thrill I felt listening to it now in such perfect quality. For the first time I understood why it was given the 1962 Grammy Award for the Best Rock 'n' Roll recording. I visualised a New Year's Eve party rocking and the incredible atmosphere coming from Chubby Checker with his invitation to dance and what it could lead to with the right crowd at the right time and place.

I suppose these were my carnal DJ motivations, a need to expose a great tune to a great audience. I played it again…

'Heeee, and round and round and up and down we go again!

and again…

Baby, make me know you love me sooooo…

and again.

And then…'

I took the record player and my precious records with me back to Olomouc. It was time to give Chubby Checker a test drive together with my precious Eddie Cochran LP.

Having treated my friends to the cakes that my mother had carefully baked for her son, I placed the record player in the entrance corridor that was isolated from the waiting room come bedroom. Placing the Chubby Checker metal disc onto the turntable I then adjusted the volume to maximum and handed over to Chubby.

'Come on everybody! Clap your hands!'

It was electric. The boys went wild for it, although it would be a couple of nights before they understood what Chubby Checker wanted them to do.

This was my first gig as a DJ playing records, a night when Radio Luxembourg took a back seat as I went through my entire record collection for the boys. Never before had I been able to play music so loud. In my home, even at half this volume, the neighbours would be battering down the door wondering what was going on. But not here, we danced at full decibels like wild boys under no supervision, one kilometre from the nearest habitation.

On the following Monday morning, the commander of our unit came from the barracks to tell us to clean the place up, as at noon the commander of our railway regiment would come with the directors of the nearby ironworks to meet us. Their newly constructed railway siding would finally start to function, which meant that we would henceforth be operating there with our loco-tractor for a two-month test run.

When they arrived, they treated us like railwaymen, not at all like subordinate kid soldiers. It was a very informal meeting where we were informed that we would be paid a little extra for our services by the ironworks.

That was good news, not just because we would earn even more money than your average soldier, but because we knew that our commanders too would be earning nice bonuses because of which, we knew we would be treated like kings.

Goodbye army drill, goodbye political lectures, hello lots of free time to do as we liked.

Army Nirvana no less.

With so much free time between us, it didn't take us long to discover the swimming pool in the centre of Olomouc. With no showers at Villa Railway station, and standard procedure being to pour cold water on oneself in the basement, the pool showers every other day became a real hygienic pleasure. One day whilst swimming alone, my attention was caught by two young beauties in swimsuits. When they were relaxing after swimming, I tried to open up conversation with a funny remark to break the ice. I asked if they were twins as they were wearing identical bathing costumes. They couldn't have been less like twins, one tall and dark haired, one a great deal smaller with mousy blonde hair.

To my surprise they laughed, which I took as an invitation to sit with them and to establish a relationship. We talked about a great many things, with music and movies high on the agenda.

When we reached the subject of the English language, I was pleased to note that the taller girl, Anička, responded as she studied English at high school. She was quite mysterious, the one I was most attracted to much more than the second girl Alena, who looked lovely also, but the chemistry in my head was in favour of the taller girl, Anička who was a medical student. While Alena was working as a nurse in hospital already, and had no chance to study English as Russian was the chosen language in her vocational stream.

I always enjoyed meeting girls by the lake or at swimming pools because without clothes, it was all down to personality, you couldn't make a fashion judgement. I decided I needed to be funny again, so I told my new friends that I was in Olomouc serving my two year compulsory duty in the army, adding that I felt they should be aware of this just in case they had any intention to fall in love with me.

This joke was also accepted with smiles and giggles.

I was glad I'd got that one out in the open as it was quite common during dance parties, when a soldier approached a girl and gave her his invitation to dance, he often heard '*I am not dancing with a soldier.*'

This was the result of countless broken romances caused by the will–o'-the wisp and fly-by-night military Casanovas.

But on this day, I just wanted to enjoy some female company for a change, so I was quite relaxed shooting the breeze with these two lovelies.

Outside, as we made to depart, I invited them to the movies the following day. Alena responded positively and immediately, but the one I really fancied, Anička, said she had to prepare something important for university and so couldn't make it.

I tried to disguise my disappointment, but I surely would have liked it better the other way round. I thought about putting tomorrow on the back burner until all three of us could go, but felt that might reveal too strongly to Anička how I felt and be too un-gentlemanlike in Alena's case. Then I asked myself how many girls, other than shop assistants, had I talked to in the past six months? That's when I decided to accompany Alena to the movies the following day.

A few seconds later, I was glad I hadn't abandoned the cinema with Alena, when Anička suggested that on Friday we could all go to a dance in a cool wine cellar with some other friends.

"If you can get a pass," she added.

Surviving Thursday with Alena was made easier now that I knew I would be seeing Anička again the following day.

I explained I had a special pass and could leave the barracks any time I wished. It was my attempt to impress them and I believe it might have worked.

The next day I met Alena in front of the cinema and it was wonderful being in the company of a girl again after so long. We watched a French movie A Man and a Woman with rather touching scenes, nice cars and beautiful music by Francis Lai. When it was over we agreed, as it was snowing and quite slippery, I would walk Alena home. It came quite natural that we should hold hands so that I would catch her if she slipped in the snow. As we were saying goodbye at her front door, she gave me a quick kiss and disappeared inside leaving me quite speechless.

The kiss kept my mind busy all the way back to our railway station. *Why* did she kiss me? Was she inspired by the French movie, which had featured quite a few amorous kissing scenes? Or could it be, God forbid, that she'd fallen in love with me? In one day? Surely not?

Suddenly there was no room for thought, other than these two new female friends. One I fancied like hell, the other who had shown such intimacy on her doorstep. Later that evening Radio Luxembourg became a background sound, overshadowed by the kiss from Alena. How was it I had the hots for Anička, and yet in spite of this, Alena had now invaded my thoughts?

Anička or Alena, Anička or Alena, Anička or Alena... Tonight I didn't need to count sheep.

The following evening, I left Villa Railway station early enough to be at our meeting point on time, as I didn't want to miss a second with my two new friends, two friends who I had obsessed over now for a day and a half. I hadn't forgotten Anička had mentioned we would go dancing with their friends and I'd considered who and how many these might be? My answer arrived with Anička herself, he was tall, a pleasant chap. I liked him.

The wine cellar itself was a pleasant place and served good wine, a great conversation aid. We talked over many subjects until the time to dance arrived. There we were, two boys with two ravishing young girls dancing to the shittiest music imaginable. On a small platform in the corner was a one-man-band, complete with organ, playing Czech favourites our parents might have responded well to.

But then, after a further bottle of wine my bubble was pricked. I was dancing with Alena, when I noticed Anička not only dancing too close to her partner for my liking, now she'd started to kiss him.

"Shit!" I thought as finally, the light came on in my naive head. Why had I only just realised they were a couple, lovers already? The swimming pool scene came back to mind. It was now plain to see that Anička was going steady, and would never have come to the cinema the following day because she had a boyfriend.

Then in the swimming pool Alena had made her choice. The wrong girl had selected me!

At this moment, watching Anička kissing her man, I didn't know what to do. Suddenly I stopped enjoying the music, or rather I stopped tolerating it. I had lost the beautiful Anička before I could get close to her, and now this horrible music just added to my suffering. Instinctively Alena knew that something was wrong, as until a moment or two ago I'd been dividing my affections equitably between both girls. Now I had lost all interest.

"What is it Jan?" she asked, and I muttered that the music was too horrible and was making me sick. Then Alena surprised me saying that she didn't like it either and that it was like something from the dark ages. This calmed me down, music I could talk about and as we did so, I was struck by lightning! Why should we continue to suffer such torture listening to this desperate middle-aged star of this wine cellar, when there were so many great records at our railway station villa?

I mentioned it to Alena, describing the place and, if they cared to make the journey, how there would only be my fellow soldier, Pepa and his girlfriend, which meant we could enjoy listening to the music at full volume.

When Anička returned from the dance floor with her boyfriend, they agreed it was a great idea. I warned them that to get to our railway station in Řepčín would require more than a kilometre walk on icy roads. They thought it very funny that I would think to describe a route they knew intimately. Řepčín was a favourite place to go during the summer, as there were two fine lakes that arose from gravel mines of old.

"We go skinny-dipping in Řepčín lakes every summer," said Anička, causing me to think of another lake in another area with another girl.

Departing with two bottles of wine, we thanked the old musician for playing for us, after all it wasn't his fault that he didn't know any Elvis, Eddie Cochran or Beatles songs. Soon however, I'd impress my new friends with my entire repertoire.

On arrival I felt like the proud owner of the building as I opened the front door with my key. I was surprised it was in darkness with no sign of Pepa and his girlfriend who, before I left, hadn't given me the impression they wanted to go out for a drink, or anything other than consume each other.

I was impatient to show off my records; however, having never been inside a railway station before, they asked for a tour. I took great pleasure in doing so and even took them to the heart of our operation, the dispatch control where all the switch turn remote controls and signal were situated.

We even descended into the cellar, where I threw open the furnace and loaded more coke to build up the heat for the girls, who had just endured a long walk in the bitter Siberian winds, and a temperature well below zero. The place was soon roasting, and off came the coats as I found the cleanest drinking vessels possible for consuming our wine. Now they were ready to rock to the Railway DJ, and I took great pleasure in displaying my entire record collection, and entertaining them with vinyl tales of extraordinary finds in mountain stores and stolen tape recorders.

Eventually I plugged in the record player, turned up the volume to full blast, and let Eddie Cochran loose in the most unconventional dance club in our country.

For all my three guests this was the first time in their lives they had heard western music played from records – Czech records they could listen to. The sound quality compared to the radio's they'd grown accustomed to, was an incredible revelation for all three of them.

I stood there enjoying their pleasure feeling 10 feet tall, having brought them to this outback railway station, our army villa, to give them this great audio experience. There was no dancing yet, they were too mesmerised by what they were hearing. Elvis' *The King*, and the real rock 'n' roll songs of Eddie Cochran, and then my solitary Beatles recording of *Rock and Roll Music*.

I turned the Eddie Cochran album over and introduced *Jeannie, Jeannie, Jeannie* explaining that unfortunately the song was not dedicated to either Anička or to Alena, but surely only because Eddie had not had the good fortune to meet them as I had. After this flattery, I quoted the first line of the song translating it into Czechoslovak, '*Well Jeannie, Jeannie, Jeannie come and dance with me.*' Eddie's voice segued mine as they obeyed me dancing around the floor, like I'd given them a military command.

Now Eddie Cochran was in command, and when we stopped for breath, someone said they wondered what Leonid Brezhnev would say if he could see his Warsaw pact army now!

We were in the middle of our laughter, reaching for more wine, I'd just dropped the needle on *House of the Rising Sun* and just as Eric Burdon sang '*There is a house in New Orleans...*', the front door started to shake and, at the same time, my bladder signalled trouble.

I was almost jailed for playing a radio in my barracks in Nový Bohumín, if this was the major or someone with rank, there would be no wriggling out of this situation. Civilians were not allowed inside military zones at any time, let alone after midnight listening to the Animals' *House of the Rising Sun*!

So I prepared myself for the worst as the door vibrated. Had we still got a pheasant on the premises I wondered? But now it was too late, the door swung open.

And there stood Pepa with his girlfriend, without coats looking like they'd just climbed from a sofa by the fireplace. Minus zero and they were glowing. "Man you scared me to death," I said. "Did you forget that the last one here on guard should leave a message if they go anywhere?"

By now Pepa had introduced himself and his girlfriend to my friends.

"Sorry Jan," he said. "It was a bit cold in here so we decided to go to a loco tractor. You know how lovely and warm they are!"

Now it was all clear to me, Pepa and his girl had wanted to have their own *chambre separé*.

Once again I reached for the needle and dropped it at the beginning of *House of the Rising Sun*, not exactly a love song, but the perfect tempo for what we all needed.

When it ended someone asked for it to be played again. Eventually, my audience requested it five times in a row, providing Villa Railway disco with a perfect 25-minute smooch!

Alena was lovely and gentle and beautiful, and I started to feel very amorous, just as everyone must have been feeling in this magic atmosphere. But something inside me wasn't quite right. I recalled Kafka and how I felt I could spend the rest of my life with her. It wasn't like this with Alena, even though dancing so close to her was quite wonderful.

The mystical evening ended, and it was Pepa's girlfriend who suggested we arrange another club night à la Villa Railway station in two weeks' time when she returned.

Everyone agreed, and then I was rewarded with warm good night kisses from both Alena and Anička.

Alena had no phone at home, so we arranged to meet one day after her day shift at hospital ended.

I knew one thing, this was my first disco in charge of the dance floor, and it certainly wasn't going to be my last.

The following week Alena and I went to the cinema to see an American movie, Wait Until the Dark with Audrey Hepburn.

Choosing a cinema was becoming more and more difficult every week as Western and Czechoslovak films dominated. There were no Soviet movies at all.

Alena and I behaved like two normal friends, with little evidence that we'd been dancing so close together just a couple of days ago. Only when a film frightened her did she take my hand and move closer to me.

Outside the little house where she lived with her mother, she gave me a warm goodnight kiss mentioning that her mum would be away for a couple of days soon, and that she would like to show me inside. In spite of my almost total ignorance where loving matters were concerned, I was smart enough to figure out that when a girl was prepared to invite a boy into a motherless home, she would have more on her mind than conversation.

Tony: Coronation Street

Back we went through the tunnel to a council estate two streets from where I'd started my journey. My career was in tatters. No Luxembourg, no BBC, no USA. But I had Christine and Daniel, and we were soon to become four, so I called on my reserves of optimism and decided to become Laurence Olivier auditioning for the Oldham Repertory Theatre, and Granada TV.

My first break came when I was cast as a DJ voice, emanating from a radio in the television series The Lovers, a popular romcom, featuring the late great Richard Beckinsale and beautiful big-eyed Paula Wilcox.

Next I played the part of a DJ for two editions of Coronation Street when teenage terror Lucille Hewitt became a go-go dancer, much to the chagrin of her parents Concepta and Harry Hewitt.

Lucille was played by Jenny Moss who held my respect, not as an actress but rather that in 1963, she'd had a couple of records out produced by the great-but-slate-loose Joe Meek. The songs were *Hobbies* and *Big Boys*, which was somewhat autobiographical for this mini-Mancunian who passed away in Scotland in 2006 after having married five times.

I don't think any DJ can claim to have ad-libbed on television's Coronation Street with legends Florrie Lindley and Minnie Caldwell, and rubbed shoulders with Ena Sharples. This experience is in my top ten of 'Did That Really Happen?' up there with meeting Elvis Presley.

In the show I was seen to introduce records from a DJ console, whilst Lucille go-go'd her tiny arse off. On the second show I had a walk-on part, where I was seen giving Minnie and Florrie a cup of *tea* in the club! Quite what they were doing in a club in the daytime, I have no idea, I was not there to wrestle with the scriptwriters, I was there to become an actor.

"Work your part Tone," encouraged actress Sandra Gough in the Granada canteen. "Yes lad, milk your line for all its worth," advised Len Fairclough, who later swapped his own acting career for paedophilia in a swimming pool.

The script read, *'Tea's up ladies'*. I spent two hours in my dressing room prior to being called to the set, practicing how I could best milk these three words?

Eventually I sauntered up to these legendary characters and said, "Tea's up ladies. Would you like milk in that?"

Shakespearean! The producer made us take it again as per script, because the retort from Florrie hadn't anticipated a question from me. Florrie and Minnie didn't like working off-script with ad-libbing DJs.

I was being paid less acting the part of a DJ than being a real DJ, and wondering what the hell I was going to do, when unexpectedly I got a call from Carl Paulson, the director of the Oldham Rep, who I had called on as soon as we'd hit Oldham. He wanted me to read the part of a blind American in the Leonard Gershe play, Butterflies Are Free.

It was a big break, there were only three or four characters in the whole play, and in America it was on Broadway.

I auditioned for Carl in an empty Oldham Rep, and he offered me the part there and then, the break every aspiring actor would dream of.

I started learning my lines and working on my American accent.

Then Radio Luxembourg's new MD, Alan Keen, called me!

"Are you ready to come back on 208?" he asked.

Pause button.

"I've got a four week summer replacement job for you."

Start button.

Ignoring the call of the greasepaint, I thanked Carl and explained my decision to take Alan's offer, and for four weeks I returned to the airways of Radio Luxembourg.

As the month drew to a close, instead of returning to England I took a job at the Blow Up discotheque. I had no pride and had decided to camp there until Alan Keen called me back full-time, a hope based on a very large supply of ego.

It took three long months before Alan finally called me.

"I've just sacked someone, when can you start?" he asked down the phone.

"What time is it Alan?"

"5pm," he answered.

"Can I go home to clean my teeth?"

At 7.30pm, unannounced, unexpected, unscripted, I opened the microphone in my old studio and said, "Hi everyone, this is yer Royal Ruler... now where were we?"

It had been a year between broadcasts.

I kept the Radio Luxembourg microphone open for 16 years.

Back as a family in the Grand Duchy, we rented a fully detached house in the village of Steinsel. We had *three* kids now, Daniel, Gabrielle and Kid Jensen who moved in with us.

On my second night back as a full-time member of the team, I was called to a DJ meeting at Paul Burnett's apartment. I was intrigued.

Paul was the spokesperson.

"We're happy you're back Tony," he began, "But it's no longer Tony Prince and the 'Luxy Lads', we're not living in your shadow anymore."

I'd only left them alone for a few months and they'd forgotten who was the lead singer at the Chez Nous. They'd forgotten the free drinks I'd negotiated, forgotten who made them piss themselves with laughter with strippers, gorillas and headstands on castle ramparts.

After only a few months without me, they expected me to rip out my genes and become... someone else!

So they had their meeting, I took it on the chin, cried a little, but come Saturday, Paul Kid and Mark were right behind me on *Mean Woman Blues* earning their free drinks.

If any of them wanted to become the lead singer, first they'd have to learn the words!

Jan: The Railway DJ

A few days after the party, suddenly lots of activity started to take place around the railway station. We were informed that our entire garrison would be leaving in May to work in Bohemia, where rails had to be changed and the track repaired on a main section of the Prague to Pilsen line.

Everyone went into training on several kilometres of track around

Olomouc. Every morning lorries arrived with a hundred soldiers from our barracks to our railway station to distribute stretcher bars on which 25 metre long rails were placed. These were then fixed together with all kinds of bolts and screws. Once they were fixed to wheels we took over moving the sections a few hundred metres with our loco tractor.

Once this was completed we'd retire to our cosy villa, whilst the poor foot soldiers completed another section.

When they eventually had a break they all came inside the railway station to drink tea and sit around.

It was only a question of time for one of them to discover my turntable and records.

"Why don't you play us some music Jan?" Someone chirped.

I tried to resist the invitation, explaining these were English tunes that might irritate our commanders but rather than be proclaimed a coward, I proceeded to play and comment on my record collection.

I tried to keep the volume low, but that wasn't possible for long, as more soldiers gathered and digested the acoustics. I noted how great it sounded at full volume with a corridor filled with soldiers, some of whom started to dance together.

This was the moment and the place where the stigma 'Railway DJ' was placed upon me so that, wherever I went in the year ahead, that's what everyone called me.

I was still afraid what might happen when our commanders appeared, but to my complete surprise they weren't at all angry, only asking, "What was making that noise in the station corridor?"

When I explained it was a record player, they didn't even question the western music pounding round the place; all they wanted to understand was why I had brought a record player with me?

Explaining this was something I had done for cultural purposes, as here at the railway station we had no access to the cinema, which they enjoyed in the barracks. I took care not to mention we'd seen more movies in more cinemas recently, than in our entire lives.

Satisfied with my answer and obviously not Eddie Cochran fans, off they went to the dispatchers office leaving us to *20 Flight Rock*. This experience brought it home to me just how our world was changing. Dozens of soldiers listening and bopping away to American rock 'n' roll songs, playing at maximum volume, with not a word of protest from our commanders, was further proof for me that our world was changing for the better. Newspaper journals changing their political leanings was one thing, but when the military became complacent about Eddie Cochran, you knew the sun was coming out in Czechoslovakia.

From today onwards, I would never again have to be afraid of anything concerning my love for western music, and my nightly intake of Radio Luxembourg.

And all this in less than two months!

Friday arrived, and whilst I'd been looking forward to my next DJ gig very much, Pepa was twice as excited as his girl would be back, and he could turn the locomotive's heater up once again.

The disco began. Both Anička and Alena proving to be excellent assistants having brought some Czech records to supplement my limited vinyl supply. I put my personal preferences to one side understanding that, after all, we lived in Czechoslovakia and where else should Czechoslovakian records be played other than in our country, at the army's first ever discotheque. I also started to appreciate how boring it might be for non-English speaking people, to continuously listen to songs in English, no matter how cool the music might be. From this knowledge on this night, I developed a career in explaining to my audiences exactly what the songs were about. As most of them listened to Radio Luxembourg, the huge majority welcomed the information, especially if it was a familiar hit they'd heard many times.

But the highlight of this music party came once Pepa and his girl had returned from their cosy loco-love-nest, when the girls started to question him about his locomotive.

"OK… who wants to be a train driver?"

We all climbed into the cabin as Pepa started the engine and I stoked up the fire.

As the loco built up speed, Pepa lectured his audience explaining that it didn't matter if you were drunk in charge of a train, because it ran on tracks, and at this time of night there wasn't another train running on this line anywhere within 100 kilometres.

With this welcome information, each of our guests became engine drivers, something so few civilians have or will ever experience. Towards 3am they all left Villa Railway laughing happily through the snow, leaving both Pepa and I to reflect on what great hosts we'd been.

The following week after I'd walked Alena home from the cinema, instead of giving me her usual good night kiss, she invited me inside, at last her mother was out of town. It was good judgement on her part not telling me sooner, she must have known me quite well by now and understood that too much thinking made Jan a dull boy.

Once inside we drank a little wine, and then Alena said she would like to show me the family album, which she placed on the sofa away from the table where we'd been chatting.

She bade me join her and I lay down next to her as she started to turn the pages, giving me a running commentary on the pictures.

I was fully aware that in this situation I could shut the album, turn Alena closer to me and make love till dawn. But I was so far from wanting to do it as my thoughts killed any chance of arousal. Here I am, a former switchman, upgraded to shunter, surviving the army years. Was I to be a typical military man, one of those who was the reason so many girls refused to dance with a man in uniform? Would I come and go?

In these few moments where crucial life-changing decisions had to be made, I compared Alena to Katka. With Katka I could talk about so many things because she was so inspiring, but we'd been too young and inexperienced and never got to the stage I now found myself in with Alena. On the other hand Alena was also lovely and gentle and witty, and surely must have loved me, as otherwise she would not have invited me to lay down next to her in this way. I was sure that she was not the type of girl who would have sexual intercourse, unless she was in love with someone.

Right now I could have wished for nothing more than to take off her dress and hold her tightly kissing every inch of her naked body, in circumstances where this divine door was opened to me.

I had decided I would not become just another soldier who used a girl while killing time in the army. I knew that, as lovely as she was, Alena was not the girl in my long-term dreams.

I made some dumb excuse about not having permission in my army book to be out tonight. Her sad eyes tortured me on the long walk in the snow back to villa railway.

If I ever wanted more proof about her love for me, I had a belly full when I met her the following week when she told me her big news. She and her mother were moving to Brno in the not too distant future. I was not very convincing when I expressed my pleasant surprise at the news.

If either of us had been materialistic, the attraction of owning a house could have become part of our courtship.

Alena and her mother owned their house, which was a high step on the ladder to success in our country. Young non-communist party couples had to wait at least 10 years for a high rent flat; whereas those in Public Safety, Secret Police, even *army officers* got a flat immediately, and for half the rent of ordinary civilians.

Alena never threw this golden opportunity into the ring, and I never considered the new advantages such materialism would bring to my life. Looking back, I see that capitalism hadn't infected either of us, regardless of the severity of our communist system.

The house must have belonged to Alena or her mother as, during those times it was not possible to have two properties, and so, letting one to be rented was not a possibility. So I could surmise they were either selling the house in Olomouc and buying a new one in Brno, or exchanging it.

If Alena had mentioned the opportunities our relationship could provide,

I would still have walked away.

Just as she would never try to win a boy's heart offering him the security of a house, the same could go for me, as I would have much preferred a new Beatles or Rolling Stones' album to a house at that time!

Perhaps just then both our souls were too clean and untarnished by all the corruption around us, and I thank God and beautiful Alena for this.

Now, had she owned a record collection…?

Tony: The Osmonds

Bell Records flew me to America to interview David Cassidy, who I'd had as a guest on the show on a couple of occasions.

Europe had a fuel shortage. My plane flew via Reykjavik, Iceland to refuel, making us eight hours late in LA.

I didn't mind, Dick Leahy the boss of Bell Records, had arranged for me to travel first class.

Because their artists used them extensively, Pan Am upgraded me. It still goes on. Airlines still want the prestige of personalities on board. It's wonderful, a £4,000 seat for economy rate, or, in my case, zilch!

A 'Special Services' manager meets you at the check-in escorting you to the first-class lounge. Here you wait, star-spotting and having to endure vintage Dom Perignon until they escort you to the flight's upper-deck where the stewardess, (usually a steward who has the mannerisms of a stewardess), calls you by your name, and feeds you in the manner in which you've swiftly become accustomed.

Delayed due to refuelling in Reykjavik, we were invited to step off the plane. No wonder they call it Iceland! Not one passenger bothered leaving after our tears froze on the top step.

A limo driver was still waiting at LA International. I'd hoped to sleep during the afternoon and interview Cass that night. Now the day was almost tomorrow, it was 3.00am and the star of The Partridge Family still awaited my arrival in his Beverly Hills mansion.

By the time I got there, Cass was stoned listening to the final mix of his own *Could It Be Forever?* but we managed to get some semblance of an interview before I was whisked back to LA International for my return flight.

Missing my connection to Luxembourg at Heathrow, I headed for London and the Speakeasy where I met Roger Holt from MGM.

"I've got an act that are going to be bigger than Cassidy," he said, when I told him where I'd been for the day.

"Ever heard of the Osmonds?"

"Early 60s, Andy Williams Show, little kids singing in tinny voices," I answered.

And so, over Speakeasy spareribs and a clasp or two of ale, we plotted the launching of the careers of Donny, Alan, Merrill, Jay and Wayne. Marie and Jimmy would come later.

Within 48 hours I was back in the USA, this time as a guest of MGM for four days at Las Vegas' Caesar's Palace where I would first chill out, watch their concerts a couple of times, lose some money and then conduct interviews with each of the five older brothers.

On day two I was on the hotel's top floor in the Caesar's health club having my jet lag pummelled out of me by a brute of an African American masseuse.

Next to me, on the adjoining slab, also being pummelled, lay a naked Donny Osmond.

I introduced myself and we chatted from massage to steam room, to work out machines, to sauna and swimming pool.

I looked at him curiously as the two of us sat in the sauna. A seven stone kid and not a bead of sweat.

"Why do you put yourself through all this Donny?" I asked. "You don't smoke or take drugs, no Coca-Cola or coffee and you haven't started to go with girls. You're not fat, you don't do anything that makes people fat, so why'd you put yourself through all this?"

"It's free", he explained logically, "Part of our Caesars Palace deal."

I'd planned to broadcast an interview with each of the brothers, the five nights leading up to their arrival in the UK.

At this stage, few in the media had heard of them, but because I received sacks of mail from the weenyboppers who religiously listened to my show at 7.30pm as they did their homework, I knew them well.

Because I wrote a column for Fab 208 magazine each week, I already appreciated an underground swell was taking place for these Osmonds.

My hunch was confirmed once I'd seen their Vegas show.

Energy *and* good looks. It was quite a combination.

The brothers danced and sang *One Bad Apple* followed by the Jackson 5's *I Want You Back*, whereupon they choreographed their way into the Temptations' *I Can't Get Next To You*.

Clean cut, cute (in Donny's case) and 'ansum; they were prime material for Fab 208, and for my radio station's early show.

That night, trying the free cocktails in the hotel lobby, Roger Holt and I ended up talking to a man called Tony Martin. When he discovered I was a disc jockey on Radio Luxembourg, he became very animated.

It was slightly embarrassing, because his music belonged in the Egerton Arms pub. Politely we humoured him as best we could, but I couldn't for the life of me recall any of his hits.

"When you get back to Radio Luxembourg," he said as we made to leave, "Go to your record library, and I guarantee you'll find more of my records than anyone's!"

"Did you leave them there?" I asked the cocktails kicking in.

"Fuck you limey," he said laughing as he walked away. "Don't forget to look now," he hollered pointing a finger gun at me.

He was right, there were hundreds and I'd never played one of them. I never would. Pete Murray and Geoff Everett's fingerprints were all over them.

Back at the station I had bigger, fresher fish to fry than my new friend Tony Martin; I now had the opportunity to finally demonstrate the never-ending power and influence of Radio Luxembourg.

I managed to persuade MGM's Press Officer, David Hughes to slip me the Osmonds' arrival time at Heathrow's Terminal 3.

"You won't give it out on air," he insisted.

"Tut tut."

Every night I let it drop.

On their day of arrival, Heathrow airport had seen nothing like it since the Beatlemania days. The Osmonds had never seen anything like it either. They had arrived.

Hundreds of screaming girls chased them through the Arrivals Terminal. Now it was time for Osmondmania.

Coincidentally the Jackson 5 arrived at Heathrow at exactly the same time as the Mormon brigade, their chart successes already well in advance of the newcomer Osmonds.

A picture of a small Michael Jackson crying with fear at Heathrow was also featured in the following day's papers. The captions said that he was frightened, but I reckon the tears were because they were chasing Donny instead of him! How things would change!

I became President of the 'Official Osmonds Fan Club' touring with them extensively during their two-year reign.

Listen to the DJ countdown intro on their Osmonds Around The World live double album, that's me at Wembley Arena in 1973, on an album that captures the moment when they called it *Puppy Love* and we rode those wild *Crazy Horses*!

It was a real adventure running the gauntlet of scream-mania from theatres to hotels to airports and tour buses, day after day.

You want fear? Be in a limo with Donny and his brothers, trapped under 200 screaming pre-pubescent girls, as it looks likely the roof will cave in.

The one drug my Mormon friends took plenty of was adrenaline!

I repeated my 'Osmonds arrival' campaign for their second trip, which would be a major national tour. The 208 weenyboppers brought down the brick parapet of the Heathrow Queens Building viewing ramparts. Luckily no one was badly hurt, but a letter arrived from the Airport Authority asking me to desist giving out arrival times of pop groups.

I wrote back to them telling them to secure the balcony brickwork, prescribing the correct values for mixing water, sand and cement!

On Donny's 21st birthday, his older brothers asked me to present him with a cake on stage at Wembley and of course we made the tabloids; the brothers and I laughing, Donny's grimace obscured by cream.

   It's not only elephants that don't forget. Two years later I was coming out of the backstage of a club in Coventry together with Christine, when two young girls stopped me, for an autograph, or so I thought.

"Tony," said one of them, "This is for Donny!"

Spludge!!

It was a banana pie. I wouldn't have minded but I hate banana, couldn't eat one to save my life. Even after towelling myself down in the back alley of the venue, I still had the detestable taste and smell in my nose, ears, and eyes all the way back to London.

"You're not amused are you?" said Christine, after I'd clocked the first 20 miles in seething silence.

   In 1973 the Osmonds invited Christine and I to their home in Utah, where we went out for dinner with Alan and Jay, together with their girlfriends. It would be a difficult dinner, we smoked like chimneys, enjoyed the odd glass of wine, they were Mormons.

   We drove up the nearby Utah mountain to Sundance, a log cabin restaurant owned by Robert Redford, where he and Paul Newman had shot sequences for Butch Cassidy and the Sundance Kid. It was a stunning setting. A waterfall cascaded down from the mountain into an icy stream that ran a babbling, silvery course beneath log-built bridges.

In the twilight, wild and free white horses roamed the grassy mountain slopes, which led majestically up to a white blanket of snow, lapping at the scene below.

Inside the restaurant Christine and I had a problem. No ashtrays and no booze!

"How about some wine?" I invited.

"This is a Mormon State Tony", said big brother Alan Osmond. "We don't drink wine."

"Do you believe in Jesus?" I asked.

"Of course," they harmonised.

"Didn't he turn water into wine somewhere?" I probed.

"Yes Tony," said Jay jumping in. "But there's non-alcoholic fruit wine."

"Yes, but do you not think they were tying one on as it was supposed to be the last supper?" I proposed.

"Not Jesus, no way," said Alan's girlfriend, horrified at such a thought.

Christine kicked me beneath the table. She hated conflict, so she went outside for a fag.

Then there was Olive, Mother-Osmond, who co-managed them with dad. When they were invited to perform at the Royal Command Performance at the London Palladium, Olive put a rider in the contract that she had to be introduced to the Queen with them backstage.

Lord Delfont agreed.

After she'd curtsied she presented our Queen with a gift, The Book of Mormon!

Head of the Church of England already! Some conversion that would have been back at the palace!

The Osmonds sold 25 million records in a couple of years and gave 10% of their winnings to the Mormon Church. Tithings they called it.

On their last tour, which I compèred, the promoter went bankrupt and I didn't get paid at all, not even 10%. No tithings of comfort and joy for the Royal Ruler!

But I was paid in memories as part of a great musical adventure, which none of us will ever forget or regret.

Over the course of time the fans seem to have forgiven me for pieing Donny on his 21st birthday, but I was the guest of honour at a fan club reunion at a Heathrow hotel some 30 years later, and very much on my guard.

Jan: Bohemia rhapsody

On 1 May we were moving lock, stock and garrison to Bohemia, so I went home during the last weekend of April to return my turntable and records back from frontline duties.

František Jemelka confirmed to me that *War is a Fool*, which he'd composed with Olda Veselý, was due for release any day now!

It was hard to believe that my friends would have a record released very soon and that, just like Elvis and the Beatles, Synkopy 61 would become recording artists, and my great friend František as co-writer would have his name printed on each and every record.

I mentioned to František and Ladislav Plch who was enjoying an early evening drink with us, how sorry I was that I'd brought my turntable back from Olomouc and so, would be unable to play 'War' the moment it was released. I then recounted the great music parties and the trouble I had in Nový Bohumín.

"You are destined to be a DJ by the sounds of things," said Ladislav.

Returning to Olomouc, Pepa told me that Alena had been to villa railway and started to cry when she learned that I'd gone home for the weekend. I just couldn't bring myself to contact her. I didn't know what to tell her to resolve how we should go on, now that we were preparing to move to Bohemia. I just had no loving or lustful feelings to drive me to her again, and decided to avoid a confrontation.

The army hired the whole train for us, while Pepa and our second engineer travelled behind us with our loco tractor. The journey took us many hours, as our unscheduled train had to keep ducking in and out of sidings to make way for the scheduled trains, so we wouldn't disrupt the network's schedule. I enjoyed the day-long journey, playing my transistor radio all the time, and I was thrilled when we came to Prague and could see our greatest city framed in our train windows.

The Prague I now gazed upon, now housed a new political gang led by Dubček and I hoped the changes I was recognising would continue towards fuller democracy under his leadership.

After half an hour, we passed a railway station with a familiar name, which I struggled to place. After a few minutes I remembered it as Černošice, the town inhabited by Michal Bukovič, the founder of the Paul Anka fan club, my generous pen friend who provided me with so many great tapes.

I'd known roughly that Černošice was not far from Prague, but never studied a map to find out where exactly it was situated. Forty kilometres later we arrived at the city of Hořovice, where our fellow soldiers had already built an enormous tented camp. It came as a blow to my unit to discover that we would have to stay here, as the nearby Hořovice railway station had no space. Staying in the camp meant that we had to obey the commanders, but above all we'd lose the food allowance, and again be in the hands of the army cooks. Even lunch would be brought out to the track.

We didn't sleep well at all that first night, and things didn't improve. We'd been spoilt rotten and were now suffering for it.

One afternoon the train dispatchers at Hořovice station gave us a guided tour around the station, and beneath a huge water reservoir created for steam locomotives, which were quickly going out of service, we spotted an area where eight beds would fit perfectly. Of course there was no toilet, but the one in the station was near enough. There was of course plenty water right above our heads, but not so easily accessed.

With a little gentle persuasion and support from the dispatchers who assured him it was crucial we were on hand for any emergency work, our commander agreed. We were heading to Villa Water Tank, and our food allowance was reinstated as soon as we moved in.

Soon we learned a method of bathing inside the tank reservoirs, it meant holding on to the edge with one hand and listening out for the water pump. Had anyone remained in the water whilst a locomotive pumped out the water, they would have been stuck in that tank until the water level raised itself, rather like a modern toilet. The moment there was any suggestion of a pump noise, we were out of there like a flash.

I phoned Michal letting him know that I was now close to his place, and before I could suggest it, he enthusiastically invited me to visit. Meeting him was like a greeting with an old friend for although we'd never met we'd exchanged many letters and tapes.

His girl, Dana, was very kind and fussed around me throughout my two-day stay, influenced, no doubt, by my uniform.

Then, finally, the time came for Michal to show me his record collection that left me quite breathless. For the first time in my life, I was gazing upon and handling real long-playing albums by the Beatles. Michal had three of their LPs and many more covetable albums, including my new hero Johnny Cash. Before now, I had no idea what he looked like, which was always the frustrating thing about listening to Luxembourg and the tapes Michal now provided.

During this memorable weekend, thanks to Michal, I could finally put a face to the singers I loved. Now I knew what my rock 'n' roll heroes Carl Perkins and Jerry Lee Lewis looked like, and I was impressed with their image. There was as much pleasure in looking at the LP sleeves as there was in listening to their content. The weekend flew by as I digested his collection, enjoying music from high quality vinyl played on his great PA system. We both enjoyed our engrossing discussions about tracks we loved and lyrics that fascinated or puzzled us. But what made our first meeting so unusual, was how we would talk to each other in English.

Dana announced dinner was ready, so we ate to the Beatles' *Please Please Me* album and drank to their *With the Beatles*.

I have never had a better meal.

What had promised to be a super weekend, turned into a veritable music lover's mini convention.

Tony: Meeting Elvis

In 1972, magic happened.

Our cavalcade of fan club busses pulled up outside the brand new Circus Circus hotel in Las Vegas, its casino roof pointing at the sky like a huge candy-striped big top. This was going to be the highlight of two weeks of thrills and dreams come true, the first ever pilgrimage by the Elvis Presley

Fan Club of Great Britain to see the King.

As Honorary President since my Radio Caroline days, I'd been invited by fan club secretary, Todd Slaughter, who now flanked me as we strode meaningfully towards the manager's office, together with David Wade, our tour organiser.

The hotel was over-booked, no room at the inn. Two hundred fans waited patiently onboard five air-conditioned buses as we went to sort the out the Mafia.

We'd arrived one week earlier treading in Elvis' footsteps, 200 from the terraces of Great Britain, most of whom had saved a lifetime, or made great personal sacrifices to be here. Extraordinary things had already happened to them in Memphis and Nashville, leaving most in a daze, but now here in East Tupelo where Elvis was born, we had a police escort from the city limits. Gun-toting Harley-Davidson outriders were taking us to meet the Mayor of Tupelo himself, right outside the Presley's two-room homestead on Old Saltillo Road.

The Women's Guild of Tupelo and the Garden Club turned out in force too, and the police were friendly, posing for photos and letting some of us ride their Harleys. Each of us walked in hallowed silence through the two sparsely furnished, baking hot rooms, and imagined Vernon the sharecropper, Gladys his wife and their son Elvis Aaron trying to squeeze into the box they had the indecency to call a house.

Some cried, I was one of them. You do on a pilgrimage, and not for the first time, the King had reached out and touched me emotionally.

Back in Memphis, we spent much time at Graceland talking with the gatekeeper, El's Uncle Vester, having photos on the steps, at the gates, everywhere.

I interviewed the silver-haired man standing on the lawn leading up to the famous paladin pillars of rock 'n' roll's most famous residence. He talked with an easy charm as a man who knew every answer, because he had met every question a hundred times.

He looked uncannily like his older brother Vernon, and I immediately felt the Presley deity. The accent, the eyes, the affection in his voice when his nephew's name came to his lips.

Here was the bloodline, third in line to the Memphis throne.

Here was the very man who taught a young Elvis his first guitar chords on frets too wide for his young fingers, on a guitar he'd received from Gladys and Vernon, when they couldn't afford to buy him the bicycle he really wanted.

How life would have changed, how earth's rock 'n' roll fables would have been so different had the bicycle been affordable, or uncle Vester had not known the two finger versions of C, F and G!

Had that bicycle been bought for the 11-year-old Elvis instead of a guitar, who's to say Eddy Merckx would have won *any* bike races with the Tupelo Mississippi Flash's feet in the pedals?
And who would have been King then? Jerry Lee Lewis? Ricky Nelson? Buddy Holly?

Beyond the scene of my interview, fans, pumped full of adrenaline, pegged each other up in a fireman's lift so they could peer over Graceland's side fencing.

Even though they knew full well that the King was in Vegas, looking over this wall was a major lifetime accomplishment for these people who had travelled from the towns and vales of the founding fathers. To actually see the field out back of Graceland, where the King rode his white stallion, Rising Sun, with Priscilla and baby Lisa Marie alongside, was as good as any drug they could get at that time in the morning.

To see anything where He had trod, to walk a green acre where He breathed this Memphis air, to touch the door behind which He laughed and played; these were the mind treasures they would keep.

Little did any of us know then, that a horror story would unfold behind that same door, not yards from where we stood posing happily for our photographs.

Not too far into the future this would be his final resting place, but today we walked a happy tour across ground that would, in the future, become hallowed.

Pragmatic souvenirs for the poorer members of our UK party, included leaves from the trees, the grass from the lawn, weeds from the doorstep, a piece of gravel from the drive, which may have once taken the King's weight as he wandered down to the gate to meet and sign autographs for his tribes.

These nameless gate fans were constantly there whenever Elvis was in residence, and had come from every conceivable corner of the globe consumed with adoration. Their arms stretched out through the wrought iron guitar-shaped gate, looking like refugees trying to get on the last helicopter out of Vietnam, beseeching his presence. A smile, a touch, a miracle.

They'll be in frames now. Bleached white grass pressed in front of the group photograph in which the highlight of their lives was captured, or in pendants, which old fans would kiss on Elvis' birthday and of course on doomsday. I suspect some of the stolen Graceland's greenery would be lodged in safety deposit boxes, heirlooms mentioned in solicitor witnessed last will and testaments. *'And your mother has bequeathed to you... a sod!'*

We were now in Las Vegas, marching across the deep pile Circus Circus casino, with what seemed like the American Armed Guard as our escorts, to meet the hotel manager.

A thousand one-armed bandits were sucking in hundreds of thousands of quarters mid-afternoon, and the crap tables, blackjack tables and roulette tables were full. Above their heads, trapeze artists fell into nets and an Elephant stood on its hind legs encouraged by a whip master.

It was cool. An air-conditioned room, the size of a stadium.

On the second-floor balcony, hundreds of kids played at sideshows hitting bullseyes, knocking things down, pinning cards to the wall. Unlike Brighton and Blackpool, if they lost there were no sad faces here, no beseeching dad for another six pence to try to win a clay model of Popeye on the second shelf.

These casino kids won every time and top shelf, because there was no bottom shelf.

These were the only folk in Vegas guaranteed to win. The Circus Circus game plan, to keep the kids happy with the stalls, and the circus performers, to encourage their parents to bring them again tomorrow.

There was a carnival atmosphere as we went by, and we watched as kids tried to leave, hardly able to carry the dozens of fluffy toys like they'd just won at 'Crackerjack' or a 'Too many cuddly toys Generation Game'. Dads followed their offspring, picking up their stuffed toy droppings as they negotiated the crowds. One sad-eyed man displayed his poverty to his wife by pulling out empty trouser pocket linings.

I drank in the scene before me, eyeing the blackjack tables whilst mentally planning to take them for a million dollars later that evening.

"We're over-subscribed," said a fat Jack Nicholson-type.

A huge, illegal Havana hung from the manager's mean mouth.

"Listen cock sparra..." I started, feigning bravado there in the bosom of the Mafia.

"I'm here to cover a Presley trip for Europe's largest radio network, 50 million listeners are looking forward to this report in Britain, Germany, France, Spain and Scandinavia. It sure won't sound good when this picks up your comments."

My microphone parried with his cigar.

The tour operator, David Wade, waded in with threats of reporting him to the American Tourist Authority, ABTA and the Royal Society for Prevention of Cruelty to Tourists!

It was Oscar-worthy.

The manager leaned back in his chair, clasping one arm behind his neck allowing his jacket to part showing first, his braces, and then the tip of a leather holster.

John fucking Wayne!

"Could you recommend anywhere else?" asked Todd meekly.

We found ourselves well down the strip at a cheap motel, a broiling 110°
walk to the Hilton for the kids who couldn't afford cabs.

But no one minded, we had a swimming pool, and by 10pm it was still
hotter than Blackpool's record temperature, and we had Elvis to look
forward to the next day.

Todd had a silver cup trophy for Elvis from the NME. I filled it with ice
placed it by the poolside cooling a bottle of Cold Duck wine, the world's
worst vino blanco.

We drank a toast to tomorrow, a big day in all our lives.

Jan: Pirates disappear

Without western magazines and media coverage available to me, music
was an enigma. There were lots of puzzles to be solved and I had to rely
on the 208 DJs to quench my thirst for information. For example, the
greatest thing I learned from Michal was that the Jordanaires were not
Elvis´ backing group, but in fact only sang vocal harmonies on his records.
The *Kid Galahad* EP Andrej gave me in Bratislava credited Elvis Presley
with the Jordanaires, so I naturally assumed they were his band, just like
the Shadows were Cliff Richard's.

I was also surprised when Michal told me that Carl Perkins was not
headlining his own shows, but that he now played guitar in the Johnny
Cash band, although Carl did have his own spot singing a couple of his
rock 'n' roll classics including *Blue Suede Shoes*. Michal remarked that Carl
might be grateful to Johnny as rock 'n' roll's popularity had been wiped out
by the Liverpool sound.

I knew that Johnny and Carl were friends who had both started to sing
in Memphis at the same time, but no one could explain to me why the
man who had written Elvis' big hit, and had three of his songs recorded
by the Beatles, was relegated to a guitar player. It was quite a realization
that a great American singer/songwriter like Carl, could have bad times
like Czechoslovak musicians, including my friends Radek Rettegy and
Pavel Váně, who were forbidden to play the clubs periodically when
their audiences showed too much enthusiasm for their western rock 'n'
roll, which was seen by the authorities as a sign of opposition against the
communist regime.

These musicians never got to make records, were never invited onto
our socialist radio stations. To say that the regime was afraid of music's
influence amongst the young, was an understatement.

Michal and I both understood the system. He, too, hid his love for western
music and had failed several times to get into university.

Whilst I was forced into the dangerous work of shunting train engines, Michal endured even more danger working for a geological company, where his daily stone grinding work was slowly destroying his lungs.

Our love for music, combined with our mutual inability to gain a university seat, was our bond. We were in agreement that providing we could listen to the wonderful music coming from the free world, we could handle pretty much anything. We also realized there seemed to be no rock 'n' roll fans amongst the white-collar workers, and so perhaps had we gone to university, music may have escaped our focus. Or was this just two of life's losers trying to justify their existence under red-rule?

Michal and his girlfriend Dana saw me off at the railway station on Sunday, and before I boarded the train, he told me that I was welcome back anytime. To me this was on a par with an invitation to visit the United States or the United Kingdom.

Back on base, to save myself from withdrawal symptoms, I once again reached for my radio noticing that something had changed down the AM frequency. A pirate station I could occasionally receive, Radio London, was no longer there. Worse still, the DJ team on Radio Caroline North had changed; there was no sign of Tony Prince or Dave Lee Travis or Bob Stewart. They'd changed presenters many times over the years, but now the Jerry 'Soopa' Leighton breakfast show was hosted by a complete stranger.

Pirate radio reception was never reliable in Czechoslovakia, especially during daylight hours; however, I loved the new style the DJs represented and tuned in when I could. Tonight Daffy Don Allen could still be heard, but it sounded to me like the rest of the pirate radio aircrew had walked the plank!

I had heard lots of anti-government statements coming from the pirates, something about a Marine Offences Bill, which I didn't totally grasp, but understood clearly that something threatened their very existence. I was bemused. How could freedom-loving Brits allow their government to rule what they listened to? It seemed almost... communistic.

Tony: Colonel Parker

Colonel Tom Parker welcomed us into his Vegas Hilton office suite, which took up most of the hotel's third floor.

After the niceties, introductions to the staff, explaining who I was, how popular Radio Luxembourg was, how the fan club was doing, the joking began.

Colonel gave Todd, his assistant Ian Bailey and I, honorary membership cards to his 'Snowman's League of America' explaining this was a great honour, and only bestowed on people who knew how to 'snow' people, a system of getting the best out of people and situations through wily means, without hurting or cheating anyone.

I tried to out-wily the king of wile.

"Colonel," I said gazing out of the large office window at Vegas below and around us, and the desert vista stretching beyond, "I couldn't help noticing that you've had every public bench in town plastered with 'Elvis at the Hilton'. That must cost a fortune!"

I pointed at the mountain range across the Mojave Desert in the distance. "Why don't you do with the Black Mountains, what they did with the presidents at Mount Rushmore? Elvis is spending so much time in Vegas these days, it'd save you a fortune long-term and become a tourist attraction forever and beyond!"

He slipped his glasses down his nose with hardly a look towards the mountains.

"Meester Preence," he began. "I can tell you are new to Vegas. I already considered this idea, but those mountains are only visible ten weeks of the year! The hotel sponsors the benches, so there's no cost to Elvis."

He pulled his cigar stub from the corner of his mouth, and looked at me like Boris Spassky after he'd made a great chess move.

"Anyway" he continued, "I don't believe I could get Elvis to pose for them there chiseller's long enough for them to do it. Elvis just wouldn't be able to sit still that long!"

Colonel's staff laughed loudly, and we all joined in.

As the pleasant afternoon continued, the Colonel told us of his days working in Tampa as a dogcatcher long before he ran into his protégés Hank Snow, Eddy Arnold and Tommy Sands, who he managed before he ran into Elvis.

"I learned the value of publicity," he expounded. "It's always been paramount in everything I've done."

He leaned back in his chair relishing telling us a bit about himself, the perpetual cigar sealed in the corner of his mouth.

"We'd been called out to rescue a pooch that had fallen down a borehole. When we arrived there were very few people and no press at all, so the first thing I did was squeeze down the hole to see how the animal was doin'. He was fine and I had him in my arms ready to climb out when I thought to myself, 'No! This will accomplish nothing.' So I sets the pooch back down and pinched it hard till the little blighter yelps and I cry out loud 'good doggy you'll be ok, your Uncle Tom is here!"

An ambitious young Tom Parker waited down below with his new friend, having whispered to his colleague at the top to let him know when the press and media arrived, and to tell them both he and the dog were now stuck.

"I stayed down that hole for over an hour covering the pooch with mud to make him look good for the cameras. When I surfaced the dog was famous, we made the six o-clock TV news!"

In full flow now the Colonel explained to we, his audience, that *this* was an example of the art of Snowmanship.

Pushing a new cigar between his lips, he flicked his Zippo, lit up and recounted his days as a hawker in the travelling fairs, of his Great Parker Pony Circus and his Dancing Chicken, which involved a record player and a hot plate, and of course a poor fucking chicken with scorched feet!

After a delightful two hours with the Colonel centre stage, magic began to happen.

The old Dutchman instructed Todd and I to select a handful of fans who would join us to meet Elvis that evening in his dressing room!

Gulp!

Then he got back to being a carnival huckster.

"What souvenirs we selling in the lobby Meester Diskin?" he asked his assistant Tom, who'd spent the afternoon feeding the Colonel lines, and reminding him of stories he hadn't yet told us. Tom Diskin then ran through a list of items that you could buy nightly in the Hilton lobby.

These included six-foot hound-dogs, puppy hound-dogs, scarves, TCB buttons, T shirts, books, scarves, the list went on as Parker wrote down the ones he thought the fans would cherish.

"Right Meester Slaughter, obviously they can't all go to meet Elvis, but I'm sure they'd like to meet Meester Diskin and I so, let's see here," he read each item again from his list of Elvis souvenirs his index finger busy on a calculator.

"That package would cost them a hundred and some odd bucks down-stairs, I'm gonna let 'em all visit us here tomorrow, meet and greet them, and you Meester Slaughter and Meester Preence can hand them their goodies."

"Tell 'em they'll get 50% off and to bring $50 each!"

"You old huckster," I thought.

Todd and I were bemused, but utterly under his spell. It was then, as he showed us to the door when I took the plunge.

"Colonel, I've been writing to you for years for permission to interview Elvis. Whatdoyoureckon?"

I'd lied of course, I'd never written to him, but I knew he wouldn't know if I had or hadn't.

"Elvis doesn't do one-to-one interviews, you should know that Meester Prince."

I didn't push it, just looked sad as the Colonel threw his arm around my shoulder squeezing me close to him as I walked through the door.

"Well I suppose if you sneak a tape recorder down there tonight, and I don't happen to see it..."

I shook the hand of God, and pushed my luck ever forward.

"One last thing Colonel," I began. "As a DJ and Honorary President of the Elvis Presley Fan Club of Great Britain, I'd consider it a career high if you'd let me introduce Elvis on stage!"

His boot urged me out of the door.

"GOODBYE MEESTER PRINCE!"

Jan: Royal Ruler returns

In April 1968, I had the surprise of my life.

Tuning to Radio Luxembourg as usual, I found my old pirate friend the Royal Ruler, Tony Prince talking to me. I checked that I hadn't tuned to 199 instead of 208 by mistake, but apart from anything else, he name-checked Radio Luxembourg and played their jingles. It was like a bolt out of the blue. It was like a reunion, and he talked like he had actually missed me.

This was the first time I had heard Tony through a full clear signal. Radio Caroline depended on atmospheric conditions to reach all the way to Czechoslovakia. Luxembourg, although troubled by medium wave atmospherics, was a lot closer and, as I would learn, their transmitter was quite enormous compared to those sitting atop ship's masts in the Irish and North Seas.

Suddenly, my favourite DJ had flown straight across the iron curtain into my bedroom.

Tony had his own way of talking and presenting the records; he was warm and seemed to be talking just to me. He was around my age too, he loved Elvis and the Beatles, I felt that night like I had won the lottery as the Royal Ruler opened the station with his masterful intro from the pen of William Shakespeare:

"Rebellious subjects! Enemies to peace! Throw your mistempered weapons to the ground... and hear the sentence of your move-ed Prince!"

So here I was under a rail steamer's water tank, listening to the latest Luxy hits presented by Tony Prince in his Palace of Peachy Platters, with all the oldies Michal played me on my visit to Černošice still hot in my memory.

I was buzzing!

April went and May arrived, and I was no longer fearful of being known as a radio head. One night, I joined my fellow soldiers in the railway station pub. A change was coming over the land, I was no longer afraid to play my radio, even in a pub, so out came my Hitachi, and within minutes people gathered around to listen and to express their admiration for the little transistor. They wanted to know how much it had cost, and where I had bought it, and as usual, were disappointed when I told them it came from the Tuzex shop in exchange for special coupons.

I found an old copy of Red Law lying at the back of the pub. On the front page was a photo of Alexander Dubček who, since 5 January had become the First Secretary of the Communist Party of Czechoslovakia. What beguiled me was that he was signing autographs to visitors who he met on the street close to Prague Castle. Until that day, I am sure not one person ever wanted a politician's autograph. Who did this guy think he was? Elvis Presley? Beneath the picture was a subtle attack on the incompetence of our government. It reported that a factory had planned to release 60,000 radio receivers, but did not have the wooden cases in which to contain them. The report also said that transistor radio production was delayed due to not having enough container handles to complete them.

So much for the Soviet Bloc leaving the capitalist countries behind, it was a devastating report of which we'd never seen before on the front page of Red Law, let alone directly beneath the picture of a major politician. A new shoot had popped up, another indication of how the times were changing and how we could hold firmly onto hope for our future.

The fact that I no longer had to be afraid of openly listening to Radio Luxembourg in front of our officers was a quantum leap of mega proportions. The officers themselves treated us amazingly well, even taking us on Sunday bus trips to places like Carlsbad and Prague.

People grouped together in Prague's Wenceslas Square and the Old Town Square, discussing freely and openly how our politics had to change. As members of the army, we were approached by good-natured people, keen to know our position. When they learned that we too wanted democratic change, they actually applauded us in the street.

The officers treated us to days out in Bohemia, because we were making them look good with the speed and quality of our work. In one day we would tear up one kilometre of old track, digging out the old wooden sleepers, cleaning the ground readying it to take the new 25 metre-long stretches of new rails.

In this way our officers would be congratulated by the Ministry of Defence, whose appreciation showed in their wage packets. Individually, we earned up to 300 crowns a month bonus, on top of our regular 75 crowns pocket money. Of course the pay was paltry compared to the equivalent output in the civilian sector, but it was big money in our circumstances, and everyone was inspired to work hard and make targets.

I had plenty of time to listen to Radio Luxembourg in the evening and, as we were now close to the West German border and the blocking of their signal seemed to have stopped, I received AFN who broadcast from Munich loud and clear throughout the day.

American radio in Czechoslovakia? Never in this world!

One warm day, I was sunbathing in my underwear, dozing on the wagon platform tuned in to AFN, waiting until we could start spreading the ballast. Suddenly I was called from below, and stood to see a group of officers who were accompanied by someone with enormous stars on his epaulets. For the first time in my life, I was face to face with a general, in what was the most embarrassing scene imaginable. I could hardly salute standing there in my underwear, with an American DJ announcing a Bob Dylan tune from my Hitachi.

I didn't wait to be questioned and I made no reference to the radio at all. "Sorry for taking a nap comrade general, but during the night we had wagons with ballast arriving late from Pilsen which slowed us down waiting for scheduled trains to pass. The work took all night to complete and we're all pretty exhausted."

"OK soldier", he smiled, saluted me and went on his way.

I caught my breath and waited for my heart rate to subside. AFN had been playing all the time and nobody said a word. At this moment, I knew that we were experiencing more freedom, not only in the press, but also in real life.

What the hell was going on?

Occasionally I tuned in to Voice of America, and once I heard that every time a listener's question was read out on air, they would win a book as a reward. I puzzled over what kind of question they would find interesting enough to feature, and decided to ask if they had trade fairs in the USA as they had in my hometown Brno?

As I had already written to the Voice of America a couple of years ago, asking for their Special English Word book which arrived safely, I had no hesitation to include my address, even though soldiers were strictly forbidden to make any contact with western countries. I now believed that the whole country was making progress towards our freedom, a belief that was reinforced a few days later when, on 27 June 1968, the weekly Literární Listy (Literary Leaves) published a proclamation, Two Thousand Words, written by reformist communist writer Ludvík Vaculík.

In it, he summarized all the bad things that the communist regime had caused so far, and called for change.

In a recent edition of Mladý Svět (Young World), Dubček was featured on the cover, showing him diving into the water from a diving tower. In our army barracks one night, we all agreed that, if only for this, we would gladly fight for him. He was without doubt the first, and probably the only communist politician capable of doing something so human.

Everyday we learned of his efforts to implement democratic change into our society, something we had never seen in our lives. He even campaigned to end censorship and in reading this alone, showed clearly he was getting somewhere.

With Dubček as our gardener, the shoots of freedom were swiftly becoming an orchard. There had been no domestic or external army intervention as the whole country embraced this dynamic politician's proposals.

We were living in the middle of what was now regarded as a civilised Europe, and quite sure no country would dare to assault Czechoslovakia as Adolph Hitler had 30 years ago. We became strong, unafraid of anything or anyone, convinced that no one in the world would be unhappy to see us breathing more freely, after all our years of suffering under communist doctrines.

Every day now was as dramatic as a football match as we watched developments. All types of newspapers and magazines came onto the market, new ones which we read cover to cover. Never before had our journals been so interesting, and never before had the press been so open, especially regarding our politics.

I was overjoyed for my friend Pavel Váně and the group Synkopy 61, who finally had their record *War is a Fool* released, another giant step, which helped to make 1968 the best in my life so far.

Tony: The King arrives

We all converged in the Hilton Showroom suffering a comedian, and not really noticing what we were eating.

The Colonel himself came down the aisle, the first of many thrills tonight for those who spotted him. He escorted our clutch of privileged Brits down below the stage, where we found Elvis' musicians sitting around the bar drinking and chatting. Colonel announced us, no Elvis yet so our posse split up, and I started chatting with his rhythm guitarist, water diviner and silk scarf changer, Charlie Hodge. I don't know what I said to him, it was small talk, a filler until…

We hadn't seen him come in, there was no fanfare, but somehow Elvis had materialised and was standing there in a black suit leaning against the wall talking calmly to the head of his Memphis Mafia, Joe Esposito. *Handsome* you ask? I agreed with Sammy Davis Jr who once said, 'From one to ten?… at least eleven!' although country singer Jerry Reed prolifically described how handsome Elvis was when he said to the King, "I kinda wish I was a girl right now!"

Fat, you ask? No sign of the overweight Elvis that would become the sickening image of his death for the tabloids in a couple of years' time.

I fiddled with my tape recorder, hidden in the travel bag over my shoulder, pulling my microphone out just as the Colonel called us over.

"OK you Brits, come and say hi to Elvis."

There were 11 of us. Eleven God-blessed Elvis fans.

Now what the hell had I planned to ask him? My mind went dry. My tongue limp.

"Hi Elvis!" said Todd's wife Vicky.

"Hello Elvis!" said someone else.

"Ow do Elvis," said a northerner.

"Great to meet you at last Elvis," said his fan club secretary from England. Everyone greeted him in their own way with a shake of his hand.

Yes, we had now touched Elvis.

People apparently all remember where they were when they heard Kennedy or John Lennon had been killed, and all recall exactly where they were as they witnessed the Moon landing or the Twin Towers nightmare. Neither will anyone who experienced it, ever forget that moment when Elvis Presley, with his hand in theirs said, "Hi there, pleased to meet you!"

In a few short years everyone would recall where they were when they heard that Elvis had died. Most people in Europe heard the news when I announced his death on Radio Luxembourg, but this isn't the moment to reflect on disasters to come, because this was a time of acute pleasure, meeting the man who, as a small boy, first fired up my love for music and changed the game for the music industry.

Whilst Elvis referred to each of us as 'Sir' or 'Ma'am', no one in our party called him Mr Presley. It just didn't accord with the way we'd all imagined this moment. To a man, we called him Elvis.

Todd gave him last night's ice-bucket award from the New Musical Express, '*For 90 trillion gold album Sales*' (or however many it was).

John, a Scottish fan, traditionally kitted with kilt and sporran caused Elvis to look down at his skirt, his lip curling into *that* smile. Then our friend, aware that Elvis collected them, gave him a Glaswegian Police Badge, with which he was absolutely thrilled.

He was so knocked out; I thought he was going to give John a Cadillac in return.

"This is Meester Prince I wuz telling you about," said the Colonel.

The emotions were scattered everywhere. Someone had spoken *my* name to Elvis, and this micro-thought was captured and stored for scrutiny later when this was all over. There were other, what would be normal, mundane events, which were so much bigger, because this was Elvis and nothing in his presence could be regarded as mundane.

I grasped the King's hand squeezing it with two hands, and saying something bloody soppy like how honoured I was to meet him. "I like your trousers," he smirked looking down. They were white covered with tin buttons the colonel had bestowed on me the day before. 'Colonel and Elvis say have a nice day'. Any other time, any other person, I'd have looked like a clown, but they made Elvis laugh, and that was some accomplishment.

Now, seeing as I was now his friend, I pulled out the microphone and saw him glance towards the Colonel who made a play act of looking away. From Colonel's response, Elvis got the message.

Then I proceeded to get my message from Elvis to his fans back home. *The microphone comes out!*

I could no longer recall the sequence of questions I'd mapped out in my mind but I remembered one, which was way down the line in my planned sequence of questions, but I needed to speak so I opened the campaign.

"Any chance of us hearing some more blues from you in the future Elvis?"

"Workin' on it," he smiled. "S'funny you should say that but... yeah, we're workin' on it!"

I checked the record level and pushed the microphone closer to those famous lips.

"Give us some of the old Merry Christmas Baby, So Glad You're Mine uh?" I suggested showing him I knew his catalogue well.

"S'right, workin' on it."

These were silly, wasteful questions from a befogged brain. David Frost, (who never got *his* Elvis interview), had nothing to worry about!

We talked about Bill Balou the guy who designed his jump suits. He wasn't wearing his stage clothes yet. He wore a smart jet-black suit with red silk trimmed pockets and a white open-necked collar shirt with black embroidery, which, on anyone else, would have looked gay. His fingers were covered in gold and diamond rings. Then I went for it, the million-dollar question.

"Elvis, this will be going out on Radio Luxembourg to some 50 million listeners, have you got any message for those listening to this show tonight?"

He bent his head down towards me, and looked nervously into the NME chrome plated cup, which he still held in both hands as if the answer may lie inside it.

"Yeah ah do," he began. "I wanna thank them for their loyalty and their devotion and I'm gonna come see 'em."

I hadn't asked that. That was the trillion-dollar question, and he was already answering the question every Elvis fan in Europe wanted me to ask.

He hesitated slightly, smiled that lip snarling grin at me giving a throaty laugh before continuing with his message, the first private message to his British and European fans he'd ever given. Or indeed would ever give.

"Mmm, ah know ah keep sayin' ah'm comin' but we will...ah mean it, we're sure gonna go come see 'em."

And that was it.

The Colonel moved quickly in there, knowing I'd just been given the greatest one-line interview in the history of music. There was no need for anything further. I had the answer. I had the headline. I had Elvis' promise.

"Showtime!" Colonel cried loudly. "Let's go now, say goodbye to Elvis."

I was utterly buzzing! Microphone off, I took Elvis' hand in mine once again.

"Thank you for everything," I said.

"Don't mention it Tony," he replied.

I was the last to leave his dressing room, making sure I also made my farewells to the rest of the room's privileged residents.

The showroom was a drone of chatter and cutlery as we sat back in our seats, the eyes of the waiting fans scrutinising us, their envy palpable as each devout Elvis fan imagined the miracles that might have happened to the lucky 11 moments ago.

Envy was natural, I'd have been envious had the boot been on the other foot, but it was obscured by 200 smiles as I pointed to my microphone with a thumbs up sign, causing the pilgrims pupils to dilate. The British posse looked like the Children of the Damned. And now their life-long dream was about to come true, the interval was almost over and not one fan would ever remember what they ate.

Back below the showroom Elvis was climbing into his white sequinned jump suit.

I was just catching my breath, ordering a very much-needed scotch and ginger ale, when Colonel Parker reappeared before me.

Something quite unbelievable was about to happen.

Jan: The girl by the pond

In the middle of July, we left our shelter beneath the steamer's water tank in Hořovice and moved to the next railway station in Zbiroh.

This was much more comfortable. We had a real room in a house that served as the station depot; we even had a railway telephone. We still didn't have a shower, but this time it wasn't a problem, a few hundred metres from the station in the middle of the woods, was a beautiful pond.

Here we kept up with everyday hygiene, swimming each day during that never-ending hot summer. On weekends, we had an added bonus when girls came through the woods to bathe in the pond.

In the middle of August, I was lucky to buy a copy of The Young World magazine at a newsstand. This popular magazine was usually sold out immediately, and therefore almost impossible to find. It was a very popular magazine amongst its target young readers, as the articles appealed, and it was all written in a much lighter style than we were used to.

The lead editorial was contained beneath the headline 'Truce', and reported on the recent visit of the Soviet Communist party boss, Brezhnev, in our border town Čierna, on the very border with the Soviet Union.

The writer remarked that it was very good to see that the press in our brotherly Eastern Bloc countries had stopped the attacks aimed at us, and so that, with this, there was a chance that the truce would turn into real peace between us.

This calmed me enormously, and I began to digest the rest of the magazine with a wonderful feeling that things were all coming together for us.

Then I got a real shock! Turning the page, I came to an extensive feature over a number of pages, all about the Frei Körper Kultur nudist movement in the German Democratic Republic. I ogled the photographs, many of naked girls and I laughed at the caption beneath the headline:

How God Created Us
'If somebody asks you to sign a moral protest against this story about nudists, please verify first if he is not the manager of a swim suit factory!'

It had always been an ambition of mine to see and swim in the ocean. Now I adjusted the ambition to swim in the Baltic Sea, where the East Germans seemed to have already made their own steps towards a certain freedom!

During the weekend, I managed to make quite a lot of eye contact with a stunningly beautiful girl. I returned on Saturday, hoping that she would appear once more, and to my great joy, after a while, I saw her floating down from the path in the woods.

After a moment, I showed her what a good swimmer I was, swimming from one side of the pond and back, in double-quick time. Then I called on my courage, telling her the water was warm enough and she should come in and in she came. In no time I had opened a conversation with her on the banks of the pond, and discovered that she, too, loved music.

I asked if she knew about John Lennon's new girlfriend Yoko, and when she exclaimed she'd not heard this big pop news, I showed her my copy of The Young World and an article about them. I had an ulterior motive to let her read the magazine of course; I wanted to see her reaction to all the nudist photographs.

As she read, I asked if she would mind if I brought my towel next to hers? So there I was once again in the company of a beautiful girl with my army mates looking on from the other side of the pond with patent envy. I pretended to be reading another magazines, but keeping one eye on her trying to estimate when she would have turned enough pages to get to the East German nudist beach feature.

Momentarily she interrupted her reading to put some suntan cream on her body, and I commented that I liked the way it smelled. She asked me if I wanted to use some, which was an offer I couldn't refuse, even though I wasn't a cream man, having learned that if you sunbathe from early summer, by high summer your body has built up its own protection. But I wasn't going to tell her such a thing when my fantasy already had her rubbing cream into my skin.

Eventually she arrived at the nudist story and I could see she took great interest.

As she read, I commented on certain statements in the article. For instance, it said it was not healthy to stay in a wet swimsuit after getting out of the water, especially for girls because their body is more susceptible to cold and wet.

"You'd better not react to that advice right here," I said which made her giggle.

I then mentioned my experiences in the Beskydy mountains at summer camp five years ago, when each evening we would leave our tents to bathe in the mountain stream with the girls and boys back to back, so we would not see each other.

"The most difficult thing I ever had to do in my life," I joked.

But I embellished on the memory, how the girls went up stream so that they got the cleaner water, and how afraid we were that their scout mistress would see us watching them frolicking in the fading dusk light. This was when she shocked me admitting that she had already bathed naked in this very pond when staying on previous occasions at her parents' chalet.

I learned that she was studying at Prague High School, and that her father was an officer who didn't want her to stay alone in the chalet, which explained why they had accompanied her on this short visit. Then she told me that next Friday 23 August they would come to stay for the whole week.

As my new friend studied English at school, I could see our common ground was expanding in a very healthy way. I asked if she listened to Radio Luxembourg, as I found it the best way to get to understand and pronounce English better?

I wasn't surprised when she told me she never listened to the station. Life as an army officer's daughter meant she would be brought up according to socialist principles set in stone in the army since 1948.

Then I made my offer.

"Come back here tonight at 8pm, I'll bring my transistor radio and you can listen to a real DJ, with luck Tony Prince will be on and you will hear what a great DJ sounds like. We can enjoy the music and turn this pond into our own private nudist camp!"

She promised to return. I felt my groins staring, but then a voice in the distance called out to her.

"Your mother and I have been waiting for you to come to lunch for hours already. You were supposed to be there by one!"

I thought I would never again have problems with officers, and now this! She gathered her things together and without a word followed her father into the woods. She did manage to glance back at me, and her face told me she would be here at 8pm.

I was beside myself with anticipation. Hadn't we looked at nudist pictures together and discussed it openly, and didn't she reveal she had already been skinny dipping in this very pond with her friends? And wasn't I now her friend? The only question now, was how would I survive the remaining five hours waiting until 8pm?

Before leaving, I surveyed the banks of the pond circumnavigating it twice to find the ideal spot for a skinny dip with a beautiful young girl.

At 7 o'clock I took my Hitachi tuned to AFN for the time being, and went to the pond to be there, well in advance of her arrival.

There were just a few people spread around enjoying the early evening sun, so I chose a free spot close to the path on which I last saw her.

I switched off the radio not wanting to be conspicuous, and laid back to wait enjoying the music of the pond as frogs and jumping fish made their presence known.

At exactly 8 o'clock I saw her approaching at rather a fast pace. Her father was mad with her for not coming to lunch on time, and had insisted she didn't go out. I was dumbfounded, looking at this gorgeous girl from Prague who obviously liked me or she wouldn't have taken the chance to come and explain.

"Does this mean we'll not share Radio Luxembourg and go skinny dipping tonight?" I asked dumbly.

She started to laugh. "If you want to risk my father killing me if I return with wet hair, then we could go skinny dipping!"

I'd have risked death at that moment to jump in that pond naked with her, but common sense prevailed, strategy was called for and I decided to protect a relationship which could still pay dividends before too long.

"When will I see you again?" I whispered above a frog chorus.

She told me once again, she would be back on the following Friday for at least seven or ten days.

Then, before leaving she added, "I'll see you in five days and we'll talk together in English and listen to your radio and..."

"Skinny dip," I interjected over-enthusiastically.

She gave an infectious giggle, came closer to me and held my hand.

"Of course we shall do some night swimming together."

Whereupon she kissed me, turned and left. My eyes followed her as my heart tried to escape from my chest. At the last moment, she turned and smiled before disappearing from the glade.

"Next Friday 8 o'clock right here," I shouted at the top of my voice.

She stepped towards me again out of the woods and waved and smiled and then, before finally disappearing shouted back "See you Friday!"

And I was alone again. Somehow I had to get through five full days. The clock was ticking... but extremely slowly!

That night in bed, with Luxembourg coming down my ear piece, I cursed myself for not even asking her name, neither had I given her mine, neither did I know which chalet her parents owned.

Insomnia kicked in as the worrying side of my brain took over. What would happen if the army told us we had to move away from Zbiroh before Friday? How then would I contact her? How would I ever again see my suncream girl? Simple, I said to myself, I would search every high school in Prague. Now, however, there was nothing left to do but wait five days and six nights, until wonderful Friday 23 August 1968 would arrive.

I reached for the radio. The DJ was Noel Edmonds. "That's about it for tonight sons and daughters," he announced. "It's coming up to 3 and we'll leave you this morning with the Buddy Holly classic That'll be the Day!"

'It sure will,' I thought turning my Hitachi off.

I was sure we would not be moved to another railway station within the coming days, as we had a hell of a lot of repairing and changing tracks to do. The fact that suncream girl and I didn't introduce ourselves by name irritated me.

Being now incredibly infatuated by my new friend, I checked the train departures for Prague that afternoon, so that she would not escape me if they did travel by train. After waiting in vain after two trains departed for Prague however, I gave up the ghost and filed my skinny-dipping away into fantasy.

I set off walking through the woods to join my friends in a pub, in a settlement called Kařez.

At that moment there was nothing in the world I wanted more than a glass of Pilsen beer. To keep myself distracted from the sun cream girl I reached for the Sunday edition of Red Law.

The front page carried the story that the Romanian communist party leader, Nicolae Ceaușescu, had left Prague after a state visit, and all the speeches published in the paper showed that Romania was not ill at ease with some of the changes now taking place in our society. Even East Germany, and the Soviet Union itself, seemed to have calmed down somewhat since the meeting with Dubček.

There was one story on the second page of Red Law that made me laugh aloud. On Friday evening a Czechoslovak Airlines plane coming from London landed in Prague. After the passengers disembarked, the dozey crew parked up in the hangar totally forgetting to unload the baggage!

Subsequently it took three hours to bring the luggage, leading to a large group of pioneer scouts, who had been on a youth exchange trip to London, missing their connections home. According to the report nobody from Czechoslovak Airlines came to apologise or offer refreshments to these kids.

What a story! But I wasn't interested in kids missing connections; I wanted to know *how the hell a trip to London had been arranged*? I'd give my eyeteeth to go to London, to visit Abbey Road and all those places I knew from the British movies and Radio Luxembourg.

The changes taking place were unprecedented in my lifetime. Red Law, the voice of communism, upholder of all things socialist, had written about kids coming back from London, like flying to the UK was nothing short of normal!

Everyone in the pub agreed with me that if we had been one year younger, we too could have visited London.

But so what? We'd been waiting all our lives so we could wait another year before our army duty was over, then London here I come on a trip which, until today, had seemed as likely as snowballs in hell.

Once again I let my fantasies flow, imagining visiting Radio Luxembourg at 38 Hertford Street, the address I heard nightly on 208, maybe meeting some of my favourite DJs. I'd go shopping down Carnaby Street and buy as many records as my baggage allowance would permit.

This Sunday, flirting with my suncream girl, drinking Pilsner brewed in their factory just 50 kilometres from the pub, listening to western radio and reading such formidable stories in Red Law, caused me to stop and think how bloody wonderful life had become and what potential for a better life now lay before me.

We all shared the euphoria, free like we had never felt before and sharing our joy by drinking to the health of our parents and families, who had endured a world war and now stood with us on the brink of a new era in a free Czechoslovakia.

It was some Sunday.

Tony: Introducing the King

"Well Meester Prince," said the Colonel. "You about ready to introduce Elvis!"

A silence fell around me.

How did I ever stand to my feet? Even as I write, my heart's tempo increases once again at the memory.

I hadn't thought how to do it. I'd only been joking with Colonel Tom. Introduce Elvis? *Never in a million years!*

What to say?

TV producers would have had a team of 10 deciding the best way for me to do this, but how could I have scripted anything? I wasn't so arrogant that I could expect this to be happening, because *this* was the nearest you get to *impossible.*

Yet, here I was following, Colonel Parker for the second time that evening, golden bricks where err I looked.

"This is Meester Prince, he's introducing the show," he said to two of the Memphis Mafia at the stage door.

Colonel had said nothing more to me from the moment I rose to my feet from my table. He gave me no instructions whatsoever as I followed like a lamb to the slaughter.

"Please, please, don't fuck this up Princey," my mind taunted.

I was escorted onto the enormous stage, passing members of the 20-piece orchestra all tuning up their instruments ready to play Elvis on to the stage. The stage was like a music village. A subdued tuning-up cacophony. J Sumner & the Stamps vocal backing group stood around shooting the breeze, eyeing me up curiously, guitarists fine-tuned their strings, trumpeters fingered their valves and the three Sweet Inspiration made last minute adjustments to their hair and make-up.

They all eyeballed me. This was an unusual event. I obviously wasn't the only one who didn't expect this to happen.

Suddenly there was no turning back as my escorts lifted the heavy golden drapes and pushed me out front.

Now I was alone.

Apart from the entire audience before me.

I wrote my script as I approached the footlights.

The audience politely stopped chattering as I lowered the microphone by one foot from the comedian's height down to my level. Then, as if that gesture was their cue, they burst into applause oblivious to whom I might be.

Then a lull as they waited.

Now it was my turn. A pregnant pause…

"GIVE ME AN 'E'...!!" I spelled out with the audience the reason we were all gathered. "Who is the King of England?" The whole room, including the Americans cried "ELVIS!"

"Ladies and gentlemen," I commenced my ad-libbing with a nervous cough and slight feedback from the microphone.

"My name is Tony Prince, I'm a DJ from Europe's number one radio station, 208, Radio Luxembourg."

I waited until they'd finished their applause; it was as if they listened to 208 every night!

"How many of you have travelled over 1,000 miles to be here to see Elvis tonight?"

Everyone enthusiastically raised a hand.

"Hands up if you've come over 2,000 miles?"

Now only the New York Staters, Canadians, smatterings from Japan and Australia and our UK party raised their hands in confirmation.

"OK then, who has travelled over 5,000 miles this week to get to Vegas?"

Two hundred hands reached for the sky.

"Ladies and gentlemen you're looking at members of the Elvis Presley Fan Club of Great Britain," said I pointing at our lot, ignoring the stragglers around the showroom who had made their way from their own far away places.

The kindly American audience gave a loud applause that could only have served to make each member of our posse feel like a star. It certainly made them feel welcomed. Accordingly each of them stood to their feet, milked their moment and waved back at the people around them.

By the time they'd settled back down and the mutual applauding had abated, I'd had time to think how to proceed from that point, to the point where I would actually bring Elvis on stage.

"Perhaps you don't realise just how lucky Elvis fans are in the United States?" I began.

"Elvis has yet to perform in Great Britain. So, if Mohammed won't come to the mountain, those 200 people you see over there represent the tip of a very enormous British mountain!"

The roof came off at that point.

It was as though the audience wanted to make up for Elvis not visiting us, or to apologise for the Boston Tea Party and for not getting alongside us earlier in the Second World War.

And then came my moment. The moment no other DJ in history would ever experience.

I introduced Elvis live on stage at the Las Vegas Hilton.

"Ladies and gentlemen, it gives me very great personal pleasure to introduce to you tonight... Elvis Presley!"

The drapes went up for me as the lights dimmed and I walked, dazed and spinning, off the stage as two things happened.

The orchestral strains of Also Sprach Zarathustra began.

And Elvis, standing in the wings, winked at me clapping his hands gently in my direction.

Holy Mother of God!

I often find myself contemplating that memory. Little did I know back in the 1950s at Oldham Municipal Art School as I covertly eyed Harry Mills' Elvis Fan Club membership card, that I would go one better.

Well, quite a few better really.

The next day, the mountain visited the Colonel.

Todd and I handed out 6ft hound dogs and parcels of goodies, taking $50 off each of our gang. (I'd loved you to have seen 200 human-sized hound dogs arriving on Heathrow's baggage carousel!)

Parker and Diskin and the rest of Elvis' management staff were magnificent hosts to our spellbound party.

No one was hurried as the Colonel recounted his funny tales and yarns, and then posed for photographs, joking with them constantly throughout the afternoon.

At the end with just Todd and I remaining he asked, "How much'd we take?"

In my heart I was thinking how he'd let himself down at the last hurdle, taking this money had spoiled the cake for an a'peth of icing. What did he want with…

"$9,650" Todd announced.

Colonel, rather than reaching for the wedge in Todd's hands, reached into his back pocket and pulled out a billfold. Peeling off a role of notes, he counted out $350 and thrust it towards Todd's stack.

"Now you've got $10,000. You're off to LA in a couple of days, and I want you to book some bands and a good venue with good food and give these lovely folks a party on Elvis!"

Over the years people have written many negative things about the Colonel. I hope I've now provided some balance.

Jan: The Russian invasion

We were in no hurry on Monday morning as we waited for the workforce to arrive, gravel-filled wagons and assembled rails at the ready when, at 11am, an express train from Prague to Paris passed by.

My plans changed there and then, I would not go to London by plane next year, but would travel by train. What a great journey that would be, travelling on a rail track that I had helped to build. Maybe then I could stop over in Paris where my Uncle Josef lived during and after the war and, who knows, I might continue my train journey and travel to Liverpool to visit the Cavern Club.

Back in the pub on Tuesday 20 August, one of the boys did some sums: There were 11 days left in August, and 30 in September so he calculated that in 41 days we would have reached 365 days, and the halfway point of our army duties. It was a stupid sum, but we all screamed with delight and ordered more beers. The atmosphere in the pub was something like Christmas; everyone was caught up in the Dubček era, the time of real change.
I had other sums on my mind too, three days to go and it would be skinny dipping time! Oh how I wished I knew her name, so that in my dreams I could call out to her.

As soon as I had put myself into sleep mode and switched off the radio, my thoughts turned to her taking me the last step into a deep and contented sleep.
I was still dreaming about her when our railway telephone rang in the middle of the night. Here at Zbiroh railway station there was no dispatcher on duty during the night as this was just a small station, so it had to be somebody from another railway station calling.
Jarek Vavřík whose bed was right next to the phone answered it. We were all awake now as we heard his dramatic reply to whoever was calling in the dead of night.
"What?" and then repeated several times "Fucking whores!! Fucking whores!! Fucking whores!!" Then he turned to us, and the bottom fell out of our world. "The fucking Russians have invaded us!"
It had been our friend, the train dispatcher on night shift duty at the next railway station in Kařez, who had heard the news on the radio, and so he phoned us immediately.
It was 2am, 21 August 1968.
Wide-awake and fearful, I tuned my Hitachi from 208 to the Radio Prague frequency where the news was confirmed and far worse than we imagined. Radio Prague informed us that huge Soviet planes were landing by the minute at Prague airport, each carrying tanks and armoured transporters.

We didn't have to question why our army didn't shoot the Russian planes down because we knew too well that our air defences were sitting on runways on the borders with West Germany and Austria. Not a single Czechoslovak plane was stationed at the borders with the Soviet Union and, of course, most of our Czechoslovak army were stationed on our western borders.

Although we were soldiers, there was nothing we could do; we were a mere railway working division without weapons. All we had were keys for locomotives sitting on the table, nothing that might stop a Soviet invasion. There was no more sleep on that night. Prague Radio continued informing us about big Soviet planes landing all the time at Prague airport, and now Soviet Infantry Divisions were advancing from the Russian, Polish and Hungarian borders, deeper and deeper into Czechoslovakia as the night became dawn.

During the night, President Svoboda asked General Dzúr what was our army doing at the eastern border that nobody noticed such a movement of foreign troops, to which he replied that his task was to guard our borders with the west not the east.

And that was it. Instead of shooting down Soviet planes as soon as they got inside our air space, we let them in. Not one army division tried to stop them on the ground, making it the simplest invasion in history.

But the people of Czechoslovakia now decided otherwise.

Prague Radio announced that the people had started to pull down road signs on crossings, so that the invaders would not know in which direction they should continue inside Czechoslovakia. It was a heroic civilian army, who now set out to stop the Soviets from fully occupying our larger cities, Bratislava, Brno and Prague itself.

The broadcasters on the radio tried to direct action amongst the public, suggesting they should destroy other signs, including names of the towns and cities on railway station platforms.

We didn't need telling twice, and immediately covered the Zbiroh shield on our station wall.

The train dispatcher arrived for work at 5am and was equally devastated. He admired our work, but now suggested we take the name shield down completely and hide it away. Afterwards we discussed whether or not the US Army would come to help as they were based nearby in West Germany? Someone reminded us that the American army under General Patton had arrived in Czechoslovakia at the end of the Second World War, reaching Pilsen and Rokycany, which was just a few kilometres away from where we now stood. This was when Patton halted any further advance because of the foolish Yalta agreement, which allowed the Soviet army to reach Prague and establish their political influence over all Czechoslovakia.

Somehow we knew that we remained a pawn between the world super powers and that we were divvied out, like in a Vegas poker game, as part of their agreement in settling the German problem of World War 2. We had no optimism that anything would have changed on this darkest of days between America and Russia.

My mind wandered, thinking how the US Army helped my father and saved his life when liberating Dachau concentration camp 23 years ago, and I wondered how my father and mother were feeling right this minute, experiencing this new violence in our land? Firstly they lost their freedom in 1939 when the Nazis came to occupy our country, then again in 1948 when communists took power and right now, at this very moment, it looked like they were losing everything for the third time. My mind joined my dear parents in Brno and I wept for them quietly as I took down the station name shield. I could handle it, but I worried the hell for them.

Wednesday 21 August was the first day of the Soviet occupation, when our officers finally came to see if we were alright and not to do anything rash should we came into contact with Soviet soldiers. They authorized us to paint over the big red star, which decorated all our diesel locomotives, as an expression of solidarity and disagreement with the occupation. Red stars were strong Soviet symbols on all their armoury and planes.

We were also told that there would be no working on the railway on this day.

"Are we on strike?" I asked.

"No," replied the officer. "You are army, we never strike, you're just not working today."

We spent the whole day huddled by the radio, and were deeply shocked when we heard that young people had been shot dead by Soviet soldiers, or run over by their tanks.

We punched the air with delight when it was reported that a Soviet tank was on fire, and as the morning progressed, we'd counted five were set ablaze. But our hearts sank, the reality of the drama hit us when a commentator estimated there were already thousands of Soviet tanks in Czechoslovakia.

We were listening to the radio intently as our country fell completely off its new track, learning that Alexander Dubček and other leaders had been arrested like criminals, and taken under armed guard to Moscow.

It was hard to believe that something like this was possible in Europe at the end of the 20th century. But still the radio kept addressing everybody to stay calm and not to interfere with Soviet soldiers. Then General Dzúr made a command to all his officers, not to partake in any attacks by the Czechoslovak army against the friendly armies of the Soviet Bloc. He ended by insisting we give them a helping hand when and if required.

This was the moment we realized that all was lost. Even though Radio Prague still talked about our Parliament protesting against the occupation, once our army announced it was tolerating the Soviet presence, it was all over. If our own army was not supporting the people, who else could?

The continuing protests by all the world's democratic countries had no effect at all.

Over 100 Czechoslovaks, mostly young, passionate kids, were killed and several hundred seriously wounded during the first days of the Soviet aggressors' visit to our country.

The following day was Thursday. We started work on the railway track in the morning and it was just like nothing had ever happened. Our officers were very reserved from that moment on, telling us we were there to work and not to discuss politics, and to leave such things to our government in Prague.

Someone remarked how could our government in Prague solve anything, when half of it was imprisoned in Moscow? To which the officer in command just said, "Keep on working, that's what we are here for."

It was a great lesson in what a difference a day makes. Yesterday this same officer was so angry about the Russians invading us, now, one day later, he was tolerating it and urging us to do likewise.

In these early days of the invasion we had to keep listening to Radio Prague to learn what was going on in our big cities. We were, after all, in a lost corner of our republic, hidden in the woods on a rural railway track but even in these darkest of moments we did not lose our sense of humour.

The funny slogans were the first to make us smile. They'd call it graffiti in years to come. Our walls were covered in hilarious messages, some of them in the Russian *azbuka* alphabet so that the invaders could read them, well the literate ones amongst them. Many of the Soviet army soldiers originated from distant Asian republics in the USSR, and were not even aware which country they had invaded! To know a continent like Europe was something way beyond their field of knowledge, which was limited to operating a machine gun and drinking beer.

Among the slogans we enjoyed the best were '*Wake up Lenin, Brezhnev has gone mad!*' and '*We have been deepening our friendship with the Soviet Union so profoundly that we finally hit the bottom.*'

The second one reflected what our own government had tried to impress on us since time immemorial, that the Soviet Union was our greatest friend, and that their friendship guaranteed peace and prosperity in our time.

With due respect to Alexander Dubček and a few others in Prague Castle who wanted real change, we had been given vivid proof that the communist system could never have anything in common with democracy and all that is decent in society.

By lunchtime the following day, our work completed, we had the afternoon off. Leaving the Hitachi with my fellow soldiers so that they could keep tuned to news from Prague, I went for a walk in the woods where all was quiet and peaceful. I came upon a little pool fed by a stream and watched with interest as two small pikes kept touching some grownup trout with their muzzles. But the pikes were too small yet to threaten the grown trout that moved quickly and calmly away, as pikes did not offer any danger. I became absorbed in the gentle interplay between the two species, and started to wonder what we had ever done to deserve the Russians' attention?

Suddenly I realised I hadn't taken a bath since the Russian invasion had rudely awoken us two nights ago. I took off my army working uniform and entered the fresh cold water, and the moment my head came to the surface, it hit me like a bolt of lightening.

My sun cream girl would be here tomorrow! Where had the five days gone? Those bloody Russians! Only now my brain, shaken into life by the cold water, let me appreciate how close I was to seeing her once again.

I started to dress, thinking about her for the first time in two days. But then, what if her father had to stay with his unit or insist she stay in Prague away from danger? We all knew what Russian soldiers were doing at the end of the Second World War, they wouldn't have changed, they would still be rapists and thieves.

I now felt that her arrival tomorrow was extremely unlikely. I left the woods blaspheming the Russians at the top of my voice.

Friday came and I loaded new batteries into the Hitachi once again and left for the pond at 6pm, very early for our 8pm date.

Even though the weather was wonderful, the sun still shining brightly through the leaves, there were only a few people there who talked quietly together. Not one of them took to the water, and the happy crowd who swam and splashed and played volleyball just one week ago, were now nowhere to be seen.

Suddenly a Sandy Shaw song came to mind and the hook kept repeating itself in my head. The song was *Girl Don't Come* written by Chris Andrews, whose own recording had started my love for record collecting. The lyrics teased me, '*You wanna see her oh yeah but girl don't come*'.

How I hated the Russians now as the clock climbed past the magic hour of 8pm. Now their invasion had affected me personally. Killing our kids, kidnapping our President and filling our squares with their troops and tanks was one thing... but ruining my skinny-dipping date was just too much for me to take! Robbed of my date with this beautiful mysterious girl whose name I didn't know, I prowled around the pond throughout Saturday and Sunday morning, until I finally accepted she would not be appearing.

On Monday, a train engineer coming from Prague gave our train dispatcher in Zbiroh a copy of *Red Law,* published in great secrecy. The paper stood firmly behind Dubček and other leaders, and was strongly against the occupation. They wrote that 10,000 people were demonstrating in Edinburgh, Scotland in front of a hall where a Soviet state orchestra was to perform. It also reported that demonstrators were burning Soviet flags in front of the Soviet embassy in London.

"Come on the Brits!" we chimed.

The news cheered us up a lot, and we even started to hope that the Russians might have to leave us soon with such international protest taking place. Red Law also expressed concern over food supply in Prague saying that, whilst there was sufficient just now, many people were buying up more foodstuffs than they required. People were panicking, stocking up with more food than they needed in the present circumstances. Radio stations also appealed to people not to buy more provisions than was necessary for their family, so that everybody could get a share.

We were lucky enough to also get the Tuesday copy of Red Law with articles explaining what was going on in Prague. We read incredibly sad stories about funeral services held for young people shot by the Russians. On the front page was an appeal for cooperative farms in middle Bohemia to deliver potatoes to Prague as soon as possible, as there was no longer any stock, a serious problem for the residents of our capital city.

I was thoroughly sickened by everything I read.

How long I wondered, would the buggers be amongst us?

With this fear I planned my own salvation knowing I should act as quickly as possible before it was too late. No matter what transpired here under Russian control there was one thing I knew for sure, I could not make it through without a tape recorder!

On the Wednesday, exactly one week after the Russians had arrived, I wrote a letter to my family, firstly expressing my hope that all went well with them.

Reassuring them that they had nothing to worry about with regard to myself, I then gave instructions to my mother to buy a tape recorder for me. It had to be either a B4 model costing 3,190 crowns, or if unavailable, the B42 costing 2,800 crowns would suffice. I emphasised the importance that it had to be a four-track recorder, as this way one could record twice as many songs as a normal two-track recorder.

Then I disclosed to mother that my savings book was hidden in the album of my spare stamps, and that the code for it was 'Allison'. My account held a little less than 5,000 crowns, and I told mother to keep the balance for herself, as money was not so important now that nobody knew what would happen in the future. I impressed on her to buy something she valued, whilst it might still be available.

All I had to do after putting the letter into the station's mail box, was to keep my fingers crossed that the savings bank would still give money to its clients, and that the tape recorder remained available.

This was an exercise in holding one's breath for a week!

Tony: Viva Las Vegas

The following year we returned on the fanclub's second, of what has subsequently become an annual trip, even more popular after Elvis' death than before.

I'd managed to arrange a trip for my Programme Controller, Ken Evans, a likeable 50-year-old Australian, and a massive fan of the King. My wife Christine was on my arm too, and a Daily Mirror manager was in tow also.

In Nashville, we did the Country Stars' Homes tour, and arrived at one with a giant guitar-shaped swimming pool. Still fuelled by class-comic syndrome, I dived in fully clothed, swimming down the neck of the guitar to give our entourage a laugh. Of course we took in the Grand Ole Opry, one of the few places where Elvis had failed to wow the predominantly country audience, who were not enthused by his treatment of *Rockabilly*.

On our way back to our hotel, we stopped at a small store to buy some cigarettes.

"Y'all interested in tickets for the Johnny Cash Show at his old school tonight?" asked the lady shopkeeper. "I have just three left here".

We couldn't believe it, what an opportunity! Cash back at school, wow!

We sat in the gymnasium watching the best in country & western, *Walking the line* with the *Boy called Sue* and his wife June Carter, helping them build a new swimming pool for the school from the proceeds.

A corridor of classrooms had been converted into dressing rooms and Ken and I used our charm on the janitor to access the area.

"Where you going?" asked Ken, seeing I wasn't following him and Christine to Johnny's dressing room.

"I've got better fish to fry," I said taking Christine by the hand into the guitarist's classroom.

Carl Perkins!

A gymnasium layered with Gods.

The man who wrote *Blue Suede Shoes*.

Top of the class!

In Memphis we stayed at the Peabody Hotel where Elvis had once stayed, and watched the ducks exiting the elevator, chaperoned down from the roof to take their daily plunge in the lobby fountain.

We visited the Sun Studios, then the King's former home in Lauderdale Courts, his school Humes High, and of course Graceland, where the lawn still suffered under fan attacks.

For the second year in succession, we were treated to a civic reception by the Ladies Guild of Tupelo where the mayor of the town welcomed us in a well-rehearsed speech filled with Elvis tales and anecdotes.

Finally, we queued to enter that sacred of all rock 'n' roll places, the birthplace of Elvis Aaron Presley.

Back in Memphis we took a trip on a Mississippi steamboat which was quite boring so I entertained the fans with an old Al Jolson medley I used to do on strict tempo nights back in Bristol with the Johnny Francis Orchestra: *'It's a treat to beat your feet on the Mississippi mud...'* which indeed it was, for everyone. The last thing I did before leaving town was to buy a shirt in Laskey's on Beale Street. If this tailor was good enough for the King, it was good enough for the Prince.

And finally, on to Vegas where things were far from well.

Todd reported that the Colonel was avoiding his calls so he'd gone on ahead to Vegas to sort things out. Colonel's secretary had lied that he was out of town but Todd had run into someone who knew Colonel and verified that the old carnival huckster was right there in Vegas.

"You go your way and I'll go mine," I said to Todd when we joined him the following day. This year the fanclub muscle wasn't flexing for us, so we each tried our own methods to secure a meeting with Elvis.

I recalled that the Colonel lunched each day in one of the Hilton's numerous restaurants just off the lobby.

I waltzed up to the Maitre D.

"I have a lunch date with Colonel Parker," I announced.

"He's at his table sir," he answered making to escort me.

"I know my way thank you," I lied and started across the room my eyes furtively seeking out Tom Parker.

The Colonel hadn't seen me for a year. I had spent a total of five hours with him and yet he instantly recognised me and stood to reach for my hand as I approached.

"Meester Prince," he welcomed chomping the butt of a cigar.

I explained I'd been lunching across the room with Ken Evans, who was keen to meet him.

Colonel's cigar moved magically from one corner of his mouth to the other. Any guilt he felt at dodging the fan club was either disguised, or he didn't have any.

"Ken's the number one honcho in radio, and I have Peter Muller from the Daily Mirror with me, and I'd love you to meet my wife."

He bought the package.

Ken, of course, was extremely important. Peter Muller however, a Mirror promotion man out on a jolly, who'd never written a line, wasn't.

"Meet me at 3pm at the Elvis booth in the lobby. I'll sort out everything."

And so he did.

That evening I escorted a party of six down to the dressing room bar, where Todd too, had chaperoned a small party including his delightful Scottish wife, Vicky.

Christine, as you can see on the snaps, was not at all enamoured with being herded around by gun toting Memphis Mafia, she snarled like Elvis.

She looked stunning in a pink dress, which we thereafter called 'the Elvis frock'.

James Burton, Elvis' guitarist, was drinking a coke leaning on the bar.

"Hey," he nudged me, "Aren't you the guy at the airport in That's the Way It Is movie?"

Elvis showed at that moment and shock-horror, Todd's wife Vicky had decided to vent her rage on the King, pissed off with the run-around they'd received since arriving.

"It's very nice of you to give Todd two minutes of your time Elvis," she chastised.

Elvis bent down towards the tiny Glaswegian viper trying to comprehend her brogue, which was Sauciehall Street thick.

It was probably the first time in history that Elvis was getting a bollocking *from a fan*.

"I'm sorry Ma'am?" said Elvis cupping an ear towards her.

"I said..." she began, but was elbowed away by a flustered Todd. You never saw Todd flustered, *ever*!

"Err this is from the NME," said Todd.

A gold record blanked Vicky's face from Elvis' view.

"Well gee... thank you very much," said Elvis pulling back from Vicky's spittle distance.

But she wouldn't let go.

"I said it's good that you..."

"And this is from the fan club..." Todd interrupted.

Elvis strained to look at the small angry woman, now jumping up and down behind his British fan club secretary.

"Ah fuck yeeeh!" said Vicky under her breath, and went to sit down by the bar sulking.

I introduced Elvis to Christine whose *'Nice to meet you Elvis'* provided the former truck driver with great relief, and as I introduced Ken and Peter, he continued to give cursory glances towards Vicky, who had now blagged a bourbon and Seven Up from James Burton, at the dressing room bar. She looked quite menacing.

Elvis had put on a few pounds, and was at the start of his slide towards the floor of his Graceland bathroom in four years time.

But even with pumped up cheeks, he still had all the ingredients of a hunk in the summer of 1973.

"Polk Salad Annie's the best thing you've done for ages," I said.

Behind us Vicky was lip snarling in the manner of Elvis, to his guitarist, her finger waggling towards Elvis.

"Thank you. Did you like See See Rider on the flip?" asked Elvis.

Vicky jumped down off her stool and advanced. Elvis couldn't see her, he was facing me, but Colonel moved to intercept before the rattlesnake bit.

"Do you still plan to come over to the UK?" asked Ken.

"That's it folks!" yelled Colonel, "It's show time!"

"Elvis Presley," began Vicky, but he didn't hear his muffled name. Nor did he see Todd dragging his wife out into the corridor, his hand clamped firmly over her mouth.

After the show, Christine was approached by a member of the Memphis Mafia in the hotel lobby. He was rounding up girls for a party in Elvis' suite.

How she refused I don't know. I wouldn't have stood in her way!

We met other girls who did go. Elvis didn't appear as they had hoped.

On the morning of our departure from Las Vegas, I ran into guitarist Charlie Hodge, the guy who supplied new handkerchiefs and glasses of water on stage to an increasingly perspiring Elvis.

I told him the comparison to last year's red carpet welcome, and this year's abysmal treatment of fans who'd invested their life savings in coming, was astonishing.

He must have carried the message to influential ears, I was about to leave for the airport when Colonel's assistant, Tom Diskin called me apologising on behalf of the Colonel and Elvis explaining that, although he couldn't be quoted, the management of the Las Vegas Hilton had told them not to encourage the 'kids from England', as he put it.

"But why?" I asked.

"Vegas was built to attract money Tony. These expensive showrooms are here to attract the big rollers, that's how they can afford Elvis, Tom Jones and Sinatra. The showroom seats have to be full of gamblers, or at least their family, whilst they lose on the craps. I'm afraid their view is that the poorer tourists do not belong in this environment."

"I'm so sorry to hear that Mr Diskin. The high rollers didn't put Elvis on that stage."

"I agree. Elvis is oblivious to such a situation, we keep him out of politics and he keeps us out of his music, it's a pretty good relationship. But I trust Tony that we showed you our true colours last year and tried our best for you all this year. Unfortunately however there are some things we don't control."

Jan: Freedom come, freedom go

Each day there was less and less hopeful news, so that our pessimism dissipated with each publication of Red Law.

In one edition, they reported that Soviet planes had distributed fake copies of Red Law across Prague. Printed in Dresden by East German communist publishers, they gave the impression that Red Law itself had capitulated. After 20 years writing totalitarian bullshit, Red Law warned the citizens of Czechoslovakia against this blatant communist propaganda in the counterfeit newspapers that fell from the sky.

During the Prague Spring under Dubček, Red Law had dramatically changed editorial policy away from communism and, for the first time since 1948, the truths had been allowed to surface. Then, on Radio Prague and through Red Law President Svoboda, Commander-in-Chief of the Czechoslovak People's Army, made a strange and confusing appeal to his military leaders.

"Only a peaceful and calm attitude can keep us on the path we embarked upon in January, under the leadership of the Communist Party of Czechoslovakia."

Our kidnapped leaders had already been forced to sign a treaty obeying Russia's commands. We were sunk! Svoboda was not Dubček. Svoboda had been a general fighting alongside the Red Army in the Second World War; he was not a man who could stand up against such powerful influences.

Our Prague Spring had passed by.

Radio Prague, our last bastion for freedom of speech, announced that a directive had been received throughout Czechoslovakian press and news media, 'recommending' journalists did nothing to besmirch the Soviet Union.

Radio Prague, now in it's final free-speech hours, read Russia's directive to us in a live broadcast in which it demanded the broadcaster's editorial could not use the terms 'occupier, occupation, and neutrality'.

Censorship was back.

International help through military aid was nowhere to be seen. America was too busy with Vietnam, President Lyndon Johnson incapable of throwing his country's weight behind our fight for democracy. The treaty of Yalta, when the super-powers divvied out the world to each other, was still firmly in place.

Each day, the number of our people angry at the Soviets was decreasing as the majority of our population capitulated, deciding it would be better to retreat so that they would not lose their jobs.

We heard key radio announcers changing tack, reconciled with the status quo and once again resigned to life under a huge red thumb.

Red Law announced it would now be allowed back into its usual publishing house, and would be returning the paper to its old size and format. They didn't mention it would return to filling its pages with poppycock.

Once again in Czechoslovakia, the race was on to impress mother Russia, and to feed well from her communist kitchen, as the race for top jobs recommenced.

We also felt a big change in attitude from the officers commanding our military railway unit, who threw a fit when they heard soldiers uttering such popular phrases as *'Fucking Russians!'*

The officers, who we had grown to like during the days of wine and roses, had families and were afraid of losing their good jobs, but their attitude towards us had changed with the pressures they were now under.

We, the work force, convinced ourselves that we were repairing the railway for our country, and were happy to receive a little extra money over and above a regular soldier's pay, so our level of discontent would never cause a revolution.

One afternoon, we waited for the green light to let us proceed with our train carrying the assembled rail tracks. The progress was slow. Often we'd have to duck into a siding with our diesel locomotive to allow a scheduled train by. It was a very fragile load and so we'd let many trains pass by, waiting then until there was sufficient time for us to move a little further up track.

As usual, I sat at the end of the train enjoying a country show called 16:05 to Nashville, on AFN. It was a nice change from listening to Radio Luxembourg each night. Many of the real western-style tunes took me back to my childhood, when I read prohibited books about the American wild west, which had been published in Czechoslovakia before the Second World War, and saved from the massive bookstore and library bonfires of 1948.

I sat alone on my railroad track in the afternoon sun, gazing on a valley that stretched below in a big green meadow flanked by woods, where birds swooped in and out, oblivious to what we humans were doing.

Suddenly my radio started to play a song that really struck me with a force so big, I can still feel it vibrate in my soul to this day. Johnny Cash started singing in his deep, gravelly voice,

'Oh, bury me not on the lone prairie
These words came low and mournfully
From the pallid lips of a youth who lay
On his dying bed at the close of day.'

It felt like the song was about me, that I was the dying cowboy because of the Soviet aggressors shattering all my dreams, robbing me of so much and not least 'Sun cream girl', my new found and lost love. The song penetrated me further at its ending which went:

'Oh, bury me not and his voice failed there
But we took no heed to his dying prayer
In a shallow grave just six by three
We buried him there on the lone prairie.'

My eyes clouded, touched by my own interpretation of the song. Could it really be so, that the world had forgotten Czechoslovakia completely? Would the free world stand by and watch our newly won democracy killed and buried by Russian invaders? What good were any of their protests if the Russian red bear refused to listen?

Just as I was about to drown in self-pity, I heard Pepa's all clear whistle. Snapping out of my morbidity, I waved my shunter flag and our train started to edge it's way forward.

It was a crucial moment as I came to terms with the truth. Locked in a communist cocoon would never kill me providing I had music, AFN during the day, Radio Luxembourg at night. In these circumstances, because of my passion for western music and love for the English language, no prison warder sent to control me from the Kremlin, would be able to beat me.

For a time, Radio Prague managed to go out on the occasional political limb keeping our spirits high. One night in the pub, we all fell silent to listen as they played a new song by Jaromír Vomáčka, someone known more for middle-aged fans and songs written with them in mind. This time he'd used the inspiration of the anti-Russian slogans written on walls by protesters. We saw them everywhere, on posters pasted to columns and pillars or hand-painted wall graffiti.

'Ivan go home, Natasha is waiting for you!' to which Vomáčka added more words to the song he sang to us. *'Go home Ivan, the girls here don't love you, go to your Natasha and don't you ever come back again!'*

What courage this middle-of-the road singer had shown. I yearned for my tape recorder, knowing that perhaps this would be the only time ever our radio stations would play this brazen protest song. In America the equivalent would be Bing Crosby singing about Vietnam, or Val Doonican in the UK protesting on behalf of the Irish. Jaromír Vomáčka was a very brave man who, because of this song, earned the admiration of a generation who, previously, were bored by his music.

This evening we skipped through the pages of Red Law in which it was clearly a reborn pro Soviet newspaper. An article reporting on East German generals and members of their Ministry of Defence visiting the East German troops, stationed in Czechoslovakia, gave the paper a golden opportunity to make a point, a point I now made in the pub.

"I wonder how many of these German generals wore Nazi uniforms the last time they visited us?" I asked my audience, drawing a huge round of applause.

But then we discussed a certain Gustáv Husák, who Red Law reported had held a meeting of the Communist Party of Slovakia in Bratislava, and came down fully against Dubček for not obeying the Soviets.

This was all too much for us in the pub, and no one could know how happy I was when the evening came so that I could finally dial Luxembourg's 208 metres.

DJ Tony Prince was talking to me, and I knew then that at least one thing was still functioning as it should, something that gave us certainty in our troubled world in the autumn of 1968. In listening to Radio Luxembourg we understood we were amongst millions also listening for their love of music and in this respect we were just as free as everyone else, until we awoke the following morning to the cruel realities that surrounded us once again.

The free world had sent us moral support thanks to their radio stations, but what I didn't appreciate whilst listening to the pirate ships and Luxembourg, was that these stations were there because the UK governments had created their own kind of communism in giving the broadcasting franchise to one governing body, the BBC. Little did I realise that when I was listening to Radio Luxembourg in the late 50s and early 60s, so too were *all* the kids in the UK and across greater Europe where radio licensing had been severely restricted. I assumed the UK basked in great music radio all day long, and that various other radio stations played Beatles and Elvis style music 24/7.

Pirate radio stations such as Caroline, London, City, England, Scotland, 270, surrounded the British Isles and it was my good fortune that with the right conditions in Brno, I could hear Radio Caroline clearly. Who would ever believe that 208, with all its English DJs, music, commercials and dialogue, was actually a business consortium made up of German, French and Luxembourg businessmen under the RTL broadcasting banner? How would we know that Radio Luxembourg used a frequency allotted to the country of Luxembourg to target UK money? Or that pirate radio was first brought onto the high seas of England by an Irishman?

During our Prague Spring, somehow we no longer needed our beloved music to provide moral encouragement. In this freedom recess in our country's history, music and radio took on a different mantle and started to be taken for granted, as something to enjoy quite openly. We may have continued to dance together in hidden spaces, but there was no longer any fear in doing so. We were quite sure then that Communist Secret Agents were no longer concentrating on western music fans, as they had before Dubček made his breakthrough.

So I'd been able to party with friends in Bratislava in the summer of '65 and celebrated New Year's Eve in an atmosphere, the likes of which we had never before experienced. Taking my record player to our army shelter in Řepčín was unheard of. Army officers watching their soldiers dancing to capitalist music on army property, was unthinkable.

Now as we saw our media capitulate, it looked like we were inexorably returning to those unthinkable times.

We had so many questions and no media to give us our answers.

How long would the Russians stay in Czechoslovakia? Would they stop broadcasting music from the west in Mikrofórum on Radio Prague? Would it again be necessary to hide somewhere when listening to Radio Luxembourg?

Something then eclipsed all my concerns. I finally succeeded in getting a phone connection to my mother, who told me she had succeeded in buying a new tape recorder for me. I was beside myself with excitement and knew I had to visit home as soon as possible. With 10 days holiday owed to me, my commander gave me permission to take my leave. I took a train to Prague, proudly knowing that I had personally helped to lay the rail we now travelled along.

I alighted in Prague, unable to resist taking a walk downtown to Wenceslas Square to see what was going on there under Soviet occupation? Prague looked much the same as I remembered it, until I came to our defaced National Museum. The facade displayed the evidence of the bombardment our people had endured. Hundreds of holes on this historical building displaying the barrage of shots from Russian tanks and armoured vehicles, now a firm reminder of the massacre that had taken place.

I gasped at the sight and cursed the stupid Russian creatures that had caused this nauseating damage. Could any cultured nation really shoot at this beautiful museum? Let alone kill unarmed people who stood between the wall and their armies?

I continued the four hour journey home to Brno, during which time I realised that having been away for more than half a year, I had missed seeing what it was like to live in a city, basking in its freedom.

Gone now was the happiness I detected in the voices of my mother and father when I phoned them before the Soviets arrived. I could see in their eyes that losing their liberty for a third time was too much for them. But they were happy to see me, and somewhat relieved that they had bought me the right four-track tape recorder.

The next thing I needed to do was to meet František and all my other friends, but when we did meet, the reunion took on the shape of a military squadron returning from battle, and counting those they had lost.

Pavel Váně, like many others had, for the first time in his life, set off to see the west. He'd left with his girlfriend for Austria, but hadn't returned. According to František, it looked like we would never again listen to him sing.

Jan Sochor, with whom we had put so many English lyrics together, had disappeared, as had others we now discussed. The Czechoslovakian WHO'S WHO IN MUSIC looked like it would become WHO WAS WHO, so many musicians had now immigrated.

I was more than happy to see Brno's top rock 'n' roll star our dear friend, Radek Rettegy, had remained with us. When I asked him why he hadn't slipped away to the free world, he replied that he would never leave our country to make way for communists, or Russians, or anyone else.

We agreed that our brief freedom experience from January to August 1968 was now at an end. But we shared the optimism that no one in power would ever again be able to fool the whole nation, as they had for so many years.

Everybody in the land, because of Dubček and his team, had tasted freedom, and everyone agreed it tasted better than anything we had tasted before. We saw movies from the west, magazines and newspapers with more western music played on our radio stations, although still almost nothing in the record shops due, I was told, to the western record companies distrust of communist companies to distribute and account royalties to them, due to currency restrictions and matters of copyright. Copyright meant individual ownership that was not recognised under communism. Neither was religion.

The most valued aspect of the new freedom, was the opportunity to travel beyond our borders, something that was virtually impossible in previous years.

František informed me that Synkopy 61 had recorded a new EP that was supposed to be released in time for Christmas, but now, with some of the members of the group, including Pavel Váně staying in the west, the record would probably never see the light of day.

During the holiday we went to see the movie Help! with the Beatles which gave us some vague hope that it might not be so bad seeing as this great movie was allowed in. But then we realized that such arrangements were made before the Russian invasion, and they would now be preoccupied sorting out western moles, and putting their supporters into key positions. But still, what a great feature Help! was to my vacation. I lost count how many times we went to see it.

I was incapable of passing by the Supraphon record shop, having spent almost half a year in the woods just dreaming of such a visit. I rifled through a small pile of Supraphon singles until I came across the Julie Driscoll & Brian Auger hit *This Wheel's on Fire*. It was played a lot on 208 at the beginning of the summer when it was riding high on the Top 20. Written by Bob Dylan, the song induced images of flower power whenever I caught it on my Hitachi transistor radio. How pleased, I wondered now, would Dylan and Julie Driscoll be, to learn that their record had slipped through the Russian invasion entering Czechoslovakia, at such a tense time in our history?

I asked the lady in the shop if she would kindly play the record across the PA out into the street, which, to our delight, she did. Now the main street of Brno sounded like Radio Luxembourg as the shop's loudspeaker above the door echoed to the lyrics.

Standing with our friends in the street, František looked at me as the record came to an end and yelled for all to hear, *"Russia nil – Jan Šesták 1!"*

I spent most of my 10-day army holidays either watching the Olympic games at František´s home, or writing lyrics from the songs we caught on my new tape recorder.

It wasn't until the very last day when we received the phone call.

"Where are you?" František shouted excitedly.

"Back in Brno, oh my God!"

František´s face, etched with excitement turned to me, "Pavel Váně is back!" After hanging up, he told me Pavel had decided to return from Austria so he could start his studies at the Faculty of Philosophy in Brno. They arranged to meet the following day so sadly I'd have to catch up with Pavel's news and stories on life outside Czechoslovakia some other time, I was heading back to the railway in the woods.

Before leaving, I expressed to František the good fortune for him personally, now Pavel would not be seen as an immigrant, so that the song *War is a Fool* co-penned by František, could now escape the media blacklist. Only last week Red Law informed readers that the rumours that Karel Gott, the most famous singer in Czechoslovakia, had emigrated were false. The report said he would return home immediately he finished his tour of West Germany.

Through our music grapevine, we heard that Karel Gott and his band really had decided to stay in West Germany but, as he was very popular in all Warsaw-pact countries it was said that the Soviet leader himself, Leonid Brezhnev, had issued a command to Czechoslovak authorities that Karel Gott and his musicians must be given permission to travel to the west anytime they wished to make a recording or tour. Quite what level of influence Gott might have enjoyed to attract such a statement from the Russian President remains a dark secret to this day.

Pavel Váně on the other hand, was a rocker, plainly an anti-establishment singer. If he had decided to stay in the west, the authorities wouldn't have batted an eyelid apart from ensuring that none of his songs would ever again be played on the radio.

Remarkably, against all the odds, Czechoslovak radio stations continued to feature *War is a Fool* somewhat frequently, and the fact that almost everybody considered this as our mantra, totally bypassed their radar.

Now every song written or sung by someone who had emigrated was banned. Actors too who had absconded, even those who had played a small part in a movie, saw their films banned forever.

No disloyal immigrant would ever again be seen in the cinema or on a TV screen throughout the Eastern Bloc.

I returned to my railway army unit in Zbiroh where we continued repairing the important Prague–Paris railway track. Soon, however, the weather became unsuitable, and it was decided we would continue this job next spring. In October we returned to Olomouc in our diesel locomotive. Passing Prague at midnight, Pepa let me drive the iron steed at speeds of 90 kilometres an hour, racing the moon as he skirted across the top of the tree line.

I was exhilarated, experiencing such absolute freedom, my first chance to drive something other than a bicycle.

But in spite of this thrill, the journey couldn't disguise the ugly truth as we sped past numerous garrisons of Soviet soldiers. How we would have loved to mow them all down.

In Česká Třebová we stopped whilst the dispatcher signed permission for our loco to continue to Olomouc. After a couple of hours he found a slot for us to continue our journey down this crowded line.

Daylight arrived and with a few kilometres remaining to Olomouc, we came across a blight on our land. In a military barracks close to the track we saw a battalion of Soviet soldiers standing near the railway.

We took this as a golden opportunity to show them eye to eye, exactly what we thought of them. Pepa sounded the loco's horn as we coasted by their shocked faces as we shook our clenched fists at them. Then I turned, dropped my trousers and mooned as we flashed by.

According to their commanders Czechoslovak soldiers were their allies. Now they knew the truth and, for the first time we felt like proper, front-line Czechoslovakian soldiers. We hugged each other screaming our delight like conquering heroes.

Arriving at Řepčín railway station, the commander confirmed that we would continue where we left off before leaving for Bohemia. This meant a pleasant lifestyle in the station house, great food allowances and extra cash working for the nearby iron foundry, whilst living in the comfortable station building.

Tony: The bum in the bush

My best memories are gilded with laughter. My philosophy was always to be original, surprise people, shock them, slap some whipped cream on their face in a posh restaurant, or stand on your head on the table during dinner at the Ivy.

The music industry is littered with people who employ this madness.

Scottish songwriter, Bill Martin, would look you deeply in the eyes and start to say '*I love you*', completely forgetting he had a mouth full of milk he hadn't yet swallowed. Bill paid no heed to the fact that he was going to ruin a suit, so long as he got the laugh. He once pushed my boss Alan Keen fully clothed into a swimming pool at an RTL music festival.

Many is the time I've been standing at a bar talking in a group with Alan, only to suddenly realise his trousers had fallen around his ankles.

The same boss was dancing with a woman at a golf club, having told her he was a gynaecologist. Fascinated she pulled him closer and whispered her confession that she had a '*sort of a wart*'.

Alan pushed her slightly away stopped dancing and looking her seriously in the eye asked, "Does it itch?"

"Well yes it does," she proclaimed waiting for his diagnosis.

"Ah," said Alan, "Here's what you have to do..."

Keen leant confidentially towards her.

"Give it a good scratch!" he whispered, and then he stretched out his palm towards her: "That'll be five guineas please!"

SLAP!!!

It's a strong impulse. Keith Moon had it in abundance. Freddie Starr was saddled with it.

Tony Ashton of Ashton, Gardener and Dyke suffered with it. Lulu's brother Billy Lawrie took some beating too.

The record promotion men such as Sony's Gary Farrow were the kings of madness. Gary rushed into my London office one day and said, "Tony there are four slags wanting your autograph and I think they're writing on your car at the front door." I rushed out to find, Mary Stavin (Miss World), Patti Boulaye, Suzie Quatro and Mia Farrow all sat on the back seat of my Panther Lima sports car!

Bell Record's David Bridger plugged David Cassidy records and came out to see us in Luxembourg regularly. A blonde lunatic with wild impulses enhanced by cocaine, once told me his habit started at school... "I always got lines," he joked.

Judd Lander, once upon a time the Jackson 5's record plugger, was another constant class comedian within the music industry.

He was the harmonica player on Boy George & Culture Club's Top of the Pops performance of *Karma Chameleon*. Judd was the original music industry chameleon and helped Noel Edmonds out on Saturday morning's Swap Shop becoming the famous Crow puppet! We joked that he spent half his time with his hand up a bird's arse.

Scottish madman, Jimmy Devlin, was also one of the funniest in record promotion, until they kicked the humour out of him by making him MD of Polygram!

I once went to an awards ceremony for Abba, a privileged guest amongst other media people, when I suddenly felt the adrenaline rush and then the trembling deep in my stomach telling me I was about to advance the art of imbecility.

Photobombing their photoshoot gave me a pride of place snapshot in which Abba are all laughing, and Agnetha is looking down at me with a knowing grin. Off camera Epic Records Press Officer is in full panic mode screaming '*Mama Mia*'!

My friend, the late great Maurice Oberstein, Chairman of SONY and the BPI, is also in the shot laughing his head off. Obie was also a major outrage player, as all M4 commuters will testify.

When he became the big cheese at Polygram he had a life-sized model of himself created by Madame Tussauds, which he placed on the balcony outside his Polygram high rise office, 25 floors above the Hammersmith flyover.

Wearing pyjamas, the Chairman of the BPI, waved at everyone who ever drove by on the Heathrow run into town. At Christmas, the Obie model exchanged his pyjamas for a Father Christmas outfit! He was the greatest rock 'n' roll chairman ever, and I miss him.

Pretty well everyone resigned from Radio Luxembourg to join the BBC, the list was endless. Of the dozens who gained admission to the hallowed studios of Broadcasting House, I was a rare species, 19 years on British radio and only ever one visit, which was with David Jacobs when it was still the Light Programme.

Before joining Radio 1, Peter Powell had been quite at home on 208 and the early evening show was perfect for him. But I had made this time slot my own, and he would have it over my dead body.

The first time Alan Keen came to Luxembourg after Peter had joined us, we finished up at my house where we threw a party. Alan's first view of Peter was his bare arse sticking out from the bushes at the side of the house, after he'd lost his way to the toilet.

Peter was very, very funny when he was plastered. Alan loved his DJ team being pissed if they weren't on air, and often joined us rocking till dawn. He was quite a boss.

Peter was quite gullible. Kid Jensen and I concocted a telex from the

Programme Director, Ken Evans instructing Peter to do the voiceover on an extremely urgent commercial that had to be transmitted that very night. Locking himself into the production facility, Peter eventually surfaced after two hours, a defeated DJ.

"There's no way I can do this Tampax ad," he cried.

The battle between Peter and I for the teenage listeners was on. I had the all-important column in Fab 208 magazine, and was president of the Elvis and Osmonds Fan Clubs. I was matey with David Cassidy, toured with David Essex and the Hollies. I was just where Peter wanted to be, although he reversed things somewhat when he joined the BBC.

Realising how successful I'd been with the Osmonds' association, Peter tied his kite to the Bay City Rollers and their manager Tam Paton, and hangers-on such as Jonathan King and DJ Chris Denning, who surfaced regularly in the Grand Duchy.

Denning had been part of the gay DJ brigade, who Eggy Lay had to offload, when Paul Burnett and I came out to the Grand Duchy. Jonathan King and Chris Denning both did time for molesting young men. Tam Paton got three years for gross indecency with young boys, and in 2007 was accused of raping Bay City Rollers' guitarist, Pat McGlynn, in his hotel room.

Peter chose the wrong crowd, and it didn't take him too long to realise this.

After stealing her off DJ Bruno Brooks, becoming her agent, marrying and then divorcing Anthea Turner, Peter morphed into one of the industry's top managers, and now makes millions representing presenters such as Philip Schofield, (a fellow Oldhamer) and Geordie superstars Ant & Dec etc.

After two decades without seeing each other, on a whim, I invited him to lunch. We chatted and laughed about the good old days in a restaurant on the banks of the river Thames.

I enjoyed it very much until the very end when Peter turned to me and said, "Well Tony, what's the purpose of this lunch?"

Peter's life had become business. He failed to appreciate that I just wanted to enjoy his company as I had in our days in the Grand Duchy, when he had shown his bare bum to Alan Keen outside my house.

I paid for the lunch and hugged him goodbye. If he reads this book: '*Peter, you owe me lunch, I'll bring Christine!*'

Jan: The cassette player

That evening I decided to visit the hospital where Alena worked to see if she would show up at the usual time, just like things were before I left.

I wanted to see her again very much, and to express my regret that I had made her weep when she learned from Pepa that I had left for Brno. Back then I was fearful that she was too serious about our relationship, knowing that I wasn't ready for such a commitment. Now, after five months I longed to touch and kiss her once again, and to take up where we left off.

I decided to keep waiting for her each evening until her shift rota would lead her to me at the end of her day shift. I stood watching the hospital entrance from a distance, not wanting to approach her in the company of her colleagues. My precaution proved to be right when, on the third night I spotted Alena leaving with another girl and an older man, who I thought to be a doctor.

My heart started to beat faster with the sheer thrill at seeing Alena again. The three talked outside the building for a while until the girl turned to leave them, whilst Alena and the man turned the opposite way alongside the hospital. In all my imaginings where I had contemplated this moment, never did this screenplay appear where Alena would leave with another man.

I was stunned by this unexpected turn of events and stood there watching them disappear, my mouth open, my expression like that of a calf left dumbstruck by a new gate in its stable.

I made a few steps towards them until he put his arm around her that made me feel quite sick. This was more than I could stand, so I turned back and decided to walk down to Olomouc, where I hoped I might come across another beautiful girl somewhere in the town centre.

I wanted to be in the company of a girl very badly.

Various thoughts were occupying my mind as I walked the streets. Who was that man with Alena? Was he her steady date, or just a doctor whom she admired?

I had heard many stories about young nurses wanting to marry a doctor. I had to accept that I had neglected Alena before I left in the spring, so she had no reason to wait for me. If I was honest with myself, I knew that had the Russian invasion not ruined my skinny-dipping date with my beautiful mystery girl, then right now I wouldn't be giving Alena a second thought. But I was giving her second thoughts and I did want to be near her again. My thoughts took me around town as I tried to distract myself by window-shopping.

I arrived at Elektra, a shop selling household electrical appliances noting that the tape recorder my mother had bought me was not on display, which probably meant they had sold out and I was lucky to get one.

But then an unusual device caught my attention with my favourite brand name 'Hitachi' on a card that described it as a *cassette recorder*. Instantly my yearning for Alena disappeared, I might never ever think of her again.

I had only read about this item in an advertisement in America's Time magazine, how the hell did it arrive in Olomouc, when only last week I had seen no sign of one in the Brno Elektra shops?

Of course I knew the answer! In Brno such an amazing new machine would have sold out instantly. I didn't even want to contemplate how come it was still here on display in Olomouc, and with a price tag of just two thousand crowns, I would have to invade my savings book at the post office and be here first thing in the morning.

As I lay in bed that night I had to bless Prague Spring once again, as I was sure that without it there would be no cassette recorder available anywhere in Czechoslovakia. So at least some fruit remained.

I didn't give Alena and her doctor friend another thought that night, now all focus was on this amazing new invention. I tuned to Radio Luxembourg to calm myself and listened to Tony Prince knowing that, if all went well in the morning, tomorrow night I would record a complete Tony Prince show with ease, and if I didn't understand something he said, or a particular song's lyrics he played, all I needed to do was press replay and replay and replay.

As Tony talked to me, my mind went to lyrics that Michal Bukovič had brought to my attention in a country and western magazine in Černošice. These were the words of Jim Reeves who had died in an air crash in 1964 wherein he said, "A stranger is just a friend I haven't met yet."

I knew well that Tony Prince, who usually opened Radio Luxembourg every night, was already my great friend. I had spent so much time with him already, be it in the days of Radio Caroline, and now here on 208 and just like this quote implied, I felt I would surely meet him one day in person.

I had felt this way for quite some time, but now with a Russian invasion standing between us and my future freedom on hold, it seemed my prognosis had to be postponed.

By noon the following day, I became one of the first people in the whole of Czechoslovakia who knew how to operate a Hitachi portable cassette player. I had to laugh over how many years I had to wait before I could buy my first tape recorder, and now I had bought a new reel-to-reel in August, and a new cassette recorder in October.

A new recorder every month, what a life!

Another interesting thing happened to me on the afternoon of 5 November 1968. I was shopping down town and very happy, having just bought a tube of imported Colgate toothpaste, an absolute novelty in our shops and something I'd been hearing sung in commercial jingles on 208 for many years.

Sitting in Olomouc's main square at 6pm, I'd managed to tune in to the

Voice of America on its medium wave frequency that was rather unusual at that time of day without the atmospheric conditions being perfect. I had tuned in to learn if there were any developments concerning Czechoslovakia. I still didn't care if someone noticed me listening publicly to a radio station in a capitalist language, as nobody seemed to give a damn. On the contrary, I would now welcome a confrontation with an officer or military patrol that might wish to know why I seemed to be enjoying a western broadcast.

I had my speech prepared just in case.

"You are <u>bothered</u> that I am listening to a foreign radio station, and you don't give a damn that we are occupied by the Soviet army, how come?" I would say.

There was never any question in my mind that pretty much the entire population of our nation wanted the Russians OUT! As these thoughts scrambled through my mind, suddenly a female announcer caught my complete attention.

"And for the listener in Czechoslovakia, we have the answer for his question about Trade Fairs."

What a thrill! For the first time in my life I had contributed to a real live broadcast, and on the same American radio station my father and uncles risked their lives to listen to all those years ago.

Now they were telling the world that the system of exhibiting new products in the US was slightly different from the Trade Fairs in Brno Czechoslovakia. I sat there in the square wanting to scream to all the passersby to come and listen to *my* broadcast.

I was supposed to receive a book as a prize for sending in my question, but I was sure that now with the Soviet arm controlling everything, nothing from the west would make it in future.

Having had a taste of broadcasting fame, I started to compose a letter that would give me an even bigger thrill, one I knew most of my friends would hear if I was successful. I would write to Tony Prince at Radio Luxembourg, and let him know how much we, in Czechoslovakia, loved his radio station and all its DJs. I would express how much we appreciated their support during these times of occupation.

I had no doubt in my mind he would dedicate a record to me if the letter reached him.

We had plenty of free time in our suburban railway station in Řepčín and with this great new recording device, life had become so much sweeter. Now I could record the Sunday night Top 20 on Luxembourg, and listen to it even when riding the locomotive. The process of recording with a cassette player was so much quicker, which meant I rarely missed the opportunity to record a favourite song. I now looked forward to returning home, and combining the ability to record from my new tape recorder and my new cassette recorder, whilst still looking forward to the reel-to-reel tapes that Michal in Černošice still generously recorded for me.

My English received an unexpected aid. In some of the larger cities in Czechoslovakia were bookstores dedicated exclusively to Soviet Literature. During Prague Spring the shops were renamed Foreign Literature, and it was in this store where one day I had the best of surprises. As usual, it was full of books in Russian and items from the Soviet Union, such as souvenirs of well-known communist characters, including Lenin statues.

I found myself staring at a shelf filled with English language textbooks. I stood there taking in these unbelievable titles and eventually purchased the Concise English Grammar for Foreign Students for a mere 20 crowns and Key with Notes and Explanations to the Exercises for 11 crowns. I also bought two books of the New Intermediate English Course, which each contained with 200 pages for 26 crowns per book. I then made my last purchase, treating myself to the hardback edition of A Book of English Proverbs. At 65 crowns, this was a little more costly, but comparing them to the price I paid for a 90-minute blank cassette costing 100 crowns, they all seemed like bargains.

I fell in love with the book of proverbs, and found it an amusing method of improving my English. Many proverbs were similar to ours so they were easy to understand, especially as they all had clear explanations so that I understood everything.

One proverb gave me consolation over my floundered love affair with Alena. It came from a collection of nursery rhymes published in 1843 and it went: *'Needles and pins, needles and pins: When a man marries his trouble begins.'*

Beneath the rhyme was an editorial note that made me laugh:

'We must not of course take the proverb as discouraging marriage and paternity.'

It seemed that the author, VH Collins, didn't want to be responsible for discouraging readers from getting married! But this proverb was like reading my story, like when Alena said she would move to Brno and that we could stay together forever and I backed off. I wasn't ready for such a definitive relationship at that time, but how different things might have been had she only left hospital alone a few days ago?

December came and we had to decide who would go home for Christmas and who took the New Year break. I myself preferred to wait for New Year, our traditional party night. I was already planning my playlist.

I left my transistor radio with my fellow soldiers, but took my new cassette recorder with me and went home for the holiday.

I found a small pile of post awaiting me, including one enormous package. There was a season's greeting card from my Japanese penfriend Mayumi

Kizara, which caused me to reflect on what a good sign it was that a Japanese letter had made it through Russian control.

But a bigger surprise awaited me in the large package that had been sent to me, post-marked Prague. I knew nobody in Prague. I had ordered nothing from Prague.

My parents watched as I ripped open the packaging, and we stood there together gazing at the biggest book I had ever owned.

The book was titled, AMERICAN MUSE (A Story of America in painting, poetry and prose - by Henry Dorra).

Turning the pages I discovered a typed letter on plain paper.

'Your question about trade fairs has been selected for an answer on the air and will be included in a program on Tuesday, 5 November, 1968 which can be heard between the hours of 1630-1700, 1930-2000 or 2130-2200 GMT.

Sincerely yours,

Shirley Shanahan

Question Editor.'

I was disappointed that the message was not printed on official Voice of America letterhead, but realised that this was so *VOA* would not put me in any danger.

How they managed to post it in Prague remains one of their tactical secrets. Neither the letter content, nor the packaging made a single mention of Voice of America, another tactic that would help to ensure delivery. Even my name and address were written by hand, as undoubtedly the station typewriter didn't reproduce the diacritic letters in our alphabet.

The book itself was enthralling, and before I set off to show it to František, I came across a cartoon from 1915 that made me bellow with laughter. It showed an army doctor with a recruit and a sign announcing: *MEN WANTED FOR THE ARMY*. The recruit was three times bigger than the doctor, huge muscles but no head at all.

Beneath the cartoon was the caption:

Army medical examiner: 'At last a perfect soldier.'

It reminded me so much of the Soviet soldiers we spotted now and then, either when passing by their barracks in our diesel locomotive, or on the streets of Olomouc where they accompanied officers who were not allowed out alone. The officers carried pistols to defend themselves in case people argued with them too much.

We realised that Russian soldiers, especially those from Asiatic USSR republics and many of their officers, didn't even know in which country they were stationed, believing Czechoslovakia to be just another republic in the Soviet Union. Like the drawing depicted, they were brainless, well this was our extremely popular belief.

František told me the big news that at last he'd travelled west, to West Berlin in fact. He was probably one of our last citizens to travel west, without approval from a university or an employer.

He also had a place to lay his head in West Berlin as Pavel Váně's mother had a good friend there, so when Pavel's sister announced she was going, František offered to accompany her, and so travelled as a family friend.

They travelled to East Berlin by train from Brno, arriving at Friedrichstraße station, the major border crossing from East to West Berlin, situated directly in the centre of East Berlin.

Walking to the checkpoint with armed East German guards at every step, František, wearing his dark glasses acted like a cool rocker, he was, after all, a successful songwriter for whom a big career in rock music was within his reach.

At that time his ambitions were to become a famous poet, as well as a successful and rich rock song lyricist. Little did he know then that within a year, his work would be banned, and none of his compositions would be permitted to be recorded for several years.

Approaching the crossing, looking like Keith Richards, the East German guards demanded František take off the glasses so they could properly identify him from his passport picture. After doing so they were motioned to proceed on their way, and within minutes had stepped into another world.

Gone were the plastic East German Trabant cars and the Soviet Volga monsters. In their place in the busy scene that greeted them were shiny Mercedes and impressive BMW's. Gone was the grey austerity of East Berlin, even the snow was whiter and the impressive buildings looked clean and well maintained. What really impacted most on František was something he had never imagined as he left the East, the people were smiling!

Something else he never dreamed of, was the sight that met his eyes when he entered a West Berlin record shop.

"I almost had a heart attack literally," he recalled. "My heartbeat increased and I started to sweat, I had to go outside and breathe some fresh air."

Never in his life had he seen so many records, albums, singles and even cassettes now contained the latest albums.

The currency restrictions when leaving for the west were quite severe. Crowns could be changed for up to $5 per day, with a $100 maximum. František was scheduled for a four-day visit with $20 spending money from which he would also have to buy food. Without a friend of a friend to stay with, these currency restrictions severely limited how many of our countrymen could ever possibly visit the west. With Christmas coming, František's potential to buy presents would be limited to the most meagre gifts.

"Standing and surveying this wonderland of music was utter torture," said František, a born storyteller. I believed his every word, and whilst I yearned to see what my friend had seen, I was so happy he hadn't emigrated like my neighbour, Jura Kameníček, who had got me the vouchers for the Tuzex shop, and so changed my life. Friendship was extremely important now. We had to stick together and make sure the Russians left our country, so we could return to our Prague Spring.

The thought passed my mind that the more our people immigrated, the easier it would be for our totalitarian rulers to control the situation here, as there would naturally be fewer people who would be in any kind of opposition.

I suddenly appreciated the precious book I'd received from Voice of America, that according to the inner cover cost $10, half of what František had to spend on his trip.

Then he really impressed me recounting his further experiences. He'd seen The Moody Blues singing their big hit *Nights in White Satin* on television, filmed to his surprise in Prague on the Charles Bridge, with some German announcer asking a question or two to each member of the group in English. The rest of the film showed them individually, as the camera followed them walking around Prague old town.

This was quite a revelation. A second British group had visited Czechoslovakia after Manfred Mann, which we had not been aware of, and perhaps shows how bad the grapevine was between Prague and Brno in those days.

But even if we had been told, would we have believed it? There were stories all the time, often hard to believe, such as the rumours that the Beatles were coming to perform in Prague's 200,000 capacity Strahov stadium.

We had to wait 22 years until a British rock group finally appeared at the Strahov stadium. The Rolling Stones performed there, but for security reasons only 130,000 spectators were permitted. Nobody then would ever forget the slogan of their show when their cavalcade came to town. It said: *'The Stones are Rolling in – The Russian Tanks are rolling out!'*

Twenty-two years would test our endurance.

František told me that some friends were angry with the Beatles for writing a song, 'Back in the USSR' that featured on their new White Album.

It just didn't sound like something we expected from them, maybe if they'd written *'Go back to the USSR from Czechoslovakia'*, we would have loudly applauded it, but this now seemed like pro-Russian propaganda and we were totally confused.

František regretted not buying this double album on his West Berlin trip, but then I revealed my new cassette recorder, on which I just happened to have recorded the song from 208.

We sat and listened carefully replaying it time and time again. Back home I listened to it many more times and finally, once I heard the last verse, I knew they couldn't be praising the Soviet Union, that wouldn't be the Beatles' style by a mile; they must have been taking the piss out of Russia, and I set about translating the lyrics to prove this was the case. The line *'Take me to your daddy's farm'* revealed to me Beatle-humour when no daddy anywhere across Russia could own a farm, and he would have to be part of a commune known as a *kolkhoze*. I also translated, *'Come and keep your comrade warm, I'm back in the USSR'* and saw it as making fun of the Soviet's addressing themselves as *comrade* all the time when in real life, in Liverpool let's say, not absolutely everyone would be someone else's comrade.

At that time, we weren't aware of the Chuck Berry song *Back in the USA* that praised American culture, neither had we been informed that this song had inspired Paul McCartney to write a parody of it.

The timing of the release was so close to the Russian invasion, Beatles fans who didn't understand the song were suddenly confused, many expressing anti-Beatles comments, such was their hatred for Russia. Everybody was by now so anti-everything, Russian people started to express dislike of all the great writers including Pushkin, Gogol, Tolstoy and Dostoyevsky, even though they had nothing in common with the Soviet Union.

I was happy to celebrate New Year's Eve again with my friends after being away for a year. Pavel Váně and František had travelled to the west for the first time, and yet I didn't feel I had missed out at all, as my affinity with the west had been established over my intensive listening to my friends, the radio stations and, even now, with the Russians camping on our doorsteps, still I could buy magazines like Time and Life regularly.

During this fleeting visit to Brno I bought a special issue of Life, and the cover said it all:

'68 Memorable Pictures of an Incredible Year'

Ten of these pages were dedicated to Czechoslovakia with very touching photographs that I had never seen before, due to our censors enthusiastically doing their job. It was though, a real surprise to me that they still did not mind importing Life and Time and a few other magazines from abroad, giving us a glimpse of our own world from their world.

Across two whole pages Life showed six young men attacking a Russian tank from very close quarters, armed only with stones. Their descriptive caption beneath the dramatic photograph read:

'A dramatic, but short-lived defiance in the streets!'

I reflected on the photograph, thinking of these brave young men throwing their lives in front of the Russian tanks on our behalf. Were they still alive? Had they been executed? Imprisoned? And, if so, where? Were they being brutalised in a Prague jail or prisoners building railroads on the Dead Road of Northern Siberia? How could we know? Who would ever tell us?

I convinced myself that it was perhaps better this way. Had our magazines printed such loathsome photographic evidence, then other kids would take up the mantle and more lives would be lost in our uneven struggle. I knew for a fact, that each of the six brave young men would far better off listening to the Beatles, than facing off with the Cossack descendants.

There were other pictures under the title 'Cruel Days of Anger and Grief', showing sad people of all ages who still refused to capitulate.

The music stopped at midnight as we joyously embraced one another. We'd made it through another year, an almost glorious year with the shittiest of endings.

We were unanimous in our cheers when someone suggested their new year's wish would be to see the Russians leave our country. Then the atmosphere dulled momentarily, and all because I had expressed my hope that they didn't take six years to leave like their Nazi predecessors had.

Someone said something about 'looking on the bright side', but then they were challenged with: *'Which side might that be?'*

We all knew the truth behind the sinister events of two days ago, when on 29 December 1968, the Czechoslovak government that had brought us to the edge of democracy after 20 years of totalitarian communism, had resigned.

Red Law was sparing with the details. It gave more space to the Czechoslovak President and Prime Minister sending congratulatory telegrams to Fidel Castro and the Cuban president Osvaldo Dorticos, on the occasion of the 10th anniversary of the Cuban revolution.

In a mere 15 lines, Red Law told us that President Svoboda accepted the resignation, and asked Prime Minister Černík to provide him with a proposal for a new government, asking him to secure that the present government remained functioning until a new one was introduced.

Alexander Dubček received no further mention in our media.

Tony: Midem madness

Christine's fear of flying was compounded by a remarkable stroke of fate. She was in Oldham visiting her family of four sisters and two brothers.

In those days if you travelled on Sunday to Luxembourg, we caught a flight to Brussels, and connected to Luxembourg on a Focher Friendship.

"I'm coming back Monday, instead of Sunday," she said down the telephone.

That meant a direct flight instead of two.

It also meant she cancelled her flight on British Airway's Pappa India, the flight to Brussels which crashed that Sunday by the Staines reservoir killing everyone on board.

On Monday she caught the train back to Luxembourg.

I remember being angry before the crash, because she'd put her phobia before getting back to me a day earlier. Tschhh!

And so Christine wouldn't fly to Cannes with me for the industries annual music bazaar MIDEM.

My boss Alan Keen and I went each year, but Christine would not have liked the 747 to Cannes this year, because halfway there it turned back with engine trouble.

If that plane had gone down, that would have been the end of the British Music Industry.

Alan and I were sat with songwriters Bill Martin and Tony Hiller.

Bill, with his songwriting partner, Phil Coulter wrote *Puppet On A String*, *Congratulations* and *My Boy* (which Elvis recorded). Tony Hiller wrote *Save Your Kisses For Me*, a Eurovision Song Contest winner.

The sound of the dodgy engine could not be heard over the rustling noises as, to a man, we opened our duty free booze.

Everyone on board was animated talking loudly and drinking heavily diverting their minds from our impending doom.

Suddenly Bill Martin stood to his feet, Dom Perignon splashing everywhere.

"The plane's going down!" he screamed as everyone turned to look at the mad Scot.

"Look," he said pointing accusingly at Dick James, the millionaire Jewish publisher, who signed the Beatles and Elton John.

"Dick James is selling his catalogue!"

The whole plane was in an uproar.

Then we encouraged Dick to stand up to sing his famous 1956 TV theme hit, *Robin Hood, Robin Hood, Riding Through The Glen*!

For a doomed flight we were pretty happy! Many of us took 24 hours to finally land!

Dick James was very familiar with Alan Keen. When Alan ran the pirate ship Radio London, the Beatles released the Sgt Pepper album and Alan inherited a pirated recording from an insider at EMI who had recorded it from the loud speakers during a staff preview. Alan called Dick and told him he had a recording and that as inferior as the soundtrack was, his station was going to give it a world premier the next day.

"That's impossible" James responded. "There are only three copies in the world. Paul McCartney has one, I have one and the third is in the EMI vaults!"

"Well, we're going to play it tomorrow on Radio London," said Alan.

"You do, and we'll sue you," said Dick, frothing at the mouth.

"Fine," said Alan. "Radio London is registered in the Bahamas, I'll give you the address."

It was a lesson for Dick. Now he knew just what pirate radio was all about! Rather than allow Alan to play an inferior recording Dick, on the understanding that Keen would never tell anyone, gave Alan his copy.

Radio London, because of Alan Keen's wile, had the world exclusive on the greatest album of its day and age.

At MIDEM, Alan stayed at the Carlton with the rest of the music industry controllers whilst I preferred the raunchier Martinez down the Croisette. After a week at MIDEM, you needed a holiday!

Here Dave Dee, Jimmy McCuloch, Lorna Luft, Bill Wyman, Jonathan King and countless other head cases from the record industry, gathered to sell their music and sign drinks to other people's rooms.

One year, a German music publisher got a bar bill for £2,000! It was unfortunate for him that he'd been allocated room 208!

Chris Yule, DJ Anne Nightingale's husband fell asleep pissed in a chair. Dave Dee, McCuloch and I, piled a pyramid of chairs over him, climbing on tables and shoulders until the stack reached the ceiling 20 feet above him.

Then Dave Dee got a soda siphon...!

Yuletide!

Someone got the idea that 12 of us should club together and draw straws for one of us to take one of the many Parisienne hookers in town, for the big take at MIDEM, to a room.

I got the short straw, which meant *my room*. The one with the largest straw got the swag.

Mike DeHavilland, a young music plugger, remained downstairs in the lobby seeking out his hooker, whilst 11 of us went to hide in my room.

Three of us were under the bed. Four in the wardrobe.

Eight shoe tips protruded from behind the curtains.

DeHavilland arrived with *two* hookers, we'd over-budgeted.

There was much rustling and French come-on talk, as a variety of the trios clothing hit the carpet. Then one of the music publishers behind the curtains laughed and the game was up.

Screams followed scream as first one, then another, laughing Englishmen appeared from behind the curtain.

Half naked, the girls were out the door before the lads in the wardrobe were out of their doors.

Halfway down the long hotel corridor, trying to dress as they ran, they turned to see the entire British music industry waving them farewell!

"You could have fucking waited!" yelled Mike DeHavilland from inside the room, looking for his underpants.

We had another whip round, this time to pay the concierge to pay the pimp to keep away from my room!

Jan: Army days end

In August 1969, my two-year long compulsory army duty was coming to an end, and I was supposed to take off my uniform for the last time by the end of September, and not before time. I was a shunter, part of the railroad army unit that repaired the main track from Prague through to Pilsen, which then continued to West Germany.

At around 11 o'clock every morning, we stood back as an express train passed by. Each coach had a beautiful sign in red letters confirming that the express had left Prague in the morning, and would pass Pilsen in a short while, and then in an hour or so would be in Nürnberg. Before the day was through, it would be arriving in the centre of Paris.

Not a single sign escaped my attention as I stood there each day, filled with envy watching the carriages go by, knowing that their passengers would soon be in the free world.

I had been to Paris many times, but only in dreams where I'd join Uncle Joseph who was stationed there as a major in the French army. In the dreams, Paris was not my final destination, I would travel on to London where I would watch the Beatles, the Rolling Stones, the Kinks and all the heroes I admired from my nightly escape via Radio Luxembourg.

In1968, for the first time in 20 years after a communist upheaval in Czechoslovakia, it had, at last, become possible for us to travel and see the free world with our own eyes.

This did not include soldiers, neither professional nor conscripted soldiers like me, so whilst there was a freedom gap for a fleeting time, I was unable to squeeze through it.

Trains going to West Germany or Austria had their own platform on every station. These platforms were crawling with customs officials, Public Safety members, and soldiers with dogs who searched the entire train controlling everyone on board, so no one could escape. Only on one occasion did anyone escape on a train, quite a few actually. In 1951, a group of escapees managed to switch the rail track to allow their passenger train down a track, normally used for freight such as timber, to West Germany.

The whole train with its cargo of 120 local commuters, many of them school children, were taken to their freedom, but only the 50 passengers who'd planned this audacious escape remained in the west, whilst the others all returned.

Our handful of freedom years was swiftly drawing to a close. Travelling abroad became more and more difficult through 1969, until finally we were back to square one, and leaving the east was impossible for another 20 years. Unless you cared to escape of course, and many did, and many failed and were killed. After the Soviet occupation the newly awakened totalitarian communists in Czechoslovakia didn't take long to impose travel restrictions on our citizens.

I had a couple of day's vacation and used it to visit my hometown, and to rendezvous with my good friend from high school, František Jemelka. As I was a more diligent Radio Luxembourg listener than František and had more time while in the army, he asked me to write down lyrics of some of the hits I heard on 208.

I did the same for Jan Sochor, and a couple of other musicians who performed original cover versions of the hits I gathered for them from *Luxy*. They also wanted to write Czech lyrics and so needed me to tell them what each song was about. I must say that I struggled with Procol Harem's *Whiter Shade of Pale*, and the meaning of Bob Dylan's songs.

By 1967, my friend František had become a well-known songwriter through his powerful lyrics to the music of Oldřich Veselý and a song they wrote together, which translated to *War is a Silly Ox*. This was a lighthearted insult, in the same way in the west you could call a friend a 'silly ass'. Pavel Váně of Synkopy 61, (who in October 2011 celebrated the band's 50th anniversary), sang the lead vocal. Loosely translated the song went:

'Somebody wrote down a few words so cool
On an old wooden stake saying war is a fool
I'm standing in front of it, eyes full of tears
I take off my cap and get down on my knees

I pray for those not seeing this stake so cool
Who never will read that war is a fool
Who never did read that war is a fool
Who aren't with me today because war is a fool'

This song which condemned war and violence became one of the biggest Czechoslovak hits of 1968, a blatant protest against Russian occupation, and a song which is still very much appreciated today. For me, it was up there with *The Eve of Destruction*, a song by Barry McGuire I'd heard many times on Radio Luxembourg during 1965.

Needless to say, it made me extremely happy and proud that my friends and schoolmates had scored this big hit with such a socially important message. But there and then it was a small prize, as František's words provided the background sound to the sins that took place in Wenceslas Square, as we all helplessly watched and witnessed our beloved Prague Spring fade away in tandem with our freedom.

And there were plenty more sins in store for us!

Tony: Singing with Paul

One day, whilst Christine, the kids and I, were touring every major British seaside resort with the 208 Summer Fun Bus, Doris, my mother-in-law, received a call for me.

"He's on tour," she answered. "Who's calling?"

"Paul McCartney!"

"Pull the other one it's got bells on!" she said in her refined Oldham accent. I'm sure he was used to these responses.

It certainly was the *Yesterday* man, and he wanted to meet with me in London. I was well intrigued and as soon as I came off the tour, I met with him and Linda over a veggie lunch at a smart Indian restaurant off Curzon Street.

It was a big day for me, Linda persuaded me to become a vegetarian.

The many times I saw her after this occasion she always said, "Still a veggie Tony?" and was always delighted when I confirmed I was still off the meat. The last time I saw Linda was just before she went to live in America, where Paul spent many months nursing her through chemotherapy.

"Still a veggie Tone?" she asked with that lovely smiling face of hers.

"Sure am, never felt better either Linda," I confirmed.

"Look out for preservatives," she whispered confidentially into my ear.

It was the last thing she ever said to me.

It transpired that Paul wanted me to conduct a number of star interviews for a radio series idea he had, which would feature Wings live recordings and stuff that hadn't made the albums.

"We're calling it 'Oo Boo Joo Boo'," he said.

"Why me?" I asked, breaking a poppadom.

"Coz you're a cheeky bugger! I want you to ask cheeky questions and I want you to record everything, including like, if you have trouble getting into the gig."

Paul left the negotiations to his manager Brian Brolly, who had no idea how much a DJ got paid for interviews. I could have really taken the piss, but asked for and got £500 and all expenses for each interview. Nice work if you can get it!

Mick Jagger in a pub by the Thames, John Entwistle in his home, Peter

Frampton in the Inn on the Park, Jimmy Page and Elton John in their studios and then... Bob Dylan's Band at Wembley!

There was no trouble getting in the gig. I was accompanied by Alan Crowder, one of Paul's managers from MPL (McCartney Productions Limited), and I knew all the security guys from the David Essex and Osmonds and David Cassidy tours.

To kill time, I started playing cards with the security team right behind the stage, an area littered with superstars. I watched Bianca Jagger and Mia Farrow eyeing up Rod Stewart and the Faces from side of stage, like two super groupies.

George Harrison arrived and disappeared into the Band's bus, which doubled as a dressing room.

I saw the Band's American manager talking to the Maharishi Harrison and pointing in my direction.

He came over to Alan, and I as I put my hot hand of cards down and switched on the microphone. I had a feeling Paul would like this.

"Harrison says there's no such thing as 'Oo Boo Joo Boo and, 'quote' Tony Prince is full of shit!"

The Band refused to be interviewed unless Paul himself appeared to confirm matters.

I stood up, mic still in hand.

"They're only Bob Dylan's fucking backing group for Christ's sake!" I said standing to leave.

I turned back waving the microphone in front of me so Paul could hear the one failed interview.

"And you can tell Harrison he's a cunt!" I called.

And then we left.

Shame really, I was holding three kings and a pair!

I'd hoped Paul would set me up to interview George. I'd have wanted to know why he believed in all the chanting and meditation and why, if his Indian teachers and prophets of Absolute Truth preached a *simple* way of life, did Swami Prabhupāda, (Bhaktivedanta Swami), Yogananda, Maharishi, Dr Radhakrishan and Mahatma Gandhi, all have such fucking *complicated* names??

Jan: Dubček

Our newly elected First Secretary of the Communist Party of Czechoslovakia, Alexander Dubček, had tried to introduce reforms, especially the decentralization of administrative authority, thus lessening the power through autonomy of central communist government. This was too much for the Soviets who sent an army of Warsaw pact troops amongst us. And so the Russian occupation began and was maintained until 1990. People flew like eagles over the border to escape, a student made the ultimate protest by committing suicide, setting himself ablaze. Alexander Dubček had lasted a mere 16 weeks.

My particular army mates and I were the great distrusted division, each from families that had somewhere along the way demonstrated that they did not support the regime. Hence in 1967, the communist officers segregated us into work groups who would never see a handgun, or be let anywhere near ammunition.

I was perfectly happy with this arrangement. Quite the last thing I wanted to do was carry a gun. For *what*? So I could shoot some poor imperialist rock 'n' roll fan wearing a German uniform?

Those whom the communists saw as their enemy were not mine, for I knew we'd more than likely have the common bond of Elvis and the Beatles and Radio Luxembourg to seal our friendship. Actually my detachment had it good. We were made up of two locomotive engineers, three to five shunters and one train chief, each of whom had extraordinary privileges when you consider why we were put into this squad in the first place. To begin with we didn't have to sleep in tents or barracks with other soldiers, as we always had to be ready on some railroad station where our loco tractor was parked. The train depots made for comfortable and warm accommodation.

Because we were constantly on the move, we were given extra money to take care of our own catering. Whilst all soldiers received a monthly stipend of 75 Czechoslovak crowns, we who lived outside barracks, received an additional 23 crowns a day.

Had we lived on pub food, this wouldn't have gone far at all but fortunately, most of the cooks cooking for some 300 soldiers in barracks, were heavy smokers, and needed money to buy their cigarettes. We took real advantage of this, making a deal of one price for every item that the army cooks provided. One crown for a loaf of bread, one crown for a lump of butter, one crown for a can of sardines, a bottle of milk and so on. All was cool, the army cooks had their cigarettes and we ate like kings for a fraction of our allowance.

Each month I spent my savings on at least two reel-to-reel Basf or Agfa tapes, plus a blank cassette or two.

I had already bought myself a reel-to-reel tape recorder just before going into the army, and in the famous spring of 1968, I'd managed to save enough to buy an absolutely revolutionary Hitachi cassette recorder. Few amongst the working class in Czechoslovakia had ever seen, let alone purchased, a cassette player. Now I could record and replay Radio Luxembourg programmes whenever I liked, and I never missed pressing the record button on Sunday nights when the fanfare would introduce the Top Twenty Show, usually introduced by DJs Alan Dell, Barry Alldis or Don Wardell. How I looked forward to the Top Twenty, the highlight of my entire week.

Hence I didn't serve in the army with a gun in my hand; instead I held a transistor radio and a cassette recorder. My only problem was the fixed price for tapes was 155 crowns, for which a four-track recording would provide me with 4 x 90 minutes of music. A cassette on the other hand provided only 90 minutes for 105 Czechoslovak crowns, but the convenience of the cassette was incredible and quite revolutionary in any nation at that time.

I was looking forward to visiting Brno for the very last time as a soldier, taking with me some song lyric transcriptions for František and the other guys.

The tape recorder had opened my world. Until the recorder came along, to write down a song's lyrics meant having to listen out for the songs I wished to transcribe, and of course, this may have been three times a night, or once every three nights, I never could tell. To hear a song in real time required a great understanding of English, and something like shorthand capabilities. I had neither. So the tape recorder was manna from heaven, and the ability to listen to a tune repeatedly lifted me spiritually, whilst the pause button transformed my life completely.

Until the tape recorder, my lyric transcriptions had been hit and miss, undoubtedly more miss than hit. I paraphrased what I *thought* I'd heard. When the song didn't come round again soon enough on Radio Luxembourg, I made up my own verses.

I probably failed to transcribe anything correctly but it mattered not, the lyrics were the framework on which the Czech musicians would hang their own Czech versions. One or two words we didn't understand made no difference.

For some unknown reason, the army officer wouldn't let us go on leave during the week leading up to Sunday 24 August, telling us that the whole Czechoslovak army was on emergency standby due to the anniversary of the Russian invasion. I was informed I could go on leave the following week.

On 21 August, we set up camp in a small railway station just outside the village of Zbiroh. There was absolutely nothing going on in this lost corner of Czechoslovakia, and so the following morning I walked down to the village and bought the communist daily Rudé právo (Red Law) to find out what the communists were writing about.

I was deeply shocked seeing the headline:

GOOD JUDGEMENT AND CALM WILL WIN.

Beneath this was a subtitle:

'*Members of Public Safety, Army and People's Militia deserve thanks and admiration.*'

The People's Militia consisted of what they called, *progressive workers* who carried guns. They were referred to in the communist media as, '*The armed fist of the working class*'.

In the third column, almost hidden, it mentioned that in Prague criminal elements were shooting at helpless citizens with machine guns, and that in the evening two young people were killed and several seriously wounded.

Whilst taking in the horror of this report, I asked myself how were Rudé právo so sure, that those two young people were killed by criminal elements, and *not* by state armed forces?

Who, I wondered, deserved 'thanks and admiration'?

The whole thing stunk to high heaven.

The following day Rudé právo printed a small note at the bottom of its second page, reporting that there were riots in Brno caused by anti-socialist elements. It stated that they had used guns and had killed Danuše Muzikářová an 18-year-old girl, and Stanislav Valehrach a 28-year-old man.

After searching for his daughter and locating her at the Public Safety offices, the father of Danuše Muzikářová took note of a bullet lying next to his daughter's body. Later, he insisted this was a pistol bullet, which came from the back of her head, through to her nose. This proved that a member of the People's Militia, or the Public Safety, had shot her because soldiers had machine guns and did not use pistols!

They had also shot her in the back as she was fleeing.

Unfortunately communist bosses hid the bullet, making it impossible to trace the true assassin, even after 1989 when many crimes against the citizens of my country were investigated.

Rudé právo reported that in my hometown of Brno, 330 people, mainly youngsters, had been arrested. I returned home a week later still deeply troubled by the reports, hoping that none of my friends would be among those arrested.

Tony: Back to England

Right out of the beautiful blue Alan Keen asked me to be Programme Director. Suddenly after a decade incarcerated in Europe, we were coming home.

We were ecstatic.

Back in Blighty we were dragging way behind the living standards of our old pals Edmonds, Jensen and Burnett, who were all doing four or five gigs a week, and housed in palaces.

Christine and I found a small white cottage in Stoke Poges, Buckinghamshire that we rented until, after only a few months, we were told that the landlord needed desperately to sell.

Somehow we managed to raise a mortgage for £37,500.

Christine went to work on the place damp coursing, breaking down walls, tarting up 'The Whitehouse'. One year later we sold it for £180,000, catching up to our old friends in one fell swoop.

For the first year, Alan Keen wanted me to continue broadcasting live as often as possible, so we agreed that I'd do one week in Luxembourg live, and two weeks pre-recorded working from Hertford Street in Mayfair.

I hit the playlist with weed-killer, if this was my station, it was going to be my fucking *great* station.

In 1987, Christine called me at MIDEM in the French Côte d'Azur, she was scared to death. She'd received a call from Richard Swainson, my assistant in the London office, telling her of a London nightclub owner who was making threats against me.

He'd tried to enter the record industry with a shite record, which I had refused to playlist.

He'd wined and dined Richard, took him to Ascot races and tried every single bit of PR to win the day, (or night in Luxembourg's case).

"He said to tell Tony to take care of his family if he doesn't make the playlist!" Richard had thoughtlessly informed Christine, whose panic button had now been firmly pressed.

I decided to return home, but couldn't get a flight until the following day. My friend Roger Holt from MGM advised me what I should do.

"Call Don Murfitt," he advised.

Don was the British record industry's Don in every respect, provider of muscle for concerts, limos for stars, and bodyguards for megastars. He was our security and I had toured with him on many occasions.

I told him of my predicament.

"Don't worry Tony, someone will pay him a visit tonight at his club," he promised.

He also put two men in a car outside my home to give Christine peace of mind until I returned.

I don't know what was said to the club owner, all Don would say was, "Take my word Tony, you won't be hearing any more from him."

We're still here to tell the story.

Thanks Don. I hope you didn't have to kill him.

In the late 60s and early 70s, Radio Luxembourg DJs such as Noel Edmunds, Kid Jensen, Paul Burnett and I, did not influence the playlist, but we did each select our own 'Hit-Pick', sometimes called a 'Sure Shot' or 'Pick-to-click'!

This tiny chink in the station's music output, was what caused pluggers and their artists to visit the Luxy DJs in their droves. Eventually also, Kid Jensen's Dimensions was as powerful an influence as John Peel's show at the BBC and Kid programmed the show himself.

The legendary 208 Top 20 Show was everyone's target on Sunday nights. When a chart show had first arrived at the station in the 50s, the hits were based on sheet music sales. In the late 50s the New Musical Express started providing their charts until finally, we took the official Music Week chart and tried to estimate and project what the records would be doing the following week.

In this way, the BBC's Top of the Pops on Thursday night, Alan Freeman's Pick of the Pops on Sunday's, would look a little stale by the time 10.30pm arrived on Sunday night.

The record pluggers became our allies, giving us background on their releases, tipping us off when a record had suddenly picked up sales, and pain of death to anyone who lied to us.

There were many great and some not so great record pluggers. You've met the dynamic duo Louis Rodgers and Colin Forsey from CBS in their gorilla skins, but CBS also employed other legendary expense account wielders. For example, Golly Gallagher who shared an apartment with Kid Jensen in Luxembourg then DJ'd in the city's Blow Up club.

His closeness to the ostracised team of broadcasters in the Grand Duchy, led to him getting a top job plugging records for CBS.

Golly was a sweet guy, the only man I've known personally who was actually stood up at the altar, a formidable accomplishment.

His record promotion career ended thanks to a set-up, wherein a television programme investigating chart hyping and radio playlisting payola at the BBC, thought they had the Head of Radio 1, Matthew Banister, hung drawn and quartered.

Golly, by this time a top independent record plugger, bragged to the 'client' that he had Banister where he wanted him.

"He owes me a few favours," stated Golly, not noticing the spy camera, which captured him promising virtually guaranteed plays on Radio 1, in exchange for over-the-top fees.

There are many freelance record promoters who lobby BBC producers, who take the piss like Golly when a naive artist's manager or would-be label mogul, walks into their office.

In actual fact, across the years, there have been only a handful of individual programmers who have been in charge of a playlist in the UK that were capable of influencing record sales.

In the 50s and 60s, the Beeb played too little pop, so they can be discounted until Radio 1 came along. Radio Luxembourg, like the eventual pirates, blatantly took payments for plays as their business model, eliminating the potential of individuals dealing in payola.

The arrival of Radio 1 saw the BBC playlist controlled by a committee of producers, all of whom were wined and dined and flattered by the attention of record pluggers, but, as individuals, not one of them had the weight that counted, other than their waistline!

Richard Park, the Programme Controller of Capital Radio, remains the only individual other than myself, who totally controlled the playlist on a radio station which was powerful enough to influence record sales and chart positions.

Richard, like me, loved radio and music far too much to allow money or favours to influence his playlist and charts.

So Golly's puffed-up promise was pure hyperbole. It had no foundation in truth. It was plain and simple bullshit, of which there is a great deal in the music industry.

When Golly turned on the TV and saw he'd been filmed, he didn't need telling that Radio 1 producers would not be taking his calls ever again! His career, as one of the nation's most successful record pluggers, was terminated.

In 18 years on prime radio, I was never propositioned to play records for money or favour, but it has to be said that the record companies fed me throughout my career.

And we all loved going out with the boys and girls from CBS, WEA, RCA, Polydor, Pye and EMI with the promise of gastronomic delights.

Eric Hall is one of my favourite pluggers. Purely by accident, he left plugging and record promotion to become one of the world's premier soccer player managers. He admits that he didn't know much about the game of soccer, but he said to me, "I didn't have to know how a record was made to persuade you DJs to play Freddie Mercury's latest release did I?"

Eric Hall brought Marc Bolan, Queen and Steve Harley out to Luxembourg, and was the man who made sure EMI accessed the airways with his personality, the most lavish dinners available and a fluid stream of bullshit.

The last time I saw Eric he was a gamekeeper, turned poacher. I became his guest on BBC Radio Essex where he'd become a DJ hosting Eric Hall's Monster Memories!

Eric Hall, one of the music industry's favourite descendent of the patriarchs, left plugging behind, when he became Elton John's Managing Director at Rocket Records.

Unfortunately, he didn't hit it off with Elton's personal manager, John Reid, who was obviously threatened by Eric, chosen personally by Elton to run his record label.

Reid sacked Eric paying him two years' salary compensation and, amazingly, it was 10 years before Elton discovered Reid had sacked Eric believing, instead, Reid's story at the time that he had resigned!

Then Eric ran into a soccer player, and his life changed totally managing the world's greatest football players, all of whom he bored to death with his ribald rock 'n' roll tales including, I'll warrant, "How Freddie Mercury wrote a love song about me!"

Dave Bridger was the wildest plugger ever to visit Luxembourg. At the time of this story, he worked for Dick Leahy's Bell Records. David Cassidy, Gary Glitter and the Bay City Rollers were amongst his scalps.

Dave had a problem with sex, drugs and rock 'n' roll. His problem was, he just couldn't get enough of any of it! He was loud, gregarious and had a joke for every situation, funny as hell, the perfect record plugger with whom I bonded out of a common driving force to be silly.

On one occasion he came to Luxembourg with a beautiful ebony girlfriend. We all went out on the town and finished up back at the Holiday Inn.

Worse for wear, Bridger escaped the developing party in the hotel bar early. When we noticed he had given us the slip, it was decided we would visit his room and drag him out for more. One thing led to another, and finally we threw him naked through his window.

It seemed a funny thing to do at the time, and fortunately his room was on the ground floor at the back of the hotel, which meant that he'd now have to walk around to the front door and pass naked through the lobby.

It was certainly not beyond the scope of Bridger's humour to do so, but David had other ideas, and suddenly he jumped towards us and smashed the window with his arm, climbing back into his room. One pint of blood and 20 stitches later, we all left the hospital and went home to bed.

It was a bad night in the annals of record promotion.

Wonderful, wild David Bridger left London for Los Angeles, which we all felt was a bit like sending an alcoholic on a tour of the Dublin pubs.

To this day I have heard no more of David Bridger, but I still see his naked white body splattered with blood, and the smirk that came on his face as the doctor stitched his arm surrounded by the nations top DJs.

"This is going to cost you fuckers at least five Power Plays!" he laughed.

He wasn't wrong!

Jan: The trials of Pavel Váně

I was shocked when František Jemelka told me our great friend, the musician Pavel Váně, the man who's voice we knew so well through *War is an Ox*, had been thrown in jail.

Pavel's first band was the Beatmongers, which he formed in 1963, covering Rolling Stones and Kinks hits. His new band Synkopy 61 had, a couple of weeks earlier, played support for the Beach Boys. Pavel was on his way to the top.

On this fateful night Pavel and František had been in the city centre, along with Radek Rettegy. Together with kids in all the big cities around Czechoslovakia, the three friends were compelled to go to the streets to protest the Russian occupation of their country. Around 3pm as they passed St Thomas' church, they ducked into the shadows from where they gazed on buses and lorries packed with soldiers, members of Public Safety and People's militia heading towards the city centre.

The three friends decided to split, František and Radek jumped on a tram whilst Pavel, who lived very close to St Thomas, waved them farewell and set off walking home.

The very moment the tram carrying František and Radek disappeared, the Public Safety and People's militia, stormed the area, shooting at will. Now, instead of protecting the people and fighting for 'peace in the world', the sites on their weapons were aimed at the sons and daughters of their own neighbours. Miss Danuše Muzikářová and Mr Stanislav Valehrach took their bullets and died on the pavement.

Just yards from his home Pavel was cornered, his long hair pulled back, a gun-butt slammed into his stomach. His explanation that he'd just got off the tram was ignored, as members of the militia accused him of throwing stones at them. His protests fell on deaf ears, and Pavel was taken to the nearby Public Safety station, where he was subjected to a vicious beating which laid him unconscious.

The station started to fill with other shit-scared kids, until they were eventually herded onto transport and taken to the prison in Brno-Bohunice. Disembarking from the bus, the protesters had to negotiate a 300-metre corridor where they ran the gauntlet of baton-wielding policemen.

One boy fainted or was knocked off his feet, falling before Pavel who reached to help him, pulling him and dragging him down the corridor as the batons rained down on him, police screaming for him to move quicker. In this vicious assault, the peace-loving singer suffered three broken ribs and concussion.

Eventually the protesters were divided 30 to a cell, each cell designed to contain just five inmates. The 30 stood side by side with no room to sit or crouch. Wardens brought old army blankets powdered with eye-watering, lice-killing powder, which caused people to cough and vomit over one another. There were no toilet breaks. They literally shit their pants.

The following morning the prisoners were called one at a time for their hearing. Those who had been wounded were checked over formally by the doctor.

When he came to Pavel who was bruised black and blue, the doctor suggested the investigators keep him in custody whilst he got into better shape. This wasn't a kindness. This was their policy not to let the public see how they treated their young people, who were only released once their wounds had healed.

The hearing was a joke, a comedy of errors. The day following the arrests, the prisoners detained in error were released. These included several members of the French national cycling team in Brno for the World Championships. An old lady who had spent the night next to Pavel was allowed to leave, together with the bag of shopping she'd been carrying when she was arrested! But the most ridiculous arrest, which my rock star friend recalled to me later, was the man who had been taken from beneath his car, which he'd been repairing.

We can laugh at these stories today. But there was not the slightest humour in it for the man beneath the car, or the old lady doing her shopping, who had been subjected to a terrifying ordeal.

After a week, the jail's capacity returned to normal, as most of those arrested on 21 August were released. Some 10% remained in jail waiting for their wounds to heal, whilst abiding by strict prison rules, which were given to each of them on a list. Every time an inmate broke a rule, they received several strikes with a baton.

Pavel remained in the same clothes he had been arrested in. He was allowed only one shower per week, on which occasion only women wardens were on duty and took their perverse pleasures in beating the naked traffic, males and females, who passed down the corridor to the shower room.

The men were shaved weekly, on a Wednesday. Pavel took note at which end the barber would begin, knowing that if he started at the far end of the line of cells, his face would be torn to pieces by the blunt razor by the time it reached his chin.

When the famous protest singer had been arrested and had not returned home, his mother started to search for him. She searched alone, because his father had immigrated immediately the Russians had invaded in August 1968.

Some years before the invasion, Pavel's father, already taking English lessons, had fallen in love with a beautiful woman, left his wife and was planning to leave Czechoslovakia once the children had grown up. He hated the communists with a passion, and the Russian invasion was the final straw. The moment they arrived, he was gone.

It was a warm summer's day as people converged around town, the scent of revolution once again filled the air. There had been no radio station or newspaper to herald the gatherings, just the student grapevine, itself a difficult network to establish, because most people went around biting their tongues, smothering their passions, afraid of upsetting a commie or the secret police, who in these days would surely sell their grandmothers for a pat on the back. Yet, as frightened as individuals were that morning, nothing deterred them from gathering, or could dilute their instinct to protest.

Groups gathered downtown where passionate and angry kids raised their voices, yelling anti-Russian slogans, whilst the more brazen individuals made speeches as in Czechoslovakia, the power of the people was about to be tested to the full.

There was never a moment of hesitation on Pavel's part to join his friends and in his search for them, found himself amongst the biggest concentration of protesters in Zelný trh, the vegetable market.

It wasn't long before the Public Safety appeared with their water cannons wielded from atop their armoured vehicles. Protesters began to build barricades constructed from garbage cans and wood from the market stalls, they piled up cobbles and bricks from the street that would soon become their arsenal.

It suddenly became frighteningly obvious to everyone gathered there that the enemy was no longer just the invading Bolsheviks, but that their very own countrymen had turned against their brothers. From behind their flimsy barricades they now faced the Czechoslovak army, including People's Militia and Public Safety who had become aggressive in the extreme, exerting their newfound political power viciously and cruelly as they dispersed the demonstrators.

Pavel became more hostile as he faced the forces who had ended his ability to roam the world as a musician, who had caused his father to flee. The famous protest singer now stood with his friends František and Radek, witnessing his song's lyrics become real, as waves of hatred coursed through his blood.

As the day progressed, instead of bricks and cobbles in their hands, they found themselves hurling Molotov cocktails, hastily created petrol bottles that smashed in flames, in most cases way short of their targets. The air everywhere was charged with adrenaline and testosterone, as the students grew angrier and angrier at what they saw before them. At least the Nazis had done their own dirty work, there was no pitting Czech against Czech in the Second World War, no People's Militia loading their guns and pointing them at their neighbours. What angered everyone was the site of older Czech citizens who had touched freedom and let it go, who should have known better, who were now bent on maiming or killing their own people.

Even in these circumstances Pavel felt great sympathy as he watched a wounded young Czech soldier whisked away in an ambulance. There was a sudden realisation that the kid was not the enemy, but someone conscripted into the army as we all were, a kid who had been following orders and would have been punished severely had he not done so.

The enemy, so far as Pavel and his friends were concerned, were the People's Militia. Those now facing them were drunk with power thanks to their loyalty to the totalitarian regime. Here they were aiming weapons at their fellow citizens, including young men and women who might well have been their next-door neighbours.

František observed certain men taking photographs, the not-so-secret police at work. He turned away quickly from a pointing lens and warned his friends. A week or two later a friend took him to a former store on Jarošova Street where Public Safety had made an exhibition of their pictures, so that it would be possible to identify demonstrators. František studied this vivid evidence and noted with enormous relief that neither he nor Radek nor Pavel featured amongst them. Had this been so, Pavel would have surely disappeared from society.

As it happened, in court, his accusers had no hard evidence against him, and he was finally released from prison, albeit under an annual house arrest order that forbade him to leave his home on the anniversary of the Russian take-over.

Whilst we should have been basking in our freedom with the rest of the world, Czechoslovak problems began when the communists took power after World War II, when they took complete political and economic control in February of 1948.

The Five Year Plan was launched to bring the Czech system and economy in line with the Russian model. When it didn't succeed they simply extended the plan year on year. They were able to do this because they could and because they had to disguise their incompetence.

The ruling party gave the choice jobs to managers who towed the party line, and those with more talent and experience were ousted in favour of the brotherhood. No one could stop them. Such was the communist system, and such was the news reporting in the communist media that we were always reading, about some enterprise beating their targets, some factory performing superhuman output, or some brave communist worker reaching 150% and setting new work records.

Enterprise directors won awards and bonuses based on fulfilment of their five-year plans, and to reach these bonuses they changed deadlines, fudged numbers and altered forecasts to suit the situation. Czechoslovakian industry was structured upon eternal cheating.

The loss of responsibility or any need to answer to anyone by the nation's leading officers saw their moral compass running completely out of control.

Now on 21 August 1969 we faced that same corruption, the same unethical officers seeking to impress their bosses as they rounded up anyone in their path, including innocents mending cars and old ladies shopping. The objective as these forces broke through the flimsy street barriers of Brno, was to make as many arrests as possible, to show their communist bosses just how smart they were in arresting so many demonstrators.

We now had Czechs killing Czechs in order to exceed a target and earn a bonus. Corruption was king, and Pavel Váně looked it straight in the eye for 20 years.

Whilst Pavel remained under lock and key, the black-hearted communist police informed his quite desperate mother that her son had been transported to Slovakia, rather than tell her he was right there in his hometown jail.

Only when it was announced that Pavel would face trial did his mother finally discover his whereabouts. A lawyer friend warned her that her son would probably be sentenced to 3-4 years, a forecast repeated to Pavel by his appointed investigator inside prison.

Under communist rule, the authoritarian enslavement our citizens suffered in this blackest of times in our troubled history, had led to an absolute big brother regime. Czechoslovakia was George Orwell's 1984.

At first hand Pavel experienced the uninvited administrators' cruel methodology of suppressing demonstrations. All around him in jail, Pavel could smell fear. Everyone held there was battered and bruised and afraid of what might come next.

Inside his confines, Pavel couldn't find a solicitor with the balls to help him, whilst on the outside his mother also struggled to find an attorney with the courage to represent him.

In the end, against all odds, not only did Pavel find himself a solicitor, he won his trial and much down to the bravery of his companions on that ill-fated night, František Jemelka and Radek Rettegy, who testified that he was with them, had just seen them off on their tram, and just wanted to go home when the arrest took place.

But this was not the end of his punishment. Even with a clean bill of health from the courts, the authoritarians made his life hell, causing his career as a musician to be seriously hindered.

Every year, as the August anniversary of the Russian invasion approached, Pavel had to keep an appointment with the Public Safety police, to confirm and swear that he would remain under house arrest on that day, and not go outside at all.

They never lightened up, never forgave him, threatening that they'd get all the enemies of socialism sooner or later, and he was on top of their list.

When he was released from prison in late 1969, Pavel continued to study psychology at Brno University, where he faced two types of professors. The new professors who'd arrived on the new totalitarian wind made things as difficult as possible for Pavel. They knew everything about him, the fact that his father had deserted the country, the fact that he wrote songs of rebellion, the fact that he had been in the riots and imprisoned, all made him a target for them to make studies difficult, and life in the University uncomfortable.

On the other hand, the older professors who came from the good old times supported him. But eventually, even though he studied psychology, things wore him down until, one day he just up and left the university to make his living as a musician.

We were bogged down by bureaucracy, every which way we turned. Questionnaires that arrived like clockwork through our letterboxes were commonplace and had to be completed, or you'd get a visit from the department in question.

When Pavel filled in the line 'Father…' he started to put the name of his mother's new husband, which in most cases avoided bringing to their attention that he was the son of an immigrant.

During the 70s he blended into various groups who provided backing for mainstream Czech pop stars. It was only towards the end of the 70s when things had started to relax, that he was once again fronting a rock band. In 1978 with his band Progres 2, he co-wrote the first Czech rock opera, Dialog s vesmírem (A Dialogue with the Universe). Even though this was undoubtedly one of the best endeavours in the history of Czechoslovak rock, the musical took two years to be released as an album and, even then, quite incomplete due to censorship.

Pavel's opera was about an astronaut who takes over a scheduled space flight to find a new planet, where he could establish a much better way of life, because he didn't like the one he'd left behind. It was of course a thinly disguised allegory, a hidden parable based on his father and those who emigrated from our country.

The opera received a 'Best Show' award in one region, whilst in another region it was totally banned. Such was the difference in censorship from one place to another, from one committee to the next. Throughout the 80s, Pavel's reputation as a writer of subversive lyrics that had a bad influence on the youth of the nation, finally led to a total ban. Now he wasn't permitted to perform anywhere. The State Booking Agency closed him down.

It now appeared that he had no way to make a living, but then during this time the greatest totalitarian music paradox happened to him.

A director of one of the Czechoslovak Army Culture unit's turned out to be a massive fan of Pavel's music, and suddenly he was doing performances in far distant army garrisons. The policy to bring culture to the army bases was to stop the young bored conscripts from spending their nights down the bars getting drunk, which is why the Army Cultural Department was introduced. The type of artists they booked fell way below anything that could captivate the young soldiers, simply because the popular and successful artists didn't need this kind of stressful gig. The boys in the army hated the mediocrity of their visiting entertainers and either boycotted their appearances, or fell asleep during their performances.

But they liked Pavel a lot, and suddenly he was back on the road. Not the one he'd dreamed of but – a road.

What was so farcical, was where the kid who had fought the Russians from behind the Brno barricade, was booked to appear. Pavel found himself in Libavá at the back of beyond, where the Russian SS20 missile arsenal was situated, something no one was supposed to know, a top secret!

One day, by mistake, the protest singer drove straight into the heart of the base!

Libavá, was and still is, a big military district, but during the occupation the Czech garrison was small, with the majority of the 2,400 square kilometres occupied by the uninvited Russian forces.

One day travelling there for a gig, after a long car journey, struggling to find helpful signs, Pavel took a wrong turn and headed straight for a Russian soldier guarding the gate.

As Russian was a compulsory language at Czechoslovak schools from the third grade, Pavel had no problems asking a Soviet soldier in his own language. He wound down the window and explained to him that he was going to the Czechoslovak barracks, and asked if he was going in the right direction. The Russian just nodded 'da da charašo' and waved him through. So Pavel thought he was going in the right direction, not realising that the Asiatic soldier probably only knew 'da da charašo' from the Russian language. Pavel continued riding the base that was 40kms long and 60kms wide, when all of a sudden he had Russians all around him.

Then he ran into the tanks on exercise in an area that announced in Russian 'посторонним вход воспрещен', but for Pavel it was too late to respect this sign meant 'No trespassing!' as he was already in the middle and there was no way back.

His car was a bright yellow Dacia, built in Romania under license from Renault. The tanks turned towards him and brought the little yellow vehicle right into their exercise, as Pavel in his four-wheeled canary zigzagged left and right as the tanks used him for target practice.

Czech soldiers witnessed the chase. They watched in horror as the bombs exploded around the little car, shrapnel cracking a passenger window, a wide-eyed pop star driving for his life.

Later when relaxing with some of the soldiers, they told him of their own captain, who a week earlier had taken a short cut to the barracks across the same area on his bicycle.

He had been shot dead.

Having escaped with his life, Pavel found himself playing in garrisons bordering Austria and West Germany, army bases where citizens could never visit unless they were checked, double checked and obtained permission from several people. However, a banned singer, known protest singer who wasn't allowed to play before the public because of his bad influence, visited some of the most secret places in Czechoslovakia!

Now we can laugh about it, but it lasted 20 long frustrating years. When we discovered Elvis and I managed to translate the lyrics to *Jailhouse Rock*, we related well to the benevolent warden who threw a rock 'n' roll party in a county jail, but we related in terms of our countrymen who had been imprisoned in the 50s, not something we, the young, would have to relate to. We thought.

Only when Pavel was imprisoned, was it driven home that one of us had been put in jail, with no evidence that he'd done anything wrong.

We were all in trouble, every kid in Czechoslovakia was done for, and there was no one who could possibly help us.

Pavel remained under the annual house arrest restriction for 12 years until, on his yearly visit to Public Safety, a drunken policeman threatened to gun him down. This didn't go down too well in the station, and this particular event turned out to be his last visit.

The freedom came too late for Pavel. His life had been ruined, his youth stolen. Even though the court had found him not guilty of breaking the law, the police took away his passport. This was the comrades exerting their power over the courts because, of course, they knew better than the courts what was good for the country. Here was the son of an immigrant, which was a big black mark against him, but he also had a girlfriend who had flown our human cage.

A person caught up in the riots whose father and girlfriend had immigrated to who knows where, was a person who would never *ever* be allowed to leave Czechoslovakia.

We were all prisoners, but none more so than Pavel Váně.

The passport was his great career killer. Musicians were amongst the gifted who somehow earned the right to travel to the west. He had friends who went to West Germany to play in the musical Hair, and it was Pavel's dearest dream to play and travel the world with a band.

For 20 years, band after band left him to work abroad. Eventually, when he applied to join a new band or formed a new group, he'd keep quiet about the passport problem, knowing his restrictions would impose themselves on the band's potential to tour abroad.

Nothing changed the inevitable; however, the moment an offer came along to work on foreign shores, he had to hold his hand up and wave them goodbye as they headed for the border with a replacement singer/guitarist.

He changed bands often, living in hope that one day they would return his passport but as time went by, Pavel began to see himself as a second level musician, and when musical problems and disagreements over the music or the lyrics arose he couldn't stand his ground, his confidence was shattered, he became schizophrenic. What good was a musician who couldn't tour?

In 1989 restrictions started to lighten up. With optimism flowing through his veins, he applied to work in Yugoslavia, but a bitter former band member he had fallen out with wrote to the authorities informing them that Pavel Váně was fully intent on immigrating. He received a letter from the Ministry of the Interior, informing him that it was not in the interest of the Czechoslovak Socialist Republic to allow him to travel outside the country.

In November 1989 the Czechoslovakian Velvet Revolution finally freed Pavel, but that could never erase the bitterness he carried through life as a kid who was not allowed to attend his father's funeral. Neither was there compensation for a life ruined, a career dashed.

He's made up for lost opportunities and has gigged all over Europe, even America, where Czech ex patriots have beseeched him to sing his songs in the Czech language, because it reminded them of the fleeting good times they enjoyed in the 60s.

Pavel was undoubtedly one of our great potentials in rock music, but he was cut down like a weed.

Imagine living in a country like that, where foreign forces take over and kill and throw young protesters into prison. A country where your only radio music came from a static-filled radio station in another country. Imagine Bob Dylan being incarcerated in America by the Nazis because they didn't like *The Times they are a Changing*, or John Lennon's talents not being heard because of communist rule in the UK and their objection to his *Revolution*. It might be hard to imagine if you have spent your life in a free world where believing in a God is permitted, even encouraged.

Pavel did make a record, an ep called Barnodaj. The record was successfully smuggled out to Luxembourg where, in 1971, DJ Tony Prince endeared himself to the youth of Czechoslovakia, by playing Pavel's record several times.

In the middle of 1968, for the first time since 1948, the authorities once again allowed the sale of certain western magazines and papers, other than those published by the western communist parties.

You could only buy them in select international hotels and, although the price was rather high because of currency exchange difficulties, I always treated myself whenever I spotted an article concerning music. So when I saw Johnny Cash on the cover of Life, dated 8 December 1969, I not only bought it, I still have it.

Beneath the large picture of Johnny Cash were the words – *'Johnny Cash sings about trains, prison and hard times.'*

Never had a headline so embraced me, a railway shunter, stuck in a communist regime with a friend who had been locked away.

I knew immediately that Johnny Cash was my man, especially when I read in the article his quote that *'Convicts feel that I'm one of their own.'*

Articles like this gave us the hope we so needed.

How things had changed since the double issue of Life Atlantic in December 1968, in which the memorable pictures of an incredible year devoted *nine* pages to 'A setback for peace in the world' depicting the shattering Prague Spring.

There and then, our citizens were all braced against the Russian intrusion but just one year later, our population was split and newborn communist Czechoslovaks didn't hesitate to kill their fellow citizens, using fear as their currency.

By the end of 1969, the distribution of western papers and magazines were stopped for 20 twenty years. Once again, all that remained as our link to the free world was the magic radio, and stations like AFN, BBC, the Voice of the America and my nightly fix, Radio Luxembourg.

Where I had radio 208, I did indeed have hope.

Tony: The King is dead

I was on one of my weeks in the Grand Duchy, and bored crazy staying in a hotel recording next week's shows during the day, and pumping it out live every night.

I stopped for a couple of glasses and a hand of poker with Chuck Klisser, a Dutch bar owner, and left a thousand Belgian francs in the hole.

It was 10.40pm when my heels beat time on the marble tiled corridor. I'd cut it a bit fine, and had to lead by example now I was the boss.

Michel, one of the friendlier engineers, greeted me and I responded in Luxembourgish with one of a half dozen phrases I'd learned,

"Moyen klangen buppet!"

He clattered past me laughing on his way to the outdoor cafes in the Place d'Armes.

It was a beautiful August night.

But not for long.

Unbeknown to me, across the English Channel, newsreader Reginald Bosanquet had opened News at Ten with a hot, breaking story.

At 10.30pm, the newsreader retracted the story, saying that they didn't know if the report could be regarded as accurate.

If it were true, it would be one of the decade's biggest news stories.

Then ITV went off the air with the entire population of Great Britain wanting to know, '*Is Elvis dead or not?*'

Whilst I was climbing the stairs in the Villa Louvigny, the nation was already searching for an alternative news source.

There was only one place to go, their radios.

As I entered the studio, our listening figures were already building to levels that had not been achieved since the 50s pre-television era, when we spent our nights learning about the 'Horace Bachelor Famous Infradraw Method!'

"Take a look at this Tone, you won't like it mate," said Mark Wesley.

In my hand was the 11.00pm news bulletin, now provided hourly via telex from the Daily Mirror newsroom in London.

My mouth dried up, I looked at my colleague who knew of my affinity to Elvis, (I'd helped to arrange a free trip with the fan club for Mark in '74).

"Is this a wind up?" I asked, hoping.

"'Fraid not Tone. I've called the Mirror and they've 100% confirmed it, although ITV have discounted it by all accounts. But it looks like it's true me old mate."

I turned away not wanting him to see my tears, marched out of the studio, ran down to the English office, opened my cupboard and pulled out a stack of Elvis albums.

I was the only DJ who stockpiled Elvis in his cupboard.

I was the only DJ who'd introduced him on stage.

Interviewed him.

Spent a lifetime loving all he stood for.

Now I was a DJ facing an enormous responsibility, the daunting task of ad-libbing a live tribute to Elvis, just minutes after hearing he was dead.

As I walked back into the studio, Mark was reading the news.

And then I started playing Elvis nonstop till 3am, cancelling not only all the play-listed records scheduled for the evening, but every commercial.

I phoned Alan Keen at home and told him what I intended doing.

"I suppose if I ask you not to drop the commercials, you'd drop your job wouldn't you?"

Thank you Alan.

The decision cost the station a lot of money, but we were richer for our principles.

And so a piece of broadcasting history commenced as listeners called in to comment, and fans shared their grief as we came to terms with the horror of that night.

Jimmy Savile stopped his Rolls Royce, and telephoned me from a Yorkshire call box to give his condolences to Elvis' family, friends and the fans. This was pre-mobile phone days, and I'd accepted a collect call as Savile hadn't enough change to call Luxembourg.

I suppose it was the first time people had heard a DJ broadcast with a broken heart. I certainly didn't have the sense of occasion to think to record the show for posterity.

Thankfully however Mike Longley, a DJ in Gloucester, recorded the whole shebang and called me to offer to dub it for any listener who missed the broadcast. All he asked was that they send him four one-hour cassettes and an SAE.

Poor Mike, he was dubbing every night for three years!

An album of the broadcast highlights was later released, and I dedicated my royalties to the Stuart Henry Multiple Sclerosis Appeal. The album has pride of place in my record library, but I still find it difficult to listen to that sad evening.

By the end of the show it was 4am in Europe, and I desperately needed a drink.

Walking down Lonely Street, I stopped in a cafe, where the town's nightclub acts go for their after-work drinks. Tonight the place was empty and the chairs were already stacked on the tables.

I threw myself on a stool at the bar.

"Give me a very large Scotch Pierre."

"Sorry Tony, we closed, me cashing up," he said fingering a wad of Belgian francs.

"Pierre, Elvis Presley died tonight, please give me a fuckin' scotch will you?" He grasped the enormity and moved to the optic without further persuasion.

Three large ones later and I walked an unsteady course the few yards back to my Heartbreak Hotel, where the first thing I did was call Christine in England; it was 5am her time.

That's when the well burst and I started to cry like a baby.

Thirty minutes, virtually none stop.

Christine cradled me to her ear gently consoling me.

Held me in her arms long distance.

A part of *me* had died that night.

B: George Brierley's living room February 1956.

D: Luxembourg Ville, 16 August 1977.

Even after all these years, a dagger still stalks my heart when I think of that lost man dropping to the floor in his Graceland bathroom, all alone without one single strong spirited adviser anywhere fucking near him!

I have my own theory as to why, on that particular night, he sank lower than he'd ever sunk.

It was the day after the anniversary of his mother's death.

Gladys had been his world.

I'll always be sorry that Elvis didn't have one good friend who could have helped him. I guess Priscila tried and failed.

Some folks say, '*It was his own fault*'.

Of course it was.

But how can we possibly know what it's like being trapped on an entire planet?

We were all his jailers.

I mean to say, even the Beatles went gaga when they met Elvis!

When Presley picked up the phone to make an appointment to see the President, the next day he was standing next to Nixon in the White House.

Presidents and Kings were genuine Elvis Presley fans!

The King's death was as big news on earth as man landing on the moon, and whilst the world had become his oyster, he couldn't move outside the shell.

What do you do when you've accomplished everything in life, can grow no bigger because there just is nothing bigger?

How do you handle depression, when you've still got to get up there on stage in Las Vegas and do two shows every night regardless of your condition?

How do you motivate your creative soul when you've been constrained for years in a contractual web of movies you know to be utter rubbish?

How can you respond or react from within that confinement, when your wife leaves you, taking your daughter to join your karate instructor, and you see her love shrivelling in that mad and restricted world into which you brought her?

Of course I'm angry and I'll always be angry with his hangers on, his Memphis 'yes' men, who were there too much for the dollar and too little for the man.

I ask myself also, what of his father Vernon and manager Tom Parker, the King's guardians, who somehow lost their influence and ultimately their control, as Elvis Aaron left his youth behind.

Couldn't they have done better for him?

Am I making excuses for Elvis? Was he too weak a vessel for the tasks he imbibed?

Would anyone have such strength?

Was it as simple as that?

I never forget also that there's a doctor in this woeful tale. A man who I would have happily pushed off the roof of the Las Vegas Hilton, given such a chance.

Doctor George Nichopolous was a pallbearer at Elvis' funeral. In the final seven months of Elvis' life, 'Doctor Nick' had prescribed him 5,684 narcotic and amphetamine pills.

In 1979, Nichopolous was watching a football game in Memphis when someone took a shot at him, narrowly missing their target.

They must have felt like I do.

A few weeks before Elvis died, Todd Slaughter had again been to the USA to present him with yet another handful of awards, which Elvis needed now like a lucky-dip lottery ticket.

It was Monday afternoon and the King was due to arrive on his private plane. Colonel Parker invited Todd to join the welcoming committee at the airport.

The custom-built Convait 880 jet landed and there was an air of expectancy as the 'Lisa Marie' taxied and parked.

You couldn't mistake Elvis' plane, his TCB (Taking Care of Business) emblem, with a lightening bolt struck through it adorned the tail fin, below the American flag.

People began to climb off. Then the stewardess, Carole Boucherre, and the crew led by Captain Elwood David.

The welcoming committee gazed upwards waiting for the King to show. There was no sign of him.

So they all made small talk patiently waiting…and waiting….and waiting. "We hung around for over an hour before he finally appeared at the top of the steps," Todd confided to me.

What he saw totally shocked him. A blowfish version of Elvis, was being helped down the steps by an aid.

"He looked extremely ill," said Todd.

Colonel Parker was pissed off with all the waiting and not a little embarrassed.

As the King touched terra-ferma Colonel gripped Todd's arm and, pointing at the award and then Elvis who was drawing closer, angrily instructed the British Fan Club Secretary to, "Give that to him!"

There was contempt in his voice.

Even in this condition, Elvis remained polite but his smile was glazed, he couldn't respond properly, like a diabetic whose sugar levels were low.

He mumbled monosyllabically, drooling his words as he thanked Todd and the fans.

Then an entourage followed him to the waiting limousines.

On the way back to town, one of Elvis' management team confided to

Todd that he felt Elvis was now in grave danger, and would die if he didn't change his act!

Yes, I'm angry sure enough. Anyway, sorry about all that, just clearing up a few old thoughts. Where was I?

Oh yes...

A number of years later whilst working again with Paul Burnett at Capital Radio in London, he had just returned from doing a memorial broadcast from Graceland for the station.

"I just can't get away from you Princey, do you know that?"

"What you bleating about now?" I asked.

"I walked into Elvis' trophy room in 'Graceland' and whose photo's hanging on the wall? Bloody Royal Ruler that's who!"

I couldn't really believe it, and didn't know what to make of it.

Then, come Christmas, Christine bought me a wonderful book titled Graceland, which contained beautiful coloured plates of each and every room in El's Memphis home.

There, on the wall, amidst all his gold discs, is a solitary colour picture of Todd Slaughter and I, standing right by the side of Elvis Aaron Presley!

Eat your heart out Harry Mills!

One last tale from the longest night in rock 'n' roll.

When I had finished my broadcast that night, as I strolled down the streets of Luxembourg seeking alcoholic oblivion, a like spirit in Holland turned off his radio and walked to his piano.

Eddie Owens, an already famous songwriter in Holland, wrote a song called *I Remember Elvis Presley*, which he released under the name Danny Mirror.

Shortly after release, he asked me if he could use my Radio Luxembourg announcement that '*The King is Dead*,' to which I agreed.

Although Eddie went gold with the single and made a King's ransom, I didn't charge him a penny, nor would I wish to capitalise on Elvis' death.

I was happy just to mark the spot for the King.

In August 2016 I went to Liverpool with the fanclub and met James Burton Elvis' guitarist and Glen D Hardin, his pianist. They remembered me from Vegas, which was cool, but one of the great pieces of previously untold insider-stories I devined from Glen, deserves telling.

Elvis auditioned his musicians himself and wouldn't let Colonel anywhere near them. He actually negotiated their pay too. On stage Elvis never stuck to any running order so the musicians had to be prepared for anything. At the end of any tour Elvis would amble down the plane handing envelopes to his musicians. Inside was a cash bonus amounting to twice what they had earned. In Vegas, after the last show they all gathered in a huge party room on their own floor of the Hilton hotel. Elvis allowed them to bring

whoever they wanted but only showed his face occasionally.
I got the definite impression they really loved Elvis.
And I love them for that.

Jan: The Beatfest

I arranged to meet František once again before returning to my unit in
Olomouc. We needed to translate more English lyrics from my Radio
Luxembourg recordings, and I was eager to hear more about his experiences
at the 1968 Beatfest, held in Prague's cram-packed Lucerna Hall, exactly
four months after the Soviet invasion. At last, the best Czechoslovak
groups had the kind of exposure bands had only dreamed of, including
Brno's own Synkopy 61 and our friend Pavel Váně. Beatfest was in its
second year, another effect of our bid to escape the grip of totalitarianism
under Dubček's leadership.

The real highlights, according to František were the Nice, with the
excellent Keith Emerson on keyboards. This was without doubt the first
UK rock act to perform live in our country, a mind-numbing experience
for the crowd. I had to suppress my envy. Having missed Manfred Mann,
now a second chance to experience a live UK band had passed me by, this
time a classic rock group, whose version of Leonard Bernstein's *America*
I had heard Kid Jensen playing on a new programme they called Jensen's
Incident, the great Luxembourg rock show, which would eventually
become Jensen's Dimensions.

I was sincerely happy for František though, and could rely on him to
recount the experience vividly. He described how Pavel and all the Czech
musicians gathered side of stage to watch in awe as this frenetic rock show
unfolded.

Whilst enjoying their unique music in close up proximity to the band,
as part of their stage show, the Nice started throwing knives into their
Leslie speakers. The Czechoslovak musicians watching were aghast and
this disregard for such wonderful equipment left their hearts bleeding.
Most of them used home made speakers and would sell their mothers for
the speakers now being trashed by the Nice.

I was happy to hear that Synkopy 61 and Pavel Váně won over the
Prague audience with many of the songs František´s had written for them,
especially *Casanova* which was a real success.

One of the concert's real highlights was not expected. Prague's Petr Novák
changed the lyrics of his emotional song *Dirty is the Paradise of the Poor
(Špinavý je chudých ráj)*, into *Dirty is the Paradise of the Reds*, which almost
brought the house down.

Two years later, this roof-lifting performance was remembered by the communist authorities, and Petr Novák was banned from public appearances, and kept under constant surveillance by the Secret Police.

In December 1968, everyone thought that the people of Czechoslovakia would stay united in our fight for freedom but by the time the third Beatfest came around in 1971, the Communist Youth Organisation controlled the festival. They were now working hand in hand with the newly organised Liquidation Squadron, a group of turncoats who pronounced that the Soviet invasion was the best thing that could have happened to Czechoslovakia. Once again the reptiles in our society came to the surface to claim their status in our grey world.

Our national pop music success beyond our borders was as restricted as our freedom. What chance did anyone have?

Zdenka Lorencová had been in Paris studying at the Sorbonne University when the Soviet troops arrived in her homeland. Signed to the Vogue label she had a modicum of success in France. Our middle-of-the-road tenor Karel Gott was loved by the older commies and popular in West Germany, but we desperately wanted someone from our country to break in the UK.

That might have happened for Bratislava's Beatmen, had they not encountered unknown forces against them. Their invitation from Manfred Mann to tour Great Britain in 1965, came in a day and age when such permission was ordained by our rigid communist bosses who, for reasons only known to them, would not allow the Beatmen to go to England.

Our biggest star, Karel Gott's break for the west came in a much more relaxed time. In 1966, he won the main prize at *Lyra*, Bratislava's pop festival when it was staged for the very first time. Although the Beatmen were sons of Bratislava, they were deemed unsuitable for this festival, which targeted easy listening musicians.

Having won at the festival, Karel Gott basked in a lot of attention, then in 1967 Supraphon took him as their prime showcase to MIDEM, the world's number one market place for buying and selling music, staged annually in Cannes.

Gott's tenor voice caused quite a sensation. In an unusual method of measuring popularity, the level of audience applause for Tom Jones registered 58 decibels, whilst Gott reached slightly less than the Welsh superstar with 54.

The German A&R managers, who already knew the singer from their visit to Bratislava, signed him to Deutsche Grammophon. The deal was signed in Cannes, and in a matter of weeks they had recorded his first album Die Goldene Stimme aus Prag, (The Golden Voice from Prague) which went on to sell 450,000 copies in German-speaking nations.

The Gott saga doesn't end in Germany. The success of his MIDEM appearance brought him an invitation to perform two shows daily for six months at the Las Vegas Frontier Hotel.

Gott's American manager boasted on billboards that he succeeded in bringing Karel Gott across the Iron Curtain, directly out of the evil Soviet Empire.

Karel Gott learned an important lesson about appearing in the Nevada dessert when, complaining about his sore throat caused by the air conditioning and his punishing two shows a night, seven days a week, the doctor said, if he wanted to go on singing, his vocal chords needed three days of complete rest. Mr Lee, the manager of the Frontier, read the medical report attentively whilst smoking a big cigar and said finally, "Which date do you want me to book your plane ticket back to Prague?" The lesson Karl took from this was that, in Las Vegas, only the death certificate gets you a night off!

Eventually Karel Gott returned to Czechoslovakia. He could have settled in America if he had agreed to stay there permanently, but told friends that emigration to the USA was the last thing he would want to do.

Much of my time that night with František was spent discussing this small clutch of successful Czechoslovak artists. We were sorry for the Beatmen who had no breaks at all abroad, and we were concerned for Zdenka Lorencová and, seeing the red grip tightening in our land, felt she might do well to remain in France.

František and I tried to forecast our future, it looked bleak, it made us mad, and so, in the end, we turned on Radio Luxembourg the only constant value in our crazy, unfair world.

We both felt that, even if the Russians remained, things could not return to square one where we had been before Dubček's influence was felt, but who could say?

Tony Prince was on the air, and we listened and chatted between his introductions, turning the volume up when a track drew our attention.

We had spent so much time with this particular DJ, his warm style and manner of speaking, suggested we had a friend.

And a friend in the west, was value indeed.

Tony: BA your DJ

Now I was guvnor of the world's greatest ever radio station.

I knew what made good pop radio and set about fighting off the enormous competition setting itself up down the FM band.

Barry Alldis was a delightful old-school Luxembourg DJ, who'd returned to the airwaves and residency in the Grand Duchy just prior to me becoming

Programme Director.

In his first term at 208 in the 50s, he'd married Fern, an elegant Luxembourg damen and was now at the twilight of an excellent career from 208 to the Beeb and back. A trick never before done, and never thereafter repeated.

For some reason, age of course, he was making too many gaffs on air. I recorded him one night and flew out to Luxembourg to chat with him, and I played him 60 errors of speech or detail in a two-hour show.

I'm sure the pressure I put poor Barry under didn't contribute much to an improvement.

And yet his research figures were constantly telling me I was wrong.

"Barry's got to go, we're a young station for God's sake," I said to Alan Keen. "If people are listening to him, they're listening to hear how many times he'll fuck up!"

Alan sympathised he knew I was right, but both of us went back to the halcyon days of 208 when Barry was a part of our nightlife, long before either of us envisioned we would one day run the station. To even think of sacking the legendary Barry Alldis was sacrilege, and we both felt uncomfortable in so much as discussing the possibility.

We thought we might start to make enquiries in the Grand Duchy about retiring Barry early on a company pension, and I returned to my office believing Alan would institute such enquiries the next time we were in the Grand Duchy for a board meeting.

One hour later Alan called me.

"Barry just fucked up for the last time Tony," he announced down the phone.

"He just dropped dead in a car showroom!"

Poor old Barry was buying a new car with Fern when his stomach ulcers perforated. According to the autopsy, the wall of his stomach looked like a sieve.

I was mortified that maybe I had contributed?

But what do you do?

The man I had admired as a young under-the-pillow listener, tuning in religiously to his Top 20 every Sunday night, had run out of programme time.

I remain deeply sorry that I may have advanced his condition but none of us, not even his family, realised he was in such need of attention.

Had we only.

Jan: The Prisoner

On this night the hypocrisy of Red Law's editors was the talk of families and friends in bars and cafés across the length and breadth of Czechoslovakia. It had been so obvious that, whilst they could not hide the tragic news under the carpet, their report was derisory and reported in the most shameful way.

Jan Palach was buried on 25 January in a famous cemetery in Prague Olšany. In 1973 his body was cremated, without informing his mother and brother, and his ashes were put into a grave in the small town of Všetaty, where Jan Palach once lived.

The totalitarian regime did not like the fact that people constantly visited his grave, which had become a shrine and a tourist attraction in Prague, and so they simply removed their discomfort to a place well away from the capital.

Even in Všetaty Public Safety prevented people from visiting Jan Palach´s grave during the anniversary of his death, at a time when people wanted to show their respects and pay homage to his bravery. Many musicians dedicated songs to the memory of Jan Palach, and among the best were two songs by Dežo Ursíny from the Beatmen. One was called *When if Not Now?* with great music by Dežo and excellent lyrics by Ivan Štrpka. Dežo Ursíny also recorded a touching Slovak version of Lennon's *Imagine*, where he paid tribute to both heroes John Lennon and Jan Palach. Of course this could never become a record. It was something he would sing live, and only then when he was secure knowing the secret police were not in his audience, for they often came snooping around concerts looking for evidence that would allow them to ban singers who did not sing according to the communist party baton. Dežo had already been harmed by the commies when the Beatmen were refused permission to join Manfred Mann on his British tour. All music lovers knew on which side of the red line Dežo stood, and we all cherished the rare opportunities when we could hear him sing proudly of Jan Palach.

In the short term, Jan's death and his greatest of sacrifices did not change much in Czechoslovakia, except perhaps he made all the honest people in our country even sadder. My own escape was my music, my transistor radio and cassette tapes. When the ABBA boys wrote *Thank you for the Music*, they wrote it for me.

One Sunday in March, when the weather became pleasant again and the sun's rays warmed our faces, the enchantment of spring called to me to visit the hospital where Alena worked. I didn't know if she still worked at the hospital, nor which shift she would be on, so I posted myself on guard at key times. Perhaps I would be luckier than the previous time, when she left the hospital with a man who had his arms around her. I was no longer concerned about the man, after several months, if they had a relationship, it could well be over by now.

As there was sufficient time before the end of the 6pm shift, I decided to take a walk downtown to look around, browse the shop windows and check if any good movies were showing.

I was lost in thoughts of re-establishing myself with Alena into a cinema maybe that very evening, thinking how much I wanted to hold hands with her again and talk as we did a year ago.

At this moment, lost in thought and studying a cinema programme poster, suddenly I froze as a voice challenged me from behind.

"Comrade soldier, let's be seeing your documents, including the soldier permit book so we can check whether you are allowed to leave the garrisons."

I turned to face an officer and two soldiers, a military control unit using that bloody condescending communist phrase 'comrade soldier'. I was nobody's fucking comrade and hated it whenever some official addressed me this way. But I stayed calm and explained to them that I had a soldier permit book with me, but no permission to leave my garrison in it, as I was staying outside the barracks for the time being as a member of a remote army railway unit. This by now was almost scripted, as I had explained to such military controls many times before, without problems.

For some reason, this time it didn't work. They informed me that I should be aware that according to military regulations, I was not allowed to leave the barracks without the written permission, duly signed by my Začátek formuláře commanding officer or sergeant. I stood before them calmly explaining how we were a special unit who went out to eat at least once a day, and to the pub on Saturday and Sunday, and so had general permission as no commander was stationed in our railway station billet. I mentioned that we had this when we first moved here months ago, and had not bothered to seek a new signature, as everything seemed satisfactory after previous military questioning.

Pointing out that the general permission should be signed each week to allow this freedom of movement now, due to disorderly drunken soldiers attacking Soviet soldiers, more severe military check-ups were in place.

I became a victim of their more officious procedures, and taken to their garrison where the officer in charge told me that I was under arrest, and would be kept in prison until Monday when soldiers from my garrison would arrive to pick me up. Then he asked me to empty my pockets and place my belongings on the table. I took my wallet from my back pocket, and then from the inner breast pocket of my heavy green army coat out came my Hitachi radio. From the side pocket of my coat, I pulled out my Concise English Grammar book of a size that fitted there snugly.

Next I had to show him what I had in my wallet, so out came my wad of 800 crowns, which really shocked him. His eyes revealed his next question, "How come you're carrying so much money around?" The military patrol boys who'd brought me in also stared at the money in amazement, which pleased me no end. Suddenly I was king. The two officers standing there probably got 50 crowns pocket money after handing over their wages to their wives. The soldiers received 75 crowns a month pocket money from the army. They'd obviously never seen 800 crowns fall out of one man's wallet before, and now they could see that the soldier they had arrested was rich compared to them.

I really enjoyed the moment and replied that it was not *that* much money for me, as I was not paid yet for my work for Olomouc Ironworks.

"This," I explained, "was just my meal allowance, as we were not accommodated in barracks like other soldiers."

Then the officer discovered a great thing with his pea brain and asked me what kind of book it was, noting that it was not Czech. I couldn't have felt better at this moment and quickly paid him a compliment, "You're quite right, this is not a Czech book, it is an English book."

I could see in his eyes an eager look. At this moment he probably thought he'd landed an American spy! He then started to browse the pages of my grammar book, something I carried with me to pass the time rather than do nothing whilst waiting for a bus, or Alena! By now the officer could see himself promoted to a higher rank for discovering a dangerous spy dealing in espionage for imperialistic powers.

He asked whether I spoke English.

"Of course I do," I replied. "After studying English for three years at high school, it would be a shame if I didn't."

My answer seemed a bit much for this officer, who I imagine was probably facing someone who spoke English for the first time in his life. I would have bet all my money there and then that he was sure I was not an ordinary soldier in the socialist Czechoslovak army, but a traitor working for some foreign enemy power.

His interrogation continued. He wanted to know what kind of book it was. I explained to him that it was a book of English grammar, which was a difficult concept to describe, because I had no doubt the poor officer, didn't even understand what Czech grammar might be.

I was explaining that the book contained such treasure as a complete list of English irregular verbs, when he threw his hands in the air and barked, "Enough!" I had, by then, plainly exceeded his pea brain's capacity.

He hadn't finished with me yet however. He wanted to know why I carried a transistor radio with me. Of course I wouldn't benefit anything in telling him the truth, that it was a one kilometre walk from the bus stop to our railway station in Řepčín, and how I loved listening to Radio Luxembourg when I walked home in the evenings. Instead I told him that I was very interested in listening to the news because I cared for the destiny of our country. Had I been honest and told him I liked listening to Radio Free Europe, the BBC and Voice of America, he would probably have executed me himself right there on the spot!

Once the questioning stopped he commanded the soldiers to take me to the prison cell. I asked him if I could take my things with me, which was when I knew I'd stepped over the line as he lost his rag altogether. He then started ranting at the top of his voice that a prisoner could have nothing at all in the cell.

How naive of me, I thought it would be fine to wile away the hours in prison listening to some great western pop music.

Survival proved difficult without the little Hitachi and the soothing music it would provide my battered spirits. Apart from the iron bars before me and three blank walls that enveloped me, all the cell offered for my night's accommodation was a chair and a metal bed with a filthy green quilt.

Left forlornly alone, I stared at the wall with nothing to do but think.

Jan Palach came to mind.

It cost him his life trying to wake up the people of Czechoslovakia but how, I wondered, could anyone like this stupid officer ever be woken from such deep slumber? Sparked into thought, I started to realise that after 1948, the communists had succeeded in brainwashing our army once they had jettisoned all the brave soldiers who could speak for themselves, who had opinions that opposed them. They rid themselves of those who had fought against the Nazis with the Allies, and were then prepared to fight on for our democracy.

Once again my parents suffering, and my dear uncle's bravery invaded my thoughts.

The last thing Moscow and its Prague puppets wanted were smart, experienced officers, preferring human fodder, stupid creatures like this officer who put me in a cell, blindly obeying their commands.

Suddenly I thought of Elvis Presley, and the soundtrack *Jailhouse Rock* played in my mind as I sat there in my own prison cell. How I would have loved to jump on a table in front of my warder, point at the officer and sing *'If you're looking for trouble - (da da da da da) - you came to the right place!'*

I fell into a deep depression and needed a distraction from my thoughts. Suddenly I made a big discovery, realising I had some half crown coins to use in the telephone booth in a little pocket down the side of my trousers. That's how stupid this officer was, he couldn't even conduct a thorough search. These coins could quite easily have been a knife!

With ten coins at my disposal, I launched into a self-made game of flipping coins in a heads or tails version of patience. The more times I got it right, the more coins I could lay down until, with an enormous run of luck, I would lay down the target I'd set of all ten coins.

By the time I was bored by this new game, I had attained six in a row.

Then my thoughts stretched to Alena and how I had probably missed her because of this situation so that, once again, the authorities had ruined my love life.

I didn't know what time it was when I rang the bell to summons the guard to tell him I needed a pee. I didn't need a pee, but I was stifled in the cell and wanted a change of scenery. The soldier said he had to ask his officer first and left to do so. Another stupid army rule, a prisoner wanted to go to the toilet, but never before an officer had given his approval.

This was the first time in my life that I had to pee under the scrutiny of a soldier with a machine gun.

When the soldier told me what time it was I was flabbergasted. I thought I'd been there four or five hours but it was actually just over an hour!

Back, locked inside the cell, I knew I had to do something or go crazy. Now I understood the effect of solitary confinement and how important friends must have been to my parents enduring such punishment in Nazi concentration camps. I could see now how any nation could breed Nazi mentality, I only had to think about the officer and his intransigent attitude towards the rules, and how he deemed to translate them, when he could plainly see that I was an innocent.

I sat there like Rodin's The Thinker trying to come up with an escape plan. I had to get out of here. But how? What should I do? Then it came to me – *money*, something they all responded to, would be my devise.

I rang the bell yet again and an irritable soldier came to inform me the officer was pissed off, but I'd anticipated this and told him be sure to explain to the officer if I didn't get back to the railway cargo depot, all hell would be let loose.

Escorted to the officer, I made my pitch.

I started to talk quickly in an agitated, worried man's voice explaining how important and necessary it was for me to be released, because there was only one engineer at the railway station, and he was incapable of moving the wagons out of the ironworks alone, as this would break all railway safety regulations. Then I played my banker, informing the officer that the average penalty for delaying one wagon a day was around 200 crowns, which could become 2,000 if there were 10 wagons, which was what I anticipated tonight. These fines were imposed on the army in a deal with the ironworks, and as I would not be there tonight, I wondered who would pay this fine when it was not our platoon's fault that I had found myself in prison after going out to eat.

I was pleased with my performance as I was returned to my cell whilst he phoned my army unit, something I had considered when concocting the plan of escape. Knowing we had no phone at our railway station in Řepčín, meant that the officer in charge of my army unit would be unable to ask somebody there if it was true that I had to be there. I then sat back, held my breath and hoped I would soon be free.

Eventually an officer from my unit arrived, and I was invited into the office to explain the day's incidents and my fictional dilemma. Turning to face the officer who had imprisoned me, he confirmed that I genuinely worked in a detached unit at the railway station and that we worked with the ironworks.

I collected my belongings, my watch, Hitachi, English grammar book and my wallet with 800 crowns. Once outside my officer offered to take me to the railway station in his jeep, but I declined, in case someone would disclose to him that there were no such things as time delay fines and that we never, ever moved wagons on Sundays!

After this very unpleasant prison experience, that night I enjoyed more than ever switching on my transistor and hearing those beautiful words, 'This is your Station of the Stars Radio Luxembourg on 208 metres medium wave.'

I suppose in my insecure world, 208 was my comfort blanket, a place to go where no one could reach me other than the friendly DJs. Tony Prince was on the air on the evening of my great escape, and my spirits lifted as each track he played took away the memory of the day gone by.

Immediately after playing Elvis' *If I can Dream* like so many times before, Tony announced details of the Elvis Presley Fan Club of Great Britain. "If you are an Elvis fan, just drop Todd Slaughter a line," he said. I knew the address by heart, as it was not that difficult to remember: PO Box 4, Leicester, England. I had often thought of writing, but I resisted as I had no means of paying membership fees with Czechoslovak currency restrictions.

The only chance you had of getting currency exchanged was to ask the bank in advance of foreign travel, which had to be approved of course. It had been much easier in 1968 when František travelled to West Berlin for four days, but now, a year later, I doubted it would be possible.

But on this occasion I had an idea. If I was sending my Japanese penfriend Mayumi Kizara gifts such as dolls in native costumes, or our latest postage stamps for which she would reciprocate with various Japanese items, why shouldn't I ask Todd Slaughter if he would barter fan club membership for stamps or dolls?

As I turned my radio off on this rather long day, I started to compose my begging letter, in which I would explain to Todd how difficult it was getting any information on Elvis, who I had admired from the first time I heard him sing so many years ago.

I went to sleep with a smile on my face, my last thought recalling how two officers today thought of me as an American spy, so why should I not now become a member of a fanclub of an American singer? That would give the pea-brains something to think about!

The next day I placed my letter in the post box inside Olomouc main post office, and left all thoughts on the matter to fate.

In May we left again to Bohemia to repair the second rail on the track from Prague to Pilsen, as we had a year ago in Hořovice, being accommodated this time without any problems beneath the station's huge water tank.

I was happy and looking forward to visiting my good friend, Michal Bukovič, in Černošice once again. But Prague Spring had moved into autumn, and the freedom we had enjoyed was fading like autumn leaves as the winds of Bolshevik change swept across the land.

The assaults and confrontations between our soldiers and the Russians led to much tighter military control, and before too long it was decided that our soldiers should not leave their barracks at all. Almost every other day our officers came to our temporary housing to make sure we were all present and correct. I decided against taking a short leave to visit Michal as I had last year. With only four months to go before I was free from the army, I couldn't risk ending up in jail again.

I had a legal two-day pass plus two days to make the journey, so with ninety days remaining before I became a civilian again, I went home to Brno.

As usual the first thing I did was to telephone František to congratulate him on the huge success of *War is a Fool*, which had become a huge national hit and was often heard on the radio. František thanked me and then asked whether I went to Prague to see the Beach Boys concert there.

I was convinced he was joking, but then I realised he wouldn't play such a cruel trick on me. He was surprised that not only had I not seen their concert, I had been completely oblivious to their visit.

First they had played in the Bratislava LYRA song contest, followed by a Prague concert and finally, just two weeks ago, here in Brno itself! I was left quite speechless. How news of such an incredible event had escaped me was all due to the incarceration of our unit and the increased barrack-pass restrictions.

I almost cried with the frustration. I had now missed Manfred Mann, the Nice, and now one of the world's truly great American bands.

Tony: The funeral

Then there was my problem with Stuart.

After having it confirmed that he had the mother of debilitating diseases, DJ Stuart Henry awaited his death for 16 years.

He wasn't the only one to suffer from his Multiple Sclerosis.

Ollie, a beautiful, tall, refined former model who had married Stu in the heady 60s, became his metabolism.

The top Scottish broadcaster would have approved of his funeral.

On a cold December day in 1995, I retraced my flight path to Luxembourg. The head steward opened a discussion with me, I was one of a handful travelling Club Class, and once he'd ascertained that I was the Royal Ruler, he became my friend.

I arrived at Ollie Henry's home with two duty free bags full of British Airway's miniature bottles of champagne, the payola given to me by the steward.

"These might come in handy next week when you have the Memorial Service," I offered.

Ollie was taught-faced. Stuart had passed away three days earlier, and she missed his ordering her about and his partnering in decision-making in all she did.

"I keep turning round to ask him what I should do," she sobbed.

As immobile and incapable of doing even the slightest thing for himself, Stuart remained the strong Scottish husband right to the end.

Fifteen years after having MS diagnosed, 14 years after the BBC recorded a memorial show in preparation of his death, 10 years after he starred on This Is Your Life and 8 years after the News of the World ran the headline '*DJ AWAITS DEATH*', the waiting was over.

Ollie and Stuart dozed off in front of the TV. Ollie awoke, glanced at Stuart who was still sleeping soundly in his wheel chair, and went to make them both a nightcap, and when she returned he was gone forever.

All her years of imagining that moment had not prepared her. Alone in their rural Luxembourg home which had been converted to accept Stuart-on-wheels, her tears flowed as she cradled him in her arms holding her final conversation with him late into the night.

I hadn't wanted to go with the cavalcade of friends and colleagues a week later when Ollie had programmed a memorial service in Luxembourg, preferring to be at the funeral.

Consequently, I was the only former colleague who'd flown out from the UK apart from Tiger, Stuart's faithful old road manager from his Radio 1 days, (who by this time roadied for the legendary Geno Washington & the Ram Jam Band).

The rest of the funeral cortege were a handful of immediate Luxembourg friends, and Ollie's sister Pam, who'd travelled from Memphis.

The one person who I expected to see there was Bunny Lewis our former agent. Sadly however, the man who became something of a father figure for Stuart was himself fighting cancer in hospital, and the news of Stuart's death was not yet given to him, for fear of causing him too much trauma.

It had been my job to sit with Stuart, beseeching him to take reign of his pride and come out of the MS closet.

By this time the disease had travelled to his larynx so that, occasionally, when fatigued, his words on-air would come out slurred.

There was only so much that the static on 208 could disguise, and I had started receiving complaints from listeners.

"Get that lush off the air!" they'd say.

"How dare you allow a drunk on Radio Luxembourg?"

I knew of course, (because Radio Luxembourg had funded his exploratory trips to German specialists who eventually diagnosed Multiple Sclerosis), that here was a super star DJ whose star was finally earth bound.

The really difficult thing was trying to tell someone who complained, that he wasn't actually drunk, but had an illness. It made them feel very small. In a media designed to bring happiness, you shouldn't be doing that to your listeners.

"Let us announce your MS to the world Stuart," I implored, "and I guarantee we will turn the complaints into compliments."

Shortly after this meeting Stuart started working with the MS Society, raising thousands of pounds for research.

They were grateful to have a well-known sufferer prepared to let his fame benefit their campaigning, and the Stuart Henry Multiple Sclerosis Appeal was born.

Later still, as the messages from his brain failed to transmit down his eroding spinal cord to his muscles and body parts, Ollie began to take on an even greater role in their partnership.

Stuart's 208 show became known as the Stu & Ollie Show.

At first she took over reading his news bulletins as lengthy speech became more difficult. Then, as banter in the studio led to Ollie chipping in more and more during the broadcast, they became a real double act.

On her own, Ollie would not have made a Radio Luxembourg *Luxembourg* disc jockey. Her accent was too plum, her demeanour too sophisticated for rock 'n' roll radio. But with her comments and her style steered by Stuart, Ollie somehow worked out quite well on what we once called, The Station of the Stars.

It was Monday morning when we gathered at Ollie and Stuart's home for the last farewell to our beloved broadcasting pal.

We were a dozen mourners.

I looked outside as someone said the hearse had arrived. All I could see was a young guy who looked like a building worker climbing from a hatch back Ford.

He had on a baseball cap, brightly coloured shirt, jeans and sneakers. A flower delivery man perhaps? A hip-hop neighbour who had parked unknowingly?

"He's the funeral director's son," Ollie explained.

"But where's the hearse?" asked a friend.

"That's it," said Ollie watching the back door of the vehicle yawn open.

"They refused to let me have the Mercedes for such a long journey!"

I looked at my grieving friend with great curiosity.

Did she think the vehicle would transport Stu all the way to heaven?

What could she have meant by 'long journey?'

Then she delivered the bad news!

"The Luxembourg Crematorium has burned down!"

There are times within great solemnity when laughter is permitted, and this was one.

Stuart would have loved all this. He was, anyway, an atheist with great Karma.

He would also have loved the rest of his last day with us...

We climbed into three vehicles, a jeep, a saloon and a sports car, and we now understood it would be a long day, for the nearest crematorium was in Liege, Belgium some 100 miles across the Ardennes.

We set off, late for Stuart's final time-slot. To make up time our cavalcade, lead by the Taunus-driven hip hop funeral director, exceeded the speed limit by some 40kms per hour. At 160kph, I turned to the English vicar who had joined us to conduct the service, and asked if he had had a quiet word with his boss before the journey?

We felt, even in a rogue convoy, safe in HIS hands.

The idea of Stuart getting a speeding ticket was beyond imagination!

We arrived at Liege Crematorium 15 minutes late. The vicar was asked to rush things as two other 'customers' were now waiting. Ollie placed two blow-up photographs next to the coffin. They were of a young pre-MS Stuart Henry taken at the height of his BBC Radio 1 popularity.

Luxembourg had inherited Stuart's talents, because the BBC defaulted in analysing what some considered a drug-enhanced stagger, as the DJ walked across Broadcasting House to and from his popular shows.

This 'sailor's gait', as Stuart himself described it, was the very earliest by-product of Multiple Sclerosis.

It got him the sack.

Stu loved a joint.

He never hid that socially and all his colleagues and producers understood this, indeed many of his BBC producers enjoyed marijuana also. Sadly however, this knowledge led the Radio 1 controllers to conclude that Stu was doing too much and needed to Beeb-gone, before he brought the Corporation's image into disrepute.

They weren't to know that their token Scot was ill.

Whilst there were many others using drugs at the BBC, so long as they kept it private and didn't reveal their leanings with a sailor's gait, they were safe.

The service came to an end.

The vicar was breathless having compressed a 20-minute speech into eight. Just when we thought we could now go back to Stu and Ollie's for a drink and a chat, another piece of bad news, Stu's ashes wouldn't be ready for another two hours!

Stuart Henry, as he was on-air for many years, was a hot property.

We sat in a café drinking thick Belgian coffee and distasteful, warm, white wine. Ollie leant over to me confidentially.

"I have to tell someone," she told me. "When I said my final farewell to Stuart back in Luxembourg I put a joint in the coffin, I know he would have appreciated it!"

It was another wonderful light relief moment in this day of grief.

"Maybe he WILL be appreciating it right now," I consoled.

Two hours later, this was confirmed as we made our way back to Luxembourg.

A stunning dusk revealed itself.

The sun, a ball of red fire was swathed in Ardennes mist before us.

The fog clung to the hollows of the valleys like lakes of grey soup.

The colours were unbelievable. It was Stu doing the light show, I had no doubt.

"Look Ollie," I whispered, pointing to the swirling masses of mist, dramatically captured by the red sun.

"I bet Stuart just gave God a toke!"

We laughed with a laughter cradled in our reverence for our long-suffering friend.

Laughter we knew Stuart would have called for...

I could hear him...

"Laugh m'friends and be joyful... for throughout my life I only ever wanted people to be happy!"

Stuart Henry did indeed make many people happy, from Radio Scotland as a young pirate DJ to BBC Radio 1 and Radio Luxembourg. And who will ever forget the Beatles singing *She's Leaving Home*, when Stuart helped to put so many runaway kids back with their families after his on-air appeals?

Farewell M'friend!

Whilst I worried my heart out for Ollie, left alone in a strange Dukedom in the centre of Europe, as I write I hear the glorious news that Ollie is happily living in the Lake District with a new partner. His name is Tom, the very professor who taught Stuart, on behalf of the Multiple Sclerosis

Society, how to use a computer.

No one deserves happiness more than this lady after her years of dedication and sacrifice for her husband.

And when we last met for a reunion in the Grand Duchy in 2015, I saw a happy Ollie and hope now that the bird of paradise flies up her nose to ensure she once again smells the roses.

Jan: The Beach Boys

Cursing my bad luck, I went to meet František to enjoy his tale telling, and his back-stage experiences at the Beach Boys concert. Synkopy 61 were one of the support bands on the tour, the other was Pavel Váně´s new band, Progres Organization. The MC introducing the Beach Boys during their Czechoslovak mini tour was František´s good friend from Prague, Petr Sís.

   Petr had the inside story, the truth behind the miracle of how the Beach Boys came to tour Czechoslovakia. He had learned that in 1969, the popularity of the Beach Boys in the United States was declining, and as they had strong relations within the American establishment, someone from the American Information Service in Washington came up with the idea that they could go to Czechoslovakia to promote American music. It was also mooted that this would get up the invading Soviet noses.

The American agency reputedly contributed to the travel expenses, as it was recognised that ticket sales alone would not be sufficient, as the purchasing power of Czechoslovak kids was very low compared to their Western European counterparts.

   I liked the story Petr described to František about the Beach Boys' Mike Love during the Prague concert. Mike Love had one of the first Moog synthesisers, from which every now and then he emitted a sound effect whilst screaming, '*To hell with Russians!*' shaping his hand in a grasp afeigning to wring someone's neck. In June 1969, you could still get away with something like that and the crowd loved it.

   The whole Beach Boys visit happened purely because the communists were too busy infighting for power to give any thought to music.

On a darker note, Petr revealed how, at the very end of their tour, he became the target for the group's wrath. The Czechoslovak State Music Agency, Pragokoncert, paid them one half in dollars, the other half in Czechoslovak crowns. They understood they had to spend this cash before leaving or it would become as valueless as Monopoly money.

The Beach Boys had heard about the high quality Czech hand-cut glass, so they asked Petr to arrange for them to purchase as much as their money would buy. Petr Sís, whilst wishing to keep the band happy, was an artistic soul with no monkey-business connections to people who could procure such a large amount of cut glass. Eventually though, through asking around, he found a man in Prague who said he could get it for them. He explained that it was not available in shops as virtually all production was exported to the west.

Petr arranged with the man to bring the cut glass to Prague airport after they returned from the LYRA Festival in Bratislava. Unfortunately a series of events took place, which could now, in hindsight, be looked on as hilarious.

Firstly the agency made a last minute booking for the band to play Brno. When they arrived at the tiny airport, Petr noticed two customs officers, which was unusual in that Brno was a domestic airport intended for inland flights only.

Although the band thought they would still be returing to Prague where they expected to hand their money over for the contraband cut glass and then go through customs, the following morning they learned of catastrophic changes to their travel plans.

Someone in authority had wanted to do the Beach Boys a favour by arranging customs officers to come to Brno airport to save them flying on their private jet to Prague, making it possible for them to leave Czechoslovakia directly from Brno.

It wasn't until they all arrived at Brno airport that all was revealed and when the Beach Boys got wind of this they rounded on Petr, angrily demanding their cut glass.

Knowing they were about to leave Czechoslovakia with a pile of money burning no hole whatsoever in their trousers, they moved into action. Petr hid in the toilets and then watched proceedings from a distance as the members of the group tried to spend their money in the tiny domestic airport lounge.

A typewriter and a gun produced in Brno's Zbrojovka factory, sat exhibited in a display showing off Czech craftsmanship. With nothing else to buy, the band insisted they buy them, but the nervous salesgirl explained it was just an exhibition and not for sale. They persisted, a senior manager was found and eventually the items were for 10,000 crowns each.

With nothing else to buy of any value, they now headed towards the bar and turned on the waitress demanding to know how much vodka she might have? The girl misunderstood what they wanted and poured them a snorter each, which made them madder.

"We need crates with full bottles of vodka, how many crates do you have?" yelled Al Jardine. She had four cardboard boxes with 6 bottles of vodka in each, and again the band unloaded 10,000 crowns for each box, twice as much as it was worth.

The Beach Boys, with money to burn, bought everything the bar had to sell. It was estimated that each girl working in the Brno airport departure lounge that morning took between twenty to thirty thousand crowns from the band, representing *two* entire years' pay per girl. Brno airport had never had it so good!

But the story wasn't over yet!

From Brno, the Beach Boys flew directly to Finland where a severe alcohol prohibition was in effect, and customs officers confiscated every bottle they had purchased for a king's ransom at Brno airport.

And this explains why, Czechoslovakia was never again to feature in a Beach Boys European tour itinerary.

When August came there were just 60 more days that were remaining until our release. During a phone call home to discuss this happy news with my folks, my mother informed me that I had received a large letter from abroad. She read me the sender's address, *'PO Box No. 4,'* and at this moment, I knew that it was from the Elvis Fan Club, and asked my mother to forward it to me as soon as she could.

After a few days, the big envelope arrived, and inside it was another envelope from THE OFFICIAL ELVIS PRESLEY FAN CLUB OF GREAT BRITAIN & THE COMMONWEALTH.

I opened it carefully to find a club newsletter dated August/September 1969 and printed and published in the UK. There was also a personal letter to me from Todd Slaughter, in which he informed me that he fully understood my situation, and that it would be OK if I sent him some nice Czechoslovak stamps, instead of the usual membership fee.

I was beside myself with joy as I browsed through my very first magazine about the King; in fact I was holding the very first printed item I had ever seen dedicated to just one singer. Until this moment, I had only ever read a little about Elvis in two sample copies of the New Musical Express. Now I had 12 pages exclusively about Elvis, with a great variety of pictures inside. It immediately became my most cherished magazine, and one I would receive every month. On the second page was news concerning an Elvis convention being held in Leicester, England on 21 September. It seemed just great to me that fans and supporters of Elvis could meet in this way, and I longed to be able to join them. Then I noticed that among the invited guests were singer Anita Harris, DJ's Jimmy Savile and Emperor Rosko... and *'RADIO LUXEMBOURG plans to fly over Tony Prince especially for the programme.'*

This was the first time I had ever actually seen the names of my favourite DJs in print. I also learned through the fan club there was such a thing as a guide dog for blind people. I had played chess with blind people as a child, but never had I seen or heard of one being guided by a dog.

The Elvis Convention was raising money in aid of the Guide Dogs For the Blind Association.
The things you learn.

Tony: Team 208

We still had a great DJ team when I returned to London. Bob Stewart was the velvet voice who stayed with RTL longer than anyone. We had reversed the BBC trend and brought Stuart Henry to the Grand Duchy plus perhaps the biggest coup, Barry Alldis who had left Australia for Luxembourg in the late 50s, left Luxembourg for the BBC in the early 60s, was now back with us in the 70s.

I employed Mike Read, Steve Wright and Timmy Mallet, giving them their first national radio break. I also employed Rob Jones from Liverpool's Radio City who left us to work a TV project with Richard Branson.

With local radio established, there was now good fishing to be had in the radio talent pool.

Timmy didn't last long. He called the listeners '*Zap-Heads*' and his show targeted kids who were already asleep when he cried "It's Timmy On The Trannie!" I recognised his powerful entertainer spirit, but he was pitching things a little too low for our radio station.

"You're not talking to the right audience," I tried to explain, but he continued zapping our listeners until, finally, I invited him to leave 208. Back in the UK, after a period on Manchester's Piccadilly Radio, he eventually found his niche working to an audience of 4-10 year olds, and became a major TV success.

Mike Read kept missing planes back to Luxembourg, and I was about to sack him after one missed flight too many, when he called me and I understood why he'd not made it to Heathrow Airport on time.

"Mike, I'm running a radio station, not a fucking railway station where the trains run late!"

He beseeched me not to sack him.

"I've got the chance of a job with Radio 1," he admitted. "It was the interview that made me late!"

How I hated the BBC throwing such ominous shadows across my life, time and time again. I promised Mike I wouldn't announce his sacking until he'd heard from them, and of course he got the job, eventually the prime breakfast show for yet another successful 208 prodigy.

How times had changed. In 1932 a memo went out from the top floor at Broadcasting House insisting that anyone, DJs or artists, working for Radio Luxembourg should not be given work at the BBC. It had all the character of a communist regime.

Now, apart from the kid from Oldham, they employed everyone we hired. We had become the BBC's DJ training ground.

Shortly after Mike left, I received a call from another of my star record spinners, Steve Wright.

"I feel insecure, can't I have a contract?"

"Steve," I said, "How can you be insecure with the kind of shows you're putting out?"

Steve used to go to the USA for his holidays, spending the entire time locked in his hotel room listening to live American radio. His mentors were the likes of Howard Stern.

208 didn't give contracts. DJs fell under the standard employees deal with RTL in Luxembourg, a deal that included a tasty annual profit-share bonus, usually the equivalent of two month's salary, plus an additional month's salary in December.

In order to receive that bonus you had to live in Luxembourg, which was the downside about working for the world's greatest commercial radio station, in what was then an extremely conservative environment. This was the reason why every DJ who ever worked there, look towards the White Cliffs of Dover and home sweet home.

Steve called me again within a week.

"Radio 1 have offered me a job."

"Take it," I advised.

"I have!" he replied.

By now I had buried any lingering hopes of ever joining our national station. I ditched the dream around this time and started to enjoy shaping the programmes, playing management and records on this legendary and wonderful radio station.

But as I put the phone down on Steve Wright, I realised that my personal envy had been replaced by irritation. The BBC was now my competitor, enemy number one.

Jan: DJ by Committee

On Wednesday, 24 September 1969, we had one big surprise when our commander gathered us around him to announce that we were to be released from the army the very next day, and that our duties were to be terminated prematurely by one whole week. Tomorrow, we would be free men once again.

What a feeling, what joy! We quickly exchanged our army uniforms for our civilian clothes and headed for the nearest pub to celebrate this unexpected gift of time. The thought, should we not bother retuning to our barracks on this last night, that no general in the world could do anything about it, was a mind trip for us all.

From childhood, we knew the day would come when we would have to serve our two years in the Czechoslovak People's Army, it was a dread for all young kids, and here we were now on the other side of that dread having just accomplished the biggest challenge in our lives. It was over, we were civilians once more and, for the first time in our lives, the dark cloud on our horizon had lifted as we toasted our future.

For the first time in two years we were drinking without uniforms, eyeing up the girls knowing that if we tried to chat them up we would never again hear, "I don't talk to soldiers."

On this unexpected night, the most important thing for us all was the feeling of freedom and enormous relief.

We held our own subtle revolt that night refusing to go near any Russian vodka, and we made a pact to boycott everything Russian henceforth. Instead we chose vodka harvested in Prostějov, a city nearby and, after the second drink, no one could tell if it was Russian or Egyptian!

Freedom was everywhere on this night, in our vodka, in our words, but mostly in our hearts.

In a few days' time my father would become 65, but I could not envisage much happiness shining from his weary face. And just as these thoughts began to depress me, I heard some great news, my friend Pavel had been released from jail just days before my return to Brno.

That first weekend back home out of the army was when my life changed. František had a surprise for me on the Saturday night and took me down Šelepova Street to a block of one-storey houses.

Luboš Rettegy, the brother of our friend Radek Rettegy, discovered the venue, it had once belonged to the army, but now it lay vacant.

In May 1969, Miloš Bernátek took the chance and started running it as a club, together with another friend of ours, Jirka Sedláček.

Thirteen years after London had its 2i's Coffee Bar, and 12 years after the launch of Liverpool's Cavern Club, Brno, at last, had its first real discotheque for young people.

Under the communist system they could not run Bav club alone, it had to come under the control of the Cultural Centre of Brno's 5th District, but whilst they were overseen by communist bureaucrats, they were free to organise events themselves.

Because our top songwriter František had toured numerous Czechoslovakian festivals with Synkopy 61 by this time, and was well connected with lots of people in the industry who respected my likable friend, Miloš put him in charge of the club's attractions and events.

I visited my first ever discotheque, and whilst I loved the atmosphere, on this occasion there was no dancing for me as conversation centred around Pavel's imprisonment and the shocking stories of his internment.

We were joined by Jindra Eliáš who, together with Luboš Rettegy, was playing DJ that night. Jindra, too, had been imprisoned on the day of the Soviet invasion and although he didn't get slapped around like Pavel, because he had been identified as a protester that day, he was expelled from the Faculty of Law where he had been studying for a year.

I recall well the anger and resentment that brewed between us that night, as we all agreed that the people running our country were all fucking bastards, right from the President down to the last policeman.

Thank God we were allowed this amazing new shelter from the world at large, Bav club, a room with speakers and lots of music, and filled with young people who loved music, in a world where there was little else to love.

Whilst Bav club was very basic as modern western clubs go, it was Nirvana to us the great naive. Inside it's walls we escaped from a world we despised. There were some very funny moments in Bav, like the time DJ Jindra was approached by two dancers protesting that he was playing the same song five or six times!

"I have to respond to requests," he explained, disguising the fact that he owned a mere handful of records. But he and Luboš were lucky that they could travel to West Germany when they could afford to do so, and here's where they unearthed the most popular tunes broadcast from Radio Luxembourg from a wish list, which I provided.

When František proposed I become the Bav club resident DJ, I inherited the exact same problem. It was one thing playing my tapes and my few eight-year-old vinyl hits to friends and workers in railway sidings, but I knew I couldn't stretch to a career with just Chris Andrews, a few Beatles tunes and an Elvis EP.

Tape recordings of Luxembourg were easily identifiable by all the static, which wasn't acceptable in a discotheque, a DJ had to play records. Of course kids understood that here, in Czechoslovakia, it would never be possible to find yourself dancing to last Sunday night's 208 Top 20, so they accepted the status quo and I knew I couldn't establish myself as a DJ with my meagre record library.

It wouldn't be until the Berlin wall came down in 1989 that music would flow like a stream in our clubs, when we could finally become professional disc jockeys pleasing our audiences and catching tunes at the same time as the rest of the world.

There would be just one singular exception to this; a night when music flowed like a live rainbow, but that was yet to come.

Whilst we occasionally borrowed records from one another, this wasn't easy either as DJs were, by their nature, competitive and their music was their key to working regularly. In most cases, serious DJs paid a lot of money for a hot record on the black market and the bigger the hit, plus the fact that it might still be featuring in the 208 Top 20 on Sunday night, the more he ruled the roost.

I was pissed off again over my personal situation. Had the army allowed me to go abroad, I would by now have built a record collection and on the coming Monday, instead of returning to the railyard for my employment again, I could have immediately become a full time DJ doing the job I could only dream of.

And yet, with František's help and optimism, I remained inspired to make this happen. The more the idea of becoming a disc jockey crystallised in my mind, the more I convinced myself that there wasn't a better man for the job in Czechoslovakia.

František, now a music consultant at Bav, forecast he would obtain records for me eventually, but in the short term I should apply for the Art Test at Brno State Agency for Concerts and Vaudville Shows. This was a socialist body made up of a Director and a committee who examined all aspiring artists, including DJs who wanted to perform in public. If you wished to be a singer, here's where you auditioned. If you wanted to be a comedian, this would be your first stand-up and now, even club disc jockeys, a new phenomenon in my country, had to prove they could do the job in front of this committee, and only then would you receive a license to work.

Of course this committee was as screwed up and bent as everything else in the public-control zone. Artists and musicians were also split into categories, with the lowest graded paid the minimum wage regardless of how many people came to see them, whilst the 'politically reliable' artists were in the top echelon of money earners – no matter how bad they were! František tipped me off that any day now Radek Rettegy would enter the Art Test, so I should wait and see how he went about it and take his advice based on his experience. As František rightly added, the most important thing in this country, so filled with rigid communist bureaucracy, was to have official permission to do something. Then, nobody could get in my way.

"And don't worry about records," said František reassuringly. "There's money to be made in discotheques, even for disc jockeys. You'll earn plenty at Bav club, there's no one better positioned to become a great knowledgeable DJ, like Jan Šesták!"

By the end of this amazing night regrouped, with my music-loving friends, my head was quite swollen, my brain abuzz with new hopes. My mouth fell open as Pavel recounted his experiences in England, and we were all in awe that he had decided to return from London simply to fulfil a gig obligation. From 60s England, right into 60s Czechoslovakia, where his own people imprisoned him and beat him mercilessly.

I knew that night that I was lucky to have this circle of friends, and that music would be our salvation. I also felt immediately that this Bav club would help us endure the communist regime, no matter how long it took to right the boat!

I got home that night and tuned in to Radio Luxembourg's last hour before the station closed down for the night. My favourite DJ Tony Prince accompanied me as I closed my eyes to plan and dream of this new road I would travel. I would do everything possible to become a disc jockey just like Tony, and fell asleep feeling a contentment I had never before felt in my life.

On Monday I went to the railway depot to make arrangements to recommence work after returning from the army, and I was asked to start that very day on the night shift.

In two years one thing hadn't changed, they still found it difficult to find people willing to earn a living by jumping on and off moving locomotives day and night, no matter how well they were paid!

At the end of the week, I met with Radek Rettegy who recounted to me all about his interview for the Art Test. I was devastated at what I might be facing, but Radek had campaigned to be an entertainer, not a disc jockey. In front of the committee he sang and performed his rather celebrated musical impressions, impersonating different nationalities by singing as a Frenchman, German, Brit, Chinese, Russian, American and Arab, all with really convincing accents. But the committee had objections, stating that it was not that funny. There he was facing the world's most unqualified X-Factor panel of judges. Who knows why they flunked him? Maybe it was because he'd impersonated a Russian singer and they were afraid that he was ridiculing our greatest 'friends and brothers'? Or perhaps his convincing British and American accents hit a nerve with them?

At the offset he'd told them that he wasn't going to make fun of anybody in particular, but to show how different we all were when we sang.

They criticized his Brno dialect as though that had anything to do with anything.

"How lucky the Beatles were that they didn't have to pass an art test with these people", I offered in sympathy. "No doubt they would have failed with their broad Liverpudlian accents!"

Radek had passed the political exam, but it had no influence on the committee. I wondered how the Beach Boys and the Rolling Stones would have gone on under this communist agency test, where *all* working class artists who wanted to entertain had to be politically aware, so that they could perform on a stage from a position of Marxism and Leninism? Maybe John Lennon and Bob Dylan would have succeeded, but I'm not so sure about Ringo or Freddie and the Dreamers!

As part of the art exam, Radek was given a question concerning the communist upheaval of 1948, something every kid in the country knew back to front. Now the only thing he had to do was to answer it in exactly the opposite way to what he really thought. Facing his jury, the auditioning entertainer explained how good it was that in the year 1948, our workers and farmers defeated the capitalists.

He could see he had impressed them, and envisaged he was now moments away from being given permission to follow his career and to sing and entertain under a part-time license, until maybe one day a full-time career might be possible.

But it was not to be. Radek's application was to perform only part-time not full time. He held down a job as a graphic designer and his wife Hana was pregnant, so full-time singing was far too risky.

If things didn't work out and he failed as a professional singer, his old graphic job would be closed to him, seen by his director to have been disloyal.

Radek wondered if he had heard them correctly? A *full time* license was offered to him.

He considered their uncalled for offer carefully, but nothing convinced him that he could maintain a family on what would at best be two gigs at the weekend. Then there was the memory of the many times he'd been banned from working, due to performing so many subversive American rock 'n' roll songs in the years before 1968. As rock 'n' roll was a big part of his act, there was no way he would give that up just for political correctness, so what then when he was banned in the future?

He couldn't get his head around why this fucking communist committee would offer him a license to be full-time, but not part-time? The opposite might have been more understandable, but then, *what* did make sense in this fucked-up country of ours?

Knowing also that the lead-comrade-director-bitch on the State Agency for Concerts and Vaudville committee, (who I was yet to meet), could withdraw his license at any time, his aspirations to become a part-time entertainer looked dismal.

In the future, Radek would fulfil his ambitions illegally which, when you consider he could have been thrown inside for this, shows the passion and will some people have to entertain.

I had now inherited the same passion wanting to become a DJ.

Working illegally, Radek's future would never see his name on a poster or promoted in advertising, if his show was questioned by the secret police who hid in the shadows, he would simply say he wasn't being paid, and had just been invited on to the stage.

Later still, as his performances grew in popularity, he was inspired by friends to make the same audition for the State Agency for Concerts and Vaudville Shows in one of the districts of Prague, where he finally succeeded to receive his license.

Later we learned where he had gone wrong with the comrade communist director in Brno. An expensive bottle of alcohol would have tipped the scales in his favour, but Radek wasn't to know and had far too much trust in human nature to believe such women existed. We understood clearly now which side of our barricades she, and others like her had stood in 1968!

I was now driven to be a DJ and confident I would blow this committee over with my musical knowledge, and how I intended to make the kids of Brno dance!

Unlike Radek, I had no graphic designer career to worry about and no pregnant wife, I wanted nothing less than a full-time job, no part-time for me, my shunting days were over!

My day of destiny arrived. I entered the office and stood before the committee, presided over by the same sour-faced comrade woman who Radek had faced.

"Yes," she said, and the room fell silent.

Confidently, I expressed my desire to be a disc jockey.

Standing to her feet, she looked me in the eye; there was no kindness in those eyes. Her words tumbled from her lips and hit me like a bolt out of the blue. She spat them at me with contempt.

"Sorry", she said, "but there is a STOP state for disc jockeys now, we have enough, no more are required. This was decided in May."

I had to change my tack, a plan B was called for, so I started to explain that I worked as a railway shunter and would quite happily work week-ends-only... but even as I spoke she wasn't listening, she was leaving her position at the centre of the committee.

"I have work to do," she said, leaving the room.

I wanted her to understand that I had been unable to apply for a DJ license, because for the past two years I had given my life to patriotically serving my country in the army.

If she'd only have listened I'm sure she would have bought it.

But she was gone... my dream with her.

As I walked towards my tram, I was glad of the heavy rainfall that disguised my tears. This was all too much. I had taken it on the chin when I had been refused a position at university. I hadn't minded when the railway turned me down as a train dispatcher due to them believing I was not politically reliable due to my family record. But now I had been turned down for something I *really* wanted, and the frustration quite overwhelmed me.

What really made me mad, was the woman hadn't even allowed me to explain what a great DJ I would make.

This woman was typical of those who had fallen into powerful positions after our Prague Spring. Many in this fleeting three-year period had visited the west, had seen the beautiful items in the shops, the splendid cars, the magnificent hotels and cafés.

Avarice had them in its grip. Bribing was now part and parcel of the communist system that indulged them. They were, of course, morally bankrupt and my awareness and that awful personal front-row experience stayed with me like a dark cloud for weeks afterwards. Her cold eyes still haunt me to this day.

Many people, even the communists who believed *too* much in the Prague Spring, were fired from their jobs when the Czech Winter returned. This included Alexander Dubček, who had tried so valiantly as our president to distance us from Russian control. For his efforts, he was sent to Turkey as our ambassador, allegedly in the hope that he would stay in the west and keep his nose out of Czechoslovakia, where too many of our people still loved him.

Dubček remained an ambassador, until in 1970, he was called back to be expelled from the communist party. After this, he became an ordinary employee in the Slovakian Forestry Service.

Just like our former President, many individuals fell foul of having been too far behind the barricades in the Prague Spring, and so the top positions became filled by those citizens who had managed to escape KGB profiling. You were either expelled from the communist party or you were scratched. Being scratched, offered you redemption, if you played your part well in your local communist party organisations.

These scratched individuals spent their life seeking support from within the party to become reinstated, whilst those expelled did everything possible to become scratched. The Prague Spring quickly forgotten, the joys of freedom behind them, all people wanted was to climb back up the commie ladder to earn more money, get better houses which were allocated by other corrupt party members. Scratch my back and I'll scratch yours was the creed now. An entire bribery network was established across Czechoslovakia, and I had the misfortune to have met one of the women who had evolved from this evil communist spawn.

What had been refreshing though, was the fact that on the two occasions that I was refused admission to university, I received the news in writing, likewise my railway boss who refused to look me straight in the eye when telling me I couldn't become a train dispatcher.

Now at least this horrible woman had met me face to face, and I had the chance to look into her eyes when she knocked the stuffing out of me. Unfortunately her eyes were soulless and she'd been in an awful hurry to get out of that room.

My convictions were reinforced – I would never again drink Russian vodka!

Tony: Ch... ch... ch... changes

I had to do *something*. I didn't like the thought of this dear station being sunk like the good ship Radio Caroline, whose function passed its sell-by date, long before she went off air.

According to Gallup Research figures, Radio 1, and now Independent Local Radio (both of which had come about because of the pirates), were whittling down our listening figures. Our static-free FM competitors were now emphasising how poor the 208 signal was.

Let's face it, before colour television, black and white seemed like a miracle. As kids we hadn't given Radio Luxembourg's static a second thought, it was just there, annoying, but hey, there was nothing else around that could compensate for the day-time pop music drought we'd had to live with. Static was not an issue, because within it was something we could only hear under those conditions.

Now however, Radio Luxembourg was finally being shown up for what she was. The King's new clothes didn't exist. 208's glory nights were in eclipse.

I had to give the listeners something that would make them put up with the extremely poor signal. Competing on a level playing field would not be good enough.

I needed something niche.

And along came disco!

Overnight I changed Radio Luxembourg to a total 'Dance Music' format, taking my cue from the upsurge in quality dance music hits arriving on my desk in the late 70s.

It was the time of *Night Fever, Rivers of Babylon, Boogie Oogie Oogie* with Philadelphia now the new Detroit, and Miami growing itself a musical reputation.

John Travolta and Olivia Newton John were the golden couple, the Bee Gees, the bee's knees. We had the movies and the media on our side, and I went to my colonel-in-chief with a battle plan.

Alan Keen, himself a veteran of the UK radio wars, agreed to let me give it a shot. He was Gallup Researched up to his gills with bad statistics, had the RTL board on his back and was relying on me to turn things around.

So we went clubbing.

No station in the world had filled the airwaves with so many bass lines. The top four best selling albums in 1978 were:

1. Saturday Night Fever
2. Grease
3. Abba: The Album
4. Boney M: Nightflight to Venus

We moved into 1979 with the likes of Chic, the Whispers, D-Train, Gloria Gaynor, Donna Summer, McFadden & Whitehead and Sister Sledge dominating our playlist.

I could see from the mail we received that we were hitting the right notes. The whole world was dancing to US imports.

After years of depressing news, Malcolm Mather, the boss at Gallup Research called Alan and I to a meeting.

I was not looking forward to it.

Then he informed us that we hadn't only stopped the rot, we had *doubled* our audience!

Ladbrokes would have given you any odds you wanted against this result. This was about as unlikely a prospect as Manchester United catching up with Arsenal in the Championship League of 2003, around November 2002!

We were just like Manchester United was, without a hope in hell. Independent Local Radio were Arsenal, cocky, way ahead of the game, unbeatable.

As all Arsenal supporters know though, shit happens!

Alan Keen and I went out to celebrate. We started at Wheelers across the road with expensive champagne together with Alan's favourite meal, egg and chips. Then up to Alan's club, Les Ambassadors on Park Lane, then... how would I know? I vaguely recall last seeing Alan in my club, Tramp.

I regained consciousness in hospital with Christine and Alan peering down at me, with grave concern etched on their faces.

Alan looked rough, but not so rough as me. At least he had a face I could recognise!

To this day, I don't know what happened or who it was I might have upset, or if it was just a genuine mugging at the club's front door.

Of course these days you're not allowed to beat people up. You can go to prison. If you're a star you can fund a photographer's retirement, simply for pushing him over.

How much a slap from Elton John or a thump from George Michael? There is no doubt that I could have made a very comfortable living down Tramp!

Towards the end of my 16 years with 208, I rekindled an old friendship with Billy Fury, the man who will now be sitting next to Elvis on their heavenly thrones.

Billy was one of the gentlest, deeply shy, rock 'n' roll giants I ever had the pleasure to know. As Billy's heart problems and numerous operations tested his mettle taking his spirit down to life's lower ledges, he kicked back.

Billy and Lisa, his Jewish princess wife, had disappeared from society as Billy indulged his love for birds and animals in a farm they bought in Wales.

Billy was very poorly indeed, and whilst heart bypasses had saved him, too much surgery had brought him to the realisation that there was no operation left that could provide him with more time.

With the sands of time running out, he suddenly got the urge to come out of retirement and climb back on board the bitch called fame, thanks to the persuasion of a life-long fan who had become his closest friend and roadie, Tony Reed.

"People still love you Billy. Your fans would all buy anything you recorded," Tony urged.

On 16 August 1982, I persuaded him to come to an Elvis Presley fan club convention to mark the fifth anniversary of El's death.

The thought horrified him; he honestly thought that Elvis' fans hated him. How wrong he was.

He walked on stage at the De Montford Hall, Leicester to sing his new single *Devil or Angel* and the roof came off.

Every one an Elvis fan, every one a Billy Fury fan!

During Billy's last few months, DJ Mike Read stayed at his Cavendish Avenue home in St John's Wood.

Here he discovered what we, his friends, had known for some time, Billy was a night-tripper.

When Lisa, his beautiful, caring wife had finally dozed off, Billy would slip out of bed, dress and go do some life squeezing before it was too late. I'm sure Lisa knew, but she'd married Billy, a very poorly pop star and this... *this* was Billy. So she slept, and closed her eyes to his life squeezing.

It was midnight when Mike went to sleep in a guest room at the same time as Billy and Lisa had retired in their Cavendish Avenue home. Mike had to get up early for the Radio 1 breakfast show.

"I was making myself a coffee in the kitchen at 5am, when I was suddenly aware of a noise," Mike told me a couple of days later.

He looked down on the kitchen floor almost tripping over Billy, who was fully dressed and drunk as a Lord, just back from a squeezing session.

Billy had everything a Mersey ferryman could dream of. Apart from his own personal wealth, his father-in-law owned half of the properties in London.

He had a farm in Wales stocked with the animals and birds he adored, a house in London next door to Paul and Linda McCartney, and a wife who would embalm his feet, if it so pleased him.

But Billy was running low on heartbeats and there wasn't much squeezing left in him. He confided this to me just days before he died.

On New Year's Eve 1982, Billy and Lisa joined Christine and I at the Regent's Park home of our good friends Jackie Gill, the UK's top female record plugger and Peter Phillips, Managing Director of ATV Music, the mighty music-publishing house. We had a lot of laughs and sang our way out of 1982. Another guest was record promoter Alan James, who was living with James Garner's daughter, Mitzie who was also bringing in the New Year with us.

At midnight, I persuaded her to call her father in LA to wish him happy New Year, it seemed surreal, Billy Fury and I chatting to Maverick as he lay on the beach!

Ian Stewart of the Rolling Stones played piano for us. Billy wouldn't sing *Halfway to Paradise*, so I did, standing right there in front of him, mimicking my friend's sexy style as I went along.

We swapped stories and talked about the good old days, and Billy told us of the time he was gigging with Gene Vincent when his act was hotter than usual.

"He'd planted his injured leg, which had a metal plate, against a stage light and couldn't understand why the fans were going wild during Summertime, which was a ballad." Billy giggled at the memory. "They were actually screaming trying to tell him his leather pants were on fire!"

Three hours into the New Year, Billy and I were getting quite sentimental, thanks to the flagons of good cheer we'd consumed. His arm was around my shoulder like we were blood brothers, rather than the DJ and the star who'd done a few concerts and interviews together, and enjoyed fun nights out in the 60s.

He put his mouth close to my ear.

"I haven't got much time left Tone," he confided tapping at his heart with his champagne flute.

"Sod off Billy!" I said looking at the champagne stain he'd made down his silk shirt.

"Seriously," he said clawing my shoulder with his spidery hand.

"I want you to get the lads together for one last wild night before it's too late!"

"Sure Billy," I said humouring him with a Stan Laurel expression.

"Don't humour me Tony, I'm serious," he said angrily like Oliver Hardy.

I scrutinised his gaunt face, he was still a very beautiful person, even though his skin now hung like tanned chamois from the protruding bones.

"Humour *you*, are you kidding me?" I gasped. "Who'd have the nerve to humour a mean bastard like you?"

And boy had he looked mean in years of yore when on television's *Thank Your Lucky Stars* after presenter Brian Matthews had introduced him, he'd look smoulderingly at the camera, and Joe Meek's music would fill the screen as he sang Johnny Ray's *Jealousy* or *Last Night Was Made For Love* or *Like I've Never Been Gone*.

The fact was though, this mean looking dude was about as shy a guy as you'd ever meet; he wouldn't swat a fly if his own life depended on it! Billy Fury, the UK's number one sex symbol, once admitted to me that he was so shy he was almost afraid to look the camera lens in the eye. So he hooded his eyes, lowered his chin and peered out from behind his turned up jacket lapel.

Curling his lips like the King.

As tough and as beautiful as James Dean but, in reality, a marshmallow man, sweet, soft and very fragile.

I took the empty champagne glass off him and made to rise for a refill.

"Fuck off Billy, you'll live longer than me," I prophesied.

He yanked me back down onto the sofa, and looked at me with those hooded eyes of his and spoke in his indelible Scouse. So indelible was the sentence, I hear him repeat it now as I write.

"Promise me you'll get everyone together for one last knees up!"

I promised.

It was a placating promise made in a champagne haze, for I had no idea that on that wonderful New Year's Eve, as Billy laughed and danced and talked to Maverick with me, he'd been posted notice by the Grim Reaper. As we drank champagne and talked about Gene Vincent, the man with the scythe was standing right beside us.

Billy was given the illusive treasures of success, wealth and mass adulation, but grew to anticipate his own early death.

Billy passed away exactly four weeks after our New Year's Eve party on 28 January 1983. At his funeral service, Christine and I stood solemnly next to Marty Wilde and his family, as Lisa was helped down the aisle towards Billy's coffin. She was overwhelmed with grief. I have rarely seen or heard grief like it.

I never fulfilled my promise to Billy to gather the clan because there just wasn't the time, but we were all at the funeral and I know he would have liked that.

I guess Billy's my favourite Scouser on a list of many, but Sir Paul McCartney is right behind him.

Further to Paul and Linda having me conduct their Oo Boo Joo Boo interviews, Paul also asked me to compere a Buddy Holly Week luncheon at the Orangery in London's Holland Park.

It was one of the best attended lunches I've ever attended, Elton John, 10cc, Eric Clapton with Patty Boyd on his arm, Freddie Mercury and the rest of Queen, Steve Harley, Roxy Music, Norman Petty who wrote all the songs with Buddy, and of course, the McCartney family.

The best power-lunch ever!

Having acquired the publishing rights to the songs of his greatest influence Buddy Holly, Paul took great pains each year to keep his hero's name alive, (I know of no other publishing company who would spend anything like Paul does on their writers, dead or alive)!

I compered the lunch annually for 10 years and I'm proud to say I never charged Paul a penny for doing it, which was my gesture and personal tribute to two people, Paul and Buddy, who enriched my life with their music. Paul and Linda always attended these lunches and, whenever we had a band, I coaxed the ex-Beatles bass player to get up and sing some rock 'n' roll tunes with me.

The best gig was London's Astoria when Paul staged a Buddy Holly Week Concert, which found Paul and I jamming with the Crickets, Mike Berry, Carl Perkins and Bobby Vee!

You *cannot* imagine what that meant to Tommy Whitehead!

At the Buddy Holly Week after Linda's death, Paul still couldn't disguise his grief.

"I just can't believe she's no longer here," he lamented to me on the balcony of the Leicester Square, Empire.

Other than the night I introduced the Beatles at the Oldham Top Rank, this was the first time in dozens of events and interviews, I'd ever seen Paul without Linda by his side.

Jan: The Beatles book

Life went on, as it does. The very next day I was walking down Česká Street when something caught my eye in the Panton shop, one of the new music publishing companies that had shot up when censorship was abolished in 1968.

There, right in the centre of the window display, was this item that just took my breath away. It was a large white book with a colour drawing of John, Paul, George and Ringo on the cover, and the title Beatles v Písních a v Obrazech, which stood for The Illustrated Beatles Lyrics by Alan Aldridge.

Printed in Finland, the sweetest book I ever owned contained 100 Beatle songs, pictures, drawings, quotations and remarks. If I had walked into a gold mine and found a seam, I could not have been more excited or indeed rich.

Lyrics which had puzzled me for years were made clear, and the translations made by František and I were finally corrected or understood, and all for a mere 54 Czechoslovac crowns.

For example in *Being for the Benefit of Mr. Kite*, the Beatles were singing, '*The Hendersons will all be there, late of Pablo Fanques fair, what a scene.*'

Now it was so simple and so obvious, Pablo Fanques was just a name, a Spanish name perhaps, how could we have known that? I bought a copy without hesitation, left the shop and was suddenly free again, as if there were no Soviet troops surrounding me, not a communist in sight.

I knew I would have a long night ahead of me as I perused this wonderful book, studying lyrics long loved, but never adequately translated. I reached the last page and turned out my light. For once, I had far exceeded Radio Luxembourg's 3am close down.

The following night I made my way to the Bav club to meet František carrying under my arm the Beatles book to keep my spirits in a state of gratitude towards the dark overlords.

This book started me thinking that perhaps sharing a life with half a million Soviet aggressors and their Czechoslovak communist supporters could just about be bearable.

'Bread and Circuses' was our subliminal treaty implanted into society to make us forget our birthright. It said: '*work for us and do our bidding then you can listen to Elvis Presley and purchase special Beatles books from the west from time to time.*'

I was on the tram now a few stops from the Bav and still the thoughts came to me. Here we were in a cage, a better cage than the one that contained us before 1968, and better than a prison. It was better than being locked away for listening to subversive western radio stations, or losing your job because you were overheard speaking in English on the telephone.

Before 1968 they put people in prison in such huge numbers, that almost every family in Czechoslovakia that showed any opposition to the Marx doctrines, had at least one member of that family in jail.

Then I remembered something that really pissed me off. Communism was a new political theory, a theory that had not been tested before Karl Marx came up with his philosophy.

We were part of his experiment. Like mice in a cage.

I climbed off the tram with the Beatles book hugged tightly under my arm as my thoughts carried me nearer to Bav club.

"What if the socialist experiment is failing?" I almost spoke the thought out loud. I stopped in my tracks and cursed our luck. "Fuck!" I shouted in English. The thought process ended there just as I arrived outside the club.

František was there all the time, taking care of the events. It was also a great place to mix with friends and the musicians, who also appeared on stage.

Pavel Váně had at last got himself together and put prison behind him, and had formed a new band the Progress Organization.

This night, as František and I poured over the Beatles' lyrics book, Pavel and the other members of his band were performing, and all the English songs they sang had been translated for them by František and I.

I was three months home from the army and was still not going steady. I talked to girls at Bav club, even invited some home, but everything ran to friendship, and amorous opportunities disappeared the moment my dear mother appeared to offer us her fresh pies and something to drink.

To be quite honest I was a little backwards coming forwards where girls were concerned, and all my conversation was about music, the Beatles and Radio Luxembourg. I hadn't yet learned the fine art of seduction.

Besides which I wasn't able to go to concerts or to Bav club as often as I would like, due to night shifts or early morning starts at five o'clock to get to the railway cargo depot.

When one of our very top singers, Petr Novák, appeared at Bav club, I had a night shift.

The following night I met František who described the evening I had missed, it was what happened after the show that really knocked me for six.

Some 50 girls wanted to meet Petr Novák and the task fell to František to select a few girls to visit his dressing room.

"We told the girls that only five of them could go backstage to see him," said František. "But, I told them that Petr would see only the girls with the most beautiful boobs, and he'd asked us to choose five of them."

At this time Petr was bigger than the Beatles to these girls.

"Twenty girls took off their blouses and lifted up their bras and Jan, we had the most terrible task choosing which five of them had the most magnificent boobs!"

My mouth fell open, what had I missed??

František had a great way of telling a story, which, in themselves, were a thrill, but this evening other shocks were to come.

I wandered out into the hall to see Luboš Rettegy, who was spinning the records as a warm up before his brother Radek came on to sing with his group.

As I rifled through his records that night I noticed an album *A Collection of Beatles Oldies* by the Beatles, and as I gently handled this diamond I had discovered, it surprised me to see the name Supraphon on the cover. "The Beatles on Supraphon, right? When did you get this?" I asked Luboš He'd had it a couple of weeks already, the first Beatles album ever released in Czechoslovakia and I was only just discovering its existence? It wasn't only the first Beatles' LP ever to be released in my country, it would also be my first Beatles' album!

The next day, I set off like the Beatles-lap-dog I had become. First stop, Supraphon on třída Vítězství.

Tony: Johnny Rotten

I was always chasing publicity for my show and ultimately for the station, and when I heard the Sex Pistols had told TV presenter Bill Grundy he was an 'old wanker' on live TV, I wanted to secure their first 'live' radio interview.

The band had ended Grundy's career because they responded to the old boozer's goading.

On the day that the tabloids gave Johnny Rotten his first front page, he and Malcolm McLaren were on a plane to Luxembourg.

"Whatdyamean you don't want me to interview him live," I cried incredulously at Alan Keen.

"Tony, you have to pre-record him, he's far too outspoken for live family radio, the entire press corps will be listening."

And that was all I needed.

"Alan tell the press I've refused to pre-record, get our Press Department to hit the phones right now, you threaten to sack me, I threaten to resign. We'll resolve it at the last minute!"

Alan played along.

We gathered a fair few column, inches from that little set-up and a pre-recorded interview with so many bleeped out expletives and profanities, it sounded like a 20 minute Morse-code message.

We'd taken Johnny and Malcolm to eat at the Holiday Inn.

Mr Lydon picked his nose, flicked his crows across the room, and played with his punk hair like monkeys do in the zoo throughout the meal.

He threw his spoon in his plate of soup, and made Malcolm laugh as the soup sprayed a table full of DJs.

"Fuckin' wankers," he breathed, not quite under his breath.

"Toss pot, cunts."

I think he spent dinner rehearsing for his next live TV spot.

"Fuckin' bastards."

McLaren was no better.

"You fuckin' out your fuckin' mind! Pre-record? What a load of fucking bollocks."

He was like a public school version of Lydon.

To this day, I'm the only person who's heard that fucking, bastard, cunting, twatting, interview in its full fuckin' glory but alas, for now, the tape remains lost in the attic. Otherwise I'd have been able to let you know some of the other swear words he came up with. But I don't believe there were many others. His vocabulary was quite limited.

It really is a talent putting in a swear word every third or fourth word, try it sometime as an après-dinner party game!

I have to close the Sex Pistols story with a genuine thank you to Johnny for the anarchy.

It was just what the puffed up music industry needed at that time, and opened the doors to some very great music!

I ran into McLaren in a New York club whilst living there in the late 90s. He said he 'vaguely remembered the interview'.

Fucking lying bastard twat!

Jan: Beatles and Bohunka

I entered the record shop rather nervously, observing the situation watching one older lady and one young girl moving behind counters, searching in the shelves for records that customers had asked for.

I didn't want to stand in a queue that would form, as a number of people arrived at the same time and I didn't want anyone listening to my line of questions.

I had convinced myself that one of the shop assistants would have put the album to one side for a friend or a relative, and I could use my charm to buy the record. I was looking for a miracle, but to discover if this might be the case, I had to have the discussion without an audience. In the communist state, a shop assistant could not be seen to release a pre-ordered product to someone, other than the person it was waiting for. That was not socialism.

Then there was the chance that someone standing behind me would report the sale to Commercial Inspection, a body set up to ensure that sales didn't go to chosen people through shop assistants' hoarding. Usually this activity involved televisions, refrigerators and cars and even bananas sometimes, for which crimes, the perpetrator would appear in Red Law under a special column called Black Chronicle. So I considered all this... it could definitely be construed that a Beatles album sold two weeks after arrival, was the subject of hoarding.

I didn't want to test this theory.

So I waited.

Then a little miracle; the first of a clutch of miracles that day. The beautiful assistant approached me with a smile asking if she could help me.

With a sad look in my eyes that of a hungry dog, I told her the full story of yesterday's trip to the Bav club to see my DJ friend Luboš. I told her how quite impossibly, I had missed the album's release but as it was now a question of life and death for me, I had come here to see if perhaps they still had one copy left?

Then, before she could utter 'sorry sold out', I added that I'd even accept a damaged copy. I had no pride.

I stopped my campaigning then, caught my breath and looked upon this lovely girl who now smiled at me. Then the miracle.

"I have one copy put aside for a friend who seems to be no longer interested, so I could let you have it."

Nobody could know how I felt just at that moment. It was the same feeling I experienced when I found two plastic singles by the Beatles and the Rolling Stones in the little shop in Zakopane, Poland on our school trip.

Still in a trance as a fresh owner of the Beatles album, I plucked up my courage and told her I would like to invite her for a drink for being so kind. Her answer floored me; it was so unexpected.

"OK," she said, "We close at six o'clock, so if you could come back around ten past six, it would be just fine."

I suppressed my delight and amazement, and with an hour and a half remaining, I went home with my precious acquisition together with the knowledge that I had a date, something as unique as the Beatles album.

Once home, I didn't know quite what to do. Normally there would be no indecision, I would simply put *A Collection Of Beatles Oldies (But Goldies!)* on my record player and play it over and over.

But tonight was nothing like normal.

With one hour to go, I made myself ready. I felt deep in my soul that tonight would be far better than anything I had ever experienced with the girls who had come into my life.

Tonight I felt my love life was due a change.

I left the precious record on the table, put on my best sweater and off I went.

It was snowing a little, which made Brno look more romantic than when it was dressed in its usual grey with neglected house facades, which is what happens when everything belongs to everybody through a socialist system. No owner, no care, simple as that. More than 20 years after the communists took power, the only houses that still looked nice were those constructed before the reds took over, houses that could stand the test of time. How such a red organisation could look so grey, was beyond me!

I arrived at the shop window some 10 minutes before closing time and when I caught her eye, she threw me a smile and a wave. God she was pretty.

I walked around a little with a look like the cat that got the cream, so that every passerby could not mistake I was indeed that cat.

She came out, we introduced ourselves, she was Bohunka. When she spoke the snow around us seemed to melt.

I caught my breath and suggested we could go to the Venus wine cellar, a very fashionable place and a favourite for myself and all our musician friends. My great hope was that some of them might be there to see me with the beautiful Bohunka and indeed the first person to greet us was František.

Every table was full and the waiter told us curtly that it did not make sense for us to wait, and that we should leave.

František got mad when he heard the waiter speak to us in this manner. Suddenly he walked over to the centre of the room and shouted at the top of his voice, "All communists are cunts!"

Then he asked if everybody had understood him and repeated, "All communists are cunts!" We stood frozen to the spot in disbelief as it registered on the faces of the customers.

Undoubtedly some thought there was some kind of provocation taking place, and wanted well away from this crazy man.

It was a genius method of making room for us.

Within minutes we were seated and being served by a very nervous waiter.

In the corner a group of young couples who had been sitting with František, were laughing at this most amazing piece of entertainment.

On reflection, we were very lucky that there were no members of State Safety in the wine bar, or that people didn't call the Secret Police. My new friend Bohunka was laughing her head off in disbelief at such an outrageous space-making stunt.

Now, knowing we both had the same political views and sense of humour, we were completely relaxed with each other.

My day of luck continued, there was one small table just for the two of us in a cosy corner.

"Do you have Bob Dylan's new album on Supraphon," she asked as we awaited our drinks.

"No," I said meekly, unaware once again that Supraphon seemed to be taking over the world.

"We have a couple of copies on the back shelf if you would like me to keep one for you?"

I stood to my feet and pinched myself.

"What are you doing?" she asked.

"I'm sorry Bohunka but I had a few drinks last night, and I just wanted to make sure I have woken up. You are my dream girl."

Bohunka spent our first date bringing me up to speed on record store politics. I learned why I hadn't known about the Beatles and Bob Dylan albums, chiefly because Red Law gave scant release information for western releases, even on our own labels.

She explained that the minute a popular album appeared in the window display, all stock swiftly sold out. Shockingly, the Beatles album was not given prime window space, since they had become a new symbol of rebellion amongst young people, who now copied their long hair and fashion... and attitude!

The record store manager would only invite the wrath of the communist customers if seen to blatantly promote the capitalist Beatles, nor would they dare to agitate passing communist bosses who would hardly appreciate long-haired western bands or American protest singers, gazing out from their sleeves cocking a snoop at our socialist society.

By now, our enthralling conversation had reached our second bottle of wine. I seemed to outmatch Bohunka on pop music history, but she held me spellbound as she indoctrinated me into the politics of our record shops.

The shop could promote how they liked jazz musician Ornette Coleman, because he was black, and therefore a symbol of oppressed Americans.

Similarly, albums released on Supraphon by Edith Piaf and Gilbert Bécaud could be placed into the shop windows, as their music was more acceptable to communists.

"We must have done something terribly wrong in our previous lives and are now being punished having to wait seven years after the Beatles released their first record before we could buy it," I said.

Bohunka then told me she had just heard that the director of the Supraphon record-pressing plant, together with his whole management team, had been fired because they had released the Bob Dylan album. Someone in the State Office of Censorship had fucked up and given permission, without listening to the lyrics or understanding what Bob Dylan was protesting about. Translating Dylan was never easy, I knew that from first-hand experience so one can assume the idiot felt an American protest singer must have been protesting about America, the Empire of Evil, without going so far as to listen and comprehend the lyrics from *Blowing in the Wind,* such as '*How many times must the cannon balls fly before they're forever banned?*'

"Nothing surprises me any more," said Bohunka showing her complete trust in me. "Since the Russian invasion, it doesn't matter if you're stupid, so long as you support the Soviet Union!"

The wine was exceptional, we had finished our second bottle by the time we had sorted out the entire political problems of our country. Looking into my lovely new friend's eyes, I knew that I would never again miss any release on Supraphon, and yet whilst this was a great realisation, I had greater aspirations for our relationship.

For the first time in my life I felt like a winner.

Bohunka ended our unusual political discussion on a surprising note.

"Your friend František was so right when he cleared Venus telling everybody what communists are like."

I offered to accompany her home, which she agreed to, and as we travelled on her tram I promised to pop by her shop the very next day for the Bob Dylan album. She also suggested we visit Bav club together soon.

I took her hand and sang the Beatles riff 'I wanna hold your hand' and she laughed, and held my hand tighter as we walked through a local park from where she pointed to a row of small family houses, at the end of the park where she rented a room.

Bohunka thanked me for a lovely evening and asked that I leave her there. I protested that I would like to see her safely to her door, but she turned to me with a gentle smile and told me she shared the room with her former boyfriend who, although he hadn't yet found a new place, was still pretty jealous.

In that moment I was crestfallen.

I told her I couldn't bear to say goodbye there and then, and after walking hand in hand to a nearby park, we fell into each others arms, kissing and hugging and embracing like the world was about to end.

The kissing and fondling of Bohunka might well have continued until dawn, had not the weather beat our mutual over-heating.

We said goodnight, sealed with a kiss, and exchanged promises to see each other the next day when I would go to get me a Bob Dylan album.

Putting my sexual frustrations behind me, I rushed home knowing the delights of my first real LP awaited me. Only Bohunka could have distracted me for so long from my Beatles album. I now regarded this as my first LP, simply because it was the first LP I had wanted and been able to buy. Eddie Cochran and Pete Seeger were fine, but I ran into them, rather than went looking for them.

LPs are like breasts; so nice to handle, however I was a little disappointed with the Supraphon packaging. I remembered how Michal's collection standing side by side had the album details printed down the spine. The Czechoslovak LP had no spine, it was flat and the detail that should have been on the spine ran on the back of the LP.

I listened many times that night playing all 12 tracks over and over again, as I closely inspected the sleeve with its wonderful coloured photographs of the Fab Four, who had so helped me through life for so long.

Nothing compared to this, playing your own vinyl album on your own record player was on the same pleasure level as sex and if on that night you'd have said to me '*Bohunka or Beatles?*', I may well have left her in the snow!

I would have liked to listen the whole night long, but as I had to go to work on the night shift the following evening, and had Bob Dylan waiting for me, I turned off the record player and then the light, and instantly fell into the arms of Orpheus.

Tony: The veggie burger

Linda McCartney took on the world's greatest burger joint, London's Hard Rock Café and won an unlikely victory.

"Are you coming to the launch of my veggie burger Tone?" she asked, "I need all the support I can get."

The Hard Rock had finally bent to Linda's persuasion, her veggie burger was going on the menu at the world's greatest hamburger joints, but the management wanted a star-studded evening to launch it.

Linda went to work, and it turned out like the Guinness Book of Hit Records had come to life, just a short walk from Radio Luxembourg's studios in Hertford Street!

It was going to be a very special occasion for me in two ways. One was amazing, the other life changing.

Mary Hopkin, who I hadn't seen since Discs-a-Gogo two decades earlier, sat with Jim Capaldi from Traffic.

Ringo Starr and Barbara Bach chatted with Linda's chum, Chrissie Hynde, from the Pretenders. Steve Harley was amongst the stars, and to cap it all, the entire McCartney family were there in force, including number one son James, who was rarely seen in public.

It was Hard Rock wall to wall!

"Long time no see," I said to Mary Hopkin, "Did we ever think that the day would dawn when we'd actually be saying to one another, *Those Were The Days My Friend!*"

"Hey Tone!" Paul chipped in from the next table. "Won't be too long now till I'm singing *When I'm '64* for real!"

It was a great veggie burger launch.

Like me, the Hard Rock Café had become one of Linda's vegetarian conquests.

Christine and I were talking to our old friends Kid Jensen, (who'd returned to being David on London's Capital Radio), and his lovely Icelandic wife, Gudron, when my heart stopped beating and the amazing thing happened. Into the Hard Rock walked the American actor Rutger Hauer escorting El's misses, Priscilla Presley!

This was too much for me to take, Christine restrained me for about 10 minutes, and then Rutger escorted Priscilla down to an area designated as the dance-floor for the evening.

I gave him 90 seconds dancing with her before I was standing behind him.

"Scuse me Rutger," I said just managing to reach his shoulder with a polite tap.

"S'my turn, excuse me please!"

And before he could even think what was happening, I was in between him and dancing with the King's dame!

Thrill?

You've no idea!

I mentioned I'd been in the Vegas Hilton the night Elvis waved to her, and their daughter Lisa Marie in 1972.

"Oh I remember that," she lied.

She saw my doubt.

"Sure I remember. Lisa Marie rarely went to the showroom."

Rutger had returned to his seat by the window, where the Hard Rock had made them into a showpiece for us all to admire.

I had her all to myself.

"We're related you and I," I yelled above the music.

"How come?" she asked her eyes showing a suspicious smile.

"We both loved the same man!"

"You were an Elvis fan uh?"

"A little bit more than that Cilla," I answered in my deepest Tupelo.

Fifteen minutes later she had my life story, and I have to say that the King sure had great taste in women.

She was a doll. Only Christine Prince, and perhaps Janet Jackson, struck me as being so superbly beautiful like Priscilla.

"Last question?"

She waited for it.

"Did that Memphis Mafia team of his get on your chest?"

"You could say that Tony," she replied with all her pretty face.

"I changed a lot at Graceland, but I could never change that!"

"Bastards" I muttered as I escorted her back to Rutger.

Jan: Bonking Bohunka

The following afternoon I went to collect my Dylan album and as it was quite busy in the store, I didn't manage to talk to Bohunka very much at all. When she handed me the carrier bag containing the album, she squeezed my hand firmly, which said it all.

I continued to meet Bohunka as often as possible, to drink a little wine or go to the movies, a great place to practise our necking, which was about as far as we were going just then. There were no 'I love you's' which made things so good between us, allowing us to talk about all subjects possible, except love.

New Year's Eve at the Bav club was on another level. With Bohunka by my side and my friends all around me and both Radek Rettegy and Pavel Váně performing the place came alive. Bav club now had its own Secret Police who kept an eye out for the Czech cops, making it the one place where Pavel could feel free to play anything he wanted. Bav club could house some 300 guests so that everybody knew everybody, and no enemy control could sneak in unnoticed.

So everyone let loose. *War is a Fool* featured live at least three times sung by various artists. First up was Pavel Váně, who had made this song one of the biggest hits in occupied Czechoslovakia. It had become the song of the year, probably the decade and for these moments in our youth, it became our national anthem, the loudest symbol of our resistance.

After a long New Year's kiss at midnight, Bohunka whispered to me that she felt it was a good time to leave. I looked at her with surprise; the party was in full swing and now promised to become one of the greatest nights ever.

Bohunka whispered in my ear that there was nobody in her room, and tonight she wanted me to show me her home. Then she added that this time she much preferred not to stay in the park as on our first date.

That was the clincher.

We took a night tram to Bohunka's place.

Once inside no words were necessary, it was as though we had known each other forever.

We awoke to a beautiful sunny, snow scene. Never before in my life had I known a new year to start with such promise. But whilst the 60s had many great moments for me, the 1970's launched in a way that every young man's New Year's Day should begin.

We'd taken a shower together, and now Bohunka placed a big towel on the carpet and handed me a bottle of body lotion, asking me to spread it across her body.

I had long dreamed of having a naked girl close to me in such relaxed and exotic circumstances. My first sexual partner, Jana, had been all smash, grab and leave. Bohunka, completely naked and damp from the shower, awaiting my massage beneath me, was in another league.

This most beautiful of all shop assistants in the world, who would make any boy crazy with lust, had laid herself out for me alone. I could not only watch her, but also touch her freely and caress every part of her body, as she guided my hand to where she wanted me to explore.

Gazing upon Bohunka's voluptuousness, doing things that have set men alight since time immemorial, I understood earth's greatest miracle and what we were put here for. And then, just as I prepared to enter her, I discovered the most wonderful things a man will ever see, a naked girl with eyes closed smiling in approval.

When our fires subsided and we lay side by side, Bohunka leaned over and kissed me.

Throughout the morning between cuddles, kisses and cups of coffee, Bohunka and I put the world to rights. We both agreed that the older generation would not experience the pleasures we did from the Beatles and our radio, and that flower power would be a concept they could never visualise let alone embrace. They had never partied to music played loudly from records and speakers, nor felt the values of the free world that were captured in western songs.

We both recognised and sympathised with our parents, the generation bludgeoned into submission by politics beyond their own borders. First by Nazi's, and now by Communist forces. They would never realise that the revolution that caused the Prague Spring, began because certain politicians began to realise that Communism wasn't working. And all anyone had to do during the 60s to appreciate this was to listen to Radio Luxembourg, where the party was in full swing every night.

Our 60s had ended well, and I promised to show Bohunka my copies of Time and Life magazines, containing photographs depicting the atmosphere of the 60s in the free world. Having just caught up with the 60s, I didn't want to let it slip away.

"But what if you were able to get the new Beatles albums as soon as they were released?" Bohunka asked. "Wouldn't you then take things for granted and not value them as you do now?"

Of course she was quite right and I told her so. When someone had nothing but crumbs, he appreciated them much more than someone that had whole loaves all the time.

"But Bohunka," I said sadly caressing her cheeks. "Why did I have to wait seven years for my first Beatles album?"

She consoled me wih her beautiful sad eyes returning my caress whereupon I stood to my feet and looked out of the window.

"What are you looking for Jan?" she asked still lying naked on the towel below me.

"I'm looking for a fucking Russian who I could snap in half," I answered.

That night I carried the overwhelming thought that there was no future anymore for me as a railwayman. I was missing too many things working nights and weekends, and not being able to see Bohunka again on this evening intensified everything.

I was earning more money than some doctors earned, but more and more I was discovering that money wasn't everything.

Then something happened to finally make up my mind.

One evening in early January, I travelled to work with one of my fellow shunters and, as usual, avoiding using the safe underpass route, we climbed up the embankment on across 12 rail lines which brought us that much quicker to out locker room housing.

With just two more tracks remaining we spotted a curious ball on the track close to the rail. As we came closer, our curiosity turned to abject terror in the realisation that the ball was a human head. Then we noticed the rest of his body some metres away.

The decapitation was that of a train chief, making his way home from work, and as there was a cargo train just leaving the depot, he wanted to run across its path as quickly as possible as such cargo trains pulled up to 50 or more wagons, taking a couple of minutes before the whole train had passed by. This poor man hurried and made it across the line easily, but what he didn't count on was that simultaneously on the very next track, a locomotive travelling at high speed with no wagons took his life.

It was a terrible sight, a traumatic experience for us.

Right there and then I knew immediately my night shift was over, I would resign my job. My resolve remained until 7am when the personnel staff arrived, and I could fill out the relative forms, giving rhyme and reason for my notice. Funnily enough, I didn't site the previous evening's experience, but rather that I had a history of poor sleep which made me a danger to myself, and my colleagues.

It was very important for me to explain it this way, so that they would not accuse me of endangering the national economy for quitting a job without a proper reason.

I had made up my mind that the next job I would apply for was to become a disc jockey and I wanted to make sure my file didn't carry any black marks that could be held against my application. At any cost, I would become a DJ once I had completed six months' notice to the railway.

I was still in shock when I went home. We should both have been sent home immediately and given some therapy, but not a thing, not even an interview to see how we were handling our meeting with a headless corpse.

Not an hour off work.

My parents took it quite well, especially when I told them of our gruesome discovery the previous night.

Tony: Saving lives & jobs

Alan Keen was eliminated by a new English board, which included Sir John Rogers, who fell asleep at board meetings, and Patrick Cox, whose father had been high up in Thames Television management.

Cox was public school. He ate spreadsheets for breakfast and made love to his bottom-lines at night.

He managed companies, just like musicians read music – no soul. He could have been managing ICI instead of Britain's lady of the airwaves.

He had me join him for board meetings in London and Paris; it was a new learning curve. Suddenly I was carrying a briefcase with management accounts and projections. If the Careers Officer could see me now!

As long as my audience ratings were OK so was I. But Cox brought an abundance of politics into 38 Hertford Street, and with Alan Keen gone, I felt vulnerable and not so insecure since the days of Geoffrey Everett 16 years earlier.

Cox's new broom was in my corridor.

I made the headlines just when Cox was starting the three-written warning's procedure. It delayed him for a while. Sir John was proud of me and said so in a letter. Gus Grass RTL's supremo sent me a well-done telegram and, well you don't sack heroes, certainly not just when they've saved someone from drowning.

Christine and I had been invited to dinner at Eton's House on the Bridge restaurant, by Neil and Jilly Ferris.

I'd first known Neil as a bright record plugger for EMI, who left them to form the country's top independent record promotion company, Ferret & Spanner.

Back then, expense accounts provided to pluggers by their labels, bought meals like the one we were enjoying that night at the House on the Bridge. This was the first time I'd been entertained by Neil since he'd gone independent, and I was concerned the meal would be a tad expensive for his new company.

"Don't worry Tony," he reassured, "I've just had my first cheque from Daniel Miller for plugging Yazoo's *Only You*," which launched Mute Records very nicely for him.

Daniel Miller was a genius, Yazoo, spawned Depeche Mode, spawned Erasure…!

He offered his Mute Records cheque for me to scrutinise.

"Whaaaat?" I said incredulously, grabbing it for a closer look.

I was looking at a cheque for £30,000!! This was in 1979!

"Daniel Miller didn't want to guarantee me a fee, so I agreed to do the plugging for a small percentage of potential sales."

Around that time independent pluggers charged something like £1,000 plus disbursements per release. They mailed out the records to local stations and telephoned the programme chiefs and DJs, and took them in personally to the BBC, Capital Radio, and to me at Radio Luxembourg.

If we didn't like it or were unsure about it they tried to talk us round, pursuaded us to listen again a few days later, took us to concerts, offered exclusive interviews, took us to dinner...

I was looking at this cheque thinking, I wish there were more honourable people in the industry like Daniel Miller, (believe me there aren't), when, suddenly, a number of waiters stampeded by our table.

Throwing open the veranda windows they disappeared outside, creating a chill in the room in more ways than one. A shiver ran down my spine as I distinguished the word 'drowning'.

Standing up, I walked across the room and out of the window onto a Thames-side boardwalk, to see exactly what was going on.

Above and to the right of us the entire Eton bridge was lined with spectators. Below me, in the dark flowing waters, a white image disappeared as I watched from the bow of a boat tied to the restaurant's mooring.

"What was that?" I said pointing to a spot in the Thames.

"Eet's a man ees a drownin'," cried an Italian waiter.

I looked around. No one moved. I looked up at the bridge. No one moved.

"Fuck!" I thought. "That only leaves me!"

I took my shoes off, and dived in fully clothed, towards where I imagined the tide may have now taken whoever was wearing a white shirt. Twenty feet out and about 10 feet down, I bumped straight into him. It was pitch dark. Gripping him round the throat in an arm lock, I looked up towards where I hoped the world would still be.

Those few seconds, as the tide tried to take me down to Teddington Lock, would replay for weeks waking me in the middle of the night in a sweat, dreaming I'd missed him.

I broke the surface and began one arm doggy paddling back towards the mooring, struggling against the tide with my half dead companion.

Meanwhile, Christine and Neil were busy throwing a rope to his also-drunk-as-a-skunk pal.

Drunk?

Who do we know who would be pissed-up enough to jump off Eton bridge, to swim to a boat on the other side of the river Thames... totally forgetting they *can't* swim??

I'd nominate these two for 'most drunk ever' in the Guinness Book of Records!

I'd lost one of my shoes, it fell into the Thames so I limped and squelched back into the restaurant to a smattering of applause.

There I was, my teeth chattering like castanets, a tablecloth draped round me for warmth. I was on my second brandy when the cops arrived.

It was a lady cop who approached me.

"Some kind of a prank was it then?" asked the blue girl haughtily.

Christine, Neil and Jilly and I all looked at each other and burst out laughing.

"You'd best ask the fellow on the floor back there in the pumping room, I'm one of the goodies!" I laughed.

A few weeks later, the lad got off with a warning.

Outside the court a member of the press asked him if he had ever met Tony Prince?

"Just the once. Underwater!" he answered.

"Have you a message for him?" asked the journalist.

"Yes," he replied, "Ask him to play *Bridge Over Troubled Waters* for me!"

Five years later, I was at a Martini reception in their Haymarket offices, when a stranger pulled me to one side.

"I believe you're Tony Prince," he said as we shook hands.

"My boss used to be very high up in Kodak, and as we knew you were coming today he asked me to pass on a long overdue thanks."

He then explained that his boss had been dining at the House on the Bridge on the same evening, and was standing behind me as the body disappeared.

He was about to dive in, when I beat him to it.

"Why would he thank me?" I asked. "Did he have his best suit on?"

"No," laughed the executive, "It was much worse than that. His wife thought he was in Paris that night but he had a romantic liaison, 'playing away' as they say. He's always been grateful that it was you who made the tabloids the next day and not him!"

Fate! Perhaps I should have been issued with more than one diploma from the Royal Humane Society? I saved a life, a marriage and my job, all in one dive!

The press were full of words like, 'hero' and 'courage' but whilst it's a very satisfying to know you have saved someone's life, I've never regarded the act as bravery. If you can swim, have had two glasses of wine for Dutch courage and in two seconds you know a person is going to die right before your eyes, you don't have time to take stock of your courage. As I discovered at the Martini reception, there was a queue behind me waiting to do what

I did.

Headlines and bravery forgotten, Cox's three written warnings eventually recommenced with the most outrageous assertion that I had 'acted against the interest of the Company'.

I had conceived a radio game, which I called Where in the World.

We hid superb prizes and asked the listeners, by a process of listening to all the clues and failed guesses, to find the exact place on the planet where the prize was hidden.

The first caller to get through to the DJ each hour could interrogate him. Every time he answered 'yes' to a question they could ask another, but if he answered with a negative, the game ended until the next caller.

I thought it was one cool radio game; the more you listened, the more clues you amassed.

The DJs and I plotted where to hide the prizes which would turn up in the corgi's basket at Buckingham Palace, on the counter of the corner shop in Coronation Street, here on the studio console in front of the DJ and so on.

"Why did you give free publicity to Harrods last night?" asked Cox through a glazed smile that also said, "Gotcha!"

"Eh?"

"You hid the prize in Santa's sack in Harrods' grotto!"

"So?"

"You gave free publicity to a potential advertiser," he said in a manner, which told me he was erecting my gallows.

This was my first official written warning.

That Harrods would ever advertise on 208 was beyond the realms of imagination, and I doubt if the Radio Luxembourg Sales Department had so much as sent them a rate-card in 208's entire 50 years!

That the mentioning on-air of Harrods could justify an official company warning for gross misconduct, revealed to me that my own Station of the Stars was on the wane.

It also showed to me that I was working for a fucking idiot!

Didn't he understand that Harrods is a British institution?

Of course he did.

But that was a technicality. The sacking process had begun.

With two warnings remaining, I made plans to leave my beloved 208 before I got busted for wishing the Queen a happy birthday, or saying 'that' instead of 'this' in a news bulletin!

Radio Luxembourg now seemed like a big old animal lying down, exhausted, ready to die.

I didn't want to be there when she did.

Jan: Independence Day

Mother was completely relaxed about my decision, but father expressed concerns and talked about security and superannuation. Then he asked what I had in mind to do after I quit the railway. There was no way I could tell him the truth. A disc jockey would not be a job to him so I told him that I wanted to do something where I could employ my knowledge of English, perhaps at the International Trade Fair grounds in Brno.

I convinced myself that this wouldn't be a bad stand-by job if I failed to make it as a DJ, on which basis I decided to learn German. First I bought a German textbook and then I took another step. As we had already a TV set, I suggested to my parents that we should acquire the antenna for Viennese TV, which both agreed to without hesitation, even though it would be totally illegal. Like radio, it was not permitted to watch a foreign enemy TV channel. My mother, in particular, was quite excited at the prospects, as she was born in Vienna in April 1915, living there until 1918, when my grandparents returned with her to Brno the moment Czechoslovakia was founded.

By early 1970, Time and Life magazines were no longer sold in our hotels, and when I asked for them, I was informed by the old lady that they just stopped sending them without an explanation. This was a characteristic of communist communications; they simply didn't need to explain anything to anyone.

The good news for me was that the Elvis Fan Club newsletter sent to me by Todd Slaughter every month from Leicester, England, kept on arriving. This also gave me more news about Tony Prince, who was closely connected to the fan club. It felt like we were one big family united through Radio Lucky Luxembourg, firstly Tony advising me to write to Todd, Todd with his generosity and the millions of Elvis fans and Radio Luxembourg with untold listeners all over Europe. I started to feel very privileged.

Unfortunately throughout the rest of January there was not the slightest opportunity for Bohunka and I to do something reminiscent of New Year's Eve. I was far from thinking about marriage, but I yearned to spend more intimate time with her. I continued meeting her every now and then after she closed Supraphon, when we would go for a drink, or take in a movie, or a concert or visit the Bav club.

Bohunka became the favourite girl amongst my friends in Bav club when Supraphon released another two great albums by the Beach Boys and Dave Dee, Dozy, Beaky, Mick & Tich, which she was able to obtain for each of us.

We all expressed surprise that Supraphon, in the climate, kept releasing records from the west, especially as the State Censorship Office had stopped the distribution of Time and Life.

"Perhaps they don't consider records as dangerous as the written word," suggested Pavel.

"Maybe someone in State Censorship has a kid who likes the Beatles," said Miloš, the owner of Bav.

One thing was for sure, everyone loved Bohunka, and not just for her pretty face!

We all had the same problem with girlfriends, because every one of us lived with our families making intimacy impossible. When I took her home all we did was chat and listen to music, as a well-meaning mother with biscuits, or a kindly father with a warm drink, would impose themselves on us without the slightest notion that we would want to be left alone.

There was consolation knowing that we weren't the only couple facing this problem, especially when warm days and nights were still many moons away.

Her former boyfriend remained in residence when Bohunka tried unsuccessfully to rent a room alone. We didn't wonder why she had failed either. Red Law admitted there were more than 400,000 families in Czechoslovakia without a flat; so one could assume this figure was far greater than the newspaper reported. Some socialist society! After 20 years since seizing power, they still couldn't house the people, and these incompetent commies certainly couldn't house Bohunka.

It was the middle of February when her former boy friend finally left again on a weekend visit to his parents.

This time, I was to spend an entire two nights with her.

Although nothing could ever measure up to our New Year's night and morning together, the weekend was quite beautiful, although perhaps less spontaneous from the first time we were together.

Deep inside, the fact that we couldn't be together constantly didn't overly bother me, as I still wished to devote a lot of time to music, listening to Luxy, or visiting the discotheques of my friends and other DJs who were lucky enough to have been given permission to become disc jockeys. I might mention there was an application process and interview by committee to go through to become a DJ. I was now studying the competition and from what I was witnessing, this interview would be a piece of cake!

With a certain satisfaction, I noted that almost none of them bothered to comment on the record, such as what the song was about, or any detail on the musicians involved.

I knew the door was open for me, and as soon as I managed to get behind the microphone and turntables, I would deliver with style, panache and… knowledge.

I learned my art through the inadequacies of most of my competitors. I understood well that a DJ could announce facts and information about the songs, especially in the early stages of a party; and that, after so many beers, words became less important than the music.

I liked to help my DJ friends carry their loudspeakers and amplifiers, and to assemble everything with them. This gave me my chance to play DJ, spinning a couple of records myself for a sound check before the first customers arrived. I never went so far as to ask them to let me play a little during their show itself, as I respected that they were in these venues with this audience as stars in their own right.

One evening, Luboš Rettegy gave me Paul Anka's *21 Golden Hits* LP, saying it was too old and saccharine, and he had never understood why I'd been so crazy for it. I went home and played it till the morning light. Although I knew all the songs back to front on the tapes Michal from Černošice had made for me, there was no comparison between a tape and the real vinyl sound.

It was clear to me that I wanted to become a disc jockey much more than I wanted to be with Bohunka. This may have been the reason it didn't concern me to know she still slept in the same room as her former boyfriend. Certainly if I had been in love with her, I might have been concerned and tried to do something about it. But I wasn't and she didn't complain either.

I did the depot a favour, and instead of quitting job on 3 July I agreed to quit on 20 July, which in fact meant that I would go to work for the last time on 3 July, taking paid vacation for the two weeks after that date. It all added up to about a thousand crowns more this way, which would come in handy as I entered the unknown.

I would finally be free on 4 July, Independence Day for Jan Šesták from night shifts and weekend shifts.

Within a couple of months, my optimism about becoming a legal disc jockey was challenged. I had reports from friends with similar career ambitions, who also met the communist dragon face to face, experiencing the same abrupt rudeness as I. Most of these wannabe DJs just gave up the dream, but I wouldn't, I just couldn't after spending years being trained by the best DJs in the world on Radio Luxembourg, Radio Caroline and AFN.

I knew what was needed, and I just had to find a way to deliver.

THE GIG

Jan: Quite a surprise

"Meet me downtown," said František down the phone. "I have some incredible news for you."

"Tell me now," I beseeched.

We met in a coffee bar before he released the bombshell.

"Pavel Černocký phoned Miloš Bernátek at Bav club asking him if he would be interested in having Tony Prince in the club for one night…"

It was too much to take at 9am.

"Tony Prince is coming to Czechoslovakia?"

Within seconds František poured cold water on me.

"Miloš rejected this offer as he has booked singer, Waldemar Matuška, for that day already."

"What? Matuška instead of Tony Prince? Is Miloš crazy or what?"

I could not believe my ears, thinking at first it was some kind of a joke, but then as Pavel Černocký, the famous Prague DJ, was part of this news it surely had some credibility, and when František suggested we go to see Miloš immediately to try to change his mind, I knew something quite amazing was in the air.

We had nothing against Waldemar Matuška, who was known as the one surely not supporting communist regime at all. In 1967 he had even beaten Karel Gott in a singing contest 'The Golden Nightingale', where people voted for the most popular singer was a poll where people voted for the most popular singer in Czechoslovakia through a poll.

As much as we liked Waldemar, there was no way in the eastern world that we would change him for Tony Prince, and I fully intended to let Miloš know what a big opportunity this would be, not just for Bav, but for Czechoslovakia.

After we arrived by tram to Bav club and I noticed Miloš sitting in his tiny office, I took a deep breath ready to start my campaign giving him a million reasons why Tony Prince had to be his first choice.

Suddenly František took my arm, looked me in the eyes and burst out laughing! I froze.

"Of course Tony Prince IS coming to Bav," he screamed with delight. "I wanted to break this news to you slowly, so that you wouldn't have a heart attack!"

I didn't know whether to laugh or cry. So I cried.

He was right of course. My emotions were out of control. Five years Tony had been talking to me, slowly teaching me not just English, but English humour and the culture of the 60s. How much music he'd introduced me to, and how much pleasure, was beyond calculation.

The Royal Ruler coming to Brno? These things don't happen in real life, not in this country anyway. As I entered Miloš' office, I still found it hard to believe.

Tony: Invitation to Rock the Bloc

Christine and I shared a number of adventures, but our trip to
Czechoslovakia in 1970 was particularly memorable and heart wrenching,
bringing home to us how bloody lucky we were in the west, and how much
Radio Luxembourg and the western music we broadcast meant to the
teens of this long tyrannised nation.

I'd been invited by Pavel Černocký, a big 208 fan, and a Prague DJ who
happened to also work for the nearest thing they could call a 'theatrical
agency', to bring my bag of records for three dates in the towns of
Brno, Carlsbad and Prague. By now I was receiving a lot of mail from
Czechoslovakia, and often gave a call out to the listeners there, especially
these days shortly after their failed revolution.

I was told by Pavel that they could only pay in Czech money, so I went
home that afternoon and asked Christine, "How would you like a holiday
amongst the Communists?"

"Won't the Russians still be there?" asked my pregnant wife, to which I
lied, "No they've all gone back to Moscow."

Had I know then how things would end, I would have gone alone. Christine's
idea of adventure was walking around Torquay or the Lake District, but
she wasn't one for high adventure, and I wouldn't have subjected her to this
adventure in her condition.

I anticipated a nice break, a holiday with the chance to shop in the city
of Prague, where we would spend the currency which had no value outside
Czechoslovakia. Little did we realize as we set off on the long journey
across Germany, what little the shops of Prague would have to offer. But
nothing was more important to me than becoming the first western DJ
to play the clubs in the Eastern Bloc, and to meet lots of these rather
wonderful 208 fans.

Leaving baby Daniel with my mother-in-law Doris in Luxembourg,
Christine, now seven months into growing our daughter Gabrielle, started
to regret her decision when, within seconds of clearing the Czech border,
the Daimler hit the first of a thousand potholes.

Looking back, it was incredibly lucky we made Prague without a puncture
or a miscarriage.

Jan: The west comes east

Miloš was already preparing a poster design he would take to the printers
where he worked. It was a big company that printed local newspapers, so
supervision was not so strict, and he could get away with printing posters

for Bav club. This time, with the name of an English disc jockey in big letters, it would make it that much riskier for Miloš, but it wasn't going to stop him.

There was no need for posters; publicity wasn't a necessity either because grapevine and word of mouth would fill two Bav clubs. We decided to slap the posters on every downtown wall and pillar we could find, just to let the people know, (and the communists especially), that there was a DJ coming to Brno, and he wasn't from Radio Moscow! This was Tony Prince, they may not have heard of him because it was quite unlawful to listen to Radio Luxembourg in our country, but we wanted them to know he was coming, and that every kid in town would be waiting for him. Then they could make their own conclusions as to the significance of this event and what this, the greatest of radio stations, meant to the kids in our country.

We decided not to use the Czech word *diskžokej* on the bright yellow poster, but to print the English translation *disc jockey* on the upper part of the poster, beneath the name Tony Prince that took up half the poster in bright red letters. Also on the poster were DJ Pavel Černocký (of Prague), together with Pavel Váně and Luboš Rettegy, who needed no introduction to the Bav club crowd.

Then my big bonus: the date, Saturday 4 July 1970 from 6pm to 23.30pm. I couldn't have programmed it any better, as this would be my first day free from the railway, the perfect setting for my new life to begin.

It became obvious as we bill-posted Brno that the inteligencia was too busy sorting their new higher status positions out, to give any notice to a bunch of guys slapping posters up around town. We at Bav club were still little fish, and here we were not even two years after the Russian invasion, with nobody bothering us as we prepared our festival of freedom, that would commence with a night with Radio Luxembourg on 4 July.

Two nights later I couldn't have had a more vivid confirmation that he was coming, than through my faithful Hitachi, when I heard Tony himself live on air calling out to all his friends and 208 fans in Czechoslovakia, saying how much he was looking forward to meeting them in July.

Tony: The tour

The silver Daimler became a spectacle wherever we went, not to mention my shoulder length hair and Carnaby Street clobber.

Here we were, hot on the tail of the historic Dubček uprising, where hundreds of brave students had faced off against the Russian army in order to redraw the Red line.

Their prisons were filled with political activists and protesters, many of them young kids who had basked in the Prague Spring under Dubček, and had Communism re-dumped on them by the invading Russian army, just when they thought they'd wiggled free.

We soon learned from our chaperones that all the Czechoslovakian kids had in the evenings, apart from 'spin the bottle' and clandestine sex, was Radio Luxembourg. Unbelievably I learned that listening to 208 had been illegal under totalitarian rule, and yet they all tuned in, regardless of threats of prison!

It was actually just like the UK before Radio Caroline sailed into town. I had enormous empathy with them.

There were no proper discotheques or clubs as we knew them, only taverns and youth centres run by the Centre of Socialist Youth, where the likelihood of hearing modern western music was zero to never. The best by far during my trip was Bav club, under the direction of Miloš Bernátek in the fifth District of Brno. The equipment was a basic, homemade-looking sound system, the lightshow non-existent. These venues were made for live musicians, few, if any Brits or American artistes had made it this far into Eastern Europe. It was like the back-end of the world so far as musicians were concerned, and if the promoters or Czech agency couldn't pay with the good old US dollar, then the managers wouldn't even mention Czechoslovakia to their artists.

Whilst we were drowning in rock 'n' roll at London's 2is coffee bar and swinging through the 60s with the Liverpool sound, the kids in Czechoslovakia and other eastern countries controlled by Communists, were culturally cut-off from all that made life so good to be a teenager in the west. Christine and I quickly learned what these kids endured and left the country understanding their plight, our heart bleeding for them.

The kids who came out to play were so star-struck with the DJ from the legendary 208 from across the Iron Curtain, I had to work extra hard to get them dancing.

The first gig was in Karlovy Vary where the entire audience just stood around the stage watching me talking after each record. DJ's didn't mix records together in these days, the extra length 12" disco records wouldn't show their A-sides and dub B-sides for another six or seven years. Motown was the floor filler, Stax and Atlantic soul records had to be high on the DJ's agenda, but he still needed to mix these with the pop and rock tracks they heard first on Radio Luxembourg.

Lulu's *Shout* rather than the original Isley Brothers version; Brian Poole & the Tremeloes' *Do You Wanna Dance* rather than the Bobby Freeman original, and a record you could play at any peak time session throughout the 70s was Jeff Beck's *Hi Ho Silver Lining*. I had all this ammunition with me, plus lots of Beatles, Stones and Elvis because you were dead without a few Presley tracks, even a decade after rock 'n' roll had dominated. Currently I couldn't get away without playing Creedence Clearwater Revival's *Bad Moon Rising* and the Archie's *Sugar Sugar*, because multiple Luxembourg plays, had sent them to the top of the charts.

And when it came to the smooch, (because every evening had to have one), out came the horny Jane Birkin and Serge Gainsburg singing *Je t'aime... moi non plus*, during which there'd be more hands on bums than you could count. After cueing up the next record, I'd put the headphones down and dance around the stage with an air guitar, or I bent down and signed autographs. I staged silly competitions on stage where the kids could win albums and t-shirts, this was more difficult here where hardly anyone spoke English, so everything had to be visual. It didn't matter what I did, they just wanted to hear the voice, we already had a relationship.

I called on my old striptease act complete with bra and babies feeding teets. People thought I was nuts and I was. The important thing for me was to either make people dance, or make them laugh. If I managed to do both, I felt I'd earned my fee. I can't tell you how touched I was by these Czechoslovak kids, I didn't see them drinking alcohol, but goodness me were they thirsty for music, I must have played the Rolling Stones' *Honky Tonk Women* four times a night and at least half a dozen Beatles' hits. I normally did just over an hour in the UK; I did a two-hour set throughout this tour, enjoying every minute as much as the audience.

Inside the baronial hotels in which we stayed, we ended the night in the hotel's own clubs, which were actually moody strip joints, where almond skinned ladies took off *every* stitch, something they never did in the UK in those days. Then, just as the g-string hit the floor, Christine would drag me away before I could even ask the resident oom pah trio if I could sing *What'd I Say* with them.

The arrival of a Radio Luxembourg DJ for the very first time in Czechoslovakia was nothing short of Beatlemania.

In Karlovy Vary, I found myself standing on stage in a theatre where row after row of kids sat *watching* me playing records. There was no dance floor as such, but after the first four bars of Free's *All Right Now* I had them out of their seats, dancing in the asles, front of stage and then on stage with me, just like the old UK rock n' roll cinema audiences when Bill Haley sang *Rock Around the Clock*.

I'd taken around 400 records with me, 100 to play and 300 to give away to the kids. It was like the feeding of the 5,000 everyone went wild, each of them starved of vinyl in a country where western music was non-existent. Before I left the country I gave the lot away. I'm sure there will be some old English DJ promo singles, sitting forgotten in a Czechoslovakian granddad's drawers that are worth quite a lot of money on eBay today.

Had I given away a DJ promo copy of the Beatles' *Love Me Do*, (which was extremely likely), this single alone would fetch £10,000 on the world collectors market! Back then in Czechoslovakia, in 1970, it was already priceless.

A pretty girl appeared at the front of stage, beckoning me and waving a handful of crumpled bank notes at me. She was screaming my name, and was plainly crying her eyes out just like teenage girls would for the Beatles or, in a few years from now, Donny Osmond and David Cassidy.

I left the record console and crouched down offering her my left ear into which she spoke in stuttered English.

It wasn't me she wanted after all - it was John, Paul, George and Ringo!

"I give you all my Deutschmark for Beatle records," she cried waving her Monopoly money under my nose, as if she hoped the smell of German money would entice me.

I gave her the Beatles' *Twist and Shout* EP, and accepted her kiss in payment.

Jan: The meeting

Because of our English knowledge, František and I were chosen to meet Tony and his wife Christine at the Hotel International, where they were accommodated. We were both flattered and quite excited to be chosen for this very enjoyable task, but no surprise, as we were the only two to have studied English at high school. We were quite apprehensive, neither of us had ever spoken English with an Englishman, we hadn't even met someone whose mother tongue was English.

We were instructed to meet at the café in the Hotel International, and wait until Tony came downstairs, when we could introduce ourselves and talk to him before taking him on to Bav Club. It was clear, with a sold out event weeks in advance, there would be little opportunity to talk at the club. I'd decided to stop by the hotel reception to ask if they had received Time or Life magazines again. The answer was negative but, as I was already at reception, I thought to enquire if Tony Prince had checked in.

Unexpectedly the receptionist not only confirmed he was here, she asked if I wished to speak with him?

Talk to Tony Prince? Talk to *Tony Prince*? Talk *to* Tony Prince? Whichever way I thought about it, it just didn't sound right, as suddenly there was no totalitarian state in Czechoslovakia, no ruling communist party, no Russian invasion, everything I had lived for focussed on this simple question, "Would you like to speak with Tony Prince?"

"OK, yes please," I said and was directed to the telephone cabin, hidden behind reception. As I approached the booth the phone started to ring.

Lifting the receiver and clutching it to my ear I heard the oh so familiar voice, one I had heard perhaps more than any other voice during the past 5 years or so.

"Hello. This is Tony Prince."

This time the big difference was that he wasn't thousands of miles away in the Grand Duchy, but right here in the very same building. I made my first conversation with him.

"Hi Tony, this is your biggest fan in Czechoslovakia speaking…"

Tony laughed and asked me to wait for him at the reception so I could take him to the café.

I was elated. Such a short conversation, but I learned that he could understand my English, and from that moment on my confidence grew and I was no longer afraid that I might fail in my task as interpreter. After all, I chuckled to myself, Tony had been my exclusive English teacher for many years, so why wouldn't we understand each other? Here was the crazy thing though, not one of us had ever seen a picture of Tony before, so we had no idea what he might look like.

The moment I saw him exiting the elevator across the lobby, I knew I was looking at the Royal Ruler. He seemed to know I was his chaperone as he walked directly towards me. Maybe I had a hat on that said 'I love 208' or I was dribbling from my mouth, but here he was extending his hand towards me…

"Well hello there Jan," he said.

"Sorry Tony," I said gathering my composure. "I just have to get used to real live Tony Prince, instead of tuning the static away from your voice!"

We both laughed loudly and walked towards the café. As we entered my childhood friend, Svatoslav Fiala, took a picture of Tony and I approaching František and the rest of our Bav club friends. Only later did František reveal how nervous everyone had been, and how angry they were becoming when I appeared to be late.

This explained the relief and shock on their faces as we approached them, laughing together like old friends who had known each other for years. Within minutes of introductions, everyone including František had the same feeling, as if they had just renewed acquaintance with a dear friend who had been away. Each of us felt we knew him well, his open personality on the air had revealed so much of himself that he was hardly a stranger to any of us.

Tony and his personality represented the essence of everything we could ever want, it was as though, when he walked into our lives, he had also brought with him the Beatles, the Rolling Stones, the Kinks and Elvis the King himself. No one else had brought them to us night after night, as did the Radio Luxembourg DJs, Noel Edmonds, Kid Jensen, Paul Burnett,

Bob Stewart, Dave Christian, Mark Wesley and Mike Hollis, and the leader of the pack who now stood before us.

We chatted away and soon learned that Tony had no intention of presenting himself as the big '*I am*' star, but a down to earth guy who really cared for us. He wanted to know everything about the young people of Czechoslovakia, how we lived, what music we liked, played and performed, how we were affected after the Russian invasion. He was interested in everything, and we chatted away over cups of tea and Coca Cola, until suddenly a new presence was felt in the room as his beautiful wife Christine, came towards us like a mini-skirted 60s vision from the west.

Now I had a second person to speak English to, and another person who immediately drew us into her confidence, as she made clear her concern for our welfare in the land of red laws and, as Christine put it, "Lots of bloody pot-holes!"

Too soon, the time came for us to make our way to Bav club where the biggest gathering of Brno kids ever, were assembled in and out of the club. In fact we were lucky that the holidays had started the previous Saturday, otherwise I couldn't imagine what the scene would have looked like. Inside, the crowd had exceeded the 300 comfort-zone capacity, 500 music-loving 208 fans had been admitted. Miloš' dilemma now was the 200 standing outside, begging to be admitted. It took me back to a certain Beatles movie many years ago.

Backstage, Tony asked me to personally chaperone Christine, perhaps the most pleasant job I have ever been given in my life. Bohunka wasn't present on this great night as she had booked a holiday with friends to Bulgaria, and so I was left completely free to devote myself to looking after this English princess.

Christine and I were given the VIP seats of honour on the upper left side of the club, from where I lorded it over the audience digesting all the looks of curiosity, admiration and a deal of male-envy directed towards me.

The atmosphere was electric, the likes of which I'd never experienced. I knew in my heart I was at last on the edge of something like Beatlemania. I noticed Christine had tears in her eyes.

"Is it too smoky for you?" I asked.

"No Jan," she replied. "I'm just moved by these wonderful kids."

The place was now like the sardine capital of Czechoslovakia; Miloš had capitulated and allowed the rest of the crowd in free of charge. Now they stood beneath us like sardines each craning their neck for a view of the stage.

When Tony walked on stage in Brno the roar was deafening. He made immediate contact with the audience and it didn't seem to matter that the huge majority spoke only a few words of English. Tony danced, screamed, punched the air and threw out 45s and photographs, which he would bend down front of stage and sign for them.

What I found to be really exhilarating were the hits he played, classic club tunes, danceable rock records and last week's hits from the 208 Top 20.

"Anyone like last week's 208 Power Play?" he asked.

And then he played Mungo Jerry's *In the Summertime*. We'd be dancing to this tune for the next 30 years in Czechoslovakia.

By midnight, Tony was stripped to the waist doing his hilarious striptease as Christine next to me, hid her face in her hands, begging him not to go any further, as by all accounts he often did in the UK. But further he went and off came the trousers that he swung through the air to almighty cheers. No one was dancing now, only the Princely Platter Player.

I was grateful that he stopped there, and that he didn't proceed with his Hide the Pound contest, or his Most Beautiful Boobs competitions, which would have undoubtedly worked going by František's recent experiences.

Tony had asked me just how raunchy he might be allowed to be in Brno, and I had mentioned although the Secret Police wouldn't get within a metre of the front door, if word of mouth were to travel outside that would worry me because it could affect the club's license.

So Tony pulled up short and delivered a show like no DJ before him had even imagined. I learned so much that night from a man who had already taught me so much, and I guess over a hundred people went home clutching one of his records including LPs, tracks that would never be released in our country, until we'd kicked the Russians out.

After the gig, the incredible *Princemania* continued outside as we fought to get him and Christine to his Daimler. Approaching midnight, and it appeared no one wanted to go home, still waiting for a closer glimpse of the famous DJ, still wanting his autograph or a record, if he had any left.

Tony and Christine were safely in the car with František and myself in the back, when the front side window gave way under the body pressure outside. Regardless, he wound down the window and patiently handed out autographs until everyone had one. And still they remained, still they pressed up against the car.

"I have to go or someone will get hurt," yelled Tony from the driver's seat slipping the car into drive and edging slowly away whilst sounding the horn.

Tony: The great escape

The next day the conflict began.

The agent had slipped in a fourth gig some 800 kilometres away in Košice up near the Polish border just past Hungary, Romania and the Ukraine, a journey of 143,000 potholes away.

In the end, with little other choice, I agreed to fly there two days later, providing they kept the Prague hotel room for my pregnant wife.

After a wonderful Prague gig, although I would be leaving early the next morning to fly to Košice, we couldn't resist an enthusiastic invite from a young artist to a party he wanted to throw in our honour in his tiny apartment.

Looking out from his living room wall was a superb metre-high pencil drawing of the great John Lennon. I stood rooted in admiration feeling, through the amazing detail in the drawing, the artist's passion to become free, just like his hero before me.

We talked politics and pop music into the night, and I wonder today how they would have responded if I'd predicted that in the not too distant future, not only would Communism fail, not only would the Berlin wall be demolished by the people of Eastern Germany themselves, but that in Russia, on a spring-like May day in 2003, Paul McCartney would perform in the burial place of Lenin, Stalin and Brezhnev, where the Beatle would be given a guided tour of the Kremlin by the future President Vladimir Putin! *Back in the USSR* in real time!

The party had arrived at the stage so many teenage parties ended up in the 60s and 70s once the wine bottle was empty. Our new friends were just starting to play 'spin the bottle' when Christine decided it was time for us to leave, graciously declining their offer to play with them.

"Can't we just watch?" I implored.

At the apartment door, our young host handed me the rolled up John Lennon drawing. I was deeply touched by a gift, which I have cherished all my life. Czech John, complete with wine stains from the party, has been on our wall wherever we've lived during the past 46 years, a vivid reminder of the time we ventured into the Eastern Bloc from where, shortly after leaving the party, we escaped over the border like spies in an Ian Fleming novel. Sadly, the artist who drew Czech John remains unknown to us to this day, even after many appeals on Facebook.

Back in our hotel, a message was waiting for me explaining that the agency couldn't get me a flight and *insisted* I travel by road. I didn't like the heavy-handed communist order, if they'd asked politely I might have taken the journey on, even though it would be an arduous two-day drive both ways. Instead, we headed the opposite way to Vienna, 200 miles away.

This would be the only gig in my life I would not arrive for. I hid my concern from Christine, wondering if my name would be on some kind of dead-man-walking list as we tried to break the Czechoslovakian/Austrian border.

We bade Pavel goodnight, saying I'd see him early in the morning. He looked very apologetic as he hugged us goodnight. We packed our bags and made our escape through the city centre, passing by the top of Prague's beautiful Wenceslas Square, taking in the magnificent National Museum where, only a short while back, the students had barricaded themselves inside revolting against the invading Eastern European armies.

The midnight moon picked out hundreds of bullet holes, eternal pockmarks, in the façade of this historic building. A constant reminder of who was in charge, left in the bricks.

Then I saw something else on a damaged museum pillar, which made me stop. There in the middle was my name on a poster promoting my Prague appearance! Christine and I were both deeply moved and fell silent as we journeyed onwards, feeling like traitors to the revolution as we passed by the Wenceslas monument, finally leaving all the wonderful kids we had met to their continuing internment.

Christine and I disguised our fear, as the stern frontier guard on the Czech side took our passports and disappeared indoors to check us out. Two young Brits, both with shoulder length hair, were hardly regular travellers through his outpost.

Returning to the Daimler, he suspiciously looked my capitalist vehicle up and down, scrutinising the broken small air-vent window now covered with cardboard and masking tape, after over-zealous fans had crowded the Daimler, breaking it as we left the club in Brno.

"Open trunk!" he ordered as a second guard arrived to flank him. I jumped out and opened the car boot shitting myself.

Perplexed, they both gazed at our booty.

We were smuggling out a wooden kitchen cabinet!

There wasn't a lot else you could buy with all my Czech crowns, that wouldn't be worth two pence outside Czechoslovakia!

I'd found Czechoslovakia to be very much like Rhyl in North Wales, a town where I'd found it difficult to find one item in one shop priced over £20.

The cabinet was lifted out and my boot strip-searched. The phone rang in their building, and the second guard left just as the first guard returned our passports and clicked his heels at me. I turned the key just as the guard inside the outpost looked towards us cradling his phone. I put my foot down and let the Daimler do what Daimlers do.

We scurried out of Czechoslovakia and cleared the Austrian border without further drama.

The dawn lights of Vienna were a most beautiful and welcoming sight, a city of gold, gleaming in the dawn sunshine.

We had made good our escape.

EPILOGUE

Jan: The End

We'd waited till the decade had slipped away for a taste of the real 60s in Brno, but it had finally happened in our city.
After Tony and Christine left, we talked about this night for two further decades, under Soviet control! It was an experience that inspired us to want our democracy back as soon as possible.
Unfortunately there would be no more squeezing through the iron curtain for DJs for another 20 years.

Tony: Let's go around again

Three decades went by before I travelled east again when, in 1989, I visited Bratislava, capital of the Slovak Republic, which was once again split from the Czech Republic, with the Russians and communism stored into their history.
I had formed a company called DMC, which published Mixmag magazine and staged the World DJ Championships, and I'd been invited to take the new DMC Champion, Cutmaster Swift, to perform. I noticed immediately how things had changed for the kids who all seemed much happier than their forefathers, having fun at last and enjoying any amount of music their hearts desired without looking over their shoulders for the Secret Police. They no longer had to listen to Radio Luxembourg, which, in one year's time, would finally close down as the long-running English Service of the giant broadcasting network RTL.
Whilst most people around the world were getting off on drugs in club-land, the kids in the East had only Coca-Cola on the tables. Their drug continued to be music, and I must say I've rarely seen a drug-free audience on such a natural high.
In 2009, through the wonders of Facebook, my old DJ friend from what was then Czechoslovakia, Jan Šesták together with Miloš, the owner of Bav club, the guys who originally invited me to Brno, invited me back for a reunion at the exact same venue I had played in their city 40 years earlier. Unbelievably the venue, Bav club, was still there and had hardly changed. The years however had changed the audience somewhat.
Jan was disappointed I hadn't taken Christine, whom he had taken such great pleasure in looking after, whilst I was on stage in 1970.
It had been a big thing then for Jan to be the escort for an English Princess

to whom he could speak and expand his English. Christine had been the very first person with whom he had held a full conversation in English. Christine was no longer keen on flying and who could blame her with her close call on the doomed Papa India flight in June 1972? She'd been back to Oldham to see her family and decided to return on Monday, rather than Sunday via Brussels. The plane came down at Staines reservoir shortly after take-off, killing all on board.

I boarded my plane at Heathrow and wondered if I was making a mistake going back to Brno 40 years later? Would I have a dance-floor filled with Zimmer frames? Would the customs officers recognise me and insist I complete my gig in Košice in Slovakia? Needless to say it was a most wonderful reunion, and an evening of conversations that inspired me to ask Jan to share his story with me, as he is doing today.

I had many forces against me in my career and lots of good fortune. The Musicians' Union, the British Labour Government, the BBC all placed career-mines before me, and of course I had to escape from my hometown before I could fly. Oldham had given me a wonderful childhood, but when I heard the King call, I had to follow Elvis like a kid from Hamlin.

But nothing I encountered compares to what Jan endured, and what all the kids in Czechoslovakia endured in their lives under house arrest, and I wanted to set our two stories side by side demonstrating to all future teenage generations what music and freedom meant to us in the mid 20th century. Understand how music and a particular radio station helped us to survive, to enjoy life, to dance to the same tunes no matter where in the world we were listening to them.

It was the spirit of the music lover Jan Šesták, of musician Pavel Váně and the student, Jan Palach, who gave his life in protest that really caused the Berlin Wall to fall.

There is no doubt in my mind whatsoever that their passion for freedom was fuelled by the nightly broadcasts from Radio Luxembourg as they heard The Beatles' *All you need is love*, the Rolling Stones' *Let's Spend the Night Together*, the Kinks, Led Zeppelin, Bob Dylan and the songs written in an environment of social freedom. It couldn't have failed to inspire them to revolt. But who amongst us in that day and age would have ever believed that the Berlin Wall would be demolished in their lifetime? I certainly didn't.

But long before the Berlin Wall was taken down by the people it imprisoned, I was privileged to meet the kids of Czechoslovakia and to understand their dilemma. I will never forget the kids of Brno, Prague and Karlovy Vary, who came to dance to the music they heard on Radio Luxembourg, and to enjoy what must have seemed like a night of freedom, when their beloved 208 finally came to town.

It was without doubt, the greatest gig of my life.

I broadcast nightly on Radio Luxembourg for 16 years, and upon my return from Czechoslovakia, from that day forth, I played many requests and dedications for the teenagers listening in the east, knowing only too well that this, the greatest of radio stations, was part of their survival kit, and each cheerful tune and dedication was a rope ladder over the east-west divide.

What happened to them after the Berlin Wall came down?

Miloš Bernátek (founder and owner of Bav club)
After the communists closed the club down in the early seventies he became a promoter in various clubs. After the Velvet Revolution in 1990, he bought the Bav together with co-founder Jirka Sedláček, making the venue blossom once again for the kids of Brno.
Miloš passed away in 2014.

František Jemelka (the songwriter)
In the early 70s František became manager of the famous Theater on a String (Divadlo na provázku), whilst continuing to write lyrics for Pavel Váně, Synkopy 61 and others. In the 90s he moved to Russia to work for the Czech commerce section for ten years. After he returned, he was active again in various cultural ventures.
František passed away in 2015.

Pavel Váně (Musician)
At last Pavel toured the world and has performed in the USA, South Africa and many parts of Europe. His recordings, uncensored at last, have all been reissued. His concerts are all sellouts.

Michal Bukovič (Songwriter)
Michal from Černošice became one of the Czech Republic's most famous lyric writers, writing lyrics in both Czech and English for famous Czech singers.
Michal passed away in 2008.

Pavel Černocký (Prague DJ)
Pavel was the person responsible for booking Tony's tour of Czechoslovakia. He continues to be a star DJ attraction in his country, and often hosts nostalgic reunion concerts in Prague.

Radek Rettegy (Vocalist)
Radek is retired, but still appears on various occasions including events at the Bav club where he performs rock and roll songs and his own popular songs about his hometown Brno.

Jaromír Hnilička (Musician)
Jaromír reaches his 85th birthday on February 1st 2017. His greatest regret is taking his colleague's advice to avoid alcohol and missing all the fun of rock 'n' roll. He still cares for his neighbours by practicing trumpet and composing in his garage. And he can still be seen performing a suite he wrote for the Brno Symphony Orchestra and Choir.

Katka (Jan's first love)
Katka became a pediatrician and still lives in Bratislava, where she has a private medical practice.
Jan says, "We see each other every now and then, *but only as friends!*"

Tony Prince
In 1983 Tony left Radio Luxembourg to launch the Disco Mix Club (DMC), a unique DJ ONLY record club that pioneered the art of music mixing. He became the publishing editor of DMC's monthly magazine Mixmag, which became the window on the modern global DJ.
As we now know, Tony's belief that the DJ was in effect a musician is clearly vindicated.
Since his pirate days, Tony has been flanked throughout his career by his wife Christine.
DMC approaches its 34th anniversary, an unparalleled accomplishment for an independent record label whilst Mixmag, no longer owned by DMC, continues to flourish.
Their son Daniel Prince lives in Ibiza, where he edits and publishes DMC's weekly online magazine whilst daughter Gabrielle, DMC's graphic designer for many years, has delivered their first grandchild Bluebell St John.
The DMC story is extraordinary and, if he can find time, Tony may well write about his further experiences as a sequel to THE ROYAL RULER AND THE RAILWAY DJ.

Jan Šesták
After the inspirational meeting with Tony and Christine Prince, Jan dodged the Secret Police for 20 years. In1975 he finally won a licence to be an unpaid amateur DJ, after which his live party sets became his vehicle through life.

With Jan holding court as night porter, in a city where nothing at all happened after midnight, Brno's International Hotel Continental became the meeting point for the city's musicians.

In 1975 Jan married Ivana and became the proud father of Šárka his daughter, who is now a doctor in psychiatry. The marriage lasted six years. In 1976, with marital status favouring his application, for the first and last time during 40 years of communist rule, Jan received permission to visit the USA. His application mentioned that he wished to study their Country and Jazz music to aid his development as a DJ.

During the trip he met many musical luminaries and attended concerts by the Outlaws (with Willie Nelson) and Waylon Jennings. The highlight of his trip however was when his original American penfriend, Dave Hogan, invited him to spin records on his morning show at WSKY Asheville NC for two weeks of his stay.

In the 80s, Jan finally succeeded in studying as a part time student at the University of Economics in Prague. With *perestrojka* and President Gorbatschov now in power, the communist bosses at hotel Continental were threatened by their non-practicing communist night porter who now had a university degree and a wide knowledge of languages. This led to a conspiracy with the Secret Police and, in September 1989, he became unemployed inheriting a fresh bad record on his Secret Police file.

Within three months the Velvet Revolution released Jan from a life long burden of communist rule. Today he is a highly respected DJ with a vast knowledge of music.

In 2015 Jan was invited by Tony Prince to Luxembourg for a three-day Radio Luxembourg reunion. At the Villa Louvigny, he met Mark Wesley, Mike Hollis and Stuart Henry's widow Ollie, people who had played such a big part in his life.